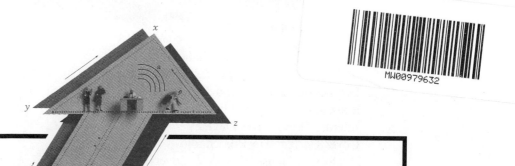

BUILDING ACCOUNTING SYSTEMS

USING ACCESS 7.0 & WINDOWS 95 • 2E

JAMES T. PERRY
PH.D. THE UNIVERSITY OF SAN DIEGO SCHOOL OF BUSINESS

GARY P. SCHNEIDER
PH.D., CPA THE UNIVERSITY OF SAN DIEGO SCHOOL OF BUSINESS

SOUTH-WESTERN College Publishing

An International Thomson Publishing Company

Team Director: Richard Lindgren
Acquisitions Editor: David L. Shaut
Production Editor: Jason M. Fisher
Marketing Manager: Sharon Oblinger
Internal Design: Joe Devine
Cover Design: Tin Box Studio
Production House: Cover to Cover Publishing

ISBN: 0-538-87494-5

2 3 4 5 6 7 8 9 D1 5 4 3 2 1 0 9 8

Printed in the United States of America

Library of Congress Cataloging-in-Publication Data

Perry, James T.
Building accounting systems : a transaction cycle approach / James T. Perry, Gary P. Schneider. -- Access ed.
p. cm.
At head of title: Access for Windows '95.
Includes index.
ISBN 0-538-87494-5 (pbk.). -- ISBN 0-538-87495-3 (CD-ROM). -- ISBN 0-538-87493-7 (package)
1. Accounting--Data processing. 2. Transaction systems (Computer systems) I. Schneider, Gary P., 1952- . II. Microsoft Access. III. Title.
HF5679.P419 1997
657'.0285--dc21 97-20713
CIP

To Nancy Perry and Cathy Cosby

PREFACE

TO THE STUDENT

Traditional methods of recording economic events and accumulating accounting information are giving way to database technology in today's accounting information systems. As we write this second Microsoft Access edition of *Building Accounting Systems*, we find that organizations increasingly depend on databases that include accounting and other operating data for mission-critical information. Accounting information systems—or the accounting views of enterprise-wide databases—contain much of the information managers use to make decisions and control operations. These databases also store the information that accountants use to prepare the formal accounting reports, such as year-end financial statements, that organizations issue to external users. As a professional accountant, you will play a central role in ensuring that the accounting systems you use, audit, and help design will deliver timely, accurate, and complete information. This book will help you learn how to perform that role effectively.

This text describes how database management systems provide the design tools that information systems professionals and accountants use to build accounting systems. The text begins by explaining how database systems are a part of your everyday life, and helps you develop a basic understanding of the theory and practice of relational database management systems. With that foundation, the book then shows you how to build the elements of accounting systems using Microsoft Access, one of the most widely available database management software packages for personal computers.

The book begins by explaining how to use the Windows operating environment. It then reviews the history and theory of relational database systems, and describes practical uses of Microsoft Access. The book explains accounting transaction cycles and shows you how to use the database theory and tools you learned in the earlier chapters to build accounting system elements for each of the four main transaction cycles: revenue, purchase, payroll, and production.

Chapter 1 provides a firm grounding in the fundamentals of the Windows 95 operating system. This chapter may be a review for some of you; for others, this will be your first hands-on introduction to Windows 95. Chapter 2 introduces Microsoft Access database management software. You will learn the basics of using tables to store information, displaying database contents, finding answers to questions with database queries, using forms to enter data, and printing database reports. Chapter 3 presents a concise, yet thorough, introduction to database theory. You will learn how to use normalization rules to structure your data in ways that avoid redundancy and data loss. This chapter also introduces user views and entity-relationship modeling. Finally, you will learn how to perform the three basic database operations that will enable you to locate subsets of table rows or columns and to collect information from several related tables in a database. Chapter 4 parallels Chapter 2's topics; however, in Chapter 4 you *create* the tables, queries, forms, and reports—tasks for which we provide step-by-step guidance. You will be happy to know that you can perform all of these database functions *without writing a single line of program code*. When you have finished Chapter 4, you will have all of the database skills you need to create basic accounting system components. Chapter 5 shows you how to add "icing" to the database "cake" with enhancements to the database elements you learned to create in Chapter 4. These enhancements include custom buttons for simplifying database operations and custom menus that replace the Microsoft Access default menu.

The remainder of the book applies database concepts and techniques to the specific challenges of building accounting information systems. Chapter 6 explains the differences between database accounting systems and double-entry bookkeeping systems, then discusses the advantages of the database approach. You will learn how to classify business activities by level of complexity. You will also learn to identify the business activities that comprise the four main transaction cycles we use in this book. In Chapter 7, you will begin your walk through the accounting transaction cycles with the revenue cycle. For example, you will learn how to use Microsoft Access tables and forms to record sales and cash collections. Chapter 8 shows database applications in the purchase cycle, which include creating purchase orders, recording the receipt of goods ordered, and paying vendors. In Chapter 9, you will learn how to build the database elements that businesses use to handle the many details of payroll accounting. You will learn how to combine records of time worked with employee information to calculate gross pay, deductions, and net pay. Chapter 10 describes the production cycle and shows you how to build accounting database elements that track materials, labor, and overhead costs into production using job order cost accumulation examples. The chapter also explains how you can extend these examples to build process, hybrid, and activity-based cost accounting databases.

We hope you will become an active participant as you read the text and work through the step-by-step examples. You will best retain what you have read by working through the book on a computer. To reinforce your learning, we have included three types of review questions at the end of each chapter:

- Multiple-choice questions, which refresh your memory about key points in the text.
- Discussion questions, which are more general and can provide a basis for interesting small group discussions of the topics.
- Exercises, which require you to use Microsoft Access to create your own accounting databases or extend the examples in the text.

By studying the text carefully, working through the examples, and using the end-of-chapter materials to reinforce your knowledge, you will learn how to use database management software to design and build accounting systems that deliver timely, accurate information to managers and financial statement users.

TO THE INSTRUCTOR

Many accounting professors feel that the accounting information systems course is the greatest teaching challenge in the curriculum. One of our goals in writing this book was to help make your job of teaching accounting systems easier. Accounting practice has evolved from manual journals and ledgers to database accounting systems—even in very small firms. At the same time, many introductory accounting courses have shifted to financial statement user and managerial decision maker orientations from the more traditional preparer orientations. Despite this decreased emphasis on the mechanics of accounting in the introductory courses, accounting majors still need to understand how accounting systems record, classify, and aggregate economic events. This book gives you a powerful tool that can help you give your students a solid introduction to database principles *and* valuable hands-on experience in constructing accounting systems. By using Microsoft Access—object-based software that features an intuitive graphic user interface—this book vastly reduces the amount of class time you must spend on non-accounting systems matters. The text's step-by-step instructions can reduce your time and drudgery in the computer lab. The time you do spend with students in class or in the computer lab will not be wasted on mundane "click here and then click there" instructing—we have filled this book with detailed instructions and examples to save you that kind of work.

We are convinced that there are at least as many different ways of teaching the accounting systems course as there are professors teaching it. Therefore, this book was designed to be flexible. In a junior- or senior-level course, the book can effectively supplement any accounting information systems text currently on the market. Most of these texts are organized around transaction cycles that are identical or similar to the transaction cycles we use in this book. Adopters of this book's earlier editions have used it successfully with many different accounting information systems texts. Some instructors have used this book as the main course text, supplementing it with readings from the current literature on internal control and systems design issues. Instructors have incorporated the book into their courses in various ways. Some cover all or part of the book in class. Others assign the book as a series of computer lab assignments or as outside reading.

Many accounting systems courses include some type of systems design project. A number of instructors have used earlier editions of this book as an effective springboard for such projects. Students can extend the book's examples or use them as analogs for the real-world systems in their projects. Students will feel better prepared to take on the challenge of a systems design project after they have experienced successes with creating the example accounting systems in this book.

Although we wrote this book with the needs of the undergraduate accounting major systems class in mind, it is flexible enough to be used in other settings. Many community colleges now offer a computer accounting course. This book would serve well as either the main text or a supplement in such a course. Instructors of graduate accounting systems courses may wish to assign this book as a project for those students who lack undergraduate systems course work—or whose undergraduate systems exposure is dated. Instructors of information systems auditing courses at the graduate level have also found the book to be a useful supplement in those courses.

The book includes a number of features that will make your teaching easier:

- A concise introduction to database theory in Chapter 3 that includes thorough discussions of normalization and entity-relationship modeling.
- An exposition of the database approach to accounting systems in Chapter 6 that includes a comparison to double-entry bookkeeping procedures.
- Step-by-step instructions in all chapters that guide the student through each example.
- Numerous figures that show the computer screen at key points in each task and that show finished forms and printed reports.
- A Companion CD-ROM that contains tables, files, queries, forms, reports, and other information to help students complete the exercises and follow along with the examples in the text.

We have taken special care to include "before" and "after" versions of database tables, forms, queries, and reports so that students can use any chapter independently of other chapters. You will find that many of the tables include comprehensive examples of significant size. By including these very large tables, we hope to give students an experience that resembles working with real-world databases.

An Instructor's Manual is available to adopters that includes detailed lecture suggestions for each chapter and solutions to all end-of-chapter questions and exercises. The Instructor's Manual also includes an Instructor's CD-ROM, which contains solutions to all computer exercises in the form of Microsoft Access tables, forms, queries, and reports. The Instructor's CD-ROM also contains the text of the Instructor's Manual, in both Word 7.0 and Adobe PDF formats, to help you create customized lecture notes, transparencies, and presentation software slide shows for classroom use.

ORGANIZATION OF THE BOOK

The text contains ten chapters. The first five chapters introduce the Windows 95 operating system, Microsoft Access, and basic database modeling. The second five chapters show students how to use the database theory and tools from the earlier chapters to build functional accounting system database elements.

Chapter 1 is an overview of Windows 95 and emphasizes fundamental operations such as launching programs, examining object properties, and manipulating windows. This chapter will help students that are computer novices attain sufficient Windows proficiency to use any Windows database management product. Chapter 2 familiarizes the student with the Microsoft Access database management system. All major database elements are discussed including tables, queries, forms, and reports. Chapter 3 presents a brief history of databases; describes the requirements for databases to be in first, second, and third normal forms; and gives students sufficient grounding in database theory to create well-designed, anomaly-free databases. Chapter 4 provides students with hands-on experience in building tables, useful queries, functional forms, and informative reports. Chapter 5 contains instructions for enhancing database systems with form buttons and custom menus. These enhancements do require the student to write macros; however, we provide step-by-step instructions that make this a pleasant exercise. Even the most computer-phobic accounting student should find writing these short code snippets tolerable.

The second five chapters of the book show students how to apply the tools and techniques from the first five chapters to the specific tasks of building accounting system elements. Since most students in the accounting information systems course will already have a solid understanding of double-entry bookkeeping, Chapter 6 describes how database accounting is different and why firms are using database accounting systems. Chapter 6 identifies firms as service, merchandising, or manufacturing and discusses the transaction cycle elements that exist in each type of firm. We use four transaction cycles in this book: revenue, purchase, payroll, and production. We define the revenue cycle to include cash receipts and the purchase cycle to include cash disbursements. Chapter 7 shows students how to track customer information, sales, and cash receipts. In Chapter 8, students get to see the purchase cycle as a mirror image of the revenue cycle. They track vendor information and record purchase orders, receipt of goods ordered, and cash disbursements. Chapter 9 presents students with a fairly simple payroll system example that they can easily extend to accommodate greater levels of complexity. Chapter 10, the production cycle, shows students how to track materials, labor, and overhead costs in a job order cost accumulation system. Chapter 10 also explains how students can extend the job order examples it presents to build process, hybrid, and activity-based cost accounting database systems.

PATHS THROUGH THE BOOK

The chapters need not be assigned in sequence. You can follow several paths through the book. If your students are familiar with Windows 95 and feel comfortable in that operating system environment, you may want to skip Chapter 1 or assign it as review reading. Chapters 2, 3, and 4 should be assigned in order, since Chapter 4 integrates the Chapter 2 introduction to Microsoft Access with the Chapter 3 treatment of database principles. Chapter 5 may be omitted. It includes some advanced database software techniques that students can use to enhance the accounting systems they build. If your students are comfortable with Windows 95—particularly if they have had some spreadsheet macro-writing exposure before this course—you should be able to assign Chapter 5 any time after Chapter 4. None of the later chapters require students to have mastered the material in Chapter 5, so you may wish to cover this material at the end of the course if time permits.

Chapter 6 presents the rationale for using a database approach to accounting systems. You may cover it any time after Chapter 3 and you should use it as an introduction to any of the chapters that follow it. Many instructors will want to cover all four of the transaction cycles, assigning Chapters 7, 8, 9, and 10 in sequence. Some instructors prefer to focus on one or two transaction cycles each semester. Chapter 7, the revenue cycle, and Chapter 8, the purchase cycle, are ideal candidates for such a focus. You can go directly to Chapter 8 from Chapter 6 if you wish. Chapters 9 and 10 are independent of each other and of Chapter 6, but students will find these chapters easier if they have first worked through Chapter 8. Although Chapter 10 includes a brief introduction to cost accounting concepts, most students will find the material in this chapter to be somewhat difficult if they have not already had a cost accounting course.

ABOUT THE AUTHORS

James Perry is a Professor of Management Information Systems at the University of San Diego School of Business. He is the co-author of nineteen textbooks and trade books and over a dozen articles on computer security, database management systems, multimedia delivery systems, and chief programmer teams. Jim is a charter member of the Association for Information Systems and a member of the Association for Computing Machinery. He holds a Ph.D. in computer science from the Pennsylvania State University and a Bachelor of Science in mathematics from Purdue University. Jim has worked as a computer security consultant to various private and governmental organizations including the Jet Propulsion Laboratory. He was a consultant on the Strategic Defense Initiative ("Star Wars") project and served as a member of the computer security oversight committee.

Gary Schneider is an Associate Professor of Accounting and Information Systems at the University of San Diego School of Business. He has written widely on accounting and systems topics. Gary's work has appeared in a number of journals including the *IS Audit & Control Journal* and the *Journal of Information Systems*. He is active in the American Accounting Association and currently serves as editor of its *Accounting Information Systems and Technology Reporter*. Gary holds a Ph.D. in accounting from the University of Tennessee, an MBA in accounting from Xavier University, and a BA in economics from the University of Cincinnati. He is a CPA and practiced public accounting in Ohio for fourteen years before undertaking his academic career.

ACKNOWLEDGMENTS

Creating a successful book is always a collaborative effort between authors and publisher. We work as a team to provide the best book possible. We want to thank the following reviewers for the insightful comments and suggestions they gave us on this and the previous edition: A. Faye Borthick, Georgia State University; Severin Grabski, Michigan State University; Mary R. Scott, Grambling State University; Jerry D. Siebel, University of South Florida. Various versions of the book's manuscript were used by students in accounting information systems classes at the University of San Diego and at Georgia State University. We appreciate the many helpful suggestions these students provided. In particular, we want to thank former students Pamela S. Drotman, for her excellent technical editing assistance on the text and accompanying digital media, Steven French, for his terrific job in generating much of the data that was incorporated into the databases, and Christa O'Neill, for producing many excellent digital movies for the Instructor's CD-ROM.

The authors especially want to acknowledge the work of the seasoned professionals at South-Western College Publishing. We thank David L. Shaut, our acquisitions editor, for his initial interest in and continual support of this project. Dave recognized an emerging need for this kind of book before any other publisher. We extend special thanks to Richard K. Lindgren, Jason Fisher, and the other members of the Accounting Team at South-Western. We appreciate the care and attention to detail with which everyone at South-Western handled the development and production of this book. We especially appreciate the efforts of Martha Stansbury, our South-Western sales representative, who enthusiastically encouraged and supported our proposal for the first edition of this book. We remain convinced that Martha is one of the best sales representatives in the business.

Finally, we want to express deep appreciation to our spouses, Nancy Perry and Cathy Cosby, for their remarkable patience as we worked both ends of the clock to complete this edition of the book on a very tight schedule. We also thank our children for tolerating our absences from their lives while we were consumed with the writing of this book.

If you would like to contact us about the book, we would enjoy hearing from you. We welcome comments and suggestions that we might incorporate into future editions of the book. You can send book-related messages to us on the Internet at **debit@acusd.edu**. For the latest information about *Building Accounting Systems* and related resources, please visit our web site at **http://www.swcollege.com/perry.html**

TRADEMARK LIST

The following trademarks and registered trademarks appear in this book:

1. Microsoft, Windows, Access, Word, Excel, Exchange, Internet Explorer, FoxPro, Paint, Office, and The Microsoft Network are registered trademarks of Microsoft Corporation. Any reference to Microsoft Windows, Access, Word, Excel, Exchange, Internet Explorer, FoxPro, Paint, Office, or The Microsoft Network refers to this note.
2. Paradox and dBASE are registered trademarks of Borland International, Inc. Any reference to Paradox or dBASE refers to this note.
3. Adobe is a registered trademark of Adobe Systems Incorporated. Any reference to Adobe refers to this note.

CONTENTS

1 Working with Windows

Objectives

This chapter presents an overview of the Microsoft Windows environment available on millions of microcomputers around the world. For those unfamiliar with Windows, you will learn the skills essential for working with it. Those familiar with Windows will probably discover some new techniques while reading this chapter. Several key Windows features are presented. In particular, you will learn how to:

- Log on to Windows.
- Understand what objects are found on the desktop.
- Open, close, maximize, and minimize windows.
- Launch an application using the Start button.
- Use a dialog box.
- Exit an application.
- Use Explorer to manage files and programs, and to launch a program.
- Create folders in Explorer.
- Get help on the current application.
- Launch multiple applications and switch between them.
- Pass data between Windows programs.
- Create and use desktop shortcuts.
- Modify the Start menu.
- Relocate the Taskbar.
- Restart Windows and log on as a different user.
- Exit Windows.

An Overview of Windows

Windows 95, like the previous versions of Windows, provides a convenient work surface from which you can run applications, manage files, and run your business. You no longer have to execute an arcane set of commands from the DOS (Disk Operating System) command prompt to accomplish the work at hand. By simply clicking on the Start button and selecting a program, you can launch Microsoft Word, Microsoft Access, or any of the large number of Windows programs available. Windows provides several other benefits that make using a computer and its programs much easier than before. One significant advantage of using Windows is that you can be running more than one program at the same time. For instance, you could be writing a memo to your sales manager using your favorite word processing program, Word. When you are ready to summarize last month's sales figures, you can quickly switch to Excel, your tried and true spreadsheet program, to review the sales figures found in last quarter's spreadsheet. Switching between applications is as easy as clicking a button.

Another advantage of Windows is that data can be transferred easily between Windows programs. Suppose you want to mail letters to customers in a particular state—Washington, for example—informing them about a special, limited time product promotion. You ask your administrative assistant to create Word documents for each customer in Washington containing details about the promotion. This might be a daunting task if your assistant actually typed each letter. However, he knows that Word can use Windows tools to retrieve information from an Access database containing your customers' names and addresses. Word and Microsoft Access work seamlessly together to deliver database information to Word documents on demand. With Windows, Word, and Access, it is a simple job to create a form letter for each customer as well as mailing labels. Figure 1.1 shows an example of a Word document (upper left), a sheet of mailing labels (Avery 5160 labels), and the underlying Access database (lower right) that dynamically supplies customer addresses to both forms. This is an example of Windows information sharing between applications employing Dynamic Data Exchange (DDE).

Another way that applications can share information is called Object Linking and Embedding, or OLE. Slightly newer than DDE, OLE actually embeds a *copy* of the data into another document. For instance, you could place a copy of the customer database, or a subset of it, into a Word document. In this example, the Word document is the *container* and the Access database, supplying the database information to the document, is known as the *server*. (You will see this container/server relationship illustrated throughout this text.)

Because of its ease of use and the advantages mentioned, Windows is a well established standard among PC users. In the sections that follow, you will learn the most important features of Windows—those skills and techniques essential to thrive in today's business world.

Starting Windows

Windows 95 automatically executes after your computer is turned on and has successfully completed some hardware tests. You will first see some introductory screens, and then the Windows desktop will appear. Depending on how you have set up Windows, you may be asked to type a user name and password. If asked

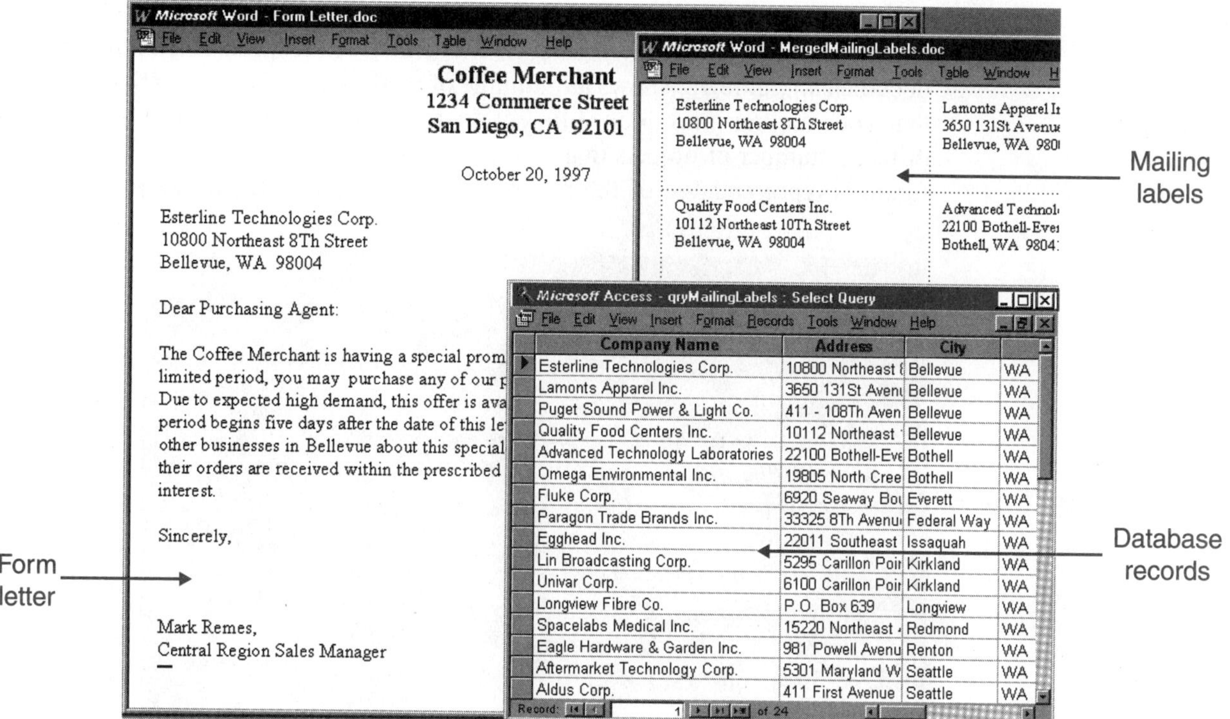

Figure 1.1 Linking database information to Word documents.

to do so, follow the steps outlined in the following section, *Logging On to Windows*.

Logging On to Windows

If your computer is in a school or corporation, you may be required to log on to Windows. After starting Windows, you will see the Windows logo on the screen followed by a dialog box requesting that you enter your user name and password in order to gain access to the computer. You may simply enter your last name and a password assigned by your instructor or supervisor. Check with your instructor or the lab supervisor. The actual process of logging on is simple once you know your user name and password. Type your user name and press Tab to place the cursor in the Password text box. Enter your password and press Enter to complete the Windows log-on process. Within a few moments the Windows desktop is displayed.

What's on the Desktop

Windows uses the *desktop* metaphor whereby the computer screen simulates one's desktop upon which rest icons and other objects. Everything on the desktop is an *object*, meaning it is a thing having properties or characteristics. Examples of objects on the desktop include My Computer, Network Neighborhood, My Briefcase, and so on. You can even add *shortcuts* to programs, printers, and documents. Figure 1.2 shows an example of a Windows 95 desktop. Keep in mind that your desktop may look different from the figure because it may contain a different number of objects that can be arranged in different ways. However, our figure is representative of the major elements found on the desktop.

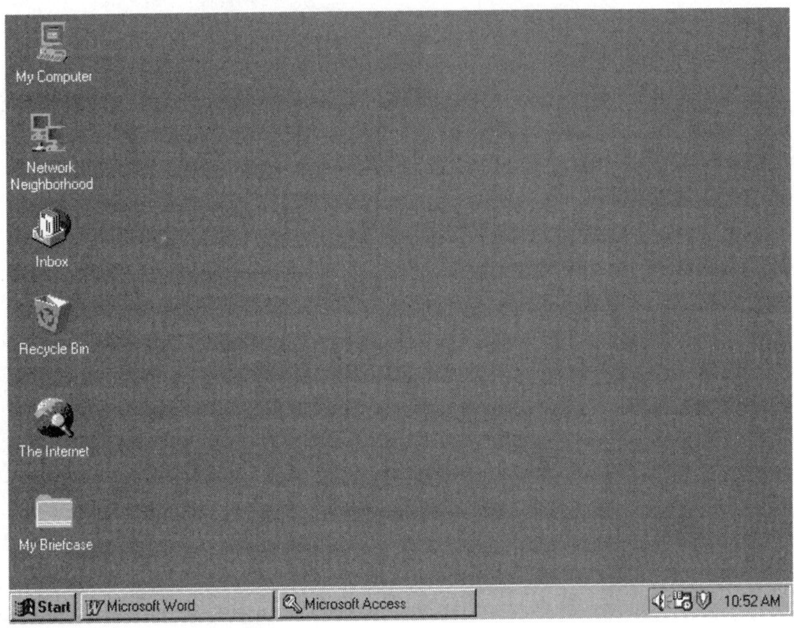

Figure 1.2 Windows 95 desktop.

The My Computer icon is the entrance to all the disk drives and files on your computer. Through My Computer you can examine the floppy disk drive, hard drives, CD-ROM drives, and the system configuration.

Inbox is the icon that represents Microsoft's Exchange program. It may or may not be on your desktop. You use Inbox to send and receive electronic mail. Exchange can be set up to work with either a direct connection or a dial-up network.

Recycle bin holds files and folders that have been deleted. Anything in the Recycle bin can either be recovered or removed permanently. Once objects have been removed, they cannot be restored.

The Internet icon provides a convenient way to access the World Wide Web (WWW) using Microsoft's full-featured Internet Explorer. Navigating the WWW couldn't be simpler, because WWW uses a page metaphor to display information.

The My Briefcase icon provides a way to keep various copies of your files synchronized and up to date whether you are working on the road, at home, or in the office. When you are finished working on a file on your portable computer, for instance, you can use Briefcase to update the file on your main computer when you get back to the office. Files are automatically and nearly effortlessly maintained so that you needn't worry about which file is the latest version and which file should be deleted.

The *Taskbar* is the gray area that normally rests on the bottom of your screen. (You can move the Taskbar to the top or sides of the screen if you wish, and you can even hide it until it is needed.) Windows 95's Taskbar contains the Start button (see Figure 1.2), which you can use to quickly find a file or start a program; buttons representing programs that are currently running; and the task tray. Two programs are currently running, and the buttons on the Taskbar indicate their names: Microsoft Word and Microsoft Access. The *task tray* contains small icons representing programs that are always in memory. For example, the task tray shown in Figure 1.2 shows three icons representing programs to control your speakers' volume, a program to schedule regularly run system tasks, and a virus protection program. At the far right in the task tray is the clock.

Using the Mouse

Before we examine Windows further, it is important to understand how to use the essential pointing device, the mouse. Although you can use Windows without a mouse, it is considerably more difficult. Five terms, describing different ways to use the mouse, occur throughout this text: *point*, *click*, *right-click*, *double-click*, and *drag*.

When we ask you to "point to Programs" or "point to Find in the Start menu," we simply mean you should move the mouse pointer so that its tip is directly over the desired object on the screen. Pointing in Windows 95 frequently opens displays, menus, or submenus.

When you are instructed to "click the mouse" or "click," press and release the left mouse button. If you are to "click on the ... button" shown onscreen, move the mouse pointer to that element and then press and quickly release the left mouse button once. Select an item onscreen by moving the mouse pointer (the arrowhead) to the item and clicking once with the left mouse button. After you select an item, you can perform various activities. For example, you can move an icon from one place on your desktop to another after you have selected it.

The action of right-clicking is similar to clicking except that you use the right mouse button. For example, if you wanted to learn about a desktop icon's properties, you would first right-click the icon to display a shortcut menu.

Frequently, we will ask you to *double-click* some object on the Windows work surface. When you double-click an icon representing a program, that program is activated. To double-click, quickly click the left mouse button twice. If you don't click rapidly enough, you will simply select the object twice, not activate it.

Another way to use the mouse is to *drag* an object. In a word processing program, for example, you might want to move a sentence from one place to another. You can do this by dragging it. To drag any object, select the object (click it), press and hold down the left mouse button and move the mouse. It takes a little practice, but you will master it quickly. Dragging is useful in several circumstances. For instance, you can enlarge a window by dragging its border or corner. You can also reduce or enlarge a Windows help frame by dragging a border toward or away from the opposite border.

BECOMING MORE FAMILIAR WITH WINDOWS

Most windows contain the same elements. The window that opens when you double-click My Computer is typical (see Figure 1.3). Each window has a frame or border, which defines the outer edges of the window. The My Computer window shown can be sized—that is, the window can be stretched or shrunk by dragging any edge. In the lower right corner is the *size grip*, which is a special handle to make obvious to the user how to resize a window. Along the window's top is a *Title bar* containing the name of the application, current topic, or current document (the current application, My Computer, is displayed in this case). When a window is active, its Title bar is a darker color than the Title bars of other windows.

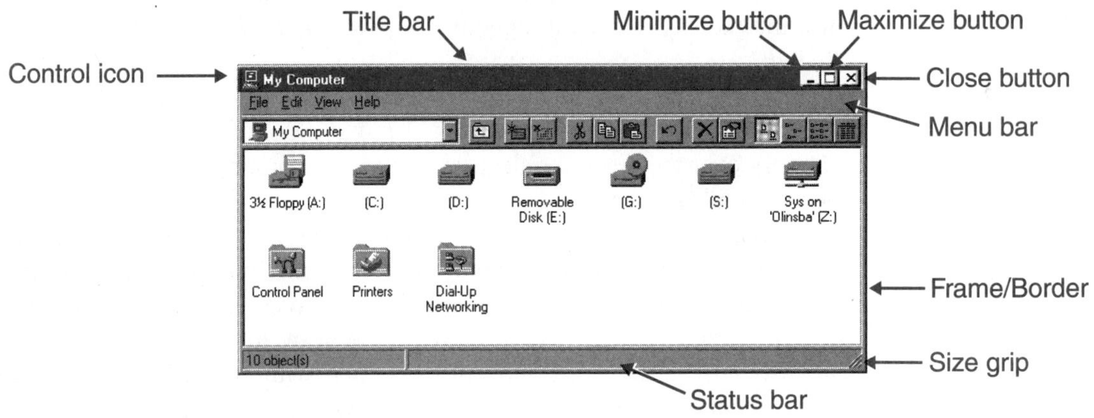

Figure 1.3 Components of a window.

Anatomy of a Window

On the extreme left of the Title bar is a *control icon*, which can be opened to manipulate the window with the keyboard. You can close a window by double-clicking its control icon, though you will find it far easier to use the mouse for most actions. Three window buttons appear on the right end of each window's title bar. These are called the Minimize, Maximize/Restore, and Close buttons. You click the *Minimize* button (the button that looks like a dash) to remove the window from view (the program remains running). If the window does not fill the screen, like ours in Figure 1.3, then the middle button, called the *Maximize* button, causes the window to fill the screen when the button is clicked. If the window is already maximized, then the middle button looks like two overlapping windows and is called the *Restore* button. When you click Restore, the window is reduced to less than full screen. You use the *Close* button in the upper right corner of a window to close the window with one click. If the window represents a program, rather than a group, then clicking the Close button terminates execution of the application.

Below the Title bar is the Menu bar. Clicking any of the menu items displays a pull-down menu, which contains commands that you can select. If you click the Control Panel's Edit menu, for instance, you will see the pull-down menu shown in Figure 1.4. A list of commands is associated with each menu of any Windows program. When you select a menu, its pull-down menu is displayed. You can select a menu either by clicking it with the mouse or by pressing the Alt key and the letter underlined in the menu name. For example, notice that the letter E in the Edit menu (see Figure 1.4) is underlined. Pressing Alt and E simultaneously displays the Edit menu. Throughout the text, we use a standard notation to indicate keys that are pressed simultaneously. For example, Alt+E connotes pressing and holding the Alt key and pressing and releasing the letter E to invoke the Edit menu. The key that follows Alt varies depending on the menu to be selected.

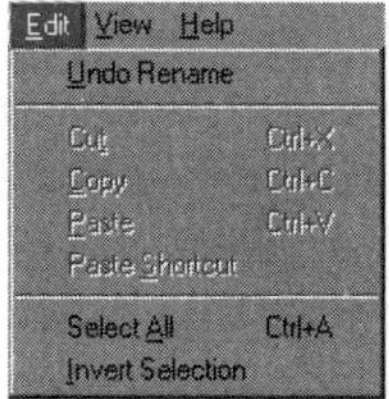

Figure 1.4 A typical Windows pull-down menu.

When you want to execute one of the commands in a pull-down menu, simply point to it. The selection bar highlights the command that the mouse points to. To execute a highlighted command, simply click the mouse. Alternately, you can use the arrow keys to move up and down the pull-down list of commands. You can press Enter to execute the highlighted command. A third way to invoke a command is to press the underlined letter corresponding to the desired command. Press the letter *a* to execute the Edit menu Select All command, for example. Some commands are inapplicable in certain situations. Whenever a command cannot be selected from a menu, it is *dimmed* (light gray). The Cut, Copy, and Paste commands are dimmed in Figure 1.4, for instance. All other commands are bold (for example, Select All).

Along the window's bottom edge is the Status bar. The Status bar displays useful information about the window such as the number of objects it holds or a description of a command you have selected when the window contains a running application.

When there is more information than can be displayed in the window, *scroll bars* automatically appear on the right and bottom window edges. By sliding the scroll boxes or using the scroll arrows, you can pan the window up, down, left, or right to see otherwise hidden parts of the object within the window.

Manipulating Windows

Like many to follow, this section actively involves you in learning several Windows features. You will manipulate program and document windows in several ways, including moving and sizing them. To help you learn and reinforce these Windows skills, we ask you to follow up your reading and actually practice each task being described. There are two types of activities in which you can participate as you read: *try it* tasks and *exercises*. Try it tasks are smaller, more easily accomplished computer activities that take only a few moments to complete. For example, a try it task might be to minimize, maximize, and restore a window; or it might be a description of how to switch between Microsoft Access to Windows Explorer using the Taskbar. We use the words ***Try it*** to mark a paragraph describing these types of activities. If the task comprises several steps, the individual steps are not numbered. *Exercises* are more comprehensive activities that are central to some ongoing and important process or project that is being described in a chapter. Exercises typically consist of two or more numbered steps whose completion help you achieve some important goal. An example of an exercise is the series of steps that illustrate how to launch several Windows applications, open document windows in each application, and copy information between open windows. Such an exercise strongly reinforces how to implement information sharing between, for example, Access and Word—an essential task in business.

Try it

Let's learn a little about the computer you're using. Double-click the My Computer icon (see Figure 1.2). What happens if you click a desktop icon only once? You simply select the icon. To activate it, double-click. The My Computer window will open, displaying icons representing hardware on your computer and your network similar to Figure 1.3. Maximize the My Computer window. Right-click the icon representing drive C. The *shortcut menu* is displayed. Locate Properties in the menu (near the bottom of the list) and click it. A tabbed dialog box is displayed, which shows the properties of the selected object. Click the General tab, if necessary, to go to the page containing a pie graph. It illustrates how much space is either occupied or available on drive C. After you have had a chance to examine the display, click the question mark button—called *What's This?* Notice that the mouse pointer changes to an arrow with a question mark attached to its right side. After clicking What's This?, you can move to any object and click it to obtain context-sensitive help. Move the mouse pointer down to the pie graph and click it. A brief explanation of the clicked object (the chart in this case) is displayed (see Figure 1.5). Click the help box to make it disappear. Finally, click the Close window button to close the dialog box. Click the Close button on My Computer to close it. The desktop reappears.

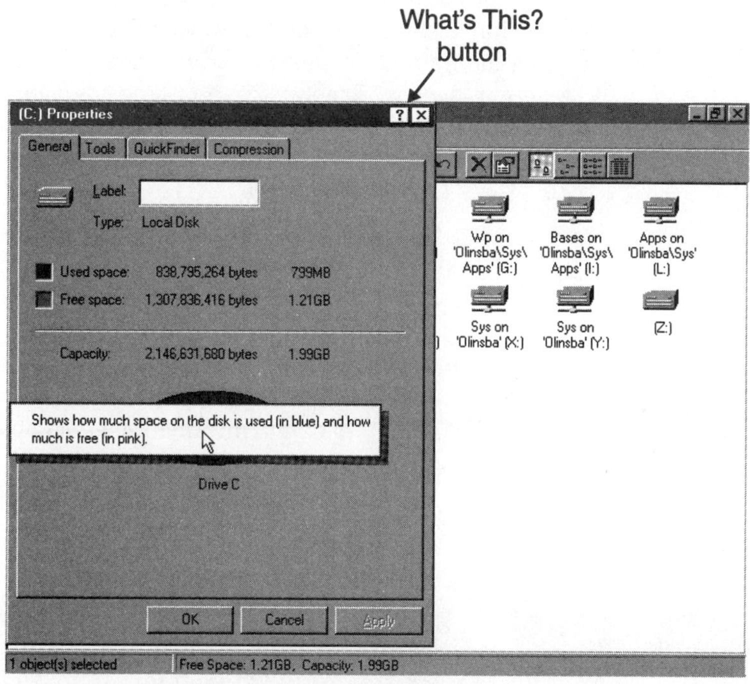

Figure 1.5 Obtaining help with the What's This? button.

Moving windows about the desktop, changing their size, and closing them is intuitive in Windows 95. We'll direct you through some fundamental window manipulation activities next.

Try it

Open the My Computer window again (double-click its desktop icon). Maximize the window, if necessary, so that it fills the screen (click the Maximize button, which looks like a small rectangle). Restore the window so it occupies only part of the work surface by clicking the Restore button (the icon that looks like two overlapping windows or rectangles located in the top right corner of the window). Make the window virtually disappear by pressing the Minimize button (the button in the top right corner of the My Computer window that contains a narrow line or dash). Where did the My Computer window go? The window disappears but its *Taskbar button* remains. When a program is minimized, a button representing it is placed on the Taskbar. By clicking the corresponding Taskbar button, you can switch from one program to another. Restore the My Computer window by clicking the Taskbar button labeled My Computer. You can change the size of a window that is not maximized. Click and drag the My Computer window's size grip away from its opposite corner to increase the window's size. Similarly, drag the size grip towards its opposite corner to reduce the window's size. There are an infinite number of window sizes you can create this way. Moving a window to a different part of the screen is also easy. Simply click and drag the window's Title bar to move the window anywhere you want. Move the My Computer window to the top left of your screen. Then, move it so it is approximately in the center of your screen. Finally, Close the My Computer window.

Getting Help

Help is available in all Windows programs in a variety of ways. Context-sensitive help provides help for almost every object on the screen. You have already used the What's This? help to obtain information about an object on the screen. *Tooltips* are another form of context-sensitive help. Tooltips are small pop-up windows that appear when you move the mouse over an object and pause it briefly. See for yourself.

Try it

Move the mouse pointer over the Start button, which is located at the left end of the Taskbar. After a second or two, a tooltip appears indicating you should "Click here to begin." Likewise, you can see the date if you move the mouse pointer to the time display located in the task tray.

Windows programs supply explicit help through a Help menu. Extensive help is available on the computer. The Windows Help system provides search features, as well as contents and indexing capabilities. An excellent way to see Help in action is to try it yourself. Windows help, available from the Start button (you will learn more about the Start button in the next section) is an excellent choice. Read the following exercise and then perform the steps.

Exercise 1.1: Getting Detailed Help

1. Click the Start button (the Start button is explained fully in the next section). The *Start menu* is displayed.
2. Choose the Help menu item on the Start menu (click it).
3. The Help Topics dialog box opens.
4. Select the Index tab.
5. Type the word ***formatting*** into the text box because we want help on formatting disks. The topic formatting is highlighted. Just below that group topic is a subtopic, disks.
6. Choose the entry *disks* immediately below *formatting* (see Figure 1.6).
7. Click the Display button to view detailed help about formatting disks. A pop-up help box describing how to format a disk is displayed.
8. Click the Close button after reading the help information. That will close and remove the pop-up box.

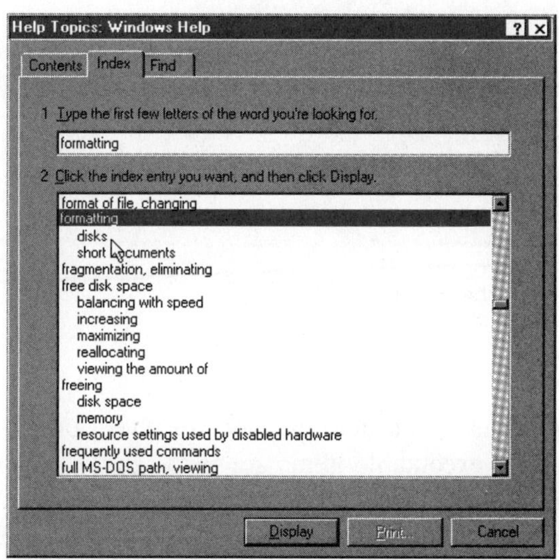

Figure 1.6 Locating help on formatting disks.

THE START MENU

The Start button, located on the left end of the Taskbar, provides the major access point for programs, documents, and other objects. The Start menu is displayed when you click the Start button, and it is a cascading menu. That is, its submenus cascade—logically flow from—the main menu items.

Opening the Start Menu

Opening the Start menu is easy. Simply click the Start button to display its menu items (see Figure 1.7). Standard menu items found on the Start menu are Programs, Documents, Settings, Find, Help, Run, and Shut Down. Some of the menu items have right arrows. These arrows indicate that the menu item leads to a submenu, which opens when you merely point to the menu item by moving the mouse over the item and pausing briefly.

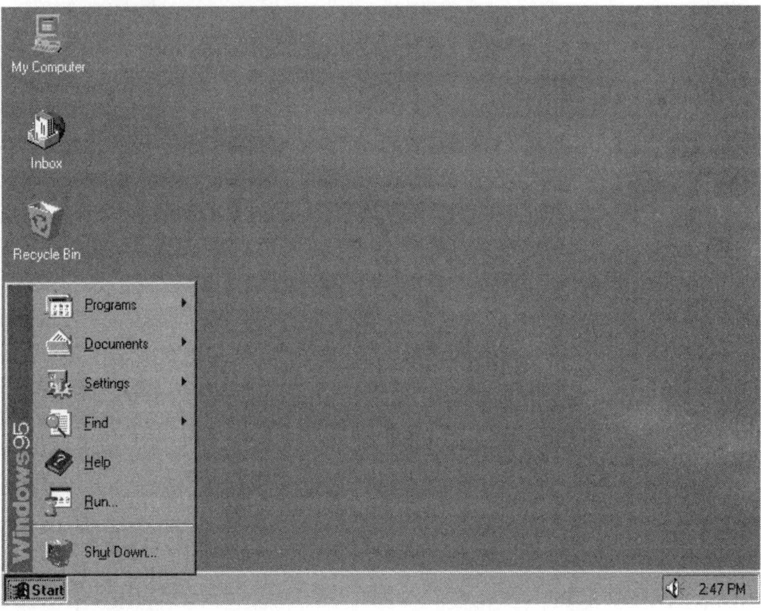

Figure 1.7 The Start menu.

The Programs Menu Item

The Programs menu item cascades to reveal program items and program group items. Only executable items are found in the program menu, not data or other non-executable objects. Program items include the MS-DOS prompt as well as Windows Explorer and other application programs. Program group items such as Accessories, Office 95, and StartUp are akin to Windows 3.1 groups that contain icons corresponding to programs. When you point to a group item, further entries are revealed. For example, Accessories is a group item that contains the usual collection of standard Windows 95 groups and programs (see Figure 1.8). You simply point to Accessories and then select a program or group item from the cascaded menu. If you have installed Windows 95 over an existing Windows 3.1 system, you will see familiar group names on the Programs menu. You can close each of the cascading menus in turn by selecting a menu item from a previous menu. Similarly, you can close all menus except the Start menu by moving the mouse pointer to one of the Start menu items that doesn't cascade such as Run or Help.

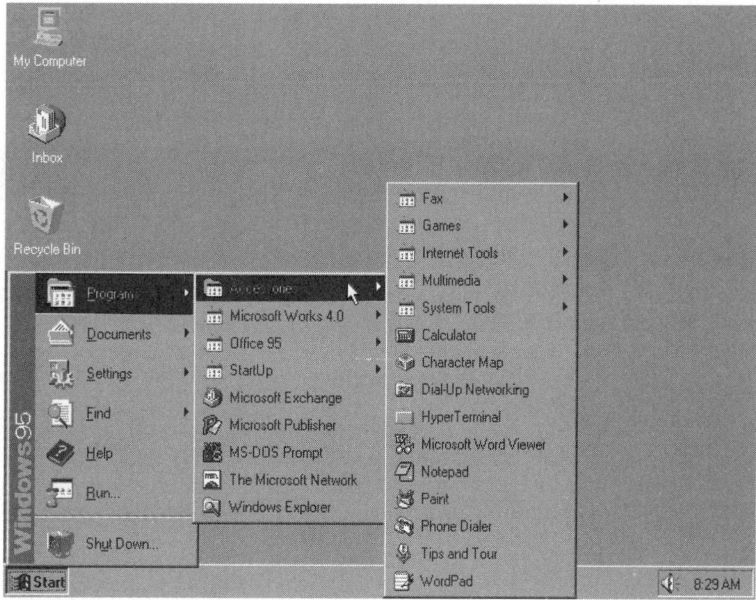

Figure 1.8 Displaying submenus of the Start menu.

Like previous versions of Windows, Windows 95 provides keyboard alternatives to the mouse. For instance, you can press Ctrl+Esc to open the Start menu. Once open, the Start menu items can be selected by using the arrow keys. The up and down arrow keys move up and down an open menu, and the right and left arrow keys move to a cascading menu or the previous menu, respectively. Press the Alt key to close all open menus.

Try it

Point to the WordPad program (but don't run it). Open the Start menu and move the mouse pointer to Programs. Pause and the cascade menu opens. Next, move to the right and point to Accessories. Move the mouse pointer down the menu items to WordPad. Finally, close all menus.

The Documents Menu Item

The Documents menu item displays a list of the 15 objects you have most recently used. If you worked on an Access database named *accounts payable.mdb* and then opened Microsoft Word to write a letter you later saved as *New customer accounts welcome.doc*, then those two document names would appear in the Documents menu item list. The Documents menu facilitates returning quickly and easily to the items you have recently been working on. For example, you return to your computer after a day's absence, start Windows, click the Start menu button, point to Documents, and then select the document you want to work on. (In this context, the word *document* refers to a variety of objects, including a word processing document, a spreadsheet, a database, or a graphic image.) This reinforces the notion prevalent in Windows 95 that you focus on the object that you want to work on, rather than worrying about which program or tool is required to load and manipulate the document—the document "knows" what program is needed to operate on it. This is called *document centric* and is orthogonal to the older Windows 3.1 notion of *tool centric* in which one first located the program needed to view or change a document and then loaded the document once the program was operational.

Try it

See what documents have been used recently on the computer you are using. Click Start and point to Documents. The cascade menu will reveal the document names or *empty* if the list has been erased. (You will learn how to erase the Documents list later.)

The Settings Menu Item

The Settings menu item allows you to change global Windows settings and options. It contains three menu items: Control Panel, Printers, and Taskbar. Control Panel contains icons representing a large number of system settings you can change and actions you can take. For example, you can add or remove programs from the Control Panel group, change your monitor's display characteristics, or alter the date and time. Control Panel contains programs similar to those found in the Control Panel of the Main group in Windows 3.1. Clicking the Printers item takes you to a group that adds, deletes, or modifies printers available to your system. Taskbar allows you to modify the structure and contents of the Start menu and provides a way to change selected properties of the Taskbar. You could choose to hide the Taskbar or hide the clock, which is customarily displayed in the task tray on the right end of the Taskbar.

The Find Menu Item

Having a document-centric system like Windows 95 is a great improvement over previous versions of Windows; however, it is not useful if you cannot locate the document you want to work on. That's when the Find menu item goes to work. You can use Find to locate files or folders on any disk drive, including floppy drives. In addition, you can find files or folders on any computer on any network to which your computer is attached. If you have opted to use Microsoft Network, you can locate files on that on-line service as well. If you cannot find a file on your hard disk, you can invoke the Find menu item to search through every file on your hard drive.

Try it

See if you can find where the Windows file called *msaccess* is located. Search for it. Click the Start menu, point to Find, and choose Files or Folders. When the Find All Files dialog box is displayed, type ***msaccess*** in the Named text box and ensure that the Look in text box indicates drive C and that the Include subfolders check box is checked. Then, click the Find Now button. Windows begins searching the hard drive for any files or folders that begin with *msaccess*. Shortly, several files are displayed in the search results window. After you have reviewed the names, click the dialog box's Close button.

The Help Menu Item

The Help menu item, which you have used earlier, provides systemwide help at the click of a button. Select Help whenever you want to find more information on a Windows topic. Product-specific help is best obtained through the Help menu of the product itself, because software product manufacturers supply rich help content along with their programs. If you want help on Microsoft Access, it is best to seek help from the Help menu within Access. Help on creating Windows shortcuts—a topic that is common across applications—can be found by using the Start menu Help menu item.

The Run Menu Item

The Run menu item provides a way to run a program easily by simply typing the program's name and pressing Enter. Usually, Run is used to launch infrequently used programs that might not be represented on the Start menu or its submenus. When you want to launch a program from the Run menu item, click Start, choose Run, and enter the program's name including the full path in the Open text box. If you don't know the program's exact location on the disk, you can choose the Browse button and search through folders until you locate it. Or, you can use Find to locate the program. If you use the latter method, then you can double-click the program within the search results list to execute it. The Run menu item serves the same function as the Windows 3.1 Program Manager's File Run command. If you find yourself using the Run command frequently for a particular program, consider placing the program in the Programs menu item or placing on the desktop a *shortcut* to the program (we will show you how to do that later in this chapter).

The Shut Down Menu Item

It is incorrect to simply turn off your computer when you are finished using Windows. In fact, Windows requires you to follow a simple procedure to shut down your computer. Doing so protects files and other data from being corrupted or saved improperly. In short, never turn off your computer while Windows is running! The Shut Down menu item provides a one-step Windows exit procedure. To shut down Windows prior to system power off, choose the Start menu and click Shut Down. A dialog box containing four options is displayed (see Figure 1.9). Choose the first option, "Shut down the computer," if you want to turn off your computer for an extended period (more that a few hours). If you want to restart (also known as rebooting your computer), then the "Restart the computer?" option is available. Choosing the "Restart the computer in MS-DOS mode?" option exits Windows and leaves you at the DOS prompt. The last option is "Close all programs and log on as a different user." This option allows you to customize the desktop for various users and save each user's custom version of Windows under a user name. Then, by selecting this option, you can restart Windows, log on as a different user, and see a unique Windows 95 interface.

Use caution. If you are using a computer in a laboratory of several computers, you probably should not shut down the computer. Always check with your instructor or an available lab assistant before selecting the shut down option. If you merely want to restore the computer desktop to its original state before leaving the lab, then select the option "Restart the computer."

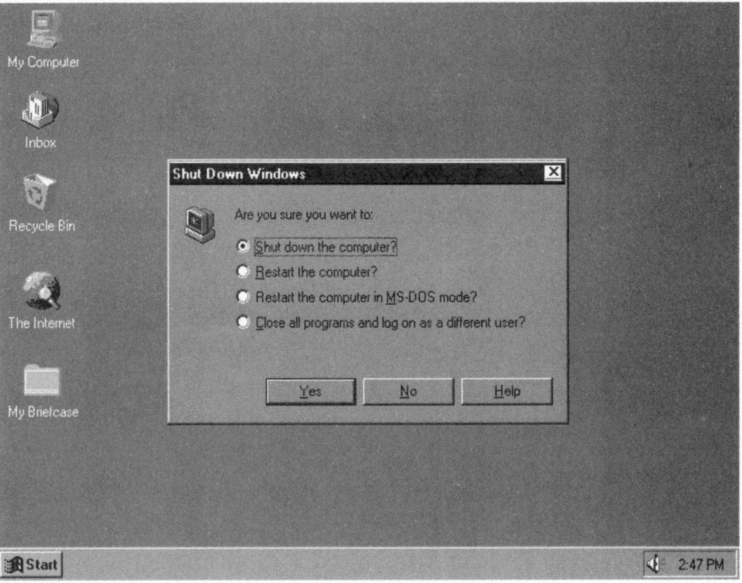

Figure 1.9 The Shut Down Windows dialog box.

WORKING WITH PROGRAMS AND DATA

WordPad is a word processor that comes with Windows 95. We will describe and use WordPad to help illustrate several mouse and keyboard techniques that can be used in other Windows products. (The term *Windows products* is used to differentiate between products designed specifically to run under Windows as opposed to programs that are designed for older, DOS-based systems.) Methods used here can be duplicated with, for example, Microsoft Access—the Windows relational database system featured in this text.

Perhaps the best way to get better acquainted with the Windows environment is to go through a complete cycle: launching a program, opening a document, altering some of the document's text, and printing the final result. We show you that process in the paragraphs that follow. WordPad, a close relative of the full-featured Microsoft Word, is featured here.

Launching Applications Directly

The following exercise guides you through the process of executing (sometimes called *launching*) the WordPad program. Subsequent exercises continue the cycle to its conclusion—a finished letter ready for mailing.

EXERCISE 1.2: LAUNCHING AN APPLICATION

1. Click the Start button.
2. Point to Programs in the Start menu.
3. Point to Accessories in the menu that cascades from Programs.
4. Locate the WordPad menu item and click it once. If necessary, maximize the WordPad window.

Next, you will use a menu to open a document and then make a change to it. Doing this gives you practice using a typical Windows application menu. To read a document from a disk or CD-ROM into the WordPad window, you *open* a document. Open is a command found in the File menu of almost any Windows application.

First, let's discuss a few disk-naming conventions we will use throughout the text. The exact names of your internal hard disk, floppy disk(s), and CD-ROM drives vary depending on the configuration of your computer. So, we adopt the following disk names to keep things simple and consistent. We refer to your floppy drive as drive A, though it could be drive A or B. We assume you have at least one hard drive, which we refer to as drive C (though you may have more than one). Finally, drive D refers to the CD-ROM drive. So simply remember: Drive A—floppy, drive C—hard disk, drive D—CD-ROM.

To prepare for the next exercise, place the Companion CD-ROM, which came with your text, into the CD-ROM drive D. If your CD-ROM drive is E, for example, simply substitute E whenever we refer to drive D.

Exercise 1.3: Opening a Document

1. Click the File menu to display its menu items. Note that you can also press Alt+F to pull down the file menu.
2. Next, select the Open command: click Open or move to Open with the arrow keys, then press Enter.

   The Open dialog box appears (see Figure 1.10). Dialog boxes require you to supply additional information, and, occasionally, make decisions by clicking various check boxes, option buttons, and other objects within the dialog box.

   A list of file names (if any) found on one of the available disk drives is displayed in the File Name list box. Notice, however, that only files with .doc extensions are displayed. Those files are stored in a form compatible with both WordPad and Word.
3. Click the arrow on the Look in drop-down list box and select the CD-ROM drive (drive D or E). A list of ten folders called Ch01 through Ch10 appear.
4. Double-click the Ch01 folder to open it.
5. Open the file *FallWashPromotion.doc* by double-clicking it. The *FallWashPromotion.doc* document is placed into the WordPad document window.

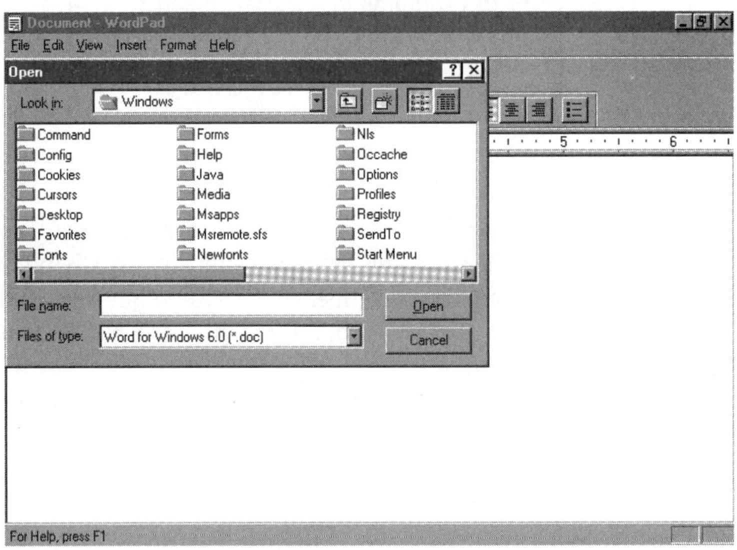

Figure 1.10 Open dialog box.

The document you see in WordPad is a letter to selected customers of The Coffee Merchant. It will be mailed to customers in the Washington state area promoting, as you can see, a special sale for a limited time. Later in this chapter you will use a slightly modified version of this letter to merge customer data—address information—directly into this letter to personalize it and make it ready for mailing. The letter now displayed in WordPad is used to illustrate a few typical Windows operations and WordPad procedures.

WordPad's Edit menu commands are similar to those found in other Windows products such as Excel or Word. With the *FallWashPromotion.doc* document still visible, let's locate and replace the two placeholder phrases *company-city* and *company-state* with an actual customer's city and state. There's no need to replace the other placeholder tags that you see in the inside address right now. We just want you to briefly experience a typical replace operation.

EXERCISE 1.4: SEARCH AND REPLACE

1. Select the Edit menu (click Edit or press Alt+E).
2. Select the Replace command (notice the shortcut key combination Ctrl+H invokes replace without first selecting the Edit menu).

   The *insertion point*, a blinking vertical bar, is in the leftmost position in the Find what text box. The insertion point indicates where typed characters will appear.
3. In the Find what text box of the Find dialog box type ***company-city*** and press Tab to move to the Replace with text box. (The characters in the Find what text box are often called the *search string*.)
4. In the Replace with text box enter the replacement string—those characters that replace any or all occurrences of the search string, company-city. Enter ***Seattle*** in the Replace with text box.

   Because the search string is long enough to be unique, there's no need to check either of the check boxes (Match whole word only or Match case). Figure 1.11 shows the completed Replace dialog box.
5. Click the Replace All button to replace all occurrences of company-city with Seattle.
6. Click OK when the search ends.
7. Repeat steps 3 through 6, replacing company-state (step 3) with Washington (step 4).
8. Click the Close button to return to the document.

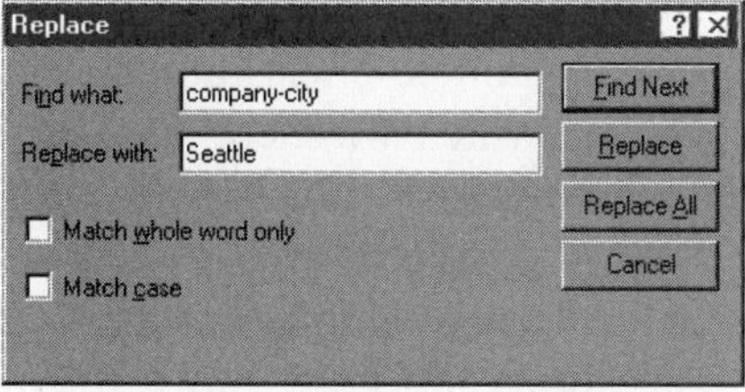

Figure 1.11 Replace dialog box.

The last exercise in this series illustrates how to print a document. The techniques shown are nearly identical for most Windows products. The Print command is normally found in the File menu.

Exercise 1.5: Printing Pages and Exiting

1. Click the File menu to display its commands.
2. Choose Print (click the Print command). The Print dialog box will be displayed.
3. Click the Pages option button found on the left side of the dialog box. The bullet to the left of *Pages* is darkened, marking it as the current choice among the three Print Range *option buttons* (also known as *radio buttons* because selecting one button clears another—much as an automobile's radio buttons do).
4. Because we want to print page 1 only, type ***1***, press Tab, and type ***1*** again. This constrains the output to page 1. The completed dialog box is shown in Figure 1.12.

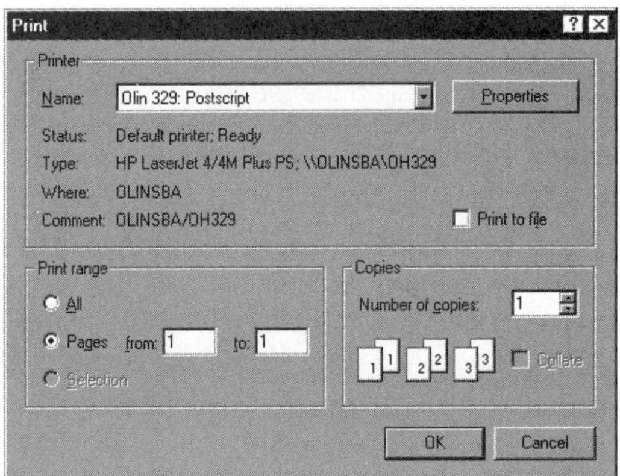

Figure 1.12 Print dialog box.

Launching an Application from a File

Launching a program by double-clicking a data file defines the concept of a document-centric system, which we mentioned earlier. In contrast, the previous section illustrated how to open WordPad and then open a document found on the Companion CD-ROM. This roundabout method exemplifies the old, *program-centric* approach to microcomputer computing. You will find the document-centric approach much faster, efficient, and error-free. In this section, we introduce you briefly to this faster method. Instead of directing you to a program and then a file to be manipulated by a program, we'll simply tell you the name of a data file on the CD-ROM and ask you to find the data and launch the program that created it. Two questions come to mind. First, how does one find the file—especially considering the size of the CD-ROM and the number of files it comprises? Second, what program must be launched in order to view or modify the data file? You'll see that the answer to question one is that you let the system search the entire CD-ROM for you. Question two's answer is that the system automatically associates a program with a data file as long as the file has a recognized *secondary name* (or extension, as it is sometimes called).

Let's try this approach to computing: find a file and load its associated program. The next two exercises show you how. In the first exercise, you will use a very helpful program called Find. Find locates files and directories on any disk by name. So, suppose you know that a particular file is stored on the Companion CD-ROM, but you cannot remember where. All you remember is part of the file name—the first part of the file name is *Olympic* and has something to do with the Olympic games.

Exercise 1.6: Finding a File

1. Click the Start button to display the Start menu.
2. Point to Find. The Find submenu is displayed.
3. Click Files or Folders, indicating you want to search for a file (or folder). The Find: All Files dialog box displays.
4. Type ***Olympic*** in the Named text box. This is the partial file name that the Find program will attempt to locate.
5. Ensure that your Companion CD-ROM is the CD-ROM drive. Then, click the drop-down arrow on the Look in text box and click your CD-ROM drive (D in our examples). Find will search only the drive you selected. However, you can select other drives if the search turns up nothing.
6. Click the Find Now button to begin the search.

Within a short time, Find displays all file or folder names it found that match, completely or partially, the file name you specify. Figure 1.13 shows it found only one file on the CD-ROM, *OlympicHostCountries.wri*.

Now that you have found the file, you want to modify it. Suppose you don't know what program was used to create the file. That's okay, because the file name extension (or secondary name) is usually associated with a particular program. Files ending with .xls, for example, are Excel files. Similarly, files ending with .mdb are Microsoft Access databases. You don't have to know these facts in order to invoke the program that created the file. The system remembers *associations* like those—file name extensions and their related programs. The next exercise

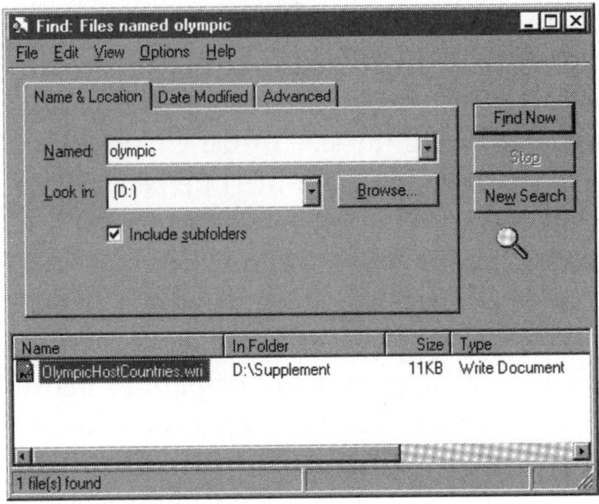

Figure 1.13 Locating a file using Find.

shows you how simple it is to execute the program associated with the file Find just located.

Exercise 1.7: Launching a Program from a Data File

1. Make sure the Find window is still available and displaying the located file, *OlympicHostCountries.wri*.
2. Double-click the file name *OlympicHostCountries.wri* located in the list of located files.
3. WordPad, a Windows-supplied word processing program, is launched and the Olympic document is displayed in a WordPad document window. The document lists information about the modern Olympics including the host countries and participant information.
4. Personalize the document by inserting your name in the upper right corner.
5. Print the document using Print from the File menu. (Leave WordPad running, because you will use it in the next section.)

The preceding exercise illustrates how easy it is to launch a program from a document. This illustrates the meaning of the term *document centric*. That is, you don't have to first load the program and then load the document. Instead, simply locate the document (*document* is used here to mean any file including a database, spreadsheet, or word processed document) you want to work on and double-click its name. That loads the required program—the one that is associated with the document.

Switching Between Applications

Windows 95 is a *multitasking* operating system, which means it is capable of running more than one program at a time. You probably will find that it is most convenient to have several programs running and at the ready at one time. Perhaps you are working with accounts receivable files with Microsoft Access and also writing letters to customers using Microsoft Word or WordPad. To appreciate how handy the multitasking capabilities are, you have to experience it. Windows 95 multitasking is smooth and intuitive. To illustrate how easy it is, you will start another program and practice switching between programs. Then, you will learn how simple it is for two applications to share information.

Exercise 1.8: Launch Another Program

1. Make sure that WordPad is still running.
2. Open the Start menu and select Programs.
3. Select Accessories.
4. Locate Paint in the Accessories cascade menu of programs.
5. Click Paint to launch it.

Paint is a graphics creation program supplied with Windows. After a brief pause, the Paint window appears as shown in Figure 1.14.

Figure 1.14 Paint and WordPad programs running simultaneously.

Now you have two programs loaded and available simultaneously: WordPad and Paint. Examine the Taskbar (usually located at the bottom of your screen). Both programs are represented by two Taskbar buttons. Program Taskbar buttons provide a convenient way to switch back and forth between programs, especially when all the programs are minimized and thus not visible. There are three ways to move from one running program to another. Each method operates slightly differently, and you may eventually select a favorite way to switch between applications. The first is using the Taskbar.

EXERCISE 1.9: USING THE TASKBAR TO SWITCH BETWEEN PROGRAMS

1. Ensure that WordPad and Paint are still running.
2. Switch to WordPad, which is probably obscured by Paint's window at the moment, by clicking the WordPad button on the Taskbar. The WordPad window becomes active.
3. Switch back to Paint by clicking its Taskbar button.

Another equally effective way to move to another program that is running but whose window is either minimized or inactive is to use the keystroke shortcut Alt+Tab. The next exercise shows you how.

EXERCISE 1.10: USING ALT+TAB TO SWITCH BETWEEN PROGRAMS

1. Press and hold down the Alt key and tap and release the Tab key. Continue holding down the Alt key for a moment. A marquee of running programs is displayed in the middle of the screen with a border around the program icon that will be displayed if you release the Alt key (see Figure 1.15).
2. Practice moving the border between the two program icons by tapping the Tab key as you continue to hold down the Alt key.
3. Release the Tab key when the border is on the Paint icon and then release the Alt key to move to that program.

Using the Alt+Tab key sequence is convenient for touch typists and it allows you to switch quickly between programs.

Finally, you may occasionally want to minimize all open windows on the desktop so that you can move to one of your desktop *shortcuts*, which are icons that represent programs. All open windows can be minimized by right-clicking the Taskbar (place the mouse in any unoccupied area of the Taskbar—avoiding

Figure 1.15 Using Alt+Tab to move between running programs.

any Taskbar buttons) and selecting *Minimize All Windows* from the context menu. Knowing this method can save you time when the desktop is filled with several windows and you want a clear shot at the desktop. The next section briefly describes how to share information between Windows applications. The particular method, called *object linking & embedding* or *OLE* for short, simplifies producing mailing labels in Word from a subset of your customers' addresses in an Access database, for example.

Sharing Data Among Applications

Data from one program can be shared with another. In the following simple but typical example, you will create a graphic in Paint and transfer the graphic to a WordPad document. The combined data—a graphic inside a document—is known as a *compound document*.

Try it

To begin, make sure that WordPad and Paint are still running. If not, launch both by clicking Start, point to the entry Programs, point to the entry Accessories in the cascading menu, and click WordPad to load it. Repeat the preceding, if necessary, to load the Paint program. Switch to Paint using the Taskbar and load the graphic file *WeRecycle.bmp* found in the Ch01 folder on your Companion CD-ROM. Click the Select tool (the dashed rectangle) and click and drag the dashed line so that it just encompasses the graphic. Then, select Copy from the Edit menu to place the graphic on the Clipboard. Next, you will send the graphic over to the WordPad document using Copy and Paste operations. Switch to WordPad and load (execute File, Open) the file called *RecycleLetter.wri*, which is also found in the Ch01 folder on your Companion CD-ROM. Insert a blank line at the top of the document where the graphic will be placed. Choose Paste from WordPad's Edit menu. The graphic is pasted into the document. If you wish, you can print the document. Figure 1.16 shows the completed compound document. When you are finished, close both the WordPad and Paint applications. The Windows desktop will be redisplayed.

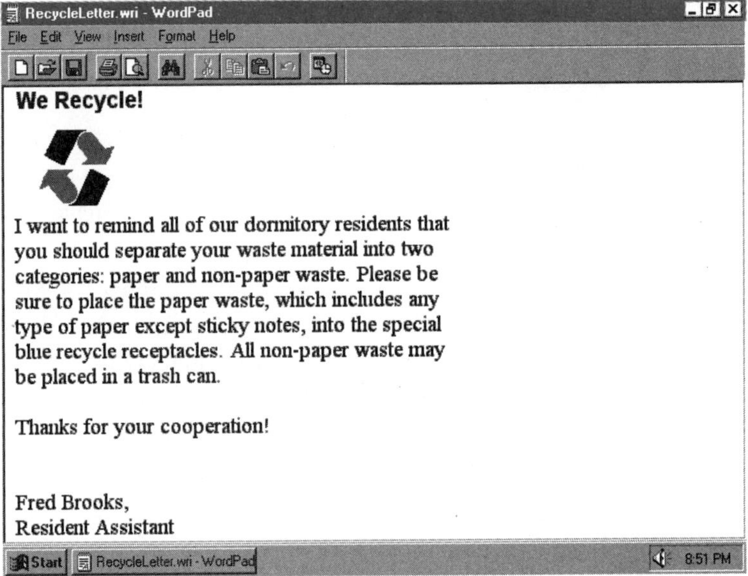

Figure 1.16 Graphic embedded in a WordPad document.

What's important to remember from the preceding example is that you pass information between Windows applications by *copying* from one application—placing the object on the Clipboard—and then *pasting* the object into the recipient (container) document. This works for virtually all Windows-compliant programs, including Access, Excel, and Word.

USING WINDOWS EXPLORER

Windows provides an advanced browser and file manager called Windows Explorer, though most experienced users simply call it Explorer. Explorer allows you to perform file management duties, open and close documents, and run programs. In fact, you may find that Explorer is the interface you use most often, because it is often more convenient to find and work with a file by using Explorer. By default, Windows Explorer is found in the Programs group of the Start menu.

Try it

Launch Windows Explorer so that you can see its interface. Click the Start button. Then, point to the Programs item. Finally, click the Windows Explorer item to start Explorer. (You can also launch Explorer by right-clicking the Start button and selecting *Explore* from the shortcut menu. This is probably the most convenient method.)

The All folders pane, also known as the *Tree* pane, presents a tree structure of your entire computer system including desktop objects. Each branch of the tree can be expanded or collapsed as you desire. In the right panel is the *Contents* pane, displaying the folders, files, and other objects found in the folder that is selected and open in the Tree pane.

Normally Explorer displays a view of your system beginning with your desktop—the "root" of the hierarchical or tree structure of files and devices. Emphasizing the outline structure of your disk file structure, each folder displayed can contain files and other folders. Figure 1.17 shows a typical Explorer window with folders and files.

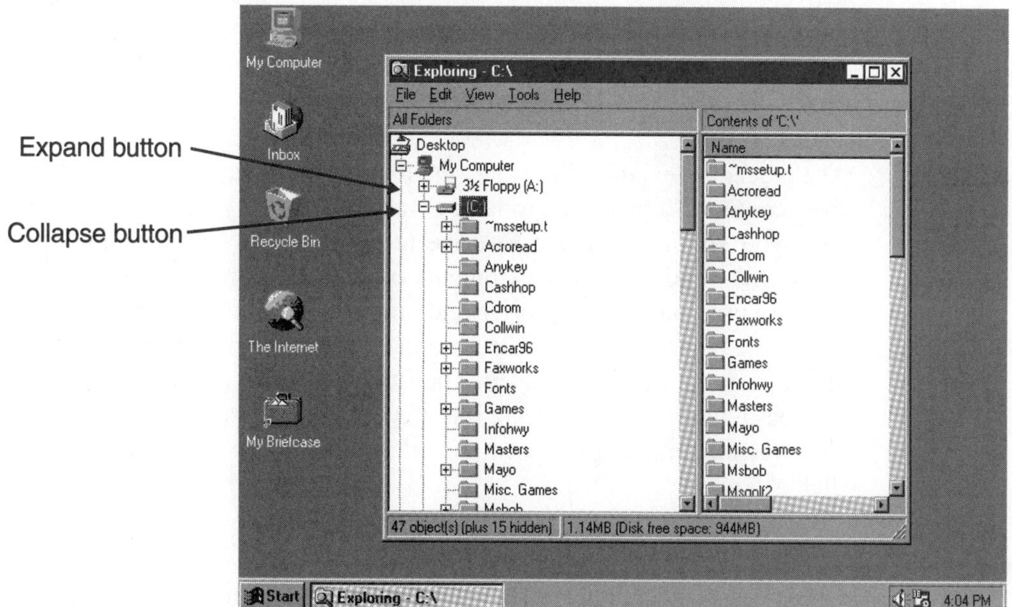

Figure 1.17 Typical Explorer window showing folders and files.

The lines in the Tree pane emphasize the relationships between folders and the folders and files that they contain. Notice, too, the plus and minus signs at the intersection of horizontal and vertical lines in the Tree pane. A small box with a plus sign—called the *Expand* button—indicates that the object contains other objects and can be expanded to reveal further detail. Likewise, boxes with minus signs are called *Collapse* buttons. Clicking a Collapse button implodes the structure, revealing less detail.

Opening Drives, Files, and Folders

The Contents pane can show only one level of detail at a time, so you must click the Expand button on the particular drive or folder until you reach the particular file or folder you are looking for. Suppose, for instance, you want to see what is on the Companion CD-ROM. Using Explorer, you can "walk" down through each of the folders and files, noting what files are stored in which folders. Practice expanding and collapsing folders in Explorer.

Try it

If Explorer is not running, start it (click the Start button, point to Programs, and click Windows Explorer). In the Tree pane, click the icon representing the C drive. Reveal more about the C drive by clicking its Expand button. Your display should resemble Figure 1.17, though the exact folder and file names on your disk may differ from the figure. Open the Windows folder on the C drive. You may have to use the Tree pane scroll bar to move down the hierarchy of folders until the Windows folder appears. Click the Windows folder to open it. The first level of folders and files in the Windows folder are revealed in the Contents pane. Note, the Tree pane never displays file names. File names are displayed in the Contents pane, however.

The preceding exercise illustrates the fundamental way you explore the disks and their contents. If you want to look at the contents of your Companion CD-ROM, then you simply click the D drive icon—the drive we are assuming is your CD-ROM—and look at the Contents pane. If you are curious about how much space is used on your disk drive and how much is left, you can use this shortcut: right-click the drive icon in the Tree pane. Then, click the Properties item on the shortcut menu that is displayed. The Properties dialog box is displayed showing a three-dimensional representation of your disk in two colors. One color represents the amount of space used; the other is the space free. Click OK to close the dialog box.

Formatting a Floppy Disk

One of the useful activities you can perform while running Explorer is formatting a disk. In particular, you can format your floppy disk, because it is highly unlikely you will want to format your hard disk(s) and you cannot format your Companion CD-ROM, which contains files, databases, and data critical to this textbook. You will want to save your database files, temporary files, and other documents you develop while reading this book and working on assignments. The logical place to save information, especially while working in a university computing laboratory, is on a floppy disk. Although the capacity of a floppy is limited, it is very portable. A floppy disk is a convenient way to transport your work from your own computer to a central computer laboratory and back. So, let's learn how to format a new floppy disk, just in case you purchase an unformatted disk.

You may already know that formatting a floppy disk prepares it for first time use. Unformatted disks have no magnetic marks identifying the beginning and ending of tracks and sectors on the disk. Tracks and sectors are the "grooves" in which all data is stored. Tracks, concentric rings on a disk, hold data. The blank spaces between concentric rings separate individual tracks. Windows Explorer can format disks quickly and easily. Once formatted, a disk can be used and reused repeatedly without ever being formatted again. You can also format a disk after it has been used. But, be aware that the formatting process erases any data that may be present on the disk. This next exercise formats a new disk so that you can use it later in the text to store data. If you have a formatted disk containing valuable data, then do not do this exercise if you want to keep the data. On the other hand, this is a good opportunity to format any new disks you have just purchased.

Exercise 1.11: Formatting a Disk with Explorer

1. Launch Windows Explorer, if necessary.
2. Place a floppy disk in drive A.
3. In the Tree pane of the Explorer window right-click the drive A icon (not the Expand button).
4. Click the Format item in the pop-up menu.
5. Select Full in the Format type group.
6. Select the *No label* and *Display summary when finished* options.
7. Click the Start button to begin formatting the floppy disk. Shortly, a summary dialog box is displayed indicating the total storage capacity of your disk.
8. Click Close twice—once to close the dialog box and a second time to close the Format dialog box.
9. Close Explorer. (You will use it soon in the next section, so you may wish to leave it running if you will be continuing with your reading.)

Creating Folders

Folders, like their physical counterparts in filing cabinet systems, are a convenient way to store and organize your files and other folders. Folders provide a way to partition and separate one group of project files from another. For instance, you may find it convenient to keep each chapter's homework, databases, and other work in its own folder whose name clearly indicates which chapter's material is stored therein (e.g., Chapter 1). The next exercise guides you through this process using Windows Explorer. To prepare for this exercise, place a floppy disk in drive A. You may want to use the disk you formatted in the previous exercise. Then complete the following exercise.

EXERCISE 1.12: CREATING FOLDERS WITH EXPLORER

1. Ensure Explorer is running and switch to it by clicking its button on the Taskbar.
2. Place a formatted floppy in drive A.
3. Click the drive A icon in the Explorer Tree pane.
4. Select File and point to New.
5. Click Folder from the cascade menu. A folder called New Folder is created and displayed in the Contents Panel.
6. With the folder called 'New Folder' still highlighted, type the folder's new name: ***Chapter 1***. Press Enter.
7. Click the Expand button on drive A to display the new folder both in the Tree and Contents pane. Figure 1.18 shows the new folder in place.
8. Click the Explorer's Close button to terminate the program.

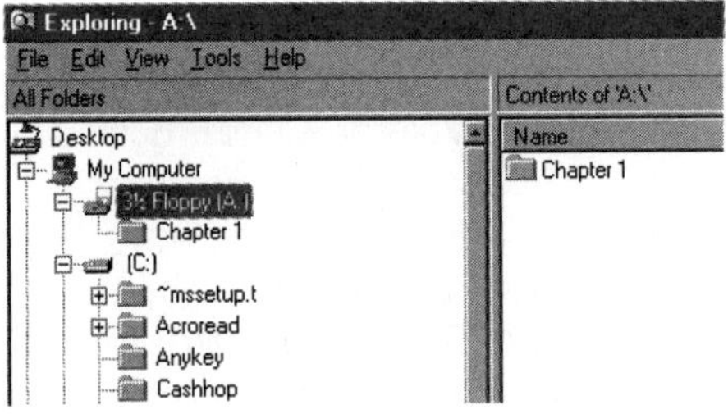

Figure 1.18 Creating a folder.

Now you know how to make new folders in which you can store files or other folders. Perhaps the most important subtlety in creating a folder is to ensure you have selected the appropriate folder or disk *before* creating a new folder. New folders are created *below* the folder or disk currently selected in the Tree pane. That is, if you wanted to create a folder labeled Chapter 2 along side the Chapter 1 folder, then first select the drive A icon. If Chapter 1 is highlighted in the Tree pane, than a new folder would be created as a subfolder of Chapter 1.

Copying, Moving, Naming, and Deleting Files

The problem with opening and using Access databases that are stored on your Companion CD-ROM is that Access prefers to open databases in a mode called read/write, whereby database records can be both read from the database and written back to it. Unless you have special software and you are "burning" a new CD-ROM, you cannot write data to a CD-ROM. You can read any data you wish from a CD-ROM. However, when you open a database on your CD-ROM, Access displays a warning dialog box instructing you that you cannot make any changes to your data. We have a simple solution to this dilemma.

Your Companion CD-ROM contains several databases, tables, and other objects that you will use as you read this textbook and work on the problems. In order for you to both read and write to Access databases, you will be asked to copy files from the Companion CD-ROM to your computer's hard drive or to your floppy disk. Then, you and Access can operate normally on the copy of the database, because it is stored on a read/write disk. That's why we want you to pay especially close attention to this section where we demonstrate using Explorer to copy a file from the Companion CD-ROM to another disk. In the following exercise, you will copy the file *FallWashPromotion.doc* from the CD-ROM to the folder you just created, Chapter 1, on your floppy disk. In preparation for the exercise, launch Windows Explorer, if necessary, insert the floppy disk you formatted in the preceding exercise in drive A, and insert your Companion CD-ROM into the CD-ROM drive.

Exercise 1.13: Copying a File from the Companion CD-ROM to another Disk

1. Prepare the Tree pane display by locating the drive A icon and click its Expand button so that the Chapter 1 folder is displayed in the Tree pane.
2. Scroll down the Tree pane display, locating the icon for your CD-ROM. Click it and click the Expand button so that the folders beginning with Ch01 are displayed.
3. Click the Ch01 folder in the Tree pane. The contents of the folder, some file names, are displayed in Explorer's Contents pane.
4. Locate the file *FallWashPromotion.doc*, select it, and then drag it from the Contents pane to the Tree pane.
5. If disk A is not visible near the top of the Tree pane, continue dragging by moving the mouse to the top of the Tree pane. It will move, revealing drive A.
6. Continue dragging the file until the dimmed file name, which represents the mouse, is directly over the Chapter 1 folder (the folder will be highlighted when the mouse is properly situated).
7. Release the left mouse button, dropping the file into the folder.

When you drag and drop a file from one disk to a different disk, the default action is to *copy* the file. However, if you drag and subsequently drop a file from one folder on a disk to another folder on the same disk, the default action is to *move* the file. You can have more control over the action by right-clicking the selected file to drag it (we call this action right-drag for short). When you drop the file into its destination folder, a pop-up menu is displayed from which you can choose either copy or move by clicking which action you'd like. Figure 1.19 shows the pop-up menu displayed when you right-drag a file.

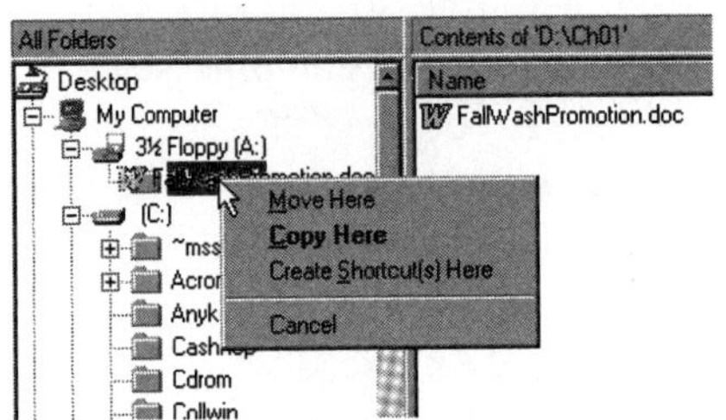

Figure 1.19 Pop-up menu displayed after right-dragging a file.

Moving a file from one place to another is a cut/paste operation. The easiest way to move a file is to right-click it and then drag it from one location to another. When you release the right mouse, a pop-up menu is displayed. From the menu you can select Move. Perhaps the fastest way to copy or move a file from one place to another is as follows:

- Locate and select (click) the file to be copied (the *source* file)
- Press Ctrl+C (to copy) or Ctrl+X (to move)
- Locate the target folder in Explorer's Tree pane and select the folder (the *target*)
- Finally, press Ctrl+V to paste the file into the target folder

Entire files or a collection of files can be copied or moved from one folder to another using copy or cut and paste keystrokes identical to those you use when copying objects between programs and the Clipboard.

Eventually, files and folders are no longer useful to you and must be deleted. The folder and file you created on disk A—the folder called Chapter 1 and the file *FallWashPromotion.doc*—have been used for demonstration purposes and are no longer needed. You can delete them. Deleted objects can be recovered once deleted if you act within a reasonable time. When deleted, files and folders are placed in a special folder called the *Recycle bin* where they remain until you empty the bin. Once you empty the Recycle bin, files are no longer recoverable. That is, when you empty the Recycle bin, Windows physically removes them from the disk. Let's see how to delete files and folders.

Try it

Open Windows Explorer, place your floppy disk in drive A, and select drive A in Explorer's Tree pane. Click the Expand button, if necessary, to reveal the folder Chapter 1. Select that folder in the Tree pane. The Contents panel reveals the file *FallWashPromotion.doc*. With the mouse positioned over the file name, right-click the file. A pop-up menu is displayed with menu items including Cut, Copy, Delete, and Properties. Click the Delete menu item and click Yes when the confirmation dialog box is displayed. The file is automatically placed in the Recycle bin.

You delete folders in the same way as files. The consequences of deleting a folder can be more significant than deleting one or more files, however. When you delete a folder, you also delete any files and folders it may contain. Make sure that the folder to be deleted contains only files and folders that you are sure you want to delete. Delete a folder by selecting it in Explorer and dragging it to the Recycle bin. (This may require you to reduce the Explorer's window so that the Recycle bin and window are simultaneously visible.)

Whenever you feel the urge, you can empty the Recycle bin, permanently removing all files it contains. Simply right-click the Recycle bin and select the option titled *Empty Recycle Bin*. Then click the Yes button.

Try it

Restoring previously deleted files is relatively simple. Right-click the Recycle bin, select the file(s) to be restored, and then select Restore from the File menu. Any selected files are restored and placed in their original locations. Minimize Explorer and locate the Recycle bin on the desktop. Double-click the Recycle bin, locate and then select the file *FallWashPromotion.doc*. Select Restore from the File menu. The document is placed back in the Chapter 1 folder on your floppy disk.

The same keystroke shortcuts you used in previous versions of Windows work for selecting files with Windows 95. For example, press and hold Ctrl and click file names to select noncontiguous files. Hold Shift and click the first and last of a group of contiguous files (those whose names appear in sequence next to one another) to select the whole group. Besides these tried and true methods, Windows 95 introduces a new selection tool: drag the mouse pointer across the Explorer's Contents window, creating a rectangular dashed line. Any file names the line touches will be selected when you release the mouse pointer. Pretty slick! (Try it.)

One way to rename a folder or file is to right-click it and then select *Rename* from the pop-up menu. Then, type in the new name. You can cancel the pop-up menu and choose to take no action by clicking anywhere outside the menu. Another, perhaps simpler way to rename a file or folder is to select it and then press F2. Or, you can *slowly* click twice (do not double-click) a file or folder name. A vertical, blinking cursor appears at the end of the object's name. You can retype the name or use the arrow keys to move the cursor left or right to make small changes in the name. Practice slowly clicking twice to get the hang of it. If you are too quick, you'll end up launching the application that is associated with the file whose name you double-clicked. Stick with one of the other renaming techniques if you have difficulty.

Setting File and Folder Properties

Files and folders have hidden attributes or properties which both limit actions you can take on the object and display information about the object. Which properties are available and can be altered depends on the type of object. Files and folders have a common set of properties that are accessible from the Windows Explorer either by right-clicking the object or selecting Properties from Explorer's File menu. Some objects such as Excel spreadsheet files and Word documents have additional properties—summary information and statistics—that reveal additional details such as the date when the object was created and last altered. Four properties that all file types and folders have in common are called Archive, Read-only, Hidden, and System. Of these, only two are important to us—the properties Read-only and Hidden.

A file or folder whose Read-only property is set cannot be easily erased. (We use the term *set* to mean "has the value of yes" or "is enabled.") When you delete a file whose Read-only attribute is set, Windows displays a dialog box asking you to reaffirm your intention to delete one or more objects. Setting a file's Hidden property makes it invisible in Explorer. Hiding files is useful when you want to reduce screen clutter by eliminating some file names from displaying while using Explorer. The next exercise shows you how to set a file's Read-only property.

Exercise 1.14: Making a File Read-Only

1. Launch Windows Explorer, if necessary, and navigate to drive A in the Tree pane so that the Ch01 folder is visible.
2. In Explorer's Contents pane, right-click the file *FallWashPromotion.doc* and select Properties from the pop-up list. The Properties dialog box is displayed.
3. Check the Read-only check box by clicking it. Notice that the Apply button, dimmed prior to your check action, is now available (see Figure 1.20).
4. Finally, click OK to affirm the changed property and return to Explorer.

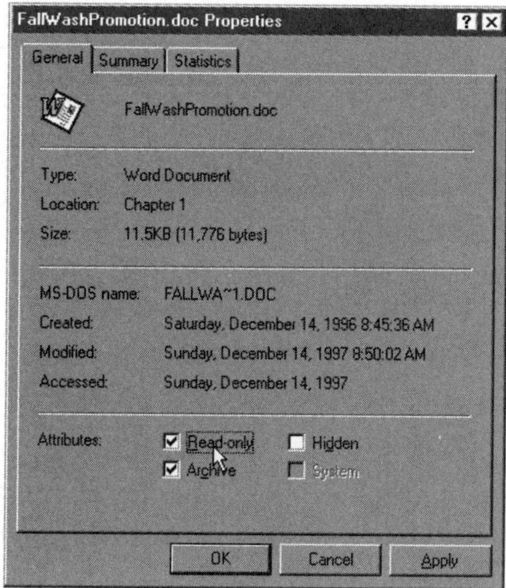

Figure 1.20 Setting a file's Read-only property.

Launching a Program from Explorer

As you become more comfortable with Windows 95, you likely will use Explorer as your default work surface for beginning your Access database work. Because most files are associated with an application, it is usually simplest to launch Explorer, locate the database file you want to work on, and then launch Access by double-clicking the file. This is a simple, efficient approach to starting a program *and* opening a file to work on. You have practiced this once already, in Exercise 1.7, *Launching a Program from a Data File*. In that exercise, you located a file using Find and then double-clicked the file name to launch WordPad. You can do the same thing in Explorer. When you locate with Explorer the database file you want to open, simply double-click its name to launch Microsoft Access. You might want to try this on your own with one of the many database files we have supplied on your Companion CD-ROM. Remember, however, to first copy the database file to your floppy disk or, better yet, to a temporary file on drive C. Then double-click the file in Explorer to run Access and open the database file.

Generally, the pattern you should follow in working with our supplied database files is to first copy the particular chapter's database file to drive C, your computer's hard drive, so that the database can be opened to both read database information as well as alter the data. That way, you will be able to make needed database modifications as you read the text and see the effects of your changes. Of course, you can open the Companion CD-ROM databases directly on the CD-ROM, but Access allows you to read the data only. You cannot post any changes to the database stored on the CD-ROM.

Exiting Explorer

Exiting Explorer is child's play. You can either choose Close from the File menu or click the Close button located in the upper right corner of the Explorer window. If you haven't closed Explorer yet, do so now using either method. The Windows 95 desktop reappears (or another application if any are still running). Make sure all running applications are closed, so that you have an unobscured view of the desktop.

CUSTOMIZING WINDOWS

You can customize the Windows 95 desktop to make it more efficient for you to use and to provide the kind of detail you like. Some customization features, such as desktop shortcuts, will yield large time savings while other changes you make simply establish the desktop—your virtual office space—as uniquely yours. Windows also provides accessibility options, which make Windows easier to use for those with physical impairments. Nearly anyone can find several good reasons to customize the Windows desktop. Only those in a university computer laboratory environment will find it counterproductive to alter the appearance and functionality of the desktop because the customized desktop cannot be saved in that situation.

Different people who use a single computer may wish to customize the desktop to their liking, changing the background wallpaper, the number and types of icons on the desktop, and so forth. *User profiles*, introduced in Windows 95, saves each user's uniquely customized desktop so that no one user affects the settings of another. Which desktop environment is selected is determined by the *user name* provided. Details of how to enable tracking multiple users on a single machine will be presented in the section titled *Restarting Windows*.

Creating and Using Shortcuts

A *shortcut* is an icon representing a program or other object and provides a quick way to get to a particular object. The Start menu items, for example, are shortcuts to programs rather than programs. This can be confusing to users new to Windows, but the distinction is important. A shortcut is analogous to a telephone number found in a typical address book. The telephone number is a shortcut to the real person who (you hope) answers the phone when you call. Like a telephone number, a shortcut can be deleted without deleting the actual object—usually a program—to which it points. Shortcuts inherit the same icon as the object to which they point, so it is sometimes difficult to distinguish between them. However, shortcut icons also contain a small arrow, which distinguishes the shortcut icon from the icon actually representing a program or other object.

The most common reason to create a desktop shortcut is quick access to frequently used applications—expedience. There is virtually no limit to the number of shortcuts you can create and place on the desktop, but we advise restraint. If you create too many shortcuts, the desktop can become cluttered and unreadable and you are almost back to where you started—unable to find a particular application or other object quickly. On the other hand, you may want to create shortcuts for lots of objects and then later cull the collection to the 20 percent of the shortcuts you use 80 percent of the time (the often observed "20/80" rule). In any case, it is simple enough to delete unwanted shortcuts later. Let's see how desktop shortcuts are created by creating one of our own. Bear in mind that your university computer laboratory may be set up to prevent desktop customization by students including placing icons on the desktop. It can't hurt to try, though.

EXERCISE 1.15: CREATING A DESKTOP SHORTCUT TO WORDPAD

1. Close any open applications so that the desktop is clearly visible.
2. Right-click any blank area of the desktop.
3. Choose New.
4. Choose Shortcut from the submenu that appears.
5. Click the Browse button.
6. Navigate to the WordPad program file, which is found in the Accessories folder of the Program Files folder on drive C.
7. Select the WordPad file (Wordpad.exe) and click the Open button. The Create Shortcut dialog box appears, and the complete directions (called the path name) to the program appears in the Command Line text box (see Figure 1.21).
8. Click Next.
9. Type ***WordPad Shortcut*** in the text box and click Finish.

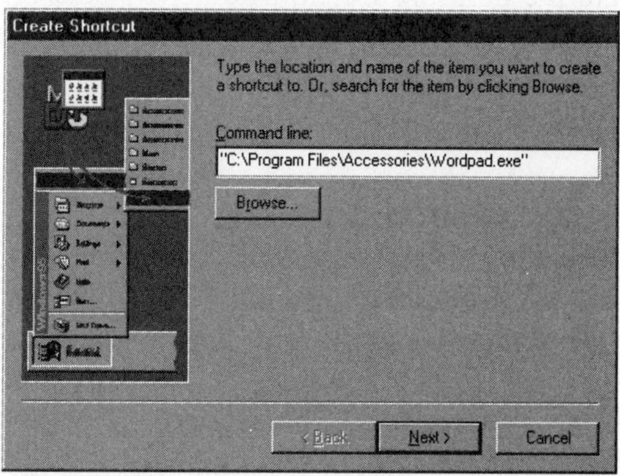

Figure 1.21 Create Shortcut dialog box.

The shortcut appears on the desktop. The shortcut icon matches WordPad's icon in every respect except that an arrow appears in the lower left corner. This identifies the icon as a shortcut (see Figure 1.22).

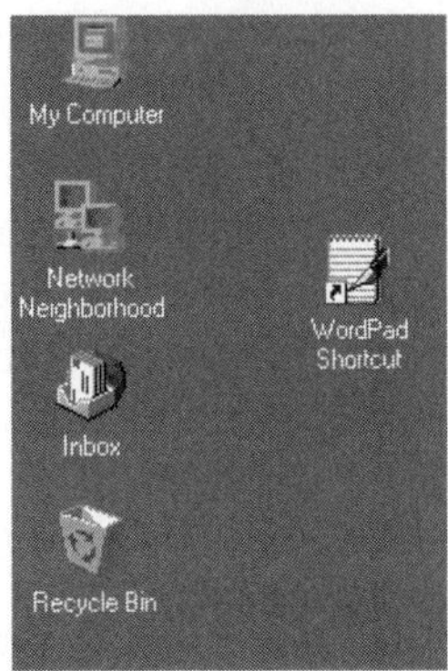

Figure 1.22 WordPad shortcut.

Use folders on the desktop to group shortcuts if your desktop becomes too cluttered. That way, you can find a shortcut by opening the folder containing shortcuts of a similar nature. Creating a desktop folder follows the same basic procedure as the first four steps of the preceding exercise. That is, right-click any blank desktop area, choose New and then Folder. Finally, type the folder's name and press Enter to finalize the operation. The folder name appears below the desktop folder. Then, you can drag shortcuts from the desktop and drop them into the folder. Because the desktop is both the source and destination of the operation, the shortcut is *moved* to a folder by default when you click, drag, and then drop it. To remove an object from a desktop folder and place it back on the desktop, double-click the folder to open it and then drag the object from the open folder onto the desktop. Delete a folder by selecting it and pressing the Delete key. Click Yes to confirm the delete operation.

Placing Shortcuts on the Start Menu

The Start menu is like any other Windows object: it can be customized. We suggest that one of the things that speeds your use of a program is to place a shortcut to the program on the Start menu directly. That way, when you click Start, the program is immediately accessible from the shortcut. Plan a bit here, though. The real estate available on the Start menu is limited. So restrict what you place there to your most often used programs. Remember, too, if you are working in a university computing laboratory, you will probably not be able to customize the Start button. The following exercise explains how to place a shortcut to Microsoft Access on the Start menu.

Try it

Locate the Microsoft Access file object (called *Msaccess.exe*). Drag the file name directly to the Start button and drop it there. The first question is how do you find the Access file object? Use the Find command on the Start menu to search for it. Click Start, click Find, and select Files or Folders. In the Named box type *msaccess.exe* and make sure that drive C is indicated in the Look In text box. Then, click the Find Now button. Shortly, the file name is displayed in the text box at the bottom of the dialog box. Select the name in the Name column of the Find dialog box and drag it to the Start button. A shortcut is available on the Start menu. Click Start and locate the shortcut at the top of the Start menu (see Figure 1.23).

Figure 1.23 Access shortcut on the Start menu.

Removing Start Menu Items

Objects including shortcuts can be removed from the Start menu. You may want to remove the Start menu shortcut to Microsoft Access you just created. Removing an item is only slightly more involved then adding an item to the Start menu. The Settings item on the Start menu is the doorway to removing a shortcut. Perhaps the simplest way to understand this process is to actually remove a shortcut. If you followed our suggestion above and added a shortcut to the Start menu, then try the following exercise to remove the item. Otherwise, simply read on as we list the steps needed.

Exercise 1.16: Removing a Shortcut from the Start Menu

1. Click the Start menu and select the Settings menu item. Three submenus are displayed: Control Panel, Printers, and Taskbar.

2. Choose Taskbar. The Taskbar Properties sheet is displayed.
3. Select the Start Menu Programs tab.
4. Click the Remove button. The Remove Shortcuts/Folders dialog box is displayed (see Figure 1.24).
5. Navigate, using the scroll box if necessary, to the item *Msaccess.exe*. (You may want to click the Programs group Collapse button to reveal the shortcut at the end of the list.
6. Select the object *Msaccess.exe*, click Remove, and click Close.
7. Click OK on the Taskbar Properties dialog box to close it.

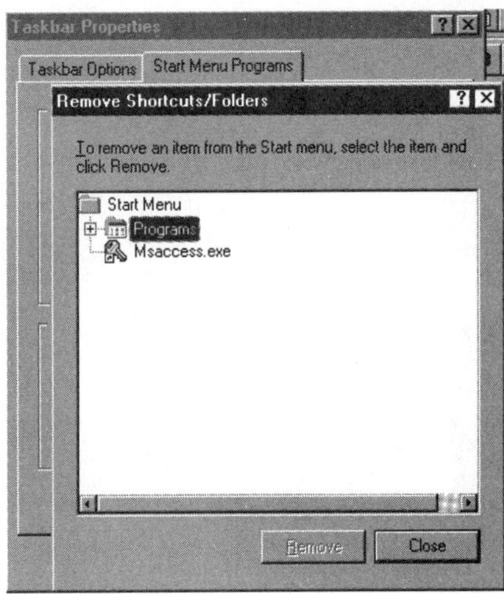

Figure 1.24 Remove Shortcut/Folders dialog box.

There's a slightly faster way to display the Taskbar Properties sheet. Simply right-click any *gray* area of the Taskbar (a gray area is any Taskbar area that is not occupied by a program button or the Status area). Then choose Properties from the pop-up menu. Remember this time saver when you deal with the Start menu or the Taskbar.

Clearing the Start Menu Documents Window

The Documents menu displays the names of the last 15 documents that you accessed. For instance, the document *FallWashPromotion.doc* appears in the Documents window because you opened that document recently. Similarly, if you open a database, the name of that database is placed in the Documents menu. When the number of document names exceeds 15, the oldest name is removed from the bottom of the list and the newest name is placed on the top. The Document window provides a quick way to return to a document you were working on recently—whether it is a Word document, Access database, or Notepad memo. This ability reinforces the notion of a document-centric system that we introduced earlier in this chapter. For example, if you wanted to work on the *FallWashPromotion.doc* document again, the fastest way to load WordPad and the document is to locate *FallWashPromotion.doc* in the Documents menu and click the name. WordPad is launched and the letter is opened automatically. How convenient.

Take a moment to look at the Documents menu on your computer to see what names appear there. To do so, click the Start button and then select Documents. A list of up to 15 documents appear in a list that cascades from the Documents menu item.

Sometimes people are sensitive about document names appearing in the Documents window. For instance, suppose you had just worked on a letter named *IncomeTaxesDue.doc* containing sensitive tax and income information. You certainly do not want an unauthorized person reading the document. It may be best to eliminate the name from the recently used names stored in the Documents menu. Clearing the names from that list is a matter of remembering a few keystrokes. The next exercise illustrates the required steps.

Exercise 1.17: Clearing the Documents Menu

1. Right-click the Taskbar.
2. Select Properties from the pop-up menu.
3. Select the Start Menu Programs tab of the Taskbar Properties dialog box (see Figure 1.25).
4. Click the Clear button. The document names are cleared from the Documents menu and the Clear button is dimmed.
5. Click the Taskbar Properties Close button to remove the dialog box.

Now if you examine the Start menu Documents menu items, you will see a single item indicating the list is empty. Emptying the Documents menu does not prevent someone from accessing your documents, but it does prevent someone else from knowing what documents you accessed recently.

Customizing the Taskbar

Some people prefer to have the Taskbar out of sight until needed. Others like the Taskbar placed in a different location on the desktop. Like the Start menu, the Taskbar can be customized to suit your needs. We show you how to alter both the location and behavior of the Taskbar. However, we want to remind you to be

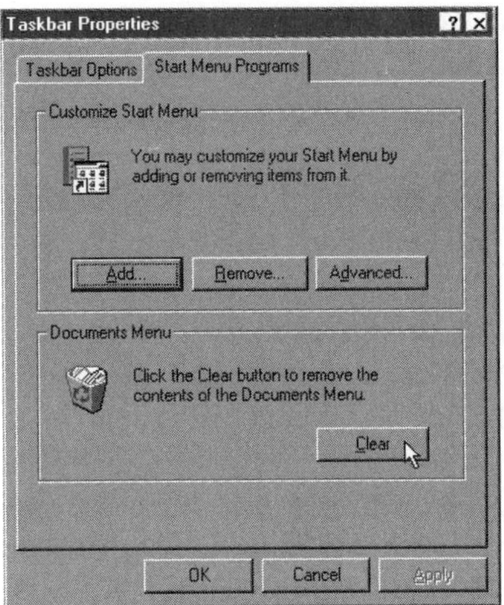

Figure 1.25 Clearing document names from the Documents menu.

considerate of others who may also use the computer. If others have access to the computer you are using, they probably expect to find a particular Windows 95 screen display. Change the Taskbar all you want, but be sure to return the computer to its original state prior to leaving the laboratory. If you hide the Taskbar, the next student who uses the computer may not know how to make the Taskbar reappear.

Changing the Taskbar's location or its size is the most obvious change you can make. To change the height of the Taskbar, move the pointer to the upper edge of the Taskbar. When the pointer changes to a double-headed arrow, you can drag the upper border towards the center of the screen to widen the Taskbar. Similarly, dragging the top edge of the Taskbar towards the edge of the screen makes the Taskbar very narrow but not quite invisible. Try altering the Taskbar's size. Widen it to almost half the height of the screen, then restore it to its standard height.

Changing the location of the Taskbar from its default position at the bottom of the screen is a straightforward procedure. Simply drag the Taskbar to one of the four edges of the screen to place it in that position.

Try it

Click any empty area of the Taskbar and drag it to the top of the screen. Notice that the Taskbar snugs itself up against the top of the display, and desktop icons automatically shift down slightly to accommodate the Taskbar. Drag the Taskbar to the right or left side of the desktop. Again, desktop shortcuts move out of the way accordingly.

Sometimes the Taskbar is unneeded and/or is using up valuable screen space. You can make the Taskbar hide until you need it by setting the Taskbar's Auto hide property. To change the Taskbar's display behavior, bring up the Taskbar Properties sheet (right-click the Taskbar and then select Properties). Click the Taskbar Options tab of the Taskbar Properties sheet that appears. Check the Auto hide check box and click OK to set the new property (see Figure 1.26). The Properties sheet closes, and the Taskbar will move off the screen until you move the cursor near the Taskbar's former location. Experiment yourself. Set the Auto hide property and then move the cursor near the edge of the screen where the Taskbar usually appears. The Taskbar reappears. Move the pointer away from the edge of the screen, and the Taskbar slips out of sight. Clearing the Auto hide property reverses this behavior. Bring the Taskbar into sight, right-click in a blank area, select Properties, and clear Auto hide on the Taskbar Options tab. Finally, click OK to establish the Taskbar characteristics.

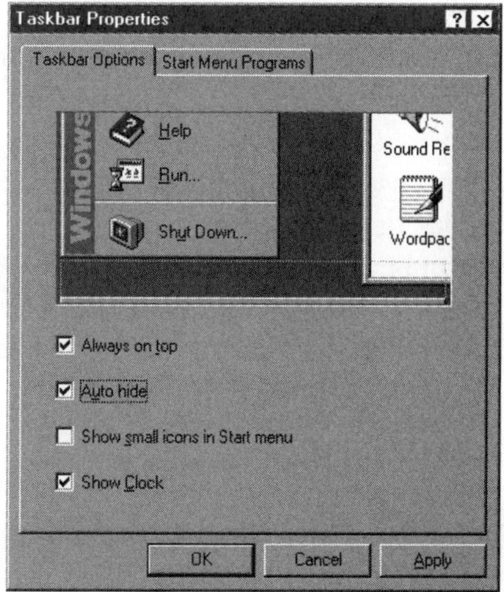

Figure 1.26 Setting the Taskbar's Auto hide property.

Another property, Show Clock, determines whether the time is displayed on the Taskbar. Clearing it removes the clock. Setting it displays the clock.

You probably noticed the Apply button on the Taskbar Properties sheet. It behaves differently from the OK button. Clicking Apply establishes the properties you have selected but leaves the Properties sheet open. You can make additional Taskbar changes if you wish. Clicking OK establishes the properties you have selected and closes the Properties sheet, precluding further Properties changes until the sheet is reopened.

RESTARTING WINDOWS

Windows may need to be restarted either because an error occurs which causes the keyboard to freeze, Windows indicates that an error has occurred and instructs you to restart, or in order to log off the network and reconnect as a different user. The first two cases are infrequent and require you to simply restart Windows but not necessarily reinitialize the entire machine. The latter case, logging on as a different user, is useful for several reasons. Whenever you restart Windows, you are asked to specify your username and password. If your computer is on a network, you must also provide a username and password to log onto the local area network. The network and Windows usernames and passwords can be the same to simplify the task of connecting to both the network and Windows. To focus our discussion on Windows itself, let's assume for a moment that your computer is not connected to a LAN (Local Area Network). Why then are a username and password required or even useful on a stand-alone Windows 95 computer? One major reason is that Windows can accommodate and keep track of multiple users' desktop preferences with usernames. That way several people, each with a self-assigned username, can log on to a particular computer. Then, Windows restores the user's desktop icons, Start menu settings, and other work environment information for each identified user. Preserved desktop settings and environment are saved in *user profiles*. User profiles provide customized desktop configurations that allow people using the computer to work most efficiently. Forcing everyone who uses a particular computer to use a fixed set of shortcuts does not aid creativity or efficiency.

User profiles can be used on computers with Windows 95, but profiles must first be enabled before they can be used. Let's examine how to enable user profiles and username tracking and then discover how to log on under different usernames.

Enabling User Profiles

You enable user profiles through the Passwords option in Windows 95's Control Panel. The Control Panel contains tools that allow you to modify virtually every aspect of your computer including the date and time, the display resolution, installed printers, hardware, and software. Among these tools is one that allows you to enable user profiles. This tool is called Passwords and the icon representing Passwords looks like a set of keys.

Access the Control Panel through My Computer or from the Start menu. That is, click the Start button, point to Settings, and select Control Panel. Or, double-click My Computer and double-click Control Panel. The Control Panel tools are displayed (see Figure 1.27).

You enable tracking and logging User Profiles by double-clicking the Passwords tool and then selecting the second option button labeled, in part, "Users can customize their preferences and desktop settings." On the User Profile

Figure 1.27 Control Panel tools.

settings section, check the options you want to preserve from one user to another (see Figure 1.28).

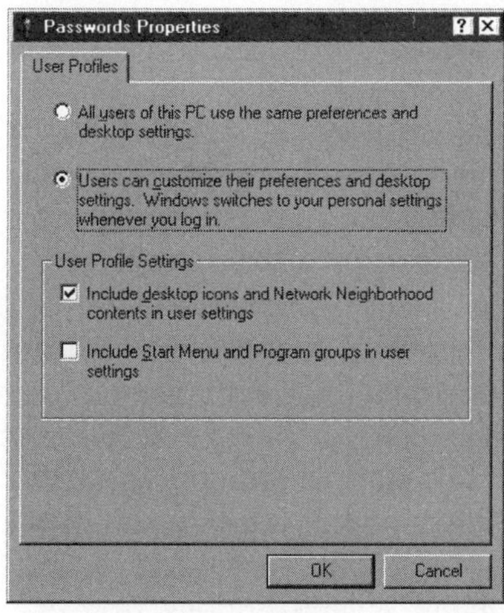

Figure 1.28 Enabling User Profiles.

Once User Profiles have been enabled, individual users' preferences are recorded when they log on with their unique usernames and optional passwords.

Logging in as a Different User

To establish your working environment, you must log on as a new user. Click the Start button and then select Shut Down from the Start menu. The Shut Down Windows dialog box appears as shown in Figure 1.29. Click the option titled *Close all programs and log on as a different user?* From the list. Finally, click the Yes button to initialize the log-on sequence. Shortly, a dialog box is displayed that requests you enter your username and password. Type in whatever username you would like (remember it!). If you want to enter a password, press Tab and type a password. Otherwise, simply press Enter to skip entering a password. Any changes you make to the desktop are noted and saved in your User Profile.

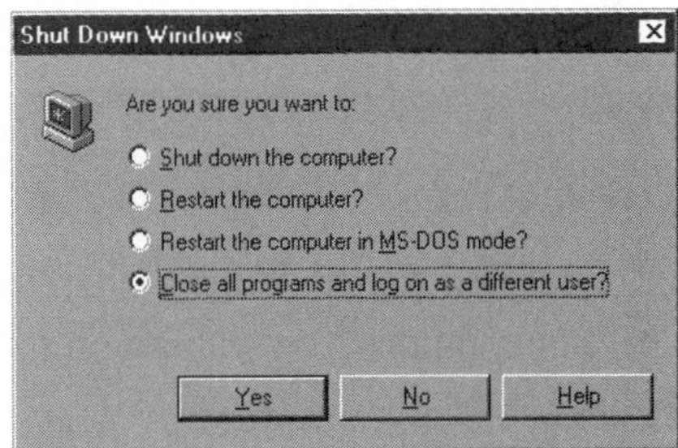

Figure 1.29 Logging on as a different user.

EXITING WINDOWS

If you are using a computer in a computer laboratory, chances are that you will not want to exit Windows. Doing so will require the next user to restart Windows or the computer from scratch. Avoid exiting Windows in this situation. However, you will want to occasionally take a break and turn off your computer. Always exit Windows *before* turning off your computer. Windows often has some clean up work to do before you can safely turn off your computer. You could lose valuable data or programs if you do not follow this admonition. Shutting down or exiting Windows is straightforward. Here's how. Click the Start button on the Taskbar and then select the Shut Down option. The Shut Down Windows dialog box appears containing several options from which to choose. Select *Shut down the computer?* and then click the Yes button to initialize the shut down process. Shortly, your screen will display a message indicating that it is safe to turn off your computer. Many computers contain internal circuitry that automatically turns off the computer after Windows completes its software shut down process.

SUMMARY

This chapter has described the Windows 95 environment. We have launched Windows, logged on to Windows, examined what is on the desktop, and used the mouse. You have learned how to use a typical Windows dialog box, and what menu items are found in the Start menu. You understand how to launch programs directly from the Start button Programs menu item. Using the more intuitive document-centric approach, you launched applications by selecting the programs they manage. You learned how to share data between running programs by embedding a Paint graphic inside a WordPad document. You learned how easily you can switch from one program to another by using the program buttons located on the Taskbar.

After working with the Windows interface, you examined Windows Explorer. You opened drives, folders, and files, formatted a floppy disk for first-time use, created a folder on your floppy disk, and copied files from the Companion CD-ROM to your floppy disk. Using Explorer, you discovered how to delete and rename files, how to set selected file properties, and how to launch applications from associated data files.

Shortcuts, you discovered, are one of the most convenient features available in Windows. You used existing shortcuts and learned how to create your own desktop shortcuts. You found that you could place shortcuts on the Start menu to provide quick, global access to your most often used programs. You learned that the Document menu's list of recently accessed files provided automatic and fast access to items you recently worked on. We illustrated how to clear the Document menu's list to eliminate the file names from prying eyes. Moving the Taskbar to other edges of the screen, you realized yet another way to customize the Windows desktop.

You learned how to enable and use User Profiles. User Profiles preserve multiple desktop settings for various users of a single computer. By tracking different desktop settings and restoring each one when a user logs onto the computer, you understood how Windows 95 provided a truly customized look and feel for multiple users. Finally, you learned how to exit Windows and shut down the computer.

REVIEW EXERCISES

MULTIPLE-CHOICE QUESTIONS

1. Using the mouse, how do you execute a program whose shortcut is displayed on the desktop?
   a. click the program's shortcut
   b. double-click the program's shortcut
   c. right-click the program's shortcut
   d. choose Execute from the shortcut's pop-up menu

2. You can click the ____ button and then move to any object on the screen and click the mouse to obtain context-sensitive help about the clicked object.
   a. Help
   b. What's This?
   c. Properties
   d. Find
3. If you want to work on a file called *MyResume.doc* but forgot where on your computer it is filed, the fastest way to locate the file is to ________
   a. use Windows Explorer.
   b. select Help from the Start menu.
   c. select Locate from the Start menu.
   d. select Find from the Start menu.
4. The Settings menu found on the Start menu contains three menu items: Printers, Taskbar, and
   a. My Computer.
   b. Control Panel.
   c. Shut Down.
   d. My Network.
5. You can either use the Taskbar to switch between Windows programs or the keystroke combination
   a. Alt+Esc
   b. Ctrl+Alt
   c. Alt+Tab
   d. none of the preceding
6. Using Windows Explorer, you can copy a file from one folder to another by
   a. dragging and dropping the selection to the target folder.
   b. pressing Ctrl+C to copy the source file(s), selecting the target folder, then pressing Ctrl+V.
   c. executing Copy and then Paste from the Explorer Edit menu.
   d. all of the preceding will work
7. Shortcuts
   a. can be created for applications but not for documents or other files.
   b. are found only on the desktop.
   c. cause the program to be deleted when the shortcut is deleted.
   d. are frequently created to provide quick access to often-used applications.
8. Which of the following statements is true?
   a. Start menu items are permanent.
   b. The Taskbar is always visible somewhere on the screen.
   c. Only one application at a time may be running under Windows.
   d. User Profiles enable desktop settings of different users to be preserved.
9. You can minimize all open windows, revealing the desktop by
   a. clicking the Minimize button on the Taskbar.
   b. right-clicking the Taskbar and selecting *Minimize All Windows*.

c. double-clicking the Taskbar.
d. setting the Auto hide Taskbar property.

10. When you exit Windows
    a. Windows performs some housekeeping chores before shutting down.
    b. you can safely turn off your computer after told to do so by Windows.
    c. the next user must restart Windows before logging on.
    d. all of the preceding are true

DISCUSSION QUESTIONS

1. Describe the advantages of Windows 95 over DOS and Windows 3.1. Limit your discussion to two topics: passing information between applications in a DOS environment versus Windows 95 and the document-centric approach of Windows 95 versus the tool-centric approach of Windows 3.1.
2. Briefly explore and describe at least five applications contained in the Accessories folder (Start, Programs, Accessories).
3. Describe two ways to create a shortcut to a program or document.
4. Describe the ways to get help on Windows 95 in general. How would you get help with cut and paste if you were using WordPad? Describe the steps you would follow.
5. Describe some of the ways you might be able to take advantage of Windows' ability to work with multiple programs and data.

EXERCISES

1. Using WordPad, write a short, two-paragraph summary of the main points covered in one of your recent classes. For instance, write about your latest accounting information systems class lecture. Be sure to include your name on the document so you can easily identify it. After you have created the document, save it on your floppy disk. Then print the document.
2. If you have a new, unused floppy disk, use Windows Explorer to format your disk. In addition, label the new disk with your last name. Next, using either the new disk or one that already has information on it, use Windows Explorer to create two folders called *Notes* and *Homework* on your floppy disk.
3. Create a new company logo using Microsoft Paint. The logo should contain at least your company's name. Try the Airbrush, Brush, Line, and Pencil tools. Change colors. Be creative. This might be your future company's logo, after all! Choose 256 Color Bitmap in the Save as type list box. Save the graphic on your disk in any folder as the file *MyLogo.bmp*. Launch the WordPad program. Start the document by embedding your logo into the new document, and then write some text on the lines below your logo. Save the document as *MyLogo.wri* on your floppy disk and print the document. Be sure your name

is either in the logo or near the top of the typed material so that you can easily distinguish your output. Finally, close both Paint and WordPad.

4. Launch the following programs, one after the other: WordPad, Paint, Notepad, and Windows Explorer. Minimize all applications so they are buttons on the Taskbar. Right-click a program's Taskbar button and select Close from the pop-up menu to stop and unload the program. Repeat the program-exiting process for all remaining programs. How many ways can you think of to exit the programs you launched?
5. Learn about Windows 95 by consulting Help. Select Help from the Start menu, select the Contents tab of Help, and select *If you've used Windows before*. Click the Display button to display the first of several Windows 95 help panels. Click the gray topic buttons to get answers to question categories such as "What happened to my program groups?"

2 Introduction to Microsoft Access

Objectives

This chapter describes the Microsoft Access database management system in detail. You will use predefined databases to browse data, use Microsoft Access menus, and create several types of information forms. The purpose of this chapter is to bring you up to speed in using Access. If you have used Access extensively, then you can skip this chapter. Important topics covered in this chapter include:

- Starting and exiting Access.
- Understanding the Access work surface icons.
- Using the Access objects, including tables, forms, queries, and reports.
- Opening and displaying database tables.
- Retrieving information by writing database queries.
- Creating and using forms to display and query tables and databases.
- Designing and using database reports.

We feature a small, fictitious stock brokerage firm to illustrate how organizations use databases to manipulate and store crucial business information. The brokerage firm must maintain a record of each client's portfolio of stocks, bonds, etc. Among the important information stored are client information, such as name and address; and portfolio information, such as the stock purchased, purchase date, number of shares bought, etc. As we work with the database package in this chapter, we will reveal various items of information kept by the stock brokerage firm. More importantly, this chapter shows you that a relational database system can be built to track and maintain critical business information and economic events.

INTRODUCTION

Modern computer-based systems, including most accounting systems, have, at their heart, a database system. An accounts receivable program, for example, frequently stores its information in a special system known as a database. The information is subsequently extracted, summarized, and displayed by a program especially adept at storing, organizing, and quickly retrieving facts stored in a database. Such systems are known as *database management systems*.

What is Access?

You will study and use one such database management system written for microcomputers, called Microsoft Access. Produced by Microsoft Corporation, Access is the most popular database management system for Windows. Once you learn the fundamentals of Microsoft Access, you will be able to create your own accounting systems with this powerful database system. (We will often use the appellation "Access" rather than the longer term "Microsoft Access.")

What is a Relational Database?

Access is a *relational* database management system. Briefly, a relational database system is founded on the rules, created and published by Dr. E. F. Codd, that collectively define a relational database management system. It is beyond the scope of this textbook to include a discussion about these theoretical foundation rules. At this point, it is sufficient for you to know that relational database products are by far the most widely accepted and easiest to use type of database management system. We will uncover some of Codd's rules for relational database systems in Chapters 3 and 4 and elsewhere when the need arises.

Access is easy to use. The fundamental storage entity for a relational database system is easy to visualize—it is a two-dimensional object having rows and columns and is called a *table*. Tables hold data, and each row corresponds to one instance of data. Columns of a table correspond to different characteristics, called *attributes*. For example, consider a table holding employee information. One row of the table might represent one employee. The table holds as many rows as the number of employees in the company, division, or department. The table's columns might hold data such as employee first name, last name, hire date, social security number, gender, birth date, and so on. Each column holds only one "fact." That is, one column always holds hire dates and nothing else; another column holds only last names.

Often, a database is comprised of more than one table. For example, the employee table might be only one of several tables that collectively describe a company's employees, their skills, and their complete productivity histories. Almost always, more than one table is used to hold information. A collection of tables that are related and collectively describe an entity is known as a *database*.

You can imagine that an accounts receivable database contains many tables that are related to one another: a customer table, a salesperson table, an inventory table (you sell goods from inventory), and so on. Although most databases contain several tables, the terms *database* and *table* frequently are used interchangeably. When a database consists of only one table, it is known as a *flat file*.

Most databases used in business and government are large and often involve hundreds of tables. We will not subject you to such a large system. However, our databases do contain more than one table and some of those tables have several hundred rows. The reason for using multiple tables to represent related information will become clear as you continue to read. To better understand the concept of tables and their relationships, begin by launching Access and looking at a few tables we have prepared.

Starting Access

Your first exercise in this chapter is to launch Access. First, launch Windows if necessary. Access is usually stored with other Microsoft Office products. Locate Access, whose file name is *Msaccess.exe*, with Windows Explorer. If you have difficulty, then use Find in the Start menu and search for the file name. Once you find it, you will be able to launch Access directly from the Find dialog box.

Exercise 2.1: Starting Microsoft Access

1. Locate the Microsoft Access program. You may wish to use Explorer or the Find menu item on the Start menu.
2. Execute Access (double-click the program name if using Explorer or the Find program). Shortly, the Microsoft Access dialog box is displayed. It contains three option buttons from which you can choose: Blank Database, Database Wizard, and Open an Existing Database.
3. Click the last option, Open an Existing Database. The Open dialog box is displayed. Normally you would locate the database to be opened and then click the Open button. In this instance, you won't specify a particular database.
4. Click the Cancel button. The Access Startup window is displayed (see Figure 2.1).

The Startup window is the principal workspace. All Access windows are opened in the Access Startup window, and they are wholly contained in it. Each type of Access window you will encounter appears in its own window. Tables are always displayed in a Table window. Forms, described in the section *Using Forms* in this chapter, are viewed in a Form window, and so on. Each window has its own distinct commands and functions that apply only to that type of window. You will

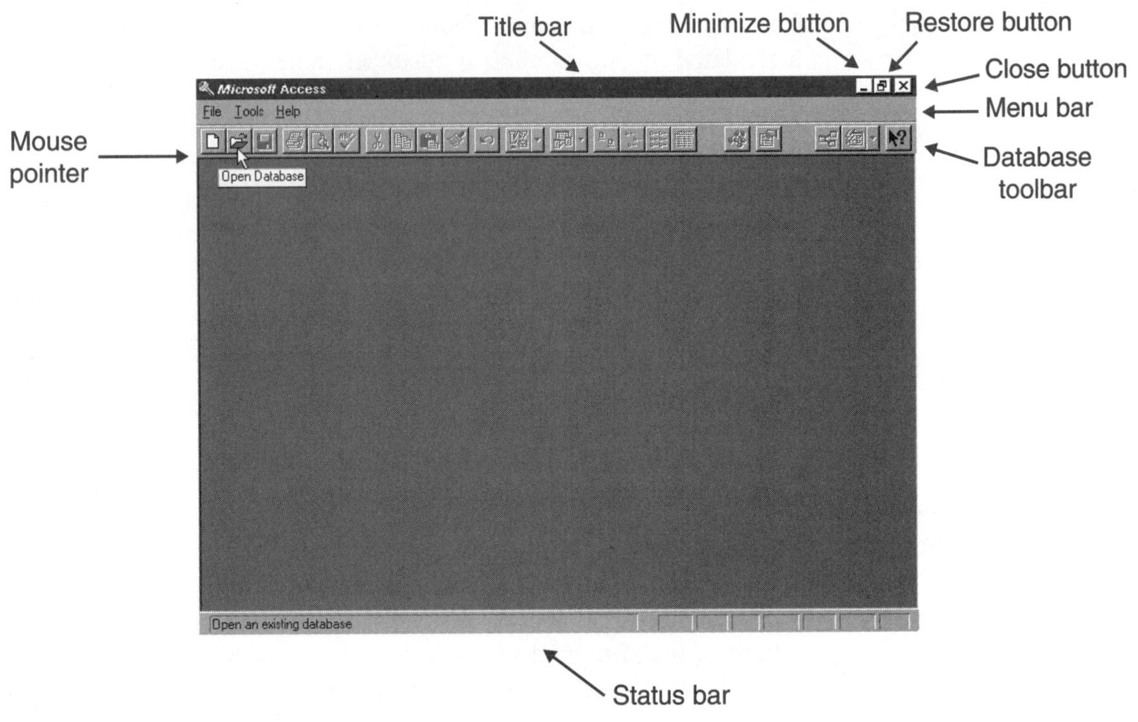

Figure 2.1 Access Startup window.

see these windows and the commands contained in them when we discuss each type of window. Take a moment to examine the Access window (see Figure 2.1 if you are not using the computer right now).

Along the top of the window are the Title bar and the Minimize, Restore, and Close buttons. Just below the Title bar is the Startup window Menu bar, containing the File, Tools, and Help menus. Below the Menu bar is the Database toolbar, displaying buttons appropriate for the current window. Notice that the mouse pointer in Figure 2.1 is positioned over a toolbar button whose name, Open Database, is displayed just below the button. When you move the mouse to other toolbar buttons their names appear after a very short delay. A brief explanation is shown in the Status bar located along the bottom of the Startup window.

Finding Help

It is important to know how to get help when you get stuck or would just like to know more about a particular aspect of Access. Let's see what help is available on creating forms. Make sure the Access Startup window is visible and active, and then do the following exercise.

EXERCISE 2.2: OBTAINING HELP

1. Select the Microsoft Access Help Topics command from the Help menu. The Help Topics dialog box is displayed.
2. Click the Index tab.
3. Type *form wiz* in the text box found near the top of the dialog box and press Enter. (Notice that you do not always have to spell the entire word or phrase for Help to recognize it.)
4. Select *Create a form* from the Topics Found list of choices and click the Display button (or simply press Enter). Help about creating forms is displayed.
5. Click the Help title bar Maximize button to enlarge the help display (see Figure 2.2).
6. After you have examined the help screen for a moment, close it by clicking the Close button on the Help title bar. The Microsoft Access Startup window reappears.

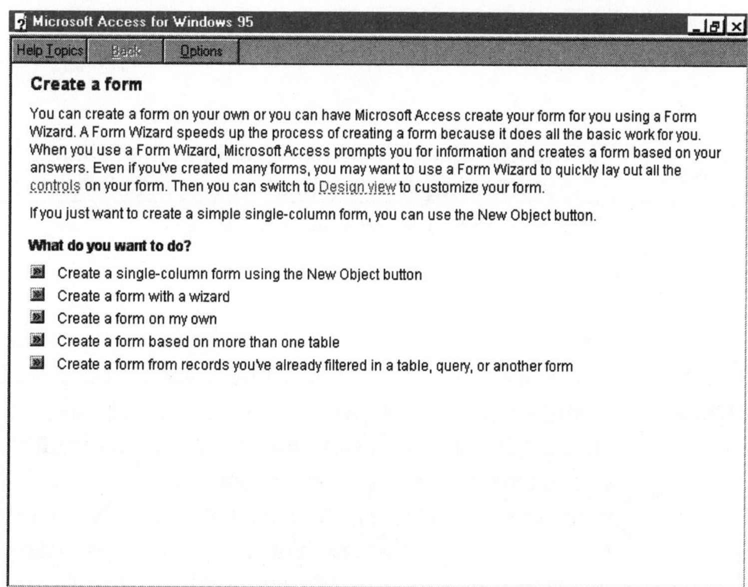

Figure 2.2 Obtaining help.

Printing Help

Occasionally, you may wish you could write down some especially important information you found in Help. Like all Windows products, help screens can be printed. By printing a few of the important help screens, you can have a handy reference within easy reach—even if you aren't near a computer. Printing help information is simple. Once you have located the help screen you want to print, select Print Topic from the Options menu, then select the correct printer and click OK. The help screen information prints out. If you wish, you can continue to other screens and print those of interest in the same way. That is all there is to it. (Print the Create a form help screen you located in the preceding exercise to ensure you understand the printing process.)

Exiting Access

After completing all of your database work, you should always exit Access. This signals Access to do its housekeeping chores such as posting any changes you have made to your database on your disk, closing other information sources, and returning to Windows. If you simply press Alt+Tab, for instance, to jump to Windows—leaving Access running—you run the risk of losing important information. You exit Access by choosing Exit from the File menu found on Access's Menu bar. Access quickly closes any open databases and returns to Windows.

EXAMINING THE ACCESS ENVIRONMENT

The Access Startup window's toolbar icons change as you move to other parts of Access. Toolbar buttons that are applicable in a particular window appear in color. Inapplicable buttons are dimmed.

Access Work Surface

The Startup window has just three menus: File, Tools, and Help. The File menu is similar to other Windows products. It contains commands that open files (database files in this case) and exit Access. In addition, the File menu contains commands to create a new database and open any hidden windows. The two File menu commands most often used are New Database and Open Database. Executing New Database allows you to create a database, whereas the Open Database command makes available an existing Access database. Figure 2.3 shows the screen display after the Open Database command is selected from the File menu.

After you open one of the available databases, Microsoft Access displays a Database window within the Microsoft Access window. The Database window is the central control point from which all database activities are conducted. Figure 2.4 shows the Database window for one of the databases, Ch02, found on your Companion CD-ROM.

The File menu changes once a Database window is open. Additional File menu commands that become available include Get External Data, Close, Save, Save As/Export, Database Properties, Page Setup, Print Preview, and Print. These

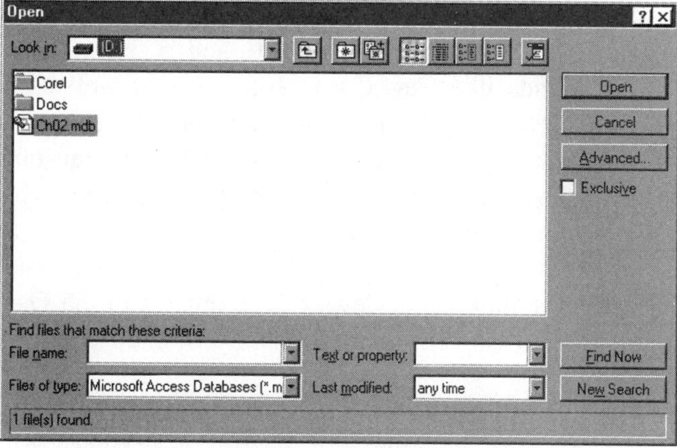

Figure 2.3 Preparing to open a database.

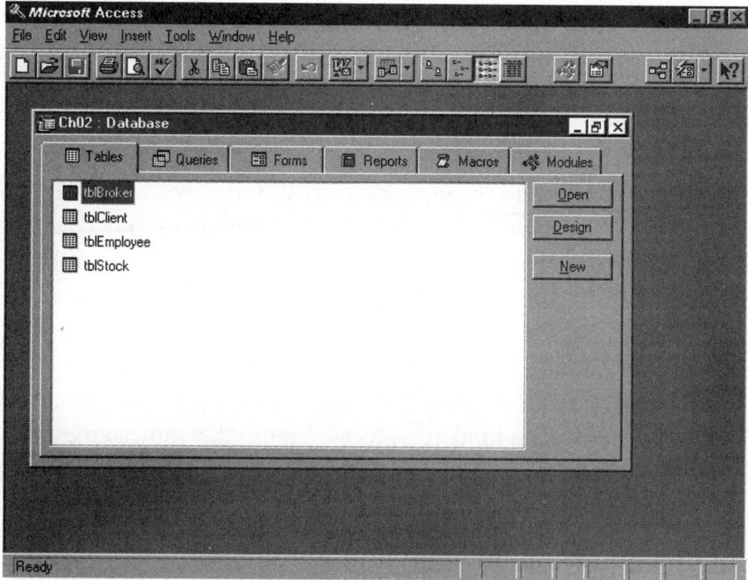

Figure 2.4 Database window.

important commands allow you to import data from other sources, close the current database, save the database, save the database under a new name or export it to another data type, alter database properties, and perform standard Windows print activities. You will use some of the File menu commands as you read this text and work through its examples.

The Menu bar also changes after you open a database (see Figure 2.4). Other menus include Edit, View, Insert, and Windows. The Edit menu contains familiar commands like Cut, Copy, and Paste as well as Create Shortcut, Delete, and Rename. The latter three commands allow you to create a desktop shortcut to any database object, delete an object, or rename an object.

The View menu lets you display different types of objects in the Database window. You can select tables, queries, forms, or reports, for instance. Another group of commands—Large Icons, Small Icons, List, Details, and Arrange Icons—provides alternative views of the objects in the Database window. The Toolbars command can be used to display or hide one or more of the several special toolbars.

The Insert menu contains commands to insert tables, forms, queries, and other database objects into the current database. AutoForm and AutoReport create a new form and a new report based on the currently selected table or query. We will use these commands in this text.

The Tools menu contains Spelling and AutoCorrect commands; Relationships, which lets you establish relationships between tables; Security, to keep your database secure; and Options, which allows you to set database-wide default values and conditions. There are other commands in the Tools menu, but they are beyond the scope of this text.

The Window menu contains six commands: Tile Horizontally, Tile Vertically, Cascade, Arrange Icons, Hide, and Unhide. Tile Horizontally and Tile Vertically arrange all Access windows so that they do not overlap one another. The orientation depends on which of the two you choose. Cascade presents windows so that only the Title bar of all open but inactive Access windows are displayed. The active window is placed on top. When Access windows are reduced to icons, the Arrange Icons command lines up the icons along the bottom edge of the Access window in the same order as it found them. Finally, the Hide command hides the active window from view, whereas the Unhide command reveals a hidden window. Figure 2.5 shows an example of several database tables. Two tables are cascaded and one is reduced to an icon and found in the lower left corner of the Access window. The Database window, Ch02, has been hidden. Later in this chapter you will look more closely at each of these three tables.

Help is the rightmost menu on the Startup window. Clicking Help displays a standard Help menu. We have presented an overview of the Help menu already, so we will not discuss it further.

Look at Figure 2.5 again. Notice the several toolbar icons. Those icons represent shortcuts to commands accessed from the Menu bar. The toolbar buttons that are unavailable in a particular situation are dimmed. Buttons that are not dimmed may be clicked to rapidly accomplish various tasks. The buttons provide a shortcut to menu commands; they do not replace the menu commands. You will use both the buttons and menus to create and modify various database objects as you read through this text.

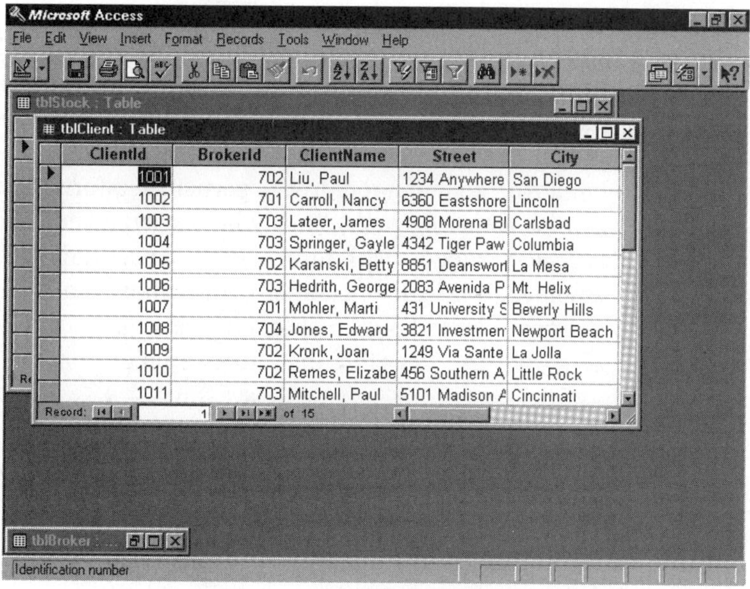

Figure 2.5 Icons and cascaded windows.

Access Objects

Access provides a plethora of ways to store, display, and report your data. The structures and methods you employ to store and display your data are called *objects*. Access objects include tables, queries, forms, reports, macros, and modules. This text tells you how to take advantage of the first five of these objects. Nearly all of your accounting information systems can be built using tables, queries, forms, reports, and macros. Only the most advanced applications—those beyond the scope of this text—require the use of modules. This section presents an overview of four of these five important types of objects and shows how each can be used in building accounting information systems. Chapter 5 describes the fifth type, macros. Sections that follow use existing objects, such as tables and forms, to illustrate further how information is organized and retrieved with a database system located at the heart of an accounting information system. You will be asked to create some tables, queries, forms, and reports for a small system. First, let's see what these objects are that are the building blocks of a database management system that you will be using to build your accounting information systems.

Tables. *Tables* are the fundamental storage structures for data, a company's information resource. Like spreadsheet models you have seen, tables are two-dimensional objects with columns and rows. Each row contains all available information about a particular item. (We will use the term *record* interchangeably with *row.*) All rows contain exactly the same number of columns, though not every row necessarily has a value for all of its columns. Consider a table holding employee information. A small company having 50 employees could store employee data—name, date of birth, hire date, etc.—in a fifty-row table. Each employee column would be a particular information *field.* (The terms *field* and *column* are used synonymously in this and other texts.) Each column contains one type (or category) of information. For example, one column contains each employee's hire date, another column holds each employee's last name, and yet another column holds each employee's birth date. Figure 2.6 shows an example of a small Access table that stores employee data.

tblEmployee : Table

Ident No	Name	Hire Date	Notes	Salary
1001	Hayes, Alice	9/1/96	Our CEO!	$142,500
1002	Cook, Fred	6/14/80	VP, Sales	$85,000
1003	Savarese, Alicia	9/1/92	Has many good	$38,750
1004	Yablonski, Carol	4/15/88	CFO, hard work	$87,000
1005	Perez, Jessie	9/17/91	Super acct exe(	$45,500
1016	Chang, Yuan	1/12/94	Shows potential	$32,000

Record: 1 of 6

Figure 2.6 Example table containing employee data.

Observe that each column holds only one type of data—an important rule to keep in mind when you create your own tables. Each row contains information about an employee, and only one row is available for a single employee. As you can see, several types of data can be stored in a table: numeric, text, date, free-flowing text (which is stored in a special *memo* field), and currency (the salary field). Access tables can also hold three other types of data called AutoNumber (generating a unique number), Yes/No, and OLE objects.

At the top of each column is the column's name, called an *attribute,* that uniquely identifies a column. Each row corresponds to one of the employees. A row is indivisible. The data in a row remains with the row, even if the rows are sorted or displayed in a different order. Though the rows are unordered, they can be organized into a more meaningful order when necessary. This is one of the advantages of a relational database system: the order of table rows is unimportant.

Similarly, the columns are placed in an arbitrary order left to right. Is there some arcane rule that states columns must be arranged in a particular order? No. We have designed the Employee table so that the employee identification number is first, but no other implicit meaning or significance exists in the columns' arrangement. You can rearrange columns so that the Salary field is second, the

Notes field is last, and so on. This is another advantage of relational databases: the order of table columns is unimportant. Access places one restriction on that rule, which you will understand more fully later. That rule is this: If a table has a unique identifier—a column value that uniquely identifies each row—then that column must be first in the table. The field *Ident No* serves that purpose. No two employees share the same identification number, so we place that field first. This type of field is called a table's *primary key*. You will learn more about primary keys later.

Queries. There are several types of queries, but the most common query is called a selection query. A *selection query* is a question you can ask about your database. (Because selection queries are the most common, they are simply called queries.) For instance, a query is "How many employees earn more than $50,000?" or "What customers' invoices are over 60 days past due?" Queries are especially helpful for combining information from several related tables into a single, cohesive result. Also, queries provide a way to reduce the data volume by returning and displaying only the subset of table rows in which you are interested. You can use queries to summarize data, displaying only the aggregate results (for example, the sum of all outstanding invoices in the accounts receivable file). Other types of queries can be used to *insert* new data into a table, *delete* unwanted data from a table, or *change* values in a table. Using Access queries, you can select which tables are the subject of your questions, designate the columns you would like to see, and specify which table rows are to be returned.

The query result, called the *dynaset*, is displayed in a Query window. Figure 2.7 shows an example of a query and its dynaset, each in its own window. In that query, only the columns appearing in the *query grid* are available in the dynaset. Check marks (✓) in the query grid Show row indicate which columns are to be displayed, and the expression **>50000**, called a *selection criterion*, filters the rows. That is, selection criteria restrict the rows that are returned to those that meet the conditions specified by the criteria—in this case, rows whose Salary field is greater than $50,000.

Forms. Frequently, it is better to work with data in your tables one row at a time. Tables are not an intuitive interface for some people, especially those who are not computer literate. Access forms solve this problem. *Forms* let you see the data from a table in a format that is easier to understand. You can see one row or many rows of a table. Figure 2.8 shows an example of a form displaying the Employee data in an attractive and intuitive layout.

As you can see, a form may be an easier way to view and change data stored in your databases. One of several records is displayed. You can move to the next or the previous record, or the first or last record, by clicking the navigation buttons, which are located in the lower left corner of the window. You can move

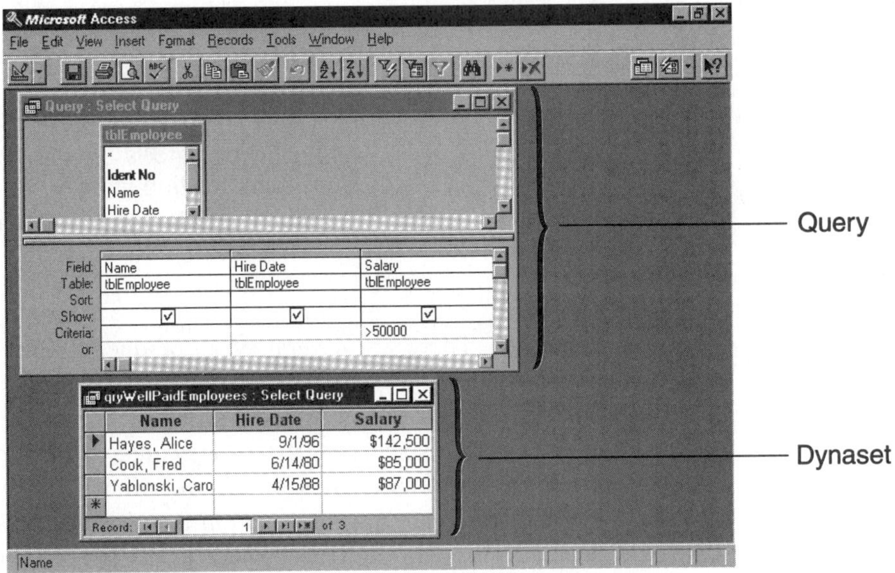

Figure 2.7 Example query and dynaset.

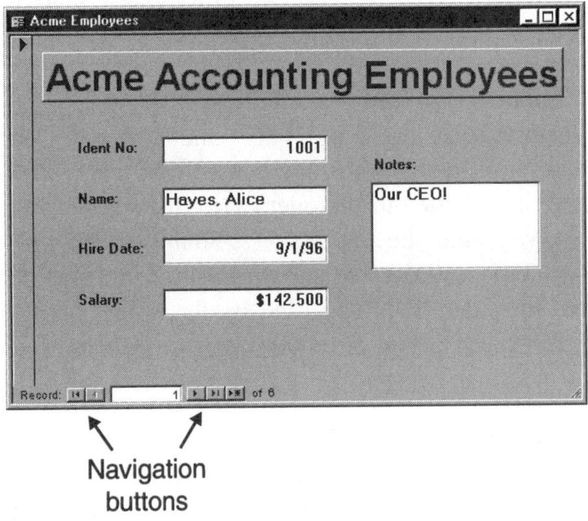

Figure 2.8 Example form displaying an Employee table row.

directly to a specific record by pressing F5 and typing a record number. The single, right-pointing arrow button moves one record at a time, displaying the next record in the form. The right-pointing arrow with a vertical line to its right moves directly to the last record. The opposite actions take place for the left-pointing navigation buttons.

Reports. Imagine showing several people in a meeting a financial statement displayed on your notebook computer's screen. That would be awkward and unprofessional. Hard copy output—a report—is a better solution. That way, the report can be distributed to an assembled group easily. Access provides a comprehensive report-producing facility.

Access reports are often the main output or result produced by a database system. While it is important to store accounts receivable information in a database and be able to query that database for answers, a far more important activity is to produce a printed output. For example, you might want a list of all receivables over 60 days past due. If there are more than a few, a printed report is the most useful output. You can scan the list, marking accounts that deserve special attention. You can also make copies of a hard copy output for distribution to appropriate departments and managers.

You can use Access's report design features and tools to customize a report to look any way you would like. A report can display data from one table or from several tables that have been linked together. Figure 2.9 is an example of a simple report employing a drop shadow around the title, a graphic (a company logo), bold column headings, and sorted employee names from the Employee table. The simple report is easy to create, and the results are professional-looking. An equivalent report produced using a programming language such as COBOL would require a few hundred lines of code and would require far more than the few minutes it takes to create the same report with Access.

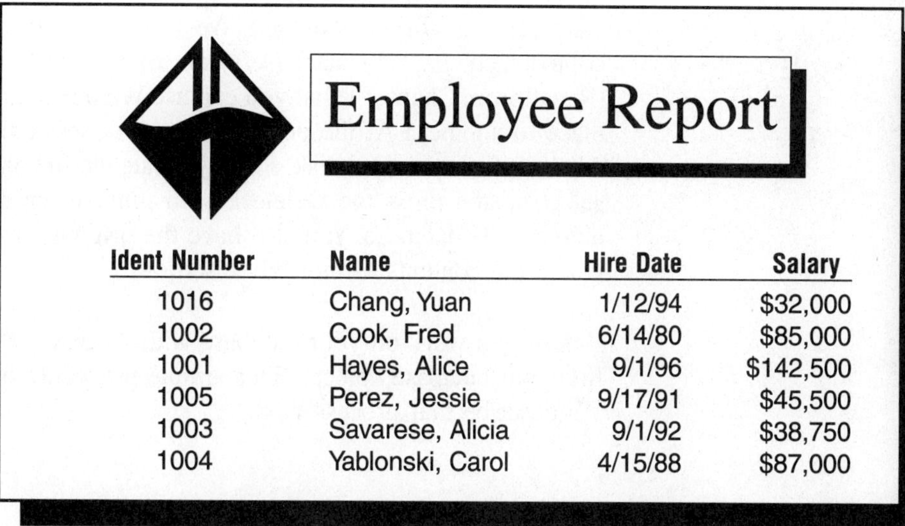

Employee Report

Ident Number	Name	Hire Date	Salary
1016	Chang, Yuan	1/12/94	$32,000
1002	Cook, Fred	6/14/80	$85,000
1001	Hayes, Alice	9/1/96	$142,500
1005	Perez, Jessie	9/17/91	$45,500
1003	Savarese, Alicia	9/1/92	$38,750
1004	Yablonski, Carol	4/15/88	$87,000

Figure 2.9 Example report.

Sections that follow describe the process of using and creating tables, queries, forms, and reports. We encourage you to participate in the exercises, because the remainder of the chapter is much more interactive. You will learn the most if you duplicate the steps we present and actually use and create the objects we do. To help you in that process, we have supplied many of the required tables, queries, forms, and reports so that you can try them out. In addition, you will create a few of your own.

WORKING WITH DATABASES AND TABLES

The foundation of any database system rests on its tables. Tables hold the data that is transformed into information. In this section you will learn how to use tables that we have provided, create your own tables, modify the order in which table columns are displayed, and link tables together.

Important Note: Before you work on the tables found on your Companion CD-ROM, you should first copy the database from the Companion CD-ROM to the hard disk, drive C, of the computer on which you are working. Do so at the *beginning* of your work session. That way, you will be able to make changes to your tables, queries, and other objects stored in the databases we supply with the textbook. You should avoid using databases directly from your Companion CD-ROM because Access limits your activities to "read-only." That means you cannot make any changes either to the structure of tables or other objects, and you cannot alter the data stored in the tables. The only database you need to copy from the Companion CD-ROM for this chapter is found in the folder called *Ch02*. The database is called *Ch02.mdb*. Copy that file to your hard disk now, before you start working with the database. We will assume from this point on that you have copied each chapter's database(s) to drive C prior to working through a chapter. (Recall from Chapter 1 that you can use Windows Explorer to copy files from one place to another.) At the end of each work session, you may want to erase the database from the hard disk. Simply locate the file on the hard disk with Explorer, select it, and press the Delete key to remove the database. Don't worry about deleting the database. You still have the original on your Companion CD-ROM, where the contents cannot be erased.

Before you work on your database with Access, be sure to tell Access where to find your database objects. This simple procedure is called *opening a database*. We describe that process next.

Opening a Database

Whether you are using a stand-alone computer (one not connected to a network of computers) or a computer in a laboratory on a local network, you must first open a database. A *database* is a collection of objects which are related, including tables, queries, forms, reports, macros, and modules. Access stores all the objects of a particular database within one file. Access fetches and stores information in whichever database is open, but only one database may be open at one time.

All exercises in this text refer to the *Companion CD-ROM* that comes with this text. (You used the CD-ROM in Chapter 1 to locate a document.) We have segregated files of all types needed for each chapter into separate databases so that you can isolate all changes and activities by chapter. Here is how the disk directories are set up. All files needed for Chapter 2 are found in the directory Ch02 (C-h-zero-two), all files needed for Chapter 3 are found in the directory Ch03, and so on. Whenever you are working with a chapter, you can locate databases and files in the associated chapter directory on your Companion CD-ROM. The next exercise shows you how to open a database that has been copied to drive C from your Companion CD-ROM so the data is available to Microsoft Access.

Exercise 2.3: Opening a Database

1. Launch Access by double-clicking the Access icon (locate it, if necessary, using the Start menu Find command as you did in Chapter 1). The Microsoft Access dialog box displays.
2. Click the option button *Open an Existing Database* and then click OK.
3. Click the *Look in* drop-down menu and select drive C. Folders and file names found on drive C are displayed in the list box (see Figure 2.10).
4. In the list box, select *Ch02.mdb* and press the Open button. (Alternately, you can double-click the database name to open it.) Microsoft Access displays the Ch02 Database window (see Figure 2.11).

The Database window displays the names of all tables in the database. There are other objects held in the database including queries, forms, and reports. The names of forms in this database can be seen if you click the Forms tab. Likewise, you can see all queries by clicking the Queries tab. If the table objects show icons or show more information, then your view setting has been changed. If your table list match doesn't match the list in Figure 2.11, select the List command from the View menu. Now the two should look alike.

Looking at Your Data through Different Windows

Access provides several ways to view your data. You can inspect your data in a Table window, which displays data in columns and rows called a *Datasheet view*—just like a spreadsheet's data. Or you can use a Form window to display one or more rows in a nontabular format. Forms provide an attractive way to view

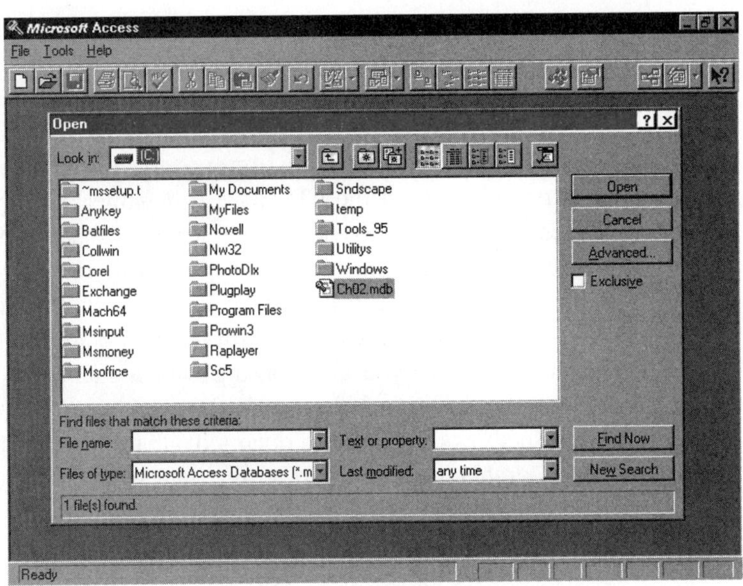

Figure 2.10 Open Database dialog box.

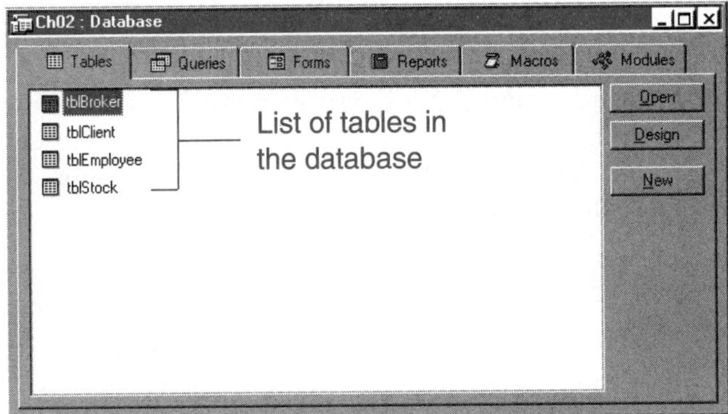

Figure 2.11 Database window.

and change data, because they can be designed to resemble paper forms with which you are already familiar. (You can also view a form in Datasheet view.) Alternately, you can view your data in a report format with the Report window. The Report window provides a preview of a printed report so that you can review it as you would a hard copy report prior to printing it.

Because each view is found in a separate window, you can display several different windows simultaneously. Figure 2.12 shows both a Table window and a Form window of the Employee table. Because the Form window is active (notice the Form window Title bar is darker), the Menu bar and toolbar are the ones used in a Form window.

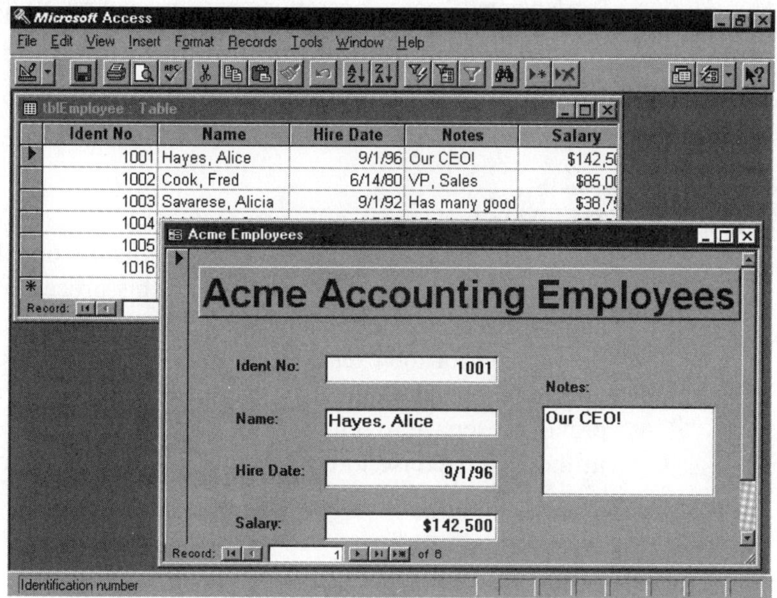

Figure 2.12 Two views of the same data.

One of the databases found on the Companion CD-ROM contains information about a fictitious stock brokerage firm. This small database consists of three related tables: Broker (*tblBroker*), Client (*tblClient*), and Stock (*tblStock*). We follow the object naming convention that all tables begin with the prefix *tbl* followed immediately by the rest of the object name. Queries begin with *qry* and the rest of the object name, forms begin with *frm* and the rest of the object name, and reports begin with *rpt* and the remainder of the name. (For simplicity, we refer to the tables in the text without their prefixes.) The Broker table contains information about four of the brokerage firm's employees, all stockbrokers. Client contains the names, addresses, and other data about selected brokerage clients. The table Stock lists the stocks currently held by each customer whose name is in the Client list. Of course, all of these tables are smaller than corresponding tables in a real brokerage house. We want you to comprehend the *process* of extracting meaningful information from the data, not marvel at the *size* of the database. It is easier to understand database concepts if we use several small tables. Client, for example, contains 15 rows, one for each customer. Broker contains 4 rows, which contain a few facts about the brokers. Finally, the

Stock table contains 173 rows. Whenever a customer purchases an individual stock, that transaction is recorded and saved in the Stock table.

You may be interested in more details about what these three tables contain. Details about each of the brokerage firm tables will be revealed as we describe fundamental Access operations and procedures in this chapter. We begin by examining the use of Access tables, the elemental building block of all database applications.

Opening a Table

The Table window is one way to view your data. When you open a table, the Menu bar and toolbar change to menus and icons that are appropriate for table operations. You can better understand this process if you open an existing table and experience firsthand how some of the toolbar buttons and menus operate. In preparation for the exercise that follows, execute Access and the Ch02 database you have copied to drive C. If you forget how to open a database, review the previous exercise to refresh your memory. Now you are ready to follow the steps in the next exercise to open one of the tables on your disk.

Exercise 2.4: Opening a Table

1. Click the Tables tab to display the list of tables in the Ch02 database.
2. Double-click the table *tblClient* found in the list of tables. (Alternatively, you can select *tblClient* and click the Open button in the Database window.) The Client table is displayed in Datasheet view (see Figure 2.13).

Take a moment to examine the Client table. Notice the Datasheet navigation buttons located at the bottom edge of the Table window. Behind the table and slightly to its left is visible part of the Database window.

Below the Access Title bar is the Table window Menu bar. The Menu bar's contents vary depending on what type of window is active (Table, Form, etc.). Below the Menu bar is the toolbar. The contents of the toolbar vary with the active window. The Table Datasheet toolbar, shown in Figure 2.14, is displayed when a Table window is active and you are viewing a Datasheet (a table). The Form Design toolbar is displayed when the Form Design window is active.

Some Datasheet toolbar buttons are familiar, because they are similar to those found in other Windows products. They are Print, Print Preview, Cut, Copy, and Paste and are the third, fourth, sixth, seventh and eighth buttons on the left side of the toolbar. The Print button is a familiar icon which you can click to print a table. Move the mouse pointer over the Print button and pause. Observe that text

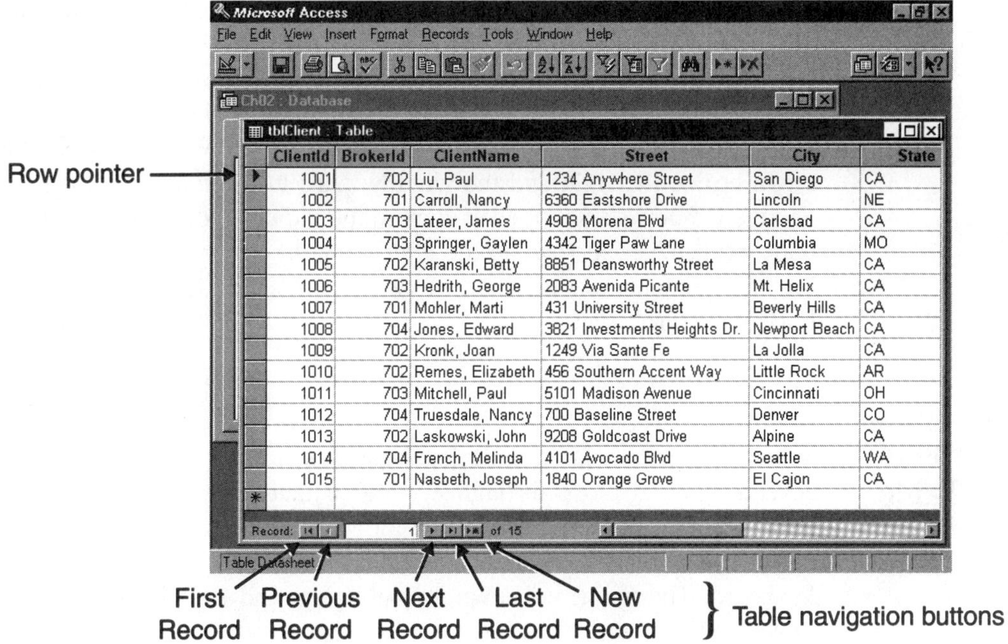

ClientId	BrokerId	ClientName	Street	City	State
1001	702	Liu, Paul	1234 Anywhere Street	San Diego	CA
1002	701	Carroll, Nancy	6360 Eastshore Drive	Lincoln	NE
1003	703	Lateer, James	4908 Morena Blvd	Carlsbad	CA
1004	703	Springer, Gaylen	4342 Tiger Paw Lane	Columbia	MO
1005	702	Karanski, Betty	8851 Deansworthy Street	La Mesa	CA
1006	703	Hedrith, George	2083 Avenida Picante	Mt. Helix	CA
1007	701	Mohler, Marti	431 University Street	Beverly Hills	CA
1008	704	Jones, Edward	3821 Investments Heights Dr.	Newport Beach	CA
1009	702	Kronk, Joan	1249 Via Sante Fe	La Jolla	CA
1010	702	Remes, Elizabeth	456 Southern Accent Way	Little Rock	AR
1011	703	Mitchell, Paul	5101 Madison Avenue	Cincinnati	OH
1012	704	Truesdale, Nancy	700 Baseline Street	Denver	CO
1013	702	Laskowski, John	9208 Goldcoast Drive	Alpine	CA
1014	704	French, Melinda	4101 Avocado Blvd	Seattle	WA
1015	701	Nasbeth, Joseph	1840 Orange Grove	El Cajon	CA

Figure 2.13 The Client table (*tblClient*).

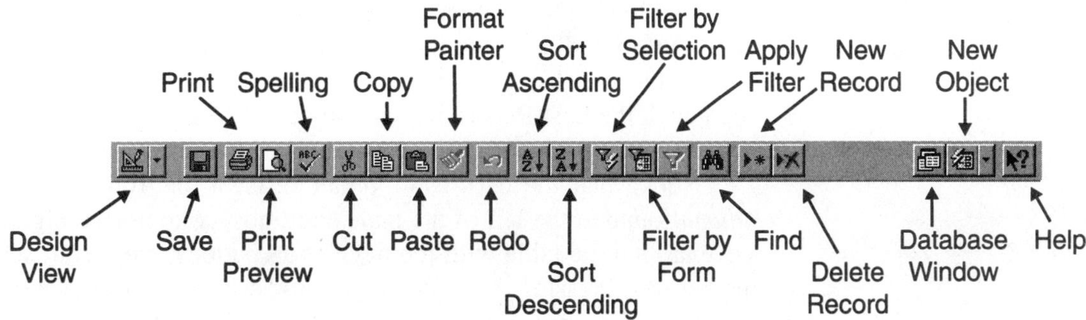

Figure 2.14 Table Datasheet toolbar.

(called a *tooltip*) appears just below the button displaying its title. The left part of the status line displays a brief explanation of the button's duties. In fact, each button's purpose is indicated in the status line as the mouse moves to or across each toolbar button.

Binoculars on the toolbar are used to search the table for particular values. Other toolbar buttons allow you to modify the table's design (Design View), sort the table into ascending or descending order, apply filter criteria to select particular records, and create forms and reports from the table. You will use some of these latter buttons later in this chapter.

A horizontal scroll bar appearing along the bottom of the Table window indicates there are table columns than cannot be viewed at once (such is the case in Figure 2.13). The scroll bar works like any other Windows scroll bar: drag the scroll box to the right and the window pans to the right; click the scroll arrows and the window shifts for each click in the indicated direction. Vertical scroll bars appear whenever all rows of the table cannot be seen at once. The vertical scroll bar, located on the right side of the Table window, operates similarly to the horizontal scroll bar.

Moving Around a Table

When you open a large table, only the first few rows are displayed. There are several ways to move through a table so that rows are displayed in the Table window. You can select one of the movement choices from the Go To selection of the Edit menu: First, Last, Next, Previous, or New. You can also use the keyboard. The up arrow, down arrow, PgUp, and PgDn keys move up one row, down one row, up one screen, and down one screen, respectively. Perhaps the easiest way to scroll through a table's rows is to use the navigation buttons (see Figure 2.13). Left to right, they move to the top of the table, up one row, to a specific numbered record, down one row, to the last record in the table, or add a new row to the table. The last button opens a new record, which is placed immediately following the last record in the table. The New Record button is a convenient way to add a new record to a table. Try the navigation buttons. With the Client table still displayed in a Table window, first go to the top of the database. Then click the Last Record navigation button to go to the last record (we use the term *record* interchangeably with the term *row*).

Notice that the dark row pointer rests in one row of the *record selector column* found to the left of the table's leftmost column (see Figure 2.13). As you move around the table with the navigation buttons, the record selector moves to another row. Pressing the right and left arrow keys moves the cursor to a different column in the same row.

Searching for a Value in a Column

Searching for a particular record in a table based on the value of one of its columns is straightforward. Though nearly all the data is visible in this small Client table example, most corporate tables contain thousands and hundreds of thousands of rows. Finding a particular client's record in such a large table would be extremely difficult without a database system. Let's imagine that the Client table contains many rows and you want to find a client whose name begins with the letters "Lasko" but you do not remember the exact spelling. Your task, in the next exercise, is to locate the client's record. If necessary open the table *tblClient* in the Ch02 database.

EXERCISE 2.5: SEARCHING FOR A ROW CONTAINING A PARTICULAR VALUE

1. With the *tblClient* datasheet displayed, click the first name in the ClientName column. That moves the cursor to the column to be searched.
2. Click the Find button (on the Table Datasheet toolbar, it looks like a pair of binoculars) and type ***Lask**** in the Find What text box. Be sure to include the asterisk, a wildcard, following the last letter.
3. Click the Current Field check box.
4. Select Down from the Search drop-down list.
5. Click the Find First button to start the search process. The arrow is moved in the record selector column to the row containing the name Laskowski, and the matching name is highlighted.
6. Close the Find dialog box by clicking the Close button.
7. Move the record pointer to the first record in the *tblClient* table by using the appropriate navigation button.

Try a few other search operations. For instance, locate the record whose City column contains "Seattle." What happens if there is no match? A dialog box is displayed indicating the search was unsuccessful.

Changing a Table's Display Characteristics

You can change the visual properties of any table you are viewing. For instance, you can move columns left or right in a table, alter individual column widths, and remove the grid lines that separate the rows and columns. You change a table's display properties by selecting an entire column and then right-clicking (clicking the right mouse button) the table column selected. Even though you may change a table's display characteristics, you are *not* changing the table's fundamental structure. For instance, if you move the ClientName column to the left of its current position, the underlying table, Client, is unaffected. Only the *display* characteristics of the Client table are affected. (Access gives you the opportunity to save a table's display characteristics permanently when you close the table.)

Let's change two display properties for the Client table temporarily. The next exercise moves the ClientName column to the first column, just to the right of the record selector column. You will also make one other visual change: you will optimize the widths of all columns so no data is obscured. Before starting the exercise, make sure Access is loaded, the database Ch02 is open, and the Client (*tblClient*) datasheet is displayed. Maximize the Table window so you can see more of the table.

EXERCISE 2.6: CHANGING A TABLE'S DISPLAY PROPERTIES

1. Move the pointer to the ClientName *field selector* (column heading). When the mouse pointer is over the column heading, it changes to a down-pointing arrow. (When the pointer is within the data of a column, it is an I-beam.)
2. Click the mouse to select the entire column (it darkens).
3. Click (again) and drag the column heading to the leftmost position in the table and then release the left mouse button. (The column remains darkened after you release the mouse.)
4. With the ClientName column still selected, right-click the mouse in the ClientName column. A pop-up menu will be displayed.
5. Select *Column Width...* from the list of pop-up menu choices.
6. Click the Best Fit button. The column resizes to the smallest width that will display both the column label and the widest column entry.
7. Move the mouse to the ClientId column field selector. When the mouse is a down-pointing arrow (as before), click and drag across all columns to select them. Release the mouse.
8. With all columns except ClientName darkened (selected), position the pointer on the right border of any field selector and double-click the mouse to produce the best fit for all the selected columns.
9. Click anywhere in the table to deselect the columns. Figure 2.15 shows the reformatted Client datasheet.

ClientName	ClientId	BrokerId	Street	City	State	ZipCode
Liu, Paul	1001	702	1234 Anywhere Street	San Diego	CA	92020
Carroll, Nancy	1002	701	6360 Eastshore Drive	Lincoln	NE	68508
Lateer, James	1003	703	4908 Morena Blvd	Carlsbad	CA	92008
Springer, Gaylen	1004	703	4342 Tiger Paw Lane	Columbia	MO	65205
Karanski, Betty	1005	702	8851 Deansworthy Street	La Mesa	CA	91941
Hedrith, George	1006	703	2083 Avenida Picante	Mt. Helix	CA	92020
Mohler, Marti	1007	701	431 University Street	Beverly Hills	CA	90210
Jones, Edward	1008	704	3821 Investments Heights Dr.	Newport Beach	CA	92221
Kronk, Joan	1009	702	1249 Via Sante Fe	La Jolla	CA	92022
Remes, Elizabeth	1010	702	456 Southern Accent Way	Little Rock	AR	88767
Mitchell, Paul	1011	703	5101 Madison Avenue	Cincinnati	OH	45227
Truesdale, Nancy	1012	704	700 Baseline Street	Denver	CO	80302
Laskowski, John	1013	702	9208 Goldcoast Drive	Alpine	CA	92014
French, Melinda	1014	704	4101 Avocado Blvd	Seattle	WA	98101
Nasbeth, Joseph	1015	701	1840 Orange Grove	El Cajon	CA	92020
*						

Figure 2.15 Changing a table's display properties.

We are finished with this exercise and do not want to permanently change the Client datasheet display characteristics, so close the table by clicking its Close button. A dialog box is displayed. It informs you that the layout characteristics for Client have changed and asks whether you want to save the new layout. Choose No to discard the table display characteristic changes you made.

Sorting Table Rows

Often, you can locate a record or group of records more quickly if the table is sorted. For instance, it is somewhat difficult to scan the Client table, as small as it is, and determine quickly whether a client named Shaut is among the list. You can imagine how difficult a client search by name would be for a much larger client list containing thousands of records, especially when the records are not sorted by name. The Client table is already sorted on one of the fields, ClientId.

There are two distinct ways to sort any table. One way is to perform a *quick sort* to organize the table on a single column. Another way is to create and apply a *filter*, which allows you to accomplish more complex, multicolumn sort operations. No matter which method you choose, the table returns to its original order once it is closed.

Some tables are automatically organized because they have *key* field(s). Client, for instance, is organized on the ClientId field because that field was designated a primary key field when the table was constructed. (Primary key fields ensure that tables contain only one record for a particular key field value.) We'll sort the Client table into ascending name order in the next exercise.

In preparation for the exercise, ensure that Access is still running and that the Ch02 database is open. Click the Tables tab of the Database window to display the list of tables in Ch02. Then, open the Client table (*tblClient*).

EXERCISE 2.7: SORTING A TABLE

1. With the Client table displayed, click anywhere in the ClientName column.
2. Execute Records, Sort, Ascending (or click the Sort Ascending button on the toolbar). The datasheet is sorted into order by clients' names.

Another way to sort a table is to create an *Advanced Filter/Sort*. When you do, you can select multiple table columns by which the table is sorted (for example, ascending order by State and then ascending order by City within each State). You can select column names from a list, place each sort column into a sort grid, and select either an Ascending or Descending sort order for each column. Once you create an Advanced Filter/Sort, you apply it by clicking the Apply Filter button found on the toolbar (it is the funnel object). You redisplay the datasheet in its original order by selecting Remove Filter/Sort from the Records menu. Experiment a bit with these. They can do no harm, because the table's actual record order is unaffected. Only the datasheet's displayed sort order is changed.

After you are done experimenting with sorting, close the Client table by clicking the Table window Close button. The Database window becomes active. Be careful not to click the Access application Close button, because the entire application will close and you will be returned to Windows.

Printing a Table

Printing a database table could not be easier. Merely select the table (it need not be open in a window to print its contents) or display the table in a Table window and select Print from the File menu. You can also click the toolbar Print button. However, be aware that you cannot control the number of pages or other print parameters if you use the toolbar Print button. Clicking the button starts printing the table immediately without any further interaction with you. We suggest you always select Print from the File menu to have greater control over the content and volume that you want printed.

When you select Print from the File menu, a Print dialog box appears (see Figure 2.16). You can choose to print all pages or a range of pages. Select a page range by entering From and To page numbers. Normally, you need only one copy of the report. However, if multiple copies are needed, simply alter the value in the Number of Copies text box. When you are ready to print the table, click the OK button. Otherwise, click the Cancel button to nullify the print process and return to the Table window.

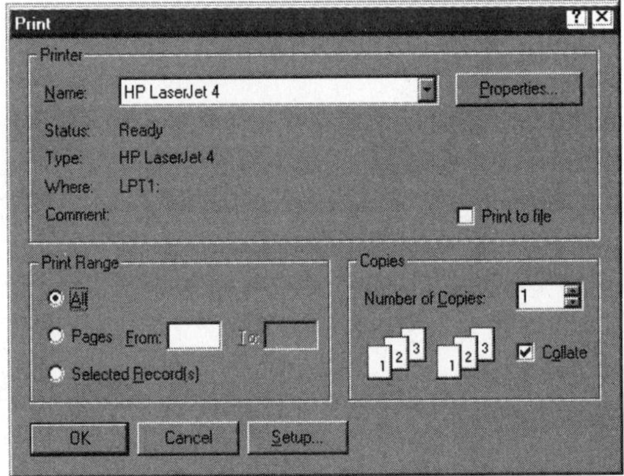

Figure 2.16 Print dialog box.

A printed table is created using a default format. Results are printed in columns with horizontal and vertical table grid lines. The date appears above and on the right side of the report, and the table's name appears centered above the table. At the bottom center of the page is a page number. Figure 2.17 shows an example of the output for the Client table.

As you can see, the table report is not beautiful by any means. Access provides tools for producing boardroom-quality reports replete with fonts, specialty features such as underlining and boldface, etc. Later in this chapter, we describe how to create and use Access reports. Reports such as Figure 2.17 are quick and easy to produce and allow you to check values in various columns quickly.

ClientId	BrokerId	ClientName	Street	City	State	ZipCode
1001	702	Liu, Paul	1234 Anywhere Street	San Diego	CA	92020
1002	701	Carroll, Nancy	6360 Eastshore Drive	Lincoln	NE	68508
1003	703	Lateer, James	4908 Morena Blvd	Carlsbad	CA	92008
1004	703	Springer, Gaylen	4342 Tiger Paw Lane	Columbia	MO	65205
1005	702	Karanski, Betty	8851 Deansworthy Street	La Mesa	CA	91941
1006	703	Hedrith, George	2083 Avenida Picante	Mt. Helix	CA	92020
1007	701	Mohler, Marti	431 University Street	Beverly Hills	CA	90210
1008	704	Jones, Edward	3821 Investments Heights Dr.	Newport Beach	CA	92221
1009	702	Kronk, Joan	1249 Via Sante Fe	La Jolla	CA	92022
1010	702	Remes, Elizabeth	456 Southern Accent Way	Little Rock	AR	88767
1011	703	Mitchell, Paul	5101 Madison Avenue	Cincinnati	OH	45227
1012	704	Truesdale, Nancy	700 Baseline Street	Denver	CO	80302
1013	702	Laskowski, John	9208 Goldcoast Drive	Alpine	CA	92014
1014	704	French, Melinda	4101 Avocado Blvd	Seattle	WA	98101
1015	701	Nasbeth, Joseph	1840 Orange Grove	El Cajon	CA	92020

Figure 2.17 Typical printed table format.

Printing information about the *structure* and *definition* of any table is a bit more complicated. Point to Tools, select Analyze, and then choose Documentor. Check the box corresponding to the name of the object (*tblClient* in this example). Then, select Print from the File menu to print detailed information such as properties, relationships, permissions, data names, data types, and sizes. A printed copy of a table's definition is good system documentation that can be handy if you are considering altering several table structures or an entire system.

QUERYING A DATABASE

One of the real power capabilities of relational databases is the ability to ask questions that return interesting and meaningful answers derived from a database. Relational database systems make asking questions particularly easy, and Access is no exception. A *query*, the usual name for a question, can be simple or complex and can involve only one table, dozens of tables, or even hundreds of tables. In a query, you specify which tables are involved in the data retrieval operation, which columns are to be retrieved, which records are to be returned, and any calculations to be performed. The result is also a table. Relational database systems are *closed* systems, because queries use tables as input and return tables as answers—tables in, tables out. A very important distinction between tables and queries, though both appear similar, is that tables are the only database object that actually holds data. Queries *do not* hold data. They are merely stored definitions that, when run, extract data from tables and return the result.

Most queries are called *selection queries*, because they retrieve selected rows from tables. There are other types of queries that do not return answers. Those queries are used to insert new records into a table, delete existing records from a table, update data in one or more columns of a table, or create new table columns. All of the examples and discussion in this section illustrate selection queries.

What are examples of the kinds of information you could retrieve with a query and why not simply print a table? Consider a larger version of the Client table. Suppose it contains information on more than 2,600 clients and your supervisor wants to know how many clients are located in California. Or, perhaps the supervisor wants to know how many clients are served by broker number 701. You probably would not print a 2,600-row client table, manually looking for the answers. That could take hours and be fraught with error and frustration. When you execute the File Print command, you cannot regulate which rows are printed (they all are) or which columns.

Queries provide a simple way to ask questions that return subsets of table rows, columns, or both. Access uses a query method called *query by example*, or *QBE*. Queries are formulated by giving Access an example of the result you want, and Access uses that model to return a result in a special, table-like structure called a *dynaset*. Let's look at an example.

Using a Query

Suppose you are a stockbroker and you want a list of all clients who are Californians. Furthermore, you want the list sorted by city. Because you are planning to mail literature to those customers, you want to see the clients' name and address fields (including zip code). However, you do not need to see the clients' identification numbers nor their assigned brokers' numbers. You would create the query by opening a Query window and showing Access an example of what you want. Figure 2.18 shows both a Query window and the resulting dynaset.

Let's try running the preceding query just to see how the question formation process works. The query shown in the Query window of Figure 2.18 has been saved in the Ch02 database under the name *qryCaliforniaClients*. That way, we can distinguish by their prefixes tables from queries and other objects when we combine them.

A note about naming objects: We follow the convention that query names have the prefix *qry* followed by the query name. No object name contains embedded blanks. Blanks in names can be troublesome and should be avoided. For example, the name *qryNewCustomers* is preferred to the name *qry New Customers,* with blanks between the words. Squash the separate words together and distinguish them by using initial capital letters for each word (except the prefix).

With that in mind, we show you how to use an existing query. In the next section we will build a new query from scratch. Set the scene before doing the next

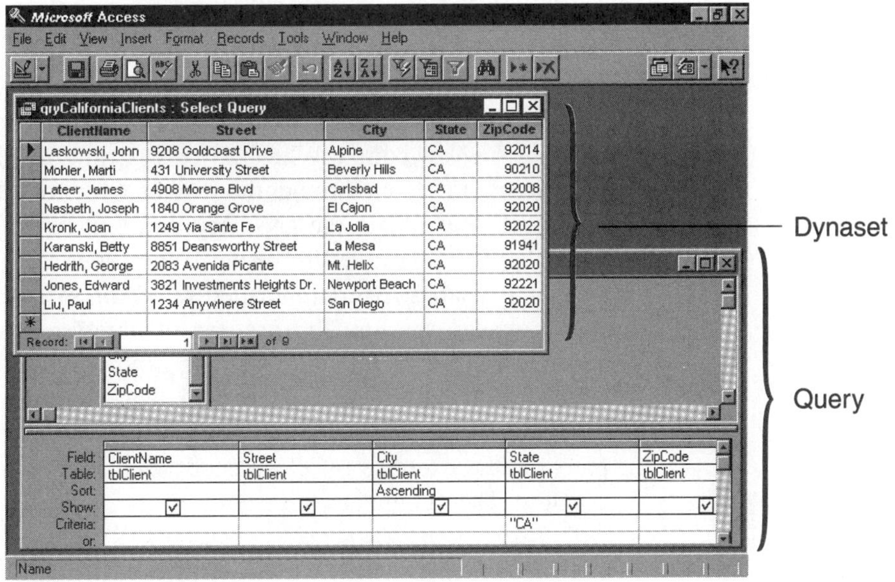

ClientName	Street	City	State	ZipCode
Laskowski, John	9208 Goldcoast Drive	Alpine	CA	92014
Mohler, Marti	431 University Street	Beverly Hills	CA	90210
Lateer, James	4908 Morena Blvd	Carlsbad	CA	92008
Nasbeth, Joseph	1840 Orange Grove	El Cajon	CA	92020
Kronk, Joan	1249 Via Sante Fe	La Jolla	CA	92022
Karanski, Betty	8851 Deansworthy Street	La Mesa	CA	91941
Hedrith, George	2083 Avenida Picante	Mt. Helix	CA	92020
Jones, Edward	3821 Investments Heights Dr.	Newport Beach	CA	92221
Liu, Paul	1234 Anywhere Street	San Diego	CA	92020

Figure 2.18 A query and resulting dynaset.

exercise: launch Access, if necessary, and ensure that database Ch02 is open. Then complete the following exercise to open and run a query.

Exercise 2.8: Running a Query

1. Click the Queries tab in the Database window to display a list of the queries stored in the database.
2. Double-click the query *qryCaliforniaClients*. Shortly, a dynaset appears displaying the query's result. (Alternatively, you can click the query name and then click the Open button.)
3. When you are done, click the Query window Close button.

The preceding dynaset displays clients living in California sorted on city. Candidate rows are drawn from a table called *tblClient.* If you are a bit curious about how the query is structured, you can click the Design View button on the toolbar. (It is the leftmost icon containing a ruler and a triangle.)

Creating a One-Table Query

You create new queries using the query by example method. For instance, suppose you want to see a list of all customer invoices that are over 60 days past due.

Printing or displaying the Invoice table would not be the answer, since all invoices would be printed. What you want is to sift through all the invoices and display only those whose invoice date is earlier than 59 days ago.

You create a query by clicking the Database window Queries tab and then clicking the New button. When the query grid is displayed, you write a query that tells Access to search through the Invoice table for all invoices more than 59 days old. Rows that satisfy the age condition will be displayed. Queries that restrict which rows are returned by using some criteria are the basis of a fundamental relational database operation called *selection*. (You specify which rows to *select*.)

Let's go through the process of creating a simple selection query that searches the *tblStock* table, returning a portion of the rows. In the exercise that follows, we will create a query that lists all stock transaction information for client number 1015. One table holds all the information we want: *tblStock*. Prepare for the exercise by closing all open windows except the Ch02 Database window. Then complete the exercise.

Exercise 2.9: Creating a One-Table Query

1. Click the Queries tab in the Database window to display the list of queries (or execute View, Database Objects, Queries).
2. Click the New button in the Database window. The New Query dialog box is displayed.
3. Select *Design View* from the list and then click OK. The Show Table dialog box is displayed (see Figure 2.19).

   Queries select information from tables, other queries, or both. You must select a table to query. A stockbroker wants to review client 1015's portfolio. So, he creates a query based on the Stock table.
4. Select the Stock table (*tblStock*), and then choose the Add button. Microsoft Access adds the Stock table to the query.
5. Click the Close button to indicate that no more tables are to be part of the query definition. The Show Table dialog box is closed. Now you can select the fields (columns) to be displayed.
6. Drag the asterisk (*) field from the *tblStock* field list to the first cell in the Field row of the QBE grid.

   The asterisk stands for all fields in the table. Dragging the asterisk saves time; you avoid dragging individual fields to the Query By Example (QBE) grid, but you lose control over the left-to-right placement of fields.
7. Drag the ClientId field from the *tblStock* field list to the second cell in the Field row of the QBE grid. (A shortcut is to double-click the field name in the list of fields to place it in the next available Field row cell of the QBE grid.) Notice that the check boxes in the Show row are checked, which means the data will be displayed in the resulting dynaset.
8. Click the check box under the ClientId column to erase the check mark. There's no need for ClientId to be displayed twice, but we want to select

only rows containing a particular value for ClientId. Therefore we include, but do not display, a separate column to hold selection criteria.

Next, we limit the search for records to those that satisfy our criteria: rows whose ClientId is 1015. That is, we want only client 1015's rows displayed in the dynaset, not all rows. We limit rows by entering the example value 1015 in the Criteria row of the ClientId column in the QBE grid.

9. Point to the cell in the Criteria row that is under the ClientId column, click the cell, and type ***1015***

   Figure 2.20 shows the completed query definition. Performing the query is simple. Once the query example is complete, you can either use the menu or click a toolbar button. Using the toolbar is faster.

10. Click the Datasheet View button on the toolbar (it is the grid-looking icon leftmost in the toolbar). The dynaset appears shortly with the results of this query (see Figure 2.21).

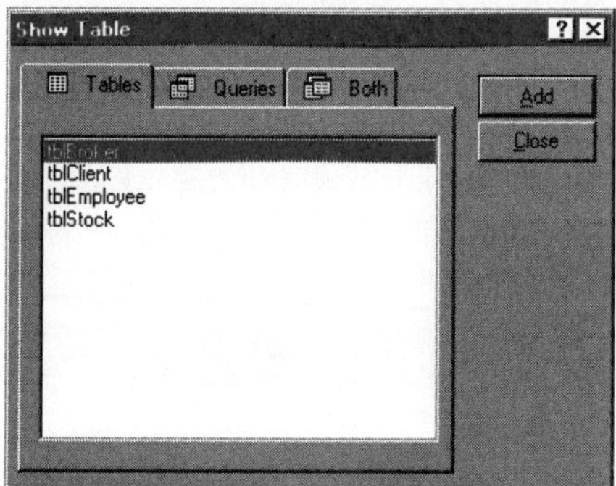

Figure 2.19 Show table dialog box.

You will be creating more queries, so you can leave the Query window open. Or, you can close the database and continue at another time.

Saving a Query

Queries can be executed periodically to produce current lists of clients, spare parts, invoices over 60 past days due, etc. It is best to save queries so that you do not have to recreate them. By saving a query, you can later rerun it to obtain accurate, timely information about data that changes over time. Note that you cannot save the dynaset, because it is not an object. It merely displays data from the underlying table that pass the criteria test. You can create a special query, called a Make Table query, which can save the dynaset as a table. We explore this and other special query types later in this chapter.

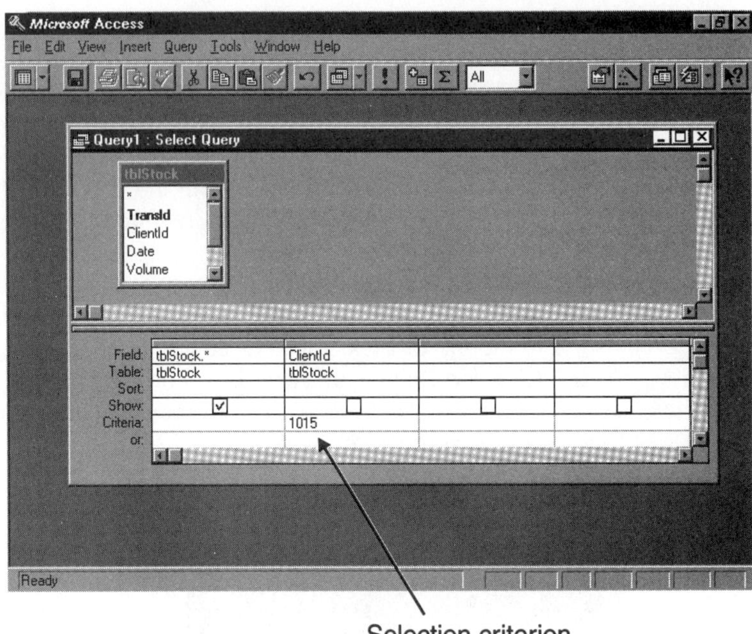

Figure 2.20 One-table query, Design View.

Query1 : Select Query

TransId	ClientId	Date	Volume	Price	StockName
20210	1015	1/8/96	100	$70.50	3M
20471	1015	3/31/96	75	$18.25	Synoptics Comm.
20476	1015	4/7/96	125	$10.50	Quantum Corp.
20575	1015	4/21/96	150	$8.38	VLSI
20725	1015	5/30/96	150	$12.50	Ask Computer
20748	1015	6/10/96	150	$21.50	Unisys
20787	1015	6/28/96	250	$10.50	Relational Tech.
20792	1015	6/28/96	125	$85.50	Compaq Computers
20941	1015	8/24/96	250	$7.50	Cipher Data Prod.
21093	1015	9/29/96	150	$91.50	Microsoft
21134	1015	10/10/96	250	$14.00	Sequent Computer
21234	1015	11/4/96	150	$37.50	Texas Instruments
21626	1015	8/25/97	125	$26.75	Comdisco
21770	1015	11/21/97	250	$1.75	Rabbit Software

Record: 1 of 14

Figure 2.21 One-table query dynaset.

Try it

You save a new query by selecting either Save or Save As from the File menu and then entering a query name in the Query Name text box. Click OK and the query is saved. Let's try it by saving the current query. Choose the Save command from the File menu. The Save As dialog box appears. Type the name ***qryClient1015*** in the Query Name text box. Click OK. The query is saved in the Ch02 database in the Queries window with the name *qryClient1015*. We have already saved the query in your database under the name *qryClient1015Stock* on your Companion CD-ROM, in case you choose not to.

For any existing query you may have altered, the procedure to save it is almost the same. Simply select Save from the File menu, and the query will be saved under the existing name in your database. Keep in mind that if there are several query windows open simultaneously, only the *active query*—the one whose window is active—is saved.

Sorting the Results

Normally, Access displays a dynaset—the result of a selection query—in order by the primary key of the underlying table. (For instance, the *tblClient* table's key column is ClientId.) If the table searched by the query has no primary key, then the dynaset's rows are displayed in no particular order. However, you can specify your own sort requirements so that dynaset rows will be in a more meaningful order. You select a sort order by selecting either Ascending or Descending beneath the appropriate column(s) in the QBE grid Sort row.

Try it

With a Query window active and displaying a query in Design view, click in the Sort row beneath the first column. Select either Ascending or Descending from the drop-down list. Continue, if necessary, selecting other columns to the right in the QBE grid. You can select Ascending or Descending for any number of columns, but the leftmost column having the Sort row cell filled is the *primary* sort column. Other sort columns' importance are determined by their *relative position* in the QBE sort grid, left to right. You may wish to drag one or more columns to the left to enhance their influence on the final sort order. Better yet, you can add columns to the right specifying sort orders for each column. Clear the Show check box of any duplicate columns so they are used to sort but are not displayed in the dynaset.

Using More Complex Selection Criteria

Suppose the manager of the stock brokerage firm wants to know how many stock transactions and the volume of each purchase that occurred in her office during the month of January 1997. She is considering sending most of her brokers on vacation for January if activity is sufficiently low during that month. Let's see how we could answer that question with a query.

To answer the preceding request, a query is formulated that returns all Stock table rows for which the value in the Date column is greater than 12/31/96 *and* less than 2/01/97. Stated like that, the criteria clearly involves two conditions—two different dates. Furthermore, both conditions must be true for a row to be returned in the Answer table. For situations like this, the criteria must use an *AND* operator. In fact, you can use the AND operator in the criteria whenever you select rows based on a range of values for a single column of a table. Let's create a new query to select all rows representing January 1997 stock purchases.

For this query we need not list all columns of the Stock table, because the manager is interested only in gross numbers of transactions, their volume, and the price of each trade. It is sufficient to list only the client identification number (ClientId), the purchase date (Date), number of shares purchased (Volume), and the purchase price (Price) columns. We are using the projection operation. A *projection* operation is one in which a subset of a table's columns are displayed. In this example, we include a subset of the Stock table's columns in the dynaset returned by the query. Projection is one of the important operations available with relational database systems such as Access. Close all windows except the Database window in preparation for the next exercise.

Exercise 2.10: Writing Selection Criteria Using an "AND" Operator

1. Click the Queries tab in the Database window and then click the New button.
2. Select *Design View* in the New Query dialog box and click OK.
3. Double-click the *tblStock* table from the list shown in the Show Table dialog box and click the Close button. (Double-clicking a table's name is a fast way to add it to a query.)
4. Hold down the Ctrl button and click, in turn, the following fields found in the *tblStock* field list: ClientId, Date, Volume, and Price. Release the Ctrl key.
5. Click inside any of the selected fields in the field list and drag the list to the first cell in the Field row. Release the mouse. When you release the mouse, the four fields are placed in separate Field row cells in the QBE grid.

   Next, create the selection criteria.
6. Click the Criteria cell below the Date column and enter the following selection criteria: ***>#12/31/96# And <#2/01/97#***

   Be sure to include > and < symbols and surround the date constants with the # symbols so that Access recognizes the enclosed values as dates rather than arithmetic expressions.
7. Click the Datasheet View button to see the results of your query (see Figure 2.22).
8. When you are finished, click the Query window Close button to close it.
9. Click No when you are asked if you want to save the newly created query. The query is saved as *qryJanuaryStockPurchases* on your Companion CD-ROM in the Ch02 database.

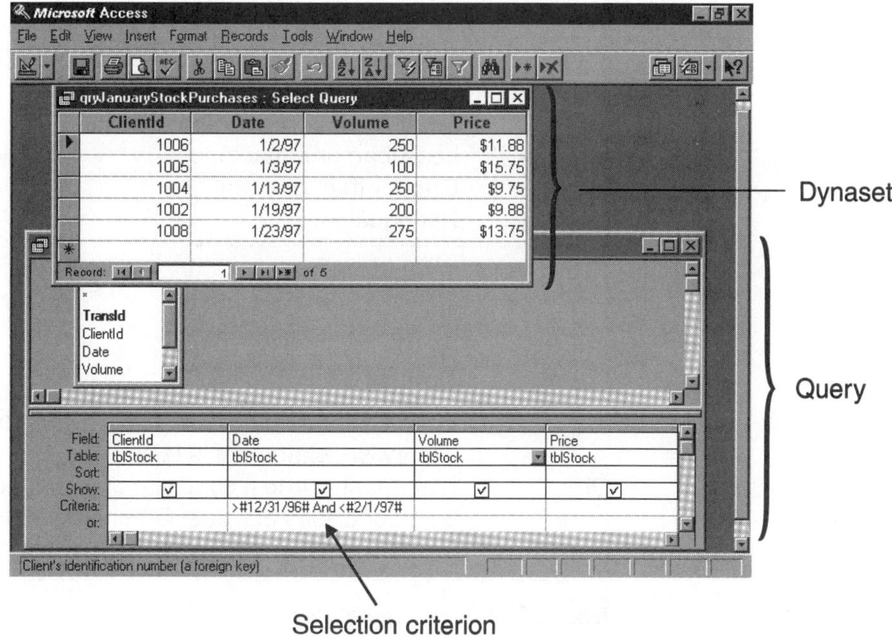

Figure 2.22 Selection and projection operations in an AND query.

Look carefully at the expression in the QBE grid in Figure 2.22 in the Criteria row of the Date column. That expression is used to filter rows, selecting only those rows whose Date value falls within the specified range.

Three new symbols and a logical operator are introduced in the criteria. The *And* separates two expressions. This indicates that the conditions to its left and right must be met simultaneously. In other words, rows are displayed only if the Date value is later than December 31, 1996 *and* before February 1, 1997. Pound signs (#) enclose each date value. Otherwise, Access would interpret a value such as 12/31/96 as the quantity 12 divided by 31 divided by 96—yielding a numerical result. (An alternate way to write an expression having the same effect is the criterion: ***Between #1/1/97# And #1/31/97#***.) You may prefer to use this expression instead. You probably are already familiar with the greater than (>) and less than (<) symbols. These are just two of the *comparison* operators which bracket the date range. A complete list of comparison operators is given in Table 2.1. Among the *logical* operators is "And." The list of logical operators is given in Table 2.2.

When you want to use criteria on two or more fields simultaneously, you place those conditions under the respective column names in the query image. For instance, suppose you want to list all stock purchases made by client 1005 in January 1997, a combination of the queries similar to those you created in previous exercises.

Operator	Meaning
<	Less than
>	Greater than
=	Equal to
<=	Less than or equal to
>=	Greater than or equal to
<>	Not equal to

Table 2.1 Comparison operators.

Operator	Meaning
And	Conditions on both sides must be true for statement to be true. Otherwise, statement is false.
Or	Statement is true if condition on either side of operator is true or if both conditions are true. Otherwise, statement is false.
Not	Unary operator negating logic it precedes.

Table 2.2 Logical operators.

Try it

Modify the preceding query—*qryJanuaryStockPurchases*—to answer your new question. Click the Criteria row in the ClientId column and type ***1005***. Running the new AND query returns rows whose ClientId value equals 1005 *and* whose Date column value is any day in January 1997. The value 1005 is an *exact match* criterion, whereas the Date criteria is a *value range* criterion. What you have learned is that AND queries involving different fields of a table are created by entering all of the criteria in the same Criteria row of the QBE grid.

More interesting queries can be created when more than one table is *joined* in one query. Frequently, queries involve several tables that are logically related. Chapter 3 contains a complete discussion of how to join tables. We defer further discussion of this important topic until then.

Creating Selection Criteria Using the "OR" Operator

You are likely to encounter queries similar to the following: "Which clients have purchased either Microsoft or Borland stock? Locate those purchase transactions and list them." A similar example is a request like this one: "List all client records whose stock purchase price is less than $2.25 or whose stock name is *Microsoft*, regardless of purchase price." Both of the preceding are questions involving two conditions, either of which is reason to list the record. That is, the criteria are called OR conditions. Unlike AND conditions in which *all* conditions must be true to select and return a row to the dynaset, only *one* of the conditions must be true for a row to be returned.

How do you form a query involving OR conditions? Let's examine the latter example in the previous paragraph and see exactly what is needed to form a query. Two independent criteria are involved. There are two basic ways to formulate OR criteria, depending on whether the criteria concern one field or different fields. If two different fields are involved (stock price and stock name, in our example), then you create a query containing two Criteria rows—one row for each condition. If a criterion involves only one field, then you can place alternate acceptable values in one field, separating them with the word *Or*.

The next exercise uses the first method, since two different fields are involved. Close any open Access windows, but leave the Ch02 Database window open.

EXERCISE 2.11: FORMING AN "OR" QUERY

1. Click the Database window Queries tab to ensure you are about to create a query, not a table, form, or some other object.
2. Select Design View in the New Query dialog box and click OK.
3. Double-click the *tblStock* table in the Show Table dialog box, and then click the Close button to close the Show Table dialog box.
4. Drag the asterisk from the *tblStock* field list to the first cell in the Field row of the QBE grid.
5. Drag the Price and StockName fields from the field list to the second and third cells in the Field row.
6. Clear the check boxes under the Price and StockName columns so they are not displayed. (They will be displayed anyway because you dragged all fields to the Field row when you placed the asterisk in the first cell.)
7. Click the first Criteria row under the Price column in the QBE grid, press Shift+F2 to enlarge the Criteria cell (this action is called "invoking the Zoom window"), and type the criterion ***<2.25***.
8. Click the OK button to close the Zoom window.
9. Click the second Criteria row under the StockName column. Type the expression ***Microsoft*** (either lower- or uppercase is fine). Access automatically surrounds text with double quotation marks. (Access ignores capitalization when searching for matches.)

   Now each Criteria row specifies an independent selection criterion. Each will return a table row whenever its one criterion is satisfied. Thus, both criteria contribute to the dynaset. However, when a row satisfies both criteria, only one copy is inserted into the dynaset.
10. Click the Datasheet View button to see the query results. The dynaset, whose rows are in TransId order (because TransId is the queried table's

primary key), is shown. Figure 2.23 shows both the query and the returned dynaset. (Normally, you can see either the query or the dynaset, since they are opposite sides of the same "coin." We have created a second query so you can see both at once.)

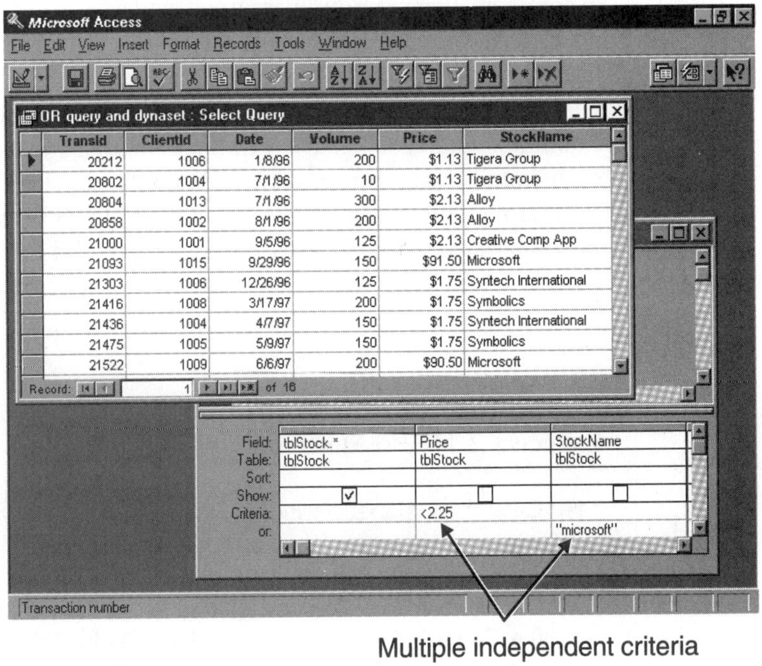
Microsoft Access
File Edit View Insert Format Records Tools Window Help
OR query and dynaset : Select Query
TransId ClientId Date Volume Price StockName
20212 1006 1/8/96 200 $1.13 Tigera Group
20802 1004 7/1/96 10 $1.13 Tigera Group
20804 1013 7/1/96 300 $2.13 Alloy
20858 1002 8/1/96 200 $2.13 Alloy
21000 1001 9/5/96 125 $2.13 Creative Comp App
21093 1015 9/29/96 150 $91.50 Microsoft
21303 1006 12/26/96 125 $1.75 Syntech International
21416 1008 3/17/97 200 $1.75 Symbolics
21436 1004 4/7/97 150 $1.75 Syntech International
21475 1005 5/9/97 150 $1.75 Symbolics
21522 1009 6/6/97 200 $90.50 Microsoft
Record: 1 of 16
Field: tblStock.* Price StockName
Table: tblStock tblStock tblStock
Sort:
Show:
Criteria: <2.25
or: "microsoft"
Transaction number
Multiple independent criteria

Figure 2.23 OR query and dynaset.

Notice that to form an OR query you have as many Criteria rows in the query grid as there are independent selection criteria. Each row contains characters, a value, or an expression below a single column. When OR conditions involve only one field, there is an alternate way to write the criteria. For example, suppose you want to display Stock table rows for anyone who has purchased either Microsoft or Borland stock. Because both criteria involve the same field, StockName, you can write both criteria in one query image row, separating the criteria with the reserved word *OR* (either uppercase or lowercase):

"Microsoft" Or Like "borland*"

Normally, when dealing with characters, capitalization is significant. However, Access ignores capitalization and locates matching rows based on spelling alone. Character matching rules vary from one database product to another, however. Be sure to experiment with it first. *BORLAND* in a query may not match *Borland* in the database if you are not using Microsoft Access.

The asterisk following the word *borland* is one of the *wildcard* characters, which can stand for none or for any number of letters. This allows a match on a string such as *borland, inc.*, *BORLAND INTERNATIONAL*, etc. The asterisk can be used on either or both ends of any query string. Whenever you use a wildcard with a character string, Access automatically inserts the word *Like* ahead of it. Of course, the order of the strings separated by OR does not matter.

What would happen if you formed a query with only one row and placed the expression <2.25 beneath Price and placed MICROSOFT beneath StockName? No rows would be returned in the dynaset, because no table rows satisfy both criteria simultaneously. The latter query is an example of specifying AND criteria. Simply stated, each Criteria row states conditions that must all be satisfied before any rows are selected by that particular criteria for inclusion in the dynaset. Of course, if there are other Criteria rows, they too may select rows to be retrieved. You should try the AND criteria as described before with Price and StockName values. Verify that no rows are returned for the data we have supplied.

Including Expressions in a Query

For most applications, it is useful to calculate values that are not stored in the database. Accounting applications are a good example. For instance, brokers keep a watchful eye on their larger accounts. One measure of a client's account size is the total purchase price of each stock a client owns. However, the Stock database does not record that value. There are two approaches to solving this problem, one is correct and the other is wholly incorrect.

An incorrect solution would be to create a new *tblStock* table column that holds the total purchase price of a stock. While this might be an acceptable solution when using a spreadsheet product, taking that approach with a database can lead to inconsistencies in the database and trouble later on. Why? Suppose that the total purchase price is calculated as the product of the Price and Volume columns (that is, purchase price is the product of price per share and the number of shares purchased). Suppose further that a mistake is discovered in transcribing the volume purchased for a particular transaction. Instead of recording 200 shares, a particular transaction involved only 100 shares. Even though the Volume value is corrected in the database record for a particular errant transaction, there is a danger that the total purchase price is not. Unlike a spreadsheet, a field value in a database row does not change automatically when other values on which it depends are changed. Here's an important rule covering this situation: *Never store in a table any value (field) that is functionally dependent on two or more fields in the record.* That's a simplification of a rule described in Chapter 3, but it merely states you shouldn't store in a database a value you can calculate or derive from the database.

So, what is the correct way to arrive at the total purchase price for each stock for every customer? The correct way is to include an *expression* in the query QBE grid to calculate the desired value dynamically—each time the query is executed. Instead of having you go through the process of creating such a query, we have provided an example for you to simply execute. You will find a query containing a calculation stored as *qryTotalValue* in your Ch02 database on the Companion CD-ROM.

Try it

Click the Queries tab in the Database window. Then double-click the query *qryStockValue*. The query displays rows from the *tblStock* table as well as each transaction's total value. Examine the query in Figure 2.24 as well as the dynaset showing the retrieved and calculated results.

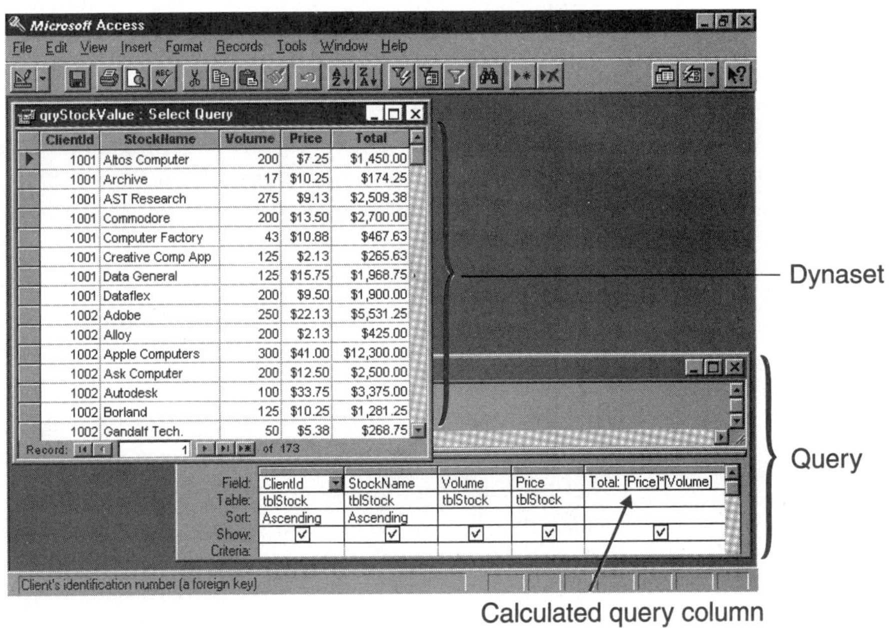

Figure 2.24 Calculating values with a query.

Click the Design View button and examine the query. Pay particular attention to the expression in the Field row. (You may have to click the horizontal scroll bar to bring the field into view.) The expression *Total: [Price]*[Volume]* is placed in the Field row. The expression computes total stock purchase price for each row in turn and creates a new column in the dynaset. The word *Total* followed by a colon and a space designates the name for the column that appears in the dynaset (otherwise, the expression is the column label). The expression variables *[Price]* and *[Volume]* reference table field names and get their values from the columns Price and Volume, respectively.

Printing Query Results

To print a query's resulting dynaset, first display the dynaset (click the Datasheet View button if necessary). Before printing, always check the dynaset to make sure it contains the results you expected. Occasionally, you may pose a query that is too broad and encompasses too many database records. Or, perhaps you inadvertently omitted a needed column. Always preview the query's result first. Print it only when you are satisfied.

Print the dynaset by choosing Print from the File menu. The familiar Print dialog box, shown earlier in Figure 2.16, appears. Make any selections necessary, perhaps limiting the range of pages to print, and then click OK to proceed. That's all there is to printing the results of a query—you simply print the dynaset.

Printing Query Definitions

You can document an object—a table, query, and so on—by printing its definition. It is very helpful to print the definitions of all your queries, because these serve as documentation for your evolving system. You might want to keep a notebook with a special section devoted to all query definitions for each database.

Printing a query's definition is a little tricky. Here's a brief overview of the steps to print the documentation for the *qryStockValue* query. Open the queries by clicking the Database window Queries tab. Select the Tools menu. Then, choose Analyze and Documentor. The Database Documentor dialog box is displayed. From the Object Type drop-down list box, select Queries. All of the query names are displayed along with check boxes. Click the *qryStockValue* check box and any other queries whose definition you want to print (Figure 2.25). Finally, click OK to preview the definition report. If you are satisfied with the report preview, select Print from the File menu to print the query definition report.

CREATING ACTION QUERIES

Besides selection queries, you can use another type of Access query called *action queries*. They provide a powerful means to make mass changes to a database. Action queries can create a new table, remove records from an existing table, update one or more fields of an existing table, and add new records to an existing table. Action queries resemble selection queries such as those discussed in the previous section. The major difference is that they *alter* the database in some way, not merely display results from the database. Action queries include make table, update, delete, append, and crosstab.

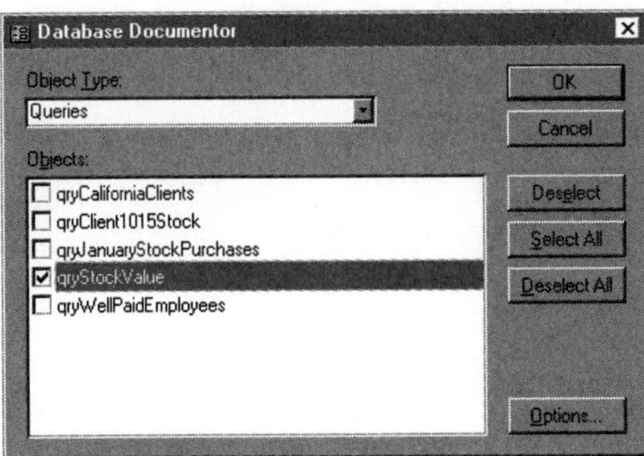

Figure 2.25 Preparing to print a query's definition.

With a make table query, you can retrieve a subset of rows from one or more tables and save the dynaset as a table. Perhaps you want to concentrate on the smaller table, or perhaps you want to export the smaller table to Excel to analyze it further. Update queries allow you to change existing database information. You can create or run an update query to increase all secretaries' hourly pay rates by 8 percent. A delete query selects and removes records from one or more tables. You could run a delete query to purge records of potential clients who have not contacted your office in over two years. With an append query, you can add new records to an existing table. Finally a crosstab query summarizes and combines data from more than one source to present a compact, spreadsheet-like result. You might use a crosstab query to sum stock sales by broker for the first quarter of 1997—a statistic that is not apparent by observing tables alone. We will present a concise description of how to create and run four of these action query types. We omit the crosstab query, because it is beyond the scope of this text. Let's begin with the make table action query.

Make Table Query

You can create a new table from existing tables by using a make table query. Suppose you want to create a new table containing only third quarter 1996 stock sales transactions from the *tblStock* table. The new table has the same structure, but contains only July, August, and September transactions. Create a make table query to deliver the information in two steps. First, create a selection query based on the *tblStock* table that retrieves all columns but only those rows whose transaction date falls between 7/1/96 and 9/30/96. Then, turn the selection query into a make table query and run it to create the desired table.

Try it

Click the Queries tab of the Database window and click the New button to create a new query. Select Design View and click OK when the New Query dialog box is displayed. Add the table *tblStock* and then close the Show Table dialog box. Drag all fields from the *tblStock* field roster to the Field row of the QBE grid. Drag another copy of the Date field to the QBE grid. Clear the Show box corresponding to the second copy of Date. In the Criteria row beneath the second copy of Date, enter the selection criteria ***Between #7/1/96# And #9/30/96#*** and select Datasheet from the View menu to preview the new table. Select Design from the View menu to return to the Design View window. Now for the new part! In the Design View window, select Make Table from the Query menu. The Make Table dialog box is displayed. Enter a new table name—the name of the table you will be creating—such as *tblThirdQuarterSales* and click OK. You can save the make table query and run it later, or you can run it now. (We have included this query on your Companion CD-ROM as *qmakQ3Sales*.) Save the query first: select Save from the File menu and name the query *qmakThirdQuarterSales*. (The prefix *qmak* can be used to indicate make table queries.) Finally, you can run the query to create a new table. Select Run from the Query menu. A warning is displayed indicating "You are about to paste 28 row(s) into a new table…" Click Yes to approve creating the new table. If you run the preceding make table query, you will find a new table when you click the Database window Tables tab. Of course, you can delete the table (you may want to save the query, however) by selecting the table, choosing Delete from the Edit menu, and clicking Yes when asked to confirm the deletion.

Update Query

With update queries, you can make changes to many records in a table. You can choose to update only one field, or you can simultaneously update several. Update queries alter individual table fields, replacing them with new values. For example, suppose we are sensitive to gender equity and want to make a mid-year adjustment to female brokers' salaries. We determine that they should receive a 5 percent raise. (Their male counterparts will have to wait an additional six months to receive a raise, if any.) An update query is what's needed to make mass changes to the table containing brokers' salaries. Of course, our table is small, but this is an example of the kind of database change that would be laborious if it were done manually, one record at a time. The following activity leads you through making an update query. You can choose to actually create and run the query, or you can simply run the one we have created called *qupdBrokerSalary*.

Try it

Create a selection query of the records to be updated, placing in the QBE grid only the fields to be updated or used for criteria. In this case, place only the *tblBroker* fields Salary and Gender in the QBE grid. (Salary is to be updated, and Gender is used to select which rows receive the update.) In the Criteria row, enter F below the QBE Gender column. Before proceeding, view the affected records to ensure your selection criteria is good: select the Datasheet View button to view the selected records. Switch back to Design View and continue. Select the Update command from the Query menu. Notice that the QBE grid changes. A new, "Update To" row is added. In the Update To row beneath the Salary column insert the expression *[Salary]*1.05* (be sure to enclose Salary in square brackets). Figure 2.26 shows the completed update query prior to execution. You can run the query to update the Salaries fields of the *tblBroker* table by selecting Run from the Query menu or by clicking the Run button on the Query Design toolbar.

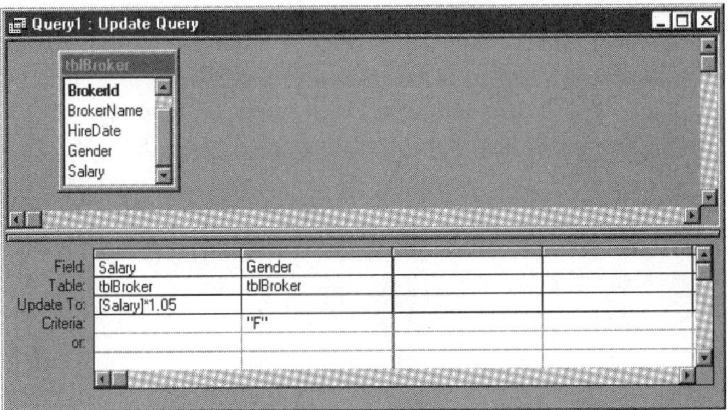

Figure 2.26 An update query example.

Bear in mind one extremely important fact about updating database tables. An update operation *cannot be reversed with Undo*. You can undo some update operations by formulating a new update query to restore updated values, but not all update operations are reversible. For instance, suppose you choose to update the location field of an employee's work address to "New York" for all employees whose city is currently Indianapolis. This will effectively move all Indianapolis workers to New York. However, you cannot easily reverse the change if other workers are already listed as living in New York. That is, it is not a matter of changing the City field of New York back to Indianapolis, because some are New Yorkers who were never located in Indianapolis in the first place! Always select Datasheet View before running an update query to check the scope of your changes.

Delete Query

A delete query is used to delete records from tables. It is *not* used to delete entire tables. To do that, simply select the table and press the Delete key. The entire table, plus data, is removed from the database. Deleting records is a much subtler activity. Suppose, for example, that you want to remove from the *tblStock* table all transactions that occurred on or before December 31, 1997. In other words, you want to "clear the books" for a new year, 1998. A delete query with the proper selection criteria will do the trick. First create a selection query and then examine its Datasheet View to ensure that proper records will be deleted when the query is transformed to a delete query. To create a delete query from a selection query, ensure the query is displayed in Design View and then select Delete from the Query menu.

Once you have properly defined a delete query, all that is left is to run it. Figure 2.27 shows an example of a delete query that removes from the table *tblStock* all stock transactions that occurred before 1998. It is also found in your Ch02 database on your Companion CD-ROM under the name *qdelOldTransactions*. Notice that the only fields that are needed in the QBE grid are those that are being used for criteria. Remember, though, that the entire record will be deleted.

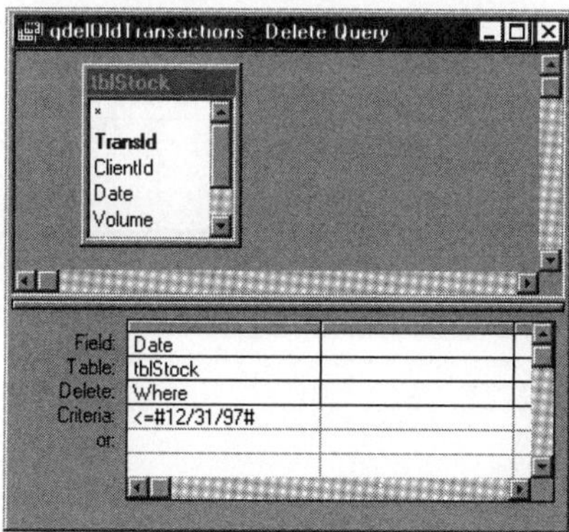

Figure 2.27 An delete query example.

Append Query

You use an append query to add records from a table or query to the end of another table. For example, you would use an append query to create a comprehensive employee table containing all employees in all divisions. The table *tblEmployee*, for example, represents only one division of a larger company. By creating an append query, you can add other divisions' employee records to the *tblEmployee* table.

To create an append query, simply create a selection query including fields from the source tables that are in the target (destination) table *and* any fields that are used as criteria. In the Criteria row of the query, establish the conditions that are used to select records from the other table to append to the current table (for example, only division 1 and division 2 employees). View the potential new records by clicking the Datasheet View button. Then, switch back to Design View and select Append from the Query menu to turn the selection query into an append query. When prompted for the target table name by the Append dialog box, enter the target table's name or select it from the Table Name drop-down list. Click OK to complete the query definition. Figure 2.28 shows an example in which a fictitious division's employee records are to be appended to the *tblEmployee* table.

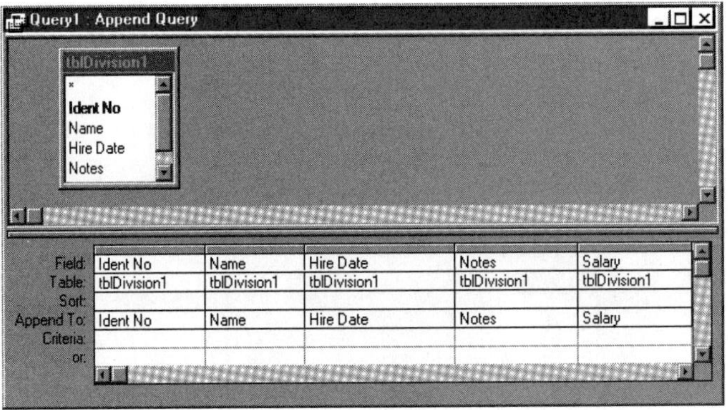

Figure 2.28 An append query example.

USING FORMS

A form provides a convenient, less cluttered work surface through which you can enter or alter information in your tables. A form can display information from one or more tables. Additionally, a form can display information from a query (that is, the query's dynaset).

One of the advantages of using a form to enter or change data is that the form can look like a paper form with which you or your clients are already familiar. When the form on the screen mimics a paper form, those using the form will intuitively know what information goes where, and they usually feel more comfortable with a familiar interface. Entering data directly into a table can be more confusing and error-prone, especially for anyone not familiar with databases in general or Access in particular. Another advantage of a form is that you can enforce a medley of validation checks on values that are entered in a table through a form.

Viewing a Table through a Form

So that you understand a form better, we have created one that displays information from the Client table (*tblClient*) you examined in Figures 2.13, 2.15, and 2.17. The form is found on your Companion CD-ROM and is called *frmClient*. (All forms on the Companion disk have the prefix *frm*.) Work through the next exercise to open a Form view of the *tblClient* table.

Exercise 2.12: Opening and Using a Form

1. Close all open windows except the Database window.
2. Click the Forms tab in the Database window to display all forms in the Ch02 database.
3. Double-click the form *frmClient* (or select *frmClient* and then click the Open button). The Client form appears (see Figure 2.29).

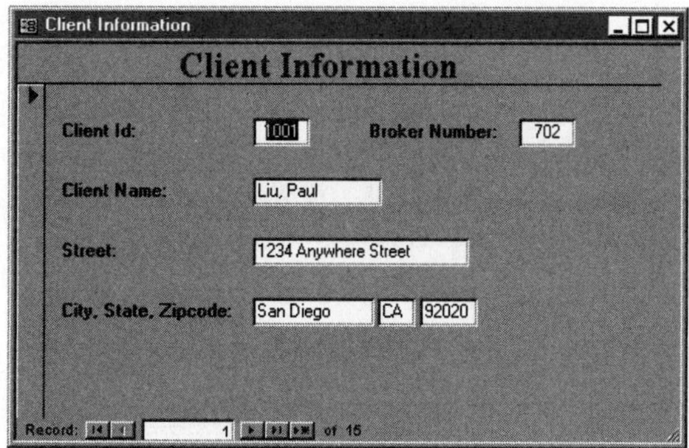

Figure 2.29 Client form.

All fields from the Client table (Figure 2.13) appear in a pleasant arrangement in the form in Figure 2.29. Client Number is darkened because it is the first field encountered in the form. Familiar navigation buttons appear along the bottom edge of the Form window. Those buttons perform the usual actions: move to the top of the table, move up one row, and so forth. The only difference is that a table row is displayed in a form. Look at the fifteen records one at a time by clicking the Next Record (Figure 2.13) button at the bottom of the Form View window. After you have moved to the last record, click the First Record navigation button to move back to the first record in the table. Notice that the form displays records in order by ClientId. The form was built from the *tblClient* table whose primary key, ClientId, maintains the table (and thus the form) rows in order by the ClientId field. If you want rows displayed in the form in name order, you could create a query that returns rows sorted on last name (specify Ascending in the QBE grid under ClientName). Then you can build a form based on the query. We illustrate a query-based form in the next section.

Several interesting design elements have been employed in the Client form so that it is at once intuitive and attractive. Along the top is a simple title, in Times Roman typeface, which identifies the form. Each form field is labeled and arranged on the form in a logical order. In the upper left part of the form is the client's identification number. It is entered first. Below it are the client's name and address. Notice that wherever information is supplied from the table—data to be changed or viewed—it is contained in a box frame that appears sunken. This helps the user visually separate labels from data. Finally, label and data fonts are different so that they can be distinguished from one another.

Viewing a Query through a Form

Forms can be created for saved queries as well as tables. It makes no difference whether the form displays a table's or a query's contents. Figure 2.30 shows a form that displays a subset of the fields from the *qryStockValue* query, which is shown in Figure 2.24. Notice that the Form window status line displays the current record and the total number of records. In this case, the total number of records depends on how many rows are selected by the query upon which the form is built. It is likely that you will create and use many forms based on queries. The form shown in Figure 2.30 is stored on your Companion CD-ROM in the Ch02 database as *frmStockValue*. Try it out yourself.

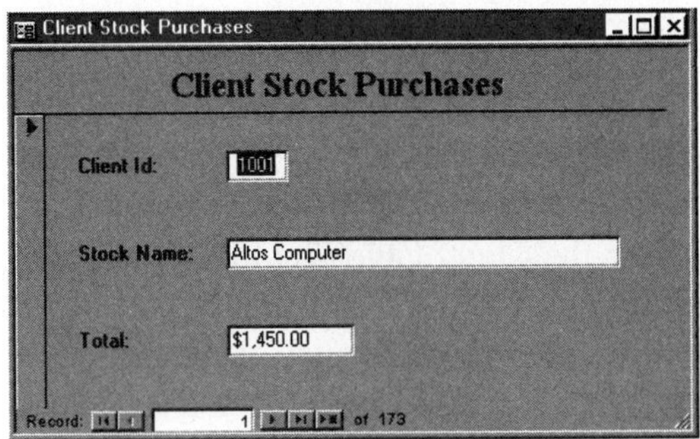

Figure 2.30 Form based on a query.

Creating a Form Quickly

When you want to enter data into a table one record at a time, your best work surface may be a form. We illustrate how easy it is to create a functional and attractive form by simply choosing a table and clicking a button. Let's create a simple form for the *tblBroker* table (on your Companion CD-ROM) through which we can observe or alter information. First, switch to the Database window (the fastest way is to click the Database Window button on the toolbar). Then, create an *AutoForm* by completing the steps in the following activity.

Try it

Click the Database window Tables tab to display a list of the Ch02 table names. Highlight the table name *tblBroker* in the list of tables. Click the New Object button on the toolbar and select the AutoForm button from the drop-down button list. (The New Object button is on the right end of the toolbar, just to the left of the What's This button.) A Form window is displayed, containing your newly created form (see Figure 2.31). The Form window Title bar contains the table name by default. You can change it later if you want. Leave the Form window open, because you will save the form in a few moments.

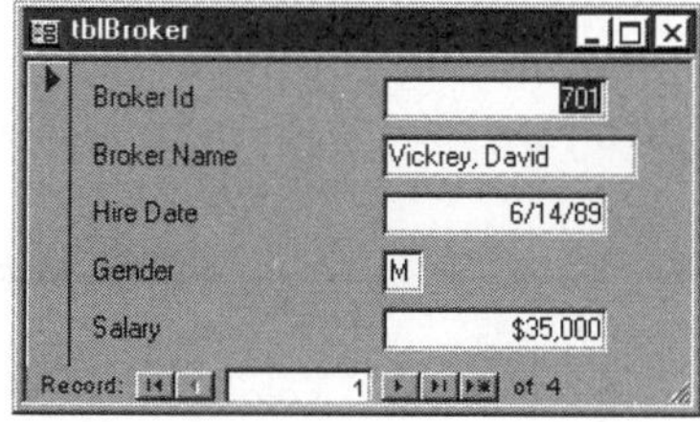

Figure 2.31 Broker form.

That's all there is to creating a form from a table. You probably agree with us that the form is attractive and functional. We show you how to modify and enhance a form in Chapter 4. For now, simply save the new form on your copy of the database.

Saving a Form

You can save a form design either by executing Save Form or Save Form As from the File menu. Then you supply the form's name. Let's save the form in your C drive copy of the database.

Try it

With the newly created Broker form still displayed, choose either Save Form or Save Form As from the File menu. Enter the name ***frmBrokerAutoForm*** in the Form

Name text box of the Save As dialog box (either upper- or lowercase is fine). Click OK to complete the form save operation. Click the Close button to close the form.

The form has been saved in your C drive copy of the current database, Ch02. We have also saved the form in the Ch02 database on your Companion CD-ROM. It is called *frmBroker*.

Editing Data with a Form

It is often easier to alter data in a table using a form. Because only one table row is usually displayed on the form, you are less likely to make mistakes.

Editing table data through a form is simple. While looking at a form in Form view (not Design view), you click the field that you want to change and make any needed changes. Let's try editing a record in the Broker table with the form. In preparation, make sure the Broker form is in Form view. Then, complete the following exercise to make one change.

Exercise 2.13: Editing Data with a Form

1. Move to the record for David Vickrey (press PgUp or PgDn or use the navigation buttons if necessary).
2. Press Tab to move to the Hire Date field. (The entire value is highlighted if you use Tab or the arrow keys to move to the selected fields.)
3. Enter the correct hire date *7/5/88*
4. Click the Form window's Close button to close the form.

Changes to a particular record are not posted to the table until you move to another record. Simply click one of the navigation buttons to store the changed record in the table. Go back to the record you changed to verify that the changed value has been saved. Keep in mind that the form merely displays table data and is not changed. Only the table data is actually changed. Changed data is automatically saved for you, and you need not save a form again unless you change the form's design.

Querying a Database with a Form

When you are looking for a particular record in a table containing many records, there's no better way to locate it than by using a form. You can load a form and then use the command *Filter By Form* or *Filter By Selection*. Additionally, you can create a more complex search using the *Advanced Filter/Sort* tool. To illustrate this process, let's use the Filter By Form command to locate all the stocks purchased by client 1013. You can imagine the daunting task this would be if you had to visually examine every row in the *tblStock* table looking for all a given client's transactions. Of course you wouldn't do it that way. Instead, you would request Access to apply a *filter*—another term for applying selection criteria so that only a subset of records is displayed—and retrieve only records of interest. Let's try it. In preparation, open your copy of the Ch02 database, if necessary.

EXERCISE 2.14: FILTERING DATA THROUGH A FORM

1. Click the Database window Forms tab to display the existing form names.
2. Double-click *frmStockValue* to open that form.
3. Select the Records menu, point to the Filter menu item, and then select Filter By Form. Notice that a down-pointing arrow appears on the Client Id data field and that the menu has changed. The Client Id has changed into a drop-down list box from which you can choose one of the unique Client Id values retrieved from the *tblStock* table Client Id column.
4. Click the Client Id drop-down list box arrow to reveal the collection of Client Id values (see Figure 2.32).
5. Choose *1013* from the list. The Client Id field displays the value 1013.
6. Select Apply Filter/Sort from the Filter menu found on the Menu bar. The first of several client 1013 records is displayed in the form. Notice that the indicator *(filtered)* appears just to the right of the navigation buttons. This indicates the form is displaying a subset of the underlying table (a filtered view), not all the records.
7. Use the navigation buttons to scroll through a dozen or so of the records.
8. When you are done, select Remove Filter/Sort from the Records menu or click the Remove Filter button (a funnel) found on the toolbar. The Remove Filter toolbar button is renamed Apply Filter when not engaged. You can toggle the filter on and off by clicking the button on and off.
9. Close the form.

You can choose to filter by any form field. Repeat steps 1 through 3 and select the field by which you want to filter. Then, clear the other fields, otherwise other field values will further restrict the records that are retrieved. Try it yourself. See if you can display in the *frmStock* form information about clients who own Microsoft stock.

Using filter by selection works almost the same way. When you choose Filter By Selection, it filters records shown in the form on selected data. To filter by selection, select a field or part of a field in a form and then click

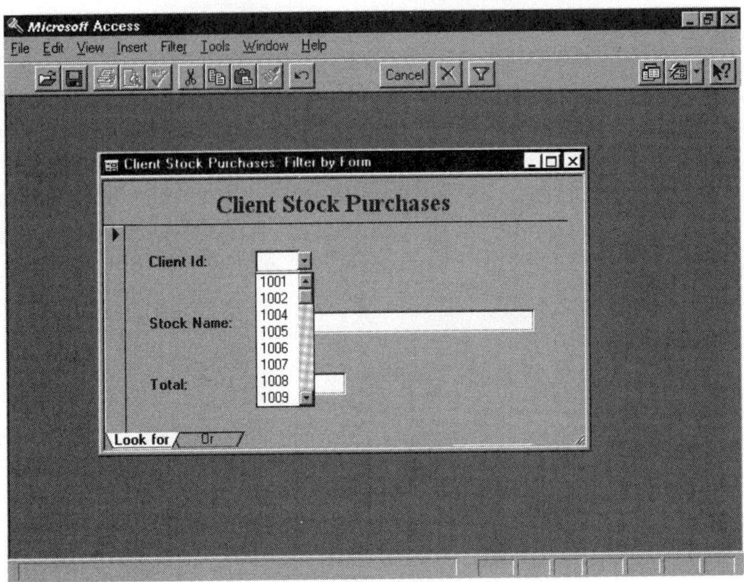

Figure 2.32 Filter by Form example.

Filter By Selection. Only records matching the selected value are displayed in the form.

Printing a Form

Though forms are best suited for onscreen work, they can be printed. To print one record, open the form, locate the record, and click the Print button on the toolbar. When the Print dialog box is displayed, click the *Selected Record(s)* radio button, and click OK.

Printing a range of records is an equally straightforward process. Select Print from the File menu, click the Pages radio button, enter the beginning and ending page numbers in the two page range boxes, and click OK. Table rows are printed in the format of the displayed form. However, you probably will not want to print more than a few records this way. There is a better way to print larger amounts of information from tables. An Access report is the most efficient way to design and produce tabular output of the records in a table or a query result. Access reports are introduced next.

DESIGNING REPORTS

Producing reports could not be much easier than the click of a button or two. Frequently, you will want either to preview a report onscreen or to produce a printed report, which you can pass around at a meeting or keep as a permanent record. Access reports are just that—reports. You can neither enter nor edit data in a report. You can create reports ranging from simple, utilitarian designs to professional-looking reports replete with attractive typefaces, drop shadows, and graphics.

Previewing a Report

Reports typically display information from either a table, a collection of related tables, or a query. We have created a report from the query you examined earlier (Figure 2.24). Though a lot can be gained from looking at the query's results onscreen, it is even more useful to have a printed report. The report you are about to preview and then print has some added features that make the information delivered by the query *qryStockValue* (Figure 2.24) more understandable and useful. First, let's learn how to open a stored report definition and preview the report prior to actually printing it. Switch to the Database window (click the Database Window button on the toolbar). Then, display a report found on your copy of the Ch02 database by completing the following exercise.

EXERCISE 2.15: LOADING AND PREVIEWING A REPORT

1. Click the Reports tab in the Database window. A list of the reports in the database appears.
2. Click the report named *rptClientStocks* and click the Preview button. A preview of the report will be displayed in the Print Preview window.
3. Click the Maximize button to display the whole window. Use the scroll bars to pan the report. Click the mouse to zoom out and zoom in. Figure 2.33 shows the report preview.
4. Close the report if you wish, or continue examining the report by following the directions in the paragraph that follows.

Use the Report window's scroll bars to move around the displayed page. To move to another page, use the navigation buttons in the lower left corner of the Print Preview window. You can also use the arrow keys and the PgUp and PgDn keys to move around the report. Take a few moments to try out the page navigation buttons. Go to the last report page, and then go back to the first. There is a brief pause as Access moves to a particular page and repaints the Print Preview window. Experiment with printing a report page.

Select Print from the File menu, click the Pages radio button in the Print dialog box, enter a page range to print, and click OK to start the printing process.

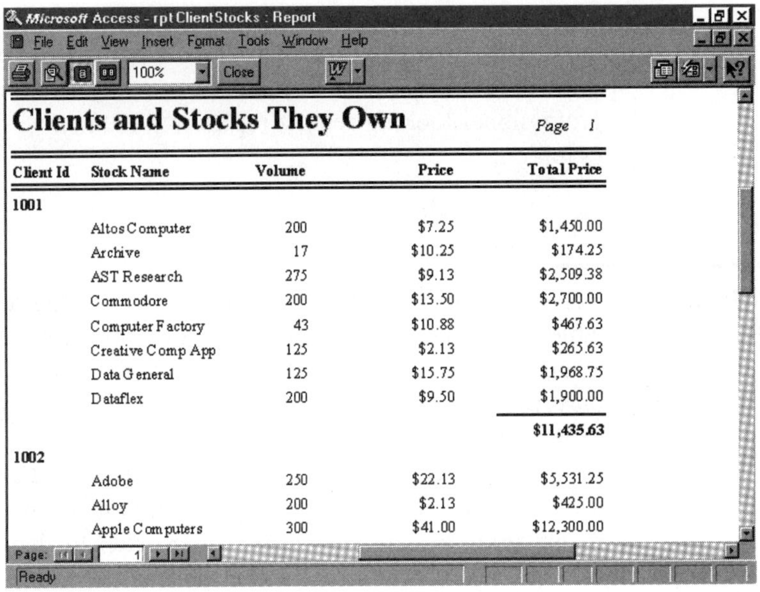

Microsoft Access - rptClientStocks : Report

File Edit View Insert Format Tools Window Help

Clients and Stocks They Own *Page 1*

Client Id	Stock Name	Volume	Price	Total Price
1001				
	Altos Computer	200	$7.25	$1,450.00
	Archive	17	$10.25	$174.25
	AST Research	275	$9.13	$2,509.38
	Commodore	200	$13.50	$2,700.00
	Computer Factory	43	$10.88	$467.63
	Creative Comp App	125	$2.13	$265.63
	Data General	125	$15.75	$1,968.75
	Dataflex	200	$9.50	$1,900.00
				$11,435.63
1002				
	Adobe	250	$22.13	$5,531.25
	Alloy	200	$2.13	$425.00
	Apple Computers	300	$41.00	$12,300.00

Page: 1

Ready

Figure 2.33 Previewing a report.

Close the report by clicking the Close button in the upper right corner of the Print Preview window. The Database window for Ch02 is redisplayed.

Now that you have seen an example of a report based on a query and how to preview and print it, let's create a simple report. It is based on the *tblClient* table.

Creating a Report Quickly

Creating a report from a table is similar to creating a form from a table. You select a table name in the Database window, click the New Object toolbar button, select the AutoReport button from the drop-down list, and the default report appears. In the following exercise you will create an AutoReport based on the Client table.

Exercise 2.16: Creating a Report Quickly

1. Click the Tables tab in the Ch02 Database window.
2. Click *tblClient* from the list of tables (highlight its name, but do not open the table).
3. Click the down-pointing arrow to the right of the New Object toolbar button to reveal a list of objects that can be created.
4. Click the AutoReport button in the displayed list. The default style report is displayed in a Print Preview window (see Figure 2.34).

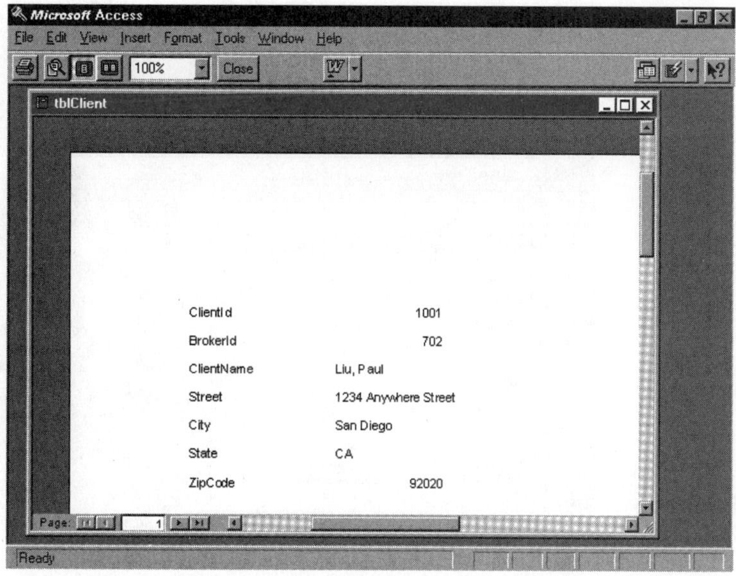

Figure 2.34 Typical AutoReport-style report.

By default, an AutoReport-generated report contains each table field arranged vertically, one above the other, with the numeric data fields right aligned and the character fields left aligned. Any of these elements can be changed or removed easily. However, you must display the report in Design View to make structural changes to it. Click the Close window button located on the Print Preview toolbar (or choose Report Design from the View menu). The report's design is displayed in the Design View window. Figure 2.35 shows the Client report design.

In the Design window, you can change a report in any way you would like. For example, you can remove a report field by selecting it with the mouse and then pressing the Delete key after the square selection handles appear surrounding the field. If you make a mistake, remember you can choose the Undo command (Undo Delete in this case) in the Edit menu.

Saving a Report

Like other file save operations described in this text, reports are saved by selecting the Save or Save As command from the File menu. Name the report in the Save As dialog box and click OK. Save your new report in your copy of Ch02 with the name *rptClientTest*. Remember to follow the convention that reports begin with *rpt* followed by the remainder of the report name.

SUMMARY

You have learned in this chapter a great deal about database systems in general and the Access database system in particular. You understand what a relational

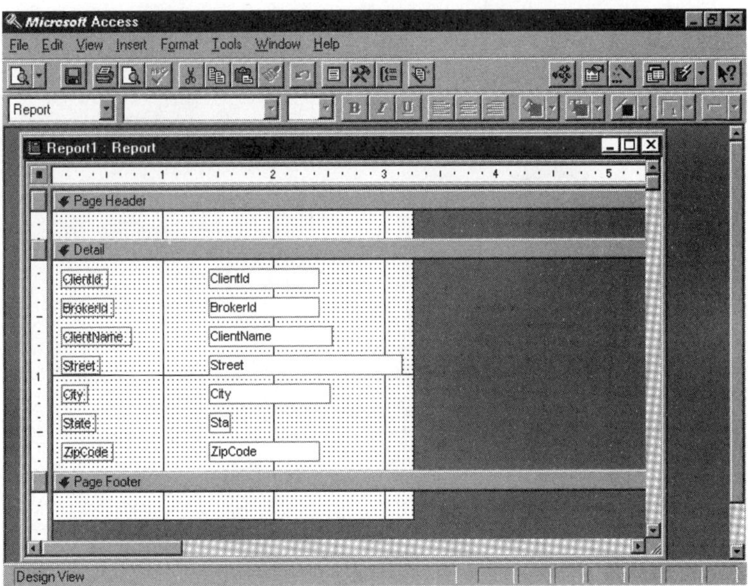

Figure 2.35 Report design.

database is and why it is the best choice for dealing with related sets of information. Tables are the building blocks of a database system and consist of columns and rows.

Tables, you found out, can be manipulated in several ways to produce the result you want. Table rows can be maintained in order when a primary key is employed. The navigation buttons in the Table window facilitate moving to various rows in a table. You can move a column in a table to another position by dragging its heading left or right. This alters the table's display characteristics but does not actually alter a column's position in the stored table.

In addition to tables, Access contains other useful objects including queries, forms, and reports. Queries, or questions, use the query by example method to pose questions about the data stored in one or more tables. Able to retrieve a subset of rows or columns, queries narrow the search for relevant information to just those elements of interest. You learned how to create queries using simple criteria as well as more complex expressions involving comparison operators. You created AND criteria in which two or more conditions must be simultaneously true. OR criteria were created by placing conditions on two or more rows of the query model.

Forms provide a simpler interface to tables, because only one row at a time is displayed. You used a form and created a quick form from a table. Forms can be made to look like paper forms encountered in a business. When a form resembles an existing paper one already in use, the computer form is rather intuitive and easy to use. You learned that by merely clicking a form entry and typing, you can change a table's data. When you move to a new record, the change is then posted to the table. And you learned that you can filter data through a table, thereby restricting which table rows are shown in a form.

Finally, you got a brief look at the hard copy output facility of Access: the report. First, you previewed an existing report. Then, you created an AutoReport for a table. Reports provide a way to print and summarize information from one or more tables in a pleasant-looking format. Reports are output only. You cannot change a table's contents with a report.

This chapter has given you the fundamental tools to begin using Access to build systems. In Chapter 3, we introduce more formal foundations of relational database management systems. In that chapter you will learn about some rules and techniques that will help you design and build accounting information systems using tables, which are well-suited for the purpose.

REVIEW EXERCISES

MULTIPLE-CHOICE QUESTIONS

1. Access is a(n) __________ database management system.
   a. algebraic
   b. flat file
   c. strictly Windows-based
   d. relational
2. Access help screens
   a. are only available when no Access table windows are open.
   b. can be printed for handy reference.
   c. only give information about Windows in general.
   d. are for advanced uses beyond the scope of this text.
3. The structure holding the result of a query is called the
   a. primary key.
   b. open query.
   c. dynaset.
   d. relational operator.
4. __________ are the fundamental storage structures for data.
   a. Forms
   b. Spreadsheets
   c. Tables
   d. Queries
5. A __________ is a question you can ask about your data in tables.
   a. help command
   b. query
   c. form
   d. request

6. You can examine your data in which of the following structures?
   a. table
   b. form
   c. report
   d. all of the above
7. A query can involve
   a. one table.
   b. two tables.
   c. three tables.
   d. all of the above
8. An example of a logical operator that can be placed in a selection criteria of a query when you want two conditions to be true at once is
   a. but.
   b. nor.
   c. and.
   d. none of the above
9. __________ provide a convenient, less cluttered work surface through which you can enter or alter table information.
   a. Forms
   b. Reports
   c. Conditional operators
   d. all of the above
10. Reports
    a. are output only—no table data can be altered with a report.
    b. can be used to change a table's information.
    c. can only be printed.
    d. all of the above

DISCUSSION QUESTIONS

1. Describe the Access work surface icons, discuss their uses, and tell how they differ from the menu commands.
2. Discuss when it is advantageous to view your data in a Table window and when a Form window is better. Explain your reasons.
3. List the steps necessary to open and display database tables.
4. Discuss why you would use database queries to retrieve information.
5. Describe the different ways to design a database report and discuss the possible situations where you might use these different designs.

EXERCISES

Note: Before doing any of the following exercises, first copy *Ch02.mdb* from your Companion CD-ROM to the hard drive of the computer on which you are working. Then, do the exercises on the copy of the database.

1. Sort the *tblClient* table on the State and City fields so that the rows are in order first by state (A to Z) and then city within each state. Print the sorted table directly from the Table window.
2. Create and execute a query based on the *tblClient* table that displays which clients are assigned broker 702. Display only the columns ClientName, ClientId, and BrokerId (in that order, left to right). The query is to sort the rows into descending order by the clients' names. Print the resulting dynaset.
3. Run the query *qryClient1015Stock* found in the query list for the Ch02 database. It produces a list of client 1015's stock purchases in ascending order by transaction identification number. Change the sort order of the rows so that query returns rows in Price order (low to high). Then modify the sort order so that the dynaset is sorted in order by the Volume column. Can you combine these sort criteria so that the dynaset is sorted first by Volume and then by Price for matching volumes? Try it! Print all three of the sorted versions of the resulting dynasets.
4. You can create an AutoForm from a query in exactly the same way you do from a table. Create an AutoForm for the query called *qryStockValue* in the query list for the database Ch02. Begin by selecting the query from the list. Click the AutoForm button. When you are done, save the form design under the name *frmAutoForm.* Turn in a printed copy of the first two pages of the form. Remember to write your name on the output.
5. Create an AutoReport report for the *tblStock* table found in the Ch02 database. Print only the first two pages of the report.

3 DATABASE FOUNDATIONS

OBJECTIVES

This chapter lays the theoretical foundation for the remainder of the text and contains practical examples of applying database theory. You will learn about the connection between accounting systems and database systems, why a relational database system is the best choice for capturing accounting information, and some of the theory and history of relational database management systems (RDBMSs). Important database design information is presented; some pitfalls to avoid in creating your tables are illustrated. Just enough theory is provided to aid you in creating efficient, optimal database objects, but the discussion avoids presenting more database theory than is needed. Important topics covered include:

- The relationship between accounting systems and database systems.
- A brief history leading to the development of database management systems.
- What duties are performed by database management systems.
- The theory and application of relational database management systems.
- Creating RDBMS objects to capture accounting events.
- Why it is important to optimize tables using normalization procedures.
- Performing database selections, projections, and joins.

Like Chapter 2, this chapter uses a real-world application to illustrate the principles we discuss. It is a classic accounting application involving processing and maintaining invoice data. A coffee bean and tea wholesaler is the focus of the illustrative application. The fictitious company, called The Coffee Merchant, purchases whole-bean coffees and teas at international auctions and sells the coffees and teas to both large and small coffee roasters. Like any business, The Coffee Merchant is concerned with keeping close track of customers who have been invoiced but who have not yet paid. Part of the relational database system is devoted to maintaining the open invoice file. Figure 3.1 shows a typical invoice for The Coffee Merchant. Invoices like the one displayed in Figure 3.1 can be generated with the Access report facility and the data in tables found in the Ch03 database of your Companion CD-ROM.

Invoice Date: *10/1/97*
Order Date: *9/6/97*
Customer PO #: *2634-63*
Sales Person: *Whitney Halstead*

The Coffee Merchant
5998 Alcala Park
San Diego, CA 92110

Sold to:

Betz Laboratories Inc.
4636 Somerton Road
Trevose, PA 19053

Item #	Qty	Description	Price	Discount	Extended
119	17	Assam Tara	13.30	10%	203 49
122	14	Ceylon Pekoe Labookelle	6.20	15%	73 78
131	17	China Keemun	10.90	5%	176 03
180	17	Vienna	3.90	0%	66 30
236	18	Rose Potpourri	6.90	5%	117 99
				Subtotal:	637 59
				Sales Tax:	0 00
				Shipping:	20 75
				Invoice Total:	658 34

Figure 3.1 Facsimile of an invoice.

Periodically, reports are generated based on both the open and closed invoices. Historic data gathered from closed invoices include information such as the total annual purchases made by each customer. Another useful report shows the total amount of each type of coffee and tea purchased by The Coffee Merchant's customers. Knowing which brands are the best and worst sellers helps The Coffee Merchant's buyers make good buying decisions in the future.

You will find the requisite tables, queries, and other database objects for this chapter in the *Ch03.mdb* database. That database is in the Ch03 folder on the Companion CD-ROM. Just as in the previous chapter, we want you to copy the database to the hard drive on the computer so that you can make changes to the database. As you know, you cannot change anything on a CD-ROM. From this point forward in the chapter, we will assume that you have copied *Ch03.mdb* to hard disk C on your computer, though any writable hard disk is fine.

A majority of the database tables are related to the invoicing needs of The Coffee Merchant. Examples throughout this chapter and exercises at the end of the chapter reference those tables. So, remember to locate and copy the Ch03 database in the Ch03 folder on the Companion CD-ROM.

Let's proceed by examining briefly the connection between accounting and database systems. That is, how did accounting come to the point of embracing relational database management systems?

ACCOUNTING INFORMATION SYSTEMS AND DATABASE SYSTEMS

Historically, accounting information has been captured in special ledgers and journals. Information about credit sales, for instance, would be recorded in a sales journal. Strict rules regarding how and where accounting information is recorded have been followed throughout time. Whenever management wanted to see an income statement, it could be produced with relative ease. Likewise, a balance sheet or other standard reports could be retrieved easily, because accounting systems were designed to produce those reports. Today's business world, however, requires more than the standard accounting reports for companies to be competitive and lean. Some reports cannot be obtained easily, if at all, using common off-the-shelf (COTS) accounting software. For example, it is probably difficult for a manufacturer to obtain ad hoc data about total monthly inventory spoilage from a traditional accounting system. Other valuable aggregations of data that provide pictures of a company's current financial or labor situation are not easily obtained with conventional accounting systems. Conventional aggregation methods provided by accounting systems have made valuable data inaccessible, except for the preparation of traditional financial reports.

Today, however, many modern accounting systems use a different approach. Database reporting is steadily replacing traditional accounting practices. Advances in accounting practice and the advent of both inexpensive and widely available computer hardware and database management software have accelerated the move toward capturing accounting information in database systems. *Events accounting* consists of storing data about an event (such as a cash sale or receipt of a purchase order) in one or more database tables. Events accounting goes beyond merely recording the associated numbers (value) of the event. Information recorded about an event—something that has happened—can include who was involved (e.g., the customer's name), why the event occurred, and so forth. There are no preconceived notions or implicit assumptions about how the information so captured is to be aggregated, output, or used. Rather, the responsibility for garnering information from accounting event data falls on the shoulders of the decision maker. An inventory manager, for example, can create (or request the creation of) a report to display current stock levels and the percentage change in stock levels from the previous month. This is a significant change from accounting information systems that made use of the debit and credit method of recording transactions. If managers need information from the accounting system to help make crucial decisions, they simply request the data they need and then review the resultant report. Managers and other decision makers need no longer rely exclusively on the standard financial statements produced by traditional accounting systems. Although some of the standard statements help managers make enterprise-wide decisions, much information is masked by traditional accounting systems.

The core of what you are studying now is accounting information systems implemented using database management systems. Because database management systems can store anything you want to record, they provide a wealth of information. Much useful business information can be gleaned from the data stored in a database's tables. As an emerging accounting information systems expert, you are on the leading edge of this significant shift to more useful accounting systems.

Next we discuss evolution of the database management systems and present some advantages and disadvantages of using database systems. We begin with a brief look at what software business tools were available before the advent of database systems.

DATABASE MANAGEMENT SYSTEMS

Database management systems (DBMSs) are valuable to business enterprises because they provide the software to store, retrieve, and modify crucial business data. DBMSs can be very cost effective, even though they are frequently costly for larger computers. Assuming that a database system is an efficient way to manage both corporate and small business data, why is it cost effective? The next section briefly describes data management and reporting prior to the advent of database management systems. Subsequent sections describe the general capabilities of database management systems—what core services they typically provide—and the advantages and disadvantages of using database management systems.

Pre-DBMS Data Acquisition and Reporting

In those adventurous years before the availability of modern database management systems, corporate data acquisition and reporting was far different from the way they are done today. Let's suppose we have traveled back in time to the late 1960s, when the Beatles were still performing together and parents were convinced that long haircuts on young men were a sign of declining morality in the United States, and assume you are responsible for ensuring that business information about The Coffee Merchant's customers is kept on the corporate computer. The Coffee Merchant, a small coffee wholesaler, has a medium-sized minicomputer on-site. The data processing department has a staff of computer programmers and support personnel to supply all the company's data processing needs.

Prior to the widespread use of modern database management systems, corporate information was kept in computer *files* on physically large disk drives (or magnetic tapes). These files, often called *flat files*, formed the core of business information processing. For instance, the accounts receivable department kept customer names and addresses in one file. When purchase orders were received, the coffee and tea order information was entered into other flat files kept on disk. An orders file contained purchase order data such as the item ordered, quantity requested of each item, whether the purchase was subject to tax (goods acquired for resale are not taxable until they are sold to a retail customer), and so on. Accounts payable kept its own set of files, which contained the names and addresses of vendors to which they owed money, invoice numbers, associated purchase order numbers, etc.

Standard, frequently requested reports were readily available. These reports summarized data held in the files. When a manager wanted to see the latest sales figures for the previous month, he could place a request with the data processing department. The requested report would be on his desk by the next morning. Finding out the current stock levels on all coffees and teas was a typical request that could be satisfied easily. Again, the data processing department would process the management request, run a program that accessed the appropriate files, and produce the report. This was typically how reports were generated for standard, traditional requests.

Custom or unusual requests and their resultant reports were a different matter altogether. While standard reports could be produced by scheduling and running programs written for that purpose, unusual report requests had to be custom-designed and written. For example, suppose the procurement office wanted to compare the inventory levels of the 20 most popular coffees and teas with the same period the previous year. Or suppose a manager wanted to see a list of the top ten wholesale customers, sorted by dollar volume. These reports would require programmers to design and write custom programs. When a special request was received, a system analyst determined what files contained the information used in the report. The analyst would also provide a program design. After the design was approved by the user(s), one or more programmers set about producing the program that would read the files, manipulate and summarize the data, and print a report. Programmers frequently wrote the program in COBOL, a high-level programming language still in wide use today. It was not unusual for a requested custom report to take several weeks before it was delivered to the requesting manager! Keeping a large pool of systems analysts and programmers on staff to supply the data processing needs of the company was (and is) expensive. Time is money, and managers could ill afford to wait weeks for critical reports.

Other problems were inherent in the pre-DBMS days. Those problems included the creation of outdated and redundant data. It was common for departments and individuals to create and maintain their own computer files, which duplicated information kept in the master files. They would do this in order to access and examine the data with their own programs quickly, rather than incurring long delays from the already overworked data processing department. Duplicate data files—files mirroring the master file data—led to inevitable data redundancy and, soon, *data inconsistency*. In a typical company, the marketing department kept its own files, sorted by zip code, of its larger customers in order to send them advertising pieces. The marketing department hired a bright young programmer to maintain the "best customer" file, and that programmer would write programs to produce mailing labels from the customer file. Problems occurred when the independently maintained customer list fell out of date. While the master list of customers was kept current by the data processing department from each month's purchase orders, the marketing department did not have access to that data. Their customer list became so out of date—old customers moved, and new customers were gained—that it was practically useless.

So you can begin to see the problems that arose. First, a wall existed between the information consumers and the information itself. That wall was the data processing department, a necessary element in the information request and receipt cycle. Second, the process tended to spawn separate islands of information that were independently maintained. This created data redundancy, which led to data inconsistency. Those are only two of the many inefficiencies inherent in the flat file system. In short, much time and money was expended to store and retrieve business data on computers prior to the advent of database management systems and accounting information systems based on them.

Functions of a Database Management System

A database management system is, simply stated, an extremely sophisticated file management system that can store and manage different types of records within one integrated system. Using a database management system's tools, a database administrator can create a sophisticated system that maintains company records, generates invoices, and in general keeps track of all a company's transactions. A *database* is the physical implementation of a particular set of records, and the database management system controls access to those records. A *relational* database management system, one of three classical models of database management systems, consists of tables containing data whose contents are related to one another through the data content of the tables. The capabilities that a database management system provides in development of an information system are the following:

- Efficient data maintenance: storage, update, and retrieval
- User-accessible catalog
- Concurrency control
- Transaction support
- Recovery services
- Security and authorization services
- Integrity facilities

One of the most important abilities of a database management system is its capacity to store, update, and retrieve data. Unlike a flat file system, you need not write and run a special program to store new data in a database. Likewise, when you want to extract information from various data files maintained by the DBMS, you can formulate a relatively simple report request in the database system's language. You need not enlist the support of a programmer to write lengthy and complicated programs to extract information. Besides, the DBMS hides all the file storage details from the user. Instead, the user is presented with an uncomplicated view of the data that the DBMS maintains.

Efficient Data Maintenance. It should be obvious that a database management system must be able to perform its most fundamental duties: store data, update data, and retrieve data. Without that capability, we have a system less capable than the COBOL programs we alluded to earlier. Implicit in the function of storage, update, and retrieval are two important characteristics. First, the database system must carry out its storage, update, and retrieval duties with great efficiency. It can employ whatever shortcuts and techniques work towards this goal. Those techniques (for example, creating and using indexes to speed access to records) must be *fast*. Second, the database management system must mask from the user the details of *how* the data is being accessed. The term *data independence* means the ability of a DBMS to hide system access details from the user, allowing the user to focus on interpreting and using their data rather than worrying about how to access it.

User-Accessible Catalog. A database catalog is itself a database comprising many tables that describe the database management system. Though it seems like a circular definition, the database catalog contains a description of the structure of all objects managed by the DBMS. Knowing the exact structure of all objects (tables and so on) is crucial for the database management system to provide effective and efficient management of the data. Some of the information contained in the database catalog includes the following:

- The names of all tables in the system
- The names and data types of every column in every table
- The range of possible values for all columns that have value limits imposed
- The inviolate relationships, when they exist, between tables (these are called integrity constraints)

Having a user-accessible catalog means that both the database management system and users can ascertain information about the structure of any data objects they own. For example, you can query the user catalog and list all tables that contain a column named Customer. Or you can retrieve the names of all tables having indexes.

Concurrency Control. *Concurrency*—use of a database by two or more users at once—must be carefully monitored by the database system. Briefly, concurrency control is enforced by the database system so two users do not attempt to alter the same piece of data at the same time. Here's an example of the problem. Suppose Ahmer and Svetlana are bank employees who are posting checks and deposits to customers' checking accounts. Let's suppose that Ahmer is working on Stirling's checking account, which currently has a balance of $100. Ahmer is about to run a transaction to add a $20 deposit to Stirling's account. At the same time, Svetlana is about to run a transaction that will deduct $40, a check she is processing, from Stirling's account. Things can go terribly wrong in a database system *without* concurrency control when the actual processing steps are performed in this (precise) sequence:

1. Ahmer's transaction reads Stirling's account balance ($100) into a work area to be processed further.
2. Svetlana's transaction reads Stirling's account balance ($100) into another work area to be processed further.
3. Ahmer's transaction adds the $20 deposit to the current amount, leaving $120 in the work area.
4. Svetlana's transaction subtracts the $40 check from her working balance, leaving a balance of $60 in her work area.
5. Ahmer's transaction concludes by posting the new balance, $120, back to Stirling's account balance in the database.
6. Finally, Svetlana's transaction concludes by posting the new balance, $60, back to Stirling's account balance in the database.

Because Svetlana's transaction was the last to occur, her transaction balance, $60, is the one that is placed in the database. Of course the correct balance after processing both transactions is $80 (a deposit of $20 and a check for $40). Concurrency controls would have prevented one transaction from being processed while another was in progress. Concurrency controls force transactions on a single record to be *serialized*—that is, to occur one after another. Though you may think a scenario like the preceding one is highly unlikely, the probability of it happening is very high in large database systems with high transaction rates—those processing thousands of transactions per minute (bank teller machines, airlines reservation systems, etc.).

Transaction Control. A *transaction* is a logical sequence of steps that accomplish a single task. More specifically, a database transaction comprises a series of steps to change one or more database entries. For instance, entering employee information into one or more tables is a transaction. Similarly, entering a purchase order into a database system's tables is a transaction. Processing a transaction frequently involves changing data in more than one table. As long as all affected entries are successfully changed, everything is fine. However, if some entries are changed but the remainder are not, then very serious problems arise—unacceptable problems.

Consider the single transaction of processing a check at a bank in which both parties have an account. Suppose Salizar writes a check to Goldstein for $200. The transaction would be as follows:

> Deduct $200 from Salizar's account; add $200 to Goldstein's account.

Suppose that the database system deducts $200 from Salizar's account and then a power outage occurs, causing the computer and the database system to crash. The remainder of the preceding transaction is lost. Later the power is restored, the computer is restarted, and the DBMS is restarted. After the database is restarted, the check is never added to Goldstein's account. $200 has disappeared into the system, benefiting the bank. *Transaction control* means that a simply stated rule is enforced: ensure that either the entire transaction is processed or none of it is. When only part of a transaction is processed prior to a failure, then the effects of the partially processed transaction must be reversed. Database management systems maintain backup records of all transactions until they are complete. Once a transaction completes successfully, its backup record is erased.

Recovery Services. When a failure occurs and the database is damaged as a result, *data recovery services* are called in to restore the database to its state prior to the failure. There are various methods employed to accomplish this. A periodic snapshot of a database's contents can be maintained along with a transaction log containing all transactions that have occurred since the last backup. The original database can be reconstructed by restoring the backup copy and then rerunning all the transactions stored in the always-current transaction log. Though failures are relatively rare, recovery services are an important function of any database management system.

Security and Authorization Services. Most large database management systems provide security and authorization services. Security and authorization services prevent unauthorized users from either accessing the system or viewing or altering any data in the database. Security services can employ encryption and views, among other techniques, to enforce security.

Encryption prevents users from actually understanding any data they might be able to retrieve, because it is transformed into apparent gibberish by the encryption program.

Views prevent users from accessing—either retrieving or altering—the hidden rows and columns they protect. Views enforce the notion of *need to know* that is frequently required by the military. For example, a sales manager whose territory includes the states of Oregon, Idaho, or Washington has a database view that constrains which rows of the Customer's table she can retrieve or even alter. The view restricts the manager's rows to those whose State field—the one containing the two-character state abbreviation—is *OR*, *ID*, or *WA*. Views can constrain not only which rows are visible to the user but also which columns are retrieved. Each person accessing a database can have his own custom view based on needs and access limitations. Further, groups of employees can have group views. Though views are very important, more details about views are beyond the scope and purpose of this text.

Authorization services enforce who can see what data. A user can authorize another access to selected information. Other users can be selectively denied access. A user who has created or otherwise is responsible for data *owns* that data. Through authorization service software, a user can either grant or deny other users access to the data owned.

Integrity Facilities. *Integrity constraints* are conditions or restrictions that must be met by data within the database. There are various types of integrity facilities, or constraint enforcement, available. What types are implemented depends on the database system itself. Typically, integrity constraints include data type, reasonable values, data format, and unique key constraints. In short, the integrity rules ensure that a table column holding an invoice date, for instance, contains values that are valid dates and fall within a reasonable range (for example, no dates before the 20th century for a computer parts inventory system).

Advantages of Database Management Systems

Some of the advantages that a database management system provides should be partially clear from the preceding material. DBMSs have other advantages over the old file and programmatic access methods. Many larger database systems provide each user with an individual view of the database. Also known as a *subschema*, a view is a pseudo table that appears to the user to be the real table. It is a definition, stored in the database, that can extract information from one or more tables and exclude selected rows and columns from being displayed. For instance, a manager might have a view of the database that displays employee data for the employees who report to the requesting manager, but no others. Views are implemented by database systems and provide a measure of security.

Data independence is another advantage of a database management system. The term *data independence* refers to a database management system's ability to hide the details of the physical storage of information from application programs that use the data. To extract information from a database, you merely request information by name and supply conditions that limit which rows are selected. The database system is responsible for translating the information request into data access statements understandable by the database system.

Changes to the structure of a database can be made transparently to the users. This is important because table designs can change over time and it becomes necessary to make changes to the internal structure of one or more tables. Frequently, table structure changes are made to provide significantly shorter database access times. When structure changes occur, those changes can be masked by using database views. The views mimic users' old perception of the affected tables' contents, and the database structure change causes no changes to users' access techniques or methods. On the other hand, imagine how much programs would be affected in a flat file system if just a few changes were made to the structure of the files they access. Programmers would have to spend a great deal of time changing all the programs that reference the files whose structure was changed. (It is no small feat to find all programs that reference a particular file or collection of files.)

Finally, database systems facilitate data sharing among users. Because corporate data is centrally stored, everyone has access to the same information and that information is always current and consistent, because there is only one copy of it. There are no duplicate versions of inconsistent data, as was often the case in the years prior to the advent of database management systems.

Disadvantages of Database Management Systems

The principal disadvantage of a database management system revolves around the large amount of secondary (disk) storage it often occupies. Consider the cost of secondary storage as you decide whether or not a database system is cost effective. Though database systems can occupy more than ten times the space required to hold the same data in flat files, DBMSs still represent a good value.

Disk storage costs are much less than the cost of maintaining data the flat file way. Programming costs have gone up rapidly in the last 15 years, whereas hardware prices have dropped sharply.

Larger database systems often require additional people such as a database administrator to keep the system running smoothly. Moreover, other database experts may be hired to handle the information needs of the company. With few exceptions, these added costs are far less than the cost of not using a database management system. Of course, smaller businesses using microcomputer-based database management packages can avoid these additional personnel costs entirely. In the latter case, only the cost of additional disk space is significant.

RELATIONAL DATABASE MANAGEMENT SYSTEMS

Database management systems can be implemented by following any of three data models in widespread use today. A *data model* is an abstract representation of a database system providing a description of the data and methods for accessing the data managed by the database. The three models in use are the *hierarchical* model, the *network* model, and the *relational* model. Throughout most of the late 1960s and early 1970s, most databases followed the hierarchical or network model. IBM's IMS database system, prevalent in the 1970s, is a prominent example of a hierarchical database management system. A DBMS that is an example of a network model is Cullinet's IDMS/R. However, in the 1970s things changed rapidly. Dr. E. F. Codd, then an IBM Fellow, introduced the relational model for database systems. Since that time, the model has evolved and changed somewhat, but the number of database systems following the relational model has exploded. Today it is the overwhelming choice for microcomputers, minicomputers, and mainframe database systems.

Compared to the other two models, the relational model provides several significant advantages. The logical and physical characteristics of the database are distinct, providing the user with a more intuitive view of the data. Using the relational model requires little training. More powerful retrieval and update operators are available, allowing even complex operations to be accomplished with concise commands. Perhaps most importantly, the relational model provides powerful tools to let us know when a database has inherent design flaws.

From this point on in the text, when we refer to a database management system, we specifically mean a *relational database management system*, or *RDBMS*.

Database Objects and Terms

Based on sound mathematical principles, the relational model is rooted in mathematical set theory, the theory of relations, and first-order predicate logic. (Don't bail out now! We will refrain from being theoretical and will not expect you to read about or understand the theoretical underpinnings of the relational model.) The model defines the conceptual view that the user has all of the objects contained by the database system. Both the data objects and the relationships between them are represented as a collection of related tables. In fact, all data—including the database table definitions and object information—exists only in tables. This provides a simple, consistent view of the database.

A relational database is a collection of relations. The primary structure in a relational model database is a relation. A table is an instance of a relation. For that reason, you will often see the terms relation and table used interchangeably (though database purists disagree). A table, or relation, consists of rows and columns, similar to a matrix or spreadsheet. Each row is technically called a tuple, though we prefer to use the less formal term row. Each column is formally known as an attribute, but we will often use the term column. Other terms used frequently in database textbooks for relation, tuple, and attribute are file, record, and field, respectively. Table 3.1 summarizes these three sets of terms.

Formal Term	Less Formal Term	Data Processing Term
relation	table	file
tuple	row	record
attribute	column	field

Table 3.1 Three sets of database terms.

Relations (tables) have the following important properties:

- The entries in each column of any row are single-valued.
- Each attribute of a given relation has a distinct name, called the attribute name.
- Every entry in a column contains a value for that column only, and the values are of like data type.
- The order of the rows is unimportant.
- The order (position) of the columns in relation to each other is unimportant.
- Each row is unique from all other rows in the relation.

The preceding relation properties are very important. Later in this chapter, we will discuss each of these in practical terms, giving examples. Figure 3.2 shows an example relation that is one of the several tables constituting The Coffee Merchant's database. Because the table is large, only a few rows are shown and only four of the ten columns are displayed—just enough for you to get the idea.

The Customer table contains 1,789 rows, in no particular order, representing the current and potential Coffee Merchant customers. Because the row order is unimportant in a RDBMS, there is no covert or implied message that one cus-

CustomerID	CompanyName	PhoneNumber	Contact
30121	Fairfield Communities Inc.	(501) 555-6079	Best, F. Stanley
30125	Alamo Group Inc.	(210) 555-1483	Maul, Duane A.
30129	Kiwi International Air Lines Inc.	(201) 555-1311	Rigas, Alan J.
30132	Republic Bancorp Inc.	(517) 555-7364	Murray, T. Peter
30136	Browne Bottling Co.	(405) 555-1168	Shelton, Carl E.
30139	Cavco Industries Inc.	(602) 555-6141	Golkin, David
30142	Bucyrus Erie Co.	(414) 555-4031	Kostantaras, Jack R. Jr.
30144	U S Office Products Co.	(202) 555-9539	Gerson, Terrence
30147	Ciatti S Inc.	(612) 555-1891	Townes, Patrick J.
30148	Tab Products Co.	(415) 555-2429	Montrone, Frank A.
30149	Diversicare Inc.	(615) 555-3354	
30153	Audiovox Corp.	(516) 555-7769	Choate, Robert
30155	Twin Disc Inc.	(414) 555-4052	Crist, Dennis P.
30158	Bay State Gas Co.	(508) 555-7017	Huff, Richard E.
30159	Fort Wayne National Corp.	(219) 555-5911	
30163	Medusa Corp.	(216) 555-4073	Hart, John M.
30164	Stv Group Inc.	(610) 555-4629	Hill, Alex W.
30168	Commercial Federal Corp.	(402) 555-9213	McMeel, John D.

Figure 3.2 The Customer relation, *tblCustomer.*

tomer is more important than another. All one can tell from the row order is that the identification number field, called CustomerID, is in ascending order. For relational databases, a row's identity is determined by its content, not its location within a table.

The table contains ten columns. (We have omitted several columns to simplify the example without altering its merit in any way.) The attributes shown in Figure 3.2 are named CustomerID, CompanyName, PhoneNumber, and Contact. However, there is no theoretical reason to list the columns in that order. Nonetheless, like some other database management systems, Access requires the primary key column, CustomerID in this example, to be the first table column. We could place the Contact column in the second column, followed by the PhoneNumber and CompanyName columns.

Within each column are particular attribute values for each row. For instance, the row identified as CustomerID 30121 contains "Fairfield Communities Inc." for its CompanyName value, "(501) 555-6079" in the PhoneNumber column, and the value "Best, F. Stanley" for its Contact value. Each row has a different value for each attribute. In particular, the CustomerID value is unique for each row. This satisfies the rule that each row must be unique. (As you know, a row is unique if any one of its columns is unique.) Said another way, the record for the first row is

30121, Fairfield Communities Inc., (501) 555-6079, Best, F. Stanley

The first column, CustomerID, is the relation's primary key. Every relation must have a primary key that uniquely identifies a given row. The primary key can comprise one or more columns. When more than one column constitutes a primary key, the individual column values need not be unique, but their combination must be. The schema of a relation for this example is the relation's name and its attributes. A compact representation of the schema for the *tblCustomer* table, using the reduced number of columns in this illustration, can be written like this:

Customer(<u>CustomerID</u>, CompanyName, PhoneNumber, Contact)

where the table's attributes are enclosed in parentheses following the table name. An underline indicates the primary key column(s).

Relational database systems have a data dictionary. A data dictionary is a collection of tables containing the definition, characteristics, structure, and description of all data maintained by the RDBMS. In other words, there is no external definition of the data structures, names of tables, column names, column data types, and so on. Instead, all that information is stored in special tables accessible by either the database administrator or the object's owner. Besides table descriptions, the data dictionary houses view definitions, object owner names, database login names (for minicomputer and mainframe database systems), and passwords. Fields in the data dictionary are automatically changed whenever an object's structure is changed. For example, if you delete a column from a table and rename another table, both operations cause changes to the data dictionary entries. A row in a table holding other tables' column names is deleted when you delete a column, and a row containing table names is updated when you rename a table (actually, several tables are affected by a rename operation). Having a data dictionary makes the job of the database management system and the database administrator more efficient, because all information needed about the system is self-contained.

Every row in a RDBMS must be distinct from all other rows in that table, or else it cannot be retrieved! This is one of the fundamental rules of a relational database management system. To ensure uniqueness, a primary key is designated for a table. A primary key, as mentioned previously, is a column (or group of columns) that uniquely identifies a given row. Therefore, the system can distinguish one record (row) of a table from another. In the *tblCustomer* table, for instance, the CustomerID column—the customer's identification number—uniquely identifies a row. There can be only one row with a particular CustomerID value. (Customer 3006 occurs only once in the table, for example.) Thus CustomerID is the primary key for the *tblCustomer* table.

Another significant key field that is very important is a foreign key. A foreign key is an attribute in one table that must match the primary key in another table. Figure 3.3 shows another table used by The Coffee Merchant to retrieve invoice data from the set of tables constituting the database.

The CustomerID column in the Invoice (*tblInvoice*) table is a foreign key, because it references a primary key found in one row of the *tblCustomer* table. Foreign key/primary key associations are important in establishing connections between related tables. Connecting two or more related tables based on their matching primary/foreign keys is a fundamental relational database operation called join. (You will learn more about the join operation later in this chapter.)

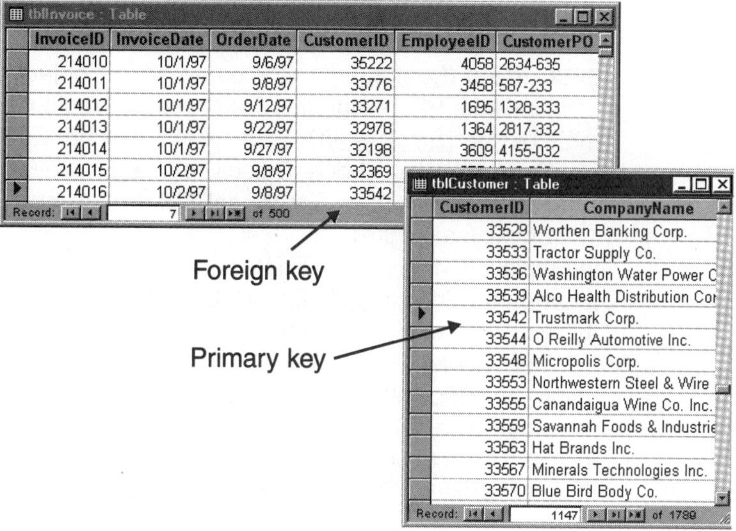

Figure 3.3 Primary key and foreign key relationship.

Invoice System Tables

In order to understand how accounting information can be organized in a database system, let's look at an example. Several of the tables contained in the *Ch03.mdb* database, which is stored in the Ch03 folder on your Companion CD-ROM, constitute invoice data for customers of The Coffee Merchant. Figure 3.4 shows schema for each table used in the invoicing subsystem of The Coffee Merchant's database.

When bits of data from each of these tables are combined in the proper way, we can build and print an invoice similar to the one shown in Figure 3.1.

The *tblCustomer* table contains vital information about each customer. Each customer is assigned a primary key—a sequence of integers beginning with any number is sufficient—so that a customer can be uniquely identified. The Invoice table, *tblInvoice*, contains a history of invoices sent out by The Coffee Merchant. Identified by the primary key InvoiceID, each row holds each customer's invoice date (InvoiceDate), order date (OrderDate), customer identification number (CustomerID), identification number of the associated salesperson (EmployeeID), and the customer's original purchase order number (CustomerPO). Of course, an invoice shows more details than these held in the Invoice table *tblInvoice*, but those additional details (such as the customer's address) are contained in another table named *tblCustomer* that is linked to the Invoice table. Figure 3.5 shows a Datasheet view of some *tblInvoice* rows.

Order lines, which contain details about individual items ordered by the customer and included on the current invoice (quantity ordered, unit price, discount, and so on), are not in the Invoice table. Instead, those details are found in

tblCountryName (<u>CountryID</u>, CountryName, ExportCoffeeBags, ExportTeaPounds)
tblCustomer (<u>CustomerID</u>, CompanyName, Contact, Address, City, State, ZipCode, PhoneNumber, FaxNumber, CreditLimit)
tblEmployee (<u>EmployeeID</u>, EmployeeFirstName, EmployeeLastName, EmployeeWorkPhone, EmployeeTitle, EmployeeCommRate, EmployeeHireDate, EmployeeDOB, EmployeeGender, EmployeeNotes, EmployeePicture)
tblEmployeeTitle (<u>TitleID</u>, Title)
tblInventory (<u>InventoryID</u>, ItemID, Caffeinated, Price, OnHand)
tblInventoryDescription (<u>ItemID</u>, Name, Beverage, Flavored, CountryID, Comments)
tblInvoice (<u>InvoiceID</u>, InvoiceDate, OrderDate, CustomerID, EmployeeID, CustomerPO)
tblInvoiceLine (<u>InvoiceID</u>, <u>InventoryID</u>, Quantity, UnitPrice, Discount)
tblSalesTaxRate (<u>StateAbbreviation</u>, StateName, TaxRate, Population, LandArea)

Figure 3.4 Schemas of tables in the invoicing system.

tblInvoice : Table

InvoiceID	InvoiceDate	OrderDate	CustomerID	EmployeeID	CustomerPO
214010	10/1/97	9/6/97	35222	4058	2634-635
214011	10/1/97	9/8/97	33776	3458	587-233
214012	10/1/97	9/12/97	33271	1695	1328-333
214013	10/1/97	9/22/97	32978	1364	2817-332
214014	10/1/97	9/27/97	32198	3609	4155-032
214015	10/2/97	9/8/97	32369	2754	912-232
214016	10/2/97	9/8/97	33542	4082	662-433
214017	10/3/97	9/22/97	34109	3370	4210-234
214018	10/3/97	9/25/97	34154	1364	1470-034
214019	10/4/97	9/5/97	31183	3370	3464-131
214020	10/4/97	9/22/97	32031	3370	2029-532
214021	10/4/97	9/29/97	33312	1301	1580-633
214022	10/5/97	9/16/97	32013	3943	1517-132
214023	10/5/97	9/23/97	31105	3943	336-231
214024	10/5/97	9/28/97	34417	3943	967-234
214025	10/5/97	9/28/97	30771	3943	1209-030
214026	10/6/97	9/13/97	35283	3943	60-535
214027	10/6/97	9/26/97	32971	3370	1927-032
214028	10/6/97	9/28/97	32130	3700	1842-332

Record: 1 of 500

Figure 3.5 Example rows in the Invoice table, *tblInvoice*.

three other tables: *tblInvoiceLine*, *tblInventory*, and *tblInventoryDescription*. Figures 3.6, 3.7, and 3.8 show sample rows from each of these tables. The *tblInvoiceLine* table may appear to be a bit odd to you. It contains only five attributes: two fields comprising a primary key and three fields containing order information. The order information fields indicate the quantity ordered, quoted unit price (which can vary for a given product depending on the customer), and discount percentage for each item on each invoice. The primary key is actually a composite primary key, meaning it consists of more than one attribute. InvoiceID and InventoryID combine to form a primary key. These two attributes identify the source invoice and inventory item number (or line) of each given invoice. The *tblInventory* and *tblInventoryDescription* tables catalog all the coffees and teas available from The Coffee Merchant (its "line card"). Only a few of the over 100 items stored in the inventory tables are shown in Figure 3.7. InventoryID identifies each inventory item uniquely, and other characteristics about the inventory item are found collectively in the *tblInventory* and *tblInventoryDescription* tables.

tblInvoiceLine : Table

InvoiceID	InventoryID	Quantity	UnitPrice	Discount
214010	1184	18	$6.90	5%
214010	1192	17	$13.30	10%
214010	1195	17	$3.90	0%
214010	1209	14	$6.20	15%
214010	1237	17	$10.90	5%
214011	1104	19	$5.30	5%
214011	1133	8	$7.90	0%
214011	1137	15	$7.00	15%
214011	1197	2	$7.10	0%
214011	1211	10	$14.70	15%
214012	1127	17	$4.50	0%
214012	1129	5	$8.40	0%
214012	1189	14	$5.30	15%
214012	1203	12	$8.10	15%
214012	1249	2	$11.90	0%
214013	1139	10	$5.30	15%
214013	1198	17	$8.10	5%
214013	1208	14	$4.50	15%

Record: 1 of 2192

Figure 3.6 Example rows in the Invoice Line table, *tblInvoiceLine*.

tblInventory : Table

InventoryID	ItemID	Caffeinated	Price	OnHand
1101	116	☑	$8.10	512
1102	422	☐	$5.30	3,190
1103	440	☐	$7.70	-130
1104	455	☐	$5.30	3,380
1105	449	☐	$7.60	3,300
1106	224	☑	$7.40	1,130
1107	113	☑	$8.80	315
1108	134	☑	$10.30	443
1109	275	☑	$8.00	354
1110	353	☐	$13.70	354
1111	314	☐	$6.40	4,390
1112	443	☐	$6.60	1,770
1113	254	☐	$8.80	456
1114	107	☑	$9.50	5,090
1115	470	☑	$15.50	354
1116	407	☐	$5.30	3,040
1117	200	☑	$8.30	141
1118	347	☑	$8.60	2,500

Record: 1 of 154

Figure 3.7 Example rows in the primary Inventory table, *tblInventory*.

tblInventoryDescription : Table

ItemID	Name	Beverage	Flavored	CountryID	Comments
101	Continental Blend	c	☐	0	100 percent Mexican Altura, ro:
104	Costa Rica Tarrazu	c	☐	45	A perfect balance of acidity anc
107	Costa Rica La Manita	c	☐	45	A standard against which all otl
110	Sumatra Mandheling	c	☐	83	An enticing favorite of many; sy
113	Assam Fancy 2nd Flus	t	☐	41	Black tea;
116	Darjeeling Badamtam	t	☐	82	Black tea;
119	Assam Tara FTGFOP-1	t	☐	41	Black tea;
122	Ceylon Pekoe Labooke	t	☐	163	Black tea;
125	Ceylon Supreme	t	☐	163	Black tea;
128	Ceylon Uva Highlands	t	☐	163	Black tea;
131	China Keemun	t	☐	41	Black tea;
134	China Yunnan	t	☐	41	Black tea;
137	Darjeeling Namring	t	☐	82	Black tea;
140	Kalgar-India	t	☐	82	Black tea;
143	Kenya Kaproret	t	☐	93	Black tea;
146	Mocha	c	☐	151	Bold, earthy, mild acidity. One
149	Costa Rica Tres Rios	c	☐	45	Costa Rican coffees are always
152	Zimbabwe	c	☐	194	Delicate, fruity aroma; medium
155	Ethiopia Mokas	c	☐	61	Earthy and winey; indigenous t

Record: 1 of 131

Figure 3.8 Example rows in the secondary Inventory table, *tblInventoryDescription.*

So, how do you get the extended price, subtotal, and other important invoice values like those shown in Figure 3.1? The answer is that you calculate those values when you print the invoice. Extended prices need not be stored in any of the tables, because they can be calculated by multiplying each invoice line's quantity and price attributes. Thus, the data in these four tables plus the Customer table, *tblCustomer*, contain all the basic information needed to produce invoices.

Now that you have been introduced to the invoice database tables, let's learn about normalization. For the moment, we will avoid too many details about the invoice tables themselves and limit our discussion to the reasons for and the definition of normalized tables.

Normalization

Unlike the past, when data was stored in flat files, we have learned that it is important to think carefully about where the individual pieces of data are stored. It is critical to design a database carefully so that its attributes are stored in the proper tables. The process of determining the correct location for each attribute is called *normalization*. Another way of thinking about normalization is this: normalizing a database is storing data where it uniquely belongs. What might happen if we choose to ignore normalization? Simply stated, unnormalized databases lead to redundant, inconsistent, and anomalous information being stored in tables.

There are numerous ways to arrange the invoice system attributes in one or more tables. However, some arrangements are better than others. A particular subset of the ways that attributes can be organized into tables is called a *normal form*, and the basis of the method to arrive at this arrangement is called normalization theory.

Researchers have identified seven normal forms. Like layers of an onion, each normal form is completely compliant with the rules of the normal forms that contain it. Correspondingly, the rules applied to achieve each normal form are successively more stringent. The least restrictive is called the *first normal form* (abbreviated as 1NF). Following that form are the *second*, *third*, *Boyce/Codd*, *fourth*, *fifth*, and *Domain/Key* normal forms. For our purposes, we discuss and use only the first three normal forms. Forms beyond this are largely of theoretical interest and do not significantly impact our work. Tables in third normal form are better than those in second normal form. Likewise, tables in second normal form are better than those in first normal form. The goal of the normalization process is to start with a collection of tables (or relations), apply normalization, and arrive at an equivalent collection of tables in a higher normal form. The process is repeated until all tables are in 3NF.

First Normal Form. A table that contains a repeating group is called an *unnormalized table*. The relational model requires that all tables be in first normal form. To achieve this, repeating data must be removed from the table and stored elsewhere. For example, suppose that an invoice table held each invoice line for all invoices in the arrangement shown in Figure 3.9.

InvoiceID	InvoiceDate	CustomerID	InventoryID	Quantity	UnitPrice	Discount	
214010	10/1/97	35222	1184	18	6.90	5%	
			1192	17	13.30	10%	
			1195	17	3.90	0%	Repeating group
			1209	14	6.20	15%	
			1237	17	10.90	5%	
214011	10/1/97	33776	1104	19	5.30	5%	
			1133	8	7.90	0%	
			1137	15	7.00	15%	Repeating group
			1197	2	7.10	0%	
			1211	10	14.70	15%	
214012	10/1/97	33271	1127	17	4.50	0%	
			1129	5	8.40	0%	
			1189	14	5.30	15%	Repeating group
			1203	12	8.10	15%	
			1249	2	11.90	0%	
214013	10/1/97	32978	1139	10	5.30	15%	
			1198	17	8.10	5%	
			1208	14	4.50	15%	Repeating group
			1216	19	7.20	5%	
			1229	5	12.90	0%	
			1249	5	11.90	0%	

Figure 3.9 Example table containing repeating groups.

Notice that for each invoice in the invoice table, there are several inventory item numbers, quantities, unit prices, and discounts. For instance, invoice number 214010 contains five items, where each item corresponds to an invoice detail item on a printed invoice. The schema representing the preceding table can be written like this:

tblInvoice(InvoiceID, InvoiceDate, CustomerID,
InventoryID, Quantity, UnitPrice, Discount,
InventoryID, Quantity, UnitPrice, Discount,...)

where the ellipsis indicates that InventoryID, Quantity, UnitPrice, and Discount can repeat any number of times—as many times as there are items listed on a single invoice.

We cannot store repeating groups (multiple values) in one table column, and we do not want to store a variable number of {InventoryID, Quantity, UnitPrice, Discount} quadruples in each row. Instead, all quadruples in repeating groups can be collected together, removed from their existing invoice table, and placed in rows of a new table. This requires that an additional column be added to the new table linking the rows of the newly formed table with the original invoice table. An example of the structure of the two tables conforming to first normal form is this (we've inserted three new fields into *tblInvoice* to conform to the actual Invoice table stored on your Companion CD-ROM):

tblInvoice(InvoiceID, InvoiceDate, OrderDate, CustomerID, EmployeeID,
CustomerPO)
tblInvoiceLine(InvoiceID, InventoryID, Quantity, UnitPrice, Discount)

The new table, *tblInvoiceLine*, contains five columns. The first two columns, InvoiceID and InventoryID, provide the requisite primary key. It is also referred to as a composite primary key because the primary key comprises two attributes.

Second Normal Form. Tables in first normal form can be placed into a relational database system, but in most cases first normal form is not good enough. Such tables are prone to several problems. Let's look at an example. Figure 3.10 shows an example of some rows of the *tblCustomer* table in first normal form (vastly different from the actual *tblCustomer* table stored in Ch03 on your Companion CD-ROM). The shorthand representation for this table is:

tblCustomer(CustomerID, CompanyName, PhoneNumber, Contact,
InvoiceID, Total)

The *tblCustomer* table contains customer information like the customer identification, company name, telephone, and contact person. The last two columns indicate the customer's invoice number and amount. Two columns, *CustomerID* and *Invoice*, form the table's primary key. Both are needed to access a row.

CustomerID	CompanyName	PhoneNumber	Contact	InvoiceID	Total
30125	Alamo Group Inc.	(210) 555-1483	Maul, Duane A.	214480	$306.80
30139	Cavco Industries Inc.	(602) 555-6141	Golkin, David	214123	$225.11
30139	Cavco Industries Inc.	(602) 555-6141	Golkin, David	214460	$315.10
30174	Thomas Nelson Inc.	(615) 555-9079	Harber, L. H.	214390	$491.96
30174	Thomas Nelson Inc.	(615) 555-9079	Harber, L. H.	214418	$185.95
30206	Matlack Systems Inc.	(302) 555-2760	Gordon, W. Phil	214334	$218.39
30212	Lilly Industries Inc.	(317) 555-6762	Choong, Jerry	214117	$152.20
30221	Mcdonald & Co. Investmer	(216) 555-2368	Bianco, Andrew R.	214249	$297.34
30225	Krause S Furniture Inc.	(510) 555-6208	Woltz, Neil G.	214087	$260.15
30228	F N B Corp. Pa	(412) 555-6028	Fancher, William F	214284	$98.35
30231	Everest & Jennings Intern:	(314) 555-7041	Gray, Robert R.	214036	$270.60
30231	Everest & Jennings Intern:	(314) 555-7041	Gray, Robert R.	214256	$165.96
30258	Lcs Industries Inc.	(201) 555-5666	Lebuhn, Eugene	214230	$895.25
30258	Lcs Industries Inc.	(201) 555-5666	Lebuhn, Eugene	214308	$541.97
30271	Wisconsin Gas Co.	(414) 555-7049	Groen, James F.	214378	$190.45
30277	Ameriserv Food Co.	(214) 555-8641	Doig, Antoino R.	214139	$139.37
30291	Southwestern Life Corp.	(502) 555-2181	Ellingboe, James	214477	$301.05
30327	Shaw Group Inc.	(504) 555-1214		214220	$430.95
30330	Packaging Resources Grc	(708) 555-6104	Horner, Tomas E.	214441	$300.63
30339	First Financial Bancorp Oh	(513) 555-4703	Gilcrest, Edward A	214369	$426.54
30343	Uniroyal Technology Corp	(813) 555-5295	Kirk, Jeffrey A.	214068	$235.00
30362	Rocky Shoes & Boots Inc.	(614) 555-1987		214450	$404.66

Figure 3.10 Example rows of the Customer table in first normal form (INF).

What can be the problem? Several potential problems exist. Suppose that the *tblCustomer* table is the only place in which customer information such as address or name is placed. What happens when you want to add a new customer and that customer has paid for an order in advance? That is, can we add a customer to the *tblCustomer* table without first generating an invoice? No, of course not! The InvoiceID value would be empty. When an attribute is empty, or has no value, it is *null*. The InvoiceID attribute cannot be null, because relational database rules do not allow the primary key, or one of its components, to be null. This situation is known as an *insertion anomaly*.

Consider this scenario. Cavco Industries pays for its two invoices, numbers 214123 and 214460 (see Figure 3.10, second and third rows), bringing its amount due to zero. The two rows corresponding to Cavco Industries are removed from *tblCustomer*. Not only are the two invoices removed, but the customer's identification number, name, phone, and contact person are deleted as well. So the deletion has a wider effect than desired—you lose knowledge of the customer entirely. Your mailing list is being destroyed! This predicament is known as a *deletion anomaly*.

Finally, the *tblCustomer* table shown in Figure 3.10 contains a great deal of redundant information. For instance, the company identification number, name, phone number, and contact person are repeated for each new invoice that is issued for a particular customer. The customer name *Cavco Industries Inc.* is entered twice, as is *Golkin, David*, the contact person. It is pure luck that both the company name and contact person's name have been spelled correctly both times. And what if you want to change the company name? You must find all occurrences of the name in the database and change each one. Yikes! What a time-consuming task that would be. This small example illustrates that tables in first normal form usually contain a great deal of redundant data.

The preceding problems can be alleviated by altering a table's structure and changing it into second normal form. A table (relation) is in *second normal form* (2NF) if it is in first normal form and none of the nonkey attributes depend on only one portion of the primary key. That is, second normal form requires that each nonkey attribute depend on the entire primary key, not just part of it. This rule applies only when you have a composite primary key—one consisting of more than one table column.

The attribute Total in the *tblCustomer* table in Figure 3.10 violates the 2NF definition. The value of Total is solely determined by the partial primary key InvoiceID. We say that Total is *functionally dependent* on InvoiceID, because a particular value of InvoiceID determines a single value of Total. On the other hand, Total does not depend on the attribute and partial primary key CustomerID, because the total invoice amount varies from invoice to invoice; no relationship exists between Total and a particular customer. On the other hand, the attributes CompanyName, PhoneNumber, and Contact each functionally depend on the partial primary key CustomerID. These two sets of functional dependencies are shown in Figure 3.11.

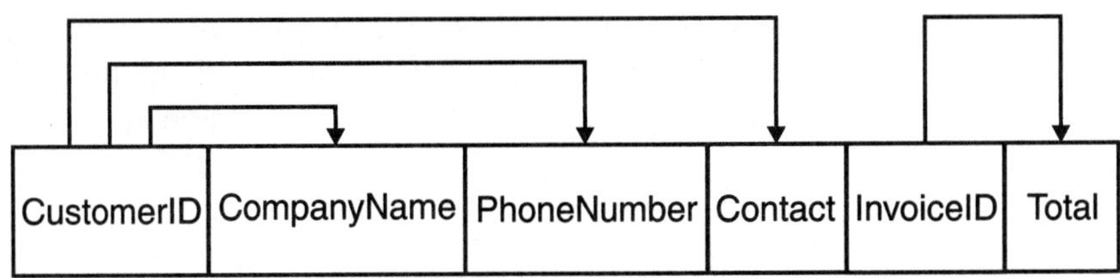

Figure 3.11 Functional dependencies in the Customer table.

The arrows lead from a primary key to another attribute. For instance, the arrow leading from CustomerID to CompanyName means that CustomerID *determines* CompanyName (or CustomerID is a *determinant* of CompanyName). It is clear that we can correct this problem by breaking *tblCustomer* into two tables. Of course, we must note the relationship between these two tables by including an extra attribute—a foreign key—linking both tables (*joining* them in database parlance) on the CustomerID key. *tblCustomer* and its related *tblInvoice* table in second normal form could be restructured this way:

tblCustomer(<u>CustomerID</u>, CompanyName, PhoneNumber, Contact)
tblInvoice(<u>InvoiceID</u>, CustomerID, Total)

where we have included in *tblInvoice* the CustomerID field as a foreign key to *tblCustomer,* thus associating these two tables.

Third Normal Form. The design goal for relational databases is to create tables that are in third normal form. A table is in *third normal form* (3NF) if it is in second normal form and all transitive dependencies have been eliminated. A *transitive dependency* exists in a table if attribute B determines attribute C, and attribute C determines attribute D.

You have probably heard an expression that can help you understand and remember the difference between 2NF and 3NF. Part of the phrase used to swear in witnesses who are about to take the stand in a trial goes roughly like this: "...to tell the truth, the whole truth, and nothing but the truth." The second normal form is analogous to "the whole truth" part of the phrase—each attribute depends on the *whole* primary key. Similarly, the third normal form is analogous to "and nothing but the truth"—each attribute depends *only* on the primary key and on no other attribute in the relation. For example, consider the Invoice table shown in Figure 3.12.

InvoiceID	InvoiceDate	OrderDate	CustomerID	EmployeeID	Contact
214010	10/1/97	9/6/97	35222	4058	Shaffer, Shaun P.
214011	10/1/97	9/8/97	33776	3458	Olbrych, Fred H.
214012	10/1/97	9/12/97	33271	1695	Yocam, William C.
214013	10/1/97	9/22/97	32978	1364	Swift, Scott C.
214014	10/1/97	9/27/97	32198	3609	
214015	10/2/97	9/8/97	32369	2754	Gosa, Myron E.
214016	10/2/97	9/8/97	33542	4082	Henderson, L. Keith
214017	10/3/97	9/22/97	34109	3370	Pirie, Thomas R.
214018	10/3/97	9/25/97	34154	1364	Ammerman, Donnie M.
214019	10/4/97	9/5/97	31183	3370	Dykstra, Bruce A.
214020	10/4/97	9/22/97	32031	3370	Mori, John F.
214021	10/4/97	9/29/97	33312	1301	
214022	10/5/97	9/16/97	32013	3943	Meyerson, Donald
214023	10/5/97	9/23/97	31105	3943	
214024	10/5/97	9/28/97	34417	3943	Tadmor, Dan
214025	10/5/97	9/28/97	30771	3943	Forney, Eugene E.
214026	10/6/97	9/13/97	35283	3943	Geddes, John G.
214027	10/6/97	9/26/97	32971	3370	Newman, Lorne R.
214028	10/6/97	9/28/97	32130	3700	Britton, Thomas W.
214029	10/7/97	9/16/97	34355	1364	Bolland, Jeffrey A.

Figure 3.12 Example Invoice table in second normal form (2NF).

The Invoice table's primary key is InvoiceID. Because only one customer may be assigned a particular invoice number (the value in the InvoiceID field), the invoice number uniquely determines the invoice date, order date, customer identification number, employee identification number, and company contact person. There are no repeating groups in the table. Therefore, it is in first normal form. Furthermore, it is in second normal form because all attributes depend on the single-attribute primary key. How about third normal form? Are all attributes functionally dependent on only the InvoiceID attribute? The answer is no. There is a transitive dependency. The InvoiceID determines the CustomerID value. CustomerID, in turn, determines the Contact column. Figure 3.13 shows the dependency in the Invoice table.

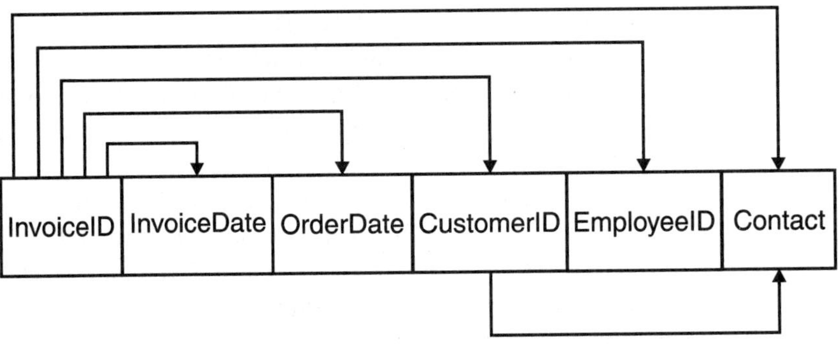

Figure 3.13 Transitive dependencies in the Invoice table.

The arrows above the attributes (represented by boxes) show the dependencies that exist between attributes and the table's primary key. Those relationships are fine. However, the arrow below the boxes shows a transitive dependency between CustomerID (the determinant) and Contact. The easiest way to remove the offending dependency is to create another table containing at least the determinant attribute (CustomerID, in this case) and all dependent attributes (Contact, in this example). Once the transitive dependency is excised, the table will be in 3NF. Of course, the field CustomerID becomes a foreign key to link the invoice to individual customer information. The new tables could be structured as follows to bring them into compliance with 3NF:

tblInvoice(<u>InvoiceID</u>, InvoiceDate, OrderDate, CustomerID, EmployeeID)

and

tblCustomer(<u>CustomerID</u>, Contact)

Third normal form enforces an informal rule stating that a table should store one fact and one fact only. Prior to decomposing *tblInvoice* into two separate tables, it housed two facts: one fact about invoices (InvoiceDate, OrderDate, etc.) and one fact about customers (Contact). After two tables are created from a single table, each new table's structure (shown above) holds only one fact.

Table Relationships. It should be clear that the process of normalizing a database's tables usually produces several additional tables. Yet the relationships between associated tables is maintained by the foreign-key-to-primary-key links. What general types of relationships exist between tables in a typical database? There are three fundamental relationships between related tables: one-to-one (1—1), one-to-many (1—M), and many-to-many (M—M). Knowing about these three is important in understanding how to reconstruct information from data stored in constituent tables.

One-to-one relationships occur frequently where a master table contains customer information, for instance, and a related table contains occasional notes about a few customers. For instance, the Customer table could have a one-to-one relationship with *tblCustomerNotes*, which might hold supplementary information about a few of The Coffee Merchant's customers. Because only a few customers have notes in the *tblCustomerNotes* table, you do not want to allocate an additional column for an occasional note. That would waste storage space. So *tblCustomerNotes* would contain the foreign key CustomerID and a Notes column. CustomerID would serve both as the primary key for the *tblCustomerNotes* table and as a foreign key into the parent *tblCustomer* table. A notation like this shows this relationship conveniently:

tblCustomer ^{1}——————>^{1} tblCustomerNotes

Very often, databases contain tables that have one-to-many relationships with each other. There are several examples in The Coffee Merchant's database. Look again at Figure 3.3. Consider the relationship between the *tblCustomer* table and the *tblInvoice* table. Each customer can have as many unpaid invoices as The Coffee Merchant permits (or none). On the other hand, an invoice row in the *tblInvoice* table can be associated with one and only one customer in the *tblCustomer* table. The relationship between the *tblCustomer* table and the *tblInvoice* table is said to be a one-to-many relationship (in that direction—customer to invoice). (Whenever appropriate, always indicate the "one" side of the relationship first.) The relationship of this type is shown this way:

tblCustomer ^{1}——————>^{M} tblInvoice

Finally, consider the relationship between invoices and the coffee and tea items found on individual invoice lines. Various coffees and teas can appear on the many lines of a single invoice. An invoice might contain a line for 10 pounds of Kona coffee and another line for 5 pounds of Columbia Supremo. Similarly, the coffee and tea items in The Coffee Merchant's inventory can appear in several invoices. For example, among the outstanding invoices there can be several that include Kona coffee. This type of relationship between the Invoice table and Inventory table is called a many-to-many relationship. We indicate this type of relationship this way:

tblInvoice ^{M}——————>^{M} tblInventory

Many-to-many relationships are difficult to represent and maintain in a relational database system. So a new table is created to help represent the M—M relationship in a more convenient way that avoids anomalies. The table is called a *relationship* table, and it combines attributes from both original tables in the M—M relationship. The relationship table makes the connection, acting as a sort of "middle man," between two M—M tables so that two 1—M relationships are created among the three tables. The relationship table in The Coffee Merchant's database is called Invoice Line (*tblInvoiceLine*), and it preserves the relationship between invoices (*tblInvoice*) and inventory (*tblInventory*). We represent this three-table relationship for the M—M relationship this way:

tblInvoice ^{1}————————>^{M} tblInvoiceLine ^{1}————————>^{M} tblInventory

Thus, it is always possible to break an M—M relationship between two tables into two 1—M relationships between three tables by using an intermediate, relationship table.

Fundamental Relational Database Operations

Relational database management systems provide several important and fundamental retrieval operations. Among the most significant are select, project, and join.

Select. The select operator chooses a set of rows from a table. Rows are selected based on a criteria, often called *selection criteria*. A new, virtual table is created by the operation. There are several ways to implement a selection operation. Some RDBMSs such as Paradox and Access provide a Query By Example (QBE), a graphical interface, in which you select example elements to specify selection criteria and check the attributes to be displayed.

Figure 3.14 shows a selection operation and the resulting dynaset, another table. The query selects rows from a smaller version of an employee table. Rows are selected in which the HireDate is after 1/1/93.

Notice that the result returns all columns of the original table satisfying the selection criterion. The result is a table, because queries in relational database systems always deliver answers in table form.

Project. The project operator returns a subset of columns from one or more tables. Columns retrieved are a result of the user indicating them, not as a result of specifying a selection criterion. Figure 3.15 shows an example of a projection of the Name and Gender columns of our example employee table shown previously in Figure 3.14.

Notice that a projection operation does not imply which *rows* are retrieved. Projections indicate only which *columns* are retrieved in the result. Of course, you can combine the selection and projection in one query to produce both a row and column subset of one or more tables.

Employee table:

ID	Name	Comm	HireDate	BirthDate	Gender
1301	Stonesifer	5%	07/06/92	03/10/62	F
1364	Pruski	4%	12/01/96	01/26/75	M
1528	Pacioli	6%	08/26/91	05/06/46	M
1695	Nagasaki	4%	01/28/96	04/10/73	M
2240	Stonely	15%	11/05/84	05/03/57	F
2318	Hunter	8%	11/16/89	01/26/50	F
2754	Kahn	5%	05/14/93	05/29/57	M
3370	Kole	9%	02/08/88	03/23/59	M
3432	English	8%	10/01/89	02/14/52	F
3436	Gates	6%	04/11/91	03/09/50	M
3458	Morrison	15%	12/13/85	07/04/52	F
3609	Chang	5%	09/16/93	03/30/73	F
3692	Ballmer	15%	05/16/81	07/13/40	M
3700	Ellison	7%	04/18/90	12/12/50	M
3892	Shoenstei	11%	09/05/86	03/06/51	M
3943	Watterson	8%	10/10/89	05/01/57	F
4012	Minsky	11%	10/13/86	04/12/55	F
4029	Manispour	11%	12/18/86	02/04/65	M
4057	Bateman	9%	02/16/88	05/01/54	M
4058	Halstead	5%	06/16/92	12/22/69	F
4082	Flintsteel	11%	03/21/86	08/22/54	F
4112	Goldman	11%	12/24/86	03/05/58	M

Result of selection operation: HireDate>1/1/93

ID	Name	Comm	HireDate	BirthDate	Gender
1364	Pruski	4%	12/01/96	01/26/75	M
1695	Nagasaki	4%	01/28/96	04/10/73	M
2754	Kahn	5%	05/14/93	05/29/57	M
3609	Chang	5%	09/16/93	03/30/73	F

Figure 3.14 Select operation on an employee table.

Join. At the center of the relational database operations is the join operation. It provides the ability to pull together data from disparate but associated tables into a single, virtual table. Usually, you join two tables together based on a matching, common attribute found in both tables. This is the role of the foreign and primary keys. In the conventional form of the join operation, one table's foreign key value

Employee table:

ID	Name	Comm	HireDate	BirthDate	Gender
1301	Stonesifer	5%	07/06/92	03/10/62	F
1364	Pruski	4%	12/01/96	01/26/75	M
1528	Pacioli	6%	08/26/91	05/06/46	M
1695	Nagasaki	4%	01/28/96	04/10/73	M
2240	Stonely	15%	11/05/84	05/03/57	F
2318	Hunter	8%	11/16/89	01/26/50	F
2754	Kahn	5%	05/14/93	05/29/57	M
3370	Kole	9%	02/08/88	03/23/59	M
3432	English	8%	10/01/89	02/14/52	F
3436	Gates	6%	04/11/91	03/09/50	M
3458	Morrison	15%	12/13/85	07/04/52	F
3609	Chang	5%	09/16/93	03/30/73	F
3692	Ballmer	15%	05/16/81	07/13/40	M
3700	Ellison	7%	04/18/90	12/12/50	M
3892	Shoenstei	11%	09/05/86	03/06/51	M
3943	Watterson	8%	10/10/89	05/01/57	F
4012	Minsky	11%	10/13/86	04/12/55	F
4029	Manispour	11%	12/18/86	02/04/65	M
4057	Bateman	9%	02/16/88	05/01/54	M
4058	Halstead	5%	06/16/92	12/22/69	F
4082	Flintsteel	11%	03/21/86	08/22/54	F
4112	Goldman	11%	12/24/86	03/05/58	M

Projection of two columns:

Name	Gender
Stonesifer	F
Pruski	M
Pacioli	M
Nagasaki	M
Stonely	F
Hunter	F
Kahn	M
Kole	M
English	F
Gates	M
Morrison	F
Chang	F
Ballmer	M
Ellison	M
Shoenstei	M
Watterson	F
Minsky	F
Manispour	M
Bateman	M
Halstead	F
Flintsteel	F
Goldman	M

Figure 3.15 Project operation on an employee table.

is used to locate a matching primary key in another table. Then the selected data from the matching rows in both tables are combined. That is, rows of one table are concatenated with those of the second table in which the common attribute matches.

For instance, suppose we want to join a slightly altered Employee table with the employee title information found in a table on your Companion CD-ROM called *tblEmployeeTitle*. In the Employee table is a number, which stands in place of an actual job title. The number is used so that the title is not misspelled when it is entered over and over in the Employee table. *tblEmployeeTitle* contains the numbers and actual job titles associated with the numbers. Normalization has produced the two tables, rather than a single table with repeating job titles, which would violate 3NF rules. The tables are joined on title number columns found in both tables. In the Employee table, this column is called *EmployeeTitle*, though it has been shortened in the illustration to simply *TitleID*. The *TitleID* column in *tblEmployeeTitle* is the primary key and contains a corresponding title field, *Title*. Joining the two tables in TitleID produces the result shown in Figure 3.16. Note that the join column *does not* have to have the same name in both tables. In the illustration, TitleID is a foreign key in the employee table, whereas TitleID is the primary key in the *tblEmployeeTitle* table. Joining is a matter of matching foreign key and primary key values.

The join illustration in Figure 3.16 is an example of the most common type of join. It is called an *equijoin*, because rows from the two tables are concatenated on matching join column values, and the join column appears only once in the result. Another join operation type combines rows from two or more tables on the join column, but rows that do not match on the join column are included in the result. A join of the latter type is called an *outer join*. Outer joins are useful for listing employees having no sales (employee join sales) or students who have or have not signed up for a particular class. We will not discuss outer joins further in this text.

There is no practical limit to the number of tables that may be joined. For instance, one of the principal results we will produce with a join operation are invoices. An invoice is created by a query that joins five of The Coffee Merchant's tables whose structures (schemas) are shown in Figure 3.4. Tables joined to form an invoice are connected in pairs on common columns, but not all on the same columns. For instance, the *tblCustomer* table can be joined to the *tblInvoice* table via their common column, CustomerID. Continuing, the *tblInvoice* table can be joined to the *tblInvoiceLine* table (individual invoice lines) over the join column InvoiceID, an attribute found in both tables. The Inventory table, *tblInventory*, is joined to *tblInventoryDescription* to link the names of each invoiced item. *tblInventory* is joined to *tblInvoiceLine* on the common column InventoryID. Figure 3.17 illustrates how the join columns of all involved tables are connected to form the single result—a dynaset. Of course, all the joins shown are equijoins.

INTRODUCTION TO DATABASE DESIGN

A well-designed database that accurately models an enterprise's operations is crucial to the success of any database system designed to maintain accounting information. On the other hand, a badly designed database that is supposed to represent a company's business can be worse than using no system at all. In the worst case, information can be misrepresented, difficult to find, or completely lost.

One very important aspect of database design is carefully choosing the rows and attributes each table comprises. This activity, often referred to as *modeling*, can be accomplished using any of several methods. We introduce you to two of

Employee table:

ID	Name	TitleID	HireDate	Gender
1301	Stonesifer	2	07/06/92	F
1364	Pruski	1	12/01/96	M
1528	Pacioli	2	08/26/91	M
1695	Nagasaki	1	01/28/96	M
2240	Stonely	3	11/05/84	F
2318	Hunter	2	11/16/89	F
2754	Kahn	2	05/14/93	M
3370	Kole	2	02/08/88	M
3432	English	2	10/01/89	F
3436	Gates	2	04/11/91	M
3458	Morrison	3	12/13/85	F
3609	Chang	2	09/16/93	F
3692	Ballmer	3	05/16/81	M
3700	Ellison	2	04/18/90	M
3892	Shoenstei	3	09/05/86	M
3943	Watterson	2	10/10/89	F
4012	Minsky	3	10/13/86	F
4029	Manispour	3	12/18/86	M
4057	Bateman	2	02/16/88	M
4058	Halstead	2	06/16/92	F
4082	Flintsteel	3	03/21/86	F
4112	Goldman	3	12/24/86	M

X

***tblEmployee* Title table:**

TitleID	Title
1	Sales Trainee
2	Sales Associate
3	Senior Sales Associate
4	Sales Manager
5	Senior Sales Manager
6	Division Sales Manager
7	Regional Manager
8	Division Manager
9	National Sales Manager

=

Result of join operation:

ID	Name	TitleID	HireDate	Gender	Title
1301	Stonesifer	2	07/06/92	F	Sales Associate
1364	Pruski	1	12/01/96	M	Sales Trainee
1528	Pacioli	2	08/26/91	M	Sales Associate
1695	Nagasaki	1	01/28/96	M	Sales Trainee
2240	Stonely	3	11/05/84	F	Senior Sales Associate
2318	Hunter	2	11/16/89	F	Sales Associate
2754	Kahn	2	05/14/93	M	Sales Associate
3370	Kole	2	02/08/88	M	Sales Associate
3432	English	2	10/01/89	F	Sales Associate
3436	Gates	2	04/11/91	M	Sales Associate
3458	Morrison	3	12/13/85	F	Senior Sales Associate
3609	Chang	2	09/16/93	F	Sales Associate
3692	Ballmer	3	05/16/81	M	Senior Sales Associate
3700	Ellison	2	04/18/90	M	Sales Associate
3892	Shoenstei	3	09/05/86	M	Senior Sales Associate
3943	Watterson	2	10/10/89	F	Sales Associate
4012	Minsky	3	10/13/86	F	Senior Sales Associate
4029	Manispour	3	12/18/86	M	Senior Sales Associate
4057	Bateman	2	02/16/88	M	Sales Associate
4058	Halstead	2	06/16/92	F	Sales Associate
4082	Flintsteel	3	03/21/86	F	Senior Sales Associate
4112	Goldman	3	12/24/86	M	Senior Sales Associate

Figure 3.16 Join operation example.

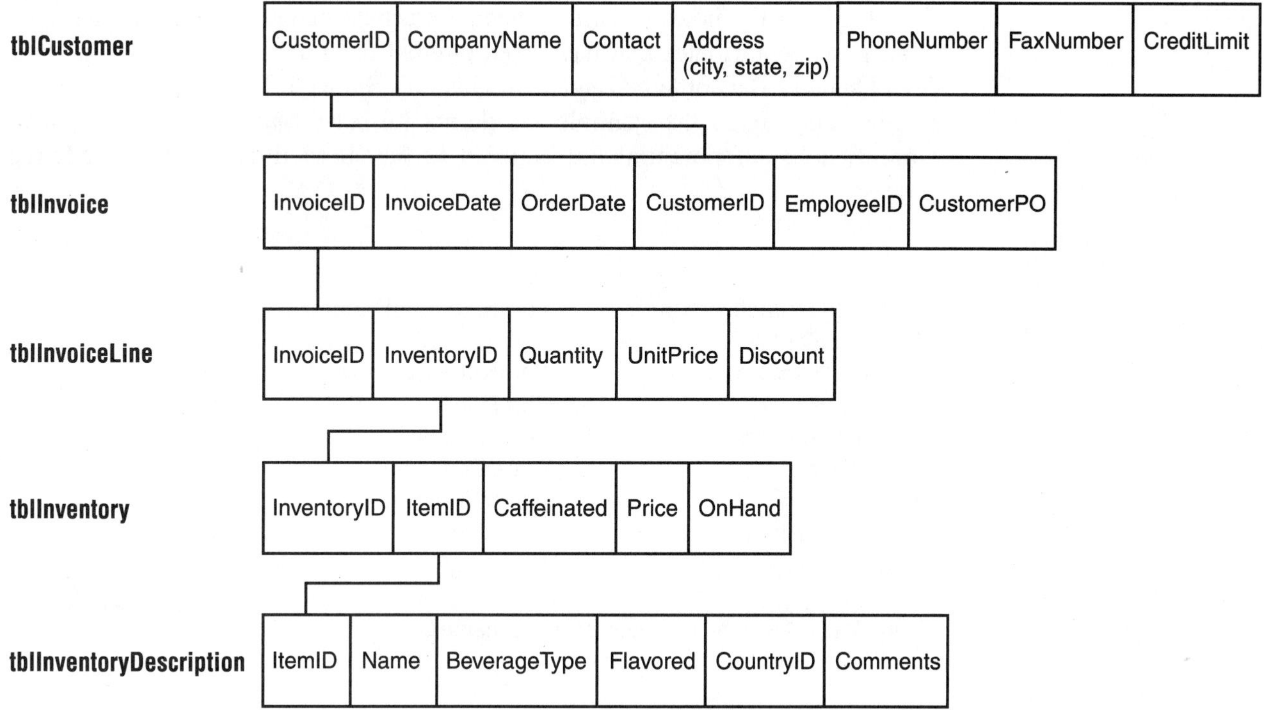

Figure 3.17 Joining Coffee Merchant tables to yield invoices.

these methods in this section. The first method we offer draws information from existing business documents. The other method, called entity-relationship (abbreviated E-R) modeling, is described in the context of The Coffee Merchant's invoice system.

Creating User Views and Relations

One way to approach designing database objects to represent a business organization is to use existing documents as a starting point. For instance, we can look at a current customer invoice, like the one in Figure 3.1. The first step is to list all the information found on the document and assign names to the attributes. Next, we can identify functional dependencies, if any. Then, the entities (tables) can be created by selecting which attributes belong in which tables. Finally, we can apply normalization rules to the tables to ensure that all tables (entities) conform to third normal form.

The first step, listing potential attributes from an existing document, is relatively straightforward. Attribute names may not be exactly right the first time, but they provide a starting point.

Figure 3.18 shows a list of potential attribute names. Of course, there are other possible attributes that have been omitted from the list such as Ship Date, Item Quantity Backordered, and Item Quantity Shipped. We have omitted these because they clutter the example and do not further illuminate the process. Our simplified list of potential attributes is sufficient to illustrate this modeling process.

CustomerContactPerson	ItemExtendedPrice
CustomerName	ItemName
CustomerNumber	ItemNumber
CustomerPhone	ItemPrice
CustomerAddress	ItemQuantity
InvoiceDate	OrderDate
InvoiceNumber	OrderNumber
InvoiceTotalAmount	SalesTax
ItemDescription	ShippingCharges

Figure 3.18 A list of potential attribute names.

Next, we identify functional dependencies. You can make good guesses as to which attributes determine the value of other attributes. Don't worry about making a mistake. Errors will be uncovered when you interact with end users. Figure 3.19 shows an example of a dependency list. Dependent attributes are listed below the attributes that determine them.

After making initial assignments of attributes, you may discover that the CustomerName depends on the InvoiceNumber, not on the CustomerNumber, in cases in which the shipping address varies from the usual customer address (a case we disallow in our example). You may determine that the price charged to a customer depends on the CustomerNumber, not the ItemNumber. The latter is true when a customer is given a price reduction based on volume or other factors contributing to a "most favored" status. Finally, results depending on fields of the database such as InvoiceTotalAmount, SalesTax, and ShippingCharges should not be stored in the database at all. Why? Because doing so would violate second normal form rules. SalesTax, for instance, depends on additional attributes besides InvoiceNumber. A change in the unit price of an item would not be reflected in SalesTax (nor InvoiceTotalAmount) automatically. As the last step in this process, you develop a revised list of attributes obeying third normal form. The attributes upon which each group depends constitute the relation's primary key, and each table's attributes are the primary key and the attributes listed below the primary key. The latter list of corrected dependencies is left as an exercise for the student (hint: see Figure 3.4).

CustomerNumber:
  CustomerName
  CustomerPhone
  CustomerContactPerson
  CustomerAddress

InvoiceNumber:
  InvoiceDate
  CustomerNumber
  OrderDate
  OrderNumber
  ShippingCharges
  InvoiceTotalAmount
  SalesTax

InvoiceNumber, ItemNumber:
  ItemQuantity
  ItemExtendedPrice

ItemNumber:
  ItemDescription
  ItemPrice
  ItemName

Figure 3.19 Tentative dependency list.

Developing Entity-Relationship Models

Another popular modeling technique is called the *entity-relationship (E-R) model.* Introduced by P. P. Chen in 1976, E-R has gained wide acceptance as a graphical approach to database design. Space limitations restrict us to introducing the topic and showing only a few examples of its use in designing The Coffee Merchant's database. For an in-depth discussion of E-R modeling, consult any database management text.

Database designers use three terms to describe a company's information: *entities*, which are objects found in the company (nouns such as invoice, purchase order, or sales receipt); *relationships*, which are the way in which distinct entities interact or are related to one another; and *attributes*, which, you will recall, describe the entities and relationships. The latter are the adjectives of an entity.

In the E-R model, entities and relationships are represented by diagrams. The diagrams contain three symbols: rectangles, diamonds, and lines. Rectangles represent entities and diamonds represent relationships. Lines are the connections between the two. A digit or letter above the line indicates the *degree* of the relationship: one-to-one, one-to-many, or many-to-many. Figure 3.20 shows an example of an E-R diagram for The Coffee Merchant's invoice system.

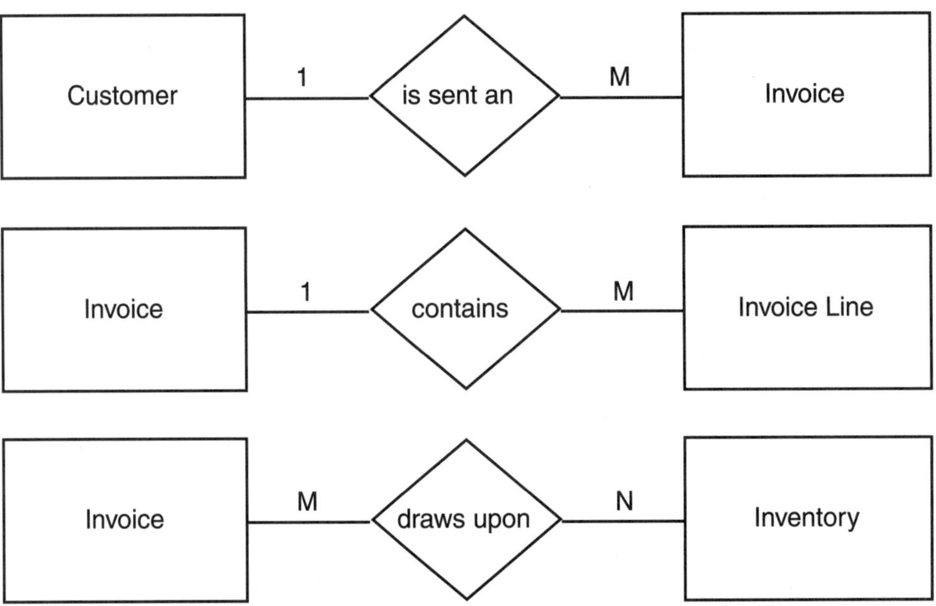

Figure 3.20 Entity-relationship diagram.

At first, the E-R model dictated that not only could entities have attributes, but relationships could as well. Attributes are listed near the relationship or entity they represent. An attribute name is attached to a line leading from the entity or relationship to the attribute. Chen later suggested a slight change to the E-R approach. The altered E-R representation proposed that only entities can have attributes, not relationships. A problem arises using the refined E-R methodology when representing many-to-many relationships. In this case, a new entity—shown with a diamond within a rectangle—is used to redraw two entities as three. The new entity reduces the relationship to three entities having a 1—M degree relationship on one side and an N—1 degree relationship on the other side (see Figure 3.21).

The newly created entity in the middle is implemented in a database as a *relationship table*, comprising the primary keys of the two entities on either side of it. This type of relationship is seen between an invoice and the inventory items that appear on invoice lines. Similarly, students and classes they take are another example of a many-to-many relationship.

After the E-R diagrams are complete, they can be combined into a single subsystem or system E-R diagram. This process is called *view integration*. For larger systems the process is started by placing the most often used entity in the center of the diagram. Then lines connect the related entities as in the original diagrams. From these entities you can identify tables. For each entity, one table is created. Primary keys for each table must be identified next. The relationships between entities, exemplified by lines connecting the entities, are maintained by

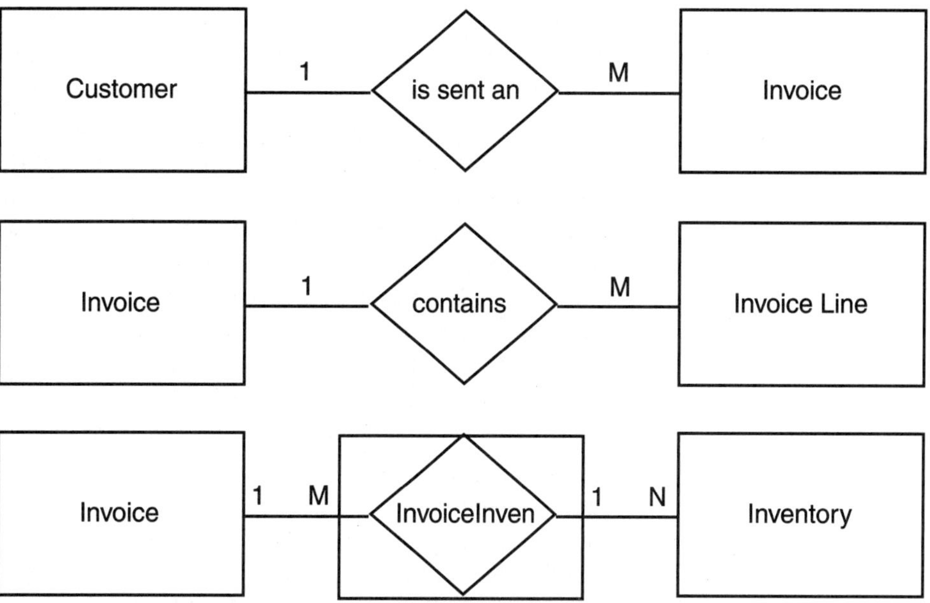

Figure 3.21 Revised entity-relationship diagram.

foreign key/primary key linkages between tables. That is, a line from one entity to another is implemented by a key in one table (a foreign key) that matches one or more primary keys in the other table. In the case of a 1—M relationship, the "one" side of the relationship has a foreign key matching possibly several rows on the many side of the relationship.

When a many-to-many relationship exists in the E-R diagram, such as the relationship between *tblInvoice* and *tblInventory*, a third table is created. Called a *relationship* table, it contains the primary keys from both tables. In other words, the InvoiceInven table contains the primary key from the *tblInvoice* table and the primary key from the *tblInventory* table. Once the relationship table is created, the three tables have a pair of one-to-many relationships. Both relationship tables and the tables to which they are related can be constructed easily. However, representing many-to-many relationships with two tables can lead to problems and should be avoided by using a relationship table.

The last step in view integration is to normalize the individual tables. For best results, all tables should be at least in third normal form to avoid the anomalies mentioned previously in the section describing normalization.

CREATING ACCOUNTING OBJECTS WITH A RDBMS

One of the important tables in the evolving invoice subsystem contains customer names, addresses, and telephone numbers (and other fields) collected from both customers and people who merely expressed an interest in receiving a catalog.

Besides periodically sending out promotional material to selected members of the customer "list," customer information appears in the "Ship to," "Sold to," or "Bill to" areas of invoices (see Figure 3.1, for instance). The Coffee Merchant sample Customer table is somewhat large (about 1,700 rows), but it is small when compared to that of a company such as Microsoft. The Customer table, called *tblCustomer*, is stored in the database called *Ch03.mdb*. The database is found on your Companion CD-ROM in the Ch03 folder. We have loaded *tblCustomer* with several rows so you can experience manipulating a non-trivial table. All of the data is real, including company names and addresses. The telephone numbers and contact persons have been randomized sufficiently to protect the privacy of individuals. You will notice that the telephone area codes are correct and correspond to the city in which the business is located.

In the next several sections we want you to create a table from scratch and enter data into it. Rather than have you be mere observers of our data, you will get involved with the whole process, from start to finish, of designing your own table. This way, you will be prepared to create quality databases after you finish reading this book and working its exercises. That's why it is instructive for you to build and fill at least one of the tables so that you see the process. If you have trouble, the Companion CD-ROM contains all the tables and other objects for The Coffee Merchant. The next section begins the process by describing how to create a mini-version of the Customer table. The section afterward describes the step-by-step process of filling (called *populating*) your table.

Defining a Table's Structure

From this point in Chapter 3 forward you will be doing a lot of work with the Ch03 database. So, now is a good time to copy the database from your Companion CD-ROM to the hard drive on your computer. Insert your Companion CD-ROM in the drive and copy the file *Ch03.mdb* from the Ch03 folder. Once the database has been copied to your disk, you can remove the Companion CD-ROM and store it away for safekeeping. Every change you make to the Ch03 database is made to the copy of the database you just created on your hard disk.

Prepare for the first exercise in this chapter using Access by launching Access. Next, select Open from the File menu and then locate and select in the Open dialog box database *Ch03.mdb*. Follow the steps in the next exercise to create an example Customer table that is a much smaller version of the *tblCustomer* table already stored on disk.

Exercise 3.1: Creating the Customer Table Structure

1. Make sure the Tables tab in the Database window is selected, and then click the New button to open the New Table dialog box.

2. Select *Design View* from the list of choices and click OK to get started. In the upper part of the Table window in Design view are columns in which you can enter field names, data types, and a description for each field. You will do this next.
3. In the Field Name column of the Table dialog box, type ***CustomerID*** (the first field name); press Tab to move to the Data Type column. Most database experts agree that column names should *not* contain embedded spaces. Some database systems disallow spaces, so your table and database cannot be ported to or used by those systems. Always follow the Hungarian notation whereby words are capitalized and concatenated together to form an object name.
4. Type *N* in the Data Type column (click the combo box if you want to see a drop-down list of all the Access data types); press Tab to move to the Description field.
5. Type the brief description ***Customer identification number***. (The Description field text appears in the Status bar on the left side whenever the cursor is positioned on the corresponding field during data entry. It helps you remember the purpose of the field.)
6. Click the Set Primary Key button on the toolbar or select Primary Key from the Edit menu. (The Primary Key button displays a small key. Move the mouse over it, pause, and the tooltip "Primary Key" is displayed confirming you have selected the correct button.) Access places a small key symbol to the left of the field name indicating that CustomerID is the table's primary key. If you need to select multiple columns for a composite primary key, simply hold down the Ctrl key and click the row selectors to the left of the fields' names. Then click the Primary Key toolbar button.
7. Press Tab to move to the next row to begin defining the next customer column.
8. Type ***CompanyName*** in the Field Name column and press Tab. Text is the suggested data type. That is fine. However, the default length, 50, is too large. Let's change it.
9. Double-click the Field Size property in the Field Properties list found in the lower half of the dialog box. Type *25*
10. Click the Description column in the Company field row and enter ***Company name***. Press Tab to move to the next row in the Table dialog box.
11. Type ***PhoneNumber***, select the text data type, change the default data length (Field Size) to *8*, and enter the description ***Telephone number***. Press Tab to move to the next row.
12. Type ***LastContactDate***, press Tab, type ***D*** to select a date type, press Tab and enter ***Date of last contact*** in the Description column.
13. Press Tab to move to a new row. Enter ***CreditLimit*** in the Field Name column, select Number data type, and enter the description ***Credit limit***
14. Enter the last field name, ***Notes***. Type ***M*** to select a memo data type. Move to the Description field and type ***Miscellaneous notes***
15. Save the newly defined table: select Save from the File menu. The Save As dialog box is displayed (see Figure 3.22). (Your field names, types, and

descriptions should match those shown in Figure 3.22. If not, simply click in the incorrect cell and change it.)

16. Type ***tblMyCustomer*** in the Table Name text box and then click OK. Your newly created Customer table, called *tblMyCustomer*, is saved in the Ch03 database.

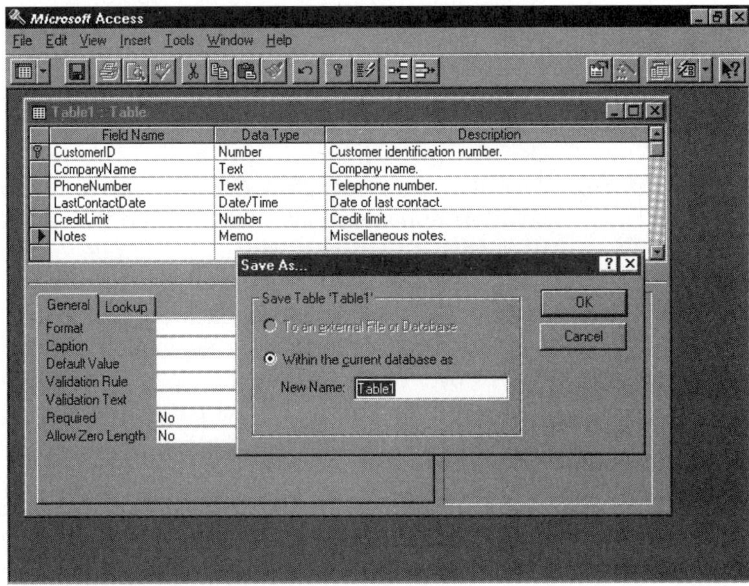

Figure 3.22 Saving a table's definition.

Note that we suggest in the last step that you save the table with the name *tblMyCustomer*, not *tblCustomer*. This is a safety feature. That way you still have the original table *tblCustomer*, which is on the Companion CD-ROM, for use in the textbook's exercises.

Next, let's place data into the table *tblMyCustomer*. This will give you experience entering, altering, and saving data—something we have not yet asked you to do in this text.

Populating a Table

When you *populate* a table, you are simply placing data into a table whose structure already exists. Entering data into a table is straightforward. First, ensure that the Ch03 database is open. Then, click the Tables tab and locate *tblMyCustomer* in the list of database names displayed in the Database window. Double-click the *tblMyCustomer* table name to open it. Maximize the Table window so that you can see the full table. Next, you will enter the first customer record. You will use three different methods to move to the next field: pressing Tab, clicking the next field, and pressing Enter.

EXERCISE 3.2: ENTERING A RECORD INTO A TABLE

1. In the CustomerID field, type ***3001*** and press Tab to move to the CompanyName field.
2. Type ***Experience Coffee*** in the CompanyName field. Move to the PhoneNumber field by clicking the cell just under the PhoneNumber field name.
3. Type ***555-1233*** in the PhoneName field. Press Enter to move to the next column, LastContactDate.
4. Type ***5/23/96*** in the LastContactDate field. Press Tab to move to the CreditLimit column.
5. Enter ***4000*** and press Tab to move to the last column, Notes.
6. Enter ***This is a good customer*** in the memo field, Notes.

Don't press any keys for a moment. Do you notice the small pencil symbol in the row selector button of the table? That indicates a record's contents are changed but not yet posted to the table. You post changes to a table simply by moving to another table record. You will do that in a moment.

If you make a mistake anywhere while entering data, simply use the arrow keys to move left or right in the field, or use the Backspace or Delete keys to delete information. Pressing a key inserts the letter into the field at the insertion point indicated by the cursor. To correct a value in a field to the left of the current field, press Shift+Tab repeatedly until the cursor arrives at the field to be changed. To display the blinking insertion point, simply press F2. Then you can use the arrow keys to move the insertion point within a field. Pressing Tab or Shift+Tab moves to another cell and selects the entire value.

Next, enter the remaining *tblMyCustomer* table data. When you move to a new row, the previous row is stored on disk. The last record you enter in a table is saved when you close the table. Or, you can simply press the up arrow key to move to a previous record to save the latest record to the table.

EXERCISE 3.3: ENTER THE REMAINING TABLE INFORMATION

1. With the *tblMyCustomer* table still displayed, click in the CustomerID column of the second table row.
2. Enter the remaining table rows. Table 3.2 shows all customer table rows. Refer to it as you enter the remaining customer records. You can enter anything you

like (or nothing) in the Notes field of each customer record. That's entirely up to you.

3. After you enter the last customer's information, click the Table window Close button to close the table. The last row of the *tblMyCustomer* table will be posted to the database.

CustomerID	CompanyName	PhoneNumber	LastContactDate	CreditLimit
3001	Experience Coffee	555-1233	5/23/96	4000
3002	Gourmet Grinder	555-1826	9/14/97	1000
3003	La Jolla Expresso	555-1919	7/9/79	5500
3004	Starbucks Coffee	555-4561	9/14/96	15000
3005	Kensington Coffee Company	555-5153	12/16/96	1000
3006	Intermezzo Espresso Bar	555-5282	8/5/96	7500
3007	Just Bean Counters	555-9646	3/15/97	2500

Table 3.2 Contents of the example table (*tblMyCustomer*).

Investigating the Invoice Table

The *tblInvoice* table, found on the Companion CD-ROM, contains information about single invoices. Its structure was shown in Figure 3.4. *tblInvoice* contains the fields invoice number, invoice date, order date, customer identification number, salesperson number, and the customer's purchase order number. Each row corresponds to an invoice, and a particular customer may have several outstanding invoices at any point. Of course, a customer may have no unpaid invoices, in which case there will be no row in the *tblInvoice* table corresponding to that customer. The primary key is InvoiceID, a unique number corresponding to the invoice number. Because each row must have a unique value in the primary key field, InvoiceID, we entered "Yes" in the Field Property called Required when we created the table (see Figure 3.23). As a matter of fact, we have marked all *tblInvoice* table columns with the Required property, meaning that all columns of a row must have something in them. They cannot be empty.

Why is the CustomerID attribute included in the *tblInvoice* table? CustomerID is a foreign key. It associates *tblInvoice* to a related table, *tblCustomer*. The *tblInvoice* and *tblCustomer* tables are linked to one another on a row-by-row basis using matching CustomerID attribute values. That is, we can *join tblInvoice* and *tblCustomer* by matching *tblInvoice*'s CustomerID foreign key to *tblCustomer*'s primary key of the same name. Foreign and primary keys do not have to have the same names. We follow that practice to help reinforce recognition of foreign keys in tables. In addition, Access will automatically join two tables on fields that are spelled identically in both.

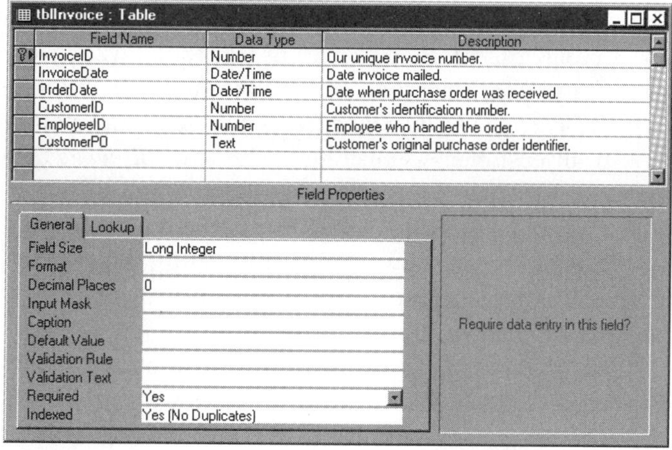

Figure 3.23 Structure of the Invoice table, *tblInvoice*.

One other important property, called *referential integrity,* has been established for the *tblInvoice* table. Though transparent to you, referential integrity guarantees that a row referenced by a foreign key will not be deleted unless all rows containing matching foreign keys are removed first. For our invoice system, this means that we cannot remove a customer from the *tblCustomer* table who still has outstanding invoices—one or more rows in the *tblInvoice* table. For this type of table-to-table linkage, the *tblCustomer* table is loosely called the *parent* table, and the *tblInvoice* table is the *child*. Referential integrity is one of the attributes you can set in the Relationships dialog box, which will be described Chapter 4.

Dealing with a Many-to-Many Relationship

The relationship between *tblInvoice* and *tblInventory* is many-to-many. Any particular invoice can contain several items drawn from inventory. From another perspective, any particular inventory item (for example, Kona coffee) may be found in several invoices. Whenever an M—N relationship exists between two tables, a *relationship* table is created. Minimally, the relationship table contains primary keys from both the *tblInvoice* and Inventory tables for every item on a particular invoice and all invoices. Figure 3.6 shows the first few rows in the relationship table *tblInvoiceLine*.

There are as many rows in the relationship table as there are invoice line items for all invoices. We have removed invoice lines from the *tblInvoice* table and placed them into the *tblInvoiceLine* table. All the items of a particular invoice can be retrieved by matching the invoice number with the InvoiceID attribute of *tblInvoiceLine*. InvoiceID is the primary key of the *tblInvoice* table, whereas the attribute InventoryID in *tblInvoiceLine* is also the primary key in the Inventory table. Thus, InventoryID in *tblInvoiceLine* is a *foreign key*. The other attributes in this table are Quantity, UnitPrice, and Discount. Quantity is the amount invoiced for a particular item (coffee or tea) for a given invoice line. UnitPrice is the price charged for this item. It can vary from the *tblInventory* Price field. Discount is the percentage discount for a line item on a particular invoice. Discounts vary from customer to customer. The two *tblInvoiceLine* table attributes, InvoiceID and InventoryID, form a *composite primary key*.

If you encounter other tables having a many-to-many relationship, which cannot be handled easily by a RDBMS, the remedy is simple. Create a relationship table containing a composite primary key that is formed from the primary keys of the two tables having the M—N relationship—just like we have done with the *tblInvoiceLine* table. Once a relationship table is in place, then one of the original tables has a 1—M relationship with the relationship table, whereas the other original table has a 1—N relationship with the relationship table. In other words, the relationship table provides the "glue" connecting two tables in a one-to-many-to-one relationship. The latter is easily maintained in a relational database management system and suffers from no anomalies inherent with other, nonnormalized tables.

PERFORMING SELECTIONS AND PROJECTIONS

A database's ability to retrieve selected rows and columns lies at the heart of its query capability, as you have learned in Chapter 2. You can display an entire table in an attempt to locate a particular customer, invoice, or inventory item, but that is inefficient, time-consuming, and error-prone. Queries, on the other hand, allow you to specify precisely which rows and which columns you wish to see. Relational database systems differ in how they deliver a query facility, but they all provide the capability. Some systems use a standard RDBMS interface language called Structured Query Language (SQL). Other systems use query by example (QBE). Microsoft Access provides both. Whichever method is available, you can have the database system search through a huge table quickly.

More about Queries

By specifying query selection criteria—conditions that attribute values must satisfy—you can retrieve information that is important to you at the moment. For instance, you can formulate a query using Access's QBE method to retrieve customer information for customers who were invoiced more than 30 days ago. Or you can query an order history table to determine the ten most popular products. In a query, you specify the table or tables you want to search, the attributes you want to display in the result, and the selection criteria used to select rows. In addition, queries can contain expressions that compute *derived* or *virtual* information from existing table data. An example of a derived value is the extended price column in an invoice line item. Extended price, though not part of any Coffee Merchant table, is an expression—the product of an item's quantity and its price. You will see how to create queries in the examples that follow and throughout the text. Queries lie at the heart of many different database results, including labels, forms, and reports.

Queries are definitions of how to retrieve information; they do not actually hold any data. Each time a query is run, a different dynaset—the result of a query—may be delivered. For instance, a query to list the passengers on flight 711 from San Diego to Las Vegas will yield different results when run on different days, because the passenger list changes from day to day.

Retrieving Selected Rows from a Table

You can create a query with the Query Wizard or manually. Once the query has been formulated, you can select Datasheet from the View menu to see the results of your newly defined query. If the query is one that will be run many times, you can save it for later use. Of course, a query will always return the same result for a static, unchanging database, but database contents rarely remain constant over time. For instance, a list of past due invoices is likely to change from month to month, so saving the corresponding query makes sense. Saving an ad hoc query that lists a company's board of directors might not be necessary, however.

To create a query, you begin by clicking the Queries tab in the Database window. After you click New, select the table(s) to be searched. The Query window will display the table(s) and a QBE grid. Once you select the fields to be included in the result, you enter the selection criteria by specifying a value or expression in the QBE Criteria row for one or more attributes. Only table rows whose attributes satisfy the criteria are retrieved.

Let's experiment with a simple query. You will formulate a query to display all flavored teas in one of the inventory tables, *tblInventoryDescription.* Open the *Ch03.mdb* database if necessary. Close all windows except the Database window. Then perform the following steps to create a query.

Exercise 3.4: Create a One-Table Query

1. Click the Queries tab in the Database window.
2. Click the New button (we are creating a query).
3. After the New Query dialog box is displayed, select Design View from the list and click the OK button.
4. Click the Tables tab in the Show Table dialog box.
5. Double-click the *tblInventoryDescription* table from the Show Table dialog box. Click the Close button, because no more tables are involved in the query. A Query window containing the table and the QBE grid is displayed.

6. Click and drag the asterisk from the *tblInventoryDescription* field list to the Field cell in the first column of the QBE grid. That will place all table fields found in the field list into the QBE grid.
7. Click and drag the BeverageType field from the field list to the Field row of the second column in the QBE grid.
8. Clear the check mark box in the Show row by clicking it (we do not want to display the BeverageType field twice).
9. Type *"t*"* in the Criteria row in the Beverage column. If you omit the double quotation marks, Access will insert them around the character automatically for you and add the leading phrase "Like" to the criteria.
10. Click and drag the Flavored field from the *tblInventory* field list to the Field row of the third column in the QBE grid. (You may have to use the scroll bar to bring the Flavored field into view.)
11. Clear the check mark box in the Flavored column by clicking it.
12. Type ***Yes*** (do *not* enclose it in double quotation marks, however) in the Criteria row below the Flavored column in the QBE grid.

Using the expression Like "t*" as a criterion for the BeverageType table column accepts spelling mistakes and variations such as *tee*, *tae*, and abbreviations such as *t*—anything that begins with the letter *t*. This broadens the selection criteria, making allowances for misspellings and abbreviations that might have crept into the table. The completed query design is shown in Figure 3.24.

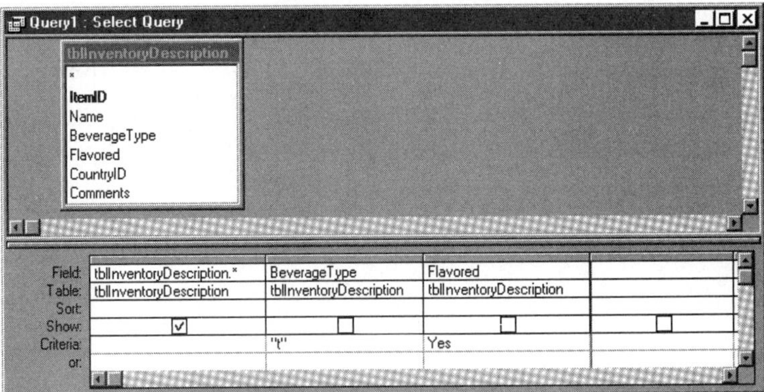

Figure 3.24 A simple query in Design view.

Now the query is ready to be executed. Click the Datasheet View button on the toolbar (or select Datasheet from the View menu) to see the resulting dynaset. It is shown in Figure 3.25. (We have optimized the width of each column in the dynaset so all columns are visible.)

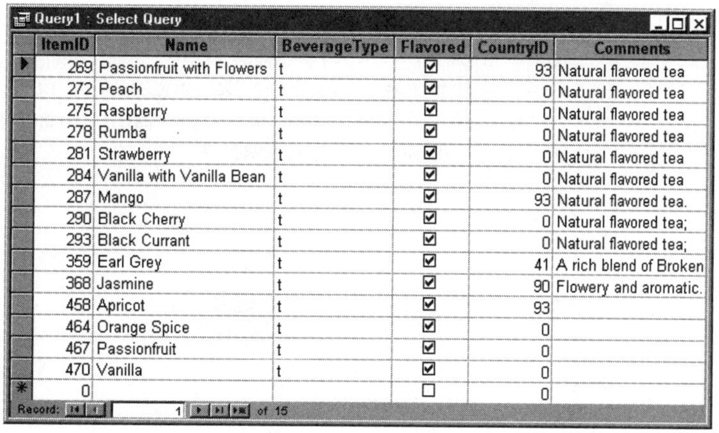

Query1 : Select Query

ItemID	Name	BeverageType	Flavored	CountryID	Comments
269	Passionfruit with Flowers	t	☑	93	Natural flavored tea
272	Peach	t	☑	0	Natural flavored tea
275	Raspberry	t	☑	0	Natural flavored tea
278	Rumba	t	☑	0	Natural flavored tea
281	Strawberry	t	☑	0	Natural flavored tea
284	Vanilla with Vanilla Bean	t	☑	0	Natural flavored tea
287	Mango	t	☑	93	Natural flavored tea.
290	Black Cherry	t	☑	0	Natural flavored tea;
293	Black Currant	t	☑	0	Natural flavored tea;
359	Earl Grey	t	☑	41	A rich blend of Broken
368	Jasmine	t	☑	90	Flowery and aromatic.
458	Apricot	t	☑	93	
464	Orange Spice	t	☑	0	
467	Passionfruit	t	☑	0	
470	Vanilla	t	☑	0	
0			☐	0	

Record: 1 of 15

Figure 3.25 Dynaset from a one-table query.

You do not need to save this query, so click the Query window Close button. Click "No" when asked if you want to save the query. For your convenience, we have saved this query as *qryFigure03-25* on your Companion CD-ROM. The Access desktop will display the Database window. You will create some more queries shortly, so leave Access running.

Extracting Selected Columns from a Table

When you wish to omit some columns (attributes) from the retrieved set, you are performing a *projection* operation. Columns are selected when they appear in the Field row of the QBE grid and their respective Show check boxes are checked. Column names placed in the Field row whose Show check boxes are not checked are not displayed in the dynaset. Unchecked columns can contain selection criteria and can be used to sort the dynaset, however. The next exercise illustrates a one-table projection.

Exercise 3.5: Projecting Attributes of One Table

1. Click the Queries tab in the Database window, then click the New button. Select Design View and click OK in the New Query dialog box.
2. Double-click the table *tblCustomer* from the list of tables, then click the Close button to close the Show Table dialog box.
3. Drag the CompanyName field from the *tblCustomer* field list to the first cell in the Field row of the QBE grid.
4. Drag the Contact field from the field list to the second cell in the QBE grid Field row. In steps 3 and 4 you have chosen only the CompanyName and

Contact columns—a projection—from the ten attributes available in the Customer table.

5. Execute the query: Click the Datasheet View button on the toolbar (or choose Datasheet from the View menu). Figure 3.26 shows the dynaset, a two-column projection of all the table rows.

Query1 : Select Query

CompanyName	Contact
Fairfield Communities Inc.	Best, F. Stanley
Alamo Group Inc.	Maul, Duane A.
Kiwi International Air Lines Inc.	Rigas, Alan J.
Republic Bancorp Inc.	Murray, T. Peter
Browne Bottling Co.	Shelton, Carl E.
Cavco Industries Inc.	Golkin, David
Bucyrus Erie Co.	Kostantaras, Jack R. Jr.
U S Office Products Co.	Gerson, Terrence
Ciatti S Inc.	Townes, Patrick J.
Tab Products Co.	Montrone, Frank A.
Diversicare Inc.	
Audiovox Corp.	Choate, Robert
Twin Disc Inc.	Crist, Dennis P.
Bay State Gas Co.	Huff, Richard E.
Fort Wayne National Corp.	
Medusa Corp.	Hart, John M.
Stv Group Inc.	Hill, Alex W.
Commercial Federal Corp.	McMeel, John D.

Record: 1 of 1789

Figure 3.26 Projection query.

We have saved the query as *qryFigure03-26* in the Ch03 database, just in case you have trouble with the preceding exercise.

Combining Selection and Projection Operations

A projection and selection operation can be united in a single query. The query can involve one or several tables. An example of such a query is one that lists from the Customer table (*tblCustomer*) the CompanyName and CreditLimit information for all California companies with a credit limit greater than $30,000. The latter part of the preceding sentence contains the selection criteria, whereas the first part contains the attributes to be displayed—the projection information.

Formulate and execute a query to retrieve the requested information. Here's an overview of how to do it. Create a query based on the *tblCustomer* table. Place CompanyName, CreditLimit, and State in the QBE grid Field row. Check the Show check boxes for CompanyName and CreditLimit in the QBE grid, but clear the Show check box for the State column. (That takes care of the projection part of the query.) Next, formulate the selection criteria. First, restrict your dynaset to

California: type *"CA"* in the Criteria row of the State column in the QBE grid. Another criterion, which must hold at the same time, is that the CreditLimit value must be greater than $30,000. Click the Criteria cell found under the CreditLimit column and enter the criteria *expression* ***>30000***. Click the Datasheet View toolbar button to see the results. Figure 3.27 shows the *tblCustomer* rows retrieved. Check the results by reproducing and running your own query against the *tblCustomer* table. This query is called *qryFigure03-27* in the Ch03 database on the Companion CD-ROM.

Query1 : Select Query

CompanyName	CreditLimit
E For M Corp.	$45,500
Earth Technology Corp. USA	$30,100
Zilog Inc.	$41,600
Harding Associates Inc.	$45,200
Sport Chalet Inc.	$49,800
Verifone Inc.	$49,500
Nellcor Inc.	$39,500
Hotel Investors Corp.	$40,100
St John Knits Inc.	$42,400
Cirrus Logic Inc.	$42,900
Good Guys Inc.	$37,800
Amgen Inc.	$40,200

Record: 1 of 12

Figure 3.27 Projection and selection combined.

Whenever *all* criteria must be true simultaneously, those criteria are entered on the *same* Criteria row of the QBE grid. On the other hand, criteria are entered on multiple lines, one criteria per row, when *any one* of the criteria being met is all that's needed to select a row. The latter is commonly called an *OR* condition, whereas the criteria stated as *California companies whose credit limit is greater than $30,000* is known as an *AND* condition (California *and* credit limit greater than $30,000).

JOINING RELATED TABLES

Earlier in this chapter we explained why table normalization is important to avoid data redundancy and inaccuracy. During the course of normalizing tables, we created two or more tables from a single table. The Coffee Merchant's database, for example, consists of nine tables in third normal form. However, only a subset of six of these are directly involved with invoice generation. With information about invoices distributed over six tables, we must be able to fuse these disparate but related tables.

Joining Two Tables

The best way to join two or more tables is to create a query containing the related tables. Then we can indicate table associations with the primary key/foreign key relationships between pairs of tables. We will join The Coffee Merchant's *tblCustomer* and *tblInvoice* tables with the field found in both that links them, CustomerID. Then we can display customer names (company names, in fact) and other invoice data from the database.

Exercise 3.6: Joining Related Tables with a Query

1. Open your copy of *Ch03.mdb* and click the Database window Queries tab.
2. Click the New button, select Design View, and click OK in the New Query dialog box.
3. Double-click the table *tblCustomer* from the list of tables to add it to the query.
4. Double-click the *tblInvoice* table name. Both tables are placed in the upper portion of the window, and a line links the like-named column, CustomerID, in both tables.
5. Click the Close button to close the Show Table dialog box.
6. Now drag four fields from the tables' field lists to the QBE Field row: Drag (or double-click) CompanyName, PhoneNumber, and Contact from the *tblCustomer* table field list to the first three Field row cells. Drag the InvoiceID field from the *tblInvoice* field list to the fourth cell in the Field row of the QBE grid.
7. Sort the dynaset by CompanyName by clicking in the Sort row in the Company column of the QBE grid. Choose Ascending (or type *a*). The dynaset rows will be sorted in ascending order by the CompanyName column. Figure 3.28 shows the Query Design window.
8. Choose Datasheet from the View menu to see the resulting dynaset (see Figure 3.29).
9. Because we have saved the query (*qryFigure03-29*) on your Companion CD-ROM, you need not.
10. Simply close all windows except the Database window, responding "No" when you are asked if you want to save the query.

Specifying Selection Criteria with Joined Tables

Our final example of a join operation involves five of The Coffee Merchant's database tables. The Coffee Merchant has decided to offer a one-time special on Kona coffee. Kona coffee will be billed at a 10 percent discount from its usual price. As a special courtesy to the customers who have been invoiced already, The Coffee Merchant will send out a corrected invoice to those who have outstanding invoices and have ordered Kona coffee. A database search must be performed to determine which customers with outstanding invoices ordered Kona. We will

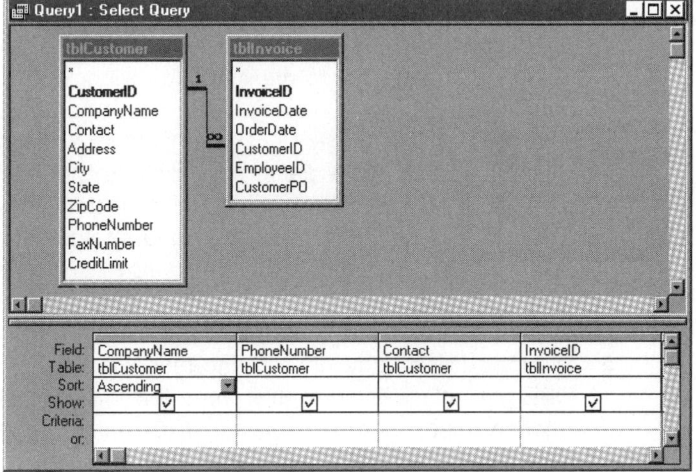

Figure 3.28 Query design for joined tables.

Query1 : Select Query

CompanyName	PhoneNumber	Contact	InvoiceID
3Com Corp.	(408) 555-5009	Marlen, James F.	214071
50 Off Stores Inc.	(210) 555-9349	Cost, Richard	214353
A H Belo Corp.	(214) 555-6670		214282
A L Pharma Inc.	(201) 555-7816	Ammerman, Donnie M.	214018
A T Cross Co.	(401) 555-1241		214023
Acme Boot Co. Inc.	(615) 555-2014	Beer, Wilber H.	214435
Act Iii Theatres Inc.	(503) 555-2241	Telang, Sudhakar A.	214203
Adc Telecommunications Inc.	(612) 555-8146	Phillips, Paul W.	214325
Adflex Solutions Inc.	(602) 555-4596	Smith, Richard C.	214106
Adobe Systems Inc.	(415) 555-4456	Weinberg, Sam	214144
Advacare Inc.	(214) 555-6198	Carver, Richard C.	214462
Advanced Technology Laborator	(206) 555-7034	Hakimoglu, Bruce	214292
Aetna Life Insurance & Annuity	(203) 555-1012	Satriale, Paul	214442
Aetna Life Insurance & Annuity	(203) 555-1012	Satriale, Paul	214206
Ag Chem Equipment Co. Inc.	(612) 555-9010	Cohen, Vincent A.	214055
Ag Chem Equipment Co. Inc.	(612) 555-9010	Cohen, Vincent A.	214415
Alamo Group Inc.	(210) 555-1483	Maul, Duane A.	214480

Record: 1 of 500

Figure 3.29 Query dynaset generated from joined tables.

build that query involving five tables and a selection criterion that restricts rows to invoice lines specifying Kona. The query is slightly more complex than others we have created, because the invoice line contains inventory item *numbers*, not inventory *names*.

Exercise 3.7: Joining Tables and Establishing Selection Criteria

1. Open your copy of *Ch03.mdb* and click the Database window Queries tab.
2. Click the New button, select Design View, and click OK in the New Query dialog box.

3. Add these tables to the query image: *tblCustomer, tblInvoice, tblInvoiceLine, tblInventory,* and *tblInventoryDescription.* (Remember how? Double-click each name.) You may want to maximize the window and drag each table by its Title bar to rearrange their display in the upper portion of the Query Design view window.
4. Close the Show Table dialog box (click its Close button). Notice that the tables are automatically linked together on their primary key/foreign key attributes. This occurs when the primary key and foreign key pairs have the same name and the same data type. (You can remove any table from a query by closing the Add Table dialog box, clicking the table's field list, and selecting Remove Table from the Query menu.)
5. Drag the following fields from the respective field lists to the Field row of the QBE grid (place them in this order, left to right): CustomerID, CompanyName, PhoneNumber, Contact (from the *tblCustomer* table), InvoiceID (from the *tblInvoice* table), and Name (from the *tblInventoryDescription* table). Whenever there are two or more sources for a field name like InvoiceID, the field can be selected from any table's field list. Now the five tables are reunited by the four links between foreign keys and primary keys. Finally, we must specify the single selection criterion, the coffee name *Kona*.
6. Click in the Criteria cell under the Name column in the QBE grid. Type ***"*kona*"*** (the character match is case insensitive) to specify the coffee name criterion. Using the wildcard asterisk before and after the name returns a name having *kona* anywhere in the name—at the beginning (Kona Extra Fancy), in the middle (Extra Kona Delight), or at the end (Extra Fancy Kona).
7. Clear the Show check box in the QBE grid under the Name column (click to clear it), because there is no point to displaying Kona and the names containing it. Figure 3.30 shows the completed query design. Examine it carefully.
8. Display the query's dynaset by selecting Datasheet from the View menu (see Figure 3.31).

Note that character strings in the Criteria row are delimited with double quotation marks, but Access supplies them automatically if you omit them. You need not display a column in order to use it to specify selection criteria (the Name column is an example). We have saved this interesting query, so you need not save it. It is called *qryFigure03-31*.

According to the query results, 15 customer invoices of the possible 500 currently saved contain an entry for Kona coffee. Close any open windows and close the Ch03 database by selecting Close from the File menu.

SUMMARY

This chapter has introduced you to the accounting information system and its relationship to database management systems. You have gotten a good grounding

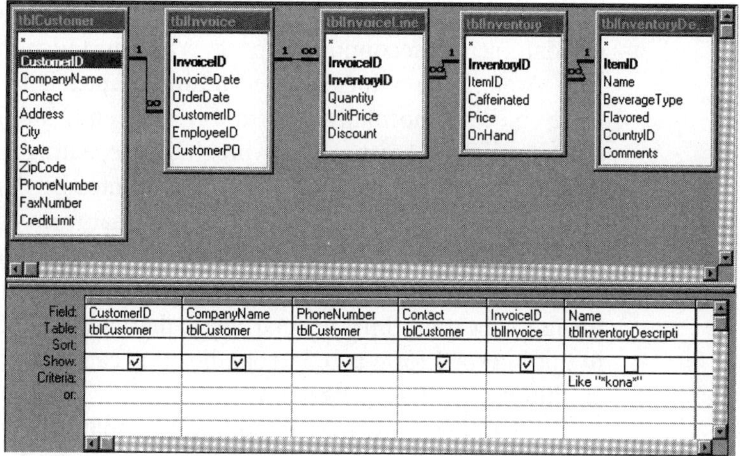

Figure 3.30 Five-table query design.

Query1 : Select Query

CustomerID	CompanyName	PhoneNumber	Contact	InvoiceID
30258	Lcs Industries Inc.	(201) 555-5666	Lebuhn, Eugene	214308
31865	Youth Services International	(410) 555-8658		214314
32031	Healthcare Compare Corp.	(708) 555-7985	Mori, John F.	214020
32513	Amdura Corp.	(203) 555-5771	Quinn, George L.	214368
32513	Amdura Corp.	(203) 555-5771	Quinn, George L.	214402
32817	Burr Brown Corp.	(520) 555-1130	Pierce, H. Randall	214401
33464	Pm Holdings Corp.	(314) 555-4179	Sehgal, Louis	214485
33799	Precision Standard Inc.	(205) 555-3023	Ferraro, John S.	214053
34112	Pope & Talbot Inc.	(503) 555-9175	Beeby, Thomas C.	214283
34137	Sps Transaction Services Inc.	(708) 555-3770	Apgar, Jacob Ergas	214237
34185	Oklahoma Gas & Electric Co.	(405) 555-3013	Larson, Earl W.	214437
34445	Coventry Corp.	(615) 555-2450		214389
34801	Kahler Corp.	(507) 555-2611	Rudd, Joseph A.	214454
34910	Terra Industries Inc.	(712) 555-1372	Cole, Fred Jones	214102
35391	Ernst Home Center Inc.	(206) 555-6780	Marshall, Samuel A.	214129

Record: 1 of 15

Figure 3.31 Five-table query dynaset.

in database theory. Increasingly, database management systems are found at the heart of many commercial applications, including accounting systems. Database systems provide several advantages over nondatabase approaches to managing data. High on the list of advantages are cost savings resulting from the centralization of all data management functions and the enforcement of data integrity and consistency by the database system. Relational database management systems provide the needed capabilities to represent accounting information. Data maintenance with a RDBMS does not require a programmer's help. Usually, you can insert, delete, and query a database system with little previous experience.

Valuable accounting information can be retrieved, and you are not limited to a standard set of accounting reports. You can tailor the output to your needs.

Among the points stressed in this chapter is the importance of representing table objects in normalized form. First, second, and third normal forms have been described. First normal form precludes repeating groups; second normal form goes further to require that all table attributes be dependent on the table's entire primary key, not just part of it. Third normal form assumes all the characteristics of second and first normal forms. In addition, third normal form tables must not contain attributes that depend on other nonkey attributes. Though other normal forms go beyond third normal form, the latter is sufficient for our needs. Tables in third normal form avoid anomalies that can destroy the accounting information credibility.

Finally, we saw how to build tables that follow the normalization rules. We created entity-relationship diagrams as an aid to developing the actual database, and we described how to handle tables having a many-to-many relationship with one another: relationship tables solve this problem. Selection and projection operations were performed using Microsoft Access. We also examined how to join tables of related information to form a composite result. The tools to join tables are queries. We used Access's query by example interface to build queries comprising related tables. These tables were linked by primary key/foreign key pairing.

REVIEW EXERCISES

MULTIPLE-CHOICE QUESTIONS

1. Prior to the advent of database management systems, business data was stored on computers in
   a. tables.
   b. flat files.
   c. programs.
   d. databases.
2. A database catalog is a database. Which piece of information is likely found in the catalog?
   a. the names of all tables constituting the database
   b. the names of all columns in all tables in the database
   c. value constraints for some columns of some tables
   d. all of the preceding
3. Ensuring that invoice dates are all reasonable is an example of what?
   a. data independence
   b. integrity constraint

   c. second normal form
   d. a subschema
4. Another name for a *tuple* is
   a. column.
   b. file.
   c. row.
   d. relation.
5. A table containing no repeating groups is at least in
   a. first normal form.
   b. second normal form.
   c. third normal form.
   d. none of the preceding
6. When a relation contains an attribute whose value is determined by another attribute that is not part of the table's primary key, the table violates the rules of
   a. first normal form.
   b. second normal form.
   c. third normal form.
   d. insertion anomalies.
7. One of the most popular methods of graphical database design is called a(n)
   a. Ernst-Relaford diagram.
   b. Codd-Chen representation.
   c. graphical user interface.
   d. entity-relationship diagram.
8. The operation in which a query returns selected columns, but all rows, of a table is called what?
   a. join
   b. selection
   c. criteria
   d. projection
9. When you retrieve related information from two or more tables in a database, that operation is called what?
   a. join
   b. selection
   c. criteria
   d. projection
10. How are many-to-many relationships represented in a relational database system?
    a. by four tables, each having a one-to-one relationship with one another
    b. by three tables, one of which is a relationship table containing primary keys from each original table
    c. by combining two tables having the many-to-many relationship into a single table

d. many-to-many relationships must be eliminated entirely, without creating any other tables

DISCUSSION QUESTIONS

1. Discuss the problems with storing data in two different places. What can this lead to?
2. Give a specific example of a table with up to seven attributes that is in first normal form but not second normal form. Describe at least one case of an insertion or deletion anomaly. Use specific field values to illustrate your example.
3. What is the significance of a transaction? Be specific. Answer by using an example. What mechanism is available by most database systems if a transaction is not completed? That is, briefly explain how a database system can compensate for one or more lost transactions via a built-in safeguard.
4. What is a primary key and why is it so important in a relational database management system?
5. Give an example of two entities that have a many-to-many relationship. Think of an example from your life such as the relationships found in classes, instructors, students, admissions officers, and so on. How are many-to-many relationships represented in a relational database system?

EXERCISES

1. List the Last name, commission rate, and gender of all male employees from the Employee table (*tblEmployee*) whose commission rate is at least 7 percent. Sort the rows by last name. Print the resulting dynaset.
2. Create and run a query that retrieves all flavored or unflavored teas whose inventory price is at least $16.00. List only Name, BeverageType, and Price in the dynaset. Print your result, writing your name and course section number on your paper.
3. Write and execute a query based on the *tblInventoryDescription* and *tblCountryName* tables that lists all products that originate from either *Ethiopia* or *Kenya*. List the name of the coffee or tea (Name from *tblInventoryDescription*) and the country name (in that order). Sort the dynaset rows by country name.
4. Formulate a query that displays all employees from the Employee table (*tblEmployee*) who are senior sales associates (*tblEmployeeTitle*). In the dynaset display each qualifying employee's last name and gender (in that order). Sort the dynaset by gender and then by last name within gender groups. (The sort will group females and then males and then sort them by last names within the group.) Print the resulting dynaset. Remember to write your name on the output.

5. You want to examine the invoices issued in November 1997. You are interested only in general information. To answer this question, form a query which joins The Coffee Merchant tables *tblInvoice* and *tblCustomer*. Display the company names, invoice dates, and invoice numbers (InvoiceID) for invoices issued only during the period 11/1/97 through and including 11/30/97. Print all pages. Save the query. (Figure 3.4 contains the schemas of all tables for The Coffee Merchant.)

4 MICROSOFT ACCESS AT WORK

OBJECTIVES

This chapter extends the knowledge you gained in Chapters 2 and 3 with more detailed information about Microsoft Access. You will learn more about creating and altering tables, forming more complex queries, defining useful accounting forms, and designing and producing revealing reports. Throughout this chapter, exercises emphasize Microsoft Access techniques critical to building accounting information systems. Similar to Chapter 2, this chapter is application oriented and contains very little theory; however, we emphasize *employing* the theory we presented earlier. In Chapter 4 you will learn how to:

- Alter a table's structure.
- Create a query involving multiple tables, derived column values, and expressions.
- Create a form replete with formatted fields and aesthetic enhancements.
- Associate a form with several tables.
- Design and print reports ranging from one-table reports to more complex multiple-table reports employing summary information.

We continue using The Coffee Merchant's invoice system as the backdrop application in this chapter. All the tables and queries created in Chapter 3 have been copied to the Ch04 folder on the Companion CD-ROM. For all exercises and examples in this chapter, we assume that you have inserted the Companion CD-ROM in the CD-ROM drive, copied the database *Ch04.mdb* to your hard disk, started Microsoft Access, and opened the Ch04 database. If not, then please be sure to do so before doing the exercises in this chapter.

ACCESS OBJECTS

The term *Access objects* refers to the several ways you can store and display information in your tables. Like most database systems, Access provides a rich variety of objects for your use. Beginning with the most fundamental, objects include tables, queries, forms, reports, macros, and modules.

Tables

All database information is stored in one or more tables comprised of rows and columns. A row contains all the information about a particular instance, or example, of an item in the table. Also called a record, a row's columns contain individual values for each attribute that characterizes the row. For instance, The Coffee Merchant's *tblCustomer* table contains a row for each current or potential customer. Columns in the Customer table hold information about ten different attributes of a customer record.

Each column can contain only one data type. Though the exact names of these data types vary from one RDBMS to another, they are all drawn from a small, common set. Data types constrain the type of information that can be entered into a column. Access supports the data types listed in Table 4.1. Of the listed types, you will probably use AutoNumber, currency, date/time, text, and number data types most frequently.

Queries

A query is a question you ask about one or more tables in your database. You use queries to locate and display a subset of the rows of a table, combine information from several tables into a single result, or perform calculations on fields. You can also use queries to make massive changes to a table, delete data from a table, or insert rows into a table.

Access uses the popular query by example (QBE) method in which you select one or more tables to query and then check off the columns you would like to see. By placing values or expressions below particular column names, you can limit the rows that are retrieved. These values or expressions are called selection criteria. By using the appropriate selection criteria, you can, for instance, list all customers who live in the Midwest. Or you can compute the total value of all outstanding invoices based on an invoice table or tables. Queries are used to reduce the amount of information that is displayed, summarizing it and giving it meaning.

Forms

Forms provide a simpler way of looking at the data in a table one row at a time. You can look at a great deal of information or only a small amount. Data displayed in a form is exactly the same data found in a table. The only difference is that you can format and enhance the data's appearance in a form. Figure 4.1 shows a form displaying data from The Coffee Merchant's Employees table. The

Data Type	Description and Use
Text	Holds characters—anything you can type on the keyboard. Data cannot be used in calculations. Employee names and inventory descriptions are examples. A text field can hold up to 255 characters.
Memo	Lengthy, variable-length text and numbers for comments or explanations. A memo field can contain up to 64,000 characters.
Number	Numeric data that can be used in calculations (unlike identification numbers, which are *not* used in calculations). Set the FieldSize property to define the specific Number type. Do not use Number type data for calculations involving money. Use Currency, instead.
Date/Time	Holds date or time information. Several formats are available, or you can establish a custom format.
Currency	Holds monetary data of up to 19 significant digits (15 to the left of the decimal point and 4 to the right). Currency fields are formatted to display a currency symbol and two decimal places. Use currency to avoid rounding errors due to calculations.
AutoNumber	A sequential, unique number that is automatically generated by Access. Numbers no longer needed are retired. The AutoNumber data type is often used for primary keys, because it guarantees unique values.
Yes/No	Yes/No, True/False, or On/Off are all examples of legitimate field values. Choose the Yes/No data type when only two values are possible (gender or invoice paid, for example).
OLE Object	Contains objects from another Windows application such as a picture, graph, or spreadsheet. When you double-click an OLE object, the program that created the object is launched so you can modify or view the OLE object. OLE objects tend to occupy a large amount of space.

Table 4.1 Access table data types.

form contains check boxes, a form header title, and sunken fields. Fields include currency, text, and number data types.

A form is especially useful for nonexperts who must enter or change data in a table. Data entry is also much easier when using a well-designed form. Helpful aids, such as drop-down lists or radio buttons, can be embedded in a form. Drop-down lists, for example, are helpful when you encounter an entry whose possible values are limited but not known to the user. By making a list available, you can choose one of a select set of values by simply clicking your choice. When you move to another row the changed information is automatically posted to the underlying table.

Form navigation buttons make moving around the data easy. You can move to the first or last row in a table, up or down one row at a time, or to a particular row. You can customize a form so that it precisely matches an existing paper form,

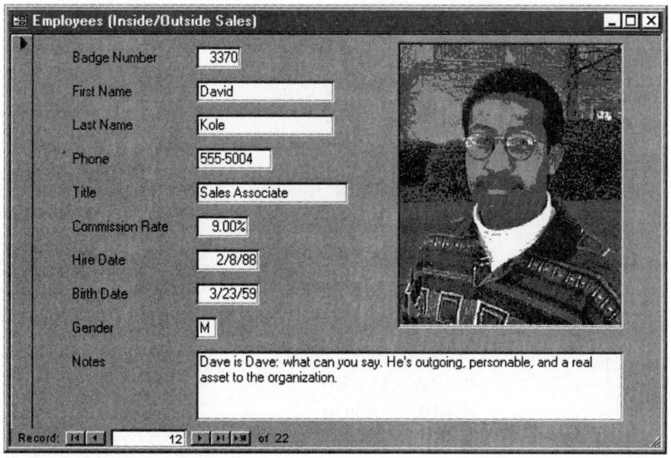

Figure 4.1 Example form.

making the computerized version less intimidating and more familiar to those who are computer novices.

Reports

While forms provide an excellent way to view and alter data in one or more tables, reports are superb for providing boardroom-quality printed, detailed, and summary information. You can sort, group, and summarize results. Reports can contain subtotals, totals, averages, and counts, all attractively printed. Like other reporting tools, you can include report headers and footers and page headers and footers. You can also create mailing labels using the Access report facility.

Like forms, reports can take advantage of Access' many design tools, including graphic import, lines, boxes, and text, to name a few. Data can be drawn from several tables and combined in one report. Figure 4.2 shows an example of a simple report that can be quickly and easily produced with Access.

Macros and Modules

Macros are Visual Basic codes that can be executed at the click of a button or when a form is opened. They define one or more actions that you want Access to perform in response to a particular event. Macros are frequently attached to objects located on a form, but you can write stand-alone code segments that can be invoked by a wide variety of objects in your applications. For example, you can write a small macro to check the value of an entry after the user moves to the next form field. If the field fails a value range test, the macro can display an error message and move the focus back to the erroneous field. We will illustrate macros in Chapter 5.

Employees by Title

Title	Name	ID	Hire Date	Birth Date	Gender
Sales Associate					
	Bateman, Giles	4057	2/16/88	5/1/54	M
	Chang, Annie	3609	9/16/93	3/30/73	F
	Ellison, Larry	3700	4/18/90	12/12/50	M
	English, Melinda	3432	10/1/89	2/14/52	F
	Gates, William	3436	4/11/91	3/9/50	M
	Halstead, Whitney	4058	6/16/92	12/22/69	F
	Hunter, Helen	2318	11/16/89	1/26/50	F
	Kahn, Phillipe	2754	5/14/93	5/29/57	M
	Kole, David	3370	2/8/88	3/23/59	M
	Pacioli, Luca	1528	8/26/91	5/6/46	M
	Stonesifer, Patti	1301	7/6/92	3/10/62	F
	Watterson, Barbara	3943	10/10/89	5/1/57	F
Sales Trainee					
	Nagasaki, Ted	1695	1/28/96	4/10/73	M
	Pruski, Kevin	1364	12/1/96	1/26/75	M
Senior Sales Associate					
	Ballmer, Steve	3692	5/16/81	7/13/40	M
	Flintsteel, Hillary	4082	3/21/86	8/22/54	F
	Goldman, Ted	4112	12/24/86	3/5/58	M
	Manispour, Sharad	4029	12/18/86	2/4/65	M
	Minsky, Barbara	4012	10/13/86	4/12/55	F
	Morrison, Alanis	3458	12/13/85	7/4/52	F
	Shoenstein, Brad	3892	9/5/86	3/6/51	M
	Stonely, Sharon	2240	11/5/84	5/3/57	F

Figure 4.2 Example report.

A *module* is an object containing custom procedures that you code using Visual Basic. Modules provide a finer degree of control and flow that allow you to write code that recognizes and traps errors—something macros cannot do. Modules are stand-alone, global objects which can be called into action from anywhere within your Access application. Defining modules means the code can be reused by all of your forms, scripts, and other libraries.

Separating Tables from Other Objects

Whether or not you are developing an application for a client server environment, you may find it convenient to separate an application's tables from queries, forms, reports, and other objects. If you choose to separate your database objects in this way, you can store tables in one database and the related nontable objects in another database. You can then create queries, forms, reports, macros, and modules based on linked tables. A *linked table* is stored in a file outside the open database from which Microsoft Access can access records. You can perform all the normal database operations on linked tables except altering their structure. That is, you can insert, delete, and update records in linked tables.

The single most important advantage of separating tables from the other application objects is application development independence. As a developer, you can continue to improve and develop the queries, forms, and reports embedded in one of the two application database files. Then when you replace a client's application with your newest version, you simply supplant the database containing the queries, forms, reports, macros, and modules with the new one. The database containing only tables remains unchanged. This way, your client's ever-changing tables are not affected. Figure 4.3 shows a graphical representation of table/object separation.

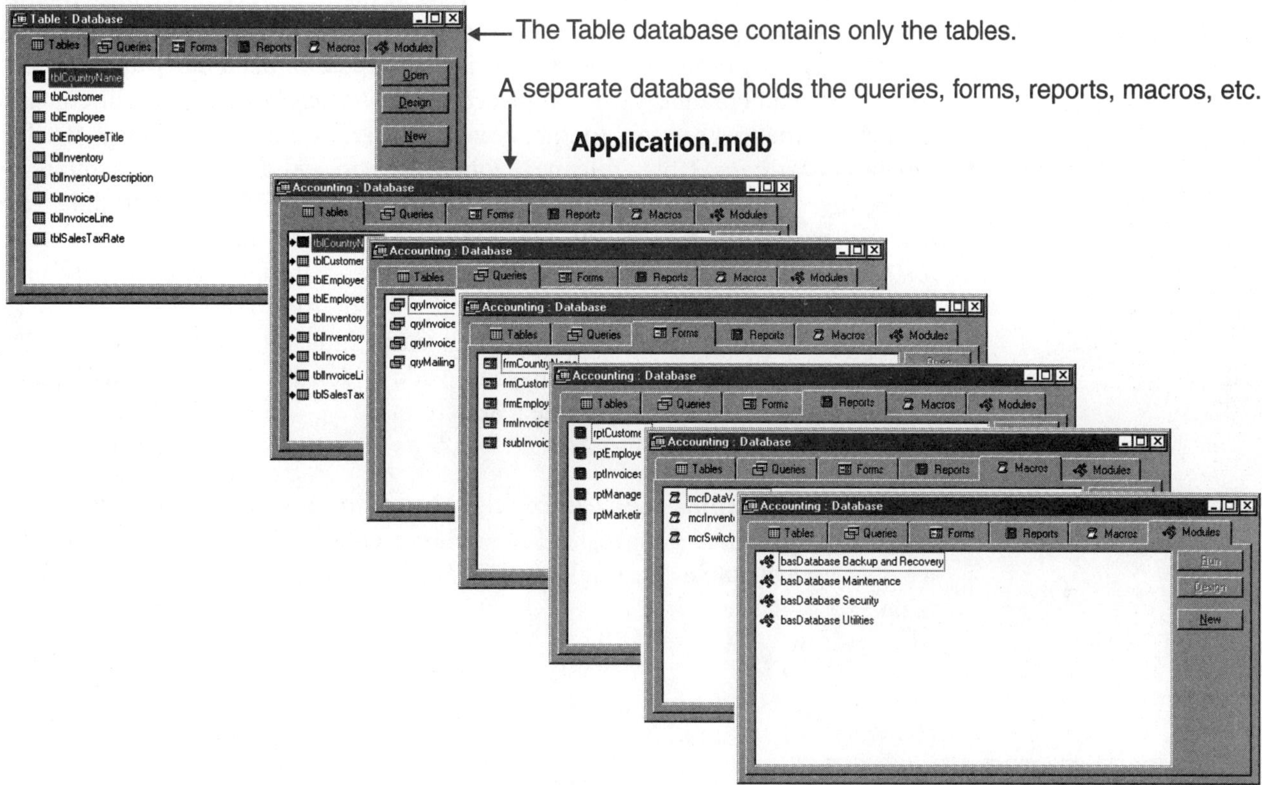

Figure 4.3 Separating tables from other database objects.

WORKING WITH TABLES

We have described tables in Chapters 2 and 3. Here we show you how to alter an existing table's structure, and how to modify a table whose rows are related to another table. Prohibiting removal of a parent table row until all the rows in another table referring to the parent table are first removed is called *referential integrity*. This is an important feature provided by most relational database management systems. Referential integrity can be enforced, and we will show you how on one of the existing tables for The Coffee Merchant. In this section we show you how to add and delete columns from a table and how to forge a permanent link between related tables. First, let's see how to add and delete table columns.

Altering a Table's Structure

The Coffee Merchant's Division Location table (*tblDivisionLocation*) contains the city and state in which each of The Coffee Merchant's divisions is located. Frequently, it is useful to place often-repeated character strings such as cities or organization names in their own table along with a unique identification number and then use the number in place of the long string in the original table. Among other advantages, this prevents one from misspelling "Cincinnati" or other city names when they occur frequently. This is the purpose of the *tblDivisionLocation* table. A related column, yet to be placed in the *tblEmployee* table, will contain a number that is related to the company division number found in the *tblDivisionLocation* table. Your next job will be to add a new table column to *tblEmployee*—a division number column—which is a foreign key field linked to the primary key of the *tblDivisionLocation* table. Once the *tblEmployee* and *tblDivisionLocation* tables are linked together, we can determine the city and state in which the employee and the employee's division are located.

Each employee row should have an entry indicating which division the employee works for. Whenever you want to add or delete a column in a table, that activity is called *altering* the table's structure.

Adding a Column. The next exercise shows you how to add a column to a table. In particular, you will add a column called *EmployeeDivisionID* to the *tblEmployee* table. That column is a foreign key to the *tblDivisionLocation* table.

EXERCISE 4.1: ADDING A COLUMN TO THE EMPLOYEE TABLE

1. Click the Tables tab in the Database window, if necessary, select *tblEmployee*, and click the Design button. Maximize the Table window to display all columns.

2. Select the entire EmployeeTitle row by clicking its row selector button and press the Insert key. (Alternatively, you can select Row from the Insert menu.) A new, empty row is added to the table's structure.
3. In the new row, select the Field Name cell, type ***EmployeeDivisionID*** and press Tab to move to the Data Type column.
4. Because the EmployeeDivisionID field will hold a number, enter ***n*** (number).
5. Select the Description field and type the description ***Identification of the division for which this employee works*** to document the field's use.
6. Select the Caption property box in the lower half of the Design view window and type ***Division ID*** (with an embedded space). The Caption property text is displayed in place of the column's name in forms, reports, and Datasheet views of tables.
7. Select Save from the File menu and click the Design view Close button. This saves the revised *tblEmployee* table structure.

To complete this operation, you need to place data in the newly created EmployeeDivisionID column. This is relatively easy. Make sure you fill in the field, because the next exercise will use the EmployeeDivisionID column values to establish a connection to the *tblDivisionLocation* table.

Exercise 4.2: Place Values in the EmployeeDivisionID Column

1. Open the *tblEmployee* table in Datasheet view and click any entry in the EmployeeWorkPhone column.
2. Select Records, Sort, Ascending (Records menu) to sort the table low to high on the work telephone number.
3. Select the topmost EmployeeDivisionID cell corresponding to employee David Kole and enter ***101*** into that cell.
4. Repeat step 3 for the next five employees. The first six employees all work in division 101.
5. In the next six EmployeeDivisionID cells, enter the value ***102***, indicating that employees Manispour through Halstead work for division 102.
6. Enter ***103*** for the next six employees' EmployeeDivisionID attributes—employees whose names are Pruski through Pacioli (yes, his great, great grandson).
7. Finally, enter ***104*** for the remaining four employees—Ellison through Flintsteel.
8. Close the table (click the Datasheet view Close button) and click No when you are asked if you want to save changes to the design of the table.

Now you have assigned divisions to each employee. Let's hope they like their new locations!

Deleting and Renaming Columns. It is easy to remove unwanted columns from any table or to give one or more columns a new name. Though you don't need to right now, here's how. To delete a column, click the Tables tab, select a table, and open it in Design view. Click the row selector to the left of the column you want to delete and press Delete. The highlighted column is removed, and succeeding attributes are moved up to close the gap. Remember to click the Save button (or File, Save) to post the changed table structure to your database.

You may decide that a column name no longer makes sense or is otherwise inappropriate. Renaming it is also simple. Display the table in Design view. Then click the Field Name cell to be changed and type over the old name with its replacement. Finally, click the Save button to store the altered table.

Establishing Referential Integrity

Access provides a way to enforce *referential integrity* whereby defined relationships between tables are maintained. Referential integrity rules prevent you from adding a record to a related table if there is no associated record in the primary table. Additionally, the rules prevent you from deleting or changing records in a primary table that would result in orphan records in a related table. For example, if you choose to enforce referential integrity between the Invoice table (*tblInvoice*) and the related Invoice Line table (*tblInvoiceLine*), you cannot delete an invoice from the parent Invoice table unless there are no related invoice line items in the *tblInvoiceLine* table.

You will do your work in the *Relationships* window, a window that displays linkages between tables for a given database. You define permanent linkages—primary key to foreign key relationships—to make forming multiple-table queries easier. You can also choose whether or not the Relationships window displays none, some, or all intertable relationships. To illustrate just how this works, you will establish referential integrity between the Employee table (*tblEmployee*) and the Division Location table (*tblDivisionLocation*). This will ensure that a division in *tblDivisionLocation* cannot be deleted until all employees (*tblEmployee*) have been reassigned to a new division or first removed completely.

Exercise 4.3: Establishing Referential Integrity

1. Close all windows except the Database window.
2. Select Relationships from the Tools menu (or click the Relationships button on the toolbar). A Relationships window is displayed, devoid of any objects.
3. Select Show Table from the Relationships menu (or click the Show Table button on the toolbar. A Show Table dialog box is displayed.
4. Double-click the *tblEmployee* table to add it to the Relationships window (see Figure 4.4).

5. Select *tblDivisionLocation* and click the Add button to place that table in the Relationships window and click the Close button, because no more tables are to be added at this time. The two tables and their attribute names are displayed in the Relationships window. (You may want to drag the bottom border of *tblEmployee* to reveal all of its attributes. Drag the right border of *tblEmployee* to reveal the longer field names.)
6. In the Relationships window, always drag the primary key field from one table to its related foreign key in the other table: click the DivisionID field in *tblDivisionLocation* and drag and drop the field onto the EmployeeDivisionID field in *tblEmployee* (see Figure 4.5). A Relationships dialog box is displayed.
7. Click the Enforce Referential Integrity check box to select that option. A check mark is placed in the check box (see Figure 4.6).
8. Click the Create button to establish referential integrity between the two tables.
9. Finally, click the Relationships window Close button and click Yes when you are asked if you want to "Save layout changes to 'Relationships'?" That preserves the newly established relationship complete with the referential integrity constraint.

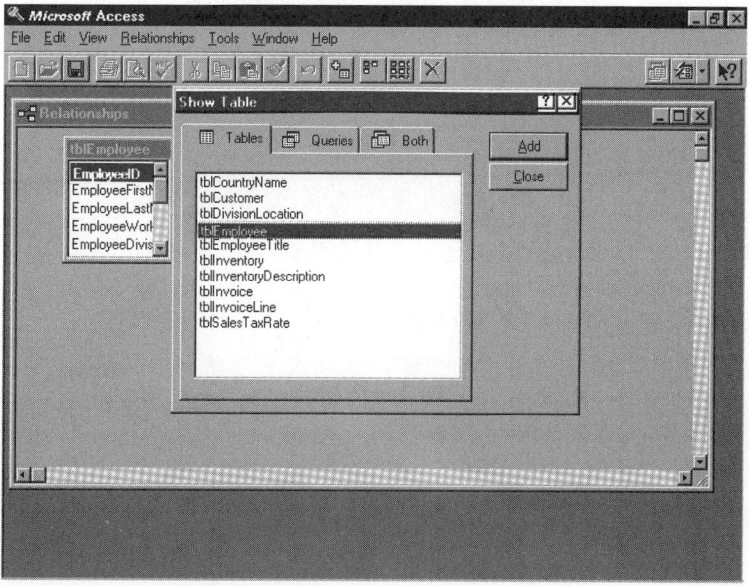

Figure 4.4 Show Table dialog box.

Editing and Removing Intertable Relationships

You can remove or edit an existing relationship between pairs of tables by a procedure similar to the preceding one. For example, you can remove referential integrity checks between *tblEmployee* and *tblDivisionLocation* by opening the Relationships window, right-clicking the line connecting the two tables, selecting

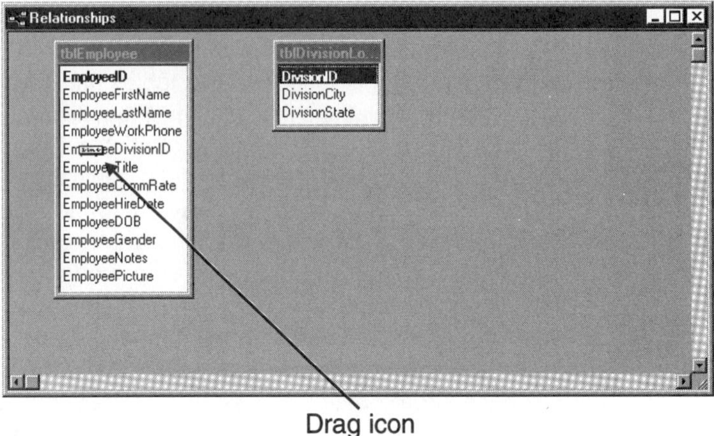

Figure 4.5 Establishing a link between tables.

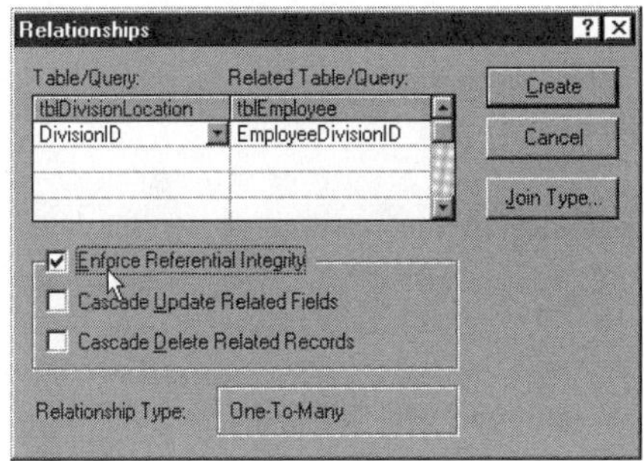

Figure 4.6 Relationships dialog box.

Edit Relationship, and clearing the Enforce Referential Integrity check box. This edits the relationship between the tables, but does not remove it. Removing a relationship is equally easy. Open the Relationships window (choose Relationships from the Tools menu), click the line that connects the two tables, then press the Delete key. Similarly, you can right-click the line connecting the tables and select *Delete Relationship* from the pop-up menu that appears. In either case, the connecting line disappears along with the explicit relationship definition. Whenever you change a relationship by editing or removing it, be sure to select Save from the File menu to preserve the relationship changes.

CREATING AND USING QUERIES

Recall that queries pose questions to the database. Unlike tables which hold information, queries actively search specified tables and return answers to your questions. For instance, you can use a query to return a list of all employees in the San Diego branch office, or a query can be used to list all invoices that are over 30 days past due. The alternative to queries is to scan the relevant tables visually, attempting to select rows relevant to your needs. This is usually an error-prone activity filled with frustration.

Another important feature of queries is their ability to join tables together. Related tables can be linked in a query definition. Then you can apply selection criteria to eliminate unwanted data. For example, you can write a query to list the names and addresses of all customers whose invoices are more than 30 days past due. The *tblCustomer* and *tblInvoice* tables are joined on the CustomerID column, and a selection criteria limits rows to those whose InvoiceDate value is more than 30 days ago.

You have experience in creating queries from the exercises in Chapter 3. Let's briefly review the steps necessary to create a new query:

- Click the Queries tab in the Database window and click New.
- Select Design View from the list and click OK.
- Add the table to be included in the query.
- Drag the fields you want returned in the dynaset to the QBE grid.
- Enter any selection criteria—either exact match values or expressions—in the Criteria row below attribute names.
- Click the Datasheet View button to display the query results.
- Revise the query if necessary to achieve the results you want.
- Save the query if you want to rerun it later.

Queries involving more than one table are built following the same basic steps outlined above except that you select additional tables in the Show Table dialog box. Of course, you must join tables by dragging the primary key field in one table to the foreign key in the other table whenever Access does not form the link automatically.

Creating a One-Table Query

Anytime you want to examine a large table looking for a group of records, it is usually best to use a query. A one-table query is easy to construct, and it whittles down to a manageable size the list you look at. We will illustrate a one-table query with the *tblInventoryDescription* table. It contains several important product descriptors including the beverage type (the allowed values are only *c* or *t*, which stand for coffee and tea), whether or not the item is flavored (yes/no), the country of origin (an identification number pointing to the *tblCountryName* table), and lively comments about the particular bean or leaf. Figure 4.7 shows some of the rows of this table.

ItemID	Name	BeverageType	Flavored	CountryID	Comments
101	Continental Blend	c	☐	0	100 percent Mexican Altura, roasted dark.
104	Costa Rica Tarrazu	c	☐	45	A perfect balance of acidity and body. Strictl
107	Costa Rica La Manita	c	☐	45	A standard against which all other Strictly He
110	Sumatra Mandheling	c	☐	83	An enticing favorite of many; syrupy, earthy,
113	Assam Fancy 2nd Flush	t	☐	41	Black tea;
116	Darjeeling Badamtam	t	☐	82	Black tea;
119	Assam Tara FTGFOP-1	t	☐	41	Black tea;
122	Ceylon Pekoe Labookelle	t	☐	163	Black tea;
125	Ceylon Supreme	t	☐	163	Black tea;
128	Ceylon Uva Highlands	t	☐	163	Black tea;
131	China Keemun	t	☐	41	Black tea;
134	China Yunnan	t	☐	41	Black tea;
137	Darjeeling Namring	t	☐	82	Black tea;
140	Kalgar-India	t	☐	82	Black tea;
143	Kenya Kaproret	t	☐	93	Black tea;
146	Mocha	c	☐	151	Bold, earthy, mild acidity. One of Arabia's old
149	Costa Rica Tres Rios	c	☐	45	Costa Rican coffees are always excellent. T
152	Zimbabwe	c	☐	194	Delicate, fruity aroma; medium body; high leve
155	Ethiopia Mokas	c	☐	61	Earthy and winey; indigenous to Ethiopia. Eth
158	Guatemala Antigua	c	☐	74	Elegant and complex. Contains hints of cocoa
161	Yemen Mocha	c	☐	191	Extremely complex aroma; spicy, cocoa, nutt
164	Jamaican Blue Mountain	c	☐	89	Extremely mellow, sweet-tasting and delightf
167	Ethiopia Sidamo	c	☐	61	Floral aroma and lively acidity. This coffee is
170	Berry Patch	t	☐	68	Fruit blend Tisanes;

Record: 1 of 131

Figure 4.7 Some rows of the *tblInventoryDescription* table.

Inventories without on hand or back-order values for each inventory item are not very helpful. The *tblInventory* table holds the price and quantity on hand information. Together, the *tblInventory* and *tblInventoryDescription* tables supply all our inventory information. They have a many-to-one relationship because each coffee listed in the *tblInventoryDescription* (for example, *Jamaican Blue Mountain*) can have both decaffeinated and caffeinated choices. In reality, the "many" side of the relationship, *tblInventory*, has at most two entries for every named coffee or tea. When necessary, we join the two tables on their common field, ItemID.

Let's create a simple query to locate and display all unflavored coffees whose beans are described as "hard bean" in the inventory. (Hard bean coffees are grown at higher altitudes than others and generally yield a better coffee.) Start from the Database window and click the Queries tab. Then click the New button on the Database window, select Design View from the list, and click OK to begin the query creation process. (When creating queries, it is often easier to *not* use the Query Wizards.) Then, do the following exercise.

Exercise 4.4: Creating a One-Table Query

1. Select the *tblInventoryDescription* table from the list presented in the Show Table dialog box, click the Add button to add it to the query, and click the Close button.

2. Drag the fields ItemID, Name, Comments, BeverageType, and Flavored from the *tblInventoryDescription* field roster to the first through fifth cells in the Field row of the QBE grid.
3. Clear the Show check boxes under BeverageType and Flavored in the QBE grid, because these fields won't be displayed.
4. Enter three selection criteria in the Criteria row: under the Comments column type ***Like "*hard bean*"*** (including the quotation marks), under the BeverageType column type ***"c"*** (with the quotation marks), and under the Flavored column type ***No*** (letter case does not matter, but *do not* place quotation marks around this criterion or any Yes/No criterion). If you omit quotation marks when entering character string data, Microsoft Access automatically surrounds them with quotation marks. Because the two selection criteria are in the same Criteria row of the QBE grid, both criteria must be true for a row to be returned. This is a classic AND criteria.
5. Click the Datasheet View button to see the query results (dynaset).

Your dynaset should look like the one shown in Figure 4.8. We have saved this query as *qryHardBeanCoffee* on your Companion CD-ROM, so you need not save yours. Simply close the query and its dynaset without saving them.

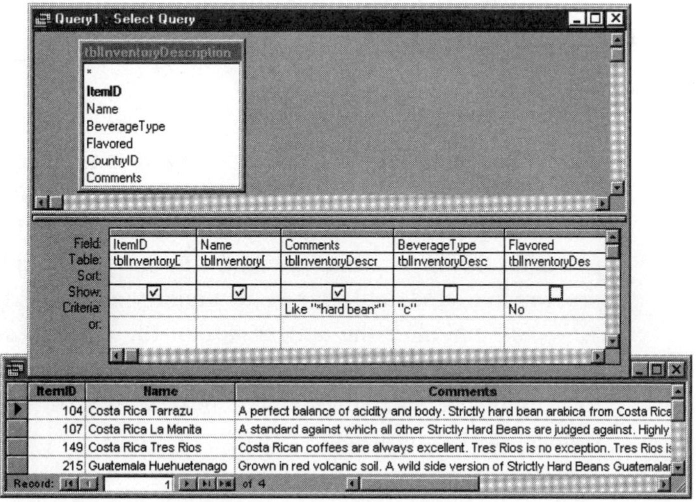

Figure 4.8 A one-table query and dynaset.

What if we wanted to see all inventory items that were either not flavored *or* are coffees? We would then place one criterion on one Criteria row and the other criterion on the "or" row just below the Criteria row of the QBE grid. (This type of query is a classical OR question.) Figure 4.9 shows the OR query and part of the result. As indicated in the status line, the query returned many rows—all flavored beverages (tea or coffee) and all coffees (flavored or not).

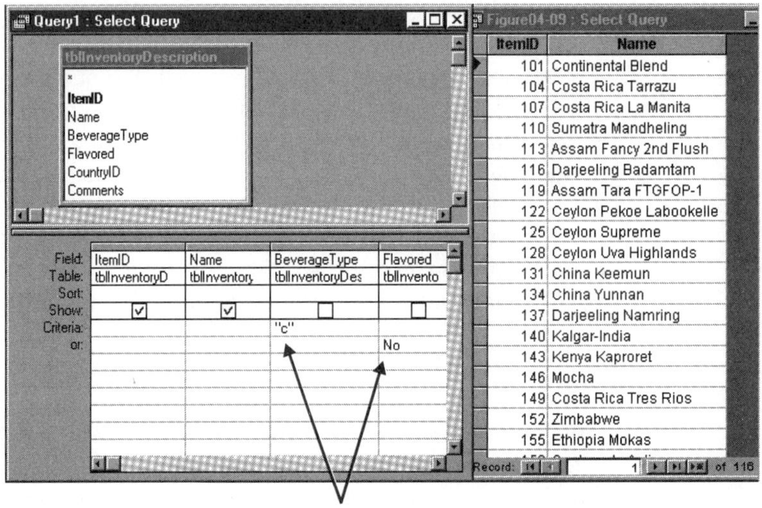

Figure 4.9 Query with multiple, independent criteria.

Working with the Dynaset

Access returns query results in a dynaset. Similar to a table in behavior and structure, a dynaset is only temporary. It is replaced every time another query is run. For most queries, you can alter information displayed by the dynaset while in Datasheet view by simply typing in new information. The new information is placed in the appropriate row and column of the underlying table. Thus, dynasets present live, updatable views of underlying table data.

You can alter the appearance of the dynaset so that the rows are arranged differently, the columns are displayed in a different order, or the columns are formatted in a special way. The next section illustrates how easy it is to make changes to the dynaset.

Producing Sorted Query Results. Suppose you want to rearrange dynaset rows so they are displayed in a more useful form. For instance, the list of coffees and teas shown in Figure 4.7 would be easier to use if it was arranged in name order. Sorting dynasets is easy. By default, Access displays dynaset records in ascending order on the table's primary key, if it has one, whether or not the primary key is displayed in the result. Creating a query to sort data in other ways is particularly useful when you want to produce a form whose results are sorted on some significant field. We'll show you how to sort the dynaset next.

Suppose you want to list all flavored teas in stock in order by their names. First, you would construct a one-table query based on the *tblInventoryDescription* table. In the QBE Field row would be the field names ItemID, Name, Flavored, and BeverageType. Only ItemID and Name would have their Show check boxes marked. Flavored and BeverageType would contain the criteria values *Yes* and *t*, respectively, to retrieve only flavored teas (both criteria must be met). How about the sorting part of it? Simple! Follow along in the next paragraph and try it.

Try it

Open in Design view the query *qryFlavoredTea*, which selects flavored teas in the dynaset. To sort the dynaset on Name, click the Sort row under the Name column—the attribute by which you want the rows sorted—and select Ascending from the drop-down list (or type ***a***). Click the Datasheet View button to see the dynaset. Notice that the rows are in Name order beginning with *Apricot* and ending with *Vanilla with Vanilla Bean.*

You can specify a sort order for more than one column. Access sorts by the leftmost field first followed by the next sort field to the right, and so on. Therefore, you should arrange the columns you want to sort, relative to each other, from left to right in the QBE grid. Note that the sort columns do not have to be the first group of columns in the QBE grid. You can sort by fields whose Show check box is cleared and thus does not display, though the reasons seem obscure at this point. We will explain later why this may be necessary.

Altering the Order and Size of Columns. You can alter the order of the dynaset table columns. The dynaset columns' order is established by the query. For instance, the first field whose Show box is checked in the QBE grid is the first column in the dynaset, but you can alter the dynaset's column order either before executing a query or after the dynaset is displayed.

To rearrange query columns, display the query in Design view and move the mouse pointer to the column selector of the field to be moved. (The column selector is the area just above the field name.) When the mouse pointer is on the column selector, it turns to a down-pointing arrow. Click the column. The entire column is darkened, indicating it has been selected. (Be careful not to move the mouse.) Release the mouse and then click and drag the column to its new location. A rectangle appears below the pointer indicating you are about to move the column. Finally, release the mouse when the column is in its new location. Columns are moved right to make room for the new column.

If necessary, you can enlarge individual columns by moving to the column selector area of a column so the mouse is over the right line of the column. When the mouse changes to a double-headed arrow, drag the right edge to the right to enlarge the column, or drag it to the left to shrink the column.

Both column order and column size can be changed in the dynaset—that is, after executing a query. When the query is displayed in Datasheet view (dynaset), you can move columns or change their size following the procedures outlined in the preceding paragraphs. If you move the cursor to a dynaset column and then select Column Width from the Format menu, the Column Width dialog box is displayed (see Figure 4.10). Click the Best Fit button to size the column so it is just wide enough for the widest entry. (The shortcut for Best Fit is to move the cursor to the right edge of the column in the column selector area and then double-click the pointer after it changes to a double-headed arrow.) Of course, you can size multiple columns at once. Drag the mouse across all the column selectors to select multiple contiguous columns. Move the mouse to the right column line of any one of the selected columns. When it changes to a double-headed arrow, double-click the pointer to optimize the column width.

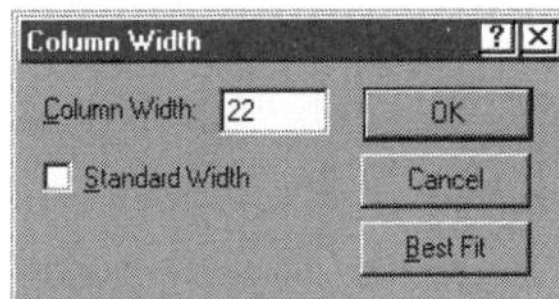

Figure 4.10 Column Width dialog box.

Altering Column Display Properties. Like other dynaset characteristics, column display formats can also be changed. First, display the query in Design view. Then move the mouse to the Field row in the QBE grid of the column whose format you want to change. When you right-click a column, a pop-up menu is displayed. Click the Properties selection. A Field Properties dialog box will be displayed. You can experiment with changing characteristics such as Format yourself. For instance, try changing the format of the ItemID dynaset column so the data is displayed in Currency format. After you are done experimenting, do not save the altered query.

Saving a Query and Printing Query Results

Saving a Query. Queries that you anticipate using more than once should be saved. Save a query by executing Save from the File menu in either Design or Datasheet view. The query design is saved in the database on your disk under the name you type (if it is a first-time save operation) in the Query Name text box. If the query has been saved before, it is simply saved under the original name, replacing the older copy.

Printing Query Results. Printing query results simply means that you print the dynaset displayed in the Datasheet view. You can select the stored query name and print it, or you can open the query and view it. In either case, you select Print from the File menu (or click the toolbar Print button) to print the dynaset. When the Print dialog box displays, make any necessary adjustments to the page range to print (or print all pages), and click OK to give final authority to print the table. Note that you do not have any control over the page headers or footers. Table and dynaset outputs are somewhat "raw" and undisciplined, especially when you compare them to Access reports.

Producing Queries Involving Multiple Tables

We created the different tables for The Coffee Merchant to normalize them in order to avoid problems such as data redundancy and inconsistent data, and to reduce data entry errors. Data is found in several related tables, and we need a way to connect the tables to retrieve information not found in a single table. When we connect tables together, we are *joining* them. Related tables are joined together by indicating which columns are common to the tables to be joined. For instance, we could join the Customer and Invoice tables on the common column CustomerID found in each table. Though these columns have the same name, they needn't. However, it is often simpler to remember the join columns by naming them identically.

Joining Tables. Linking two or more tables is not difficult. You indicate how tables are connected by drawing join lines between them. In many cases, Access can automatically determine how tables are connected when tables to be joined have identically named fields or they have been joined permanently using the Relationships window. If Microsoft Access does not create join lines for you automatically, you can join tables manually.

You join tables manually by creating a query and adding all the related tables to the query in the Show Table dialog box. Then create a join line between each table pair by selecting the primary key field in one table and dragging it to the equivalent foreign key field in the other table.

Conditional Queries Using Comparison Operators. Queries containing conditions are very useful. A *condition* provides a way for you to specify a range of values, or minimum or maximum values. For example, perhaps you would like to locate all inventory items which are back-ordered.

The coffee buyer is preparing to order more coffee and tea from the ranches around the world. One of the important questions to be answered is what products are back-ordered. In our system, a product is back-ordered when the OnHand field in *tblInventory* is negative. The buyer wants to see the product identification number, the product name, and the back-order volume columns. Two tables are involved and must be joined. These tables are *tblInventory*, the Inventory master table, and *tblInventoryDescription*. We will use a comparison operator to create the selection criterion. A *comparison operator* is a special symbol that compares one value to another. The comparison operators are shown in Table 4.2. In particular, we will use the less than (<) comparison operator in the selection criterion of the exercise that follows. It answers the buyer's question concerning items to be ordered that are back-ordered. We begin condensing things a bit by combining several separate steps into one numbered step.

Operator	Meaning
<	Less than
<=	Less than or equal to
>	Greater than
>=	Greater than or equal to
=	Equal to
<>	Not equal to
Between	Test for a range of values where two extreme values are separated by the And operator
In	Test for "equal to" any member in a list
Like	Test a text or memo field to match a pattern string

Table 4.2 Comparison operators.

Exercise 4.5: Writing a Two-Table Query Using Comparison Operators

1. Create a new query joining the tables *tblInventory* and *tblInventoryDescription* (select the Queries tab, click New, select Design View, click OK, and add the two tables from the Show Table dialog box).
2. Link the tables on their common attribute ItemID (Access should do this automatically for you).
3. Drag the columns ItemID, Name, BeverageType, and OnHand to the Field row of the QBE grid.
4. Write the selection criterion in the OnHand column: click in the Criteria row below OnHand and type *<0* (a conditional expression containing the less than (<) comparison operator).
5. Click the Datasheet View button to display the dynaset. Figure 4.11 shows both the query and the dynaset. Your screen may be arranged differently, but

the dynaset should show the same rows as the figure. (This query is named *qryStockOut* on the Companion CD-ROM.)

6. After observing the result, click the Datasheet view Close button and click No when you are asked if you want to save changes to the query.

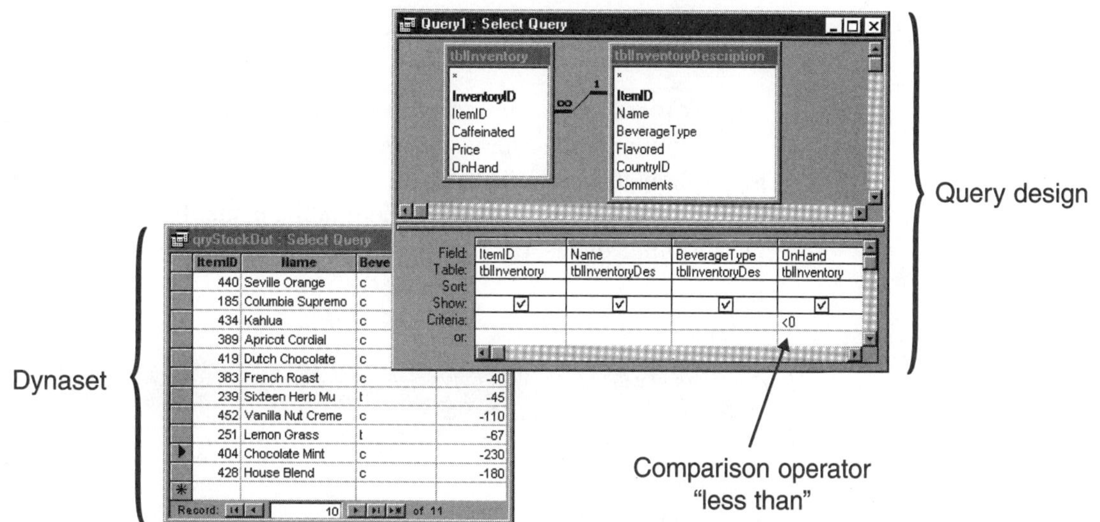

Figure 4.11 Two-table query using a comparison operator.

Using Wildcards in Query Criteria. A *wildcard* character allows you to find information when you are unsure of the complete spelling of an alphanumeric field. Used with the Like operator (see Table 4.2), the wildcard characters define positions that can contain any single character, a single number, or zero or more characters in a text string match pattern. There are three Like operator wildcard characters in Access. They are shown in Table 4.3. Here's an example of how they can be used. Suppose you want to check The Coffee Merchant's stock for any beverages whose name contains the word *chocolate* (for example, Dutch Chocolate). You are interested in how much is available, if any. You can use the * (asterisk) wildcard character and the partial word *choc* to return any beverages whose Name field contains *choc* anywhere within it.

The preceding query involves two tables, Inventory and Invenamt. Further, the key search criterion is the wildcard expression *choc*. This is placed in the Criteria row just below the Name column in the QBE grid. (After you type the preceding expression, Access automatically surrounds it with double quotation marks and precedes the entire phrase with the comparison operator *Like*.) The

Wildcard Character	Meaning	Example Pattern Matches
?	Any single character	*b?lk* matches balk or bulk
*	Zero or more characters	**or* matches door, floor, and matador *or** matches ordinary, order, and organize **or** matches bored, category, and fluoride
#	Any single digit	*6#4* matches 604, 644, and 664

Table 4.3 LIKE wildcard characters.

asterisk preceding *choc* indicates that any word or phrase can appear before the word. Similarly, the asterisk following *choc* indicates that any characters or words may follow the word. That is, the search criterion requests any rows in which the partial word *choc* is found anywhere in the name. Figure 4.12 shows a query and the resulting dynaset.

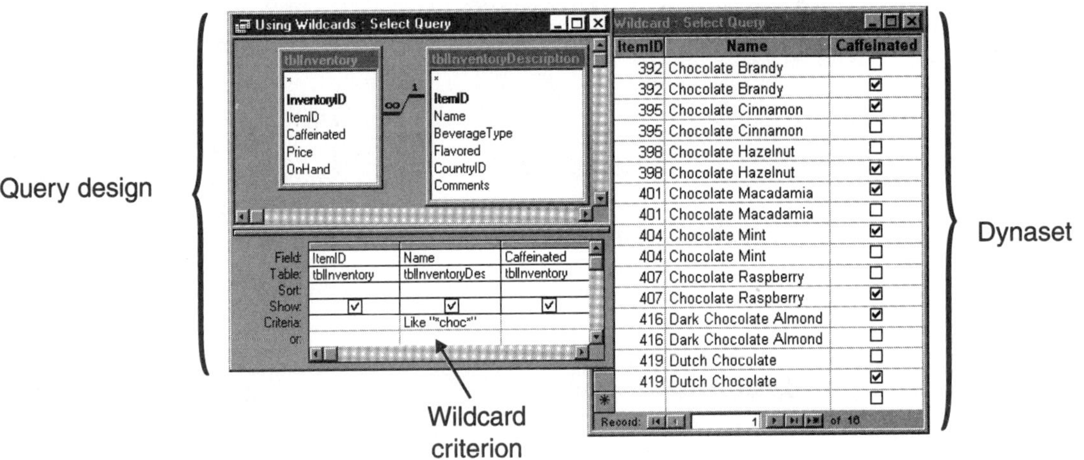

Figure 4.12 Query using a wildcard.

Using Logical Operators in Query Criteria. Some other useful operators helpful in forming selection criteria are called logical operators. *Logical operators* provide a way of bonding two comparison or wildcard criteria. There are several logical operators, but the ones used most often are AND, OR, and NOT. Using the AND operator, you can specify a condition in which two criteria must be true simultaneously. For example, suppose you want to examine the invoices issued during the first week of July 1997. A temporary employee was used to process the invoices that week, and you heard that some invoices were handled incorrectly. You can use the AND operator to bound the range of invoice dates you want to inspect. Specifically, you write the criterion expression ***>=#7/1/97# And <=#7/7/97#*** in the Criteria row below InvoiceDate in the QBE grid. This selection criterion states a range of acceptable invoice dates. The range encompasses dates that are greater than or equal to July 1, 1997 *AND* (simultaneously) less than or equal to July 7, 1997. (The # characters are used to surround dates so that Access doesn't confuse dates with arithmetic expressions. Do not confuse this use of the pound sign with the wildcard character used to match a single digit.) Thus, the criterion limits rows from the Invoice table to invoices issued during the first week. An equivalent way of writing the preceding criterion using the Between comparison operator is ***Between #7/1/97# And #7/7/97#***. Any dates between or matching the two dates satisfy the criteria.

Performing Calculations with Queries

Recall that in Chapter 3 we emphasized the importance of omitting from a table information that can be calculated or derived from other columns in the table. For instance, good database design and normalization rules preclude the inclusion of a column of extended prices in any of The Coffee Merchant's invoice tables. This is because the extended price is calculated from the fields Quantity, UnitPrice, and Discount already in *tblInvoiceLine*. Therefore, the extended price can be calculated. It should not be stored in the table. Why? Suppose the extended price is stored in *tblInvoiceLine* along with Quantity, UnitPrice, and Discount. What if we discover a mistake in the Quantity or UnitPrice values in one or more invoices? Changing either renders the extended price value inaccurate (we call the data *inconsistent*).

That leads us to this question: How do you produce the extended price and other useful calculated results? One answer is that you include any calculations in a query. Access allows you to write expressions that sum, average, and count values as well as those involving the arithmetic operators, fields, summary operators (we will discuss these in the next section), numeric constants, and comparison operators. The arithmetic operators are the familiar ones: +, -, *, and /, and you have been introduced to comparison operators. You reference other query or table fields by enclosing their names in brackets. To compute a result and display it in a query, you simply write an expression in its own Field row cell.

Let's write an expression to see exactly how to calculate results that are displayed in the dynaset. In this next exercise, we will join the *tblInvoiceLine*, *tblInventory*, and *tblInventoryDescription* tables and display invoice line items for invoices in the database. Among the columns displayed will be the extended price, which is computed with the following formula:

[Quantity]*[UnitPrice]*(1-[Discount])

For example, if someone ordered 20 pounds of a particular coffee priced at $10.00 per pound and received a discount of 5 percent, then the extended price would be:

20*10*(1.00-0.05)

(Though the Inventory table, *tblInventory*, contains a price field, Price, for each item carried, customers may or may not be charged that *suggested* price. The actual price charged is stored in UnitPrice, an invoice line field (*tblInvoiceLine*), and may vary from one customer to the next.) The extended price calculated by the preceding expression is $190.

Exercise 4.6: Writing Expressions in Queries

1. Close all windows except the Database window.
2. Create a new query, adding the tables *tblInvoiceLine*, *tblInventory*, and *tblInventoryDescription* to it. Access will draw join lines connecting the three tables on their respective primary and foreign keys. Close the Show Table dialog box.
3. Drag the fields InvoiceID, ItemID, Name, UnitPrice, Quantity, and Discount to the first six Field row cells in the QBE grid (in the order listed).
4. Next, write the expression for Extended Price: click in the seventh cell in the Field row—the first empty cell—and type the following expression: ***Extended Price: [Quantity]*[UnitPrice]*(1-[Discount])***
5. Right-click the cell containing the preceding expression and select *Properties* from the pop-up menu that appears.
6. Select Format and then select Currency from the drop-down list (see Figure 4.13). Doing this will format the calculated expression to display the result rounded to two decimal places and will include a currency symbol and commas (if necessary).
7. Click the Datasheet View button to see the dynaset (see Figure 4.14). We have saved the query as *qryInvoiceLineItem* on the Companion CD-ROM.
8. Close the query without saving it (or save it under a name different from the preceding one) once you are finished examining the results.

Step 4 shows an example of an expression—the product of three fields, Quantity, UnitPrice, and Discount. Whenever you refer to table field names, always enclose them in brackets. Otherwise, Access becomes confused. The expression has been renamed with *Extended Price*, which precedes the expression. To rename a column (an expression in this case), simply begin with the new name (it can be several words) followed by a colon and a space. Then write the expression. If you

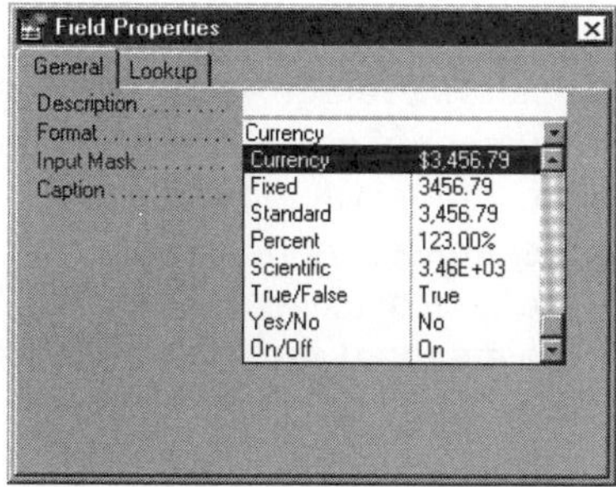

Figure 4.13 Formatting a calculated column.

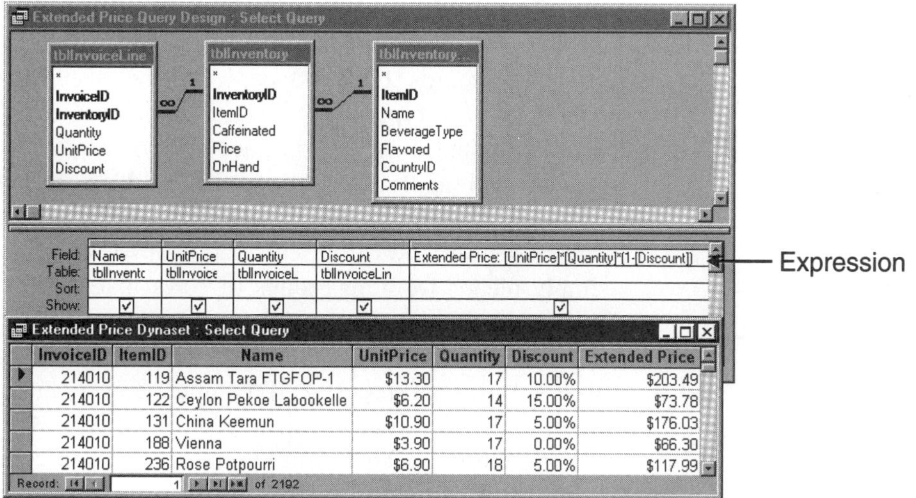

Figure 4.14 Query design and dynaset containing a calculation.

had not renamed the resulting column, then the unpleasant-looking label *[Quantity]*[UnitPrice]*(1-[Discount])* would be displayed in the dynaset column label.

Producing Summary Results

Summary information can reveal situations that are not obvious from examining detailed data. Access provides nine functions that produce aggregate information for data groups or an entire table. The functions are listed in Table 4.4 along with a brief description of what each does. Of the listed functions, the most useful to those of us in the accounting profession are Avg, Count, Max, Min, and Sum.

Function	Meaning
Avg	Computes a field's average value (ignores null fields)
Count	Counts the number of non-null (empty) items in a field
Max	Computes the largest value in a field
Min	Computes the smallest non-null value in a field
Sum	Computes the total of all items in a field
StDev	Computes the standard deviation of non-null values in a field
Var	Determines the variance of non-null values in a field
First	Determines the field value from the first record in a table or query
Last	Determines the field value from the last record in a table or query

Table 4.4 Access aggregate functions.

Sometimes you may want statistics for all rows of a table or joined set of tables. At other times, however, you will need summary statistics on smaller groups of records. For instance, it may be revealing to know the total number of pounds of each type of coffee and tea ordered each month. This would disclose the more popular choices. Or, accounts receivable might be interested in a gross statistic such as the average number of days, by customer, between sending an invoice and receiving a payment. When summary information is calculated for several sets of rows, that calculation involves *grouping*. Grouping information simply means forming groups of rows that share some common characteristic such as having identical values for a client name or other given attribute.

Frequently, the summary functions are used in queries (but they can also be used in forms and reports). To compute an average of a numeric field in a query, simply click the Totals toolbar button and type *Avg* in the QBE grid Total row beneath the field. Then, run the query. You can compute multiple summary statistics on a particular field as long as you include multiple copies of the field name in the QBE grid Field row.

Let's try some of the summary functions. The next exercise is quite simple. Using the *tblInvoiceLine* table you have examined previously, we will write a query to compute the total of each invoice in the database for all invoices. Prepare for this exercise by closing all windows except the Ch04 Database window and click the Queries tab.

Exercise 4.7: Using Summary Functions in a Query

1. Create a new query, add the table *tblInvoiceLine* to the query, and close the Show Table dialog box.
2. Select Totals from the View menu to add a new line, Total, to the QBE grid. (You can also click the Totals button on the Design View toolbar.)

3. In the second cell in the Field row enter the expression shown previously for Extended Price:
   Extended Price: [Quantity]*[UnitPrice]*(1-[Discount])
   You may want to press the F2 function key to produce a larger view of the cell. Called the *Zoom box* by some, the larger display makes it easier to see the whole expression. When you are finished writing the expression, press F2 again to reduce the field cell back to its normal size.
4. Click in the QBE grid Total row beneath the second cell—the expression you just typed—and select the Sum function from the drop-down list (click the list box to display the list of summary functions).
5. Set the format of the second cell, the expression, to Currency by right-clicking the Field row cell containing the expression, selecting Properties, and selecting Currency from the drop-down list in the Format box of the Field Properties dialog box.
6. Close the Field Properties dialog box.
7. Click the Datasheet View button to see the results. Figure 4.15 shows both the query and its dynaset.

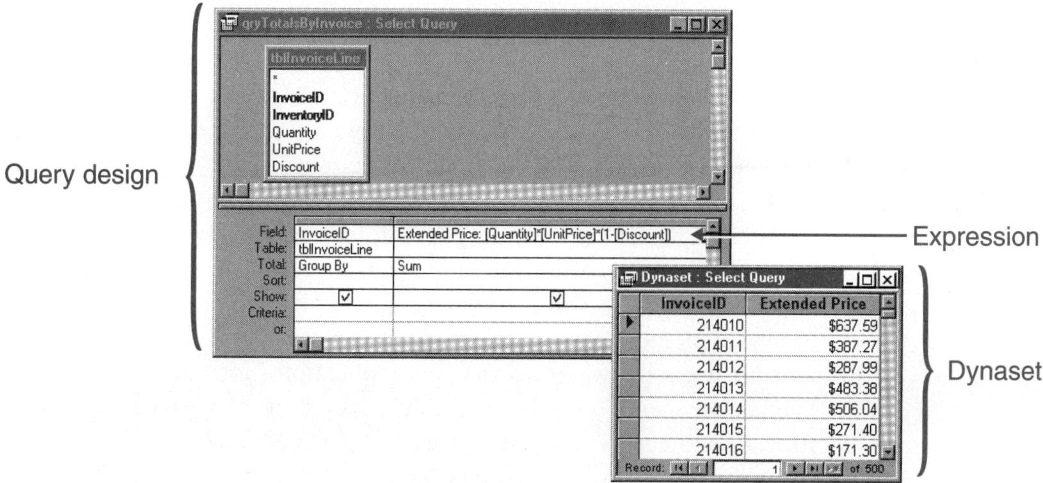

Figure 4.15 Invoice totals created with an aggregate function.

The dynaset clearly shows the totals for the first 7 of the 500 invoices in the database. Switch back to the query Design view in preparation for a little experiment. (*Do not* discard this query yet.)

Can we see the grand total of all invoices that are in the database? In other words, is it possible to sum all the individual invoices in a query? The answer is yes. As a matter of fact, you can make a simple change to the query you created in the preceding exercise to yield the grand total.

Try it

Display the previous query's design. Move the mouse pointer just above the Field row of the InvoiceID field in the QBE. When the pointer changes to a solid, dark, down-pointing arrow, click it to select the entire QBE grid column. Press the Delete key to delete that column. Click the Datasheet View button to see the grand total of all invoices in the database. Your altered query should display a single row with the value of $176,729.37—a good deal of money.

Keep the following in mind whenever you use the summary functions. Place the summary function in the field for which the computation is to be performed (beneath an expression in our previous example). Rename a summary column when desired by typing the new name, a colon, a space, and then the field name. (It works equally well when creating aliases for fields as well as entire expressions.)

BUILDING FORMS

A form displays information from one or more tables in an easily understood and attractive format. Unlike a Table window, a Form View window typically shows you one row of a table at a time. Forms have several advantages as mentioned earlier, but one of the most compelling is that a form can be sculpted to look like any of a company's existing paper forms. When database forms match paper forms, the computer forms are almost always intuitive and familiar to those using them. And because the computer forms look familiar, they are not intimidating to new computer users. Forms make up an application's primary interface. As far as your users know, forms *are* the application (not the tables and other objects behind the scenes). Forms can be used to store and pass information from one form to another or from one phase of your application to the next.

Forms can have a plain but functional design, or they can be elaborate, with drop-down lists, built-in help, attractive field designs, and buttons that activate predefined activities when they are clicked. Like queries, forms do not store database information. They simply display information retrieved from one or more tables. Data exhibited in a form can be pulled from a single table or from multiple tables joined on a common key field. Forms can also display data directly from a query of arbitrary complexity. Any of the queries we created in the previous section could be the basis of a form.

We begin our exploration of forms and their utility by creating a rather simple form from a single table. Then we will create a form whose data is derived from multiple related tables. The last form will be created from a query.

Designing a One-Table Form

It is much easier to enter data and alter data in the Customer table using a form. The next exercise shows you how to create an *AutoForm* from the Table window. Subsequent exercises will enhance the form's appearance. First, start with a clean slate. Launch Access if necessary and open your copy of *Ch04.mdb*. Close any open windows except the Database window. Then create a form by executing the steps in the following exercise.

EXERCISE 4.8: CREATING A FORM FROM A TABLE QUICKLY

1. Click the Tables tab in the Database window and click the Customer table, *tblCustomer* (you do not need to open it, but you can).
2. Select AutoForm from the Insert menu. Quickly, a default form is created and displayed (see Figure 4.16).
3. Save the newly created form by choosing Save from the File menu and typing ***frmMyCustomerForm*** in the Form Name text box of the Save As dialog box. Click OK to store the form in the database. (The string *frm* is the customary form name prefix—one of the database world's rules that is equivalent to accounting's "GAAP.")

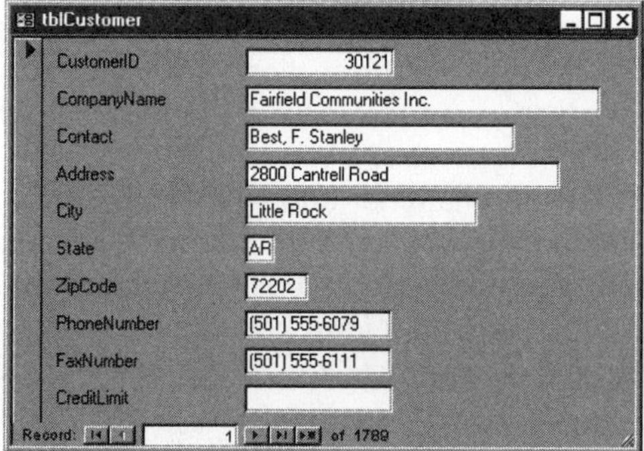

Figure 4.16 AutoForm generated for the Customer table (*tblCustomer*).

Try it

Notice that the first row of *tblCustomer* is displayed. Click a navigation button, located at the bottom of the form, and view different customers' information. Click the Last Record navigation button to view the last customer's information. Click the Design View button to examine the form's *design*. Close the form. Click the Forms tab to see the new form's name, *frmMyCustomerForm*.

Whenever you want to create a form to enter or examine data in a table, the easiest way is to first create an AutoForm. Then, you can alter the default form to suit your needs, making it more attractive and functional. One of the fundamental operations you will use in the Form Design window is moving and sizing fields and other form objects. To move an object, you first select it and then drag it to its new location. When you select an object, small square handles appear around it. Passing the pointer over any of the object's handles causes the pointer to change shape. By dragging a handle, you can enlarge or shrink the object by dragging the handle away from or towards the object, respectively.

You can move several objects at once by selecting them and dragging the entire group. As with other Windows programs, you select multiple objects by pressing the Shift key and then clicking each object in turn. With Microsoft Access, you can simply drag the mouse so that the dashed line touches or surrounds all objects you wish to select. When you release the mouse, all objects are selected. Let's rework the default form by first changing the title. Ensure that the form you created in the previous exercise, *frmMyCustomerForm*, is displayed in Design view. Click the Maximize button on the Form window to make it as large as possible.

Exercise 4.9: Altering a Form's Title

1. Add a form header: select Form Header/Footer from the View menu. Form Header and Form Footer sections are added to your form.
2. Choose Toolbox from the View menu to display the Toolbox on the work surface (see Figure 4.17). You can also click the Toolbox button found on the toolbar—it has a hammer and wrench on it—to display the Toolbox. You can move the Toolbox anywhere on the screen by dragging its Title bar.
3. Click the Label button to add a title to the form; move the mouse to the upper left corner of the form header, and drag it down and to the right until the outline is approximately 0.25" by 2.0". Release the mouse.
4. Type the label ***Coffee Merchant Customers*** in the label box. Click outside the label box to see the text.
5. You can, if you wish, remove the Toolbox from the screen by clicking its Close button. Or you can drag it to the top, left, right, or bottom of the screen to dock it there.
6. Right-click the label box in the form header and select Properties from the shortcut menu that pops up. (Alternatively, you can click the Properties button on the toolbar.)
7. Select Properties. A property sheet is displayed.
8. Click the Format tab.
9. Scroll to the last entry in the sheet, the Text Align property, and type ***Center*** (or select it from the drop-down list) in the Text Align box.
10. In the Font Size box type ***14*** to indicate you want a point size of 14. Close the property sheet by clicking its Close button.

11. If the title is not entirely visible in its text box, move the mouse to any corner. When the pointer turns to a double-headed arrow pointing at an angle, double-click it. The box enlarges (or shrinks) as needed to accommodate all the text.
12. Click the Form View button to see the altered form.

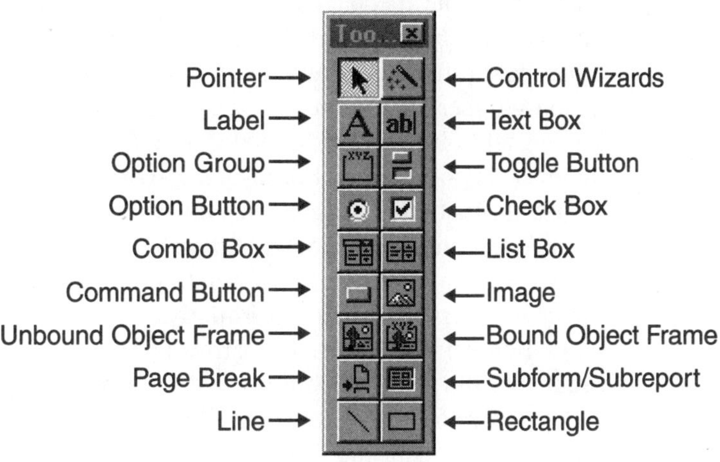

Figure 4.17 Microsoft Access Toolbox.

Your revised Customer form should resemble the one shown in Figure 4.18. We have saved it as *frmCustomer* on the Companion CD-ROM.

tblCustomer

Coffee Merchant Customers

CustomerID	30121
CompanyName	Fairfield Communities Inc.
Contact	Best, F. Stanley
Address	2800 Cantrell Road
City	Little Rock
State	AR
ZipCode	72202
PhoneNumber	(501) 555-6079
FaxNumber	(501) 555-6111
CreditLimit	

Record: 1 of 1789

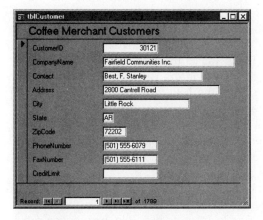

Figure 4.18 Altered Customer form.

Using a Form

Through using a form, you will realize that data entry with a form is more intuitive and easier than entering data directly into a table. We have created a simple form called *frmOrder* (remember to use the prefix *frm* for all your form names) that will introduce you to the look and feel of a typical form. The Order form found on the Companion CD-ROM provides a convenient work surface to enter new orders into the tables comprising the order database. The form provides all the requisite mechanisms to automatically place order information into two tables called *tblOrder* and *tblOrderLine*. Furthermore, the form supplies a helpful table lookup feature in two key locations: the Customer No. (customer identification number) field and the Sales Rep. (sales representative) field.

A table lookup field is helpful to anyone entering information with which he or she is not familiar. For instance, if you do not know a customer's number—a normal situation—you can click the *combo* box (a combination of a text box and a list box) to display customer names. When the cursor is on the customer number entry, you can click the down-pointing arrow to peruse the list of existing customer numbers and names. Similarly, you can look up a sales representative's name by clicking the *list* box arrows associated with the field. Let's enter one order into the system using the order form.

Prepare for the next exercise by launching Access, if necessary, and closing all windows except the Database window. Click the Forms tab and double-click *frmOrder* found in the list of forms. An order entry form is displayed. Follow the steps in the next exercise to enter and save information in an existing order entry table.

Exercise 4.10: Using the Order Entry Form

1. Click the Order form's Maximize button so the form fills the window and then type *5678* (or any four-digit number) into the Order No. form field. Press Tab to move to the next field.
2. Enter a date in the form mm/dd/yy (for example, *7/11/97*) into the Order Date field. Press Tab to move to the next field.
3. With the cursor in the Customer No. field, click the combo box arrow on the right side of the field to display a list of customer numbers and names (see Figure 4.19).
4. Scroll through the list of customers until the company name *Cheesecake Factory Inc.* appears. Click that name. After you select the name, its corresponding customer number is inserted into the field and thus the underlying table.
5. Click the down arrow on the Sales Rep. list box and select (click) the name *English, Melinda* when it appears in the window.
6. Press Tab to move to the Sale Type option group. Notice that a dashed line appears around the *Wholesale* label. The Wholesale/Retail options are

known as *radio buttons* because clicking one check box places a check mark in it and deselects all others in the group—like the buttons on a car radio.

7. Press Tab to accept the default check box value, Wholesale. After a few moments, the form cursor (sometimes called the *focus*) will be displayed in the first row of the line item subform, directly below the Inventory label.
8. Enter ***1128***, press Tab, and enter ***20*** in the Quantity column. Press Tab to move to UnitPrice.
9. Enter ***8.50*** and press Tab twice. The cursor moves to the next row. Notice that the ItemID, Name, and Price are automatically inserted into the form; the extended price, Extended, is calculated and inserted also. Discount takes on its default value, 0.00, if you do not enter a value.
10. Figure 4.20 shows an example of a completed order entry form. Continue entering values, if you wish, to match those shown in the figure. Besides entering Inventory, Quantity, and UnitPrice values for each row, remember to type ***5%*** and ***15%*** (type the percent sign) in the Discount column for the last two entries, respectively.

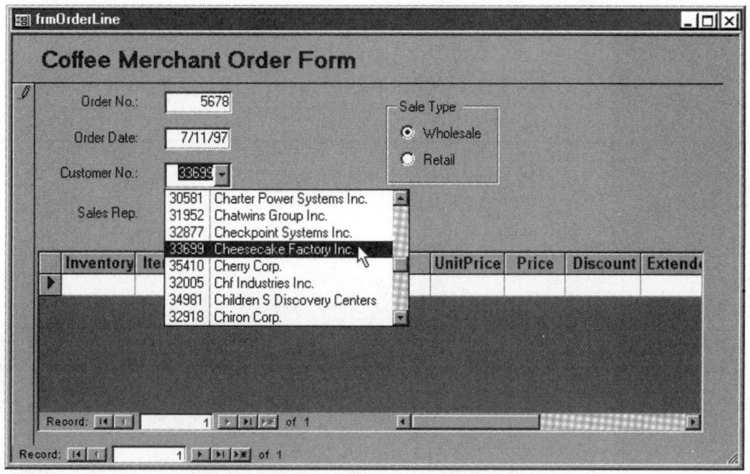

Figure 4.19 Using a combo box to make a selection.

If you want to try the form again, first clear it by clicking the Next Record navigation button located at the bottom of the form. By moving to another record, you cause the current form data to be posted to the various database tables and the form to be cleared, ready for another entry. When you are done entering information, click the form's Close button. Don't be concerned that you might lose data. Microsoft Access automatically posts any newly entered data to the database when you move off the current record or close the form.

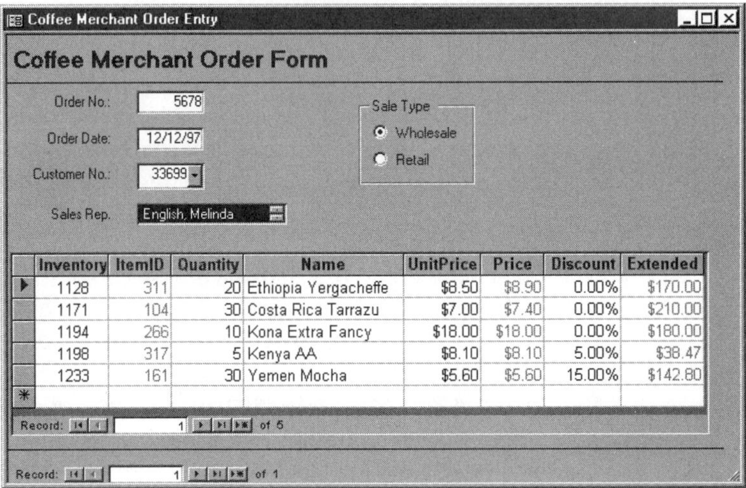

Coffee Merchant Order Entry

Coffee Merchant Order Form

Order No.: 5678

Order Date: 12/12/97

Customer No.: 33699

Sales Rep. English, Melinda

Sale Type

Wholesale

Retail

Inventory	ItemID	Quantity	Name	UnitPrice	Price	Discount	Extended
1128	311	20	Ethiopia Yergacheffe	$8.50	$8.90	0.00%	$170.00
1171	104	30	Costa Rica Tarrazu	$7.00	$7.40	0.00%	$210.00
1194	266	10	Kona Extra Fancy	$18.00	$18.00	0.00%	$180.00
1198	317	5	Kenya AA	$8.10	$8.10	5.00%	$38.47
1233	161	30	Yemen Mocha	$5.60	$5.60	15.00%	$142.80

Record: 1 of 5

Record: 1 of 1

Figure 4.20 A completed order entry form.

Viewing a Form's Master Table. You can easily examine the master table associated with your form. First, open the form in either Form view or Design view and click the Datasheet View button on the toolbar (or execute the Datasheet command from the View menu). Whichever method you choose, the master table for the current form will be displayed in a Table window. This way you can see how and where the master table information (in our case, the customer and sales representative information) is stored. Close the Table window by clicking its Close button.

Scrolling through the Data. You have used a Table window's navigation buttons to view the data in a table. Similarly, you can examine all the order data—from multiple tables—through a form. Assuming you have entered additional orders, you can click the First Record button to go to the first order you entered, or click the Last Record button to go to the last order entered in the system. Other navigation buttons work in a familiar way. Try them.

Editing Data. Editing data couldn't be simpler. In a Form View window, click on any field you would like to change and type the change. For form fields using lookup tables (fields having list boxes or combo boxes), click the arrow near the field to display the list of values; then enter a new value or select one of the displayed entries. It is best to use a lookup table when available, especially for noncontiguous values like sales representative identification numbers. As budding form designers, you should incorporate lookup tables for fields whose values are limited to a specific and small list of acceptable values. This saves a lot of frustration and confusion on the part of form users.

Filter By Form and Filter By Selection. With forms, you can view particular records or groups of records using either the Filter By Form or Filter By Selection techniques. Though we mentioned these two techniques previously, let's review them here. When you filter something, you are restricting what is displayed to some subset of the objects available. Filtering records being viewed through a form is no different. You simply specify the criteria—similar to query criteria—which are used to restrict your view of the records and then select Apply Filter/Sort from the Filter menu. Records are displayed in the usual way in the form, but you will notice that only a select group of records are available. The total number of records in the filtered set are indicated to the right of the navigation buttons at the bottom of the form. Try it yourself.

Try it

Display the form *frmCustomer* found on your Companion CD-ROM. Notice that there are 1,789 customer records. All are available for viewing. Next, click the Records menu, select Filter, and select Filter By Form from the Filter cascade menu. Let's see how many customers there are in Montana and who they are. Click the State form field and type ***MT*** in either upper- or lowercase. Select Apply Filter/ Sort from the Filter menu. Voila! Apparently there are only two customers located in Montana. Using the navigation buttons, you see that they are *Buttrey Food and Drug Stores Co.* and *Montana Power Co.* Select Remove Filter/Sort from the Records menu (notice the Filter menu is unavailable while viewing filtered records). The form indicates all records in the table are available again.

Filter By Selection works in almost the same way as Filter By Form. You select a field, such as City, which has an entry by which you would like to filter and then choose Filter By Selection from the Records menu. Only records whose fields match that of the selected field are displayed. Try it.

Try it

Display *frmCustomer* again. Move to the first customer in the Customer table, Fairfield Communities, Inc. Click the City form field and drag the cursor across the entire city name to select it. Let's see how many other customers we have in the selected city of Little Rock. Click the Records menu, select Filter, and select Filter By Selection from the Filter cascade menu. It looks like there are six customers in Little Rock. Select Remove Filter/Sort from the Records menu. The form indicates all records in the table are available again.

You can do more with Filter By Form and Filter By Selection. However, those details you will have to discover on your own. We have a lot more to cover on other topics. So, let's move on.

Creating a Multitable Form and Subform

Many forms involve more than one table. The Coffee Merchant's Order form is an example of a multitable form, because data such as the order number, order date, and sales representative number are stored in a table called *tblOrder*, whereas the details about the items ordered (item id and quantity ordered) are stored in another table called *tblOrderLine*. The Inventory table, *tblInventory*, is also referenced by The Coffee Merchant's Order form, although no new inventory items can be entered via the form. Finally, the *tblCustomer* table is consulted to locate and display customer numbers in the Customer No. field. Four tables are joined and referenced by The Coffee Merchant's Order form.

Although using The Coffee Merchant's Order form is an informative exercise, you will benefit much more from *building* a form from scratch. Once you create a form, it is only a short time until you will be designing elaborate forms for your own applications. Figure 4.21 shows you an example of a multitable Invoice Entry form referencing many of The Coffee Merchant's tables. That form has the look of the finished form we are striving for in this section. When finished, your form should start to resemble the one in Figure 4.21.

Coffee Merchant Invoice

Invoice ID 214010 | Contact Person Shaffer, Shaun P.
Invoice Date 10/1/97 | Address 4636 Somerton Road, Trevose, PA 19053
Order Date 9/6/97
Customer's PO# 2634-635 | Phone (215) 555-3336
Company Name Betz Laboratories Inc. | Sales Rep Whitney Halstead

ItemID	Name	Price	Quantity	Discount	Extended Price
119	Assam Tara FTGFOP-1	$13.30	17	10.00%	$203.49
122	Ceylon Pekoe Labookelle	$6.20	14	15.00%	$73.78
131	China Keemun	$10.90	17	5.00%	$176.03
188	Vienna	$3.90	17	0.00%	$66.30
236	Rose Potpourri	$6.90	18	5.00%	$117.99

Record: 1 of 5

Record: 1 of 500

Figure 4.21 Example Invoice Entry form.

The Invoice form that you will build in this section is actually two forms: a main form and a subform. The main form displays one record from the *tblInvoice* table. Simultaneously, the subform displays several related records that are the individual items that have been billed on that invoice. Information on the subform includes item number, item name, quantity ordered, unit price, discount, and extended price. Subform information is synthesized by a query you created previously called *qryInvoiceLineItem*.

Creating a Form Containing a Subform. Access allows you to create design documents (a form or a report) that use data found in more than one table or query. The best way to create a main form and its subform is to use a Form Wizard. The following exercise outlines how to create an invoice form. Prepare for the next exercise by closing all open windows except the Database window and clicking the Forms tab.

EXERCISE 4.11: CREATING AN INVOICE FORM AND SUBFORM

1. Click the New button on the Forms page of the Database window. Access displays the New Form dialog box.
2. Select *Form Wizard* from the list of form choices and type ***qryInvoiceMain*** in the list box found just above the Cancel button. (When creating forms with subforms, it is normally best to use the Form Wizard.) You base the top half of the form on the table or query that contains the data to appear on the main form (the data on the "one" side of the one-to-many relationship). In this case the main form will contain customer invoice information. The subform will contain invoice detail lines with products, quantities, prices, etc.
3. Click the OK button to begin the form-building process. The first of several Form Wizard dialog boxes is displayed.
4. Click the chevron button (">>") to move all fields on the Available Fields list onto the Selected Fields list. The latter list contains the fields that will be displayed on the form.
5. Add the subform fields to the form: click the drop-down list arrow next to the Tables/Queries list box to display the queries and tables in the database.
6. Locate *qryInvoiceLineItem* in the list and click it. The list of fields supplied by the query are now listed in the Available Fields list (see Figure 4.22).
7. Click the chevron button (">>") to move all the subform fields onto the Selected Fields list.
8. In the Selected Fields list, locate and select the field called *qryInvoiceLineItem.InvoiceID*.
9. Click the less than button—the one displaying "<"—to remove the extra InvoiceID field, moving it from the Selected Fields list back onto the Available Fields list. (Alternatively, you could select each field in turn, clicking the ">" to place each onto the Selected Fields list. The way we suggest here is faster.)
10. Click Next to proceed to the next step.
11. When the next dialog box appears asking you how you want to view your data, click Next again to accept the suggested default.
12. Select the Datasheet layout for your subform by clicking the Datasheet option button. Click Next to go to the next step.
13. Accept the suggested default "Standard" style and click the Next button to proceed. Be careful on the last Form Wizard dialog box. Be sure to change the form and subform names by altering them in the text boxes. If you do not do it here, it is *much* more difficult to do so later.

14. In the Form text box type ***frmInvoice2*** and ***fsubInvoice2***. (Be sure to enter the prefix *fsub* for the subform. This prefix indicates a form is a subform and is the accepted standard for naming subforms.)
15. Click the Finish button to conclude the form-building process.

Access takes a few moments to build both the form and subform and then opens it for your use (see Figure 4.23). Scroll through the records to experience how the form works. Occasionally, you may want to scroll through the subform to display all the invoice items for a particular invoice. Keep in mind that the outermost set of navigation buttons page through whole invoices, while the inner set skip from line to line on invoice details in the subform.

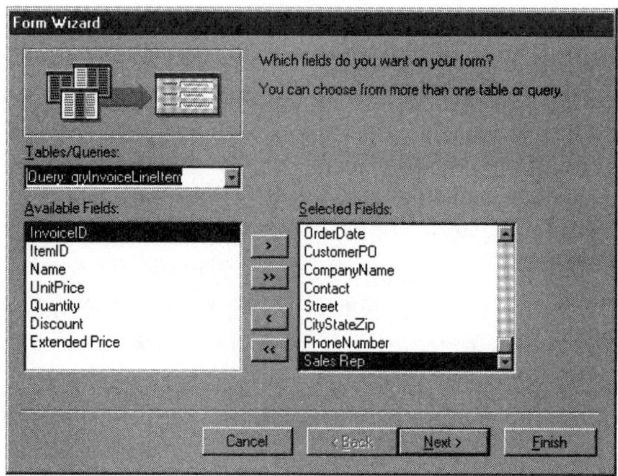

Figure 4.22 Selecting main form and subform fields.

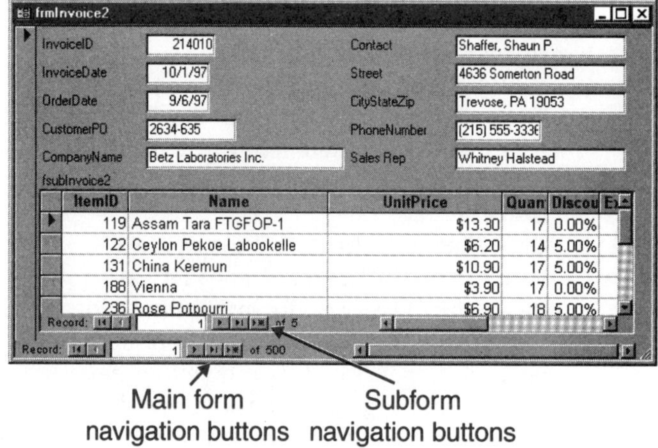

Figure 4.23 Main form and embedded subform created by the Form Wizard.

Modifying a Subform's Column Widths and Labels. Some of the subform's fields are not sufficiently wide. Consequently, some fields are completely visible while others are not. For example, notice in Figure 4.23 that none of the Extended Price values are visible. Similarly, the UnitPrice column seems far too wide. Let's modify the widths of some subform columns so that they are just large enough to display their information but not too large. Then, we will change the subform column label from *UnitPrice* to *Price*. The next exercise shows you how to accomplish these tasks. Prepare for this exercise by closing all windows except the Database window. Next, click the Forms tab to display the list of forms in your database. Do you see *frmInvoice2* and *fsubInvoice2* in the list?

Exercise 4.12: Modifying a Subform's Column Widths and Labels

1. Double-click the subform *fsubInvoice2* to open it. If necessary, click the Datasheet View button on the toolbar so the information is displayed as a datasheet, not a form.
2. Alter all the columns to an optimal width: move the mouse to the leftmost column label, ItemID. When the mouse turns to a down-pointing arrow, drag it to the right until all columns are selected. (Selected columns are displayed in black.) Release the mouse button.
3. Move the mouse to any border between two columns in the label area or move it to the rightmost border of the rightmost label. When the mouse pointer changes to a double-headed arrow with a vertical line dissecting it, double-click the mouse. All columns change size, adjusting to the smallest width that is wide enough to display the largest values or column labels.
4. Click anywhere to deselect the columns. Now the columns display the widest values without truncating them. If you wish to further customize individual column widths, you can do so by dragging the line to the right of a column's label when the mouse pointer is a double-headed arrow. Dragging the right column line to the right widens the column; dragging to the left narrows the column.
5. Switch from Datasheet view to Design view by clicking the (what else!) Design View button found on the toolbar.
6. Double-click the UnitPrice field in the Detail section of the form to display its property sheet. (If you find this difficult—double-click timing is everything—then right-click the field and select Properties from the pop-up list.)
7. Click the property sheet tab labeled *Other*, double-click the value displayed in the Name property, and type ***Price*** to replace the UnitPrice name.
8. Click the dialog's Close button to close it.
9. Close the *fsubInvoice2* subform (click the form's Close button) and click Yes when asked if you want to save the changed design.

You will do additional work on this form, but it is always a good idea to preserve the partially complete work. That way, you don't risk losing a large amount of work if something should happen to the power to your computer.

There are several controls on the forms with which you are working. *Controls* are all the objects that appear on forms or reports. For example, the label *InvoiceID* is a control as is the field displaying the value 214010 in the InvoiceID field. There are three types of controls in Access: bound controls, unbound controls, and calculated controls. A *bound control* has as its data source a field in an underlying table. The invoice date field in Figure 4.23 is a bound control. An *unbound control* has no data source and is used to display a title or label on forms and reports. The invoice date label (*InvoiceDate*) in Figure 4.23 is an example of an unbound label. A *calculated control* has as its data source an expression rather than a table field. The Extended Price field is an example of a calculated control. We use the term *control* frequently when referring to objects on forms or reports.

Altering a Subform's Column Formats. When you want to alter an item's property such as its display format, you summon the item's property sheet and make the necessary changes. The property sheet is used to set, view, or change the properties of a table, query, form, report, or control. Available in the Design view of a Table, Query, Form, or Report window, the property sheet is displayed whenever you click the Properties button on the toolbar. It remains on the work surface, even when you select other controls or objects, until you close it. You can also display the property sheet for a selected object by right-clicking the mouse and then choosing Properties from the pop-up menu.

The next exercise illustrates how to change the way two numeric values are displayed in the subform *fsubInvoice2.* Currently, the Price and Extended Price columns display their values in currency format. This may not be desirable in some situations. Let's change the display format for the two columns so that no currency symbols are displayed. Prepare for the next exercise by opening *fsubInvoice2* in a Design window.

EXERCISE 4.13: CHANGING A COLUMN'S DISPLAY CHARACTERISTICS

1. Select both the UnitPrice and Extended Price controls (*not* their labels) by pressing Shift and then clicking each one.
2. Click the Properties button on the toolbar. The property sheet appears with the Title bar displaying *Multiple selection*, which indicates more than one object will be affected.
3. Click the Format tab. The subset of properties associated with the way data appears when displayed are its Format properties.

4. Click the Format property box, click its combo box arrow, and locate and select *Standard* (see Figure 4.24).
5. Close the property sheet.
6. Close and save the subform (click the subform's Close button and click the Yes button to save the changed subform).

If you wish to verify the last property changes, simply open the form in Form view. Notice that the currency symbols are absent in both the Price and Extended Price fields.

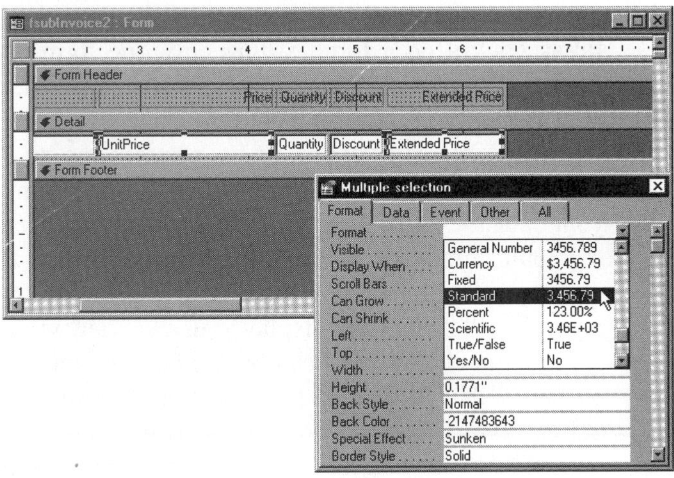

Figure 4.24 Changing objects' properties.

Rearranging Form Fields. You can easily rearrange controls on a form by selecting them and then dragging them to a new location. For example, you can move the CompanyName control closer to the customer's address controls on the right side of the form. Move controls by displaying the form or subform in Design view. After you click the bound control, you can move the hand over the selected control. When the pointer changes to a small hand, click and drag the bound control and its attached unbound control (its label) to a new location. If you want to move a group of controls, simply Shift-click each of them and then move them as a group. To deselect controls, simply click outside the selected control or group of controls.

If a subform's data is not fully visible because the form is not wide enough (a likely case), click the Design View button, click the subform frame to select it, and drag the right border handle to the right to widen the entire frame. (You may have to switch back and forth between Design view and Form view until you have adjusted the subform frame to your liking.) Though your form does not exactly match our Invoice form, it is very close. Only a few embellishments remain to make them identical. You can do that on your own, if you wish.

Printing a Form

Printing a form is a good way to keep track of the forms you have developed for an accounting system. Printing a form is probably the easiest task of all. First, select the form from the list on the Forms sheet of the Database window. Then select Print from the File menu (or click the Print button on the toolbar). When the Print dialog box displays, select the range of pages to be printed and click OK. You may be surprised to see more than one form on a single page. Access prints the current form and any others that will fit on the page. You can insert a Page Break control on a form so that only one form per page is printed. We won't discuss those details here, but if you wish to try it, open a form in Design view, display the Toolbox, and locate the Page Break control.

You can print out properties, permissions, and design information for database objects, including your forms' designs. Printing the design characteristics of your database objects helps you document your database's design or the accounting application you create. Select Tools, Analyze, Documentor. Then, check the objects about which you wanted printed definition information. Click OK and the report is formulated and displayed in a preview window. If you decide to print the report, simply click the Print button on the toolbar. If not, click the Close button on the toolbar to discard the report and return to the Database window. Try it. Select *frmInvoice2* and print its design definition report.

When you want to see a comprehensive list of information from one or more tables, then printing forms is not adequate. Instead, you need a report. Reports and how to produce them are described next.

CREATING REPORTS

Reports provide the mechanism to produce high-quality printed database information. While you can use a form for viewing or altering information in the database, you cannot enter or alter information in a report. Reports are strictly for output. Like forms, reports are based on information found in tables or generated from queries. Unlike forms, reports allow you to group information from one table. With forms, you must join two or more tables to group information by using a form/subform combination.

Using Report Wizards

Microsoft Access provides two ways to create reports. You can create a report from scratch, starting with a blank form, or you can use a Report Wizard. We

ɪrefer using Report Wizards because the process is easier
g a report from scratch.
offer several styles of reports, including Columnar
ıtoReport, Chart, mailing labels, and summary reports.
ds create preformatted, single-column (Columnar) or
eports with very little involvement from you. Other r-
s, produce more interesting results including subtot s
mple.
t Wizard from the Database window after clicking he
cting New. You designate a table or query which ro-
d in the report. Then you select one of the report t pes,
om the list displayed in the New Report dialo box.
port generation process. Simply follow the eport
respond to its questions. Within a few secon after
to complete the process, an attractive repor is dis-
window.

Exa

views: Design view, Print Preview, d Layout
o change the layout and design of a port. Print
e data and its appearance in the re ort. Layout
ont, layout, and general appearance f the report.
pend most of your time, because you create and
A printed report is simply a matter of placing
from the database into the proper predefined locations in the report and printing the merger.

All reports are based on data supplied by tables or queries. An Access report is divided into *sections*, which appear at particular places when the report is printed. There are seven different types of sections, but a report does not have to include all seven sections. Each section appears once in Design view. When you print a report, some sections are repeated as needed. Figure 4.25 shows an example of a report's design.

The Detail section is required in each report. However, the other sections are optional and may be omitted. Beginning at the very top of the report is the Report Header section. It is printed once at the beginning of the report. The Page Header's contents are printed on every page. The Group Header's contents are printed every time the grouping field value changes. Contents of the Detail section is printed for each record selected from the underlying table(s) or queries. The Group Footer prints at the end of each group. The Page Footer prints at the bottom of each page. The Report Footer prints on a page at the end of the report.

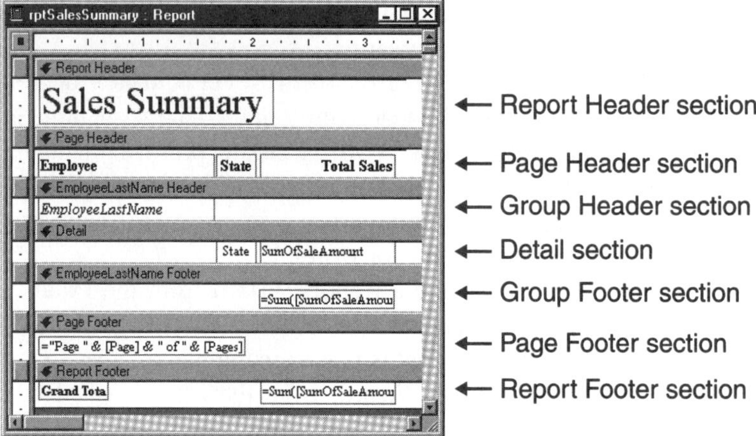

Figure 4.25 Report sections.

Creating a Tabular-Style Report

In many ways, creating a report resembles creating a form. Designing a report, including its field layouts, headings, and other details, occurs in the report Design View window. When you want to see the report replete with data—a facsimile of the printed report—you click the Print Preview button on the toolbar. We introduce report creation by illustrating how to build and print a tabular-style, one-table report.

Using the Report Wizard. The Employee table is a good table to practice on. Suppose we want a printed list of employees and associated information sorted by the employees' last names. All the requisite information is found in one table, *tblEmployee*. Follow the steps in the next exercise to create a report with the help of the Access Report Wizard. As usual, prepare by clearing the work surface: close all windows in Access except the Database window.

Exercise 4.14: Creating a Report

1. Click the Database window Reports tab and click the New button.
2. Select *Report Wizard* as the method to create the report and click the drop-down arrow to display all the database's tables and queries.
3. Click *tblEmployee* and then click OK to start the Report Wizard. A new dialog box is displayed in which you choose which fields will appear on the report.

4. From the Available Fields list, double-click the following fields, one at a time, to move them onto the Selected Fields list: EmployeeID, EmployeeLastName, EmployeeHireDate, EmployeeDOB, and EmployeeGender (see Figure 4.26). Click the Next button when you have entered all fields. (You can also select a field and press the ">" button to move a field onto the Selected Fields list, but it is faster to double-click the names.)
5. The Report Wizard displays several more dialog boxes. The next one asks whether or not you want to create a grouping level. Because you do not, click Next without making any changes.
6. The next dialog box asks if you want to sort the report records. Because we want the report to display the employee information in name order, click the drop-down arrow next to the first sort box and select *EmployeeLastName* from the list of report fields. Click the Next button to proceed.

   Note: If you discover you have made a mistake on some earlier Report Wizard dialog box, you can simply click the Back button repeatedly until the dialog box containing the mistake is reached. Make any changes and then click the Next button to go back to where you left off.

7. Ensure that the Tabular option (in the Layout option group) and the Portrait option (in the Portrait Orientation option group) are selected. Click the Next button.
8. Accept the default Formal report style by pressing the Next button.
9. Type ***Coffee Merchant Employees*** in the text box. Click the Finish button to finalize your choices and generate your report.

   Note: The report title is also used to name the report—not a good situation. You should rename the report *rptMyEmployeeReport.* To do this, select the report name, press F2, type the new report name, and press Enter. You can rename any object that way. We have saved this report as *rptEmployee* on the Companion CD-ROM in case you want to see our report.

10. After reviewing the report preview, click the Close button on the toolbar (*not* the Close window button) to view the report's design. Finally, click the Design view Close button to close and save the report.

Access creates the report and displays it in Print Preview (see Figure 4.27). The report lists employee records in name order. Did you notice that some report column labels such as *Badge Number* and *Last Name* are different from their table column names? The reason for this is that we included less cryptic names for them in the Caption property of the table design when we created the *tblEmployee* table. (To verify this, you can examine the Employee table in Design view.) Print the report, if you wish, by selecting Print from the File menu.

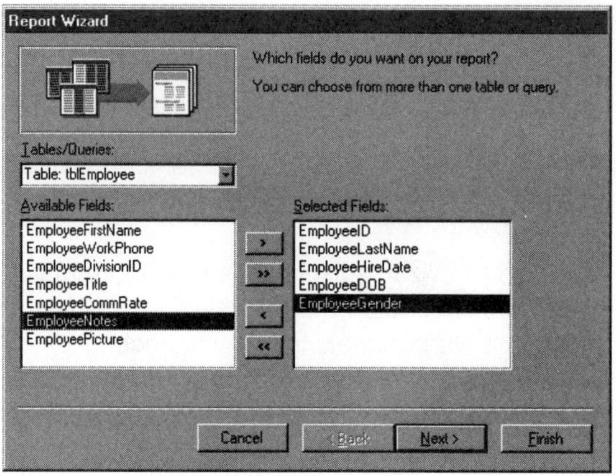

Figure 4.26 Selecting fields for a report.

Coffee Merchant Employees

Last Name	Badge Number	Hire Date	Birth Date	Gender
Ballmer	3692	5/16/81	7/13/40	M
Bateman	4057	2/16/88	5/1/54	M
Chang	3609	9/16/93	3/30/73	F
Ellison	3700	4/18/90	12/12/50	M
English	3432	10/1/89	2/14/52	F
Flintsteel	4082	3/21/86	8/22/54	F
Gates	3436	4/11/91	3/9/50	M
Goldman	4112	12/24/86	3/5/58	M
Halstead	4058	6/16/92	12/22/69	F
Hunter	2318	11/16/89	1/26/50	F
Kahn	2754	5/14/93	5/29/57	M
Kole	3370	2/8/88	3/23/59	M
Manispour	4029	12/18/86	2/4/65	M
Minsky	4012	10/13/86	4/12/55	F
Morrison	3458	12/13/85	7/4/52	F
Nagasaki	1695	1/28/96	4/10/73	M
Pacioli	1528	8/26/91	5/6/46	M
Pruski	1364	12/1/96	1/26/75	M
Shoenstein	3892	9/5/86	3/6/51	M
Stonely	2240	11/5/84	5/3/57	F
Stonesifer	1301	7/6/92	3/10/62	F
Watterson	3943	10/10/89	5/1/57	F

Tuesday, April 14, 1998 Page 1 of 1

Figure 4.27 Tabular-style report.

Modifying Data Alignment. You can enhance the appearance of a control's data or label by adjusting its alignment (its Text Align property). Some of the data columns in the Employee report do not line up well with their column labels. For example, the Badge Number label is far to the left of the actual identification number column values. Similarly, the Gender data values appear misaligned with their respective column label. You alter the alignment of labels (unbound controls) or data (bound controls) to achieve a pleasing appearance. Briefly, we will illustrate how to alter the data alignment in the next exercise. Prepare for the exercise by displaying the Employee report (*tblMyEmployeeReport*) in Design view. Then follow the steps in the next exercise to alter the data alignment for several report column data controls.

Exercise 4.15: Altering Data Alignment

1. Move the cursor to the Detail section and select the EmployeeID and Gender bound controls (hold the Shift key and click each one).
2. Select Properties from the View menu (or click the Properties button found on the toolbar) to display the property sheet.
3. Click the Format tab to reveal that collection of related properties.
4. Scroll the property list to its very bottom and click the Text Align property text box. (The properties are arranged alphabetically within each tabbed sheet.)
5. Select *Center* from the four alignment choices (see Figure 4.28).
6. Close the property sheet and select Save from the File menu to save your design changes.

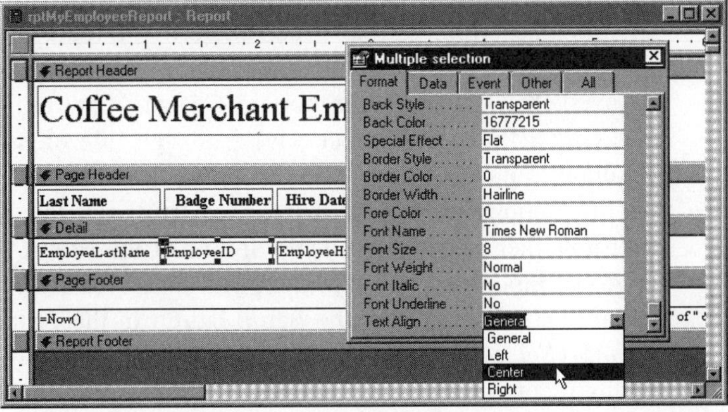

Figure 4.28 Altering simultaneously the layout properties of several controls.

Deleting Controls and Report Sections. Because the *rptMyEmployeeReport* report (or *rptEmployee* in our case) is so short, we will delete the Page Footer section (it contains a single control that displays the current page number). This activity is straightforward, so we will skip a formal exercise and simply describe the steps.

Try it

Before eliminating the Page Footer section, you must first remove all its controls. There are three controls in our example: two calculated controls and an unbound control. Using the horizontal scroll bar, move to the left edge of the report and locate the control in the Page Footer section containing the Access function *=Now()*. Select it (handles appear around it when it is selected) and press Delete to remove it. In a similar way, remove the second control that resides in the Page Footer. Move to the right edge of the report and locate the Page Footer control containing the expression *="Page " & [Page] & " of " & [Pages]*. Select the control (a rather long expression) and press Delete to remove it. Finally, select the thin line (the unbound control) appearing near the top of the Page Footer section. Press Delete to remove it. Once all controls in a section are gone, you remove the section by dragging up the bar below the section. In our case, you move the mouse to the *bottom* of the Page Footer section until it turns into a double-headed arrow pointing up and down and dissected by a small horizontal line. Then drag the arrow up until the Page Footer section is eliminated. Release the mouse button. In effect, you have reduced the height of the Page Footer section to zero. That removes it. Removing *both* the Page Header and the Page Footer is much simpler. Simply click *Page Header/Footer* in the View menu to remove its check. The two sections are removed simultaneously, and any controls in both are removed automatically. Save the altered report by selecting Save from the File menu. Close the report after it is saved.

Saving and Printing a Report. Any reports you want to run periodically should be saved. You have also been saving reports and other objects periodically during their development. Special purpose reports used only once need not be saved. You can save a report in Design View or Print Preview view. Just like saving a form, you select Save from the File menu. For new reports, you must supply a name prior to the report being stored in the database.

Reports exist to be printed, so let's print this report. You can print a report from either the Design View window or the Print Preview window. You can alter global report settings like margins, page orientation (portrait or landscape), and paper size by clicking the Setup button in the Print dialog box. Print the report *rptMyEmployeeReport* so you have a copy of its final form. We will not be using this report further, so you can either save it or delete it from the database.

Can we produce a report similar to *rptEmployee* or *rptMyEmployeeReport* in which the rows are sorted into order by division location and by employee names within each division? The answer is yes—by using the Report Wizard to form report groups.

Using a Query to Produce a Grouped Data Report

You learned that either tables or queries can be the basis of any forms you create. The same is true for reports. When you base a report on a query, you can alter the query's selection criteria, save the query, and run another report. For example, we could create a query that selects invoices that are 30 days past due, base a report on that query, and then run and print the report. Printing a list of invoices that are 31 to 60 days past due would then be easy. Simply modify the existing query to select rows whose invoice date is 31 to 60 days ago, save the modified query, and rerun the report.

Another advantage of basing reports on queries rather than tables is that you can introduce calculated fields into the report that can be summed by a field defined in the report. You cannot do that with a report based on one or more tables. For instance, the query to calculate extended price shown in Figure 4.14 can be used to create printed invoices. You can see that query-based reports are more versatile than reports directly based on tables. In this section we show you how to create a report that groups employee records together on their division location (city). The data that is displayed in the report is produced by a query joining the *tblEmployee* and *tblDivisionLocation* tables on matching Division ID values. In *tblEmployee*, that foreign key is called *EmployeeDivisionID*. The corresponding primary key in the *tblDivisionLocation* table is called *DivisionID*. The completed report displays employee information grouped by location city and sorted by employee name within each location. We begin the process by describing the query, which is stored on the Companion CD-ROM, that produces the data upon which the report is based.

Examining the Report's Query. Building a report that lists employees and their division locations begins with a query. We use a query because we can eliminate the location identification number and can apply query selection criteria to produce location-specific reports or a company report—whichever is needed. Joining the *tblEmployee* and the *tblDivisionLocation* tables, we select the DivisionCity field from the *tblEmployeeLocation* table and select the remaining fields from the *tblEmployee* table. Then, if Access does not do so automatically, we drag the DivisionID field from the *tblDivisionLocation* table and drop it on top of the EmployeeDivisionID field in the *tblEmployee* table to join them. (Remember to always drag from the primary key to the foreign key when joining tables.) When tables have identically named fields and one of them is a primary key, Access will automatically join the two tables on those key fields. (You can also join tables in the Relationships window to forge a permanent bond between them.)

The *report* definition will organize the report alphabetically by ascending city names, so the query need not. (In fact, sorting a query's results on one or more fields does not affect the sort order produced by a report based on that query in any way. So don't bother unless you run a query alone or use it to display data in a form. Identify the sort fields in the report definition process.) The query in Figure 4.29 will be the basis of our report. Found on the Companion CD-ROM, the query is called *qryEmployeesByLocation*. Because the information in each row is unique without the employee ID being present, there is no danger that any rows will be eliminated because they are duplicates.

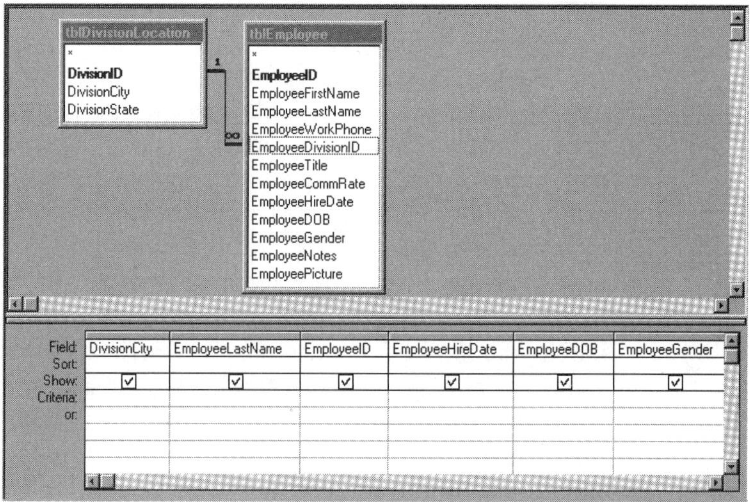

Figure 4.29 Two-table query used by a report.

Now we can create an employee report based on the query. This time we do not list each step. Instead, we describe the initial steps that you should take.

Creating the Initial Report. Begin creating a new report by clicking the Reports tab and then selecting the New button. Select *Report Wizard* from the list of choices and click the drop-down arrow on the text box located below the list of report types. Select from the alphabetized list of tables and queries the query name *qryEmployeesByLocation* and click OK. Select all the fields from the Available Fields list, moving them to the Selected Fields list by clicking the chevron (">>") button. Click Next to go to the next step. Access recognizes the one-to-many relationship between the tables and suggests that DivisionCity be the grouping field. Accept that advice by clicking the Next button to go to the next step. The next step asks if you want to add any grouping levels. In some reports you might want to, but not on this one. Click Next without making any changes to move to the next step. We want the records within each group to be sorted on employees' names. Therefore, click in the first sort list box—the only one available at the moment—and select *EmployeeLastName* from the list of report fields. Notice that *Ascending* is the default sort order. Click Next to move to the Layout and Orientation options screen. Both the suggested default options, Stepped Layout and Portrait Orientation, are fine, so click Next. Again, the Formal report style is fine, so accept that suggested default by pressing Next. In the final Report Wizard screen displayed, change the report's title by typing ***Employees by Location*** in the text box found at the top. Click the Finish button to generate the report and preview it. When finished examining the report, close the Preview window. Remember that the report is saved as the name you typed for the report title—a nonconforming database object name. Be sure to rename the report to something such as *rptEmpLoc*. For your convenience, we have place the report on your Companion CD-ROM as *rptEmployeesByLocation*. Examine that report, or print it if you wish. Figure 4.30 displays the one-page employee report.

Deleting Unwanted Controls. Reports created by an Access Report Wizard sometimes contain controls that are not wanted in the final report. For example, the Report Wizard inserts expressions into a Page Footer section that display the current date, *=Now()*, and the current page number, *="Page " & [Page] & " of " & [Pages]*. You can remove unwanted objects from a report by selecting them and then pressing Delete. Remove those expressions from the Page Footer so you experience how to remove controls from a report. You can delete all objects at once by pressing Shift and clicking each object, then pressing Delete after all objects are selected. Save the altered report design before continuing with your work. Saving your work periodically is a good idea.

Adding a Group Footer. A *Group Footer* is displayed just after the grouping element, the employee's city in our example, changes. Currently, our report does not have a Group Footer because, in part, we have no numeric fields whose sums or averages need to be displayed after a complete group is printed. We add a Group Footer to illustrate how it's done. Display the report in Design view and click the *Sorting And Grouping* button located on the toolbar. When the Sorting and Grouping dialog box appears, click the row selector to the left of the entry *DivisionCity* to select it. Then double-click the Group Footer list box located below in the Group Properties area. This will change the value from "No" to "Yes," which means a Group Footer will be displayed (see Figure 4.31). Close the Sorting and Grouping dialog box. Notice the new Group Footer section in the report.

Adding a Page Break. A *page break* causes the printer to skip to the top of a new page. You can place a page break in any section. For instance, we can place

Employees by Location

DivisionCity	Last Name	Badge Number	Hire Date	Birth Date	Gender
Bridgewater					
	Chang	3609	9/16/93	3/30/73	F
	Ellison	3700	4/18/90	12/12/50	M
	Flintsteel	4082	3/21/86	8/22/54	F
	Watterson	3943	10/10/89	5/1/57	F
Cincinnati					
	English	3432	10/1/89	2/14/52	F
	Halstead	4058	6/16/92	12/22/69	F
	Manispour	4029	12/18/86	2/4/65	M
	Morrison	3458	12/13/85	7/4/52	F
	Shoenstein	3892	9/5/86	3/6/51	M
	Stonely	2240	11/5/84	5/3/57	F
San Diego					
	Gates	3436	4/11/91	3/9/50	M
	Goldman	4112	12/24/86	3/5/58	M
	Kahn	2754	5/14/93	5/29/57	M
	Minsky	4012	10/13/86	4/12/55	F
	Pacioli	1528	8/26/91	5/6/46	M
	Pruski	1364	12/1/96	1/26/75	M
West Lafayette					
	Ballmer	3692	6/16/81	7/13/40	M
	Bateman	4057	2/16/88	5/1/54	M
	Hunter	2318	11/16/89	1/26/50	F
	Kole	3370	2/8/88	3/23/59	M
	Nagasaki	1695	1/28/96	4/10/73	M
	Stonesifer	1301	7/6/92	3/10/62	F

Tuesday, February 24, 1998 Page 1 of 1

Figure 4.30 One-page employee report.

a page break in the Group Footer section. That way, each city listed along with those employees in that city are printed on their own, new page. To insert a page break, display the Toolbox (click the Toolbox button if needed), click the Page Break button, move the mouse to the left side of the report within the Group Footer section. Click the mouse to drop the page break into the report's Page Footer section.

Go ahead and place a page break in the *rptEmployeesByLocation* report so that each group prints on a new page. Figure 4.32 shows the report in Design view with the Toolbox visible and the page break in place. You can remove a page break by selecting it and then pressing Delete.

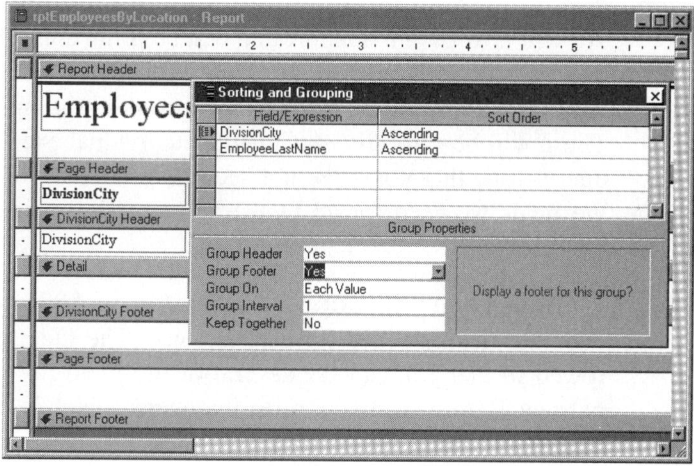

Figure 4.31 Inserting a Group Footer into a report.

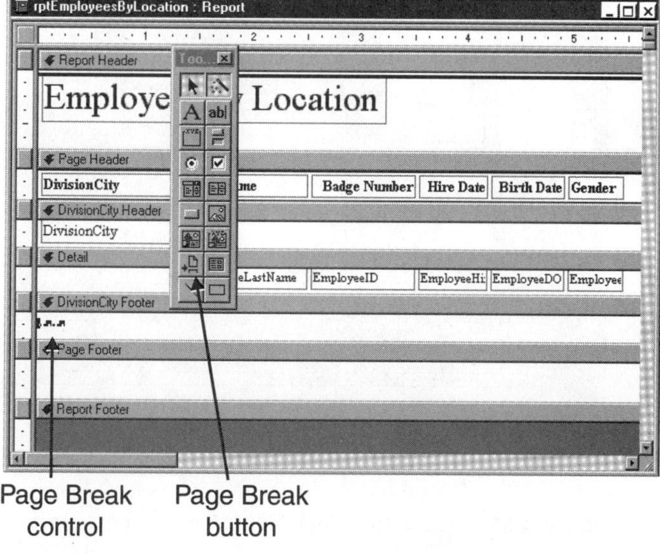

Figure 4.32 Report design with a page break control in place.

Save the report again and print the first two pages to examine the result. Close the report but leave the Database window open. We are done tweaking the design of the *rptEmployeesByLocation* report.

Building Reports with Queries and Expressions

We will next design a report that can be printed as an invoice. You will do a good deal of the work, and some of the procedures we will merely outline. You are familiar with all of the steps needed to build the Invoice report except for a few. These will be carefully explained in individual exercise steps. We begin with the query—one that you have not seen before—that joins six tables to assemble all the fields we need for an industrial strength invoice.

Using a Query to Supply Data. Figure 4.33 shows the query that will produce the fields needed for each invoice. The QBE grid columns have been narrowed so that you can see several of the Field row entries, though most are out of view. Before going on, open the query, which is the foundation of our Invoice report, and study it carefully. The query is saved on your Companion CD-ROM as *qryInvoiceReport*. Observe how the tables are joined.

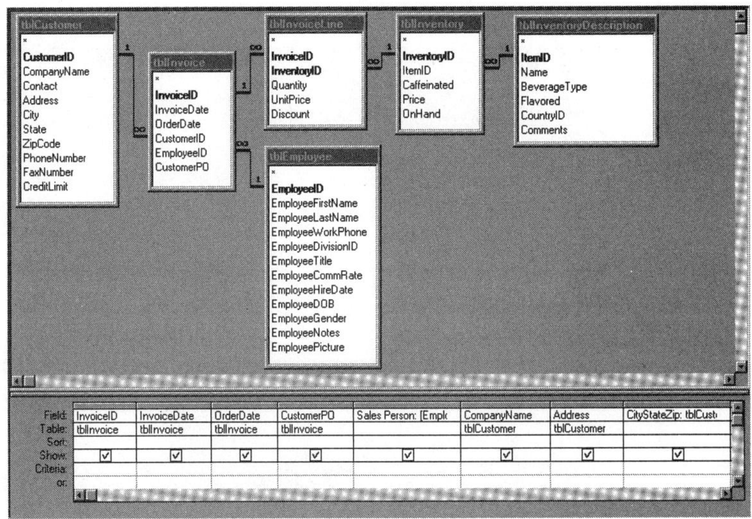

Figure 4.33 Query to select fields for Invoice report.

The *tblCustomer* and *tblInvoice* tables are joined on the column CustomerID. The table *tblInvoice* is joined to the table *tblInvoiceLine* on the column InvoiceID found in both tables. Other joined tables are *tblInvoice* to *tblEmployee* on EmployeeID fields, *tblInvoiceLine* to *tblInventory* on the column InventoryID, and *tblInventory* to *tblInventoryDescription* on the key column ItemID. Thus, the six tables are joined by five sets of primary key to foreign key pairs.

Figure 4.34 shows a typical invoice that we would like to produce with Microsoft Access. The report (one invoice per page) is ready to be mailed to customers.

Invoice

Invoice Number: 214010
Invoice Date: 10/1/97
Order Date: 9/6/97
Customer PO #: 2634-635
Sales Person: Whitney Halstead

The Coffee Merchant
5998 Alcala Park
San Diego, CA 92110

Sold to:
Betz Laboratories Inc.
4636 Somerton Road
Trevose, PA 19053

Item #	Qty	Description	Price	Discount	Extended
119	17	Assam Tara FTGFOP-1	$13.30	10%	203.49
122	14	Ceylon Pekoe Labookelle	$6.20	15%	73.78
131	17	China Keemun	$10.90	5%	176.03
188	17	Vienna	$3.90	0%	66.30
236	18	Rose Potpourri	$6.90	5%	117.99
				Subtotal:	$637.59
				Sales Tax:	0.00
				Shipping:	20.75
				Invoice Total:	$658.34

Figure 4.34 Invoice report.

We begin by generating the initial report using the Access Report Wizard. However, before we proceed, examine this brief list of the general steps needed to create the Invoice report from the *qryInvoiceReport* query:

- Use the Report Wizard, which will automatically group data on the InvoiceID value, to produce the initial report with data supplied solely from the query *qryInvoiceReport.*
- Move selected report fields from the Page Header into the InvoiceID Group Header.
- Move selected report fields from the Report Header into the Page Header.
- Delete the Report Header, Report Footer, and Page Footer sections.

- Create expressions in the InvoiceID Footer that calculate the invoice subtotal, sales tax (if any), shipping, and invoice total amounts for each invoice.
- Add miscellaneous graphics and other labels as needed to embellish the invoice.

Creating the Report's First Draft with the Report Wizard. It is almost always best to create the first draft of a report with the Report Wizard. It is a nasty business creating a report with no help, and the Report Wizard is new and refined for Windows 95. The Wizard determines we need a report with groups because the data is produced from a query whose tables are joined in a one-to-many relationship. That's just what we want. In particular, we want all the invoice detail lines—the item name, quantity, price, discount, and total price—in any given invoice grouped by invoice number.

Let's begin building the first version of the Invoice report. Ensure that the database *Ch04.mdb* is open. Click the Reports tab in the Database window. Then follow the steps in the exercise to create a new report.

Exercise 4.16: Using the Report Wizard

1. Click the New button on the Database window, select Report Wizard, and click the arrow on the Tables/Queries text box to display a list of tables and queries in your database. Click *qryInvoiceReport*, then click OK.
2. Make these choices as you go through the remaining dialog boxes:
   - Select all available fields from the query to appear on the report.
   - Choose to "view your data" by the *tblInvoice* grouping.
   - Select no other groupings.
   - Choose to sort your records in ascending order by the ItemID field.
   - On the sort field dialog box, click the *Summary Options* button and check the box under the Sum column of the Extended row to sum that field, for both detailed and summary fields.
   - Accept the Stepped report layout in portrait orientation.
   - Accept the default Formal report style.
   - Type the report title ***Invoice*** in the text box on the last dialog box.
3. After reviewing the draft report, close it.
4. Rename the report by selecting *Invoice* from the list of reports, pressing F2, and typing ***rptInvoiceCut1***. This name allows you to keep each successive, improved version so you can compare and contrast them.
5. Reopen the just-saved report in Design view.

Figure 4.35 shows the initial report in Design view. Notice that we have removed the rulers and enlarged the window so you can see more of the report. (You can remove the rulers by clicking Ruler in the View menu. The check mark beside the Ruler choice is removed, indicating the rulers will not display. This item is a toggle: select it again to reestablish the rulers.)

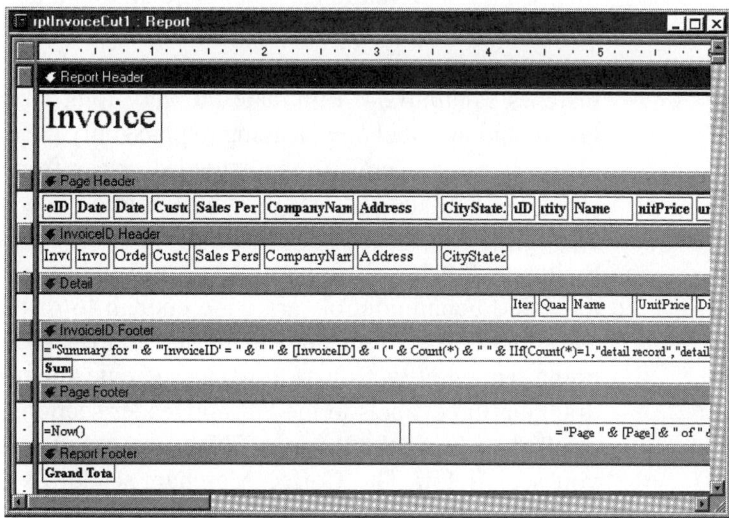

Figure 4.35 Initial Invoice report layout.

Rearranging and Deleting Report Fields. The next major step is to move selected text fields from the Page Header to the InvoiceID Header. Follow the discussion as we outline how to rearrange fields. All the fields in the Page Header will be either moved or eliminated. First, we must make room in the InvoiceID Header. Drag the bottom of the InvoiceID Header area down until the group is about two inches tall. Then, select all fields in the Page Header section (they are all labels). Remember, you first press the Shift key and then click each field in turn to select all of them. Drag the selected fields down into the InvoiceID Header area and release the mouse. Click anywhere to deselect the items. In the Page Header, delete the horizontal lines (select each and press Delete). Move the large label *Invoice* and its attendant horizontal line from the Report Header section to the Page Header section.

Move the ItemID, Quantity, Name, UnitPrice, Discount, and Extended text labels down so that they are just above the bar labeled Detail and about one inch in from the left edge of the report border. With those six controls still selected, move the pointer to the right side of any one object and double-click its side handle to enlarge all labels so their full names are visible. (Label controls are bold, whereas you notice that bound controls displaying field values are not bold.) In a similar way, select the Detail section bound controls and spread them out from one another a bit. With all Detail section controls selected, drag any one of the bound controls' right selection handles to enlarge all selected controls. Delete the labels *CompanyName*, *Address*, and *CityStateZip*. Be careful to not delete the bound controls of the same name! They contain the actual customer information.

Continue to rearrange bound and unbound controls. Do not worry when the labels and associated bound controls do not line up horizontally or vertically. You can fix that later. For now, simply rearrange objects so their approximate location matches Figure 4.34. Eliminate the very long character string in the InvoiceID Footer and the label *Sum*, leaving in place only the expression *=Sum([Extended])*. (The expression sums up the extended prices from each invoice line's extended price, yielding the subtotal.) Using Figure 4.34 as a guideline, rearrange each of the Group Header labels and bound controls so they resemble the layout shown. Switch to Preview view periodically to see how the data and labels line up and to ensure bound controls are wide enough to display the data.

The Coffee Merchant's name and address shown in Figure 4.34 are bold, 12 point, Times New Roman typeface. Create them by opening the toolbox and dragging three labels to the Group Header section, change the Format properties of all three using the Property Sheet, and type the name and address information you see. Below The Coffee Merchant's address is the customer's address. It consists of four bound controls referring to the fields *CompanyName*, *Address*, and *CityStateZip*, which are all supplied by the query. The latter is a concatenation of the three *tblCustomer* fields City, State, and Zipcode. The expression found in the query that "glues" these three fields together is:

```
[City] & ", " & [State] & " " & [ZipCode]
```

where the ampersands are character string operators that "add" one group of characters to the end of another. Once your design is fairly close to Figure 4.34, be sure to save your newly altered design. Name it ***rptInvoiceCut2***.

Now you can simplify the report by eliminating the Report Header, Report Footer, and Page Footer. These contain unneeded lines and summary information—information that is unsuitable for our Invoice report. It is simple to eliminate entire report sections, and you don't need to remove any fields from the sections beforehand. Remove the Report Header and Footer first by clicking the Report Header/Footer selection in the View menu. Click OK when the warning dialog box is displayed. Because you want to retain the Page Header, you cannot use the same technique to eliminate the Page Footer. Instead, simply delete all controls in the Page Footer. This removes the Page Footer itself because nothing prints there or below that band.

Modifying Existing Labels. Notice in Figure 4.34 that the label to the left of the invoice number is *Invoice Number:* (with a colon), not the original label matching the field name, *InvoiceID*. It is easy to alter labels. Click the label you wish to change once and the entire label is selected. Click a second time (do not double-click the label) and an insertion point style cursor is placed in the string so you can add and delete characters. If you find the activity of clicking twice slowly a bit difficult to master, you can use an alternate technique. Double-click the label to bring up its property sheet. Then click the property sheet's Format tab and type in the Caption property text box the corrected label. You can close the property sheet or leave it open. Leaving it open makes it simpler to change other labels' Caption properties. Change all labels in the InvoiceID header to match Figure 4.34. Now is a good time to save your design. A lot of work has gone into the invoice since you last saved it. Select Save As from the File menu to save the invoice under a new name (if you want to track the generation changes). Select a name such as *rptInvoiceCut3* to indicate version three.

Creating Calculated Fields. Calculated fields are created by writing an expression involving arithmetic operators, numeric or character constants, table field names, and report objects. For example, we created an expression in the *qryInvoiceLineItem* query, which provides information for a form, that is the product of the quantity, price, and discount fields. You can create calculated controls, or expressions, in reports as well. For example, Subtotal, Sales Tax, Shipping, and Invoice Total in Figure 4.34 are calculated fields. They are not values stored in tables, because that would violate normalization rules and lead to inconsistent data.

Because the Subtotal, Sales Tax, Shipping, and Invoice Total fields are calculated, their values change with each invoice printed or displayed on the console. The Subtotal report field in the InvoiceID Footer was automatically created by the Report Wizard when you selected Summary Options and checked Sum for the Extended field. The calculated control computes the sum of the Extended Price fields for every invoice. Let's rename the subtotal calculated control so we can refer to it by an appropriate name in subsequent calculated controls such as Invoice Total. Other fields such as Sales Tax and Invoice Total will reference the field holding the summation of Extended Price. Here is how you rename an existing control.

Try it

Click the field in the InvoiceID Footer that sums the Extended Price field. Display its property sheet (double-click the control or click the toolbar Properties button). Select the tab labeled *Other*. Type ***ctlSubtotal*** in the Name property text box, replacing the current entry. Close the property sheet. Prefixes such as *ctl* identify the source of the value—a report control, not a table field. Giving objects names such as ctlSubtotal, ctlSalesTax, and so on accomplishes two important goals.

First, the names document the meaning of the fields you create on a design document (report or form). Second, names are mnemonic and easy to remember when you construct other calculated expressions.

Creating a new field that contains an expression is straightforward. The next exercise explains how to create the ctlSalesTax and ctlShipping calculated controls that are placed just below the Subtotal field in the InvoiceID Footer. First, create more room in the InvoiceID Footer so that it can accommodate the three additional fields, ctlSalesTax, ctlShipping, and ctlInvoiceTotal. Move the mouse to the bottom edge of the footer. When the pointer changes to a double-headed arrow, drag the bottom report edge down so that the InvoiceID Footer is approximately two inches deep.

Exercise 4.17: Creating a Simple Sales Tax Calculated Control

1. Display the Invoice report in Design view, display the Toolbox, and click the Text Box button in the Toolbox.
2. Move the mouse to a position just below the subtotal control in the InvoiceID Footer and drag the mouse to create a control that is the same size as the ctlSubtotal control.
3. Display the control's property sheet and change the control's name: type ***ctlSalesTax*** in the Name property. (Remember, click the *Other* tab to locate the Name property.)
4. Click the property sheet Format tab, select the Format property, and type ***Standard*** (or select it from the drop-down list).
5. Click the property sheet Data tab.
6. Click anywhere inside the Control Source property text box and then click the Build button (it has three dots—an ellipsis) that is subsequently displayed at the right side of the Control Source property. The Expression Builder dialog box is displayed.
7. Because our customers are wholesale customers, we will not charge sales tax (a simplifying assumption). In the Expression Builder box, type ***=0*** and then click OK to close the dialog box. (Notice that Access expressions are just like Excel spreadsheet expressions. They begin with an equal sign and are followed by an arbitrarily complex expression, though just a constant in our example here.)
8. Edit the label to the left of the sales tax control: click it twice and enter ***Sales Tax:***
9. Click the Format tab and change the label's Text Align property to *right*. (Text Align is the last entry in the list of Format properties.)

Leave the property sheet open for the next expression you will build. Next, let's construct the expression to calculate the shipping cost. To keep things relatively uncomplicated, we make the simplifying assumption that shipping is a linear function. It costs $0.25 per pound for every shipment. The number of pounds is determined by summing the Quantity bound control, because Quantity is recorded in *pounds*. The next exercise runs you through building this next expression.

EXERCISE 4.18: CREATING A SHIPPING CALCULATED CONTROL

1. Assuming the Design view of the Invoice report is still displayed, display the Toolbox and click the Text Box button.
2. Move the mouse to a position just below the sales tax control, ctlSalesTax, in the InvoiceID Footer and drag the mouse to create a control that is the same size as the ctlSubtotal control.
3. Change the control's name: type ***ctlShipping*** in the Name property.
4. Click the property sheet Format tab, select the Format property, and type ***Standard***
5. Click the property sheet Data tab, click inside the Control Source property text box, and click the Build button.
6. Type the expression ***=0.25*Sum([Quantity])*** to calculate shipping costs (see Figure 4.36).
7. Click OK to close the dialog box.
8. Edit and right-align the label to the left of the shipping calculated control: enter the text ***Shipping:*** into the label.

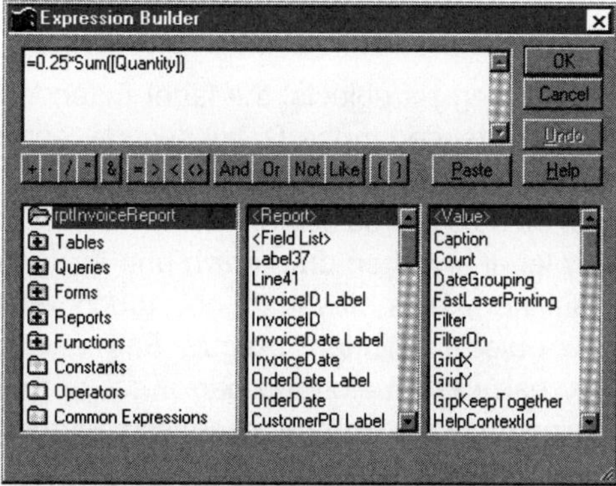

Figure 4.36 Writing an expression.

Click the Print Preview button to verify that the subtotal, sales tax, and shipping values are correct. Click any of the navigation buttons to verify other invoices display correct values for the three controls you have created so far. Switch back to Design view to complete the remaining work on your report. If you haven't already, create a label to the left of the subtotal calculated control and type the text ***Subtotal:*** in the label.

Following the two previous exercise examples, create the Invoice Total calculated control. Name it ***ctlInvoiceTotal***, enter the expression *=[ctlSubtotal]+[ctlSalesTax]+[ctlShipping]* for the Control Source, and choose the Currency format. Edit and right-align the label to the left of the Invoice Total control, typing ***Invoice Total:*** for its Caption property. Though labels attached to text boxes are bold by default, you can bold other controls' contents by selecting the control(s) (Shift-click if more than one) and then changing the Font Weight property (found on the Format sheet) to Bold. Save the report once again to preserve your work.

Aligning and Sizing Fields. It is important to know how to align report controls (fields) and size them so that your report has a pleasant and professional look. Up to this point you have not been concerned with how labels and data are aligned. For instance, we have ignored the fact that the Extended label in the InvoiceID Header appears far to the left of the actual prices in the detail lines below it. A simple exercise will illustrate how to align one column of values. Once you have aligned and sized one column, you can repeat the same steps for other labels and values.

In preparation for the next exercise, ensure that the report *rptInvoiceReportCutx* (where *x* is the number corresponding to your latest version of the report), is displayed in Design view.

EXERCISE 4.19: ALIGNING AND SIZING MULTIPLE FIELDS

1. Select the following six objects: the label Extended in the InvoiceID Header, the bound control Extended in the Detail section, and the four calculated controls ctlSubtotal, ctlSalesTax, ctlShipping, and ctlInvoiceTotal. Release the mouse when all six objects are selected. Hint: Select all the objects by clicking above the topmost label and then drag down and through the objects. Keep the rectangle outline narrow so you do not "touch" other objects (see Figure 4.37).
2. With the six objects selected, execute Format, Size, to Narrowest. All six objects are resized to match the narrowest of them all.
3. Align all objects on the right by executing Format, Align, Right. All objects snap into vertical alignment on the rightmost object of the six.
4. Click outside the objects to deselect them.

Repeat the preceding four steps for the label/value pairs ItemID, Quantity, UnitPrice, and Discount. However, the Name column must not be narrowed,

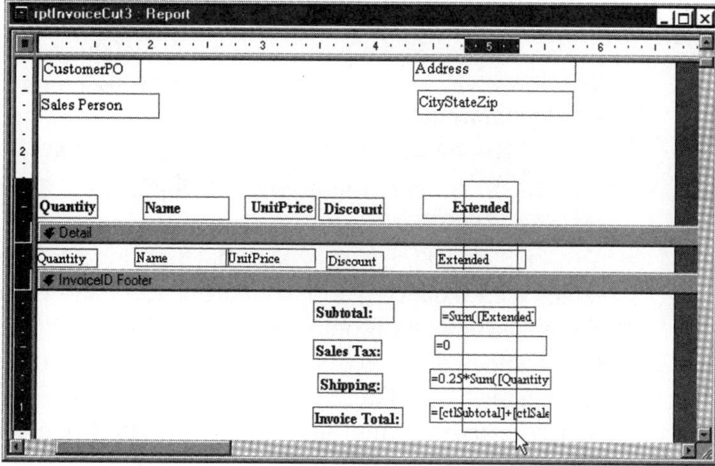

Figure 4.37 Selecting multiple objects across report sections.

because it displays rather long names of coffees and teas. Instead, size the Name label and value controls by executing Format, Size to Widest. The Name label in the header widens to match the values in the Detail section. If necessary, you can widen both controls later to accommodate long descriptions.

Finally, place a Page Break control near the bottom of the InvoiceID Footer, below all existing InvoiceID Footer controls already in place. Be sure to place the page break far enough down so that it will fall below the Shipping and Invoice Total controls. Save your report one more time.

Preview your Invoice report in the Report window. Your screen should resemble the one shown in Figure 4.34. There are several small embellishments you need to add to spruce it up, but you can fine tune your invoice any time you wish. So that you will have a good base from which to understand this report, we have saved the complete Invoice report and named it *rptInvoiceReport* on your Companion CD-ROM. You can improve on your design, or you can study ours.

SUMMARY

This chapter has emphasized using Access to create tables, queries, forms, and reports. You have learned how to create and populate tables and to establish referential integrity for selected attributes. The importance of selection and specification of primary keys has been stressed. You know how to write and save queries that involve both single and multiple tables. Queries can contain expressions comprised of comparison operators, arithmetic operators, example elements, and wildcard characters. Using queries, you can focus on the data elements important to you.

You crafted forms for several tables that display a friendlier, more intuitive interface between the form user and the database. You learned how to select tables and join them, how to add columns to forms, and how to change the properties of fields on the form.

Lastly, you have had a lot of exposure to Access reports. You built a tabular-style report using a Report Wizard. You learned that reports can receive their data from both tables and queries. One of the reports you built contained a query. You also created an invoice report that tied together six of The Coffee Merchant's tables with a query. Various report headers and footers were described including group headers and footers, and you added calculated controls to the group footer that computed invoice subtotals, sales tax, shipping, and total invoice values. Having read this chapter, you can work with the four major Access components—tables, queries, forms, and reports—to build richly featured accounting database systems that serve the needs of your users.

REVIEW EXERCISES

MULTIPLE-CHOICE QUESTIONS

1. If you want to list all male employees in the Accounts Receivable department, which object would you use to reduce the possible results to just the requested persons?
   a. table
   b. form
   c. query
   d. report
2. If you wish to add a column to an existing table, you must
   a. first enter Edit mode.
   b. display a table in Design view.
   c. change the table's Datasheet view properties.
   d. disable referential integrity checks.
3. A query involving more than one table must indicate how the tables are related to each other by
   a. minimizing them.
   b. displaying their property sheets.
   c. linking them.
   d. drawing link diagrams.
4. While displaying the property sheet of a control on a form, you can change the control's
   a. size.
   b. font size.

c. orientation.
d. position.

5. The easiest way to create a default form for a single table is to open a Table window and then
   a. right-click the Form button.
   b. click the Query button.
   c. right-click the Table button.
   d. click the AutoForm toolbar button.
6. One advantage of using a query as the foundation of a report is that
   a. a query is the only way to join multiple tables.
   b. different reports can be run from a query by changing the query's selection criteria and rerunning the report.
   c. tables cannot be used to create a report.
   d. a query is protected from unauthorized access.
7. A report can be used to
   a. change data in a table.
   b. print information found in one or more tables.
   c. input information into multiple tables.
   d. none of the preceding can be accomplished with a report
8. What is the expression to form a subtotal of a control called Extended Price?
   a. =Sum(Extended Price)
   b. =Sum[Extended Price]
   c. =Sum([Extended Price])
   d. Sum[Extended Price]
9. Information that is unsorted can be organized into related groups in a report by
   a. creating a page footer.
   b. creating a sort footer.
   c. creating a calculated field.
   d. creating a group header or footer.
10. You can align objects that lie in different sections or bands of a report. After selecting the objects to be aligned, you execute what?
   a. Format, Size All
   b. Format, Align
   c. Format, Snap to Grid
   d. View, Align

DISCUSSION QUESTIONS

1. Discuss the advantage(s) of providing a list box or a combo box in a form. How does it help a user? What possible disadvantages are present when using a list box control?

2. Explain why referential integrity is so important when dealing with a database, such as The Coffee Merchant's, involving several related tables. Give a scenario in which the lack of referential integrity could cause problems. Be specific.
3. Discuss the problem with storing an extended price (an invoice item quantity multiplied by the item's wholesale or retail price) in the *tblInvoiceLine* table. Why could you not simply add a column called ExtendedPrice to the Invoice Line table?
4. What advantages are there to using a form to view or update data in a table? Are there any disadvantages to using a form rather than viewing the table directly?
5. Explain why you might want to use a form to search a database. Can you change values in underlying tables through a form? Explain.

EXERCISES

1. Add a column called RepAddress to the *tblEmployee* table. Enter any address information up to 20 characters in the new column for the first six sales representatives. Use any data you wish. Print the altered *tblEmployee* table and the table's structure.
2. Create a query to list the ItemID, OnHand, and Name values for all inventory items whose on-hand amount is between 1 and 139 pounds, inclusive. Sort the result in descending order by the OnHand value. Print your result. (You should have fewer than a dozen rows in the dynaset.)
3. Write a query to display invoices with an invoice date between December 5, 1997 and March 10, 1998 (inclusive). Display the *tblInvoice* table fields InvoiceID, InvoiceDate, and CustomerID. Also display the CompanyName and Contact person from the *tblCustomer* table. Print the resulting dynaset.
4. Create a query that produces invoice information from The Coffee Merchant's tables: *tblInvoice*, *tblInvoiceLine*, *tblEmployee*, *tblCustomer*, *tblInventory*, and *tblInventoryDescription*. Display the following columns: InvoiceID, ItemID, Quantity, UnitPrice, Discount, InvoiceDate, OrderDate, CustomerID, EmployeeLastName, CompanyName, and PhoneNumber. Write the expression for extended price **Quantity*Price*(1-Discount)**, and rename the resulting column **Extended Price**. After you have completed the query, run it and then print the result.
5. Create and print the report shown in Figure 4.2. The report displays information from the two tables *tblEmployee* and *tblEmployeeTitle*. The latter contains two columns, title identification numbers (the primary key) in the first and job titles in the second. Include a title at the top of each page, and include your name, course number, and section in the report band. You do not need to include a page break.

6. Create a report that lists employee last name, employee first name, and their sales in order of the employee's last name. Employee sales data is stored in the table *tblSalesTransactions.* The foreign key in that table linking it to employees is EmployeeID. Once you get the query right, produce a report showing all sales transactions for the employees whose last names are Pacioli, Hunter, or Ellison. Include an unbound control containing your name. If your instructor requests it, include other unbound controls (labels) indicating other identification information such as the course name and section number.

5 AUTOMATING PROCEDURES AND MANAGING DATA

OBJECTIVES

Chapter 5 explains the art of automating commonly used procedures and how to use selected Access data management procedures. You will learn how to write macros and attach them to command buttons. You will also learn how to use other macros to create your own customized drop-down menus that operate just like other Windows menus. You will not learn how to program; that would be both pointless and beyond the scope of this book. This chapter teaches you how to create useful and professional-looking enhancements that make using your forms and reports even easier. In particular, you will learn:

- What events are and how they propagate throughout your application.
- How actions are recognized and triggered by events.
- How to write macros and attach them to buttons.
- How to create form navigation buttons.
- How to create automatic data validity, range, and reasonableness checks in a form.
- How to write a specific procedure to ensure that inventory stock levels are sufficient to fill an order.
- How to copy, rename, and delete Access database objects.
- How to link tables to your database.

INTRODUCTION

Access contains a powerful tool: the macro. A macro is a single action or a series of actions stored as an object. Macros help you automate and simplify the use of tables, queries, forms, and reports. You can automate nearly every task with a macro, reducing the effort to carry out a task to just a few mouse clicks. Macros can be used to create complete turnkey applications, or they can be used to simply enhance an application with small code segments performing specialized duties. Though entire applications can be automated using macros, doing so would be beyond the scope of this text. Our objective here is to introduce you to a few useful language elements that can simplify the use of your applications and automate sometimes arcane procedures. Then you can use these representative examples in your applications, applying the techniques you learned to specific situations you encounter.

When you click a button on the Access toolbar, you change the state of that button. It changes from unclicked to clicked. Similarly, whenever you use a keyboard or a mouse, you are changing the state of something within the computer. An object's state is its list of characteristics, and Access keeps track of each object's set of possible states. For instance, one state a button can be in is *enabled*. Otherwise, it is *not enabled*. Access knows that if a button's state is not enabled, then an application cannot click the button. Furthermore, Access displays the button's "not enabled" state by dimming it. The importance of Access and the states of objects is that Access provides you the opportunity to interrupt processing that follows each change of state. For instance, Access recognizes when a button is clicked by the user and looks for a user-written bit of code that reacts to the button being clicked. Any change of an object's state is called an *event* and one type of program that reacts to an event to perform processing is called a *macro*. A macro can determine how an object behaves after a triggering event occurs. That is, when you attach a macro to an object, the macro can "listen" for an event on that object and react to the event in a prescribed way.

Here's an example where a macro simplifies a process for anyone using a data entry form. You know that to delete data stored in the tables constituting the Sales Order system shown in Chapter 4 (Figure 4.20), you must first delete the order lines from the subform. Once you delete the individual order lines, then you can delete the main order record (the main form in Figure 4.20). However, someone using your accounting system may not know much about database systems generally or Microsoft Access particularly. Therefore, you cannot expect those using your accounting system to know, for example, which keys to press to delete a record or even that you must delete the subform data first.

You can eliminate this and similar difficulties by creating intuitively labeled buttons that carry out the required actions. A button might execute a series of steps to accomplish an action such as editing a data field or searching a database for a particular item. For instance, you can simplify the process of deleting information by creating a button labeled *Delete Record* and placing it on a form. The button invokes a macro that implements an action when the button is clicked. After clicking the button (causing a *click* event), the macro selects a complete record, executes the Select Record command, and then executes the Delete command. By automating frequently used procedures with buttons, you minimize users' keystrokes; they do not have to choose sequences of commands from menus. One button performs a series of steps that accomplish some database task. Those using your accounting system will be happy that they do not have to study and learn the database commands. Instead, they can concentrate on the accounting task at hand.

Figure 5.1 shows an example of a form containing buttons with macros attached to them. When a user clicks the Save Record button, the database is updated with the new record. Similarly, the Cancel Changes button contains a macro that cancels the most recent changes made to the data.

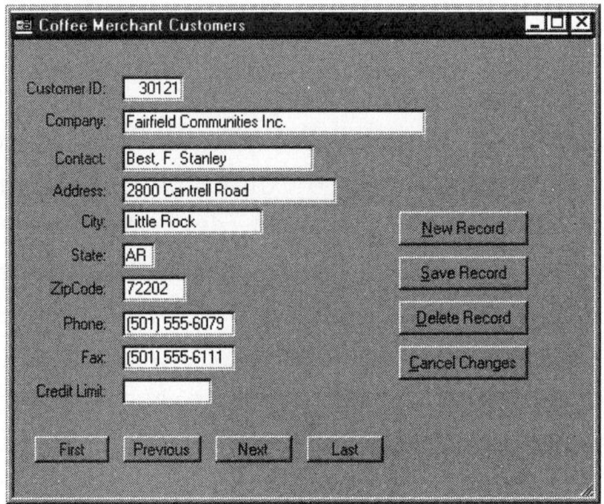

Figure 5.1 Example of a form with action buttons.

A good example of the utility of a button and its attached macro is the New Record button on The Coffee Merchant's Customers form. The New Record button contains a macro that is part of a larger unit called a *macro group*. The macro associated with the New Record button is called NewRec and it contains several steps. Figure 5.2 shows the NewRec macro and surrounding macro definitions that are part of the larger family of related macros.

What is the macro doing? It has four steps or actions: Echo, GoToRecord, another GoToRecord, and GoToControl. The Echo command freezes the screen while the macro is running to avoid displaying messages and actions in quick sequence. The next two GoToRecord commands move to the last record in the table and then move to the (empty) record following the last one. Finally, the GoToControl moves the focus back to the first field in the form, CustomerID.

Do not be concerned if the meanings of the lines in Figure 5.2 are not apparent to you. You will learn the purpose of each of the statements later in this chapter. The example merely illustrates a typical macro.

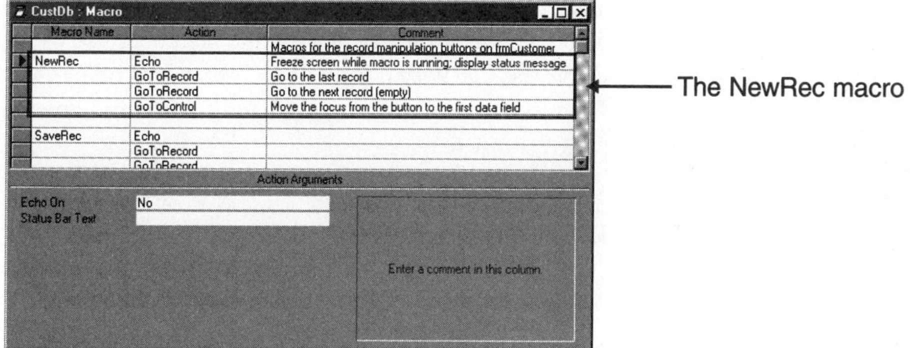

Figure 5.2 The NewRec macro.

Macros can be attached to objects other than buttons on your design documents. You can attach a macro to a form itself. For instance, you can embellish a form with a macro that prompts users for a password whenever the form is opened and before displaying database information. Form fields can have macros attached to them as well. You can modify a form field so its value is validated before the cursor is allowed to pass to the next field.

AUTOMATING FORMS WITH COMMAND BUTTONS

You develop macros by planning them, attaching them to the object whose behavior is to be affected, and then testing the macro to ensure that it works correctly. To understand macros and their usefulness, we will add a few buttons to the Customer form, *frmCustomer.* That form is used to display The Coffee Merchant's customer information and update it. To begin, start Windows and load Microsoft Access. Copy the database *Ch05.mdb* found in the Ch05 folder on your Companion CD-ROM to your hard drive. Once the database is copied, open the database *C505.mdb.*

Creating a Command Button

Let's make things a bit easier for your users by creating on-form database navigation buttons. Though navigation buttons are available in the Form window, the ones we design will be larger and easier to locate. (We have set a form property so that the traditional navigation buttons are not displayed.) Together, we will create a button that will move to the first customer record in the database and display it. After we create that button, you can create three other navigation buttons using the first one as a model. The other buttons move to the next record, the previous record, and the last record. First, we create a button (command button). Then we create a macro that causes an action to occur when the button is clicked. Follow the steps in the next exercise to create a button object and place it on the Customer form, *frmCustomer*.

Exercise 5.1: Creating a Command Button

1. Click the Form button to display the form names in the Database window.
2. Select (click) the form called *frmCustomer* and then click the Design View button to load the form and display it in a Design window. Maximize the form so it fills the window. (The form is a slightly improved version of the Customer form you saw in earlier chapters.)
3. Place the Toolbox on the work surface: select Toolbox from the View menu. Drag the Toolbox to the right edge of the window so it is out of the way.
4. Click the Toolbox Command Button tool (see Figure 5.3). Then move the mouse pointer below the CreditLimit field in an open area. Click the mouse to drop the button onto the form. If the Command Button Wizard dialog box is displayed, simply click the Cancel button located near the bottom of the dialog box. (We do not need the Wizard's help to create our first button.)
5. Click the newly created button twice *slowly* until a vertical bar (the *insertion point*) appears within the button's label.
6. Using the Backspace and Delete keys, remove the current button label (*Button25*, for example) and type ***&First*** in its place. Click outside the button to deselect it.
7. Select Save from the File menu and type ***frmCustomer1*** in the New Name text box of the Save As dialog box. Doing so establishes a new form name so you can revert to the original form *frmCustomer* if you need to start over. (Leave the form on your screen, because you will continue to make changes to it.)

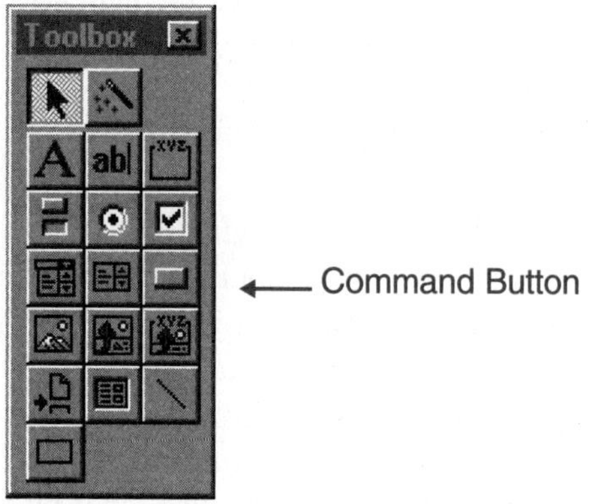

Figure 5.3 Toolbox showing Command Button.

Now that you have a button on the form, switch to Form view and try out the new button. Click it and notice that it seems to do nothing except appear sunken when it is clicked. That is because no macro (an action) has been assigned to the button's *On Click event.* Next, we will give the button some work to do.

Creating a Macro and Attaching It to a Button

To change the way a button behaves when you click it, you attach a macro to one of the button's event properties (it has several). Because you want the button to react and do work when it is clicked, you associate a macro with the button's *On Click event*. You associate a macro with a button's On Click event by displaying the command button's property sheet and writing the macro's name into the text of the Click property. First, though, you must *create* a macro that performs the duties of going to the first record in the database being displayed by the form. Once the macro is created and saved, you can then attach it to an event property.

The next exercise creates the macro that is invoked when the First navigation button (see Figure 5.1) is clicked. Ensure that the form *frmCustomer1* is still loaded and displayed in Design view.

Exercise 5.2: Creating a Database Navigation Macro

1. Maximize the form, click the First button to select it (selection handles appear around the button), and display the button's property sheet (click the Properties button). Drag the property sheet to a location where you can see both it and the navigation button labeled First.
2. Click the property sheet's Other tab, double-click the Name property, and type ***cmdFirst*** (this changes the button's internal name).
3. Display the button's event properties by clicking the property sheet's Event tab. Click inside the On Click property text box. An arrow and a Build button (...) are displayed on the right side of the text box.
4. Click the Build button. When the Choose Builder dialog box is displayed, double-click the Macro Builder choice. The Save As dialog box is displayed.
5. Type the macro name ***CustNav*** and click OK. The Macro Design window is displayed.
6. Move the insertion point to the second row, first (Action) column (each macro instruction is called an *action*). Click the arrow to display the *action list.*
7. Scroll the list until the action *GoToRecord* appears. Click that action to place it into the Action column.
8. Click the comment column to the right in the same row and enter the comment ***Move to the first record*** in that cell.
9. In the bottom portion of the display, specify the arguments for the action: Click the Record row in the argument list, click the arrow, and select *First*

from the list. The hint box to the right is displayed when you click an action argument box. It gives you information on what to specify for the action argument.

10. Select Macro Names from the View menu to display the Macro Name column.
11. Type the name ***FirstRec*** in the Macro Name column of the same row containing the action.
12. Click the Macro window Close button and click the Yes button when prompted to save the changes.

The completed macro is called FirstRec. It is shown in Figure 5.4. Your macro should look like that one.

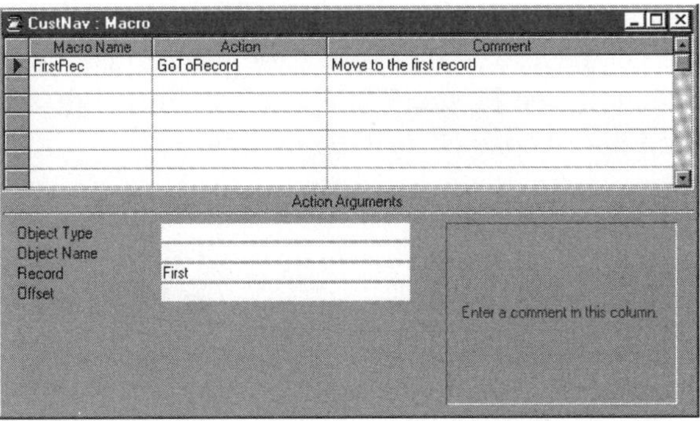

Figure 5.4 Macro window showing the FirstRec macro.

You have just created a macro group. A *macro group* is a macro which contains one or more macros. When you use a macro group, it is easier to keep track of related macros like the navigation button macros. They are contained in one macro rather than stored as several separate macros. Over time, creating individual macros causes their numbers to soar and makes them very difficult to manage. Creating macro groups is no different than creating single macros. The advantage of a group is organization. Related macros can be placed under one "roof" so they can be easily located later. This is especially helpful when you have an application with hundreds of macros.

Although you have attached the CustNav macro—a *group* macro name—to the First button's On Click event, the actual macro name must be changed to FirstRec. After all, FirstRec is the name appearing in the Macro Name column of the CustNav macro group. FirstRec contains the code to move to the first database record. So, let's change the macro name associated with the First button's On Click event. The next exercise shows you how simple this change is.

Exercise 5.3: Attaching a Macro to a Button's On Click Event

1. With the form in Design view, select the First button and display its Event properties.
2. Click within the On Click text box and then click the down arrow that appears on the right side of the text box (see Figure 5.5). (Be careful to not click the Build button, because that will display the macro itself, not the list of macro names.)
3. Click the choice *CustNav.FirstRec* in the selection list. (You refer to a particular macro that is part of a macro group by specifying the macro group name, a dot, followed by the macro name.)
4. Click the property sheet's Close button.

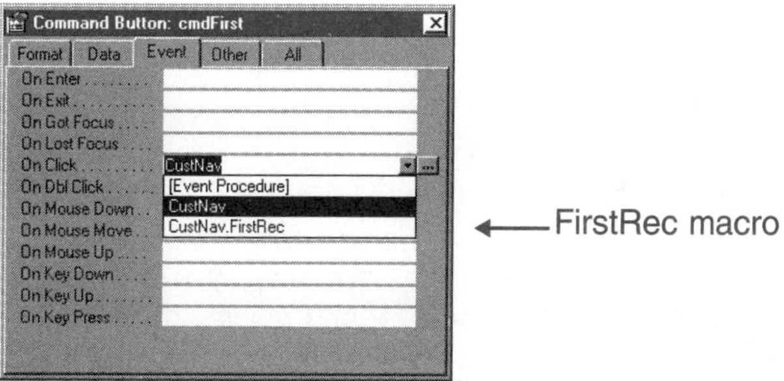

Figure 5.5 Selecting a macro to attach to an On Click event.

Try out the new button. First, return to Form view and then select Edit, GoTo, Last to move to the last customer record. Now, click the First button. The first record is displayed! In the next section, you create the remaining three navigation buttons by building additional macros housed in the CustNav macro group.

Creating Other Form Navigation Buttons

Creating the remaining navigation buttons, which mimic the duties of the form's traditional navigation buttons, is relatively simple. You have created the first of these already. The procedure is similar for the Previous, Next, and Last navigation buttons. To save a little time, you can select the First button, copy it to the Clipboard, click any open area of the form, and paste the copy onto the form. Then, change each button's label and create and attach a new macro to it. Changing the label is simple for you by now, but you may wonder how to create a new macro—one that is part of the CustNav macro group—and attach it to a new button. We guide you through the process of creating a second navigation button. Then, we ask you to produce the other buttons on your own.

If you haven't done so already, clone the button labeled *First* by copying it to the Clipboard and then pasting it back onto the form. Then, change the button's name. Click the newly cloned button a second time so the insertion point is displayed within the label. Erase the current label and enter ***Previous*** in its place. Repeat this process, cloning and labeling the buttons ***Next*** and ***Last***. When you are done, you will have four buttons (First, Previous, Next, and Last) displayed on your *frmCustomer1* form. All the navigation buttons currently activate the same macro (FirstRec), however.

The next exercise describes the process of adding three more macros called *PrevRec*, *NextRec*, and *LastRec* to the CustNav macro group. When completed, the CustNav macro group will have all the required navigation button macros. All that will remain to be done is to attach each macro to the appropriate navigation button.

Exercise 5.4: Adding a Macro to the CustNav Macro Group

1. With the *frmCustomer1* form displayed in Design view, right-click the Previous button, select Properties, and display the properties in the Event tab.
2. Click inside the On Click event text box and then click the Build button. The CustNav group macro is displayed in the Macro window.
3. Click in the second empty row below the last line of the FirstRec macro. Type ***PrevRec*** in the Macro Name column. (This gives a name to the macro.) Be sure there is a blank row between the FirstRec and PrevRec rows. The blank row is not necessary, but it provides visual space between successive macros.
4. Press Tab to move to the Action column, click the down arrow, and select the GoToRecord action from the drop-down list.
5. Press Tab and type ***Move to the previous record*** in the Comment column of the same row.
6. In the Action Arguments panel, select *Previous* from the Record argument list (click the Record text box and then click the drop-down arrow to display the list of possible arguments).
7. Repeat steps 3 through 6 twice more, entering the NextRec and LastRec macros. With the Macro window displayed, move to the fifth row and enter ***NextRec*** in the Macro Name column. Select the GoToRecord Action, and select the Record argument *Next.* Enter the comment ***Move to the next record*** in the Comment column. Finally, enter ***LastRec*** in the seventh row's Macro Name column. Select the action GoToRecord with the Record argument *Last.* Enter the comment ***Move to the last record*** in the Comment column. Your CustNav macro group should resemble Figure 5.6.
8. Save the completed CustNav macro by clicking the Macro window Close button. Press the Yes button when you are asked if you want to save your

changes to the CustNav macro. Microsoft Access stores the CustNav macro in the Database window on the tab marked *Macros*. Click the Database window Macros tab to see the macro name in the list.

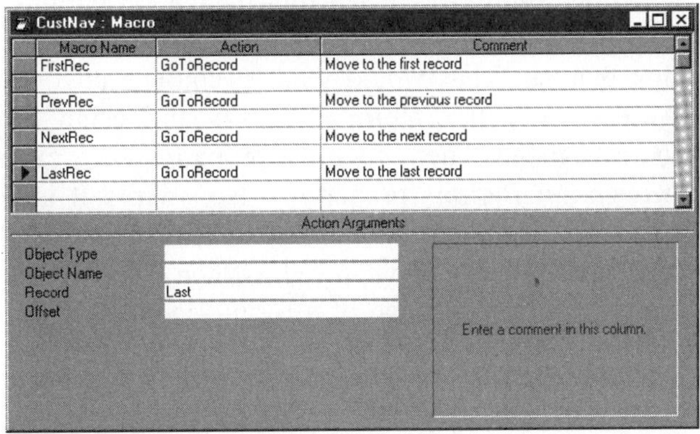

Figure 5.6 Completed CustNav macro group.

Complete the process of building navigation buttons by attaching the three new macros in the CustNav group to their respective buttons. You have already done this task in Exercise 5.3; repeat those steps to attach the PrevRec macro to the Previous button, the NextRec macro to the Next button, and the LastRec macro to the Last button. Remember that you do not have to close the property sheet after changing each button's On Click event. Simply click another button and change its On Click event property without closing the property sheet. After you do these three tasks, be sure to save the *frmCustomer1* form to preserve your work.

If you want to size the navigation buttons so that they match Figure 5.1, take a moment to complete the next exercise.

Exercise 5.5: Optimizing Button Sizes

1. In Design view, select all four database navigation buttons.
2. Execute Format, Size, to Fit. This optimizes the button lengths to be just long enough to display the buttons' names.
3. With the four buttons still selected, make them all the same length but no longer than the longest button by executing Format, Size, to Widest. This step sizes the buttons to a uniform width.
4. Finally, grab one of the handles in the middle, top edge of a button and drag it toward the bottom edge to reduce the height of all the buttons slightly. Ensure that you can still see the buttons' labels, however.

5. Rearrange the buttons so that they appear side by side as shown in Figure 5.1.
6. Save the form (select Save from the File menu).

Now that you have created four navigation buttons of your own, you can eliminate Access' built-in navigation buttons. There's no need for two sets of navigation buttons. That would tend to confuse anyone using your form. Eliminate Access' navigation buttons this way. In Design view, choose Select Form from the Edit menu. Then, open the property sheet, click the Format tab, and set the *Navigation Buttons* property to No. While it is convenient, let's also set the *Record Selectors* form property to No by double-clicking the Record Selectors text box until No is displayed. (When Record Selectors is set to Yes, an arrow appears in the left edge of a form—something we don't need on our form.)

Printing a Macro or Macro Group

You should always save a macro prior to testing it. The FirstRec macro of the CustNav macro group created in Exercise 5.2 was saved when you closed the Macro window and clicked the Yes button when prompted to save the macro. If you have made changes to your macro but have not yet saved it, Access displays a dialog box to remind you to save the macro. You can choose Yes to save the changes (or No to bypass saving the changes).

One part of documenting your developing or completed system is to maintain a printout of all macros you have written. Perhaps you will keep these in a notebook along with printouts of forms, reports, queries, and other relevant documents. To print a macro, display it in the Macro window and select Print from the File menu. Then, click OK when the Print Definition dialog box displays. That's all there is to it. You must repeat this process for *every* macro you want to print because, unfortunately, there is no way to print more than one macro at a time. This is another reason for grouping related macros together in a macro group—you can print several macro definitions at once by printing the group macro containing them.

IMPLEMENTING DATABASE MANIPULATION BUTTONS

Other useful buttons that can save time for your users and simplify their work include those that update a record, insert a new record in the database, delete an unwanted record, post all changes to a record to the database, and cancel (negate) any changes made to a record. While these tasks can be accomplished by using the Access menus, those menus can be intimidating to anyone not familiar with

Microsoft Access. So, we show you how to create the buttons and associated macros to accomplish these important database tasks. We continue to use The Coffee Merchant's Customer form. When you are done with this section, your form (*frmCustomer1*) should resemble Figure 5.1, and all the form's buttons should work correctly.

Creating the Save Record and New Record Buttons

Users want to be able to easily save a record and add new records to a database. You can facilitate these two operations by providing buttons that perform those functions. Saving a record is implemented neatly with a macro. The Save Record button saves all changes to the current record by moving to the next record and then moving back to the changed record. Moving "off" the altered record causes Microsoft Access to write the record to the database before moving on to the next record. It is as simple as that.

Let's examine how to build the macro to be attached to the Save Record button. As with creating the navigation buttons, two major steps are involved. First, place a button on the form; second, create a macro to carry out the action and place its name in the button's On Click event property text box. Create the Save Record button by repeating Exercise 5.1, steps 4 through 6. This time, type the button label ***&Save Record***, being sure to include the leading ampersand. (The ampersand causes the character following it to be underlined, and this allows the user the alternative of pressing Alt+S to save a record.) You may have to lengthen the button to make the entire label visible, or execute Format, Size, to Fit. Change the button's internal name: click the Other property sheet tab and type ***cmdSaveRecord*** in the Name property text box. Close the property sheet. Then, follow the steps in the next exercise to create a new macro group called *CustDb*. The first macro in the group, named *SaveRec*, is created next.

Exercise 5.6: Creating the SaveRec Macro

1. Display the Database window. Click the Macros tab and then click the New button to create a new macro.
2. Select Macro Names from the View menu to open the like-named column in the Macro window.
3. Move to the first row of the macro grid under the Macro Name column, type ***SaveRec***, and press Tab to move to the Action column.
4. Enter the values in the Action column and the Action Argument values indicated in Table 5.1. (Each Action/Argument pair goes in the Action Arguments panel, found in the lower portion of the Macro dialog box, in the same order as in Table 5.1.)
5. Close the macro and save it as ***CustDb***.

Action	Argument	Argument Setting
Echo	Echo On:	No
GoToRecord	Record:	Next
GoToRecord	Record:	Previous

Table 5.1 SaveRec macro actions and arguments settings.

To invoke the SaveRec macro, its name must appear in the On Click event of the Save Record button. Redisplay the *frmCustomer1* form in Design view, display the Save Record button's property sheet, select the Event tab, and click inside the On Click event text box. Attach the newly created SaveRec macro by clicking the down arrow on the On Click event text box and select the macro named *CustDb.SaveRec* from the drop-down list (see Figure 5.7).

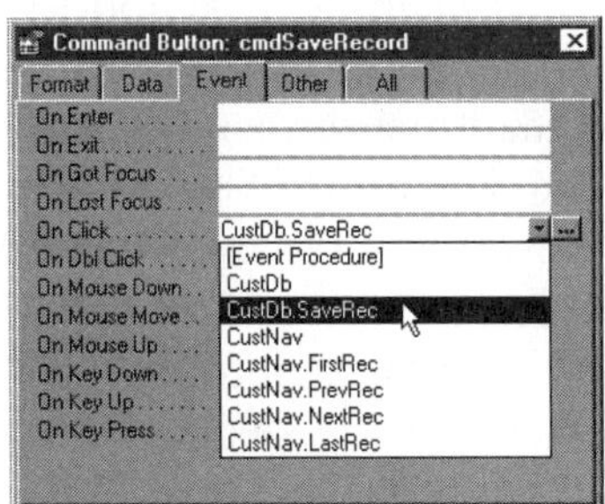

Figure 5.7 Selecting a macro for the Save Record button.

To try out the new Save Record button, let's create a new customer record. First, click the Form View button. Next, use the navigation buttons to move to the last record. Finally, open a new, completely blank record by clicking the Next navigation button. Enter any data you would like, but be sure to assign a CustomerID that is greater than 36,000 (don't type the comma, of course). That way, you will not inadvertently change an existing customer record. Now click the Save Record button. Satisfy yourself that the record was actually posted to the database by alternately pressing the First and Last navigation buttons. After you press the Last button, your new record will be displayed. Figure 5.8 shows an example of a new record after the Save Record button has been pressed. (We will soon create and use a Delete Record button to remove the record you entered so that the Customer database remains unchanged.)

The New Record button is equally simple to implement. Create a new button like you did in Exercise 5.1 (or simply copy and paste the Save Record button). Change the button's label to ***&New Record***. Change the button's internal name to ***cmdNewRecord*** (the Name property found on the Other property sheet tab).

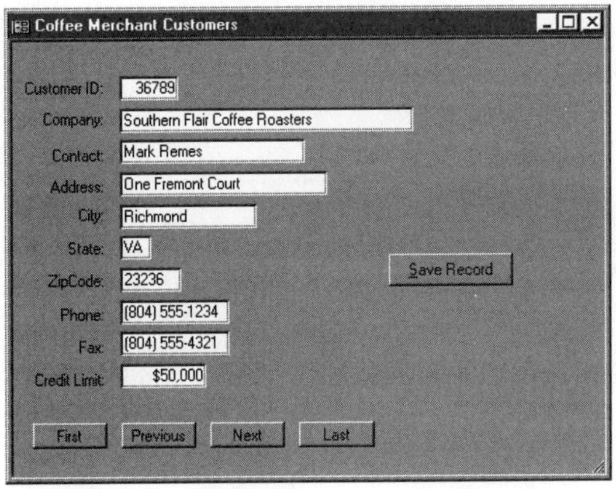

Figure 5.8 Example of an added record.

Add a macro to the CustDb macro group by right-clicking the New Record button and selecting *Build Event* from the pop-up list. The CustDb macro group is displayed. Add the NewRec macro by clicking in the Macro Name column in an empty row. Leave a blank row between the NewRec macro row and any other macro rows. This provides a visual separation between macros. (Execution of a macro halts when a new name is encountered in the Macro Name column.) Enter the actions and action arguments shown in Table 5.2 for the NewRec macro. When you are finished, close and save the CustDb macro group. Figure 5.9 shows you the two macros currently constituting the CustDb macro.

Action	Argument	Argument Setting
Echo	Echo On:	No
GoToRecord	Record:	Last
GoToRecord	Record:	Next
GoToControl	Control Name:	CustomerID

Table 5.2 NewRec macro actions and arguments settings.

To invoke the NewRec macro, its name must appear in the On Click event of the New Record button. Redisplay the *frmCustomer1* form in Design view, display the New Record button's property sheet, select the Event tab, and click inside the On Click event text box. Attach the newly created NewRec macro by clicking the down arrow on the On Click event text box and select the macro named *CustDb.NewRec* from the drop-down list.

Here's what the lines of the NewRec macro accomplish. The Echo action with the *No* argument freezes the screen while the remainder of the macro runs.

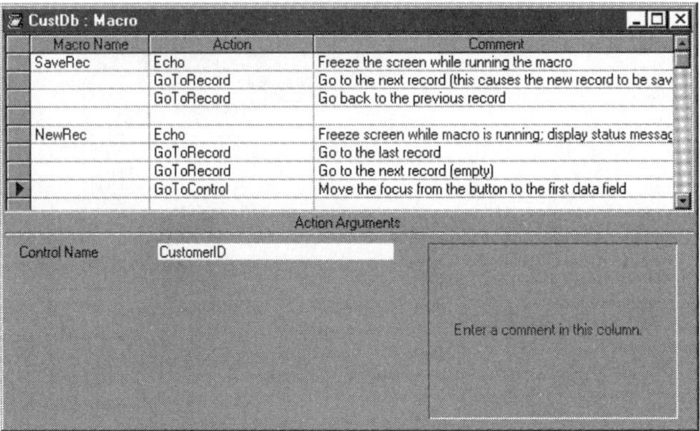

Figure 5.9 The CustDb macro group containing two macros.

This prevents the screen from appearing jumpy during the macro's execution. The first GoToRecord command moves to the last record in the table. The second GoToRecord moves to the next (empty) record. Finally, the GoToControl moves the focus (cursor) to the CustomerID column so that data may be entered immediately.

Creating the Delete Record and Cancel Changes Buttons

The Delete Record button deletes the currently displayed record from the database. In contrast, the Cancel Changes button discards any changes made to the current record, restoring the original record. The difference between the two actions is that the Cancel Changes button restores the original values of a record that has not been posted (saved) in the database. That is, it allows you to rescind any changes to the current record *before* the record is saved to the database. On the other hand, the Delete Record button irrevocably *removes* a record from the database.

Begin building the two buttons by copying and pasting the SaveRec button twice—once for each button to be created. Change the labels on the newly cloned buttons to ***&Delete Record*** and ***&Cancel Changes***. Change the buttons' internal names to ***cmdDeleteRecord*** and ***cmdCancelChanges***, respectively. Resize the buttons, if necessary so each is the same width but only as wide as needed.

The Delete Record Button. Following the same general procedure described earlier, we show you how to create a macro called DeleteRec and how to attach it to the Delete Record button. Follow along in the next exercise as we guide you through the process.

Exercise 5.7: Adding DeleteRec to the CustDb Macro Group

1. Switch to the Database window and click the Macros tab. Select CustDb from the list. Then click the Design button to display the macro group's design.
2. Click in the empty row that is two rows below the last row of the NewRec macro and type ***DeleteRec*** in the Macro Name column. (That is, ensure that there is at least one blank row between the last row of the NewRec macro and the row containing the DeleteRec macro name.)
3. Using Table 5.3 as a guide, fill in the DeleteRec macro Actions and Action Arguments. (You can add comments to each Action row if you wish.)
4. After you complete the four-row macro, click the Macro window Close button to close the window. Click the Yes button when the dialog box appears asking if you want to save the macro design changes.
5. Switch to the *frmCustomer1* Design View window (click the Forms tab, select *frmCustomer1*, and click the Design button) and right-click the Delete Record button. Select Properties from the pop-up menu.
6. Select the property sheet's Event tab and click the On Click text box.
7. Click the down-pointing arrow and select *CustDb.DeleteRec* from the list of macro names.
8. Close the property sheet.

Figure 5.10 shows the DeleteRec macro. Notice that one of the DoMenuItem commands and its Action Arguments are displayed. Examine that figure and Table 5.3 to understand exactly how to enter the correct macro information.

Action	Argument	Argument Setting
Echo	Echo On:	No
DoMenuItem	Menu Bar:	Form
	Menu Name:	Edit
	Command:	Select Record
DoMenuItem	Menu Bar:	Form
	Menu Name:	Edit
	Command:	Delete
GoToControl	Control Name:	CustomerID

Table 5.3 DeleteRec macro actions and arguments settings.

Let's briefly examine the DeleteRec macro code (see Figure 5.10). As before, the Echo with the No argument freezes the screen until the entire macro has completed. The DoMenuItem action provides the mechanism to execute any of the Access commands. The Action Arguments indicate which window's menu, menu name, and command are to be executed. The first DoMenuItem command

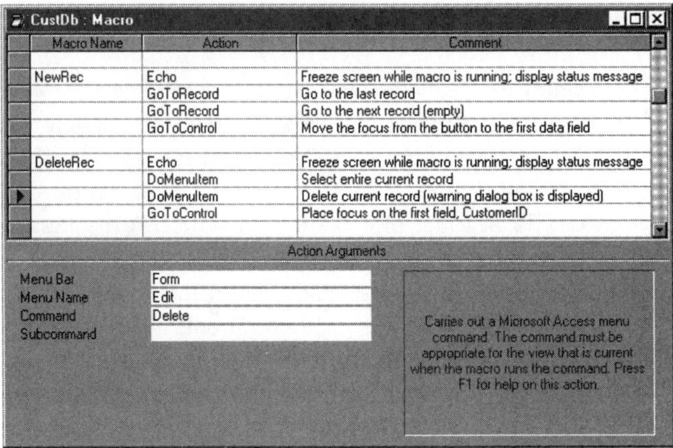

Figure 5.10 The DeleteRec macro.

executes the Select Record command of the Edit menu, displayed whenever a form is displayed. Similarly, the second DoMenuItem command executes the Delete command in the Edit menu of the Form Menu bar. After the Delete command is executed, Access automatically displays a warning dialog box (see Figure 5.11). You have the opportunity to confirm or cancel the delete operation. Last in the four-command macro is GoToControl with the CustomerID Control Name argument. This causes the focus to move from the Delete Record button to the CustomerID field after the current record is deleted. That way, users can immediately return to altering information in the data record, beginning with the CustomerID field.

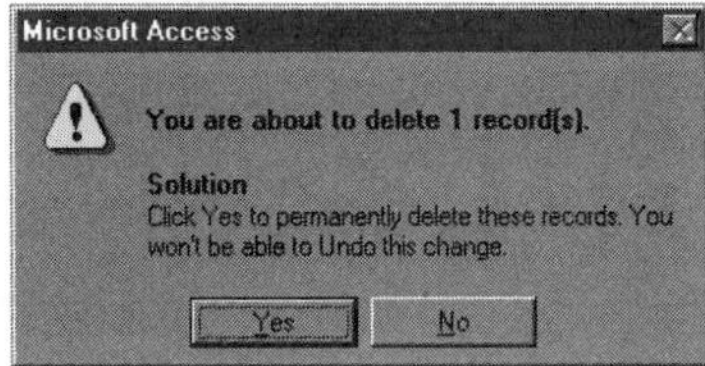

Figure 5.11 Delete record warning message.

The Cancel Changes Button. The macro attached to the On Click event of the Cancel Changes button is similar to the DeleteRec macro. You already have the Cancel Changes button on your *frmCustomer1* form. Cancel Changes will simply negate any changes you have made to the current record.

Create the new macro called *CancelRec* in the CustDb macro group. Repeat Exercise 5.7 to create the CancelRec macro, making these changes: in step 2, type

CancelRec for the macro name and insert the three macro steps shown in Table 5.4 in the macro; in step 5, right-click the Cancel Changes button; and in step 7, select the macro *CustDb.CancelRec* from the drop-down list. Figure 5.12 shows the entire CustDb macro group, including the CancelRec macro and its (optional) comments. The only change in the CancelRec macro is the action argument command *Undo Current Record.* Executed from the Edit menu of the Form Menu bar, Undo Current Record cancels all changes made to the current record. The original record values are restored.

Action	Argument	Argument Setting
Echo	Echo On:	No
DoMenuItem	Menu Bar:	Form
	Menu Name:	Edit
	Command:	Undo
GoToControl	Control Name:	CustomerID

Table 5.4 CancelRec macro actions and arguments settings.

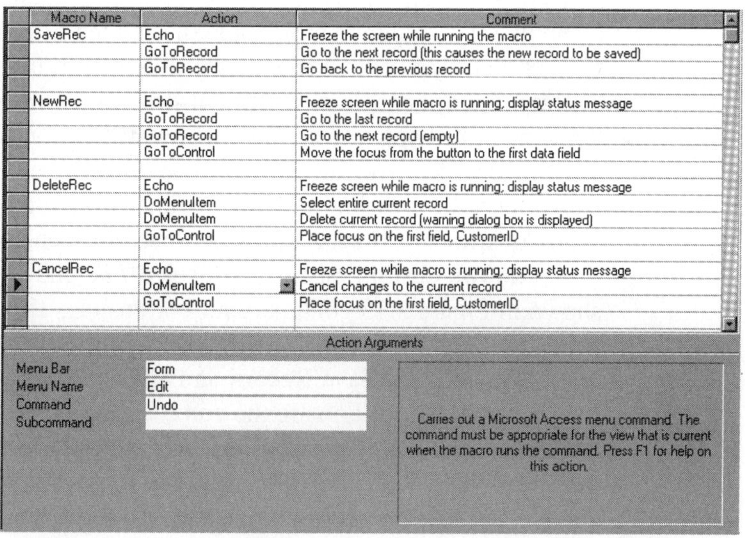

Figure 5.12 The CustDb macro group of four macros.

Try it

Check out the new Cancel Changes button. Switch *frmCustomer1* to Form view, make a few changes to the current record, and click the Cancel Changes button.

All the changes you have made will be rescinded, and the record will be restored to its original form.

This is a good time to save your form, because you have made several changes to it. From the Design View window, select Save from the File menu to save the latest changes to the *frmCustomer1* form.

CREATING ACTION MENUS

Another valuable technique for helping users is the creation of custom menus that replace the Access menus. By creating your own menus, you simplify the command structure and limit the commands available to your users. Custom menus that operate like familiar Windows menus are best, because users are accustomed to the menu and drop-down command style.

This section shows you how to create a custom Menu bar containing two menus. Once you create a few of the menu selections and learn how to display and process them, you can create your own menus. Use these menu-creation techniques as a guide to building menus suited to your own database applications.

Both of the custom menus we illustrate in this section have four command choices. Each menu is a traditional drop-down menu (sometimes called a pull-down menu). When you create a menu system for your application, the development process involves building the menus, displaying the menus, and processing (activating) the selected menu command. Figure 5.13 shows you one of the two drop-down menus displayed for the custom menu we develop in this section.

The two custom menus are labeled *File* and *Database*. The Database menu shown in Figure 5.13 contains four commands. These commands accomplish the same things as the like-named buttons in the form shown in Figure 5.1. The first two commands are Save Record and Cancel Changes. Grouped below the Database menu separator line are the commands New Record and Delete Record. The File menu contains commands that are more global (see Figure 5.14). File menu selections deal with the form, not the database. From the File menu you can choose to close the form, print the form, set up printing parameters, or exit Microsoft Access.

Begin creating a new Customer form by first cloning *frmCustomer1* so you can preserve all your work. (If you make a mistake in any of the ensuing steps, you can always fall back on *frmCustomer1* and begin again.) The simplest way to copy a form is to copy it to the Clipboard and paste it back into the database. Here's how it is done. Click the Form button in the Database window and select *frmCustomer1*. Then select Copy from the Edit menu. Select Paste from the Edit menu. Type the form name ***frmCustomer2*** when the Paste As dialog box is

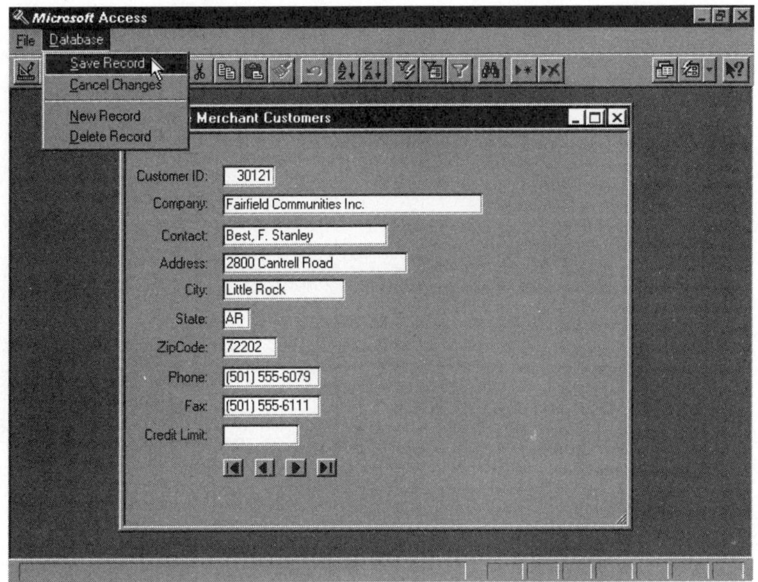

Figure 5.13 Customer form with custom Menu bar.

File	Database
Close Form	Save Record
Print	Cancel Changes
Print Setup	New Record
Exit	Delete Record

Figure 5.14 Custom menu structure.

displayed and click the OK button. Now you have a copy of the *frmCustomer1* form to work with.

Did you notice that the navigation buttons in Figure 5.13 look different? That's because we have changed their appearance to a more familiar look. If you wish to do this to your navigation buttons, then do the following.

Try it

Display *frmCustomer2* in a Form Design window, right-click the button labeled First, and select Properties. Select the Format tab on the property sheet and then click the Picture property text box. (The Picture property displays *(none)*). Click the Build (...) button displayed on the right side of the Picture property text box. The Picture Builder dialog box will be displayed. Drag the Available Pictures scroll box down until the entry *Go To First* appears (there are three entries labeled that way). Select the *first* Go To First entry (see Figure 5.15). Click the OK button to replace the button label *First* with the arrow graphic.

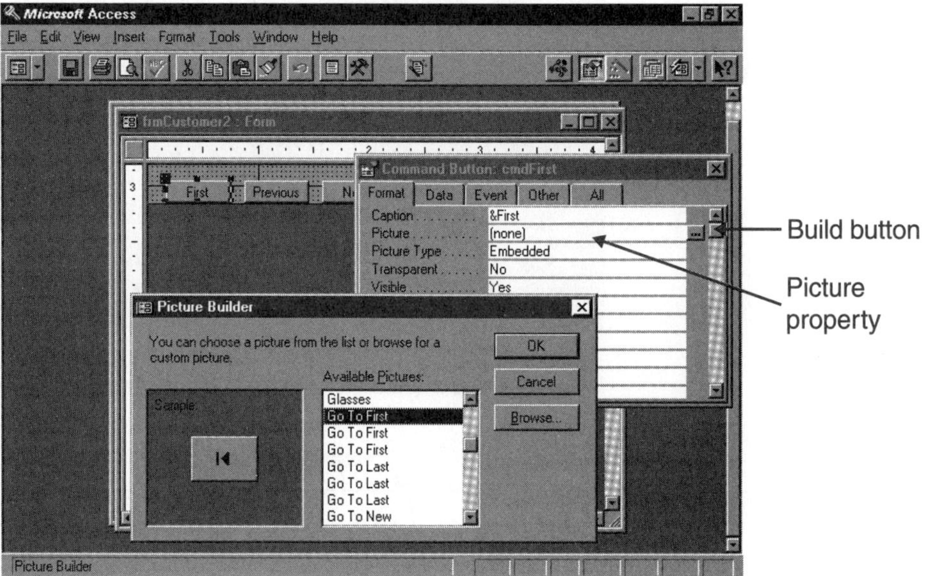

Figure 5.15 Selecting a picture for a button.

Before closing the property sheet, click another navigation button and change its Picture property in a similar way. Do this for the remaining three navigation buttons with text labels. Search for and select the pictures called *Go To Previous*, *Go To Next*, and *Go To Last* in the Available Pictures list. Select arrows that match those shown in Figure 5.13. Then you can close the property sheet and size all the buttons using the Format, Size, To Fit command. Finally, move the buttons into position below the database information controls on the *frmCustomer2* form.

Delete the four buttons labeled *New Record*, *Delete Record*, *Save Record*, and *Cancel Changes* from the *frmCustomer2* form. (Don't worry. Most of the work that went into creating the buttons—building the macros that perform the function—will be preserved!) Those buttons are no longer needed, because their functions will be invoked through menu selections. You delete a button as you would any other object: select the object (a button) and press Delete. Alternatively, you can hold down the Shift key, select all four buttons at once, and press Delete to remove them in one operation. Now we are ready to begin the menu-building process.

Creating a Menu that Mimics Access Commands

There are two distinct types of menus you can display in your application: a global menu or an individual form menu. If you create a *global* menu, it appears throughout your application (though it can be replaced by individual form menus). A *form menu* is one that is attached to an individual form; this type of menu does not persist from one form to another. When another form is opened, the original Microsoft Access menu is displayed.

The general procedure for creating either a global or form menu is the same. You use the Microsoft Access *Menu Builder*, a command located in the Add-ins cascade menu of the Tools menu. The Menu Builder is the easiest way to build your custom menus. An overview of the procedure is as follows: you select Tools, Add-ins, Menu Builder. Then either clone an existing Access menu system or build one from scratch. (We will build ours from scratch.) You establish the menu and command structure, using a special notation to indicate which entries are commands and which are menu names. Simultaneously, you fill in the names of macros and existing Access commands that carry out the actions for each command you create. Building a menu is not a difficult procedure, and the result provides your users with just the commands they need to use your application.

First we build the two menus and their eight commands, indicating which macros and Access commands will carry out the commands. Subsequently, we attach the menu to the *frmCustomer2* form. This way, the commands are *local* to the form, not global. The custom menu is automatically displayed whenever you open the *frmCustomer2* form. When you leave it, the standard Access menus are reinstated. In Exercise 5.8 that follows, you will learn how to build the File menu and its drop-down commands and how to attach macros and existing Access commands to your custom commands. Prepare for the exercise by displaying *frmCustomer2* in a Design View window.

Exercise 5.8: Creating the Custom File Menu

1. Choose Tools, Add-ins, Menu Builder. The Menu Builder dialog box appears. To create a new menu, click New.
2. Choose *<Empty Menu Bar>* from the list of Menu bar templates displayed and click OK. (Of course, you could select the Form menu and begin your menu with that template. However, the process of deleting the many unwanted commands and menus is more work than creating a menu from scratch.) Figure 5.16 shows the Menu Builder dialog box displayed after you click OK.
3. Type ***&File*** in the Caption text box and click the button labeled Next. That places the File menu into the topmost position and moves the insertion point down one row.
4. In the Caption text box type ***&Close Form*** and click the indent (right-pointing) arrow. This inserts a set of three dots to the left of Close Form, indicating it is a command *under* the Form menu.

5. Click the down arrow to the right of the Action text box and select *DoMenuItem* from the drop-down list.
6. Click the Build button (...) appearing to the right of the Arguments text box. The DoMenuItem Arguments dialog box will display.
7. Click the down arrow to the right of the Command text box in the DoMenuItem Arguments dialog box. Choose the Close command from the drop-down list. Click OK to finalize the menu selections (see Figure 5.17).
8. Click the Next button to move to the next menu level.
9. Next, insert a Separator line: Type a hyphen (-) in the Caption text box, press the indent (right-pointing) arrow, and click the Next button.

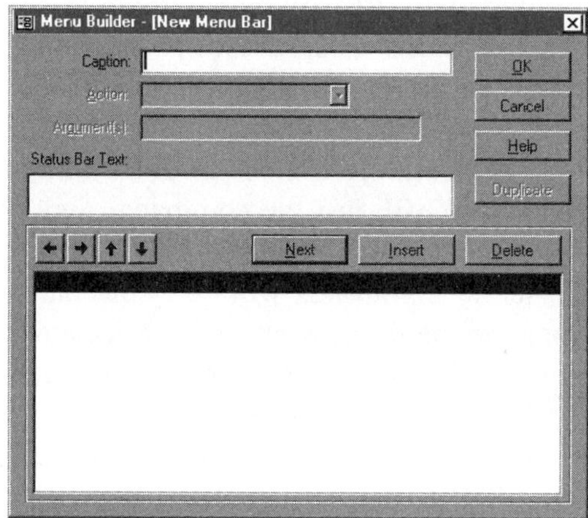

Figure 5.16 Menu Builder dialog box.

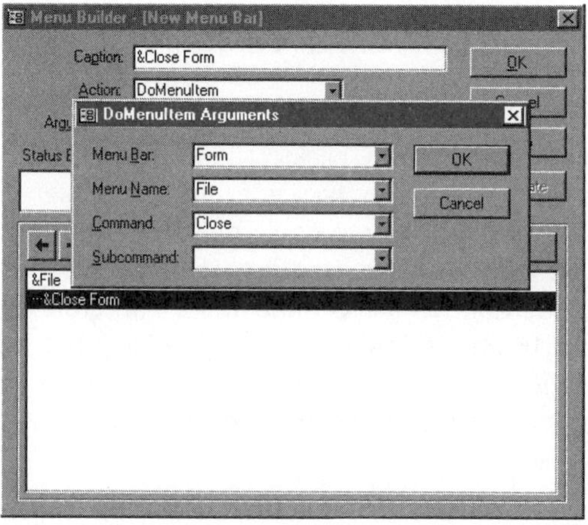

Figure 5.17 DoMenuItem Arguments dialog box.

Add the three remaining commands and separator line following the same general steps listed. Continue building the menu by entering the Print, Print Setup, and Exit commands. Each command uses the DoMenuItem action. Table 5.5 lists exactly how each command is typed and the DoMenuItem Arguments. Be sure to include the ampersands in the indicated position in each command. Doing so allows the user to access the menu or command by typing Alt plus the underlined key instead of using the mouse. Whenever possible, offer your clients alternative choices and methods.

Menu Command	Action	Argument	Argument Setting
&Close Form	DoMenuItem	Menu Bar:	Form
		Menu Name:	File
		Command:	Close
&Print	DoMenuItem	Menu Bar:	Form
		Menu Name:	File
		Command:	Print
Print &Setup	DoMenuItem	MenuBar:	Form
		Menu Name:	File
		Command:	Page Setup
E&xit	DoMenuItem	Menu Bar:	Form
		Menu Name:	File
		Command:	Exit

Table 5.5 File menu commands and their DoMenuItem arguments.

Figure 5.18 shows the Menu Builder dialog box with the completed custom File menu. Save the menu to preserve your work. You will modify the menu later. To save the menu, click the Menu Builder dialog box OK button. Then, type the name ***mnuCustomerMenu*** (no spaces) in the Menu Bar Name text box of the Save As dialog box. Click the OK button to save the macro. This names the customer menu and supplies the prefix name for all macros that are automatically generated to carry out the menu commands. (Click the Database window Macros tab after you save the menu to see the new macros stored there.)

Examine the Menu Builder dialog box carefully as we explain its contents. The File menu structure is similar to an outline. At the topmost level is *&File*. The ampersand precedes the hot key for the menu or command. When the menu is displayed, the letter is underlined. Notice that three dots precede *&Close Form*. This indicates a submenu or command that is a child (subset) of the menu above it and to its left. Every time you press the right (indent) arrow, three dots are added to the left of the entry. That is, indentation indicates where an entry lies in the tree-like hierarchy. An entry which is at the lowest level in a particular menu is a command. Any entry which is a hyphen preceded by dots represents

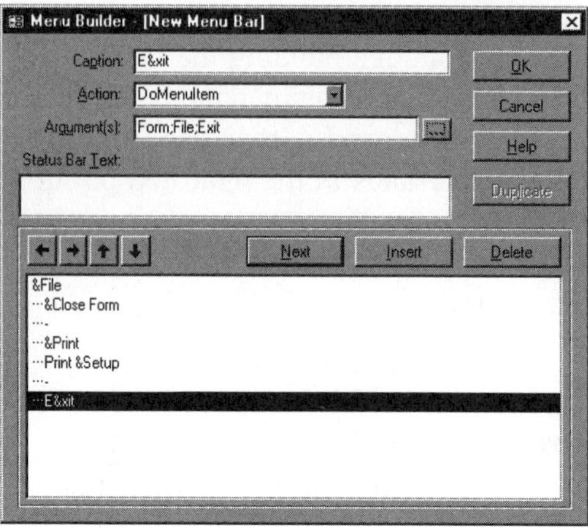

Figure 5.18 Menu Builder dialog box with completed File menu.

a separator bar. It can occur anywhere below the main menu entries in the hierarchy. Figure 5.19 shows how the custom File menu will look when it is activated. Compare the menu to the Menu Builder dialog box to better understand the role of indent, separator bars, and the menu and commands that have been created.

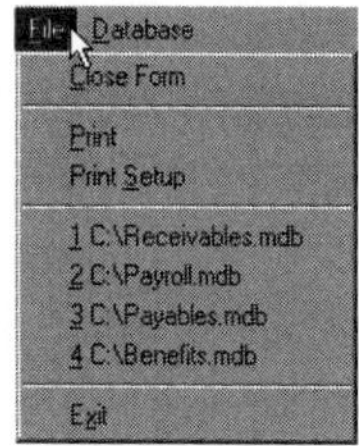

Figure 5.19 The File menu.

Creating a Menu that Uses Macros

Building the custom Database menu is nearly identical to the procedure described in Exercise 5.8. The only real difference is that we will associate our four CustDb database macros with the individual Database menu commands. (Recall that we used *existing* Access commands to implement the custom File menu.) Continue by executing Tools, Add-ins, Menu Builder (the *frmCustomer2* form need not be open while you work on the menu). Select *mnuCustomerMenu* and click the Edit button. The Menu Builder dialog box is displayed (see Figure 5.18). Execute the steps in the following exercise to create the Database menu and complete the custom menu-building process.

Exercise 5.9: Creating the Custom Database Menu

1. Click the mouse below the Exit command to move the dark bar. Type ***&Database*** in the Caption text box and click the Next button.
2. Type ***&Save Record*** in the Caption text box and then click the right-pointing (indent) arrow.
3. Click the arrow to the right of the Action text box and select *RunMacro* from the drop-down action list.
4. Click inside the Argument(s) text box, then type ***CustDb.SaveRec*** and click the Next button. The preceding makes use of the SaveRec macro we wrote earlier. Recall that SaveRec is part of the CustDb macro group.
5. Type ***&Cancel Changes*** in the Caption text box, click the right-pointing (indent) arrow, and type ***RunMacro*** in the Action text box.
6. Type ***CustDb.CancelRec*** in the Argument(s) text box and click the Next button.
7. Type a hyphen (-) in the Caption text box, click the right-pointing (indent) arrow, and click the Next button.
8. Repeat steps 5 and 6 but this time enter ***&New Record*** in step 5 and enter ***CustDb.NewRec*** in step 6.
9. Repeat steps 5 and 6 once more, entering ***&Delete Record*** in step 5 and entering ***CustDb.DeleteRec*** in step 6.
10. Click OK to save the completed custom menus.

After you have completed constructing the Database menu, your Menu Builder dialog box should resemble the one shown in Figure 5.20.

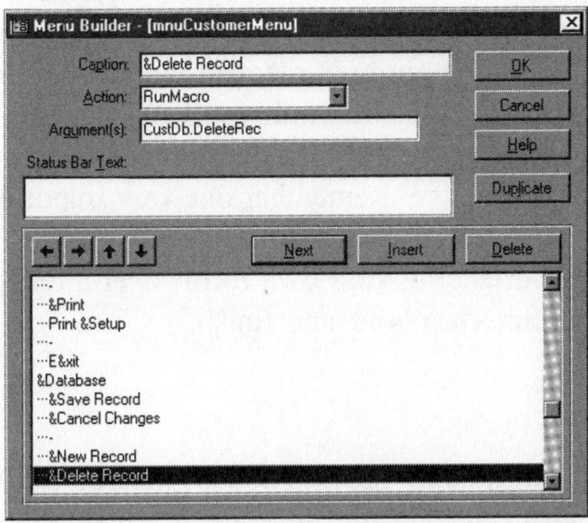

Figure 5.20 Menu Builder dialog box with Database menu.

Attaching a Menu to a Form

Building drop-down menus and their action macros is a major part of creating a functioning menu system, but there is one other task to complete the menu. The custom menu must be attached to the form. This is an uncomplicated procedure. The next exercise leads you through the final step of connecting the *mnuCustomerMenu* menu to the *frmCustomer2* form.

Exercise 5.10: Gluing a Menu to a Form

1. Open the *frmCustomer2* form in Design view.
2. Double-click the form's *form selector* to display the form's property sheet. The form selector is the square button that lies in the upper left corner of the form (Design view) at the intersection of the horizontal and vertical rulers.
3. Select the *Other* tab and click the Menu bar's property text box. An arrow is displayed in the right end of the text box.
4. Click the down arrow and move the scroll box (if necessary) until the name *mnuCustomerMenu* comes into view. Select *mnuCustomerMenu* by clicking it.
5. Save the altered *frmCustomer2* form.

That completes the process of building a custom menu. Try out one or several of the menus. Display *frmCustomer2* in Form view, click the Database menu, and select the New Record command (you can click New Record or type ***n***). Try out the navigation buttons. When you are done experimenting, be sure to close the *frmCustomer2* form. Do not close the database, unless you want to stop for now, because we are not yet done with it. Move to the Database window.

We realize that the particular menus we chose to show you may not be exactly the type of menus you want for your accounting applications. The point is, of course, that you now know how to implement a menu of your own design. Use our menu and techniques as a model for designing your own menus. You may notice that we chose not to implement the navigation buttons with a menu. After a little experimentation, we think you would agree that moving around the database by repeatedly using a menu is tedious and time-consuming. Buttons are a much better alternative. Remember one very important part of building a system: testing. Be sure to try out your creations before releasing them to your user audience. Experiencing your own forms over a test period will reveal any weaknesses in the interface's fit and finish.

AUTOMATING INTERNAL CONTROL FEATURES

Most database systems provide some inherent validity checking whereby input values are checked to ensure they are acceptable. Microsoft Access is no exception, providing a Validation Rule for tables, forms, and controls. For example,

Access can prevent you from entering a number such as 67.89 in a date field on a form, because Access automatically applies data validation based on a field's data type. If you attempt to enter data that does not match the field data type, Access displays an error message. However, even though Access's validity checks are powerful in a general way, they simply cannot handle the more specific checks. Using a form's date field as an example, what do you suppose Access would do if you entered an invoice date such as 10/17/2020 and pressed Enter or Tab? Although that date is probably not reasonable, Access allows you to enter it without issuing an error message.

You *can* detect and prevent erroneous dates as well as prevent other types of data entry errors that would pass Access's fundamental validity tests. Central to validating data are macros attached to events associated with a field or form to be validated. Access macro statements provide powerful features that make elaborate, inter-field validity checking easy to implement.

Macro validation methods are also useful in automating internal controls involving databases external to the application. For example, it is not difficult to write a short macro that checks available inventory of an item as the sales order quantity is being entered. When a sales order line item exceeds stock on hand, a macro can detect the condition and issue a warning message. Additionally, a macro can reduce on-hand quantities to the appropriate value based on the quantity that was entered into an order form. This stock-checking internal control is a business rule that can be enforced best by writing a macro and attaching it to a field.

We show examples of validating a field and enforcing business rules in the two sections that follow. You can use these as models to create your own validity checking and rule enforcement procedures for your accounting applications.

Validating User Input

One example of application-specific data validation is checking a date value immediately after it is entered on a form to ensure it is reasonable. Of course, "reasonable" is a temporal measure and depends on the application. Though we might implement this type of date validation at the root—with the built-in Validation Rule property available for each field in the table itself, writing a macro makes more sense when you want to *share* the validation procedure across forms and applications within the same database. Macro techniques can detect certain errors immediately. Frequently, Access does not identify a mistake until you move off the current record. Depending on automatic validity checks provided by Access can delay recognizing mistakes, which can sometimes frustrate users who have keyed in a lot of data in the meantime.

Chapter 4 introduced an Order Entry form, which is shown in Figure 5.21. Recall that the form fields Customer No. (customer number) and Sales Rep. (sales representative) use either a combo box or a list box to look up and display a list of acceptable values for their respective form control fields. In the case of list box controls, data validation occurs automatically because you must select one of the items from the list.

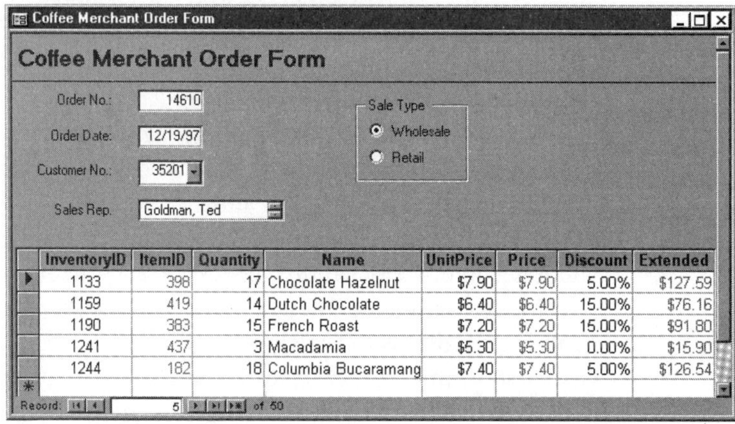

Figure 5.21 Coffee Merchant Order form.

Let's create a macro that checks the Order Date form field to ensure it is acceptable. We will attach the macro to one of the events of the Order Date field. (An *event* is an action recognized by an object such as moving a mouse, leaving or entering a field, and so on.) The particular event that we attach the date validation macro to is the *BeforeUpdate* event. If we associate the macro with the BeforeUpdate field property setting, then it is triggered whenever the focus moves from the control whose value has changed. Moreover, the macro springs into action just *before* Microsoft Access accepts the change. Therefore, an ideal way to check a field's contents is to test it when the value changes—when the BeforeUpdate event is triggered.

The ValidDateCheck macro checks the Order Date field to ensure it is valid. If it is, the cursor is permitted to move to the next field. If the date value does not conform to the rules you have established, then the cursor does not move and an error message is displayed. We will accomplish the data validation process in two steps. First, we will write the data validation macro. Second, we will associate the macro with the BeforeUpdate event for the Order Date form field.

Writing a Macro with Conditions. The date validation rule we wish to implement is this: any order date entered into The Coffee Merchant's Order form must be plus or minus five days of today's date (inclusive). All other dates (those outside that range) are invalid. This rule, though arbitrary, allows data entry persons the flexibility of back-dating or post-dating the order up to five days. This may not always be a good policy, but we implement this rule simply to show you how to enforce it. You are free to tighten such rules as you see fit. When an invalid date is recognized, an information message should be displayed and then the user is allowed to reenter a correct date.

Prepare for the next exercise by closing all Access windows except the Database window for the database *Ch05.mdb.* Then click the Macros tab and click the New button to begin the process of writing a new macro.

Exercise 5.11: Creating a Date Validation Macro

1. Select Conditions from the View menu to open the Condition column in the Macro Design window.
2. Click in the topmost Condition column cell and enter the following expression: ***[OrderDate] Not Between Now()-5 And Now()+5***
3. Click in the Action column to the right of the cell containing the previous condition. Click the down-pointing arrow, then scroll through the list of actions until *MsgBox* appears and select it.
4. Click in the Message text box of the Action Arguments found in the lower half of the Macro window. Enter in the Message text box the following informative message:
   Date must be between five days ago and five days from now
5. Choose *No* for the Beep value, choose *Warning!* from the Type drop-down list, and type ***Date Error*** in the Title text box of the Action Arguments.
6. Click in the second row of the Condition column and type ... (three periods in a row).
7. Click the Action column in the second row (the cell just below MsgBox) and type ***CancelEvent*** in that cell. Figure 5.22 shows the Macro window with the MsgBox action selected. (The Condition column has been enlarged to reveal the entire condition.)
8. Click the Macro window Close button to close the macro. Click the Yes button to save changes, enter the macro name ***ValidDateCheck***, and click OK when the Save As dialog box appears. The macro is saved as *ValidDateCheck* and the Macro window is closed.

What is the Condition column in a macro and how does it alter the way the macro works? Sometimes you want a macro to spring into action only under certain circumstances. For example, the macro ValidDateCheck should check the date after the user moves the cursor from the Order Date field. Then, *if* (and only if) the date is outside the acceptable range of possible dates, the macro should display a warning message and cancel the event that led to the date being checked.

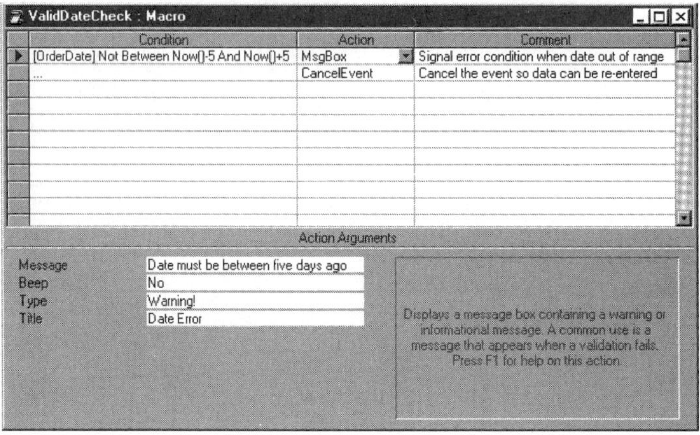

Figure 5.22 ValidDateCheck macro.

If the date is acceptable, the macro should proceed with its next step. In this case, the macro halts.

A condition that must be met for a macro action to occur is placed to the left of the Action column statement. If *several* actions are to occur when *one* condition is true, then you place an ellipsis (...) in the Condition cell to the left of each of those actions. For the ellipsis to work, however, the actions marked with the ellipsis condition must appear immediately below the original condition in an unbroken series. (Actions that have no ellipsis are always executed by the macro.)

Look at Figure 5.22 again. The condition that must be true to execute the MsgBox action statement is *[OrderDate] Not Between Now()-5 And Now()+5*. The second action, *CancelEvent*, is executed only when the condition is true, because there is an ellipsis in the Condition column indicating the preceding condition is continued to the current action. The CancelEvent action cancels the event that caused Access to run the macro. That is, CancelEvent prevents Access from attempting to update the record in the database. After all, we do not want erroneous data to be posted to the database *after* we recognize the error. That would defeat the reason for data validation in the first place.

You can test multiple conditions, known as *cases*, by placing multiple conditions in separate rows. Each condition is tested in turn, and the associated action is executed if the condition in the same row is true. Macro execution halts, in any case, when it encounters the end of the macro or a macro name, which signals the beginning of another macro.

Once the macro has been constructed, you can attach it to the field, form, or other object to complete the process. Next, we describe how to attach the ValidDateCheck macro to the Order Date field of The Coffee Merchant Order form.

Associating a Macro with an Event. The second step that completes the process of implementing data validation for a field is to attach the macro to a particular event of a field that will cause the macro to execute. Because we want the macro to check the Order Date form field just after the user enters a value and tries to move to the next field, the appropriate event to which we should attach the macro is called *BeforeUpdate*. This event, or internal signal, occurs (as mentioned previously) after a value is entered but before Access has a chance to update the field. The next exercise illustrates how to bind the ValidDateCheck macro to the Order Date field's BeforeUpdate event.

EXERCISE 5.12: ATTACHING A MACRO TO AN EVENT

1. Display *frmOrder* in Design view.
2. Right-click the Order Date form field (not its label) and select Properties from the pop-up menu to display the control's properties.
3. Click the Event tab and click inside the Before Update property text box.
4. Click the arrow that appears in the text box to display a drop-down list of macros (there should be several macros by now).
5. Use the scroll bar if necessary to locate and select (click) the macro named *ValidDateCheck* from the list. (The list of macro names is displayed in alphabetical order, so ValidDateCheck is at the end of the list.)
6. Close the property sheet and save the form; be sure to respond Yes when asked if you want to save the changes.

Try it

The process of creating a data validation macro and attaching it to an object is complete. Now it's time to test your macro. Display the form *frmOrder* in Form view and select Data Entry from the Records menu. A blank record is displayed. Now, enter an order number larger than 14999 and move to the Order Date field. First, enter a correct date to ensure the macro does nothing: type any date that is plus or minus five days from the current date and press Tab. If your ValidDateCheck macro is working properly, the cursor will move to the Customer No. field without incident. Next, test what happens when a disallowed date is entered. Press Shift+Tab to move back to the Order Date field and type ***10/17/96***, a date which is outside the permitted range for this field. An error message should be displayed like the one shown in Figure 5.23. If not—if the cursor moves to the next field without incident—then the macro is incorrect. Examine the macro's design carefully and make needed corrections. Ask your instructor for help if necessary.

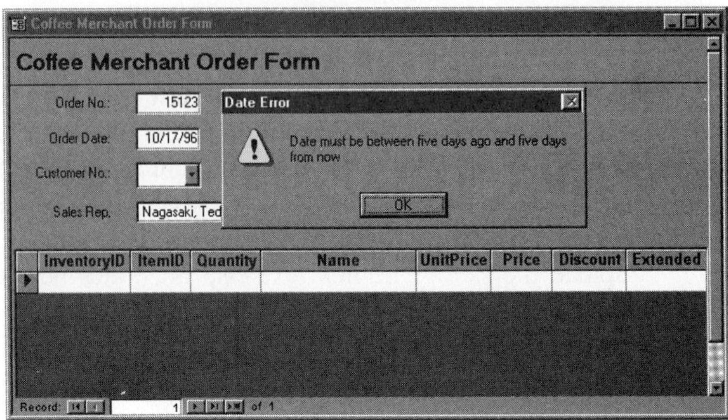

Figure 5.23 Data validation error message.

Cancel the actual database update process and return to the Database window by double-clicking OK in response to the error message. Click OK when the "...value in the field or record..." message is displayed. Click the Close button and click OK once again when the "you cannot save this object at this time..." message is displayed.

Access's response to the invalid date error condition, detected by your macro, is to prevent the cursor from leaving the Order Date field until the user enters a valid date. When a valid date is entered, the macro is executed and the date is found valid. Control returns to the user so he or she can continue entering order information.

The date range chosen in the validity test is arbitrary. We are illustrating how to write data validation routines. You can choose to validate dates, numeric values, and even character strings for any number of form fields using the same techniques shown here. Use the date validation method as an example to create similar form field validation tests.

Enforcing Business Rules

Other rules regarding how a business operates can be enforced using Access macros. Such rules can include the stipulation that a sales order being entered be checked against the customer's payment history file. Another example is requiring that a sales representative's number be included on each sales order form. Neither of the preceding rules validates data input, because the form fields involved are not subject to range or reasonableness tests. Rather, the tests performed are more subtle and involve information that is not linked to the current form. We show you in this section how to construct this type of business rule test.

It is important, when entering a sales order, to check that there is sufficient stock to be able to supply the item being entered. Look at Figure 5.21 for a moment. If a line for 17 pounds of Chocolate Hazelnut is entered, the requested amount should be checked against stock on hand. If less than 17 pounds are on hand, then an action should be triggered. At the very least, the data entry person should be notified that insufficient stock exists for the particular item. Then, the order being entered can indicate "back-ordered," or some alternate inventory source can be searched. Additionally, the system should automatically generate a purchase request for additional stock. That purchase request could be an entry in another table that is printed daily to see what stock should be ordered.

We will show you how and where to place a check to ensure stock ordered is available while the order is being processed. For illustration purposes, we will keep the reaction to a stock shortage brief: the process will merely warn the data entry person of the shortage. Later, you can embellish the macro to include a mechanism that creates a purchase order or that simply inserts an appropriately identified row in a purchase table.

The exercise that follows checks each line item quantity value just after it is entered (but before it is placed into an order table). Checking is conceptually simple: the quantity ordered is compared to the item's OnHand value stored in the *tblInventory* table. If the ordered amount just entered exceeds available stock, a warning message will be displayed on the screen. The macro that performs the comparison between requested quantity and the actual quantity available is attached to the Quantity column of the *fsubOrderLine* subform. The subform is embedded in the master form, *frmOrder* (see Figure 5.21). Prepare for Exercise 5.13 by closing all windows in the Ch05 database except the Database window.

We begin by creating the macro, called *OrderLookupQty*, that performs the stock check. In writing a macro with a condition, we will use an Access function called DLookUp to look up and return the amount of stock on hand for a particular item. The macro will generate a warning message if DLookUp determines that the amount of the item in stock is less than the quantity requested in the order. Otherwise, the macro returns control to the Order Entry form.

Exercise 5.13: Writing a Macro to Check Stock On Hand

1. Create a new macro (click the Macros tab and then click New) and select Conditions from the View menu to open the Condition column in the Macro window.
2. Click in the Condition cell of the first row. Press Shift+F2 (press and hold the Shift key and tap the F2 key) to enlarge the data entry area so that you can more easily see the text you are about to type. A Zoom box opens.
3. Carefully enter the following statement. (Enter the expression as one long line.)
   [Quantity]>DLookUp("[OnHand]","[tblInventory]","[ItemID]= Forms![frmOrder]![fsubOrderLine].Form![ItemID]")

4. Click OK to close the Zoom box and then click the Action cell to the right of the condition you entered. Select *MsgBox* from the list of choices displayed when you click the arrow.
5. Fill in the Action Arguments for the MsgBox action as follows:

   Message: ***Less inventory available than required for order. Enter 0 (zero) in the quantity field to move on.***
   Beep: ***No***
   Type: ***Critical***
   Title: ***Stock Out Warning!***

6. Place an ellipsis in the Condition column in row 2; enter ***CancelEvent*** in the Action column of the second row. (Enter a comment in either or both macro rows if you wish.) Your macro should resemble the one shown in Figure 5.24.
7. Click the Macro window Close button and click Yes to save the macro. Enter the macro name ***OrderLookupQty*** in the Save As dialog box.

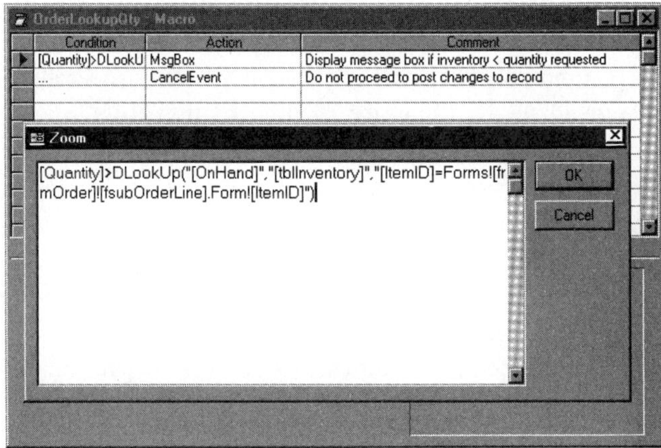

Figure 5.24 OrderLookupQty macro.

This completes the definition of the macro that performs a stock check. All that remains to be done is to attach the macro to the *fsubOrderLine* Quantity control. You have done this previously in Exercise 5.12. As before, we want to enter the macro's name in the Before Update property of the Quantity control so that the macro is triggered whenever an entry is made in the Quantity field. Briefly, the steps are these: open the *fsubOrderLine* form in Design view, display the Quantity control's property sheet, select the Event tab, click the Before Update property text box, and type ***OrderLookupQty*** (or select it from the list of macros displayed after you click the arrow). Close the property sheet and save and close the changed *fsubOrderLine* form.

Here's an explanation of the OrderLookupQty macro you just entered. Whenever a Quantity is entered in the subform, the macro jumps into action. The condition in the first row is somewhat complex. The DLookup function has the general form:

DLookup(expression, domain, criteria)

The actual version used in your macro contains *"[OnHand]"* for the expression argument. This is the column value that is located and returned from the Inventory table. The Inventory table name is the second argument of the DLookup function. The second argument is *"[tblInventory]"*, which names the table to be searched for the stock quantity. Finally, the third argument indicates which row of the *tblInventory* table to look for. A match between the ItemId of the *fsubOrderLine* form and the matching item in the Inventory table is the inventory row containing the stock on hand we seek. That criteria argument is the rather lengthy expression:

"[ItemID]=Forms![frmOrder]![fsubOrderLine].Form![ItemID]")

where the notation beginning after the equal sign is the standard way to name a subform field embedded within a form. It requests a match between the order line item identification in the order entry and the inventory item whose primary key is also ItemID.

After DLookup returns a single number, the OnHand value for the chosen inventory item, it is compared to the Quantity value. Simplified, the condition is the following:

[Quantity]>quantity retrieved from the inventory by DLookup

If the preceding condition is true—more inventory is requested than is available—then the Action associated with the Condition is executed. In this example, a MsgBox statement is issued displaying a warning message. The second row, containing the CancelEvent statement, is executed. That's all there is to the OrderLookupQty macro. Yet, it illustrates that you can search other tables for information that is not part of the current form.

There are alternative actions that you could take if there is not sufficient stock to fulfill the current order. You could update the OnHand column of the *tblInventory* table to reflect how much of the item was taken from stock (negative amounts mean a back-order situation exists). Or, you could halt processing. We have shown you one way to deal with the situation—display a warning message.

Now that you have a fundamental understanding of the macro attached to the Quantity form control, let's see it in action. Experiencing the macro in action (triggering a warning message) really drives home how this process enforces a fundamental business rule.

Try it

Display the *frmOrder* form in Form view and click the First Record navigation button. Click the form Maximize button. The first sales order is displayed. Execute each of the following steps to see exactly how your newly created business rule catches an attempt to order more of an item than currently exists in stock. Move the mouse pointer to the Quantity column in the last row of the subform corresponding to the *Ethiopia Sidamo* entry. Double-click the current Quantity entry to highlight it. Type the new quantity value, ***5000***, and press Tab to enter the value. A warning message is displayed because there are only 3,440 pounds of Ethiopia Sidamo (item 167) in stock, not the requested 5,000 pounds (see Figure 5.25). Click OK to remove the message box, then change the quantity back to its original value, ***4***. Close the form.

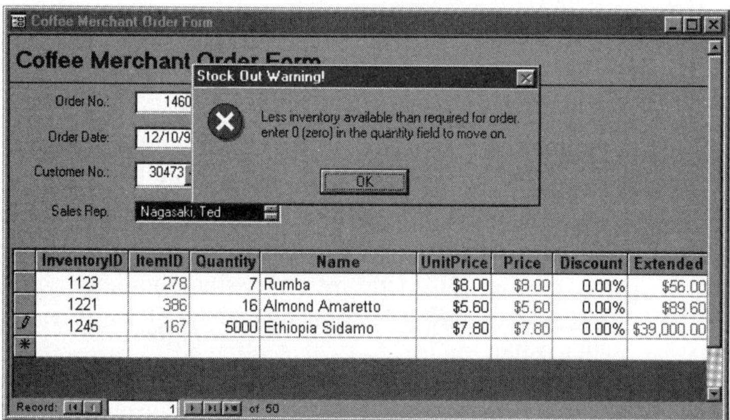

Figure 5.25 The stock check macro in action.

MANAGING DATA

This last section describes how to do light maintenance on your database objects and how to link tables from other databases to your database. First, we discuss copying databases, local tables, and tables not in the present database. You learn how to rename and delete tables, and finally we show you how to use a table stored in a different database without physically housing the table in your database. That action is called linking tables.

Copying Data

You may sometimes need to copy a table, query, or other Access database object from one location to another, or you may decide that you would like a duplicate of a table saved under a different name in the same database. Copying a table from another database is accomplished by the Import command of the Get External Data command found in the File menu. You clone an object such as a table by using the Copy command found in the Edit menu. We describe each activity separately.

Copying an Entire Database. Suppose you have been developing an accounting subsystem at work and you want to take home some of the database files and work on the system there. You have database software both at work and at home, but the database changes frequently, and the only current copy is on your office computer. One solution is to copy the entire database replete with tables, queries, and other objects to your floppy disk and then reverse the process on your home computer system (copy the database from the floppy disk to your home computer). Copying the entire database solves the problem when it can completely fit on a floppy disk. If not, then you can copy selected database objects to your disk and work with those objects at home. The simplest way to copy the entire Access database to your floppy disk is to use Windows Explorer (see Chapter 1). Simply right-click and drag the database file from your hard disk to the floppy disk in Explorer. If the database is larger than the capacity of a floppy disk, then you should use one of the widely available data compression programs to reduce the database's size to fit your disk.

Cloning a Table. Suppose the purchasing department wants to experiment with a different way to handle inventory, and they want to experiment with the *tblInventory* table. You anticipate that they will alter the table structure in their quest to streamline inventory management. You decide the only safe thing to do is give the purchasing department a copy of the Inventory table saved under a different name. That way, any changes the purchasing department makes to the table are insulated from the rest of the business. The process of creating a copy of a table is the same for any database object. Here's an exercise to show you how.

EXERCISE 5.14: MAKING A COPY OF A TABLE

1. With only the Database window of the Ch05 database open, click the Tables tab and select *tblInventory*.
2. Select the Copy command from the Edit menu.
3. Select Paste from the Edit menu. The Paste Table As dialog box is displayed. If you are pasting a table, you can choose to copy the table's structure only, its structure and data, or append the table's record data to one of your existing tables.

4. Type *tblInventoryCopy* and click the Structure and Data option button. Click OK to complete the procedure. The Inventory table (*tblInventory*) structure and data is copied into the Ch05 database and renamed *tblInventoryCopy*.

Importing a Table from Another Access Database. Any database objects, including tables, which are part of another Access database can be copied to the current database using the Import command. Suppose you want to copy a table called *tblStock* from a database named *Ch02.mdb* into the current database, *Ch05.mdb.* Unlike what was done in Exercise 5.14, you are not copying a table within the current database, nor are you copying an entire database. This request is somewhere between these two extremes. The next exercise shows you how to do this.

Exercise 5.15: Importing a Table from Another Access Database

1. Open the Ch05 database if necessary.
2. Select File, Get External Data, Import.
3. Locate and then double-click the Ch02 folder on your Companion CD-ROM. Select the *Ch02.mdb* database and click the Import button.
4. Select the Tables tab in the Import Objects database window.
5. Click the table name *tblStock* and click OK to import the table into your database. Figure 5.26 shows the Import Objects dialog box just prior to clicking the Import button.

The *tblStock* table is placed among the tables in your Ch05 database. Prior to clicking the Import button, you can select as many objects from the database as you like, including Tables, Queries, Forms, and Reports. All objects are imported in a single, speedy operation.

RENAMING AND DELETING TABLES

Other database housekeeping duties include renaming objects (tables, forms, etc.) and deleting objects from the database. Rename an object by editing its name directly. Delete a database object by selecting it and pressing the Delete key.

Renaming a Table. Let's rename the *tblStock* table you imported into Ch05 in Exercise 5.15. Simply click the Tables tab and select the *tblStock* table. Click the

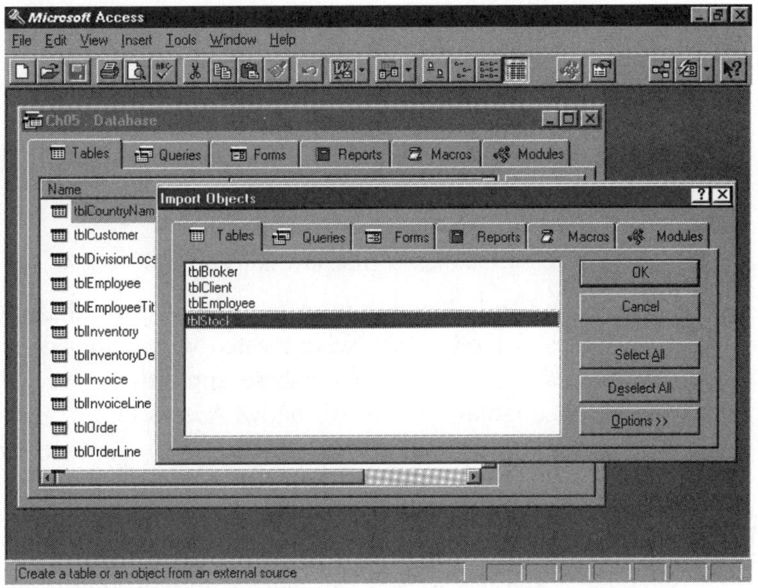

Figure 5.26 Importing a table from another Access database.

name again and type the new name, ***tblCompanyStock***. The table is renamed just that simply. Of course, you can rename any Microsoft Access object. Remember, however, that the renamed object may be referenced by another object such as a query or form. Make sure you make any necessary changes to other affected objects. Otherwise you will get an error message when you use affected objects.

Deleting a Table. Deleting an object is as simple as renaming it. However, because it removes objects from the database irrevocably, you want to think before you act. It is safe to delete the *tblCompanyStock* table, because it is not used by any part of The Coffee Merchant enterprise. Select the *tblCompanyStock* table and press Delete (or select Delete from the Edit menu). A confirmation request dialog box is displayed. Click OK to give permission to delete the selected table. The table is removed from the database. You can select Undo Delete from the Edit menu if you delete the wrong table, but you must act immediately.

Linking Tables

If your company already has data stored in a computer and you want to access that data in your database application, then you can *link* the remote tables to your database. You can link tables that are not in Access format. For example, the following database formats can be linked to an Access database:

- dBASE III, dBASE IV, and dBase 5
- Microsoft FoxPro
- Paradox
- Excel spreadsheets
- Text files, both delimited and not delimited
- Access databases that are not currently open

When you link one or more tables to your database, you have full access to those tables as though they were created within your database. The original tables are still available to other database applications, as well as your Access database. Linked tables behave like native Access tables, and you can do almost anything to them *except* alter their structure. You can enter and update data, use existing queries, forms, and reports, and you can develop new objects that reference the linked tables. You can even rename linked tables to follow the table naming conventions established for the home database.

Because Access can work with non-Access database formats, you can manipulate data stored in Paradox tables from within Access. That is, you can lash together tables in different formats and treat them as though they were all native Access tables. This serves your data needs by allowing you to extract information from a dBASE IV table, while leaving intact the original dBASE application and data. Others can continue using the same dBASE tables. Another important advantage of linking tables is that you can revise an ongoing Access-based accounting system using linked copies of all required tables. This allows you to work with "live" data being maintained in another database while you develop new software in your developmental database. This clean separation of data from procedures that manipulate the mission-critical data is very desirable. When it is time to switch to a newer version of the accounting system database, you simply replace the original database's non-table objects (forms, queries, and so on) with the latest version. The tables are *not* replaced.

Our final exercise demonstrates how to link a table found in another Access database that is not currently open. You can think of the table as being located on a remote server connected to your system. In fact, the table we ask you to link to the Ch05 database is located in a different database found on the Companion CD-ROM.

EXERCISE 5.16: LINKING A TABLE FOUND IN ANOTHER DATABASE

1. Open the Ch05 database—the one which will use the linked table.
2. Select File, Get External Data, Link Tables.
3. In the Link dialog box, locate and then select the *Supplement* folder found on your Companion CD-ROM.

4. Select the database *Zipcodes.mdb* and click the Link button to open the database. The Link Tables dialog box is displayed.
5. Select the only table found in the list, *ZipCodes*. Click OK to link the table to the database *Ch05.mdb.*

The linked table appears in the list of tables in your Ch05 database (see Figure 5.27). To the left of the table is an arrow indicating the table is linked to this database, not a part of it. After you have linked a table, you can rename it following the Access convention for naming objects.

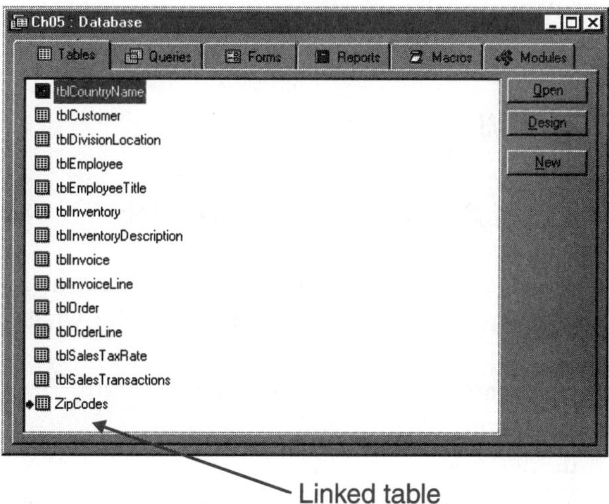

Figure 5.27 Linked table, *ZipCodes*.

Deleting a linked table couldn't be simpler. Select the linked table and press Delete—just like you would delete any other Access database object.

SUMMARY

You have learned how to use Access macros to automate database procedures and how to copy, rename, delete, and link tables. You created buttons and linked macros to them so that they perform a series of steps. With navigation buttons, you simplified moving around the database rows displayed on a form. Other database activities can be simplified by making buttons that modify database rows, create new rows, save changes, and cancel changes. Though creating buttons is more work initially, these buttons spare users from learning details about the database system and its interaction language.

You created action menus that provided another way to present choices and actions to your users. Menus can be built so that they replace the Access Menu bar and are displayed automatically when a form is opened. When a user clicks a menu choice, an event is triggered that is subsequently processed by the macro you associated with the menu command.

You also learned that you can use macros to automate internal control features. The controls you read about and implemented included validating dates entered in orders and checking stock on hand to ensure that an order can be filled.

Finally, we described several data management functions including copying a database, copying a table, and importing a table from another database. Other useful data management methods included in the discussion were renaming, deleting, and linking tables.

REVIEW EXERCISES

MULTIPLE-CHOICE QUESTIONS

1. You can create small program segments which alter the behavior of objects. These program segments are known by what general name?
   a. subprograms
   b. events
   c. actions
   d. macros
2. When you click a button on a form, it causes which event from the following list to occur?
   a. Open
   b. GetFocus
   c. MouseOpen
   d. Click
3. A macro containing other macros is called a
   a. procedure macro.
   b. group menu.
   c. macro group.
   d. menu cluster.
4. You can display a dialog box with an informative or warning message with which of the following macros?
   a. MessInfo
   b. InfoBox
   c. Message
   d. MsgBox

5. When creating custom pull-down menus, you attach the custom menu to which form property so that the custom menu is displayed automatically when the form is opened?
   a. the Pop Up property
   b. the Menu Bar property
   c. the On Load property
   d. the Before Update property
6. You can attach a validation macro to what property to prevent the cursor from moving off the current form field just prior to Access updating the data?
   a. canMove
   b. Before Update
   c. After Update
   d. On Enter
7. What symbol, placed in a Macro window Condition column, is used to indicate that a macro line is to be executed as part of a previous Condition?
   a. colon
   b. semicolon
   c. ellipsis
   d. period
8. What macro statement is commonly used to execute one of the standard Access commands?
   a. DoMacro
   b. ExecuteMenu
   c. RunCommand
   d. DoMenuItem
9. The last row in a macro should be ______ to separate it from other macros in the group.
   a. empty
   b. filled with asterisks
   c. filled with the command END
   d. filled with three hyphens
10. When you want to use the data found in a Paradox table for an Access application and the Paradox table must also be available for a Paradox application, the best way to handle this is to do what?
    a. Import the table into your Access database.
    b. Copy the table into your Access database.
    c. Link the Paradox table to your Access database.
    d. Abandon all hope of using the Paradox table.

DISCUSSION QUESTIONS

1. What are the advantages, if any, of using custom-designed buttons to automate a procedure that can be executed by using existing Microsoft Access menus?

2. Describe what advantages, if any, would accrue by attaching a field validation macro to check whether a field is empty or not. After all, you can check the Required property in the table's Design view to accomplish the same thing. What is the difference in these two approaches?
3. Discuss the meaning and relationship between events and event properties. List at least five form event properties and briefly describe the event properties. Use Access Help and search for the definition or use of the event properties you choose to describe.
4. Why did we attach the File menu (shown in Figure 5.19) to the form? Wouldn't it be simpler to attach the menu to the entire application? What are the implications of the latter choice—a custom menu for the application?
5. Describe in detail the DLookUp function (four or five sentences will do). Start by defining its general format: what are its arguments? Then, describe concisely the purpose of the function and where it might prove useful.

EXERCISES

1. Create a form that allows you to view information in both of the inventory tables *tblInventory* and *tblInventoryDescription* at once. Then create four navigation buttons labeled *First Record*, *Last Record*, *Next Record*, and *Previous Record* with associated macros that implement the record navigation. Create a group macro that contains all four macros. Print an example of the form (choose any inventory item) and print the definition of the group macro. Be sure to write your name on each page of output.
2. Modify the *frmCustomer2* form you created containing menus in the following way. Add a menu called Navigation that contains four selections: First, Last, Previous, and Next (in that order from top to bottom). The menu should appear between the File and Database menus. Of course, the menus should be operational. Delete the navigation buttons found on the *frmCustomer2* form. Save this form under a new name of your own choosing. Turn in printouts of all new or modified macros and label them appropriately.
3. Modify The Coffee Merchant's Order form so that the Order No. and Order Date fields are validated by macros. The validation rule for the Order No. field is this: the Order No. must not be less than 15000 and not greater than 99999. The validation rule for the Order Date field should be changed to this: the date must be between 30 days ago and today's date, inclusive. Print the validation macros as well as the form.
4. Create a macro that is used in the *frmCustomer* form. The macro prevents the user from leaving the CustomerID field if an invalid value (or none) is entered. A customer number is considered invalid if it is one of the existing customer numbers. Print this modified macro. Be prepared to demonstrate the modified form to your instructor.

5. Write a macro that is used in the *frmCustomer* form which validates the ZipCode field. The macro prevents the cursor from leaving the ZipCode field unless a valid, existing Zipcode is found in the *Zipcodes.mdb* database found in the folder named *Supplement* on your Companion CD-ROM (see Exercise 5.16). Ensure that the entered Zipcode corresponds to the correct city and state abbreviation by consulting the *Zipcodes.mdb* database. Include a warning message dialog box that displays if an invalid Zipcode value is entered. The warning dialog box should display the message *Incorrect Zipcode entered.* Print the macro. Be prepared to demonstrate this new macro to your instructor.

6 Accounting Databases in Transaction Cycles

Objectives

This chapter introduces the second part of the book, in which you will learn how to build accounting information system components using the database software skills you learned in the first five chapters. In this chapter, we will

- Explain the differences between double-entry bookkeeping and database accounting systems.
- Examine the advantages and disadvantages of database accounting systems.
- Define business activity classifications.
- Describe transaction cycles.

This chapter will help you understand the differences between double-entry bookkeeping and database accounting. We use business activity classifications and transaction cycles to provide a framework that will help you apply the database skills you learned in earlier chapters to the task of building accounting database components.

Introduction

You probably learned the mechanics of accounting for economic transactions using the tools of manual double-entry bookkeeping such as journals and ledgers. This chapter begins with a discussion of the differences between database accounting systems and manual double-entry bookkeeping systems. We then explain the advantages and disadvantages of using a database approach to building accounting systems. This chapter's discussion of business activity classifications then introduces three levels of complexity that accountants use to classify firms. These classifications will help you understand when to incorporate particular database features into your accounting database system designs. Finally, the chapter describes transaction cycles, which provide a way for accountants and others to classify economic events into related categories.

The four chapters that follow this one each describe how to use database software to build accounting system elements for a specific transaction cycle. In this chapter, we show you which economic events and database tables each transaction cycle includes. In subsequent chapters, we describe details of the database table fields and show you how to create forms, queries, and reports to accomplish accounting tasks in each of the four transaction cycles.

DATABASE ACCOUNTING SYSTEMS

In Chapter 3, we introduced database theory and explained how firms could use relational databases as part of their accounting systems. Much of the interest in using databases for accounting systems arose as businesses saw the advantages of relational databases for all their information processing needs. Researchers such as William McCarthy and George Sorter developed events-based approaches to accounting theory that provide a solid theoretical underpinning for the use of relational databases to perform accounting tasks. These events-based approaches argue that accountants should strive to store all relevant attributes of economic events in a readily accessible form. Relational databases accomplish that objective.

Double-Entry Bookkeeping vs. Database Accounting

Double-entry bookkeeping provided an excellent way of recording transactions for many years. It satisfied accountants' need to capture the essence of each transaction. When double-entry bookkeeping was first developed over five hundred years ago, the costs of gathering and storing information were very high. Recording transactions with pen and paper was a time-consuming task—double-entry bookkeeping gave accountants a valuable tool that quickly identified essential elements of transactions. Therefore, double-entry bookkeeping let businesspersons capture key attributes of transactions in a highly aggregated form. This kept the cost of information gathering and storage to a minimum. Also, the debit-credit balancing check provided an important internal control feature in manual accounting systems.

Try it

If you would like to see how far we have come in replacing manual accounting systems with database systems, take a trip to your local office supplies store and try to find a pad of two-column accounting paper. If you have trouble finding it, ask a salesperson for help. He or she will probably look up the product's location—in the store's inventory database.

Computerized transaction processing has released accountants from the limitations and drudgery of manual accounting systems. Using computers, we can now capture a wide variety of information about each transaction quite easily. For example, supermarkets and other retail stores routinely read bar codes at their checkout stations to capture the date and time of purchase, the identity of the item purchased, the store location, the checkout station number, and the cashier number. Even more important is that they obtain all of this information with one quick swipe!

Technology, such as bar code readers and optical scanners, has played a major role in reducing the cost of acquiring and storing multiple attributes of each economic event. To see more clearly how double-entry bookkeeping and database accounting differ, let's consider a sales transaction. A typical sales transaction begins when a customer sends us a purchase order. If we have the goods in stock and the customer's credit is acceptable, we ship the goods and invoice the customer. A double-entry bookkeeping system would record this transaction with the following journal entry:

Date	Account	Debit	Credit
Date	Accounts Receivable	*Amount*	
	Sales		*Amount*
	Explanation		

This journal entry includes five items of information:

- Transaction date
- Names of the accounts debited
- Names of the accounts credited
- Transaction amount
- Explanation of the transaction

If we had posted this journal entry to a subsidiary ledger, the journal entry would include a sixth item of information, the customer's account code. If the sale had been recorded in a sales journal instead of the general journal entry shown the format would differ—for example, the account names might be implied by the transaction appearing in the sales journal rather than being explicitly stated—but the information recorded would be the same. To summarize, a double-entry bookkeeping system records five or six transaction attributes and records one of them, the amount, twice.

Now let's consider how a relational database accounting system might handle the same transaction. We might record the transaction in a set of database tables similar to those that appear in Figure 6.1.

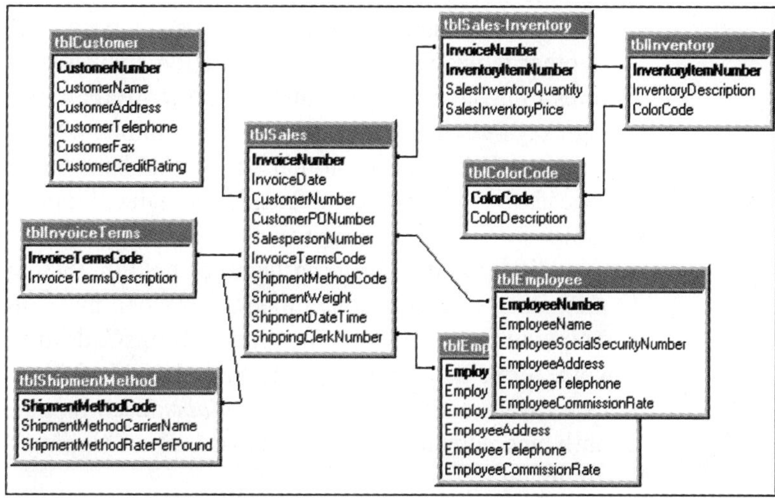

Figure 6.1 Sales transactions stored in a database accounting system.

The database system shown in Figure 6.1 stores attributes of the sales transaction in the *tblSales* table. However, it also stores attributes of the sales transaction in the seven other tables that appear in Figure 6.1. The database accounting system can store many more attributes of the sales transaction than the journal entry could. Note that the database system stores these attributes in an atomic form, scattered throughout the tables. These tables, constructed according to the normalization rules you learned in Chapter 3, are linked to each other through their primary key fields.

The database system stores 10 transaction attributes in the *tblSales* table and a virtually unlimited number of attributes in the other tables. For example, if the invoice included 20 items, the *tblSales-Inventory* table would store 40 attributes (20 item quantities and 20 item prices) of the transaction. Contrast this with the information stored in the double-entry bookkeeping journal entry. The journal entry does not even tell you how many items were on the invoice, much less tell you anything about those items!

Not only does the database accounting system store many more attributes than the double-entry bookkeeping system, it does so efficiently. Recall from Chapter 3 that normalization in database table design reduces or eliminates the storage of redundant information. Let's take a look at what we have stored in each table, how the tables are linked, and how we might extract information from this sales system.

The primary keys appear in bold type in Figure 6.1. The primary key of *tblSales* is InvoiceNumber. The other attributes of the sale that are stored exclusively in this table include the invoice date, the customer's purchase order number, the shipping weight of the items sold, and the shipping date and time. The other five fields in *tblSales* are foreign key fields. These foreign keys link *tblSales* to other tables that contain information about the sale. We use these foreign key links to avoid recording information more than once. For example, the first foreign key field in *tblSales* is CustomerNumber, which links *tblSales* to *tblCustomer*. Instead of storing a customer's name, address, and other information in *tblSales* repeatedly for every invoice, this normalized database design lets you store customer information once for each customer and link it to individual sales by including just the CustomerNumber field in *tblSales*. The other foreign keys in *tblSales* are SalespersonNumber, InvoiceTermsCode, ShipmentMethodCode, and ShippingClerkNumber. The InvoiceTermsCode links each sale to a table of invoice terms that might include cash, 2/10 net 30, 1/15 net 30, and net 30. If these terms were entered directly in *tblSales*, each input clerk might enter them differently and corrupt the sales database. The ShippingMethodCode performs a similar function.

Try it

With several other members of your class, see how many different logical ways you can devise to record the names of several shipping firms. You might be surprised at how many variations are plausible.

The SalespersonNumber and the ShippingClerkNumber foreign key fields contain the identification numbers for these two employee participants in sales transactions. Note that Figure 6.1 shows *tblEmployee* twice to accommodate these two links, however, the firm actually has only one Employee table. The primary key of *tblSales*, InvoiceNumber, participates in a link to *tblInventory* as part of the composite primary key in *tblSales-Inventory*. Recall from Chapter 3 that the only way to link two tables that have a many-to-many relationship is through a relationship table. In a sales transaction, each invoice can have many inventory items. Also, each inventory item can appear on many different invoices. In this sales system, *tblSales-Inventory* is the relationship table that models the many-to-many relationship between *tblSales* and *tblInventory*.

Note that the database system directly records only some of the items that the double-entry bookkeeping system records. The database system directly records the date of the sale, the customer number, and the nature of the transaction as a sale. The database system does not directly record the transaction as an element of accounts receivable. Since sales transactions comprise the left side of the accounts receivable account, storing information about sales in the tables that appear in Figure 6.1 is sufficient. To calculate the amount of a particular invoice—the amount that the double-entry bookkeeping system recorded twice in the journal entry—an accountant using a database system would run a query that linked *tblSales* with *tblSales-Inventory* and *tblShipmentMethod*. The query would obtain the SalesInventoryQuantity and SalesInventoryPrice for each InventoryItemNumber in *tblSales-Inventory* for the InvoiceNumber. The query would also obtain the ShipmentMethodRatePerPound from *tblShipmentMethod* and the ShipmentWeight from *tblSales*. The query would multiply the SalesInventoryQuantity by the SalesInventoryPrice for each InventoryItemNumber and multiply the invoice's ShipmentWeight by the ShipmentMethodRatePerPound for the ShipmentMethodCode on the invoice. Finally, the query would sum these products to determine the amount of the invoice. Although pure database theory prohibits the storage of calculated fields in relational databases, many accounting databases store intermediate results of calculations such as this invoice amount calculation to increase the efficiency of processing repetitive transaction data. We do strive to avoid storing calculated fields because of the functional dependency problem discussed in Chapter 3.

The database approach can do anything that double-entry bookkeeping can do and more. Accountants can use the database tables in Figure 6.1 to calculate invoice amounts and generate the same accounts receivable records and financial statement amounts that they could with journals and ledgers. If, however, a manager wanted to know how many green-colored inventory items the firm sold during March of the previous year, the journals and ledgers would be virtually useless. Using the database, we could quickly provide the manager with an answer that included number of items and sales in dollars. We could even offer to generate subtotals by customer or geographic location for both number of items and sales in dollars.

Try it

Examine Figure 6.1 carefully. Identify interesting facts about the firm's sales and sales-related activities that you might find or calculate by searching the database tables and combining the information attributes they contain.

As you can see, relational databases record far more information for each transaction than a traditional double-entry bookkeeping system can record. A database accounting system also provides a flexible web of information relating a firm's economic events to each other. In Chapter 3, we discussed some of the advantages and disadvantages of database management systems. The next two sections extend that discussion to accounting database systems.

Advantages of Database Accounting Systems

Manual double-entry bookkeeping systems are very efficient; however, computer implementations of double-entry bookkeeping use a flat file processing design. In manual systems, the dual nature of the accounting debit and credit model provides a built-in error correction mechanism. In automated systems, this same duality is inefficient and serves no real control purpose.

Database accounting systems store data only once. This feature leads to a number of advantages over flat file double-entry accounting systems. A database accounting system can:

- Lower data storage costs.
- Eliminate data redundancy.
- Eliminate data inconsistencies.
- Avoid duplicate processing.
- Ease add, delete, and update data maintenance tasks.
- Make data independent of applications.
- Centralize data management.
- Centralize data security.

Database accounting systems offer greater flexibility in extracting data than flat file double-entry accounting systems. This flexibility leads to other advantages. For example, a database accounting system can:

- Ease report modifications and updates.
- Provide *ad hoc* query capabilities.
- Facilitate cross-functional data analysis.
- Permit multiple users simultaneous data access.

Database accounting systems also provide data entry and integrity controls as part of the database management system. These controls are embedded in the structure of the tables as they are created, thus eliminating the need to program controls into every application that uses the data in that table. We will now explain how some of these advantages work.

Because a database stores data only once, the storage costs will be lower than for a flat file system that requires redundant storage. By avoiding the need to store data in multiple locations throughout the system, a database accounting system prevents data inconsistencies. For example, when a customer notifies us of an address change, we can enter that change once, in the Customer table. Every application that uses customer addresses—which may include invoicing, billing, sales promotions, marketing surveys, and sales summaries—automatically uses the updated address as soon as it is entered. Data inconsistencies can be a source of many potentially embarrassing problems for businesses. Since data is entered only once, the tasks of adding, deleting, and updating records can be accomplished more efficiently. By avoiding data redundancy, a database approach also ensures that the data items used in accounting applications will have the same field names, field lengths, and data types as other applications.

Centralizing data management and security lets businesses fix responsibility for these functions on one person or group. By concentrating this activity, a database approach enables the person or persons responsible for data management and security to develop valuable expertise in this function. When a firm adopts a database approach to managing its data, it usually hires a database administrator. The database administrator holds ultimate responsibility for the specifications and structure of all database tables in the information system. The database administrator is also responsible for enforcing security, making backups, and coordinating contingency plans for emergency situations.

Having the best collection of data in the world will not do managers any good if they cannot access it. A major advantage of database accounting systems is that they facilitate users' access to accounting data. By providing intuitive, graphically based report generators, database management software allows accountants to easily change the structure and format of their reports. Traditionally, one of the most difficult challenges of designing an accounting system has been trying to anticipate every report that the accountants and managers using the system would ever want—before the system even exists! The powerful query languages built into currently available database management systems make this crystal ball unnecessary. Queries let users ask database accounting systems for information by combining data tables and performing calculations in ways the systems' designers never imagined. Further, these user-designed queries and reports can access more than accounting data. For example, tables containing marketing and production information can be combined with accounting information tables to create truly cross-functional reports.

Finally, database accounting systems implement many important data input and data integrity controls at the database level. In the next four chapters, you will learn how to create accounting data tables that include validity checks, existence checks, reasonableness checks, and limit controls. By implementing these controls as part of the database, you avoid the need to include the controls in every application that uses the data.

Disadvantages of Database Accounting Systems

Despite the lengthy list of advantages outlined in the previous section, database accounting systems do have some disadvantages. The increased functionality of a database system does not come free—the higher price tag for a database system includes the costs of:

- Greater hardware requirements.
- The database software itself.
- Employing a database administrator.

Centralizing management and security control functions creates several drawbacks:

- The system operation becomes critical.
- Incorrect data entry corrupts many users' work.
- Territorial disputes over data ownership may arise.

One last disadvantage—a disadvantage that is more psychological than real—is accountants' distrust of any single-entry accounting system. Double-entry bookkeeping is so pervasive in accounting education and practice that most accountants automatically question and fear anything else.

The increased cost of a database accounting system is often offset by reduced needs for data storage and reduced programming costs. The elimination of data redundancy in a database system reduces the data storage capacity required. Since the data table structures can include many data entry and integrity controls, application programming is simplified—and simpler programming takes less time and costs less money.

The centralization of data and security control is a double-edged sword. Centralization puts all of a firm's information eggs in one basket, and that increases risk. However, it also allows a focusing of resources on contingency planning, security, backup, and recovery that can actually reduce risk levels.

Many firms have decided that the advantages offered by database accounting systems outweigh the disadvantages. The vast majority of new accounting system implementations are database systems. We expect this trend to continue as database management software becomes less expensive, more capable, and easier to use.

BUSINESS ACTIVITY CLASSIFICATIONS

Different businesses require different kinds of accounting information systems. The size of a business determines part of its accounting information requirements. Larger businesses, for example, process more transactions and require greater computing capacity than smaller businesses. The complexity of a firm's business activities also has a significant effect on its accounting system design. Accountants classify the complexity of firms' business activities using three broad categories: service, merchandising, and manufacturing. Not all businesses fit neatly into one of these categories, but the categories provide a good beginning reference point when considering accounting information system options.

Service Firms

Service firms comprise the simplest form of business activity. They provide their customers or clients with a service for which they charge a fee. Service firms' accounting information systems track revenues and expenses only—they do not need to track inventory information since service firms do not have inventory. Examples of service firms include:

- Accounting firms.
- Barbershops.
- Advertising agencies.
- Entertainers.
- Interior decorators.
- Law firms.
- Management consulting firms.
- Physicians.
- Realtors.
- Trucking companies.

You can see the simplicity of service firm accounting system requirements by examining the income statement in Figure 6.2.

This income statement shows revenues and expenses. The expenses are shown in one list—they are not broken down into categories of expenses.

Merchandising Firms

Merchandising firms are the next step up in complexity from service firms. The goal of merchandising firms is to buy goods at a low enough cost and sell those goods at a high enough price to earn a margin that will cover other expenses and provide a profit. Examples of merchandising firms include:

- Computer stores.
- Department stores.
- Discount merchandise chains.

Example Service Firm
Income Statement
Year Ended December 31, 1998

Revenue		$353,150
Expenses:		
Advertising	$ 42,170	
Depreciation	27,640	
Insurance	9,420	
Salaries	94,210	
Rent	106,400	
Other	62,180	342,020
Net income		$ 11,130

Figure 6.2 Example Service Firm income statement.

- Food markets.
- Hardware stores.
- Health food stores.
- Mail-order merchandisers.
- Office supply stores.
- Shoe stores.
- Wholesalers.

Merchandising firms' accounting information systems must track revenues and expenses, just as service firms' systems. However, the largest expense for merchandising firms is the cost of the goods that they have sold. Since firms often buy goods in one period and sell those goods in the next period, their accounting systems must also track inventory. Figure 6.3 contains an example of a merchandising firm's income statement.

Note how the merchandising firm income statement uses beginning and ending inventory in the cost of goods sold calculation.

Manufacturing Firms

The most structurally complex type of firm is the manufacturing firm. In addition to the activities that merchandising firms undertake, manufacturing firms produce the goods that they sell. Examples of manufacturing firms include:

Example Merchandising Firm
Income Statement
Year Ended December 31, 1998

Sales		$822,370
Cost of goods sold:		
Beginning finished goods inventory	$ 59,530	
Purchases	472,930	
Less: Ending finished goods inventory	(63,240)	469,220
Gross profit		$353,150
Selling and administrative expenses:		
Advertising	$ 42,170	
Depreciation	27,640	
Insurance	9,420	
Salaries	94,210	
Rent	106,400	
Other	62,180	342,020
Net income		$ 11,130

Figure 6.3 Example Merchandising Firm income statement.

- Automobile manufacturers.
- Canneries.
- Construction firms.
- Farmers.
- Machine tool manufacturers.
- Meat packers.
- Oil refineries.
- Pharmaceutical firms.
- Restaurants.
- Steel mills.

All manufacturing firms engage in similar classes of activities. Manufacturing firms must:

- Purchase raw materials and labor.
- Incur other manufacturing costs.

- Process the raw materials, labor, and other manufacturing costs into finished goods.
- Sell the finished goods.

A manufacturing firm's accounting information system must track information about all four of these activities. These include service firm and merchandising firm activities plus the additional burden of tracking costs through the production activity. Figure 6.4 contains an example of a manufacturing firm's income statement.

Example Manufacturing Firm
Income Statement
Year Ended December 31, 1998

Sales				$822,370
Cost of goods sold:				
Beginning finished goods inventory			$ 59,530	
Cost of goods manufactured:				
Beginning work-in-process inventory		$ 44,900		
Direct materials:				
Beginning inventory	$ 26,270			
Purchases	98,910			
Less: Ending inventory	(28,360)	96,820		
Direct labor		153,460		
Manufacturing overhead		210,600		
Less: Ending work-in-process inventory		(32,850)	472,930	
Less: Ending finished goods inventory			(63,240)	469,220
Gross profit				$353,150
Selling and administrative expenses:				
Advertising			$ 42,170	
Depreciation			27,640	
Insurance			9,420	
Salaries			94,210	
Rent			106,400	
Other			62,180	342,020
Net income				$ 11,130

Figure 6.4 Example Manufacturing Firm income statement.

The manufacturing firm's income statement reflects the increased complexity of its activities. The merchandising firm's *Cost of goods sold* section has expanded to include the three manufacturing costs: direct materials, direct labor, and manufacturing overhead. These costs, adjusted by beginning and ending work-in-process inventories, are shown on the income statement in Figure 6.4 as the *Cost of goods manufactured*. The cost of goods manufactured was $472,930. The cost of goods manufactured is analogous to purchases on a merchandising firm's income statement.

Now that we have seen how the different levels of complexity in the three business activity categories affect their income statements, we can discuss accounting information system requirements for each category. These accounting information system requirements are often expressed in terms of transaction cycles.

TRANSACTION CYCLES

Most accounting information systems and auditing textbooks are organized around business cycles. Some authors refer to these cycles as transaction cycles or accounting cycles. This framework—structuring accounting systems around cycles rather than financial statement accounts—is consistent with a database approach to accounting systems. A diagram of commonly used transaction cycles appears in Figure 6.5.

You can see how the transaction cycles relate to each other in Figure 6.5. In the revenue cycle, firms sell finished goods for cash or the promise to pay cash. This cash enters the financial cycle. Cash flows out of the financial cycle and into the purchase and payroll cycles. In the purchase cycle, the firm exchanges cash for materials. In the payroll cycle, the firm exchanges cash for labor. The production cycle converts materials and labor into finished goods, completing the cycle.

These exact cycle definitions are not universally accepted. For example, some accountants and systems designers include payroll activities in the purchase cycle since both payroll and purchase cycles culminate in writing a check. However, most accounting information systems texts treat payroll separately because payroll transaction processing is more complex and requires tables and calculation queries that the purchase cycle does not require. You may also see the revenue cycle decomposed into separate sales and cash receipts cycles. Similarly, the purchase cycle can be divided into separate purchase and cash disbursement cycles.

A firm may not have all of the transaction cycles depicted in Figure 6.5. For example, service and merchandising firms do not have a production cycle. The purchase cycle in a merchandising firm acquires finished goods for resale, not materials for production. For many service firms, the purchase cycle is unimportant.

In later chapters, we will explicitly discuss all of the cycles except the financial cycle. We include the major transaction processing elements of the

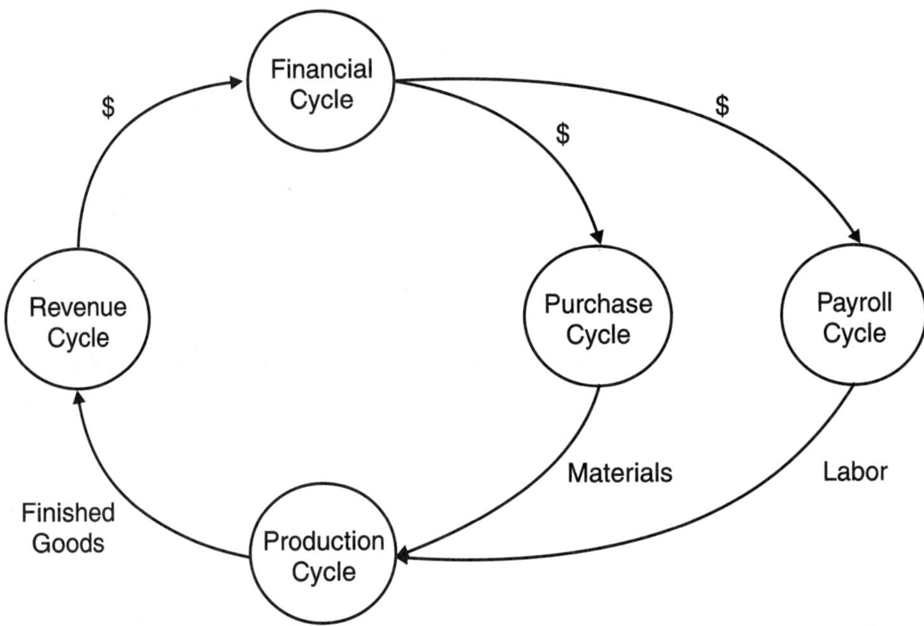

Figure 6.5 Transaction cycles.

financial cycle—cash receipts and cash disbursements for routine transactions—in our discussions of the revenue, purchase, and payroll cycles. Most accounting information systems courses avoid extensive treatment of the transactions specific to the financial cycle because these transactions are few in number. Auditing classes do spend significant time on financial cycle transactions because they are unusual and often involve large dollar amounts. The transactions that occur only in the financial cycle, such as stock issuances and large borrowings, are interesting but do not require highly complex information systems in most firms because of their infrequent occurrence.

Some accounting systems books describe a general ledger or financial reporting transaction cycle. When using the database approach, the financial reporting activities of a firm do not comprise a separate set of transactions. These reporting activities merely query and summarize the data stored while the business conducts its revenue, purchase, payroll, and production activities. Therefore, we do not treat financial reporting as a separate cycle in this book. The remainder of this chapter provides a brief introduction to the revenue, purchase, payroll, and production cycles.

Revenue Cycle

The revenue cycle includes all sales and cash collection activities. The three main transactions that we must record in the revenue cycle are:

- Customer orders.
- Sales.
- Customer payments.

We must also record the shipment of goods if it occurs separately from the sales transaction. The revenue cycle accounting system must be able to generate documents and reports that include:

- Sales order reports.
- Invoices.
- Shipping documents.
- Remittance advices.
- Cash receipts summaries.
- Sales analyses.
- Balances owed by customers.

Manufacturing, merchandising, and service firms all have similar revenue cycles. They all sell goods or services to customers and they all expect customers to pay them. A typical revenue cycle database would include the following data tables:

- Cash receipt
- Customer
- Finished goods inventory
- Sales
- Sales order
- Salesperson

The database design would also include necessary relationship tables, such as a Sales-Finished Goods Inventory table. We will explain how to build revenue cycle tables, forms, queries, and reports in Chapter 7.

Purchase Cycle

A manufacturing firm's purchase cycle includes all activities related to ordering raw materials from vendors, receiving the materials ordered, and paying for the materials. A merchandising firm's purchase cycle includes the activities related to ordering, receiving, and paying for goods acquired for resale. If a service firm has a purchase cycle system, it will record the purchase of materials incidental to providing services, such as office supplies. The main transactions that we must record in the purchase cycle are:

- Purchase orders.
- Receipt of goods ordered.
- Payments to vendors.

The purchase cycle accounting system must generate documents and reports that include:

- Purchase orders.
- Receiving reports.
- Checks.
- Backorder reports.
- Purchase summaries.
- Goods received summaries.
- Balances owed to vendors.

A typical purchase cycle database would include the following data tables:

- Cash disbursement
- Purchase order
- Raw materials inventory
- Raw materials inventory receipt
- Vendor

The database design would also include necessary relationship tables, such as a Purchase Order-Raw Materials Inventory table. We will explain how to build purchase cycle tables, forms, queries, and reports in Chapter 8.

Payroll Cycle

The payroll cycle includes the system elements needed to calculate employees' gross pay, deductions, and net pay. The payroll cycle must comply with a complex set of government regulations. The payroll cycle is closely related to the human resources management system in all firms—some firms have even integrated the two systems. The main transactions that occur in the payroll cycle are:

- Employees earn pay.
- Payments to employees.
- Payments of payroll taxes and taxes withheld from employees' pay.

The payroll cycle must generate documents and reports that include:

- Employee time reports.
- Employee commission reports.

- Checks.
- Payroll registers.
- Employee earnings records.

Manufacturing, merchandising, and service firms all have similar payroll cycles since they all have employees. A typical payroll cycle database would include the following data tables:

- Cash disbursement
- Employee
- Time worked

We will explain how to build payroll cycle tables, forms, queries, and reports in Chapter 9.

Production Cycle

A manufacturing firm's production cycle converts raw materials and labor into finished goods. The production cycle accounting database must record the use of materials and labor in production and must record the allocation of manufacturing overhead costs to units produced. Merchandising and service firms do not have a production cycle. The production cycle's main transactions are all cost flows:

- Materials inventory costs flow into production.
- Labor costs flow into production.
- Overhead costs are allocated to production.
- Total production costs flow into finished goods inventory.

The production cycle accounting system must generate documents and reports that include:

- Bills of materials.
- Job cost reports.

A typical production cycle database would include the following data tables:

- Finished goods inventory
- Job
- Raw materials inventory
- Time worked

The database design would also include necessary relationship tables, such as a Job-Raw Materials Inventory table. We will explain how to build production cycle tables, forms, queries, and reports in Chapter 10.

SUMMARY

In this chapter, we discussed database accounting systems, business activity classifications, and transaction cycles. We explained why double-entry bookkeeping was an excellent system for manual accounting tasks for many years, but we then argued that database accounting systems have advantages over computerized double-entry bookkeeping systems. Our discussion of business activity classifications showed you how to categorize firms as manufacturing, merchandising, and service businesses. We then explained how these classifications can help you match particular database features to accounting applications. We concluded the chapter with a discussion of transaction cycles and introduced the next four chapters of the book.

REVIEW EXERCISES

MULTIPLE-CHOICE QUESTIONS

1. A double-entry bookkeeping system records each transaction
   a. twice.
   b. as an abstraction.
   c. in a relational database.
   d. on the day it occurs.
2. The events-based approach to accounting theory
   a. classifies businesses in terms of their complexity.
   b. requires validity checks on all accounting events that are entered into the database.
   c. supports the use of relational database accounting systems.
   d. supports the use of double-entry bookkeeping systems.
3. The CustomerNumber field in *tblSales* (see Figure 6.1) is a
   a. foreign key.
   b. composite primary key.
   c. relationship key.
   d. primary key.
4. To find the amount due on an invoice, a database accounting system would
   a. look up the InvoiceAmount field in *tblInvoice*.
   b. look up the InvoiceAmount field in the sales journal.
   c. print an Invoice Totals report from *tblSales*.
   d. query several tables and perform calculations.
5. The primary key in *tblSales-Inventory* (see Figure 6.1) is
   a. the SalesInventoryQuantity field.
   b. the InvoiceNumber field.
   c. the InventoryItemNumber field.
   d. a combination of a and c.

6. Database systems store data only once. This feature
   a. makes *ad hoc* queries possible.
   b. eliminates data inconsistencies.
   c. facilitates cross-functional data analysis.
   d. permits multiple users simultaneous data access.
7. One disadvantage of database accounting systems is that they
   a. make data more dependent on applications.
   b. often require duplicate processing.
   c. can be more expensive to install and operate.
   d. fail to adequately control data entry errors.
8. The term *cost of goods manufactured* on a manufacturing firm's income statement is similar to
   a. *cost of goods sold* on a merchandising firm's income statement.
   b. *revenue* on a service firm's income statement.
   c. *purchases* on a merchandising firm's income statement.
   d. *gross profit* on a merchandising firm's income statement.
9. A time worked table would normally appear in a
   a. payroll cycle application.
   b. revenue cycle application.
   c. production cycle application.
   d. both a and c.
10. The purchase cycle includes
    a. manufacturers' ordering and receipt of raw materials.
    b. merchandisers' ordering and receipt of goods for resale.
    c. both a and b.
    d. none of the above.

DISCUSSION QUESTIONS

1. Why is double-entry bookkeeping better suited to manual accounting systems than to computerized accounting systems?
2. What prevents accountants from using a database model to automate a double-entry bookkeeping system?
3. In which of the business activity classifications described in this chapter would you include a hospital? Why?
4. Consider the statement, "Database accounting systems may be fine for large corporations, but they don't make sense for small firms." Do you agree? Write a brief statement that supports your position.
5. Centralizing management control and data security was both an advantage *and* a disadvantage of database accounting systems. Explain how you would determine whether the advantages of centralization outweigh its disadvantages for a particular firm.

EXERCISES

1. Describe the tables that a grocery store would use in its revenue cycle. Be sure to include all necessary relationship tables and foreign keys.
2. Using the tables and fields shown in Figure 6.1, describe how a database accounting system could use a query to print an invoice.
3. Assume you are working for a manufacturing firm that operates 14 factories, each with 16 departments. What tables would you add to those listed in this chapter for the payroll cycle to track employee time worked by factory and department?
4. Redraw Figure 6.5 for a merchandising firm.
5. Describe how a merchandising firm could use the purchase cycle tables described in this chapter to calculate the amount it owed to a particular vendor.

7 Revenue Cycle

Objectives

Revenue cycle activities include accepting orders from customers, recording sales, invoicing customers, recording cash received from customers, and maintaining records of these events. In this chapter, you will learn how to use Microsoft Access to design tables, queries, forms, and reports that can help you:

- Create and maintain customer records.
- Create and maintain finished goods inventory records.
- Record sales orders.
- Record sales/shipment information.
- Print invoices.
- Record payments received from customers.
- Summarize and report cash receipts information.

INTRODUCTION

This chapter describes the revenue cycle elements of accounting information systems. We illustrate many of these components using example data for the Pipefitters Supply Company, a merchandising firm. The revenue cycle includes those activities related to the sale of goods or services. Whether firms are manufacturers, merchandisers, or service businesses, their revenue cycles are similar. For example, manufacturing and merchandising firms sell products to customers; service firms perform services for customers. In both cases, customers place orders for the product or service that they are purchasing. The selling firm then ships the product or performs the service. At this point, the selling firm will send the customer an invoice that shows details of the sale. Customers then, pursuant to the terms stated on the invoice, usually pay the amount due shown on the invoice. Some customers will pay on receipt of a monthly statement that lists all of the invoices for that month. The practice of paying the statement amount once each month is a holdover from the days when running batch computer processes or manually writing checks was a cumbersome ordeal. Most businesses now find it more convenient to print checks daily and, therefore, pay from invoices rather than from monthly statements.

In addition to handling orders, invoices, and incoming payments, the revenue cycle accounting system must maintain a permanent record of customer information and provide tools for updating and revising that customer information. As we discussed in Chapter 6, a key feature of database accounting systems is their ability to store much more information about each transaction than a traditional double-entry system stores. To take full advantage of this feature, users must be able to access the revenue cycle information stored in the system to perform sales and cash flow analyses. Users must also be able to perform update and maintenance tasks on finished goods inventory information. Finally, the revenue cycle system should give financial accountants the information they need to create ledgers, journals, and financial statements.

CUSTOMER INFORMATION

Customers are the lifeblood of any business; therefore, accounting system database tables must include many details about each customer. At a minimum, firms want to know where their customers are located, what they have purchased, and when they purchased it. Businesses also want to track when their customers pay and the amounts of the individual payments. Some businesses do not record information about their customers' identities. For example, businesses such as retail stores, fast-food restaurants, and amusement parks seldom record individual customers' names and addresses. Customers of these businesses pay cash and would not tolerate the time it would take to record their identities. These businesses do, however, keep careful records of customer traffic by day, hour, and location. Increasingly, these types of firms are developing ways to obtain information about their customers' identities. Many supermarket chains now offer their customers an identification card that gives them a discount on merchandise. The discount is the price that these supermarket chains are willing to pay to obtain customer identity information.

Customer information appears on many documents that businesses create and use. Invoices, shipping documents, and end-of-month account statements require customer names and addresses. For example, the marketing department might want a list of customers that includes the name and telephone number of customer contact persons or a set of mailing labels for a particular group of customers. To ensure that customer information is consistent wherever it is used, many firms keep all customer information in one database table. Any document or report that includes customer information obtains it from that table. If, for example, a customer moves to a new location, the customer's address needs to be changed only once. A relational database accounting system stores customer information in a *customer table*.

The Customer Table

The first table in the revenue cycle that we will describe is the Customer table. The Customer table provides a central location for storing all information about each customer. This makes adding, deleting, or changing customer information easy and efficient. Copies of all tables, forms, queries, and reports that appear in this chapter are included in the *Ch07.mdb* database on your Companion CD-ROM. Feel free to copy that file to your hard drive and experiment with it as you work through this chapter.

To create *tblCustomer*, start Microsoft Access as you learned in Exercise 2.1. Once you are in the Database window, click the New button and double-click Design View in the New Table dialog box that appears. Figure 7.1 shows the Table window open in Design view on the Microsoft Access desktop.

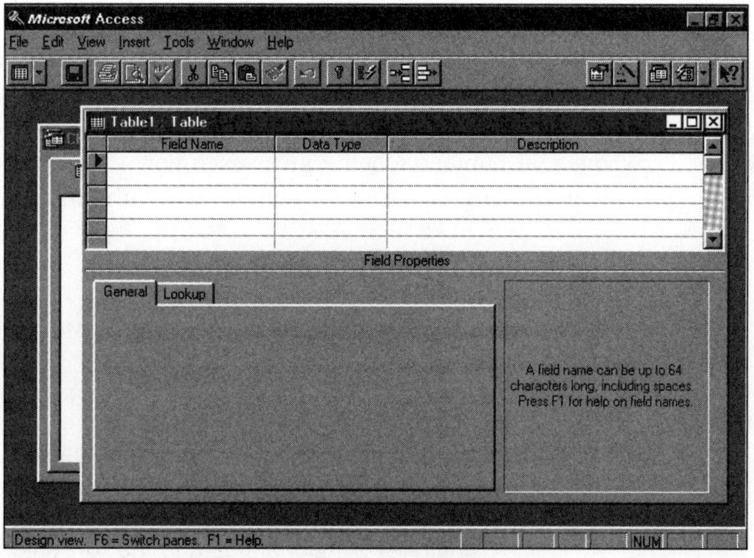

Figure 7.1 The Table window open in Design view.

The top part of the Table window includes the grid in which you will enter the Name, Data Type, and Description for each table field. The bottom half of the Table window includes a tabbed section in which you will specify Field Properties and a panel that provides context-sensitive help. In Figure 7.1, the Database window is behind the Table window. Remember, you can switch between windows on the Microsoft Access desktop in three ways.

Try it

The three ways you can switch between windows on the Microsoft Access desktop are:

1. Click the Window Menu item at the top of the desktop and select a window from the list of open windows that appears.
2. Press Ctrl+F6 to switch from one window to another.
3. Click an exposed, but empty, part of the background window to make it the active window.

The first field in the Customer table will be its primary key, the customer number. When the Table window opens, the cursor is in the first row of the Field Name column. We want to enter the name of the field, set it to an appropriate Data Type, and make it the table's primary key. You learned in Chapter 3 that the primary key field must be a unique identifier that exists for every record in the table. Firms use a variety of coding schemes to create customer numbers that will have these characteristics. For example, some firms use alphanumeric codes that combine the first four letters of the customer name with the first four digits of the customer address to create a unique customer number. To ensure that each CustomerNumber is unique, many firms assign a sequential number to each new customer. A sequential number scheme gives each new customer a number that is one greater than the largest customer number that currently exists.

Exercise 7.1: Creating the CustomerNumber Field

1. Type the name of *tblCustomer's* first field, ***CustomerNumber***, and press Enter.

   The first row in the Data Type column changes into a combo box and the Field Properties list appears in the bottom pane of the Table window.
2. Click the Primary Key button on the toolbar to make the CustomerNumber field the primary key for *tblCustomer*.

   A small key symbol appears in the row selector box to the left of the first row in the Field Name column. Since you will not be using CustomerNumber in any calculations, you can set its data type to Text. The Data Type combo box contains *Text* as its default selection.
3. Press Tab to accept the Text default selection.

   You can use the Description column to store a description of the CustomerNumber field if you wish. The Description column is a built-in documentation tool that is especially useful for storing explanations of complex or potentially confusing fields. Next, you can set the remaining properties of the CustomerNumber field.

4. Press F6 to switch to the Field Properties pane. The cursor will highlight the default Field Size value of 50.
5. Press Delete to erase the highlighted default value.

   If you use a sequential number scheme, the size of the CustomerNumber field will depend on how many customers you expect to have. For example, to start with a customer number of 10001 and accommodate up to 89,999 customers, you would set the Field Size to 5.
6. Type *5* in the Field Size column and press Enter.

   The panel on the right side of the Field Properties pane provides detailed instructions for each step in the property-setting process. Figure 7.2 shows the dialog box for the new Customer table after completing Exercise 7.1.

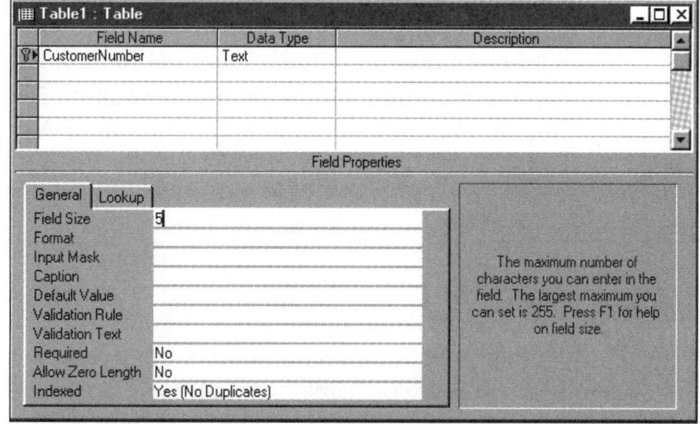

Figure 7.2 The CustomerNumber field in *tblCustomer*.

Now we will explain how to set the remaining properties for the CustomerNumber field. The Caption property is very useful and easy to set.

Try it

Press the Tab key three times to move the cursor to the Caption property box or click the mouse in the Caption property box to select it. Type ***Customer Number*** in the Caption box. This Caption property setting will cause *Customer Number*, rather than *CustomerNumber*, to appear as the default text for form and report controls that reference the CustomerNumber field. This can be quite a time saver when you are building reports and forms that use the CustomerNumber field.

The sixth field property in the lower half of the Table window is the Validation Rule property. The Validation Rule property provides a useful internal control feature at the table level. You can use this property to limit the values that a user can enter for a table field. This feature can help prevent data entry errors. For example, CustomerNumber is a five-digit field. The Validation Rule property lets you limit data entered into the field to numbers that are exactly five digits long.

EXERCISE 7.2: SETTING THE VALIDATION PROPERTIES

1. Press the Tab key twice or use the mouse to select the Validation Rule property box by clicking it.
2. Type the expression ***Like "#####"*** in the Validation Rule box to prevent a user from entering anything other than exactly five digits in the CustomerNumber field. For example, this Validation Rule would prevent a user from entering *JTP46* (which contains non-digit characters) or *9244* (which contains four, not five, digits) in the CustomerNumber field. You can make this data input internal control feature even more useful by entering Validation Text to accompany the Validation Rule.
3. Press Tab to move the cursor to the Validation Text property box.
4. Type ***Invalid entry. You must enter a Customer Number of exactly five digits.*** This text will appear in an error message dialog box whenever a user attempts to enter a CustomerNumber value that violates the Validation Rule.

Since CustomerNumber is the primary key of *tblCustomer*, you will want to ensure that each table record always has a value in the CustomerNumber field. Press Tab to move the cursor to the Required property combo box, click the box's arrow button, and select Yes. The Validation Rule property setting will override the Allow Zero Length property. The Indexed property was automatically set to Yes (No Duplicates) when you made CustomerNumber the table's primary key. Figure 7.3 shows the Table window with all of the above property settings for the CustomerNumber field.

You can create fields for the rest of the customer information by following the same general procedures you used to create the CustomerNumber field. To create a field for customers' names, type ***CustomerName*** in the second row of the Field Name column and leave its Data Type set to Text. The appropriate size for CustomerName will vary from firm to firm, but you should set it to accommodate the longest customer name you anticipate. For this example, set the CustomerName Field Size property to ***25***.

When you use the CustomerName field in forms and reports, the context will usually indicate that you are referring to a *customer* name. Press the Tab key twice, then set the Caption property to ***Name***. Of course, the Caption property

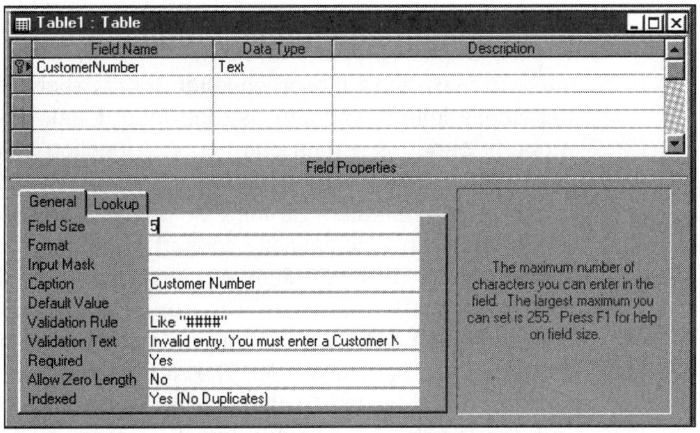

Figure 7.3 Property settings for the CustomerNumber field.

only sets the default, so if you need to clarify the label in a particular form or report, you can change the control's text in that form or report. You do not need to set any other CustomerName properties. Note that this firm's customers are business entities. If the customers had been individuals, we might have stored the customer name by creating separate fields for CustomerFirstName, CustomerMiddleInitial, and CustomerLastName.

Next, you can enter CustomerAddress1 and CustomerAddress2 fields with property settings that are similar to those of the CustomerName field. The CustomerAddress2 field lets the table accommodate customers with a second address line, such as a suite or office number. In the sample form, we set the Caption property to Address for both of these fields.

Now you can create three more fields for the rest of the customer address. By storing the three address elements—CustomerCity, CustomerState, and CustomerZipCode—in separate fields, you will help users more easily search and select records from the database on values of those elements. Make CustomerCity a Text Data Type with a Field Size property of ***25***, then set its Caption property to ***City***.

The CustomerState field is an excellent candidate for an input mask, since all U.S. state abbreviations are two capital letters. In the following exercise, we will show you how to create the CustomerState field and control the date entered into the field so that it conforms to the U.S. Postal Service's abbreviation convention.

Exercise 7.3: Creating a Custom Input Mask for CustomerState

1. Enter a Field Name of ***CustomerState***
2. Set it to a Text Data Type.

3. Set the Field Size property to *2*
4. Set the Caption property to ***State***

   To make sure these two-letter abbreviations are stored in the table as uppercase letters, you can use the Input Mask property. The Input Mask property performs a data entry control function similar to that of the Validation Rule property. However, a pattern set in the Input Mask property can insert and change characters as the field value is entered. For example, you can use this property to automatically convert lowercase letters to uppercase letters. Unfortunately, the Input Mask property does not allow you to customize the error message that appears when an entry is incorrect. You should carefully consider whether to use the Input Mask property or the Validation Rule property for a particular field. The next step shows you how to set the Input Mask property for the CustomerState field to limit the data entered to letters, limit the length of the field to two characters, and automatically convert any lowercase letters to uppercase.
5. Type *>LL* in the Input Mask box. The > symbol converts lowercase letters to uppercase letters and the *LL* placeholders in the expression limit the entry to two letters. Any other value entered will generate an error message.

Using an Input Mask property setting for the next field, CustomerZipCode, also works well. Setting the CustomerZipCode Field Size property to 10 accommodates the U.S. Postal Service's five-digits-plus-four Zip Code format. When you Tab into the Input Mask box, a button with an ellipsis label, called the Build button, appears to the right of the Input Mask box. Clicking the Build button starts the Input Mask Wizard, which can create input mask templates for commonly used fields.

Exercise 7.4: Using the Input Mask Wizard for CustomerZipCode

1. Click the Build button to open the Wizard. A Microsoft Access dialog box appears informing you that you must save the table before proceeding. Save the table with the name ***tblCustomer*** and open the Input Mask Wizard dialog box.
2. Select Zip Code from the list of Input Mask Names and click the Next > button.
3. Click the Next > button to accept the default placeholder character, the underscore.
4. Click the option button to change the data storage default of not storing the hyphen so that Access stores the hyphen as part of the field contents, then click the Next > button.
5. Click the Finish button to return to the Table window. The Wizard will create the Input Mask property setting of 00000\-9999;0;_ for the CustomerZipCode field.

This setting includes three parts; each part is separated by a semicolon. The first part contains the template. The Zip Code template includes the placeholder *00000*, which requires the user to enter five digits in this field. The backslash character tells Microsoft Access to recognize the next character, a hyphen, as itself. The *9999* placeholder permits, but does not require, the user to enter another four digits. The *0* in the second part of the setting, between the first and second semicolon, tells Access to store the hyphen along with the digits in the CustomerZipCode field. The third part of the setting makes the underscore character the default placeholder that will appear in CustomerZipCode field controls on data entry forms. To complete the Field Properties settings for the CustomerZipCode field, enter ***Zip Code*** as its Caption property.

The last three fields in *tblCustomer* store each customer's telephone number, credit limit, and the name of a primary contact person. Create the CustomerTelephone field with a Data Type of Text and a Field Size property setting of ***14***. You can use the Input Mask Wizard to set the Input Mask property to the pre-defined *Phone Number* setting as shown in Figure 7.4. In our example database on the Companion CD-ROM, we elected to store the telephone numbers with mask characters and we set the CustomerTelephone Caption property to Telephone.

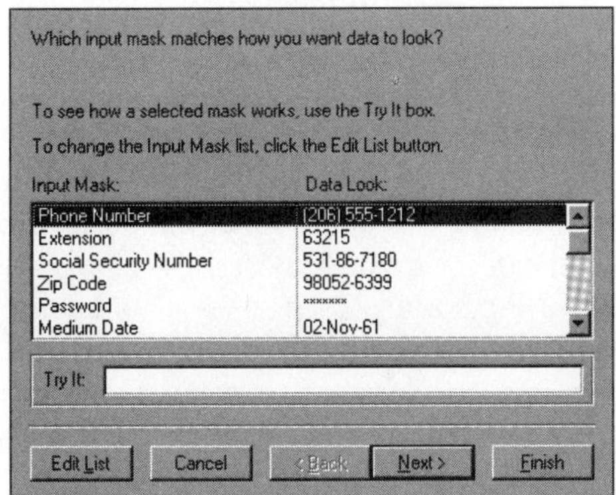

Figure 7.4 Using the Input Mask Wizard to select a *Phone Number* setting.

Enter ***CustomerCreditLimit*** in the next open row of the Field Name column. Set its Data Type to currency by typing ***Currency*** over the default setting, Text. Currency is a number Data Type that displays dollar signs automatically. To restrict credit limit amounts to integer values, change the Decimal Places property to 0. Set the Caption property to ***Credit Limit***.

Try it

Another way to choose Currency is to click the Data Type cell and select Currency from the list. Selecting a Currency Data Type automatically sets the Format property to Currency and the Decimal Places property to Automatic.

Enter the last field in *tblCustomer*, ***CustomerPrimaryContact***. Use your own judgment in setting the Data Type, Field Size, and Caption properties for this field. At this point, you can either close the Table window or open the table in Datasheet view to enter data. If you close the window, a dialog box will appear and ask you if you would like to save your changes. To open the table in Datasheet view, click the first toolbar icon. This icon toggles between Datasheet view and Design view for tables.

If you open the table in Datasheet view, you may notice that the toolbar at the top of the screen has changed; it has become the Datasheet toolbar. This toolbar provides buttons that can help you perform data entry, editing, and viewing tasks. You may also notice that the title of each table column in Datasheet view is the Caption property value you set. The *Ch07.mdb* database on your Companion CD-ROM includes a *tblCustomer* table with sample data that you can use to populate your table.

Try it

Note that we used a number of different characters in the Input Mask properties of the fields in *tblCustomer*. If you would like to review a complete list of characters that you can use in customizing Input Mask properties, use the Microsoft Access on-line help feature. Select Help, Microsoft Access Help Topics from the menu, click the Index tab, and type ***input masks***. Click the Display button, then double-click the words "InputMask Property" that appear in the Topics Found dialog box. This help topic includes a complete list of available characters and explains how to use them in the Input Mask property's syntax.

The Customer Information Form

You could enter customer information in *tblCustomer* while it is open in Datasheet view. However, the number and size of the fields in the table makes this a difficult task. Depending on your screen resolution, only six or seven of the table's ten fields will be displayed in the Datasheet view window. Entering customer information in Datasheet view would require a user to scroll back and forth to enter all the field values for each record. In this section, we will show you how to create a form for *tblCustomer* that will make entering, changing, and deleting customer information much easier.

You can create a form for *tblCustomer* by using the procedure you learned in Exercise 4.8. First, make sure you have selected *tblCustomer* under the Tables tab in the Database window. Then you may either choose Insert, AutoForm from the menu or click the New Object button's down arrow and select AutoForm as shown in Figure 7.5.

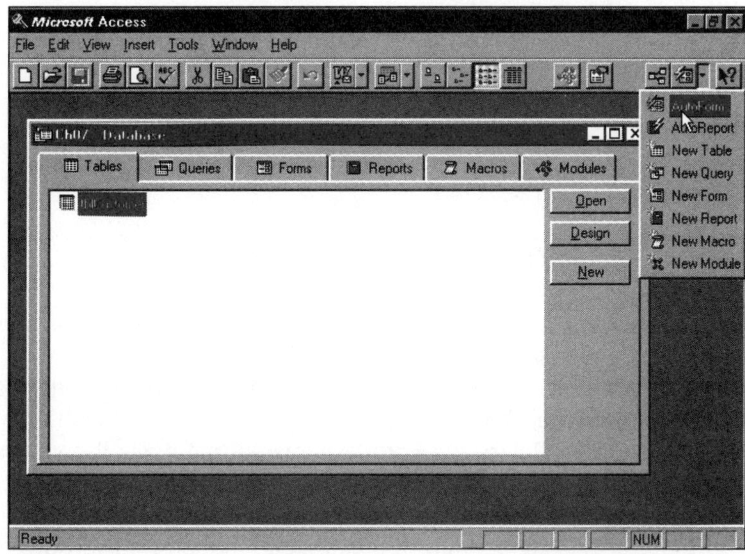

Figure 7.5 Selecting AutoForm from the New Object button's menu.

The AutoForm action examines the selected table and creates a form that accommodates many of the table's field characteristics. AutoForm is quick, easy to run, and often creates a usable form. Even when it does not create an ideal form, it often creates a form that you can edit to meet your specific needs. The results of the AutoForm action appear in Figure 7.6.

Although AutoForm did a good job of creating a usable form, you can improve the appearance of the form and enhance its usefulness. We will show you how to do this in the following exercise.

Exercise 7.5: Improving the Customer Data Entry Form

To modify the form, you will need to work in Design view. To enter Design view while the new form is displayed:

1. Click the Design View toolbar button (the first button on the left of the toolbar) or select View, Form Design from the menu.

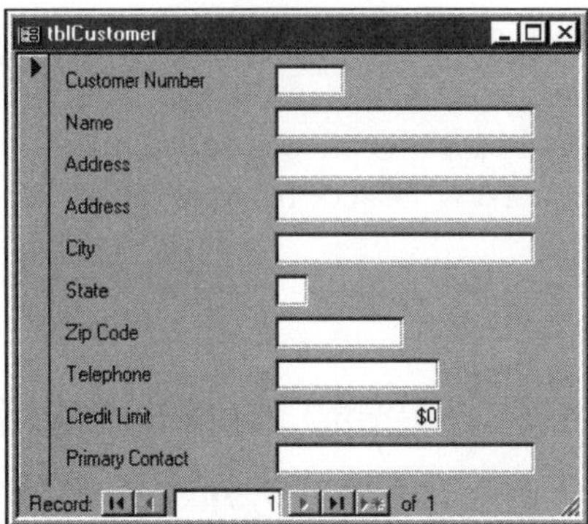

Figure 7.6 The AutoForm-generated Customer Data Entry form.

Here are some improvements that you might want to make in your Customer Information form. First, let's make a little working room on the form by performing the next three steps.

2. Click and drag the right side of the Form window to make the window wider.
3. Click and drag the right edge of the form background to the new right edge of the window.
4. Resize the Form window so that it fills the vertical space on the desktop.

   The Form Wizard sets the text of all the bound controls to an 8-point MS Sans Serif font. This font is often too small for many users to view comfortably. You can make the form easier to read and fit all of the controls on one screen by performing the next two steps.

5. Position the mouse cursor in the Detail area of the form just above the Customer Number control, then click and drag a marquee, or selection rectangle, around all of the controls on the form. Click the Font Size toolbar button and select 10 from the list.
6. While the controls are still selected, choose Format, Vertical Spacing, Decrease from the menu.

   Next, you can adjust the appearance and alignment of the controls.

7. Select the CustomerNumber label by clicking the box in its upper-left corner—the mouse cursor will change to a hand with a pointing index finger—and carefully drag the label toward the CustomerNumber text box control to its right. Only leave one or two grid dots exposed between the label and the text box control.
8. Click and drag a marquee around the label controls only and select Format, Align, Right to right-justify the label controls.
9. While all of the labels are still selected, drag the left edge of the CustomerNumber control label (it's the widest label) far enough to the left to expose all of its text.
10. Click the Align Right text formatting toolbar button to align the label text within the controls.
11. Click the Bold text formatting toolbar button to format the labels as bold text.

12. Right-click the CustomerCreditLimit control and select Properties. In the property sheet, click the Format tab and change the Text Align value from General to Left. Close the property sheet.

    Finally, you can complete the modifications to the form by changing some of the form's properties.

13. Select the form by choosing Edit, Select Form from the menu or clicking the small gray box in the upper-left corner of the form.
14. Open the form's property sheet by choosing View, Properties from the menu or clicking the Properties toolbar button.
15. Click the Format tab in the property sheet and change the value of the Caption property from *tblCustomer* to ***Customer Information***. You can also change the value of the Record Selectors property from Yes to No, the value of the Scroll Bars property from Both to Neither, and the value of the Auto Resize property to No. Close the property sheet.
16. Adjust the widths of the bound controls to accommodate the longest possible field contents.

    This last step may require some trial and error adjusting. You can use the Form View and Design View toolbar buttons to switch between the two views. Note that as you switch back and forth, the form changes size because the Design View rulers and the Detail section indicator bar disappear when you open the form in Form view.

Try it

You cannot eliminate the Detail section bar from the Design View window, but you can remove the rulers. Select View, Ruler from the menu. Note that this action operates as a toggle; if you repeat the action, the rulers will reappear. This little trick works in the Design View window for reports, too.

You can make additional adjustments to the form's look to satisfy your own sense of aesthetics. For example, you may want to make the text box controls taller to accommodate the larger font. Alternatively, you could reduce the size of the font in the text box controls. Figure 7.7 shows a finished version of the Customer Information form. To save the Customer Information form, select File, Save from the menu or press Ctrl+S and enter ***frmCustomer*** as the Form Name in the dialog box. You can close your Customer Information form with the menu command File, Close or you can press Ctrl+W.

Maintaining Customer Records

Now that you have created a Customer table to store customer information and a form that makes using that table easy, you can efficiently and effectively maintain customer records. First, you will want to create records for new customers.

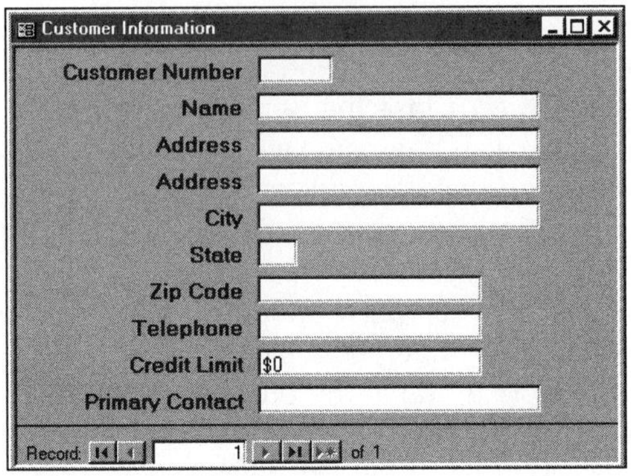

Customer Information

Customer Number
Name
Address
Address
City
State
Zip Code
Telephone
Credit Limit $0
Primary Contact
Record: 1 of 1

Figure 7.7 The Customer Information form in Form view.

Second, you will occasionally delete customer records you no longer need. Third, you will need to update the table as customers move, get new telephone numbers, and change other information that you have entered in *tblCustomer*.

You will want to keep your file of customer information current. Remember, one advantage of using a relational database model for an accounting system is that you only need to add, delete, or change information in one place. For customer information, *tblCustomer* is that place.

To use *frmCustomer* to add customers to *tblCustomer*, open the form by clicking the Form tab in the Database window and double-clicking *frmCustomer*. To enter customer information, just begin typing. Press Enter after typing the information into each control field. Notice how the Input Mask and Validation Rule properties that you set for *tblCustomer* help you avoid data entry errors in the CustomerNumber, CustomerState, CustomerZipCode, and CustomerTelephone fields.

After entering all of the information for the first customer, press Enter to go to the next record. After you have entered a number of customers, you can move backward and forward through the table using the PgUp and PgDn keys or the navigation buttons at the bottom of the form.

Deleting records from *tblCustomer* is a dangerously easy operation. Open the Customer Information form by clicking the Form tab in the Database window and double-clicking *frmCustomer*. To delete a record, move to that record using the navigation buttons at the bottom of the form, then choose Edit, Select Record from the menu. Press the Delete key to delete the record. Microsoft Access gives you a warning message that asks you to confirm the deletion. This deletion is not reversible. You can delete individual fields in a record using the Delete key while you are in Form view. Individual field deletions are reversible by selecting Edit, Undo Delete before you move to another field. After you move to another field, you can reverse *all* field deletions in the current record by selecting Edit, Undo Current Field/Record from the menu or pressing Esc. If you want to reverse changes you have made to a field *and* changes to other fields in the record, press Esc twice. All other deletions are permanent.

Deleting records in accounting databases is an action you will always want to consider carefully. Data in accounting tables is usually related to data in other tables. For example, if you examine a record in a Sales Order table, it will contain a customer number. The only place you will find that customer's name and address is in the related Customer table. If someone has deleted that customer's record in the Customer table, you may never find out who the customer was!

Keeping existing customer records current to reflect address changes, new telephone numbers, and other changes is an easy and straightforward task using *frmCustomer*. Open the Customer Information form by clicking the Form tab in the Database window and double-clicking *frmCustomer*. Use the navigation buttons at the bottom of the form to move to the customer record you want to change. Any changes you make to field contents will be limited by the Input Mask and Validation Rule property settings for *tblCustomer*, just as though you were entering data for the first time.

Try it

You can move through the individual fields of the displayed record by using the Enter or Tab keys. The Shift+Tab key moves backward through the record. The up and down arrow keys also move the cursor through the form.

Useful Variations on the Customer Information Form

The Customer Information form you just created is an attractive, functional data entry screen. However, you can improve its usefulness by adding more features to the form. For example, you could use the Command Button tool in the toolbox to create buttons on the form that would make it easier to use.

Try it

Click the Design View toolbar button, click the Toolbox toolbar button, then click the Command Button toolbox button. Draw a new Command Button on the form to open the Command Button Wizard. The first Command Button Wizard dialog box provides three categories of buttons that might be useful on this form. The Record Navigation Category includes buttons that can help users navigate the table more easily. The Record Operations Category includes buttons that can help users add, delete, and undo changes to records more easily. The Form Operations Category includes buttons that perform other form operations and filter database records. You can refer to Chapter 5 for more information regarding how to use the Command Button Wizard to make forms easier to use.

You may also want to create separate forms for entering and modifying different portions of each record. For example, you may want only the credit department to be able to set and modify customers' credit limits. You could then create two versions of the Customer Information form, one for general data entry and the other for the credit department.

In the general data entry version of the form, you can prevent access to the CustomerCreditLimit control by changing its properties. You can remove a control from the form's tabbing sequence and prevent it from being selected or edited. To modify the CustomerCreditLimit control's properties, complete the following exercise.

Exercise 7.6: Preventing Edits of the CustomerCreditLimit Field

1. Open the Customer Information form in Design view by clicking the Form tab in the Database window, selecting *frmCustomer*, and clicking the Design button.
2. Right-click the CustomerCreditLimit control and choose Properties to open its property sheet.
3. Click the Data tab and change the Enabled property to No, then change the Locked property to Yes.
4. Click the Other tab and change the Tab Stop property to No. To indicate to users that they cannot change this field, you can modify the control's appearance.
5. Click the property sheet's Format tab and change the Back Color property to the light gray color of the form background. To change the color, select the Back Color property and click the Build button that appears to the right of the property box. You can make your color selection from the dialog box that appears. If you prefer, you can enter the number of the light gray color, ***12632256***, directly into the Back Color property box.
6. Change the Special Effect property to Flat.
7. Change the Border Color property to the light gray color of the form background.
8. Change the Border Style property to Transparent.

The CustomerCreditLimit control now blends in with the form's background, suggesting to users that they will not be able to select or change a customer's credit limit. Try to enter the field you have protected. You will find that you cannot select the field by clicking it, tabbing into it, or using the arrow keys to move to it. You can save this form by switching to Design view and selecting File, Save As/Export and entering ***frmCustomerGeneral*** as the New Name in the Save As dialog box.

Just as you do not want the persons that enter and edit customer information to be able to access the credit limit field, you will also want to prevent persons in the credit department from changing customer attributes such as name and phone number. To create a version of this form for the credit department, you can change the properties of every control on the form *except* CustomerCreditLimit. To do so, complete Exercise 7.7.

Exercise 7.7: Creating a Credit Department Version of the Customer Form

1. Open the Customer Information form in Design view by clicking the Form tab button in the Database window, selecting *frmCustomer*, and clicking the Design button.
2. While holding down the Shift key, click each control except CustomerCreditLimit, then click the Properties toolbar button to open a property sheet for all the selected controls.
3. Click the Data tab and change the Enabled property to No, then change the Locked property to Yes.
4. Click the Other tab and change the Tab Stop property to No.
5. Click the property sheet's Format tab and change the Back Color property to the light gray color of the form background, 12632256.
6. Change the Special Effect property to Flat.
7. Change the Border Color property to the light gray color of the form background.
8. Change the Border Style property to Transparent.
9. Click the Format tab in the property sheet and change the Caption property to ***Customer Information - Credit Department***. Select Edit, Select Form from the menu, and then click the Properties toolbar button.

   You can save this form by switching to Design view and selecting File, Save As/Export and entering ***frmCustomerCreditDepartment*** as the New Name in the Save As dialog box.

Now you have a Customer table that contains information about customers. The table relates each piece of information to a particular customer through the CustomerNumber primary key field. All information about a particular customer appears in one row of the Customer table. You also have built two versions of a form that facilitate entering, deleting, and changing customer information.

INVENTORY INFORMATION

Customer information is very important to any business, but potential customers will only become actual customers if a firm has something to sell them. *Inventory* is a generic term for what firms sell to their customers. Inventory, broadly defined, may include products, services, or both. For example, a hardware store sells products, an accounting firm sells services, and an auto repair shop sells both products and services.

In our revenue cycle discussion of inventory, we are interested only in the goods or services available for sale to customers. We discuss the acquisition of inventory or inventory components in Chapter 8, and the conversion of materials and labor into finished products or services in Chapter 10. Firms need information about the inventory they have for sale in the revenue cycle because they must track which inventory items they sell, at what price they sell them, when they sell them, and to whom they sell them.

To ensure that inventory information is consistent wherever they use it, firms try to keep all inventory information in one database table. Any document, report, or transaction that needs inventory information must obtain it from that one inventory table.

The Inventory Table

The revenue cycle requires an inventory table that contains at least two fields. The first field should be the primary key, a number or code that uniquely identifies the product or service. For products, this field might contain an item number, item code, part number, catalog number, UPC (universal product code), or SKU (stock-keeping unit) number. For services, this field might contain a labor code, task code, or service number. The second field should contain a description of the product or service.

Some firms use a third field to store inventory selling prices in the inventory table. If a firm has fixed selling prices for each inventory item, it can store those selling prices in the inventory table. Firms that sell the same product or service at different prices to different customers must store selling prices in a sales-inventory relationship table. Firms that offer discounts from the list price to certain customers or classes of customers can store the list price in an inventory table and store the discount percentage in their customer table.

One problem that firms face when they store their inventory prices in the inventory table occurs when they change their prices. For example, if a firm recalculates and prints an invoice from last year with this year's prices, they will obtain an incorrect result. Possible solutions to this problem include storing the selling price in a sales-inventory relationship table or creating aggregate records of invoices that include the inventory prices in effect at the time of the transaction. Some firms store prices in an inventory table and copy them to the sales-inventory relationship table when a sale occurs.

Before accounting and inventory control systems were automated, the primary key often contained encoded descriptive information about the inventory item. For example, a women's clothing retailer might have used the mnemonic code *WSk-10-Br-HM* to identify a size 10 brown wool skirt supplied by Hometown Mills. A sales clerk could easily become familiar with many of the codes and not need to look up item descriptions—often a time-consuming task in a manual system. Some firms now assign sequential numbers to their inventory items. However, if employees without easy access to the automated system perform warehousing or shipping tasks, coding inventory items according to some logical mnemonic plan still makes sense.

Let's consider some alternatives for creating a simple inventory coding and description scheme for the Pipefitters Supply Company, a plumbing supply business that sells pipe and fittings. They sell only copper and brass pipe and offer a limited number of pipe lengths, diameters, and types of fittings. Table 7.1 shows the composition, type, and diameter of the inventory items. The table also shows mnemonic codes that might be used for each inventory attribute.

Composition	Code	Type	Code	Diameter	Code
Brass	B	4' pipe	4	.25"	025
Copper	C	8' pipe	8	.50"	050
		Cap fitting	C	1.0"	100
		Elbow	L	2.0"	200
		T-connector	T	3.0"	300
				4.0"	400

Table 7.1 Inventory items.

Note that even this fairly simple inventory will fill 60 rows (2 compositions × 5 types × 6 diameters) in a database table. Therefore, each alternative we consider should accommodate these 60 inventory items and logical additions. For example, the firm might decide to carry plastic pipe and fittings in all types and diameters that they currently sell. This would add another 30 records to the Inventory table.

One coding scheme that might work for the Pipefitters Supply Company inventory is to assign sequential numbers to the inventory items. For example, using a sequential code with a size of three characters and starting with *101* would accommodate up to 899 inventory items. An alternative is to create a code that uses letters and numbers in a systematic way. For example, we could create a coding scheme that would assign *BT-200* to the 2" Brass T-connector shown in Table 7.1. This second coding scheme would help warehouse and shipping employees identify inventory items even if they do not have ready access to the computer system on the warehouse floor or the shipping dock.

Once we have decided on a coding scheme, we must determine how best to store the inventory descriptions in the table. One alternative would be to use one field for the entire inventory description. This field would contain, for example,

2" Brass T-connector. This alternative requires strictly enforced standards for entering the descriptions. For example, you would not want to have one description entered as *2" Brass T-connector* and another description entered as *Elbow, 1" Copper*. In practice, such standards can be difficult to monitor. A better alternative uses separate fields for each description element. Using separate fields makes it easier to create effective input validity checks. Using separate fields also lets users search, query, and generate reports from the table more easily. In the next exercise, we will show you how to create an Inventory table for the plumbing supply company data that demonstrates a mnemonic coding scheme and separate description fields.

Exercise 7.8: Creating an Inventory Table

1. Click the Table tab in the Database window, then click the New button.
2. Double-click Design View in the New Table dialog box.
3. To create the item code field, type ***InventoryItemCode*** in the first row of the Field Name column. Leave its Data Type set to Text.
4. Click the Set Primary Key toolbar button.
5. Press F6 to move the cursor to the Field Properties pane of the Table window, set the Field Size to *6*, then press the Tab key twice to move the cursor to the Input Mask property line.

   Our mnemonic coding scheme uses the first character to indicate product composition, the second character to indicate product type, and a string of three characters to indicate product diameter. To implement this coding scheme, you can use an Input Mask property that requires the first character to be a letter, capitalizes the first two characters, inserts a hyphen automatically, and requires the last three characters to be numbers.
6. Type ***>LA\-000;0;_*** in the Input Mask property box. The > converts all subsequent characters to uppercase, the *L* requires entry of a letter in the first position, the *A* requires entry of either a letter or a digit in the second position, the \- automatically inserts a literal hyphen, and the *000* requires entry of three digits following the hyphen. The *;0* tells Access to store the hyphen in the Inventory table and the *;_* makes the underscore character the placeholder on input forms.
7. Set the InventoryItemCode Caption property to ***Item Code***
8. Since this InventoryItemCode is the Inventory table's primary key, you should set the Required property to Yes.

   Now you can create the three inventory element description fields. The first field is InventoryComposition. All current inventory items are either *Brass* or *Copper*. You can prevent errors and ease data entry by creating a field that accepts only these field values. Another thing you can do to make data entry easier is to have the form automatically capitalize the first character.
9. Enter a Field Name of ***InventoryComposition*** and leave its Data Type set to Text.

10. Press F6 and change the Field Size to ***6***
11. Press Tab twice and set the Input Mask property to ***>?<?????***
12. Press Tab and set the Caption property to ***Composition***

    You can use the Validation Rule property to ensure that the field accepts only one of the two correct values and issues an appropriate error message when a user attempts to enter an incorrect value.
13. Press Tab twice and set the Validation Rule property to ***="Brass" Or ="Copper"***
14. Press Tab and set the Validation Text property to ***You must enter either Brass or Copper in this field.***
15. Enter a Field Name of ***InventoryType*** and leave its Data Type set to Text.
16. Press F6 and change the Field Size to ***11*** (the longest value for this field is the 11-character string, *T-connector*).
17. Press Tab twice and set the Input Mask property to ***>C<CCCCCCCCCC***
18. Press Tab and set the Caption property to ***Type***
19. Press Tab twice and set the Validation Rule property to ***="Cap fitting" Or ="Elbow" Or ="T-connector" Or ="4' pipe" Or ="8' pipe"***
20. Press Tab and set the Validation Text property to ***You must enter one of the following in this field: Cap fitting, Elbow, T-Connector, 4' pipe, or 8' pipe.***
21. Enter a Field Name of ***InventoryDiameter*** and leave its Data Type set to Text.
22. Press F6 and change the Field Size to ***4***
23. Press Tab three times and set the Caption property to ***Diameter***
24. Press Tab twice and set the Validation Rule property to ***Like ".25?" Or Like ".50?" Or Like "1.0?" Or Like "2.0?" Or Like "3.0?" Or Like "4.0?"*** to limit the field so that it accepts only correct values.
25. Press Tab and set the Validation Text property to ***You must enter one of the following values in this field: .25", .50", 1.0", 2.0", 3.0", or 4.0".***

Notice that the InventoryDiameter field contents presented us with a special challenge because they included quotation marks. We solved the problem by using the question mark as a wildcard character. This is not a perfect solution—if someone were to enter *2.0Q* in this field, the Validation Rule would detect the error—but it allows the Validation Rule property to check the first three digits of the field. We could have solved the problem by storing only the number portion of the diameter description in the table and adding the quotation marks when we used the field contents on forms or reports; however, the quotation marks present even greater problems in those settings. Therefore, we decided to face the problem here at the table level.

The Inventory table's structure is now completely defined, so you can save the file by selecting File, Save and entering a Table Name of ***tblInventory***. Figure 7.8 shows the populated *tblInventory* that we have included in the *Ch07.mdb* database on your Companion CD-ROM.

To enter data into *tblInventory*, click the Table tab in the Database window and double-click *tblInventory*. The table will open in Datasheet view, ready to

tblInventory : Table

Item Code	Composition	Type	Diameter
B4-025	Brass	4' pipe	.25"
B4-050	Brass	4' pipe	.50"
B4-100	Brass	4' pipe	1.0"
B4-200	Brass	4' pipe	2.0"
B4-300	Brass	4' pipe	3.0"
B4-400	Brass	4' pipe	4.0"
B8-025	Brass	8' pipe	.25"
B8-050	Brass	8' pipe	.50"
B8-100	Brass	8' pipe	1.0"
B8-200	Brass	8' pipe	2.0"
B8-300	Brass	8' pipe	3.0"
B8-400	Brass	8' pipe	4.0"
BC-025	Brass	Cap fitting	.25"
BC-050	Brass	Cap fitting	.50"
BC-100	Brass	Cap fitting	1.0"
BC-200	Brass	Cap fitting	2.0"

Record: 1 of 60

Figure 7.8 The populated Inventory table in Datasheet view.

accept data. As you enter data, notice how the Validation Rule properties you incorporated in this table make the job easier. You should also try to enter some invalid data. See what types of errors your data input controls detect—and which errors slip through.

The Inventory Form

Although you can enter data directly into *tblInventory* more easily than you could enter data into *tblCustomer*, you can make data entry and update tasks easier and less error-prone by creating a Data Entry form for *tblInventory*. In our example firm, we restricted the inventory composition, type, and diameter. Although this is somewhat unrealistic, it gave us an opportunity to illustrate table-level controls. It also let us illustrate some form design techniques that you will find useful in many different accounting applications.

You can create a Data Entry form for *tblInventory* by clicking the Form tab in the Database window and then clicking the New button. Since *tblInventory* has only four small fields, we do not need to use a columnar form. We can display a number of records at one time by using a tabular form. Type ***tblInventory*** in the table box or select it from the drop-down list and double-click AutoForm: Tabular in the New Form dialog box. As you can see in Figure 7.9, AutoForm creates a fairly good-looking form that we can modify to meet our specific needs for entering inventory data efficiently and effectively. This version of the form is included as *frmInventory1* in the *Ch07.mdb* database on your Companion CD-ROM.

Of course, we can improve the usefulness of this form. In this section we will provide several exercises that you can follow to improve the appearance and functioning of the form. You can use these techniques in many applications other

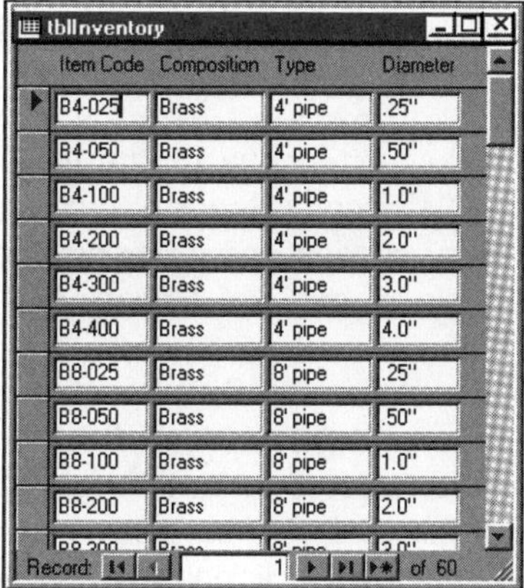

tblInventory

Item Code	Composition	Type	Diameter
B4-025	Brass	4' pipe	.25"
B4-050	Brass	4' pipe	.50"
B4-100	Brass	4' pipe	1.0"
B4-200	Brass	4' pipe	2.0"
B4-300	Brass	4' pipe	3.0"
B4-400	Brass	4' pipe	4.0"
B8-025	Brass	8' pipe	.25"
B8-050	Brass	8' pipe	.50"
B8-100	Brass	8' pipe	1.0"
B8-200	Brass	8' pipe	2.0"

Record: 1 of 60

Figure 7.9 The Inventory Data Entry form created by AutoForm.

than inventory forms. Our first exercise includes some general improvements to the form. The results of this exercise, in Form view, appear in Figure 7.10. You can use this figure as a guide while you work through the steps in the exercise.

Inventory Data Entry

Item Code	Composition	Type	Diameter
B4-025	Brass	4' pipe	.25"
B4-050	Brass	4' pipe	.50"
B4-100	Brass	4' pipe	1.0"
B4-200	Brass	4' pipe	2.0"
B4-300	Brass	4' pipe	3.0"
B4-400	Brass	4' pipe	4.0"
B8-025	Brass	8' pipe	.25"
B8-050	Brass	8' pipe	.50"
B8-100	Brass	8' pipe	1.0"
B8-200	Brass	8' pipe	2.0"

Record: 1 of 60

Figure 7.10 An improved version of the Inventory Data Entry form in Form view.

EXERCISE 7.9: MAKING GENERAL IMPROVEMENTS TO THE INVENTORY FORM

1. Click and drag a marquee around all of the text box and label controls on the form to select them, then click the Font Size drop button on the toolbar and select 10.
2. Select the label controls in the Form Header and click the Bold button on the formatting toolbar.

3. Drag the right side of the form and the gray backgrounds in both the Form Header and Detail sections to the right to provide more working room in the form.
4. Increase the horizontal spacing between the fields. You can do this by repeatedly selecting Format, Horizontal Spacing, Increase from the menu with all of the fields selected or by clicking and dragging each control separately.
5. Resize the label controls in the Form Header section to display the larger, bolded text.
6. Resize the text box controls in the Detail section to display the full contents of the fields. This will require that you toggle back and forth between Design view and Form view. Be sure to scroll down through all of the table records when checking the width of the controls. You can match the width of the text box controls to the label controls by clicking each while you hold down the Shift key and then selecting the Format, Size, to Widest menu command.
7. Use the toolbar text align buttons to align the headings and column contents as you see fit. We centered the Item Code and Diameter fields and left-justified the other fields.
8. Choose Edit, Select Form from the menu, then click the Properties toolbar button to open the property sheet for the form. Click the Format tab and change the Caption property to ***Inventory Data Entry***
9. To prepare for the next exercise, open the toolbox by clicking the Toolbox button on the toolbar. The toolbox will open in whatever position in which it was last closed, so you may need to drag it to a more useful position and shape.

The results of Exercise 7.9 appear in Figure 7.11. Note how we have arranged the form to the left of the desktop and the open toolbox to the right so that we may easily work with both. This version of the form is also included as *frmInventory2* in the *Ch07.mdb* database on your Companion CD-ROM.

You learned in Chapter 4 that a combo box control is a combination of a text box and a list box. In this exercise, we will show you how you can make the form a more efficient data entry device that also helps prevent input errors by replacing three of the text box controls with combo box controls.

Exercise 7.10: Adding Combo Box Controls to the Inventory Data Entry Form

1. The first step in this exercise is to remove the text box controls for the three fields that you will be replacing with combo box controls. While holding down the Shift key, click the InventoryComposition, InventoryType, and InventoryDiameter text boxes. Then press the Delete key.
2. Now you can use the Combo Box Wizard to create new controls for these three fields. Click the Combo Box button in the toolbox and draw a new control in the Detail section of the form just below the *Composition* label.

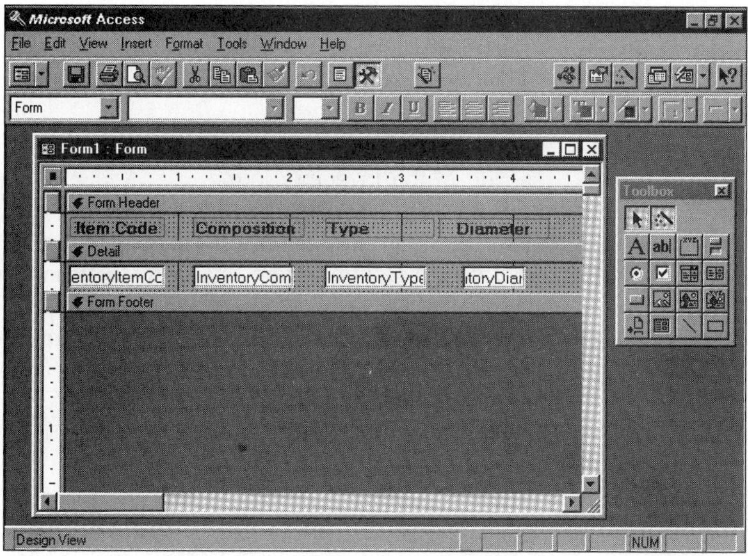

Figure 7.11 The improved Inventory Data Entry form in Design view.

3. In the first Combo Box Wizard dialog box, click the "I will type in the values that I want." Option button, then click the Next > button.
4. Enter ***1*** in the Number of columns box and then press the Tab key.
5. Type ***Brass*** in the first row, press Tab, then type ***Copper*** in the second row.
6. Move the mouse cursor to the right edge of the *Col1:* column header. When the cursor becomes a thick vertical bar with a horizontal double-arrow, click and drag the right edge of the column to the left. Decrease the column's width so that it accommodates the widest text, Copper. Click the Next > button to open the next dialog box.
7. Click the combo box arrow button and select the InventoryComposition field. Click the Next > button to open the last dialog box, then click the Finish button. The Wizard creates a combo box control according to your specifications and places it on the Inventory form.
8. To test the new control, click the Form View button, then click the InventoryComposition combo box arrow button to display the two choices, Brass and Copper.
9. To delete the label and change the text font to match the other controls on the form, begin by clicking the Design View button. The new combo box should still be selected. Click the Font Size toolbar button and select 10. Select the label by clicking its upper-right corner handle. Press the Delete key. You may wish to adjust the size and position of the control to match the text box control it replaced.

Next, we will show you how to create combo box controls for the InventoryType and InventoryDiameter fields. You could use the Combo Box Wizard to create controls for these fields; however, another approach is to make copies of the existing combo box, then modify the new controls to suit the requirements of these two fields.

10. Select the InventoryComposition combo box, press Ctrl+C, then press Ctrl+V twice.
11. Drag the two new combo boxes into their correct positions in the Detail section of the Inventory form.
12. With the new InventoryType combo box selected, click the Properties toolbar button to open the control's property sheet and then click the Data tab.
13. Change the Control Source property to ***InventoryType*** and the Row Source property to ***"4' pipe"; "8' pipe"; "Cap fitting"; "Elbow"; "T-Connector"***
14. Close the property sheet and switch to Form view to test your new InventoryType combo box. At this point, the Inventory Data Entry form should look like the one in Figure 7.12.

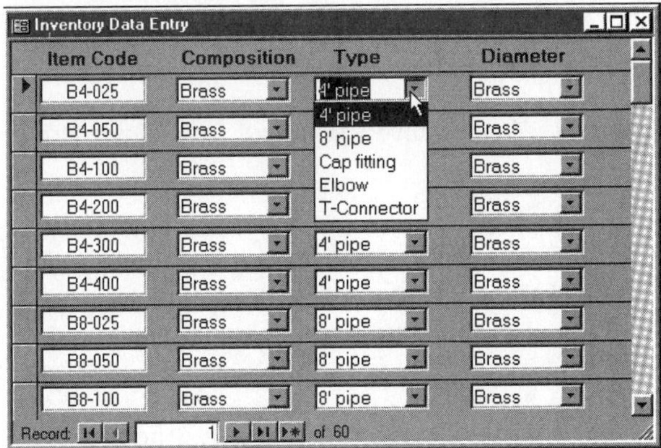

Figure 7.12 Testing the InventoryType combo box control in Form view.

The InventoryDiameter combo box presents a slightly more difficult design challenge. Entering the double-quote characters (the inch-marks) in the Row Source property would confuse Microsoft Access since it uses double-quote characters as string enclosures in that property. One way to work around this problem is to have the Row Source property look up the combo box values in a table. So, take a break from your form-building task—you may close or minimize the Inventory form—and create a simple table that contains the InventoryDiameter values by following the next six steps.

15. Click the Tables tab in the Database window and click the New button. Double-click Design View in the list that appears in the New Table dialog box.
16. Enter a Field Name of ***InventoryDiameter*** and click the Set Primary Key toolbar button.
17. Change the Field Size to ***4*** and select View, Datasheet from the menu.
18. Click the Yes button to save the table and enter ***tlkpInventoryDiameter*** as the Table Name in the Save As dialog box.

19. Enter the six valid values in the InventoryDiameter column as shown in Figure 7.13. You can return to the Inventory form by selecting File, Close from the menu.

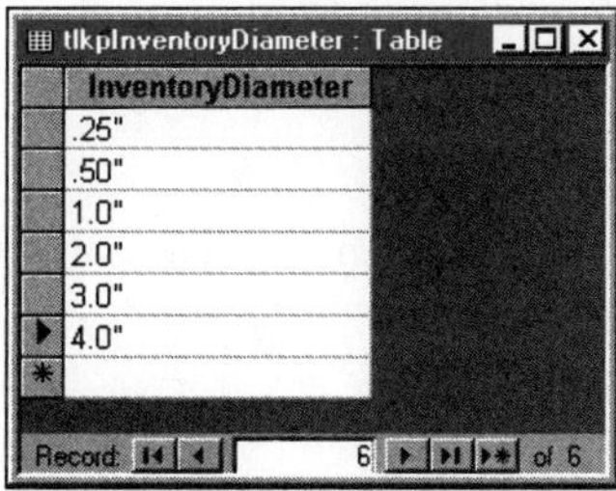

Figure 7.13 Entering values in the Inventory Diameter Lookup table.

20. Reopen *frmInventory2* on the desktop. We can now continue to modify the InventoryDiameter combo box control.
21. Select the InventoryDiameter combo box control and click the Properties toolbar button.
22. Change the Control Source property to ***InventoryDiameter***, the Row Source Type property to ***Table/Query***, and the Row Source property to ***tlkpInventoryDiameter***

You can switch to Form view and test the operation of the Inventory Data Entry form. This version of the form is provided as *frmInventory3* in the *Ch07.mdb* database on your Companion CD-ROM. Note that the Validation Rules you built into the underlying *tblInventory* still operate in the form, no matter how you change the controls. You should always be careful not to create rules in your forms or controls that conflict with the rules you built into the underlying tables. If you are not paying close attention to these details, it is possible to create a table-form combination that will prevent you from entering any data at all! When you create controls on a form, it is a good idea to give them a descriptive name. We use the prefix "cbo" for combo box controls, so you may want to go into the property sheets for these new controls, click the Other tab, and set the Name properties for the controls to ***cboInventoryComposition***, ***cboInventoryType***, and ***cboInventoryDiameter***, respectively.

SALES ORDERS

When customers decide to buy products or services, they communicate this desire by sending a purchase order form, sending a letter, making a phone call, or telling a salesperson. Each of these actions can comprise a *purchase order*. The firm that receives the purchase order often records it in some way as a *sales order*. No matter whether the order arrives as printed paper in the mail, a verbal order over the telephone, or a digital signal through a telecommunications link, all sales orders contain common components that identify:

- When the sales order occurred.
- Which customer placed the order.
- Which inventory item(s) the customer wishes to purchase.

To record these sales orders, we will need a Sales Order table, *tblSalesOrder*. To identify which customer placed each order, we will include a customer number field in *tblSalesOrder* that is linked to the *tblCustomer* table that we created earlier in this chapter. To track the individual inventory items that the customer has ordered, we will create a link to *tblInventory*. Since the link between *tblSalesOrder* and *tblInventory* is a many-to-many link—each sales order may contain many items and each item in the Inventory table may appear on many different sales orders—we cannot use a foreign key link. As you learned in Chapter 3, we must create a separate relationship table to model this link. We will show you how to create a relationship table, *tblSalesOrder-Inventory*, that will handle that job here.

The Sales Order Table

Since each sales order comes from only one customer, and a sales order needs a customer to exist, you can build the customer-sales order link into the Sales Order table. The primary key in *tblCustomer*, CustomerNumber, will become a foreign key in *tblSalesOrder*. Of course, the Sales Order table will need its own primary key and a field for the date of the sales order. Since customers may send purchase order forms to indicate what they want to buy, you should consider including a field to store customers' purchase order numbers. We will include a customer purchase order number field in our example. Therefore, *tblSalesOrder* will have four fields: a primary key, a date, a foreign key link to *tblCustomer*, and a record of the customer's purchase order number. Exercise 7.11 shows you how to create this *tblSalesOrder*.

Exercise 7.11: Creating a Sales Order Table

1. Click the Tables tab in the Database window, then click the New button. Double-click Design View in the New Table dialog box.
2. First, create the primary key field. Enter a Field Name of ***SalesOrderNumber*** and click the Set Primary Key toolbar button. Leave the field's Data Type set to Text.

3. Press F6 to move to the Field Properties section of the window and change the Field Size to ***6***. This size will accommodate 899,999 sales orders with a starting number of 100001.
4. Set the Input Mask property to ***000000;;_***
5. Set the Caption property to ***Sales Order Number***
6. Next, create a field for the sales order date by entering a Field Name of ***SalesOrderDate*** and a Data Type of Date/Time.
7. Set the Format property to Short Date.
8. Set the Input Mask property to ***99/99/99***. If you prefer, you can use the Input Mask wizard by clicking the Build button that appears to the right of the Input Mask property box. If you use the wizard, select the Short Date option.
9. Set the Caption property to ***Date***

   The next field, CustomerNumber, is the foreign key link to *tblCustomer*. Although the field's name in this table need not match its name in *tblCustomer*, it is a good idea to use the same name. We follow this convention in our examples here and on your Companion CD-ROM. More important is that the Data Types of these two fields must be compatible. The easiest way to ensure Data Type compatibility is to make the fields an exact match. The primary key in *tblCustomer* is CustomerNumber, a Text field with a Field Size of 5. Follow the next steps to create the CustomerNumber foreign key field in *tblSalesOrder*.
10. Enter a Field Name of ***CustomerNumber***, leave the Data Type set to Text, and set the Field Size to ***5***
11. Set the Input Mask to ***00000***

    Recall that we used the Validation Rule property instead of the Input Mask property when we created the CustomerNumber field in *tblCustomer*. The Input Mask property is sufficient in *tblSalesOrder* because we will later create a *referential integrity* link back to *tblCustomer* on this field. As you learned in Chapter 4, a referential integrity link places a much more powerful limit on field contents than does a Validation Rule property setting. We will show you how to create this referential integrity link after we finish creating the tables we want to link.
12. Set the Caption property to ***Customer Number***

    The fourth and final field in the Sales Order table is the customer purchase order number field. This field must allow any combination of numbers, letters, and symbols that customers might decide to use in identifying their purchase orders. Since we cannot anticipate the characteristics of this field we cannot build any data entry internal controls into the table for this field.
13. Enter ***CustomerPONumber*** as the next Field Name, leave its Data Type set to Text, and set its Field Size property to ***15***. Set the Caption property to ***Customer PO Number***

This completes the design of *tblSalesOrder* except for the referential integrity link that we will show you how to add later in this chapter. To save your work, select File, Save As/Export from the menu and enter ***tblSalesOrder*** as the table's New Name. The table that appears in Datasheet view in Figure 7.14 is included as *tblSalesOrder* in the *Ch07.mdb* database on your Companion CD-ROM.

tblSalesOrder : Table

Sales Order Number	Date	CustomerNumber	Customer PO Number
100001	1/14/98	10001	101-PR-753979
100002	1/16/98	10003	26754
100003	1/16/98	10007	BP-8666789
100004	1/17/98	10005	276-555438
100005	1/17/98	10010	985553
100006	1/18/98	10005	276-555497
100007	1/18/98	10006	DD-78725-NC3
100008	1/19/98	10001	101-PR-754007
100009	1/20/98	10002	8779465QW
100010	2/20/98	10004	B-462-121894

Record: 1 of 10

Figure 7.14 The Sales Order table in Datasheet view.

The Sales Order table identifies when an order was received, records which customer placed the order, and assigns the sales order a unique identifying number as its primary key. You can enter only part of the sales order information in this table since *tblSalesOrder* does not store information about which inventory items customers have ordered on specific sales orders. This would require *tblSalesOrder* to have repeating fields, a violation of the normalization rules you learned in Chapter 3. To store this additional information, we need a relationship table to link *tblSalesOrder* and *tblInventory*.

The Sales Order-Inventory Table

If Pipefitters Supply Company accepted orders for only one inventory item at a time, it would not need this table. We could add fields for inventory item code and quantity ordered to *tblSalesOrder*. Most businesses would find this policy to be too restrictive, since it would require their customers to send a separate sales order for each item they wanted to buy. The Sales Order-Inventory table we will now show you how to create, *tblSalesOrder-Inventory*, is a relationship table that records the many-to-many link between *tblSalesOrder* and *tblInventory*. Therefore, the Sales Order-Inventory table needs four fields to store:

- The primary key of *tblSalesOrder*.
- The primary key of *tblInventory*.
- The quantity of each inventory item that appears on each sales order.
- The price of each inventory item that appears on each sales order.

Exercise 7.12 will show you how to create *tblSalesOrder-Inventory* with these four fields. Before you begin, close any open tables.

EXERCISE 7.12: CREATING THE *TBLSALESORDER-INVENTORY* RELATIONSHIP TABLE

The primary keys from *tblSalesOrder* and *tblInventory* will combine to form the composite primary key in *tblSalesOrder-Inventory.* In Microsoft Access, you create a composite primary key by creating two separate fields, one for each entity table's primary key, then designating *both* fields as primary keys. If you are using the Microsoft Access help screens, you may notice that Microsoft uses the term *junction table* instead of *relationship table* in their on-line help and other documentation.

1. Click the Table tab in the Database window, click the New button, then double-click Design View.
2. Enter a Field Name of ***SalesOrderNumber*** and leave its Data Type set to Text.
3. Press F6 and change the Field Size property to ***6***
4. Set the Input Mask property to ***000000;;_***
5. Set the Caption property to ***Sales Order Number***
6. Set the Required property to Yes.
7. Set the Indexed property to Yes (Duplicates OK).

   The Indexed property setting must allow duplicates because a field that is part of a composite primary key may contain duplicate values. Remember that when you use entity table primary keys as part of the composite primary key in a relationship table, you always want an exact match on Type and Size. You will simultaneously enter values into the SalesOrderNumber fields in this table and *tblSalesOrder* using the Sales Order Entry form that we will describe later in this chapter. The other half of the composite primary key is the primary key of *tblInventory*, InventoryItemCode.
8. Enter a Field Name of ***InventoryItemCode*** and leave its Data Type set to Text.
9. Press F6 and change the Field Size property to ***6***
10. Set the Input Mask property to ***>LA\-000;0;_***
11. Set the Caption property to ***Item Number***
12. Set the Required property to Yes.
13. Set the Indexed property to Yes (Duplicates OK).

    The next field in *tblSalesOrder-Inventory* will store the quantity of each inventory item a customer orders on a particular sales order.
14. Enter a Field Name of ***SOInvQuantity*** and set its Data Type to Number.
15. Set the Field Size property to Long Integer and the Decimal Places property to ***0***

    The integer property setting assumes that Pipefitters Supply Company does not accept orders for fractional units. The long integer property setting will allow the company to record a quantity of up to 2 billion units for any one inventory item on any one sales order.

16. Set the Caption property to ***Quantity***

    The last field in *tblSalesOrder-Inventory* will store the price that the customer agrees to pay for each inventory item on each sales order.

17. Enter a Field Name of ***SOInvPrice*** and set its Data Type to Currency.
18. Leave the Field Size property set to Currency and set the Decimal Places property to ***2***
19. Set the Caption property to ***Price***

If you followed the steps in Exercise 7.12 carefully, you will have created most of the structure for *tblSalesOrder-Inventory*. Note that we have not shown you how to set the composite primary key in this table. We will show you how to do this in Exercise 7.13. To begin this exercise, you should have *tblSalesOrder-Inventory* open in Design view.

Exercise 7.13: Creating a Composite Primary Key for *tblSalesOrder-Inventory*

1. While pressing the Ctrl key, click the row selectors for SalesOrderNumber and for InventoryItemCode.
2. With both fields selected, click the Primary Key toolbar button. The primary key symbol should appear in the row selectors of both fields as shown in Figure 7.15.

This completes the basic design of *tblSalesOrder-Inventory*. To save your work, select File, Save As/Export from the menu and type ***tblSalesOrder-Inventory*** as the New Name in the Save As dialog box. A version of this table that includes data for the Pipefitters Supply Company is included in the *Ch07.mdb* database on your Companion CD-ROM.

We have shown you how to create *tblCustomer*, *tblInventory*, *tblSalesOrder*, and *tblSalesOrder-Inventory*. Now you are ready to model the relationships among these tables. You learned how to create relationships among tables in Exercise 4.2. We show you how to create relationships for the Sales Order and related tables in Exercise 7.14.

In Exercise 7.14, you will establish relationships among four tables. If the tables do not contain any data, you should not have any problems as you follow the steps. If the tables do contain data, you must make sure that the data in key fields are compatible before you begin the exercise. For example, if you have

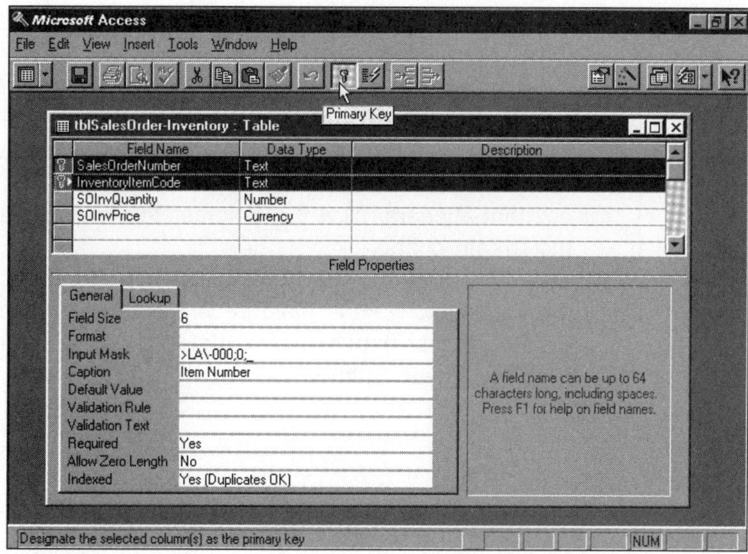

Figure 7.15 Creating a composite primary key for *tblSalesOrder-Inventory*.

entered any CustomerNumber values in *tblSalesOrder*, those exact values must exist in the CustomerNumber field in *tblCustomer*. Similarly, any values you have entered in the SalesOrderNumber or InventoryItemCode fields in *tblSalesOrder-Inventory* must exist in the corresponding fields of *tblSalesOrder* and *tblInventory*, respectively. If corresponding values do not exist in these fields, Access will not permit you to establish referential integrity on those links.

Exercise 7.14: Creating Relationships Among *tblCustomer*, *tblInventory*, *tblSalesOrder*, and *tblSalesOrder-Inventory*

1. Close any tables that are open on the desktop.
2. Select the menu command Tools, Relationships.
3. In the Show Table dialog box select *tblCustomer*, *tblInventory*, *tblSalesOrder*, and *tblSalesOrder-Inventory* by clicking their names while holding down the Ctrl key.
4. Click the Add button, then click the Close button.

   The tables you have chosen should appear in the Relationships window. You may wish to resize and rearrange the tables in the Relationships window using Figure 7.16 as a guide.
5. Click and drag the CustomerNumber field from *tblCustomer* to the CustomerNumber field in *tblSalesOrder*.
6. In the Relationships dialog box that appears, click the Enforce Referential Integrity check box, then click the Create button.

Enabling the referential integrity option provides an internal control on the CustomerNumber field in *tblSalesOrder*. This referential integrity link will prevent users from entering customer numbers in *tblSalesOrder* that do not already exist in *tblCustomer*.

7. Click and drag the InventoryItemCode field from *tblInventory* and drop it on the InventoryItemCode field in *tblSalesOrder-Inventory*. In the Relationships dialog box that appears, click the Enforce Referential Integrity check box, then click the Create button.
8. Click and drag the SalesOrderNumber field from *tblSalesOrder* and drop it on the SalesOrderNumber field in *tblSalesOrder-Inventory*. In the Relationships dialog box that appears, click the Enforce Referential Integrity check box, then click the Create button.

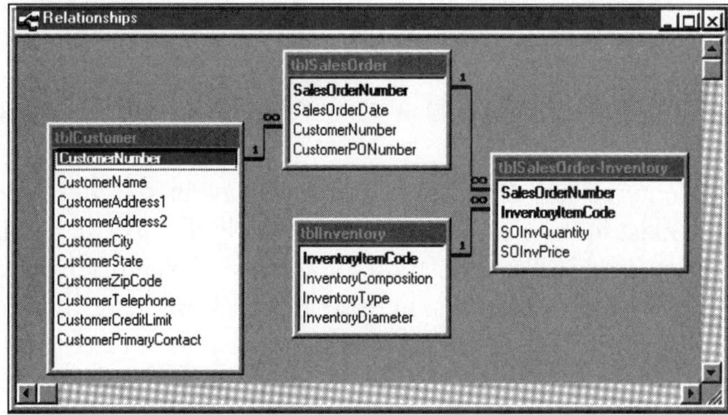

Figure 7.16 Relationships among *tblCustomer*, *tblInventory*, *tblSalesOrder*, and *tblSalesOrder-Inventory*.

The Relationships window showing all of these links appears in Figure 7.16. We have moved and resized the table representations in the Relationships window to make the table fields and the links easier to see. Select the File, Close menu command to return to the Database window. Now that you have established the necessary links, you can create a Sales Order Entry form.

The Sales Order Entry Form

The sales order entry task requires a more complex form than either the tasks of customer information entry or inventory information entry required. To enter all of the information contained in customers' sales orders, we will need a form that links:

- *tblSalesOrder* table to *tblCustomer*, to obtain information such as the customer's name and address.
- *tblSalesOrder* to *tblSalesOrder-Inventory*, to obtain a list of the inventory item numbers, quantities, and prices for each item on each sales order.
- *tblSalesOrder-Inventory* to *tblInventory*, to obtain a description for each item on each sales order.

A Sales Order Entry form that meets these objectives will use four tables. The form must read from *tblCustomer* and *tblInventory* and write to *tblSalesOrder* and *tblSalesOrder-Inventory*. Since this form will read data from *tblCustomer* and *tblInventory*, you must have data entered in these tables. Recall that the *Ch07.mdb* database on your Companion CD-ROM includes populated versions of these tables that you can use or from which you can copy data to work through the form-building exercises that follow.

Exercise 7.15: Creating a Sales Order Entry Form

1. Be sure that you have closed all tables. Click the Forms tab in the Database window, then click the New button.
2. Double-click Form Wizard in the New Form dialog box.

   First, we must select the fields that will appear on the form. Since some of the fields have the same name, it is important to select each field from the correct table. For the Sales Order Entry form, we will want to select the SalesOrderNumber and CustomerNumber fields from *tblSalesOrder* and the InventoryItemNumber field from *tblSalesOrder-Inventory*.
3. Select Table: *tblSalesOrder* from the Tables/Queries combo box in the Form Wizard dialog box and click the >> button to move all of the *tblSalesOrder* fields to the Selected Fields box.
4. Select Table: *tblCustomer* from the Tables/Queries combo box and click the >> button to move all of the *tblCustomer* fields to the Selected Fields box. Select *tblCustomer.CustomerNumber* in the Selected Fields box and click the < button to move that one field back to the Available Fields box. Alternatively, you could have selected each field in the Available Fields box *except* CustomerNumber and clicked the > button to place them individually in the Selected Fields box. Select the CustomerPrimaryContact field in the Selected Fields box before going to the next step. This will ensure that the next field will be added to the end of the list and will help the Wizard properly create the form.
5. Select Table: *tblSalesOrder-Inventory* from the Tables/Queries combo box. Select the InventoryItemCode field name in the Available Fields box and click the > button to place it in the Selected Fields box. Repeat this procedure for SOInvQuantity and SOInvPrice.

6. Select Table: *tblInventory* from the Tables/Queries combo box. Select the InventoryComposition field name in the Available Fields box and click the > button to place it in the Selected Fields box. Repeat this procedure for InventoryType and InventoryDiameter.

   Now that we have selected the fields that will appear on the form, we can give the Form Wizard further instructions that it can use to create the form.
7. Click the Next > button. The Form Wizard should indicate that it has chosen to view data by *tblSalesOrder*, to create a Form with subform(s), and to arrange the fields as shown in Figure 7.17.
8. Click the Next > button to accept the Form Wizard's proposed design.
9. Click the Tabular option button, then click the Next > button.
10. Click the Next > button to accept the Standard Style.
11. Enter ***frmSalesOrder*** and ***fsubSalesOrder*** as the Form and Subform titles, respectively. Click the Finish > button to have the Form Wizard go to work creating the Sales Order Entry form-subform combination.

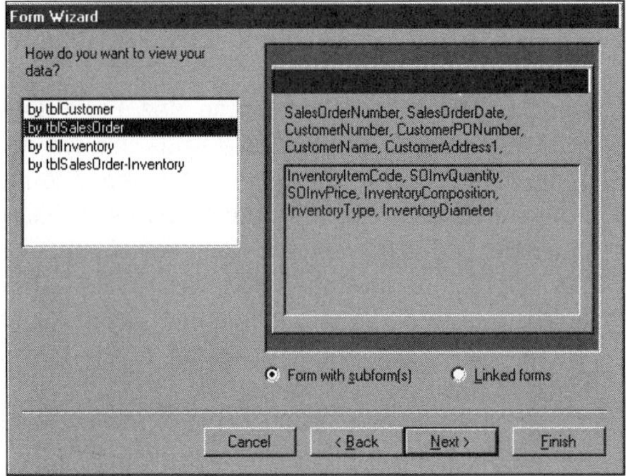

Figure 7.17 The Form Wizard's proposed design for the Sales Order Entry form.

The Form Wizard may take some time—over a minute on slower computers—to generate the forms. When it has completed its work, it will display the finished Sales Order Entry form as shown in Figure 7.18. Remember that this form is actually two forms, a subform nested inside a form. The Form Wizard has already saved these objects under the names we gave them in the preceding exercise.

Although this Wizard-generated form is certainly usable and includes all of the controls needed to enter, delete, and modify sales order information, you may

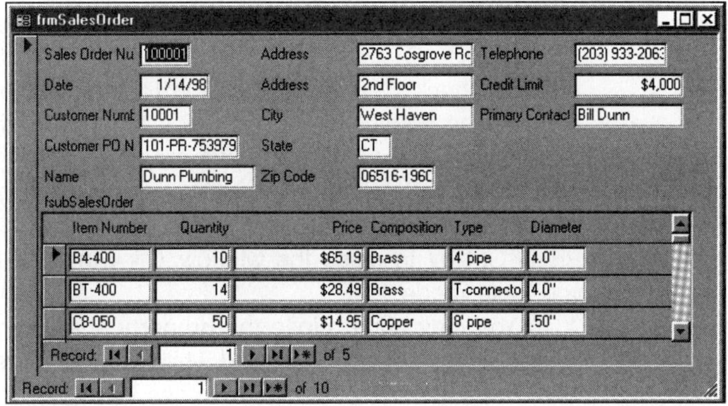

Figure 7.18 The Sales Order Entry form generated by the Form Wizard.

see some ways to improve it. The next two exercises show you how to make some improvements that make the form and the subform more effective and easier to use. You might identify other improvements or alternative ways of making the improvements we suggest. We encourage you to experiment, since form design is as much an art as a science. Just remember that you are designing a form that an input clerk might be using eight hours a day, so avoid bright colors and other design features that might irritate the user.

EXERCISE 7.16: IMPROVING *FRMSALESORDER*

Whether you have created the Sales Order Entry form using tables that contain data or you have entered data in the form after you created it, you will notice that the form does not scroll through the sales orders in numeric order. The Form Wizard did not include a sorting rule in the query it built behind *frmSalesOrder*. This is fairly easy to fix.

1. Open *frmSalesOrder* in Design view, choose Edit, Select Form from the menu, then click the Properties toolbar button to open the form's property sheet.
2. Click the property sheet's Data tab, then click the Record Source property's Build button to open the Query Builder window for the query behind the form.
3. Type ***Ascending*** in the SalesOrderNumber field's Sort cell in the QBE grid.
   While the Query Builder window is open, you can create a new field, CustomerAddress3, that combines the CustomerCity, CustomerState, and CustomerZipCode fields.
4. Use the scrollbar at the bottom of the QBE grid to move to next open grid column and press Shift+F2 to open the Zoom box.

5. Type ***CustomerAddress3: [CustomerCity] & ", " & [CustomerState] & " " & [CustomerZipCode]*** in the Zoom box, then click the OK button.

   To check your work, click the Run toolbar button—the button with the exclamation point—and scroll to the far right of the resulting dynaset. Examine the new field you have created, CustomerAddress3. It should show each customer's city, followed by a comma and a space, state, followed by a space, and zip code.
6. Press Ctrl+W to close the window. Click the Yes button to save the changes you have made.

   You may either close the property sheet or drag it to the bottom of the screen so it is out of your way while you do more work on the form. The next steps include cosmetic changes to the form's layout that make it easier to use. These are only recommendations; feel free to use your own judgment as you make these changes. You may find it helpful to refer to Figure 7.19, which shows the form modified using the steps we outline below.
7. Select the CustomerCity text box control with the property sheet open. Click the Data label and change the Control Source property to ***CustomerAddress3***
8. Delete the CustomerState and CustomerZipCode controls (both the labels and the text boxes).
9. Delete the *fsubSalesOrder* label on the Subform/Subreport object.
10. Consider deleting the labels for those text box controls that are self-explanatory and in which you will not be entering data on this form. We chose to delete labels for CustomerName, all of the customer address fields, and CustomerTelephone.

    Next, you can set the properties of the information display controls so that they blend in with the background of the form and so that data entry persons cannot use them to change data in *tblCustomer*.
11. Select the information display text box controls with the property sheet open. Click the Format tab and change the Back Style property to Transparent, the Special Effect property to Flat, and the Border Style property to Transparent.
12. Click the Data tab and change the Enabled property to No and the Locked property to Yes.
13. Click the Other tab and change the Tab Stop property to No.

    Finally, you can make the following appearance adjustments. As you fine-tune the form, you will find the Format menu commands—Align, Size, Horizontal Spacing, and Vertical Spacing—to be quite helpful. For making small adjustments to form controls, the Ctrl+arrow keys and Shift+arrow keys are also useful. The Ctrl+arrow keys move the selected object(s) and the Shift+arrow keys change the size of the selected object(s).
14. Resize and rearrange the controls so that the data entry controls (SalesOrderNumber, SalesOrderDate, CustomerNumber, and CustomerPONumber) are separated from the information display controls.
15. Use the tools on the Formatting toolbar to set the labels' typefaces to Bold. You can also use the Formatting toolbar tools to change the justification of the text box control contents.

16. Choose Edit, Select Form from the menu, click the Format tab, change the Caption property to ***Sales Order Entry*** and the Record Selectors property to No.

The results of these modifications to *frmSalesOrder* appear in Figure 7.19. This form is included as *frmSalesOrder* in the *Ch07.mdb* database on your Companion CD-ROM. You can close the form by pressing Ctrl+W in either Form or Design view. Click the Yes button to save your changes.

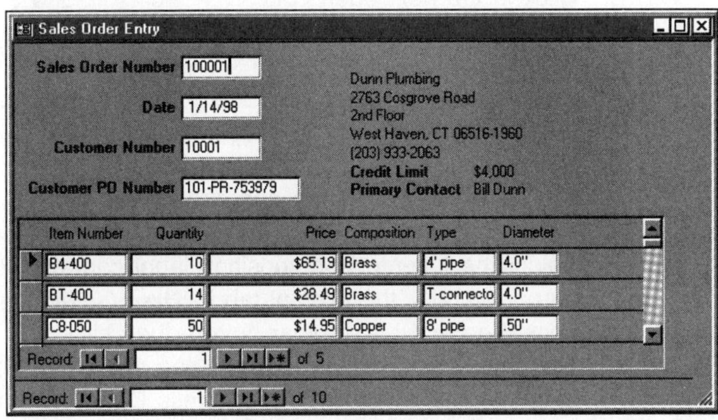

Figure 7.19 The modified *frmSalesOrder* in Form view.

In the next exercise, we will show you how to make similar modifications to the subform, *fsubSalesOrder*. Be sure you have closed all tables and forms before beginning. You may wish to use Figure 7.20 for guidance as you work through the exercise.

EXERCISE 7.17: IMPROVING *FSUBSALESORDER*

1. Click the Forms tab in the Database window, select *fsubSalesOrder*, then click the Design button.
2. Delete the InventoryType and InventoryDiameter controls.
3. Rearrange the remaining controls and their labels in the following order: InventoryItemNumber, InventoryComposition, SOInvQuantity, and SOInvPrice.
4. Click the Properties toolbar button and select the InventoryComposition text box control. Change its properties as follows: click the Format tab and set the Back Style property to Transparent, the Special Effect property to Flat,

and the Border Style to Transparent; click the Data tab and set the Enabled property to No and the Locked property to Yes; then click the Other tab and set the Tab Stop property to No.

Next, we will show you how to open the query behind the form and create two new calculated fields that you can use on this form.

5. Choose Edit, Select Form from the menu. Click the property sheet's Data tab, select the Record Source property, then click its Build button to open the Query Builder window.
6. Select the first open column in the QBE grid and press Shift+F2 to open the Zoom box.
7. Type ***Description: [InventoryDiameter] & " " & [InventoryComposition] & " " & [InventoryType]*** in the Zoom box and click the OK button.
8. Click in the next open column in the QBE grid and press Shift+F2. Type ***Extension: [SOInvPrice] * [SOInvQuantity]*** in the Zoom box and click the OK button.
9. Press Ctrl+W to close the Query Builder window. Click the Yes button to confirm that you want to save your changes.
10. Select the InventoryComposition text box control with the property sheet open. Click the Data tab and change the Control Source property to ***Description***
11. Select the InventoryComposition label control and change its Caption property under the Format tab to ***Description***
12. Click the Field List toolbar button, then click and drag the Extension field to the Detail section of the form to the right of the other controls. Select the Extension field's label control, press Ctrl+X to cut the label, click the Form Header section bar, then press Ctrl+V to paste the label in the Form Header. Use the Ctrl+right arrow key to align the label control over the Extension text box control.
13. Using Figure 7.20 as a guide, use the tools on the Formatting toolbar to adjust the font characteristics and alignment of the fields on the form.

The results of these modifications to *fsubSalesOrder* appear in Figure 7.20. This form is included as *fsubSalesOrder* in the *Ch07.mdb* database on your Companion CD-ROM. You can close the form by pressing Ctrl+W in either Form or Design view. Click the Yes button to save your changes. You should open *frmSalesOrder* and make sure that your revised subform still fits in the *fsubSalesOrder* subform object on *frmSalesOrder*. You can modify either or both forms to obtain a precise fit. Unfortunately, Microsoft Access has not automated this task, so you must do some trial-and-error fitting to get a good result. Figure 7.21 shows *frmSalesOrder* adjusted to fit the modified *fsubSalesOrder*.

As you learned in Chapter 5, you can further enhance this form by adding buttons that make navigation easier. You can also add error-checking macros to the form. For example, you could write a macro that would test whether a par-

fsubSalesOrder

Item Number	Description	Quantity	Price	Extension
B4-025	.25" Brass 4' pipe	20	$21.95	$439.00
B4-100	1.0" Brass 4' pipe	10	$34.79	$347.90
B4-400	4.0" Brass 4' pipe	10	$65.19	$651.90
BC-025	.25" Brass Cap fitting	50	$5.25	$262.50
BL-100	1.0" Brass Elbow	100	$10.45	$1,045.00
BL-100	1.0" Brass Elbow	15	$10.45	$156.75

Record: 1 of 37

Figure 7.20 The modified *fsubSalesOrder* in Form view.

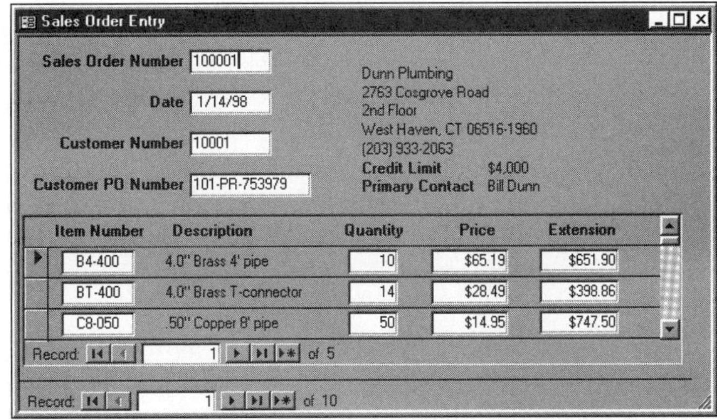
Sales Order Entry

Sales Order Number 100001
Date 1/14/98
Customer Number 10001
Customer PO Number 101-PR-753979

Dunn Plumbing
2763 Cosgrove Road
2nd Floor
West Haven, CT 06516-1960
(203) 933-2063
Credit Limit $4,000
Primary Contact Bill Dunn

Item Number	Description	Quantity	Price	Extension
B4-400	4.0" Brass 4' pipe	10	$65.19	$651.90
BT-400	4.0" Brass T-connector	14	$28.49	$398.86
C8-050	.50" Copper 8' pipe	50	$14.95	$747.50

Record: 1 of 5

Record: 1 of 10

Figure 7.21 Adjusting *frmSalesOrder* to contain the modified *fsubSalesOrder* in Form view.

ticular sales order would exceed a customer's credit limit. We encourage you to experiment with some of the techniques you learned in Chapter 5 to enhance this form and other sales order forms you create for your own projects or client applications.

RECORDING SALES

After the credit department approves the sales order and the goods are ready to be shipped, the system must create an invoice and shipping documents. Shipping documents, such as bills of lading or packing slips, vary greatly in appearance and design. However, they always contain a subset of the information that appears on the invoice. In this section we will show you how to create an Invoice report. You can easily modify this invoice to create shipping documents that suit a particular application. The invoice is a very important record in the revenue cycle;

it summarizes each sales transaction for accounting and includes valuable marketing information. To create an invoice, you will need two new tables: a Sales table and a Sales-Inventory relationship table. You will also use the *tblCustomer* and *tblInventory* objects that you have already created.

The Sales Table

Since each sale transaction occurs with only one customer, and a sale needs a customer to exist, you can build the customer-sales link into the Sales table by making the primary key of *tblCustomer* a foreign key in *tblSales*. The Sales table will need its own primary key and a field for the date the items were shipped. We will also include a SalesOrderNumber field in our example. We will not, however, create a foreign key link to *tblSalesOrder* on SalesOrderNumber. If we created such a link, which would be consistent with database theory, Microsoft Access would not always respond correctly because the links from *tblSalesOrder* and *tblSales* to *tblInventory* might conflict. Therefore, *tblSales* will have four fields: a primary key, a shipment date, a foreign key link to *tblCustomer*, and SalesOrderNumber. Exercise 7.18 shows you how to create *tblSales*.

Exercise 7.18: Creating a Sales Table

1. Click the Tables tab in the Database window, then click the New button. Double-click Design View in the New Table dialog box.
2. To create the primary key field, enter a Field Name of ***InvoiceNumber*** and click the Set Primary Key toolbar button. Leave the field's Data Type set to Text.
3. Set the Field Size property to ***6***
4. Set the Input Mask property to ***000000;;_***
5. Set the Caption property to ***Invoice Number***
6. To create a field for the invoice date, enter a Field Name of ***InvoiceDate*** and a Data Type of Date/Time.
7. Set the Format property to Short Date.
8. Set the Input Mask property to *99/99/99*. If you prefer, you can use the Input Mask Wizard by clicking the Build button that appears to the right of the Input Mask property box. If you use the Wizard, select the Short Date option.
9. Set the Caption property to ***Date***
10. Next, enter a Field Name of ***CustomerNumber***, leave the Data Type set to Text, set the Field Size to *5*, set the Input Mask to ***00000***, and set the Caption property to ***Customer Number***
11. Enter ***SalesOrderNumber*** as the next Field Name, leave its Data Type set to Text, set its Field Size property to *6*, set its Input Mask property to ***000000;;_*** and set its Caption property to ***Sales Order Number***

This completes the design of *tblSales*. We will add referential integrity links to *tblCustomer* and the relationship table that connects *tblSales* to *tblInventory* after we create that relationship table in the next exercise. To save your work on the Sales table, select File, Save As/Export from the menu and type ***tblSales*** as the New Name in the Save As dialog box. An example *tblSales* is included in the *Ch07.mdb* database on your Companion CD-ROM.

The Sales-Inventory Table

This table is very similar to *tblSalesOrder-Inventory*. It provides the many-to-many link between *tblSales* and *tblInventory* and stores the quantity and price of each inventory item on each invoice. Exercise 7.19 will show you how to create *tblSales-Inventory* with four fields: InvoiceNumber, InventoryItemNumber, SInvQuantity, and SInvPrice. Before you begin, close all tables and open the Database window.

Exercise 7.19: Creating the *tblSales-Inventory* Relationship Table

1. Click the Table tab in the Database window, click the New button, then double-click Design View.
2. To create the first half of the composite primary key, enter a Field Name of ***InvoiceNumber*** and leave its Data Type set to Text. Set the Field Size property to ***6***, the Input Mask property to ***000000;;_***, the Caption property to ***Invoice Number***, the Required property to Yes, and the Indexed property to Yes (Duplicates OK).
3. To create the second half of the primary key, enter a Field Name of ***InventoryItemCode*** and leave its Data Type set to Text. Set its Field Size property to ***6***, its Input Mask property to ***>LA\-000;0;_***, its Caption property to ***Item Number***, its Required property to Yes, and its Indexed property to Yes (Duplicates OK).
4. While pressing the Ctrl key, click the row selector for InvoiceNumber and then click the row selector for InventoryItemNumber. With both fields selected, click the Set Primary Key toolbar button. The primary key symbol should appear in the row selectors of both fields.
5. Next, enter a Field Name of ***SInvQuantity*** and set its Data Type to Number.
6. Set the Field Size property to Long Integer, the Decimal Places property to ***0***, and the Caption property to ***Quantity***
7. Enter the last Field Name of ***SInvPrice*** and set its Data Type to Currency.
8. Leave its Field Size property set to Currency, set its Decimal Places property to ***2***, and set its Caption property to ***Price***

This completes *tblSales-Inventory*. To save your work, select File, Save As/Export from the menu and type ***tblSales-Inventory*** as the New Name in the Save As dialog box. A version of this table that includes data for the Pipefitters Supply Company is included in the *Ch07.mdb* database on your Companion CD-ROM.

Exercise 7.20 will show you how to model the relationships needed to record sales for the Pipefitters Supply Company. In this exercise, you will model the relationships among *tblCustomer*, *tblInventory*, *tblSales*, and *tblSales-Inventory*. If you have entered data in the tables, be sure that the data in the tables' key fields are compatible, otherwise Access will not permit you to establish referential integrity links on those fields.

Exercise 7.20: Creating Relationships Among *tblCustomer*, *tblInventory*, *tblSales*, and *tblSales-Inventory*

1. Close any tables you have open on the desktop.
2. Select the menu command Tools, Relationships. The Relationships window will appear and display the relationships you established in Exercise 7.14. Since we are going to add more tables to the window in the exercise, you may want to click and drag the edges of the window to make it larger.
3. Select the menu command Relationships, Show Table. Select *tblSales* and *tblSales-Inventory* by clicking their names while holding down the Ctrl key.
4. Click the Add button, then click the Close button. The tables you have chosen will appear in the Relationships window. You may wish to resize and rearrange the tables in the Relationships window using Figure 7.22 as a guide.
5. Click and drag the CustomerNumber field from *tblCustomer* to the CustomerNumber field in *tblSales*. In the Relationships dialog box that appears, click the Enforce Referential Integrity check box, then click the Create button.
6. Click and drag InventoryItemCode from *tblInventory* to *tblSales-Inventory*. In the Relationships dialog box, click the Enforce Referential Integrity check box, then click the Create button.
7. Click and drag InvoiceNumber from *tblSales* to *tblSales-Inventory*. In the Relationships dialog box, click the Enforce Referential Integrity check box, then click the Create button.

The Relationships window showing these links, along with the links you created in Exercise 7.14, appears in Figure 7.22. We have moved and resized the table representations in the Relationships window to make the table fields and the links easier to see.

Select the File, Close menu command and click the Yes button to save your changes to the Relationship window. Now that you have established the necessary links, you can create a form in which you can enter sales information.

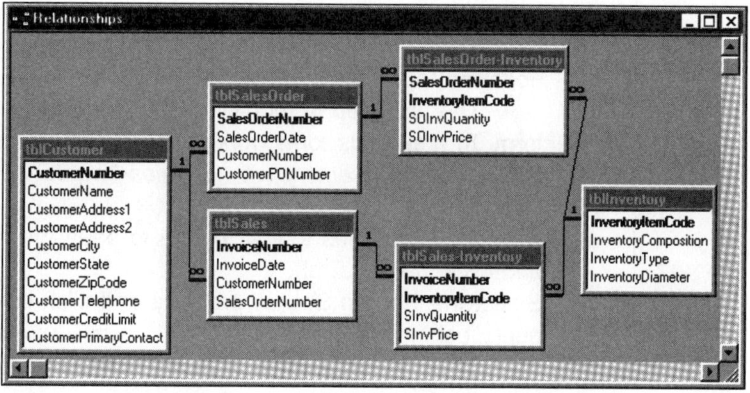

Figure 7.22 Relationships among *tblCustomer*, *tblInventory*, *tblSales*, and *tblSales-Inventory*.

The Sales Entry Form

The Sales Entry form resembles the Sales Order Entry form you created earlier. The Sales Order Entry form lets you enter the items that customers order. The Sales Entry form lets you enter the items actually shipped to customers. If our example firm, Pipefitters Supply Company, was certain that it would always have all items in stock, we could generate invoices from the Sales Order table. Unfortunately, this assumption is not realistic for most companies. To enter sales information, we will need a form that reads from *tblCustomer* and *tblInventory*. The form must write to *tblSales* and *tblSales-Inventory*. Since the Sales Entry form will read data from *tblCustomer* and *tblInventory*, you must have data in these tables.

Since the Sales Entry form is so much like the Sales Order Entry form we showed you how to build earlier in this chapter, you can modify that form to become a Sales Entry form instead of starting all over again. Exercises 7.21 and 7.22 describe how you can edit the objects in *frmSalesOrder* and *fsubSalesOrder* to create a form-subform combination for sales entry, *frmSales* and *fsubSales*. You can also learn more about how forms are constructed by working through these exercises. The Form Wizard, when it created *frmSalesOrder* and *fsubSalesOrder* for us, hid some of the more interesting elements of Access forms from you. Whenever you work with form-subform combinations in Access, you should always start with the subform. Therefore, we will modify *fsubSalesOrder* in the first of these two exercises.

Exercise 7.21: Modifying *fsubSalesOrder* to Create *fsubSales*

1. Click the Forms tab in the Database window and select *fsubSalesOrder*. Press Ctrl+C to copy the form object, then press Ctrl+V to paste it back into

the Database window. Type *fsubSales* in the Paste As dialog box and click the OK button. With the new form object selected, click the Design button to open the form in Design view.

The first step in modifying the form is to change the query behind the form. To make this form work as a Sales Entry subform, you must replace *tblSalesOrder-Inventory* with *tblSales-Inventory* and change the query's field references.

2. Click the Properties toolbar button to open the property sheet for the form and click the Data tab.
3. Select the Record Source property and click its Build button to open the query behind the form.
4. Select Query, Show Table from the menu and double-click *tblSales-Inventory.* Click the Close button.
5. Click anywhere in the *tblSalesOrder-Inventory* object to select it and press the Delete key.
6. Click and drag InvoiceNumber from *tblSales-Inventory* to the first Field cell in the QBE grid. All of the existing columns will move to the right when you release the mouse button. Set the InvoiceNumber field's Sort order to Ascending.
7. Click and drag InventoryItemCode from *tblSales-Inventory* to the second Field cell in the QBE grid. Be careful to select this code from *tblSales-Inventory*. If you select the InventoryItemCode field from *tblInventory*, the form will not work properly.
8. Repeat this procedure by clicking and dragging SInvQuantity and SInvPrice to the third and fourth Field cells, respectively.
9. Using the scroll bar at the bottom of the QBE grid, move the grid so the Extension field is visible. Select the Extension field and press Shift+F2 to open the Zoom box.
10. Edit the expression to read ***Extension: [SInvPrice]*[SInvQuantity]***
11. Press Ctrl+W to close the Query Builder window, then click the Yes button to save your changes.

    You have changed the underlying query of the form, so you must change the Control Source properties of the text box controls on the form that no longer refer to an existing field in the query.
12. Select the SOInvQuantity text box control. If the property sheet is not open, click the Properties toolbar button. Click the Data tab and change the Control Source property to ***SInvQuantity***
13. Select the SOInvPrice text box control. Click the property sheet Data tab and change the Control Source property to ***SInvPrice***

You can save the form by pressing Ctrl+W and clicking the Yes button to save your changes. Next, we will show you how to turn *frmSalesOrder* into the main form component of a working Sales Entry form. Be sure you have closed all forms and tables before proceeding.

EXERCISE 7.22: MODIFYING *FRMSALESORDER* TO CREATE *FRMSALES*

1. Click the Forms tab in the Database window and select *frmSalesOrder*. Press Ctrl+C to copy the form object, then press Ctrl+V to paste it back into the Database window. Type *frmSales* in the Paste As dialog box and click the OK button. With the new form object selected, click the Design button to open the form in Design view.

   The first step in modifying the form is to change the query behind the form. To make this form work as a Sales Entry subform, you must replace *tblSalesOrder-Inventory* with *tblSales-Inventory* and change the query's field references.
2. Open the property sheet and click its Data tab. Select the form's Record Source property and click the Build button to open the query behind the form.
3. Select Query, Show Table from the menu and double-click *tblSales*. Click the Close button.
4. Click anywhere in the *tblSales-Order* object to select it and press the Delete key.
5. Click and drag InvoiceNumber from *tblSales* to the first Field cell in the QBE grid. The existing columns will move to the right when you release the mouse button. Set the InvoiceNumber field's Sort order to Ascending.
6. Click and drag InvoiceDate, CustomerNumber, and SalesOrderNumber from *tblSales* to the second, third, and fourth Field cells in the QBE grid, respectively.
7. Press Ctrl+W to close the Query Builder window, then click the Yes button to save your changes.

   You have changed the underlying query of the form, so you must change the Control Source properties of the text box controls that no longer refer to existing fields in the query.
8. Either by typing directly in the text box controls on the form or by editing their Control Source properties in the property sheet, change the following Control Source properties:
   - SalesOrderNumber to ***InvoiceNumber***
   - SalesOrderDate to ***InvoiceDate***
   - CustomerPONumber to ***SalesOrderNumber***
9. Change the Caption properties of the accompanying labels for these controls to match. You may wish to refer to Figure 7.23 as a guide.
10. Click the *fsubSalesOrder* Subform/Subreport object at the bottom of the form and click the Data tab on the property sheet. Change the Source object to *fsubSales*. Change both the Link Child Fields and the Link Master Fields properties to InvoiceNumber.

You can save your modified *frmSales* by pressing Ctrl+W and clicking the Yes button to save your changes. The completed form, showing both *frmSales* and *fsubSales*, appears in Figure 7.23 in Form view.

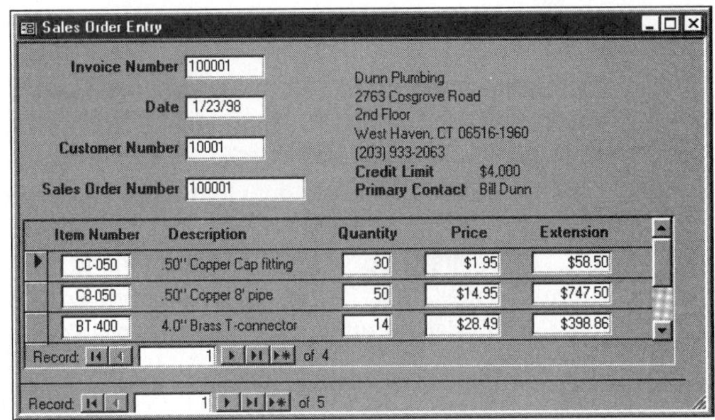

Figure 7.23 The completed Sales Entry form in Form view.

The Invoice Report

The Sales Entry form we have just described facilitates the entry of information about sales into the Pipefitters Supply Company revenue cycle accounting system. When Pipefitters ships a customer order, they will want to send an invoice. Although more firms are using electronic data interchange every day, many customers will want an invoice printed on paper. As you learned in Chapter 2, the Microsoft Access *report* objects provide nicely formatted printed output. In this section, we will show you how to create a printed invoice. The first step in generating an Invoice report is to build a query that will gather the information we have stored about the sales transaction in *tblSales*, *tblCustomer*, *tblInventory*, and *tblSales-Inventory*. In Exercise 7.23, we show you how to build just such an invoice query.

Exercise 7.23: Building an Invoice Query

1. In the Database window, click the Queries tab and then click the New button to open the New Query dialog box. Double-click Simple Query Wizard.
2. Select Table: *tblSales* in the Tables/Queries combo box and click the >> button to move all of that table's fields to the Selected Fields box.
3. Select Table: *tblCustomer* and use the > button to move the CustomerName, CustomerAddress1, CustomerAddress2, CustomerCity, CustomerState, and CustomerZipCode fields to the Selected Fields box.
4. Select Table: *tblSales-Inventory* and move the InventoryItemCode, SInvQuantity, and SInvPrice fields to the Selected Fields box.
5. Select Table: *tblInventory* and move the InventoryComposition field to the Selected Fields box.
6. Click the Next > button to move to the next Query Wizard dialog box, then click the Next > button in that dialog box to accept the Detail query default.

7. Name the query ***qryInvoice***, click the option button to select "Modify the query design," and click the Finish button. The new query will open in Design view.
8. Set the QBE grid Sort cells for InvoiceNumber and InventoryItemCode to Ascending.
9. Scroll to the first open column in the QBE grid, select the Field cell, press Shift+F2 to open the Zoom box, and type ***Description: [InventoryDiameter] & " " & [InventoryComposition] & " " & [InventoryType]***

   Note that this is the same expression we used in *fsubSalesOrder* and *fsubSales*. If you prefer, you may cut and paste this expression from one of those forms' queries instead of typing it again. The next two expressions are the same as those we used in *frmSalesOrder* and *frmSales*, so you can cut and paste instead of typing them, too.
10. In the next QBE grid Field cell, open the Zoom box and type ***Extension: [SInvPrice]*[SInvQuantity]***
11. In the next QBE grid Field cell, open the Zoom box and type ***CustomerAddress3: [CustomerCity] & ", " & [CustomerState] & " " & [CustomerZipCode]***

You can click the Run toolbar button to run the query and examine the dynaset it produces to check whether you entered the expressions correctly. Press Ctrl+W to close the Query Builder window. Click the Yes button when prompted to save your changes to *qryInvoice*. Now we will show you how to use this query as the basis for an Invoice report.

Exercise 7.24: Creating an Invoice Report

1. In the Database window, click the Reports tab, then click the New button. In the New Report dialog box, select Report Wizard and choose *qryInvoice* in the combo box. Click the OK button to proceed.
2. Click the >> button to move all of the query's fields from the Available Fields box to the Selected Fields box. Click the Next > button to continue.
3. In the next dialog box, click the Next > button to accept the default viewing by *tblSales*.
4. Click the Next > button since we do not need to specify any additional grouping levels.
5. Enter ***InventoryItemCode*** in the first sorting box, then click the Summary Options button. Click the check box to Sum the Extension field, click OK to return to the previous dialog box, then click the Next > button.
6. The next dialog box gives you a choice of Layout options. We used Align Left 1, but you can choose any of the options that you prefer for the look of the printed invoice.

7. The next dialog box gives you a choice of styles. Again, you may choose any one that you prefer. Our choice was the Formal style. Click the Next > button to continue.
8. Type ***rptInvoice*** in the title box and click the option button to select "Modify the report's design." Click the Finish button to generate the report.

   The report generated by the Report Wizard is fairly close to being a usable document. We have made a number of adjustments to the report's appearance. One page of the finished Invoice report appears in Figure 7.24. The design elements appear in the partial image of *rptInvoice* in Report Design view shown in Figure 7.25. We discuss several important changes you should make to *rptInvoice* in the following steps, but we encourage you to use Figure 7.24, Figure 7.25, and your own judgment to create an attractive, useful Invoice report.

Invoice

Pipefitters Supply Company
5998 Alcala Park
San Diego, CA 92110

Invoice Number 100001
Date 1/23/98
Sales Order Number 100001

Sold to: Dunn Plumbing
2763 Cosgrove Road
2nd Floor
West Haven, CT 06516-1960
Customer Number 10001

Item Number	Quantity	Price	Description	Extension
B4-400	10	$65.19	4.0" Brass 4' pipe	$651.90
BT-400	14	$28.49	4.0" Brass T-connector	$398.86
C8-050	50	$14.95	.50" Copper 8' pipe	$747.50
CC-050	30	$1.95	.50" Copper Cap fitting	$58.50

Invoice Total $1,856.76

Figure 7.24 A printout from *rptInvoice*, the Invoice report.

9. Move the label control that includes the text *rptInvoice* and the line object from the Report Header section to the InvoiceNumber Header section.

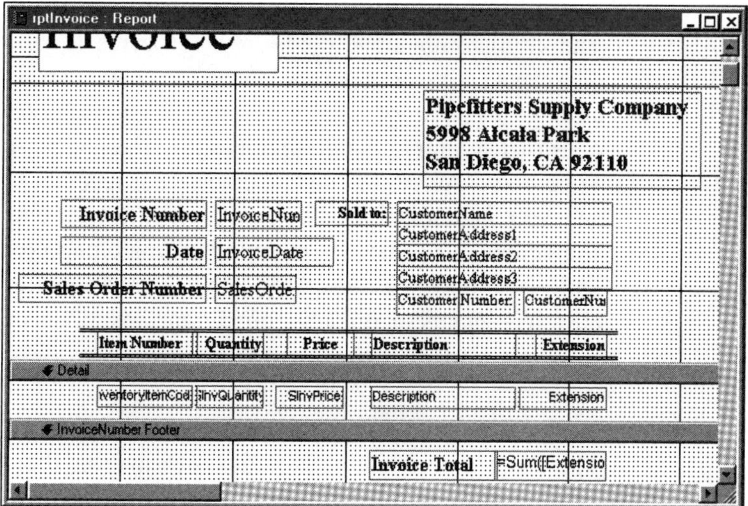

Figure 7.25 The bottom portion of *rptInvoice* in Report Design view.

10. Select View, Report Header/Footer from the menu to delete these sections. Click the Yes button to confirm this deletion. Delete the Page Header/Footer using the same procedure.
11. To print one invoice per page, click the InvoiceNumber Footer and click the Properties toolbar button to open its property sheet. Click the Format tab and set its Force New Page property to After Section.
12. Click the Toolbox toolbar button to open the Toolbox. You can use the Label tool to create a label control for Pipefitters Supply Company's name and address.

Try it

When you are typing text in a label control you will find that the Enter key does not create a carriage return, it just accepts the changes you have made to the control. To place a carriage return in a label control, you must type either Shift+Enter or Ctrl+Enter.

This invoice is only one possible design, of course. Different businesses and other organizations use other document designs and include slightly different information items on their invoices. Note that with a few minor modifications, this Invoice report could become a shipping document.

RECORDING CASH RECEIVED FROM CUSTOMERS

The ultimate objective of the revenue cycle is, of course, to receive customers' payments for the goods or services they have purchased. Firms need to record the amount and date of each incoming customer payment. We will explain how to construct a simple cash receipts table that tracks cash receipts by customer. A more elaborate system would track cash receipts by invoice number and permit an exact matching of customer payments to specific invoices. Since customers sometimes do not pay by invoice, this matching process can be difficult to design and execute. You can satisfy many business information needs with the basic customer payment tracking procedure described in this section.

The Cash Receipts Table

The Cash Receipts table includes information about the payments received from customers. A tempting candidate for the primary key is the preprinted check number that appears on checks that Pipefitters receives from its customers. Unfortunately, this customer check number is not a good primary key because we cannot be certain that the number is unique. Pipefitters could easily receive two different checks from two different customers that have identical preprinted check numbers. Most firms use a *remittance advice number* as the primary key for their Cash Receipts tables. You have probably seen remittance advices, but you may not have known what they were called. For example, the portion of your credit card statement that you tear off and return with your payment is a remittance advice. Businesses usually prepare remittance advices for, or assign remittance advice numbers to, every check they receive.

In addition to the remittance advice number primary key, we will want to include fields for the date that the check was received, the check number, the amount of the check, and the customer number. CustomerNumber will be the foreign key that we will use to link the Cash Receipts table to the Customer table. The next exercise shows you how to build a Cash Receipts table.

EXERCISE 7.25: BUILDING A CASH RECEIPTS TABLE

1. Click the Tables tab in the Database window, then click the New button. Double-click Design View in the New Table dialog box.
2. Enter ***RemittanceAdviceNumber*** as the first Field Name. Click the Set Primary Key toolbar button to make this field the table's primary key. Leave the Data Type set to Text, but set the Field Size property to ***6***
3. Set the Input Mask property to ***000000***, the Caption property to ***RA #***, and the Required property to Yes.
4. Enter ***CashReceiptDate*** as the next Field Name. Set its Data Type to Date/Time. Set its Input Mask property to ***99/99/99*** and its Caption property to ***Date***

The next field in the Cash Receipts table will store the customer check number. Although most firms' checks use only numeric characters in their check numbers, some may include other characters. Therefore, this field must allow any combination of numbers, letters, and symbols that might appear on a customer check. Since we cannot anticipate the characteristics of this field, we cannot build any input mask or validation rule data input controls for this field into the Cash Receipts table.

5. Enter ***CustomerCheckNumber*** as the next Field Name, leave its Data Type set to Text, set its Field Size property to *15*, and set its Caption property to ***Customer Check #***
6. To create the foreign key field, enter ***CustomerNumber*** as the next Field Name with a Text Data Type, a Field Size of *5*, and an Input Mask property of ***00000***. Set its Caption property to ***Customer Number*** and its Required property to Yes.
7. Enter ***CashReceiptAmount*** as the last Field Name, set its Data Type to Currency, its Decimal Places property to *2*, and its Caption property to ***Amount***
8. Save the table you have created by selecting File, Save As/Export from the menu and typing ***tblCashReceipts*** as its New Name in the Save As dialog box.

Your Companion CD-ROM includes *tblCashReceipts* in the *Ch07.mdb* database. Figure 7.26 shows the Cash Receipts table in Datasheet view. Note that the column titles show the text we entered in the Caption properties for each field.

tblCashReceipts : Table

RA #	Date	Customer Check #	Customer Number	Amount
100001	1/28/98	10207	10010	$2,000.00
100002	1/28/98	33256	10005	$631.20
100003	1/28/98	4927	10001	$1,856.76
100004	1/29/98	108755	10007	$781.00
100005	1/30/98	10256	10010	$122.50
100006	1/30/98	4952	10001	$84.75
				$0.00

Record: 1 of 6

Figure 7.26 The Cash Receipts table in Datasheet view.

The final step in creating *tblCashReceipts* is to establish a referential integrity link to *tblCustomer* on the foreign key, CustomerNumber.

9. Click the Relationships toolbar button to open the Relationships window. Click the Show Table toolbar button, select *tblCashReceipts*, click the Add button, then click the Close button.
10. Click and drag CustomerNumber from *tblCustomer* to *tblCashReceipts*.
11. Click the Enforce Referential Integrity check box, then click the Create button.

The Cash Receipts table, linked to *tblCustomer* on CustomerNumber, is included in the Relationships window that appears in Figure 7.27. The Cash Receipts table is the last table we will include in this chapter's revenue cycle accounting system. Therefore, Figure 7.27 shows a complete picture of the relationships among all revenue cycle tables.

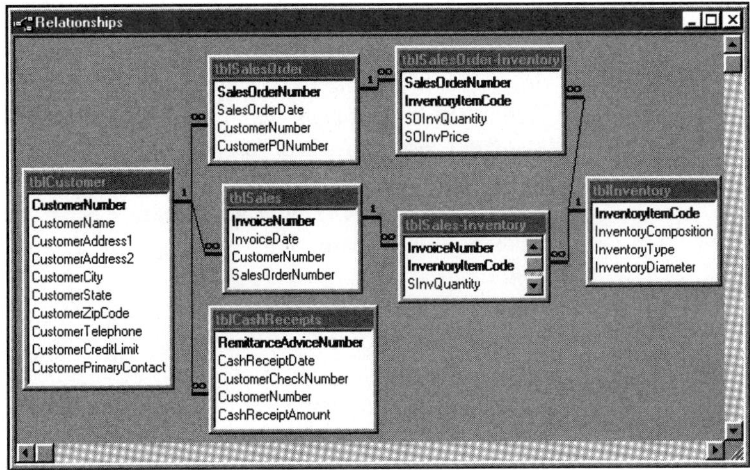

Figure 7.27 Relationships among the revenue cycle tables.

The Cash Receipts Entry Form

The construction of the Cash Receipts form is simple and straightforward. The form works with only one table, *tblCashReceipts*, and that table has few fields. Exercise 7.26 shows you how to create the Cash Receipts form, *frmCashReceipts*.

Exercise 7.26: Building a Cash Receipts Form

1. Click the Forms tab in the Database window and click the New button. In the New Form dialog box, select Form Wizard and choose *tblCashReceipts* in the combo box. Click OK to proceed.
2. Click the >> button to move all of the fields to the Selected Fields box, then click the Next > button.
3. Click the Tabular option button, then click the Next > button.
4. In the next dialog box, click the Next > button to accept the default Standard style.
5. Enter the form name, ***frmCashReceipts***, click the "Modify the form's design" option button, then click the Finish button to have the Form Wizard generate the form.

6. With the form in Design view, you can make a few minor adjustments to the form's appearance, such as bolding the titles, increasing the horizontal spacing between the fields, changing the alignment properties of the text box and label controls, changing the form's Caption property to ***Cash Receipts Entry Form***, and changing the form's Scroll Bar property to Neither.

The completed *frmCashReceipts* in Form view appears in Figure 7.28. You can use this figure as a guide in fine-tuning your form. Save your edits and close the form by pressing Ctrl+W and clicking the Yes button to confirm the changes.

Cash Receipts Entry Form

RA #	Date	Customer Check #	Customer Number	Amount
100001	1/28/98	10207	10010	$2,000.00
100002	1/28/98	33256	10005	$631.20
100003	1/28/98	4927	10001	$1,856.76
100004	1/29/98	108755	10007	$781.00
100005	1/30/98	10256	10010	$122.50
100006	1/30/98	4952	10001	$84.75
				$0.00

Record: 1 of 6

Figure 7.28 Completed *frmCashReceipts* in Form view.

Cash Receipts Reports

Standard reporting forms for cash receipts do not exist, so you may create your own report designs to meet the needs of your or your clients' specific businesses. Some firms may want reports of cash receipts by customer, by date, or by geographic region. Although aggregate cash receipts information is important, the details are seldom as interesting as, for example, details of sales transactions.

One useful cash receipts report is the Daily Cash report. Many businesses follow the internal control procedure of depositing all cash receipts intact each day. The Daily Cash report provides the check figures for the bank deposit.

Exercise 7.27: Creating a Daily Cash Report

1. In the Database window, click the Reports tab and then click the New button.
2. In the New Report dialog box that appears, select Report Wizard and enter ***tblCashReceipts*** in the combo box. Click the OK button to continue.

3. Click the >> button to move all of the fields to the Selected Fields box. Click the Next > button to continue.
4. Click CashReceiptsDate in the list of fields on the left side of the dialog box, then click the > button. The Wizard will insert a grouping level titled *CashReceiptDate by Month* in the report template. Click the up-arrow button above the word *Priority* to move the new grouping to the top of the template.
5. Click *CustomerNumber* in the template, then click the < button to remove CustomerNumber as a grouping level.
6. Click the Grouping Options button. Enter ***Day*** in the Grouping intervals combo box and click the OK button. Click the Next > button to continue.
7. Enter ***CustomerNumber*** in the first sort order box, then click the Summary Options button.
8. Click the Sum check box for the CashReceiptAmount field, click the OK button, then click the Next > button to continue.
9. Select the Align Left 1 Layout and click the Next > button.
10. Select the Corporate style and click the Next > button.
11. Enter a report title of ***Pipefitters Supply Company Daily Cash Report***, click the option button to "Modify the report's design," then click the Finish button.
12. Using Figure 7.29 as a guide, make any minor modifications you wish to the form. Save the form by selecting Save As/Export from the menu, entering ***rptDailyCash*** in the New Name box, and clicking the OK button.

OTHER REVENUE CYCLE COMPONENTS

In this chapter, we have created sales order reports, invoice reports, and cash receipts reports. Our purpose was to demonstrate how to generate useful reports from revenue cycle accounting data tables. This section discusses some other revenue cycle reports that you might want to create or adapt to specific business needs.

Customer Statements

Many firms send their customers a statement of account activity at the end of each month. The statement shows a beginning balance, lists each sale and cash receipt, and calculates an ending balance. This statement lets customers review their purchases and payments regularly. It also lets customers reconcile their accounts payable records with the statement. As we noted earlier in the chapter, many firms now pay from invoices rather than from monthly statements. Systems designers use two general approaches for combining sales and cash receipts tables in one monthly statement report. One approach requires the use of a common field, such as a sequential transaction number. You can easily modify the *tblSales* and *tblCashReceipts* tables we created in this chapter to include a transaction number field for this purpose. That will, however, de-normalize both tables. A second approach is to use queries to summarize and place sales and cash receipts data into an accounts receivable table that has no primary key. This also

Pipefitters Supply Company Daily Cash Report

For Internal Use Only

Cash Receipts for: *Wednesday, January 28, 1998*

Customer Number	*RA #*	*Date*	*Customer Check #*	*Amount*
10001	100003	1/28/98	4927	$1,856.76
10005	100002	1/28/98	33256	$631.20
10010	100001	1/28/98	10207	$2,000.00
		Total		*$4,487.96*

Cash Receipts for: *Thursday, January 29, 1998*

Customer Number	*RA #*	*Date*	*Customer Check #*	*Amount*
10007	100004	1/29/98	108755	$781.00
		Total		*$781.00*

Cash Receipts for: *Friday, January 30, 1998*

Customer Number	*RA #*	*Date*	*Customer Check #*	*Amount*
10001	100006	1/30/98	4952	$84.75
10010	100005	1/30/98	10256	$122.50
		Total		*$207.25*
		Grand Total		*$5,476.21*

Figure 7.29 Printout of *rptDailyCash.*

violates the normalization rules; however, it does so in an aggregate table, rather than the tables that store the originally entered transaction data.

Sales Analysis

Database accounting information systems include much information that is useful to nonaccountants. Traditional accounting records contained only the date and dollar amount of each sale and cash receipt. A database accounting system contains much more information about each sale and cash receipt. The Sales, Sales Order, Inventory, and Customer tables we described in this chapter can be combined in many ways to provide useful information to the marketing and strategic management functions. For example, you could combine our Customer table, Sales table, and Inventory table to generate reports that show sales by customer, inventory item code, customer city, time period, or any combination of these. If Pipefitters' sales manager wanted to know what dollar amount of brass fittings they sold in North Dakota during last December, you could easily create a query that would provide the answer.

Sales and Accounts Receivable on the Financial Statements

The traditional function of accounting systems has been to capture and store the information needed to prepare financial statements in accordance with GAAP. We presented a database approach to developing a revenue cycle accounting system that provides much more than the minimal level of information contained in financial statements. The database approach still provides basic debit-and-credit accounting information. For example, to obtain the general ledger entry credit to Sales and debit to Accounts Receivable, you can simply add a control to *rptInvoice* that sums the sales totals in its Report Footer. You can create subsidiary ledger debits and credits by adding a CustomerNumber grouping level to *rptInvoice* and including a control that sums the sales totals in the CustomerNumber Footer. You can follow similar procedures to obtain the general ledger debit to Cash and credit to Accounts Receivable using the numbers generated by the *rptCashReceipts* report we illustrated earlier in this chapter.

SUMMARY

In this chapter we described how to construct the tables, forms, queries, and reports commonly used in the revenue cycle of accounting information systems. Tables are the basic building blocks of the revenue cycle. Forms make data entry, editing, and deletion easier. Queries can extract data from several tables at once to help answer complex questions about revenue cycle activities. Reports include invoices and shipping documents; they also may contain summaries of revenue cycle activities for internal management use.

The revenue cycle begins with customer records and finished goods inventory records. As sales orders arrive, we must record information about which customers want to buy which inventory items. When goods are shipped to customers, we create invoices and shipping documents. We record customer payments when we receive them. Finally, we summarize all of these activities and create reports and journal entries that allow the preparation of financial statements.

REVIEW EXERCISES

MULTIPLE-CHOICE QUESTIONS

1. The revenue cycle includes all of the following except
   a. keeping customer information current.
   b. recording the cost of merchandise purchased.
   c. recording payments received from customers.
   d. summarizing sales information.
2. The revenue cycle uses an inventory table to provide
   a. descriptions of products sold.
   b. purchase cost of products sold.
   c. names of vendors that supplied the products sold.
   d. quantity of products sold.
3. The CustomerNumber field in *tblCustomer* is a
   a. composite primary key.
   b. foreign key.
   c. primary key.
   d. relationship key.
4. A good policy would be to delete a record in a customer table only when that customer
   a. files for bankruptcy court protection from creditors.
   b. moves its offices out of the country permanently.
   c. has not made a purchase within the past twelve months.
   d. is no longer related to any other database tables.
5. Fields in data entry forms that only display data should have their Locked and Tab Stop properties set as
   a. Locked = Yes, Tab Stop = Yes.
   b. Locked = Yes, Tab Stop = No.
   c. Locked = No, Tab Stop = Yes.
   d. Locked = No, Tab Stop = No.
6. A mnemonic inventory item coding scheme
   a. helps experienced employees identify inventory quickly.
   b. helps data entry clerks enter inventory codes quickly.
   c. is required by generally accepted accounting principles.
   d. is easier to design than a sequential number coding scheme.
7. A Sales Order-Inventory table would most likely be
   a. an entity table.
   b. a referential integrity table.
   c. a query table.
   d. a relationship table.

8. The link from *tblSales-Inventory* to *tblInventory* on the InventoryItemCode field is a
   a. one-to-one relationship.
   b. one-to-many relationship.
   c. many-to-one relationship.
   d. many-to-many relationship.
9. A slightly modified copy of an invoice report can often serve as a
   a. sales order.
   b. shipping document.
   c. customer record.
   d. cash receipts record.
10. A good primary key for a cash receipts table would be the
    a. customer check number.
    b. invoice number.
    c. cash receipt number.
    d. remittance advice number.

DISCUSSION QUESTIONS

1. The examples in this chapter assumed that Pipefitters Supply Company was doing business only in the United States. What changes would you make if Pipefitters had many customers from other countries?
2. Service businesses, such as real estate agents, law firms, and accounting firms, do not have inventory. What table would a service business have instead of *tblInventory*?
3. Restaurants do not usually record customers' names and addresses or send out invoices. What tables, forms, queries, and reports might you use in the accounting information system for a restaurant's revenue cycle?
4. How would you decide whether to enforce referential integrity for a foreign key link?
5. Describe how you might create a customer statement that showed sales and cash receipts from customers on one report.

EXERCISES

1. Change *tblCustomer* so that the CustomerState field will accept only legal state abbreviations. Hint: you should consider adding another table to the revenue cycle system to accomplish this task.
2. Many firms keep track of which salespersons handle particular sales. Modify the revenue cycle system in this chapter to include a salesperson entity.

3. Create a report that shows sales by customer with sales by product grouped under each customer.
4. Modify the revenue cycle system presented in this chapter to include a *ship to* address on the invoice.
5. Create a report that shows the month-end general ledger entries for sales and cash receipts.

8 PURCHASE CYCLE

OBJECTIVES

The purchase cycle includes placing orders with vendors, recording purchases, recording payments made to vendors, and maintaining records of these activities. In this chapter, you will learn how to design Microsoft Access tables, queries, forms, and reports that can help you:

- Create and maintain vendor records.
- Create and maintain materials inventory records.
- Print purchase orders.
- Summarize and report purchase order information.
- Record the receipt of ordered materials.
- Print checks and record disbursements to vendors.
- Summarize purchases and accounts payable information.

INTRODUCTION

This chapter shows how to use Microsoft Access to build the purchase cycle components of accounting information systems. In this book, we define the purchase cycle to include acquisition of goods and services and payment for those goods and services. We noted in Chapter 6 that payroll accounting systems, which could be considered a part of the purchase cycle, are often sufficiently complex to merit separate treatment. Therefore, we cover payroll accounting systems in Chapter 9 as the payroll cycle.

In manufacturing firms, the main focus of the purchase cycle is ordering, receiving, and paying for materials—including both direct and indirect materials. In a merchandising firm, the main focus of the purchase cycle is the acquisition of goods for resale. Since materials acquisition is not a major concern for service firms, their purchase cycle is somewhat less important to them than it is to manufacturing and merchandising firms. However, all businesses—even service firms—must acquire goods and services that support their selling and administrative functions. This acquisition activity takes place within the purchase cycle. Therefore, all three types of firms need accounting systems that can record purchase cycle activities.

In a manufacturing firm, the purchase cycle process begins when one of the production departments prepares a materials requisition document. In some manufacturing systems, this document is automatically generated by the computer when materials inventory falls below a predetermined reorder point. For example, in a materials requirement planning (MRP) system, the computer can use the master schedule to generate timely materials requisitions without human intervention. In a just-in-time (JIT) production control system, materials requisitions are generated frequently—often daily or weekly. The materials requisition document goes to the purchasing department and is their authorization to prepare a purchase order. In many automated MRP and JIT systems, the computer generates the purchase order directly.

In many merchandising firms, particularly retailers, the demand for goods is highly unpredictable. Manufacturers often have the luxury of planning production; retailers must react quickly to shifts in consumer demand. Ability to accommodate this rapidly fluctuating demand is often the difference between success and failure for a retailer. Therefore, retail merchandisers delegate purchasing decisions to highly skilled buyers who have authority, within a predetermined dollar budget, for purchasing a particular category of merchandise. These buyers use daily sales reports, inventory reports, market research, and their intuitions to make their inventory purchase decisions. To record their purchase decisions, buyers create either purchase requisition documents or purchase orders.

All three types of firms need to acquire and pay for the goods and services that accountants classify as selling and administrative expenses. For example, merchandising, manufacturing, and service firms all purchase office supplies, pay for advertising, and reimburse employees for travel expenses. A responsible individual, such as an office manager or department head, creates a purchase requisition document to authorize purchase of and payment for such items.

In all three types of firms, the purchasing department uses materials or purchase requisitions as its authorization to place purchase orders. Purchasing agents then try to find the best price and delivery dates offered by approved vendors. In some industries the purchasing agent is a skilled negotiator with considerable latitude in making decisions. Whether it is the result of spirited deal making or is generated automatically, the purchase order is sent to the vendor by the purchasing department. In the past, purchase orders have been paper forms; however, many firms now use electronic data interchange (EDI) to send purchase orders to vendors.

The purchasing department sends a copy of the purchase order, with quantities omitted, to the receiving department or makes similar information available electronically. When shipments of ordered goods arrive, the receiving department completes a receiving report. Accounting must compare the receiving report, the purchase order, and the vendor's invoice. If the details on all these documents match, accounting prepares a check for the amount due. The check is then forwarded to the treasurer with supporting documentation. This documentation typically includes the purchase order, the receiving report, and the vendor's invoice. The package of supporting documents is often called a voucher. The treasurer signs the check, marks or mutilates the voucher and the supporting documents so they cannot be used to authorize a second payment for the same purchase, and sends the check to the vendor.

The purchase cycle system must generate summary reports of purchase and cash disbursement activities for management's use. The system should also generate information that financial accountants can use instead of their traditional double-entry bookkeeping debits and credits to create ledgers, journals, and financial statements.

In this chapter, we will show you how to build the components of a purchase cycle system for the Electric Controls Company, a firm that manufactures custom electrical control panels for industrial customers. You can think of electrical control panels as larger and more complex versions of the metal box that contains the circuit breakers at your house or apartment. Electric Controls buys components such as switches, circuit breakers, and relays to assemble these control panels.

VENDOR INFORMATION

Firms need easy and quick access to information about their vendors. Purchasing agents need vendor names, addresses, and telephone numbers. They also need to know for which inventory items a particular vendor has been approved. Vendor information appears on many business documents such as purchase orders and checks. To ensure that vendor information is consistent wherever it is used, firms keep all vendor information in one database table. Any document that needs vendor information obtains it from that one table. If, for example, a vendor moves to a new location, the vendor's address need be changed only once. In a relational database accounting information system, vendor information resides in a vendor table.

The Vendor Table

The first purchase cycle table that we will build is the Vendor table. This table provides a central location for storing all information about each vendor, which makes adding, deleting, or changing vendor information easy and efficient. Many firms also include information about *potential* vendors, firms they might buy from in the future, in a vendor table. Remember that examples of all the tables, forms, queries, and reports that we use in this chapter are included in the *Ch08.mdb* database on your Companion CD-ROM.

Exercise 8.1: Building a Vendor Table

1. To create a Vendor table, which we will title *tblVendor*, start Microsoft Access as you learned in Exercise 2.1. Once you have the Database window open, click the New button and double-click Design View in the New Table dialog box that appears. Figure 8.1 shows the Table window open in Design view.

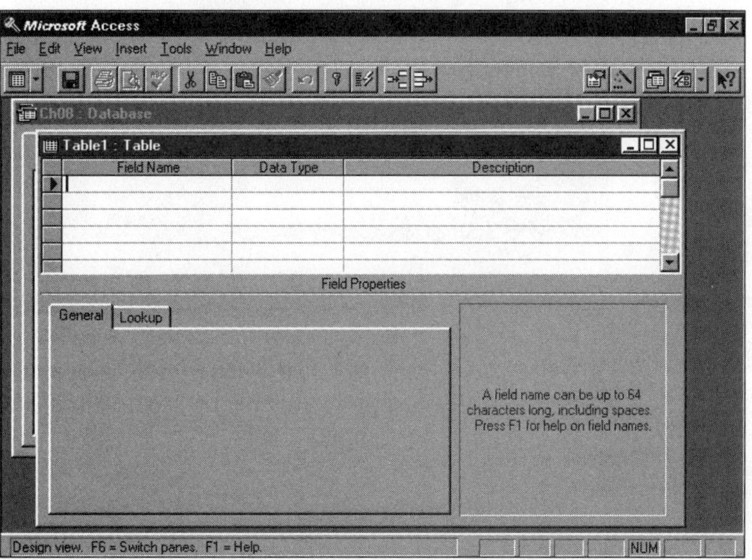

Figure 8.1 The Table window open in Design view.

The top part of the Table window includes the grid in which you will enter the Name, Data Type, and Description for each table field. The bottom half of the Table window includes a tabbed section in which you will specify Field Properties and a panel that provides context-sensitive help. In Exercise 7.1, we showed you how to create a CustomerNumber field for *tblCustomer*. Some of the Vendor table fields are similar to those in *tblCustomer*, so we will be using many of the same techniques to build *tblVendor*.

2. Enter ***VendorNumber*** as the first Field Name, leave its Data Type set to Text, and click the Primary Key toolbar button to make this field the table's primary key.

3. Press F6 to switch to the Field Properties pane of the Table window, then set the Field Size property to *4* and the Caption property to *Vendor Number*. We will use a sequential number scheme for VendorNumber starting with 1001. This four-digit Field Size property allows the Electric Controls Company to store 8,999 vendors in the table.
4. Set the Validation Rule property to the expression *Like "####"*
5. Set the Validation Text property to ***Invalid entry. You must enter a Vendor Number of exactly four digits.*** Figure 8.2 shows the Table window displaying the VendorNumber field's property settings at this point.

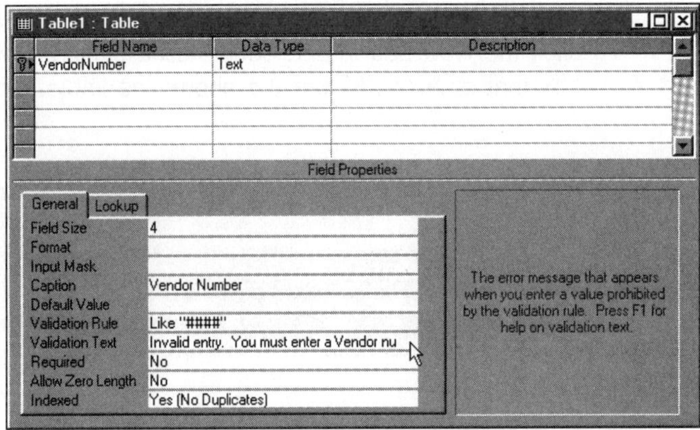

Figure 8.2 The VendorNumber field property settings.

This Validation Rule will prevent a user from entering anything other than four digits in the VendorNumber field. The Validation Text property makes this internal control feature even more useful. It lets us customize the error message that will appear in a dialog box whenever a user enters a VendorNumber value of anything other than four digits. Recall that we can use either an Input Mask property setting or a Validation Rule property setting to control data input. Each method has its strengths and weaknesses. The Input Mask property operates on each character as it is entered, but issues only a standard error message. The Validation Rule property operates on the field as a whole, so it does not warn users of errors until they try to exit the field. A Validation Rule does, however, allow us to customize the error message.

Try it

You can obtain more information about the Like Operator and its syntax by selecting Help, Microsoft Access Help Topics from the menu, clicking the Index tab and entering ***like operator*** as the search term. You can also learn more by entering ***ValidationRule Property*** or ***ValidationText Property*** in the Help Index window.

6. Enter ***VendorName*** as the next Field Name. Leave its Data Type set to Text and set its Field Size property to ***25***
7. Set the VendorName field's Caption property to ***Name***, since it will usually be obvious from the context on forms and reports that we are referring to a vendor's name.
8. Create VendorAddress1 and VendorAddress2 fields to store vendors' street addresses and office or suite numbers, respectively. Use your own judgment in setting the properties of these two fields.
9. Enter ***VendorCity*** as the next Field Name. Set its Data Type to Text, its Field Size property to ***25***, and its Caption property to ***City***
10. Enter ***VendorState*** as the next Field Name. Set its Data Type to Text, its Field Size property to ***2***, and its Caption property to ***State***
11. Set the Input Mask property for the VendorState field to ***>LL***. The > symbol converts lowercase letters to uppercase letters and the *LL* placeholders in the expression limit entry to two letters. Any other value entered will generate an error message. For more information on setting an Input Mask for U.S. state abbreviations, see Exercise 7.3.
12. Enter ***VendorZipCode*** as the next Field Name. Set its Data Type to Text and its Field Size property to ***10***. This setting will accommodate the U.S. Postal Service five-digits-plus-four Zip Code. Set the Caption property to ***Zip Code***
13. Set an Input Mask property for VendorZipCode of ***00000\-9999;0;_***. This requires five digits, allows the extra four digits as an option, automatically inserts the hyphen as the user enters the data, stores the hyphen as part of the field contents, and uses the underscore character as a placeholder. For more information on this property and how to set it with the Input Mask Wizard, see Exercise 7.4.
14. Enter ***VendorTelephone*** as the next Field Name. Set its Data Type to Text, its Field Size property to ***14*** (this will provide enough space to store the seven-digit number, a three-digit area code, the two parentheses, one hyphen, and a space), and its Caption property to ***Telephone***. Click the Input Mask property Build button to have the Input Mask Wizard create an input mask of !(999) 000\-0000;0;_ for this field as shown in Figure 8.3. Access will require that you save the table before using the Wizard. You can save it with the name ***tblVendor*** when prompted. Be sure to choose the option of storing the literal characters (the hyphen and the parentheses) with the number.
15. Enter ***VendorPrimaryContact*** as the last Field Name for *tblVendor*. Set its Data Type to Text, its Field Size property to ***25***, and its Caption property to ***Primary Contact***

This completes our *tblVendor* design. At this point, you can either close the Table window or open the table in Datasheet view to enter data. If you close the window, a dialog box will appear and ask you if you would like to save your changes. To open the table in Datasheet view, click the first toolbar icon. This icon toggles between Datasheet view and Design view for tables.

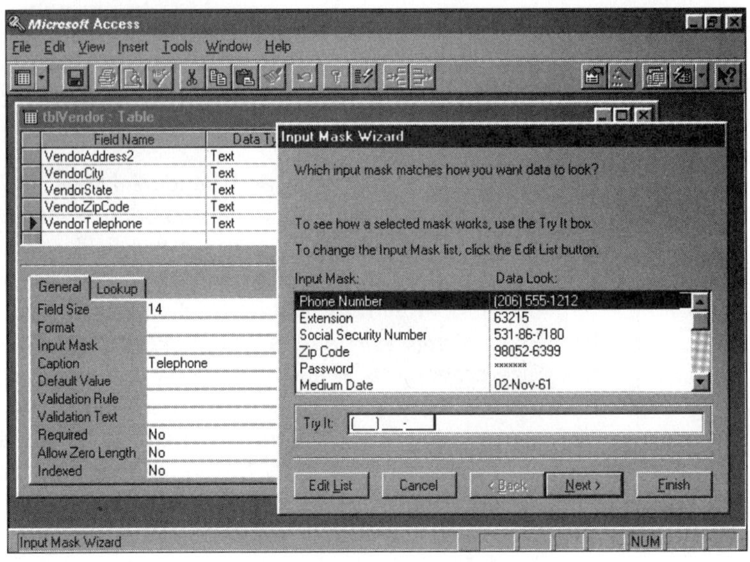

Figure 8.3 Using the Input Mask Wizard for the VendorTelephone field.

If you open the table in Datasheet view, you may notice that the title of each table column is the Caption property value you set. The *Ch08.mdb* database on your Companion CD-ROM includes a Vendor table, *tblVendor*, that includes sample data for the Electric Controls Company. This table appears in Datasheet view in Figure 8.4.

tblVendor : Table

Vendor Number	Name	Address1	Address2	City	State	Zi
1001	Square P Corporation	14532 Electron Way		Middletown	OH	450
1002	Bolden Wire and Cable Co.	2798 Larsen Road	Suite 400	Flint	MI	485
1003	Witchita Relays, Inc.	5764 Dawkins Drive		Witchita Fall	TX	763
1004	Allied Electrical Supply	58927 South Wacker Drive	2nd Floor	Chicago	IL	606
1005	Bomac Sheet Metal Co.	2788 Waterson Parkway		Long Beach	CA	908
1006	Billiter Extrusions, Inc.	7076 Sherwood Road		Carson	CA	907
1007	US Electrical Controls	14878 Freemont Avenue	Suite 1800	St. Louis	MO	631
1008	Mayberry Switch & Control	1946 Mabry Hood Road		Knoxville	TN	379
1009	Haskins Hardware Co.	9478 Jackson Drive		Chester	PA	1901
1010	Pirozolli Supply, Inc.	1746 Hurley Place		Rock Hill	SC	297

Record: 1 of 10

Figure 8.4 The Vendor table, *tblVendor*, in Datasheet view.

Users could enter records directly into *tblVendor* in Datasheet view, but as you can see in Figure 8.4, the *tblVendor* fields do not all appear on the screen at once, even if we display the table in a very small font. Entering data would quickly become a tiresome task, requiring the user to scroll back and forth to view and enter the values in each record. You can make data entry and data viewing tasks much easier by creating a form for *tblVendor*.

The Vendor Information Form

A form for the Vendor table will make entering, changing, and deleting customer information much easier than using *tblVendor* in Datasheet view. We will show you how to use the general procedure you learned in Exercise 4.8 to create a form, then we will show you how to modify the form to make it more useful.

To run the AutoForm tool, open the Database window, click the Tables tab, select *tblVendor*, then choose Insert, AutoForm from the menu. The result appears in Figure 8.5. This compact form is quite usable. Note that AutoForm examined the fields and determined that a columnar presentation would be necessary for this form. This form is included as *frmVendor1* in the *Ch08.mdb* database on your Companion CD-ROM.

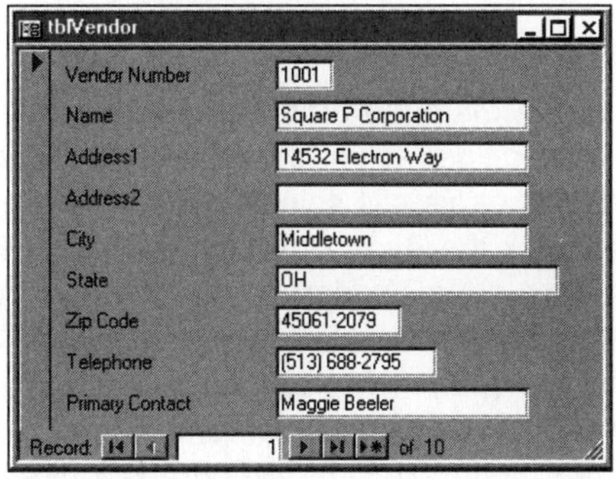

Figure 8.5 The Vendor Information form created by the AutoForm tool.

Although the AutoForm tool has produced a usable form, some of its shortcomings are obvious. For example, the Microsoft Access default for font size in form controls is 8 points. This is often too small for users to see clearly and quickly, especially near the end of a long day of repetitive use. Exercise 8.2 guides you through changes that will make the form more attractive and easier to use. To begin the exercise, have the AutoForm-generated Vendor Information form open on the Microsoft Access desktop.

Exercise 8.2: Modifying the Vendor Information Form

1. Select View, Form Design from the menu.
2. Click and drag the lower-right corner of the form to make it larger in both dimensions.

3. Click and drag the gray Detail section background to fill the now-available space.
4. Click and drag a marquee around all of the controls on the form to select them.
5. Click the button on the Font Size combo box on the Formatting toolbar and select or enter ***10***
6. With the controls still selected, press Shift+down arrow four times to stretch the controls vertically to accommodate the larger font.
7. With the controls still selected, choose Format, Vertical Spacing, Increase from the menu to restore the vertical distance between the controls.
8. Using Figure 8.5 as a guide, adjust the size of the text box controls.

Try it

You may find the commands under the Format menu helpful. For example, you might set the width of one control, then Shift+click the other controls whose width you want to increase. While the controls are selected, choose the Format, Size, to Widest menu command.

9. Click and drag a marquee around the label controls to select them. Using Figure 8.5 as a guide, adjust the size of the label controls.
10. With the label controls still selected, click the Bold button on the Formatting toolbar, then click the Align Right button on the Formatting toolbar.
11. Change the text in the VendorAddress1 label control to ***Address*** and delete the text in the VendorAddress2 label control.
12. Since the form displays one record at a time, the record selector on the left side of the form serves no useful function. To delete it, choose Edit, Select Form from the menu, click the Properties toolbar button to open the form's property sheet, click the Format tab, and change the Record Selectors property to No.
13. While the property sheet is open for the form, change its Caption property to ***Vendor Information Form***

    The completed form appears in Figure 8.6, displaying the information for vendor number 1001 in our Electric Controls Company sample data. To save your form while in Design view, select File, Save As/Export from the menu and enter ***frmVendor*** as the New Name in the Save As dialog box. This form is included as *frmVendor2* in the *Ch08.mdb* database on your Companion CD-ROM.

Maintaining Vendor Records

We have shown you how to build a Vendor table to store vendor information and a Vendor Information form that makes it easy to enter and view data in that table. With the Vendor Information form, you can:

Vendor Information Form

Vendor Number	1001
Name	Square P Corporation
Address	14532 Electron Way
City	Middletown
State	OH
Zip Code	45061-2079
Telephone	(513) 688-2795
Primary Contact	Maggie Beeler

Record: 1 of 10

Figure 8.6 The improved Vendor Information form, *frmVendor.*

- Create records for new vendors.
- Delete records for vendors that have become inactive or have gone out of business.
- Update Vendor table records as vendors move, get new telephone numbers, and change other items of information you have stored in your Vendor table.

You will want to keep your file of vendor information current. A key advantage of the relational database model is that you only need to add, delete, or change information in one table. To use the Vendor Information form to add vendors to *tblVendor*, open *frmVendor*. As you enter values, notice how the Input Mask and Validation Rule properties you set in *tblVendor* limit the values you can enter in the VendorNumber, VendorState, VendorZipCode, and VendorTelephone controls. Try entering out-of-range values in these fields to test the internal controls you built into the table.

Try it

Deleting records from the Vendor table is very easy. Open the Vendor Information form by clicking the Forms tab in the Database window and double-clicking *frmVendor.* To delete a record, move to that record using the navigation buttons at the bottom of the form, then choose Edit, Delete Record from the menu. Microsoft Access gives you a warning message that asks you to confirm the deletion. This deletion is not reversible. You can delete individual fields in a record using the Delete key in Form view. Individual field deletions are reversible by selecting Edit, Undo Delete before you move to another field. After you move to another field, you can reverse field deletions in the current record by selecting Edit, Undo Current Field/Record. You can also press Esc repeatedly to reverse deletions.

Be careful when deleting records in accounting databases. Data in one accounting table is usually related to data in other tables. For example, if you examine a record in a purchase order table, it will contain a vendor number. The only place that vendor's name and address is stored is in the related vendor table. If someone deletes that vendor's record in the vendor table, you may never be able to identify the vendor.

Keeping existing vendor records current to reflect address changes, new telephone numbers, and other changes is straightforward. Use the navigation buttons at the bottom of the form to move to the vendor record you want to change. You can move through the individual fields of the displayed record using the Enter or Tab keys. The Shift+Tab key moves backward through the record. The up and down arrow keys also move the cursor through the form. Any changes you make to field contents will be limited by the Input Mask and Validation Rule property settings for *tblVendor*.

MATERIALS INVENTORY

In Chapter 7 we described how to track finished goods inventory in the revenue cycle. In this section, we will explain how to build tables and forms that can help you track materials inventories—both the goods that manufacturing firms purchase for resale and the raw materials that manufacturing firms purchase and then convert into finished goods. We will explain how to record the conversion of materials and labor into finished goods in Chapter 10. Firms record and monitor materials inventory information in the purchase cycle because they need to know which vendors sell what inventory items. Firms also use materials inventory records to provide inventory descriptions on purchase orders, receiving reports, and other documents. To ensure that materials inventory information is consistent wherever it is used, firms keep all materials inventory information in one database table. Any document, report, or transaction that needs inventory information must obtain it from that table.

The Materials Inventory Table

The purchase cycle requires a materials inventory table that includes at least two fields. The first field must contain the primary key, a number or code that uniquely identifies the inventory item. This primary key field might contain an item number, item code, part number, or catalog number. In some industries, these inventory item identifiers are standardized; for example, some firms use UPC (universal product code) or SKU (stock-keeping unit) numbers as the primary keys in their materials inventory tables. The second field should contain a description of each inventory item. The description may include information about an item's size, weight, shape, color, hardness, or other qualities. Alternatively, a firm may decide to store these inventory item attributes in separate fields.

Few firms can store inventory purchase prices in the materials inventory table—that would require the firm to know, in advance, exactly what price it would pay for each item. A firm could store the vendor number of the vendor that supplies each item in the materials inventory table, but only if just one vendor would ever supply that item. If more than one vendor might supply a particular item and any particular vendor might supply more than one item, the inventory and vendor entities have a many-to-many relationship. We will show you how to use a materials inventory-vendor table to model that relationship.

Since each vendor is likely to have its own inventory part number, you should store that vendor inventory number in the materials inventory-vendor table. However, you would not want to use vendors' inventory numbers as the primary key for your table. Two different vendors may use the same number for different inventory items. To model the purchase of particular materials inventory items at different prices, you should store purchase prices in a purchase order-materials inventory relationship table.

The Electric Controls Company has decided to use a two-field description scheme in its Materials Inventory table. Electric Controls classifies the parts it uses to build control panels into six categories:

- Circuit breakers
- Connectors
- Relays
- Sheet metal
- Switches
- Wire

The Electric Controls Company materials inventory description will include two fields. One field will identify an item's category; the second field will store details about the particular item. Exercise 8.3 will show you how to build the Materials Inventory table.

EXERCISE 8.3: BUILDING A MATERIALS INVENTORY TABLE

1. Choose the Tables tab in the Database window, click the New button, and then double-click Design View in the New Table dialog box that appears.
2. Enter ***MInvStockNumber*** as the first Field Name and click the Primary Key toolbar button. Leave its Data Type set to Text and set its Field Size property to ***3***, its Input Mask property to ***000***, and its Caption property to ***Stock Number***.

   Some firms might use a descriptive coding scheme for this field as we did in the finished goods inventory example in Chapter 7. However, the Electric Controls Company purchasing department personnel who will be using materials inventory information have ready access to the computer system.

This reduces the benefits of using mnemonic coding schemes. Therefore, we have chosen to use a sequential number scheme for the MInvStockNumber field. The three-digit field will allow Electric Controls to maintain records on as many as 899 different materials inventory items.

3. Enter a Field Name of ***MInvCategory*** for the first description field. Leave its Data Type set to Text.
4. Set its Field Size property to ***16*** to match the number of characters in the longest inventory category name.
5. Set its Input Mask property to *>L<CCCCCCCCCCCCCCC*. This setting will automatically capitalize the first letter entered in the field, thus making data entry easier, and will ensure that any other characters entered are either lowercase letters or spaces.
6. Set the Caption property to ***Category***
7. Enter ***MInvDescription*** as the third Field Name. Leave its Data Type set to Text.
8. Set its Field Size property to ***25*** and its Caption property to ***Description***
9. Press Ctrl+S to save your work. Enter ***tblMaterialsInventory*** as the Table Name in the Save As dialog box.

Figure 8.7 shows *tblMaterialsInventory* in Datasheet view displaying the data for the Electric Controls Company. These data are included in *tblMaterialsInventory*, which is part of the *Ch08.mdb* database on your Companion CD-ROM.

tblMaterialsInventory : Table

Stock Number	Category	Description
101	Sheet metal	1/8" Steel 4x4 sheet
102	Switch	DPDT 240v 100a
103	Wire	500' Copper #22AWG
104	Sheet metal	1/4" Steel 4x4 sheet
105	Switch	SPDT 240v 100a
106	Relay	SPDT 120v 40a Silver
107	Circuit breaker	240v 40a
108	Relay	TPST 240v 100a Mercury
109	Sheet metal	1/8" Aluminum 4x4 sheet
110	Wire	500' Copper Twin #18AWG
111	Connector	F 240v 100a solderless
112	Switch	DPST 240v 50a
113	Connector	M 120v 40a clip
114	Sheet metal	1/4" Aluminum 4x4 sheet
115	Circuit breaker	120v 40a

Record: 1 of 15

Figure 8.7 The Electric Controls Company *tblMaterialsInventory* in Datasheet view.

The Category Table

The Input Mask property setting for the MInvCategory field in *tblMaterialsInventory* capitalizes the first letter and limits the field to 16 characters. However, this setting does not limit the values entered to the six specific categories. As we explained in Chapter 7, you can specify a Validation Rule property that will restrict the values entered to the six categories.

An alternative to setting a Validation Rule property is building a separate table that contains the permitted values, then enforcing referential integrity on a link between the category field in *tblMaterialsInventory* and the category field in the new table. If there are more than four or five permitted values, this separate-table technique can be more efficient than setting a Validation Rule property. When the permitted values are in a separate table, the tasks of adding, altering, and deleting values are much easier than when they are buried in a Validation Rule property setting. Exercise 8.4 shows you how to create a Category table and enforce referential integrity on a link to *tblMaterialsInventory*.

EXERCISE 8.4: BUILDING A MATERIALS INVENTORY CATEGORY TABLE

1. Choose the Tables tab in the Database window, click the New button, and then double-click Design View in the New Table dialog box that appears.
2. Enter ***Category*** in the first row of the Field Name column.
3. Click the Primary Key toolbar button to make this field the primary key.
4. Leave its Data Type set to Text.
5. Set its Field Size property to ***16***
6. Press Ctrl+S to save your work. Enter ***tblCategory*** as the Table Name in the Save As dialog box.
7. Select View, Datasheet from the menu to open the table in Datasheet view. Enter the six category values shown in Figure 8.8.

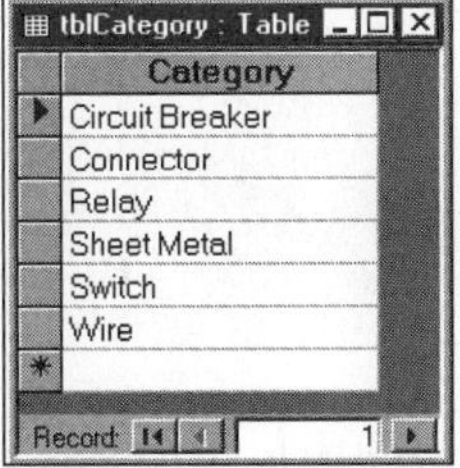

Figure 8.8 The Category table in Datasheet view.

Figure 8.8 shows *tblCategory* in Datasheet view displaying the six categories that the Electric Controls Company uses to classify its materials inventory. This table is included in the *Ch08.mdb* database on your Companion CD-ROM. Tables like *tblCategory* are sometimes called *lookup tables* because the main table field looks up entered values there to determine their validity. In Exercise 8.5, we show you how to create a lookup link and enforce referential integrity on that link.

EXERCISE 8.5: ENFORCING REFERENTIAL INTEGRITY ON A LOOKUP TABLE

1. Close all open tables. With the Database window displayed, choose the Tools, Relationships menu command. Click the Show Table toolbar button.
2. Click the Tables tab in the Show Table dialog box, then select (click while pressing the Ctrl key) *tblCategory* and *tblMaterialsInventory*.
3. Click the Add button, then click the Close button.
4. Adjust the size and location of the tables displayed in the Relationships window using Figure 8.9 as a guide.
5. Click and drag the Category field from *tblCategory* to the MInvCategory field in *tblMaterialsInventory*. When the Relationships dialog box appears, check it carefully to make certain that you dragged the field to its proper destination.
6. Click the Enforce Referential Integrity check box, then click the Create button.

The Relationships window showing the two linked tables appears in Figure 8.9. To return to the Database window, press Ctrl+W, then click the Yes button to save your Relationships window layout changes.

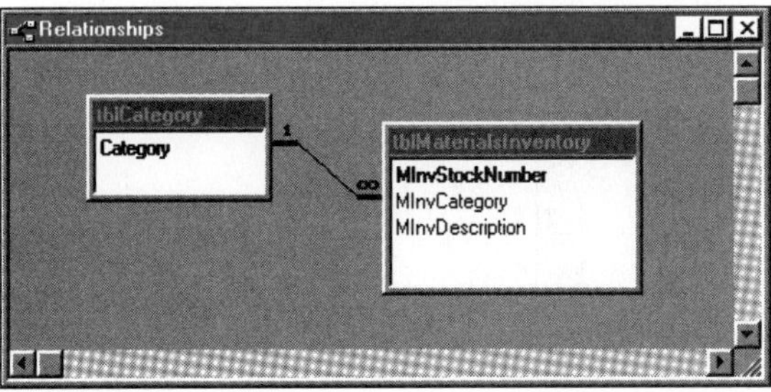

Figure 8.9 Linking *tblCategory* and *tblMaterialsInventory*.

The Materials Inventory Form

The Materials Inventory form will let users enter inventory records easily and accurately. The form will also provide a convenient way for users to view, update, or delete existing inventory records. Exercise 8.6 shows you how to create *frmMaterialsInventory*, a Materials Inventory form.

EXERCISE 8.6: USING AUTOFORM TO CREATE A MATERIALS INVENTORY FORM

1. Click the Form tab in the Database window, then click the New button.
   Since *tblMaterialsInventory* has only four small fields, we do not need to use a columnar form. We can display a number of records at one time by using a tabular form.
2. Type ***tblMaterialsInventory*** in the table box or select it from the drop-down list in the New Form dialog box.
3. Double-click AutoForm: Tabular in the New Form dialog box.
4. To save the form, press Ctrl+W, click the Yes button to confirm that you want to save changes to the form's design, and enter a Form Name of ***frmMaterialsInventory*** in the Save As dialog box.

As you can see in Figure 8.10, AutoForm creates a fairly good-looking form that we can modify to meet our specific needs for entering the contents of *tblMaterialsInventory* efficiently and effectively. Note how the tabular format lets users view more than one record at a time. This version of the form is included as *frmMaterialsInventory1* in the *Ch08.mdb* database on your Companion CD-ROM. The database also includes *tblMaterialsInventory*, which includes the records displayed in Figure 8.10.

tblMaterialsInventory

Stock Number	Category	Description
101	Sheet metal	1/8" Steel 4x4 sheet
102	Switch	DPDT 240v 100a
103	Wire	500' Copper #22AWG
104	Sheet metal	1/4" Steel 4x4 sheet
105	Switch	SPDT 240v 100a
106	Relay	SPDT 120v 40a Silver
107	Circuit breaker	240v 40a
108	Relay	TPST 240v 100a Mercury
109	Sheet metal	1/8" Aluminum 4x4 sheet
110	Wire	500' Copper Twin #18AWI

Record: 1 of 15

Figure 8.10 The Materials Inventory form created by the AutoForm tool.

Although the AutoForm tool has made a good start toward creating a usable form, we can improve the appearance and usefulness of the form. To modify the form, click the Design View toolbar button. To make the design tools more accessible, click the Toolbox toolbar button before you begin Exercise 8.7, which shows you how to improve the design and appearance of *frmMaterialsInventory*.

Try it

You can click and drag the toolbox around the Design window as you work, but you might find it useful to move the toolbox to the top of the Design window. When you do this, the toolbox icons become slightly larger and arrange themselves across the top of the work area just below the toolbar. You can see this in Figure 8.11, which shows the Materials Inventory form in Design view with the toolbox moved to the top of the Design window, just under the Formatting toolbar. We usually work with the property sheet open, too. To open the property sheet, click the Properties toolbar button. As you can see in Figure 8.11, we often keep the property sheet just partially exposed on the desktop, off to one side or below the form on which we are working.

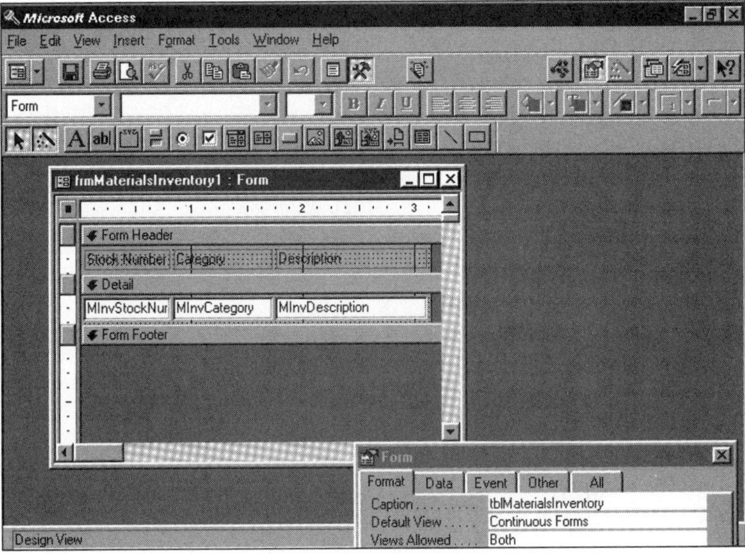

Figure 8.11 The Materials Inventory form in Design view with the toolbox and property sheet opened.

Exercise 8.7: Improving the Materials Inventory Form

1. Choose Edit, Select Form from the menu, click the Format tab in the property sheet, and change the form's Caption property to ***Materials Inventory***
2. Click and drag the right edge of the form to make it wider, then click and drag the edges of the gray Detail section background to fit the enlarged frame.
3. Select the label controls in the Form Header section and click the Bold button on the Formatting toolbar. You may also want to click the Center button on the Formatting toolbar to center-align the labels and use the

Shift+right arrow key to make the labels a little wider and expose all of the labels' text.

4. Click and drag a marquee around all of the controls (in both sections of the form) and repeatedly select Format, Horizontal Spacing, Increase from the menu to increase the space between the controls.

   You can use Figure 8.12 as a guide. Remember, you may need to switch back and forth between Form view and Design view to obtain your desired results.
5. Select the MInvCategory text box control in the Detail section and press the Delete key.

   We will show you how to replace this control with a combo box control. We used a similar form design procedure to modify *frmInventory* in Exercise 7.10.
6. If the Control Wizards button in the toolbox is not depressed, click it. Click the Combo Box tool button in the toolbox and draw a combo box control in the Detail section to replace the MInvCategory text box you just deleted. This will start the Combo Box Wizard.
7. In the first Combo Box Wizard dialog box, click the Next > button to accept the default of linking the combo box to a table or query.
8. Double-click *tblCategory* in the list box. This action also moves the Wizard to its next dialog box.
9. Double-click Category, then click the Next > button.
10. In the next Combo Box Wizard dialog box, click and drag the right edge of the Category column header to the left until the column just accommodates the widest text, Circuit breaker. Click the Next > button.
11. Click the option button to "Store that value in this field," then select or enter ***MInvCategory*** in the combo box.
12. Click the Next > button to open the final Combo Box Wizard dialog box and click the Finish button.

    When the Wizard returns you to the Design View desktop, select the new combo box control's label and delete it. The easiest way to do this is to use the Select Object combo box control on the Formatting toolbar to select the new combo box label (it will have a suffix of _Label) and press the Delete key.
13. Name the control by changing its Name property under the Other tab in the property sheet to ***cboMInvCategory***
14. To save the form, press Ctrl+W, click the Yes button to confirm that you want to save changes to the form's design, and enter a Form Name of ***frmMaterialsInventory*** in the Save As dialog box. Note that this will overwrite the form you created in Exercise 8.6 if you saved it using the same name. This form is included as *frmMaterialsInventory2* in the *Ch08.mdb* database on your Companion CD-ROM.

To test this new control, select View, Form from the menu, then click the cboMInvCategory control's arrow button. The combo box should display the six choices from *tblCategory* as shown in Figure 8.12.

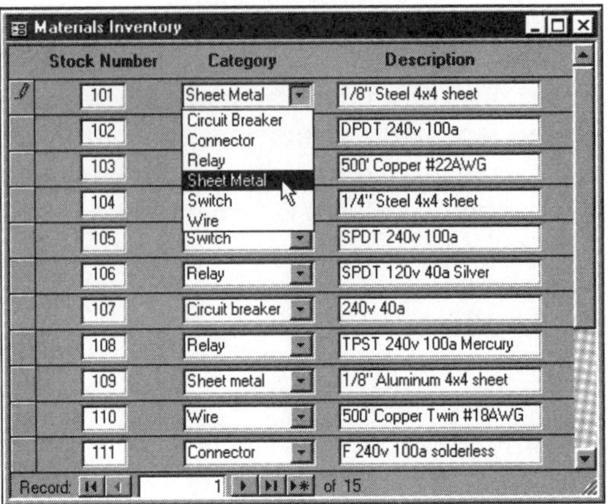

Figure 8.12 The cboMInvCategory control on the Materials Inventory form.

Try it

The Combo Box Wizard actually writes a query that accesses *tblCategory* and inserts the six values from the Category field in that table. To examine this query, click the MInvCategory combo box in Design view with the property sheet open, click the Data tab, select the Row Source property, and click its Build button. It is a simple query, but it does the job!

The Materials Inventory-Vendor Table

The Electric Controls Company could identify vendors that supply particular materials inventory items by including the vendor number as a foreign key in the Materials Inventory table. Unfortunately, a foreign key field only works if each inventory item is supplied by just one vendor. To accommodate the far more common situation in which more than one vendor supplies a particular item, most firms need a materials inventory-vendor relationship table to model the many-to-many relationship between the two entities. Further, since each vendor will have its own inventory stock number, Electric Controls will want to connect vendors' stock numbers with its own inventory stock numbers in *tblMaterialsInventory*. For example, vendors will expect Electric Controls to use *their* stock numbers when they send purchase orders. The Electric Controls Company can use a Materials Inventory-Vendor table to relate each vendor's stock number to the stock number in *tblMaterialsInventory*. A field for vendor stock number in *tblMaterialsInventory-Vendor* will model this relation.

Note that the relationship table we are creating here is completely independent of purchase order records. The relationship between the vendor entity and the materials inventory entity is that vendors have *offered* these items for sale. It does not mean that the Electric Controls Company has purchased items from each of the vendors that offer those items. Another point worth noting is the difficulty of keeping this relationship table updated. Electric Controls deals with a small number of suppliers, and those suppliers have maintained the same item numbers for years. In a less stable setting, or in a business with many vendors, maintaining this relationship table can become very time-consuming. With the advent of electronic commerce, more firms are offering their catalogs on CD-ROM and online over the Internet. The easiest way to keep a materials inventory-vendor table current is by using automatic updates from such sources. If Electric Controls had vendors that changed their part numbers often, they might still maintain this table, but they probably would not enforce referential integrity on its links to the Materials Inventory and Vendor tables.

In Exercise 8.8, we show you how to create a Materials Inventory-Vendor relationship table for the Electric Controls Company. We also show you how to link the table to *tblMaterialsInventory* and *tblVendor.* Finally, we show you how to enforce referential integrity controls on the links among these tables.

Exercise 8.8: Building a Materials Inventory-Vendor Table

1. Choose the Tables tab in the Database window, click the New button, and then double-click Design View in the New Table dialog box that appears.

   To begin, create the two fields that will constitute the composite primary key. We will use the primary key fields of the two entity tables in the relationship, *tblMaterialsInventory* and *tblVendor*, to accomplish this task.
2. Enter a Field Name of ***MInvStockNumber*** and leave its Data Type set to Text.
3. Set its Field Size property to ***3***, its Caption property to ***Stock Number***, and its Indexed property to Yes (Duplicates OK).
4. Enter a Field Name of ***VendorNumber*** and leave its Data Type set to Text.
5. Set its Field Size property to ***4***, its Caption property to ***Vendor Number***, and its Indexed property to Yes (Duplicates OK).

   These settings exactly match those of the MInvStockNumber field in *tblMaterialsInventory* and the VendorNumber field in *tblVendor.* We will not set Input Mask properties for these fields since we are planning to create links back to the entity tables and enforce referential integrity on those links. We do, however, need to indicate that these two fields will combine to form the *tblMaterialsInventory-Vendor* composite primary key.
6. While pressing the Ctrl key, click the row selectors for each of the two fields to select them.
7. While the two rows are selected, click the Primary Key toolbar button. The primary key symbol should appear in both row selectors.

The third field in *tblMaterialsInventory-Vendor* will store the stock numbers that the vendors use for each inventory item. Note that different vendors will likely have different stock numbers for the same item.

8. Enter a Field Name of ***MInvVendorStockNumber*** and leave its Data Type set to Text.
9. Set its Field Size property to ***20*** and its Caption property to ***Vendor Stock Number***
10. Press Ctrl+S to save your work. Enter ***tblMaterialsInventory-Vendor*** as the Table Name in the Save As dialog box.

The *Ch08.mdb* database on your Companion CD-ROM includes *tblMaterialsInventory-Vendor,* which appears in Datasheet view in Figure 8.13. This table contains the Electric Controls Company's inventory-vendor information. The last work we must do to finish this table is to create links back to the entity tables and enforce referential integrity on those links.

tblMaterialsInventory-Vendor : Table

Stock Number	Vendor Number	Vendor Stock Number
101	1005	18S44-279632
102	1007	240-100-SW284
103	1002	22C-SS-500
103	1004	29733-22
104	1005	14S44-279677
105	1007	240-100-SW184
106	1003	87R9643
106	1008	SPDTSil20743
107	1001	276-RT-774692
107	1007	240-40-CB108
108	1003	92R3371
108	1008	TPSTMerc17764
109	1005	18A44-279619
109	1006	844A3650
110	1002	18C-DS-500
110	1004	86412-18
111	1009	65497289
111	1010	263F417
112	1007	240-50-SW236
113	1009	12931662

Record: 1 of 25

Figure 8.13 The Materials Inventory-Vendor table in Datasheet view.

11. Press Ctrl+W to close the table.
12. Select Tools, Relationships from the menu. The Relationships window will appear with a display of the relationship we created earlier between *tblCategory* and *tblMaterialsInventory.*
13. Click the Show Table toolbar button.
14. While pressing the Ctrl key, click *tblMaterialsInventory-Vendor* and *tblVendor,* click the Add button, then click the Close button. You may want to resize and rearrange the tables in the Relationships window using Figure 8.14 as a guide.
15. Click and drag the MInvStockNumber field from *tblMaterialsInventory* to the corresponding field in *tblMaterialsInventory-Vendor.* Click the Enforce Referential Integrity check box, then click the Create button.

16. Click and drag the VendorNumber field from *tblVendor* to the corresponding field in *tblMaterialsInventory-Vendor*. Click the Enforce Referential Integrity check box, then click the Create button. The completed set of relationships appears in Figure 8.14.
17. Press Ctrl+W and click the Yes button to confirm the changes you have made. This will close the Relationships window and return you to the Database window.

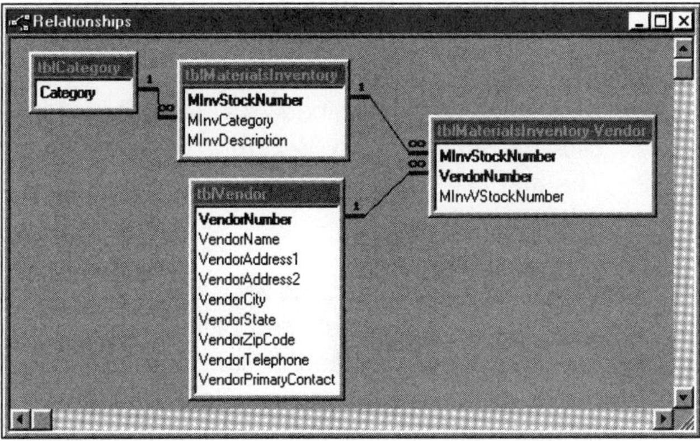

Figure 8.14 The links from *tblMaterialsInventory-Vendor* to *tblMaterialsInventory* and *tblVendor*.

A Materials Inventory Query and Report

Purchasing department personnel can use information in *tblVendor*, *tblMaterialsInventory*, and *tblMaterialsInventory-Vendor* to make their jobs easier. For example, suppose you are a buyer and must obtain price quotes on sheet metal materials. To perform this task efficiently, you would like to have:

- Names of vendors that supply sheet metal products
- Vendor stock numbers for sheet metal products
- Vendor telephone numbers
- Name of the person you will talk to when you call

In the next two exercises we will show you how you can create a query, *qrySheetMetal*, and a report, *rptSheetMetal*, that will provide this information for the Electric Controls Company. The query will extract information from *tblMaterialsInventory*, *tblVendor*, and *tblMaterialsInventory-Vendor*. We will then show you how to build *rptSheetMetal* based on the query. These exercises illustrate a frequently used method of exploiting the data stored in relational tables. As you learned in Chapter 4, a query allows us to retrieve information from a relational database in ways we had not considered when we designed the database.

The following exercises assume that you are using the Electric Controls Company data from the tables included in the *Ch08.mdb* database on your Companion CD-ROM. If you have entered your own data in the tables, the examples will still work; however, the query results and reports will display your records rather than the ones shown here.

Exercise 8.9: Building the Sheet Metal Query

1. Click the Database window's Queries tab, click the New button, then double-click on Simple Query Wizard in the New Query dialog box.
2. The first field we will include in the query is the MInvCategory field from *tblMaterialsInventory*. Select Table: *tblMaterialsInventory* in the Tables/Queries combo box.
3. Click MInvCategory in the Available Fields list box, then click the > button to add it to our list of Selected Fields.
4. The next fields we need in our query are in *tblMaterialsInventory-Vendor*. Select Table: *tblMaterialsInventory-Vendor* in the Tables/Queries combo box and click the >> button to move all three of its fields to the Selected Fields list.
5. The last table we need in *qrySheetMetal* is *tblVendor*. Select Table: *tblVendor* in the Tables/Queries combo box.
6. Using the > button, move the VendorName, VendorTelephone, and VendorPrimaryContact fields from the Available Fields list box to the Selected Fields list box. The Simple Query Wizard dialog box showing the complete list of selected fields for *qrySheetMetal* appears in Figure 8.15.

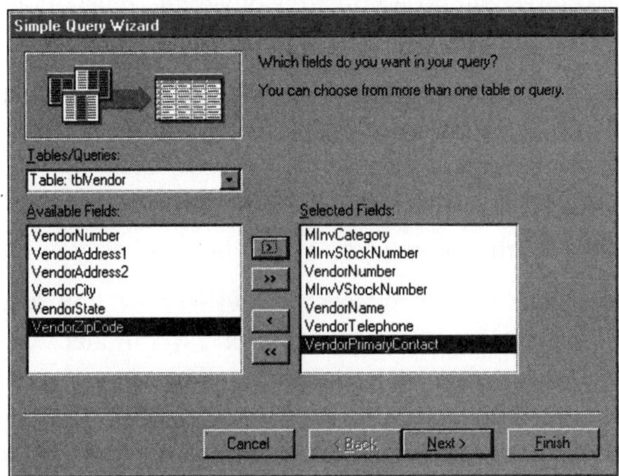

Figure 8.15 A Simple Query Wizard dialog box with field selections for *qrySheetMetal*.

7. Click the Next > button to open the next dialog box. Click the Next > button in that dialog box to accept the default of having the Wizard generate a detail query.
8. Enter a title of ***qrySheetMetal*** for the query, click the "Modify the query design" option button, then click the Finish button to have the Wizard create the query to your specifications. The Wizard-generated query appears in Query Design view in Figure 8.16. We have adjusted the size of the Query Builder window and the table objects to show you more clearly the work that the Wizard has performed.

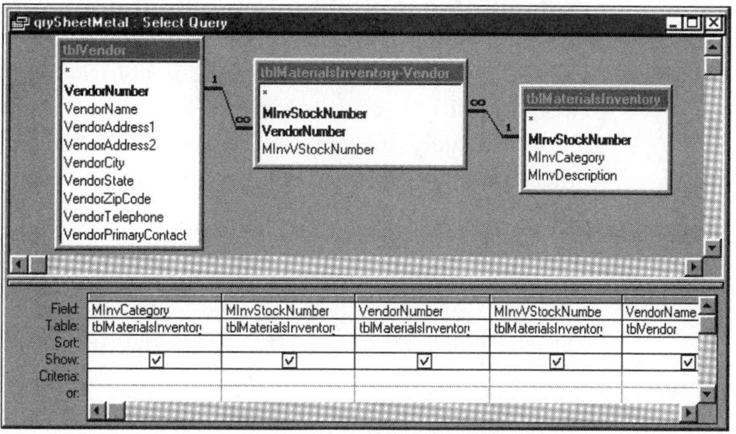

Figure 8.16 The Simple Query Wizard-generated *qrySheetMetal* in Query Design view.

9. To have the query select only the vendors that supply products in the sheet metal category, enter ***Sheet metal*** in the first Criteria cell in the QBE grid, under MInvCategory. When you run the query, Access will enclose the words in quotation marks because MInvCategory is a text field.
10. Since we do not want to include the category in our results (we want just the vendors that supply sheet metal products; we do not need the words "sheet metal" included on each line of our dynaset), click the box in the first Show cell in the QBE grid to remove the check mark.
11. Enter ***Ascending*** in the VendorName QBE grid Sort cell to arrange the resulting dynaset in alphabetical order by vendor name.
12. Select Query, Run from the menu to have the query generate a dynaset of results. The *qrySheetMetal* result in Datasheet view appears in Figure 8.17.
13. To close the query and save your changes, press Ctrl+W and click the dialog box Yes button. The query we built in this exercise is included as *qrySheetMetal* in the *Ch08.mdb* database on your Companion CD-ROM.

The *qrySheetMetal* dynaset provides all of the information that we wanted; however, we need to change the dynaset column headings and make some other

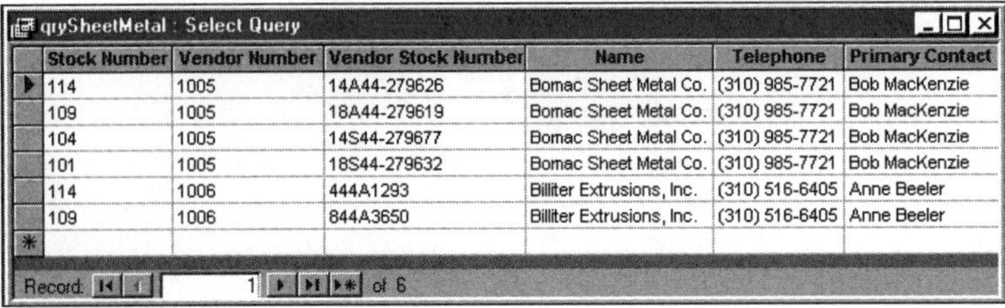

qrySheetMetal : Select Query

Stock Number	Vendor Number	Vendor Stock Number	Name	Telephone	Primary Contact
114	1005	14A44-279626	Bomac Sheet Metal Co.	(310) 985-7721	Bob MacKenzie
109	1005	18A44-279619	Bomac Sheet Metal Co.	(310) 985-7721	Bob MacKenzie
104	1005	14S44-279677	Bomac Sheet Metal Co.	(310) 985-7721	Bob MacKenzie
101	1005	18S44-279632	Bomac Sheet Metal Co.	(310) 985-7721	Bob MacKenzie
114	1006	444A1293	Billiter Extrusions, Inc.	(310) 516-6405	Anne Beeler
109	1006	844A3650	Billiter Extrusions, Inc.	(310) 516-6405	Anne Beeler

Record: 1 of 6

Figure 8.17 The results dynaset of *qrySheetMetal.*

modifications to make the output more useful. Consider how difficult it would be to use this output if we had generated a list of 50 or 100 vendors instead of just two. The repetition of vendor name is not too cumbersome in our example, but it would rapidly become so as the number of vendors and items in the dynaset grew. Fortunately, we can use this query as the basis for a report that we can tailor to meet virtually any user requirement. In the next exercise, we show you how to create a report, *rptSheetMetal*, that is based on *qrySheetMetal*.

Exercise 8.10: Building the Sheet Metal Report

1. Click the Database window's Reports tab and click the New button to open the New Report dialog box.
2. This dialog box has two data entry areas, a list box and a combo box. Enter ***qrySheetMetal*** in the combo box, then double-click on Report Wizard in the list box.
3. Move the VendorName, VendorPrimaryContact, VendorTelephone, MInvStockNumber, and MInvVStockNumber fields from the Available Fields list box to the Selected Fields list box by clicking the field name, then clicking the > button, for each field. Be sure to move the fields in exactly this order because the Wizard makes decisions about the report design based on field order. Note that we did *not* include VendorNumber in the Selected Fields list. The Report Wizard dialog box with the fields selected in this order appears in Figure 8.18.
4. Click Next > to open the next Report Wizard dialog box. The report template that appears in the window should show the VendorName, VendorPrimaryContact, and VendorTelephone field names in the Report Header and the two stock number fields in the Detail section of the report. If your template has this information, click the Next > button to open the next dialog box. If your template does not have this information, click the Back < button and check your Selected Fields list with the list shown in Figure 8.18.
5. Click Next > to accept the default grouping level settings.
6. Enter ***MInvStockNumber*** in the first sort order combo box, then click the Next > button.
7. Click the Stepped Layout option button, then click the Next > button.

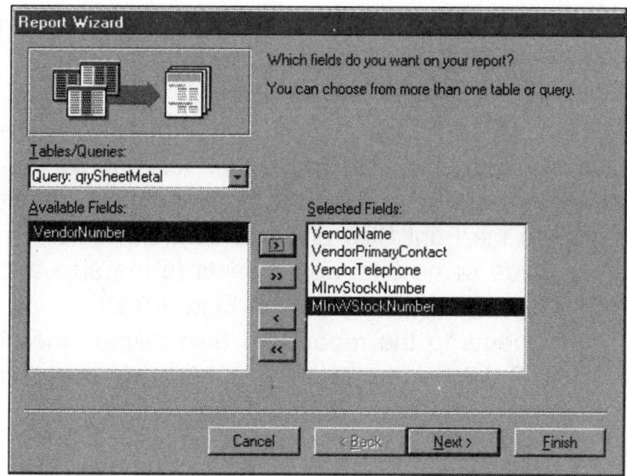

Figure 8.18 Selecting fields for *rptSheetMetal* in the Report Wizard.

8. Click the Corporate style, then click the Next > button. We liked the Stepped Layout in a Corporate style for this report, but we encourage you to experiment with different layouts and styles as you build your report.
9. Enter ***rptSheetMetal*** in the report title box. This entry creates the name of the report and tells the Report Wizard what text to enter into the title label control on the report. Our report name does not make a very good report title; however, you can easily edit the title label control text after the Report Wizard finishes its work.
10. Click the option button for the "Modify the report's design" choice, then click the Finish button to have the Report Wizard generate the report and open it in Report Design view as shown in Figure 8.19.

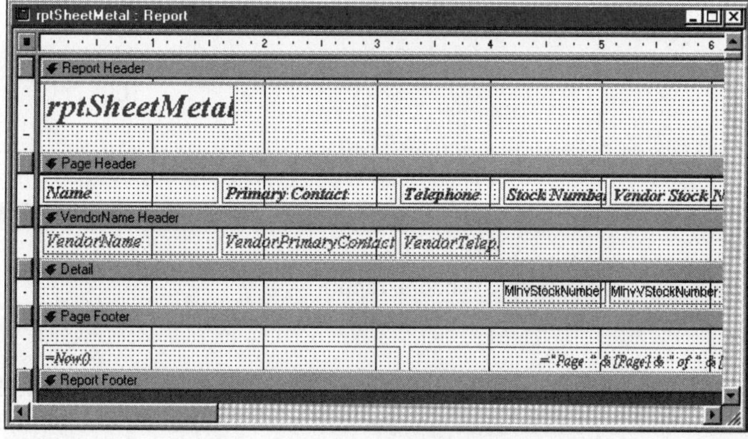

Figure 8.19 The Report Wizard-generated Sheet Metal report in Report Design view.

11. Change the text of the label control in the Report Header section to ***Electric Controls Company - Sheet Metal Vendors***
12. Change the text of the MInvStockNumber control to ***Our Stock Number***
13. Select all of the label and text box controls in the Page Header, VendorName Header, and Detail sections by clicking and dragging a marquee around them. Use the Formatting toolbar Font Size combo box to change the Font Size of these controls to 10.
14. We made some final adjustments to the size and placement of the controls to obtain the report shown in Figure 8.20, which you may use to guide your adjustments to the report. We also deleted the controls in the Page Footer.
15. Press Ctrl+W and click the Yes button in the dialog box to save your changes and close *rptSheetMetal*.

Electric Controls Company - Sheet Metal Vendors

Name	*Primary Contact*	*Telephone*	*Our Stock Number*	*Vendor Stock Number*
Billiter Extrusions, Inc.	*Anne Beeler*	*(310) 516-6405*		
			109	844A3650
			114	444A1293
Bomac Sheet Metal Co.	*Bob MacKenzie*	*(310) 985-7721*		
			101	18S44-279632
			104	14S44-279677
			109	18A44-279619
			114	14A44-279626

Figure 8.20 The completed Sheet Metal Vendors report.

The Sheet Metal Vendors report that appears in Figure 8.20 is included as *rptSheetMetal* in the *Ch08.mdb* database on your Companion CD-ROM. The report we have created is just one example of many possible designs; however, it illustrates how you can turn a query dynaset into an attractive, useful report.

PURCHASE ORDERS

Now that you have built tables and forms that a firm could use to enter and maintain records of vendors and materials inventory, you can build the system components that facilitate ordering inventory items from vendors. A purchasing department receives materials requisitions from production departments that show materials descriptions and quantities needed. The purchasing department then must:

- Identify vendors that provide these materials.
- Select a vendor.
- Send a purchase order to the chosen vendor.

The format of materials requisitions varies with the firm's industry, size, and the skill level of the production department personnel that prepare materials requisitions. The format also depends on the nature of the firm's production cycle. The form of purchase orders also varies from firm to firm; however, all purchase orders must contain the following:

- Order date
- Vendor name and address
- Identification of the inventory item(s) to be purchased
- Quantities and prices of the inventory item(s) to be purchased

The purchase order also frequently contains shipping information, including an expected shipping date. To identify the vendors and inventory items, you can link the Vendor and Materials Inventory tables to a new table, the Purchase Order table. However, connecting purchase orders to the specific inventory items on each purchase order will require a separate relationship table to model the many-to-many link.

The Purchase Order Table

In this section, we will show you how to create a Purchase Order table, *tblPurchaseOrder*. Since only one vendor will be associated with any specific purchase order, you can include *tblVendor's* primary key, VendorNumber, as a foreign key in *tblPurchaseOrder* to establish the needed link. Of course, *tblPurchaseOrder* will need its own primary key and a field for the order date. To keep our example simple, we will omit specific shipping data and just record an expected shipping date, the date the vendor agrees to ship the ordered items, on the purchase order. Therefore, *tblPurchaseOrder* needs four fields: a primary key, an order date, a foreign key link to *tblVendor*, and an expected vendor ship date. Exercise 8.11 provides step-by-step procedures you can follow to create a Purchase Order table for the Electric Controls Company example data we have provided.

EXERCISE 8.11: BUILDING A PURCHASE ORDER TABLE

1. Click the Tables tab in the Database window, click the New button, and then double-click Design View in the New Table dialog box that appears.
2. Type ***PurchaseOrderNumber*** as the first Field Name. Leave its Data Type set to Text.
3. Click the Primary Key toolbar button.
4. Set PurchaseOrderNumber's Field Size property to *6*, its Input Mask property to *######*, and its Caption property to ***P.O. Number***. This primary key field will accommodate 899,999 purchase orders if we use a starting number of 100001.
5. Enter a Field Name of ***PurchaseOrderDate*** and set its Data Type to Date/Time.
6. Set PurchaseOrderDate's Input Mask property to *99/99/00;0;_* and its Caption property to ***P.O. Date***

   The next field is the foreign key link to *tblVendor*. After we finish building *tblPurchaseOrder*, we will show you how to establish a link on this field to *tblVendor* and how to enforce referential integrity on that link. We will design this field to exactly match the primary key of *tblVendor.*
7. Enter ***VendorNumber*** as the Field Name and leave its Data Type set to Text.
8. Set VendorNumber's Field Size property to *4* and its Caption property to ***Vendor Number***

   We will not enter a value for the VendorNumber field's Input Mask property because the referential integrity link to *tblVendor* will ensure that values entered will be those that already exist in *tblVendor*.
9. Enter a Field Name of ***PurchaseOrderExpShipDate*** and set its Data Type to Date/Time.
10. Set this field's Input Mask property to *99/99/00;0;_* and its Caption property to ***Expected Ship Date***
11. Press Ctrl+W and click the Yes button to save your changes and close the table. Enter ***tblPurchaseOrder*** as the Table Name in the Save As dialog box.

    The last step in building *tblPurchaseOrder* is to create a link on VendorNumber to *tblVendor.*
12. While in the Database window, click the Relationships toolbar button. The Relationships window will open and display all of the purchase cycle table links we created in earlier sections of this chapter.
13. Click the Show Table toolbar button to open the Show Table dialog box.
14. Double-click *tblPurchaseOrder*, then click the Close button.
15. Click and drag the VendorNumber field from *tblVendor* to the VendorNumber field in *tblPurchaseOrder*.
16. Click the Enforce Referential Integrity check box, then click the Create button. The Relationships window showing the new link among the existing relationships appears in Figure 8.21. To close the Relationships window, press Ctrl+W and click the Yes button to save the changes you have made.

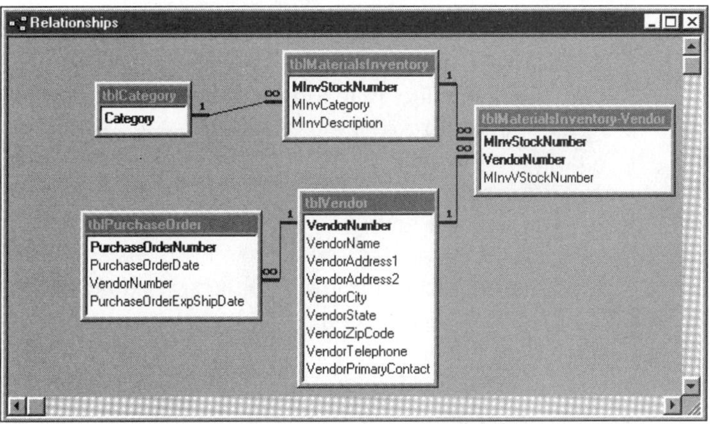

Figure 8.21 Adding a link from *tblVendor* to *tblPurchaseOrder* on the VendorNumber field.

A copy of *tblPurchaseOrder* is in the *Ch08.mdb* database on your Companion CD-ROM. This completes the job of building *tblPurchaseOrder*; however, you cannot enter purchase orders in this table yet. The Purchase Order table does not identify which inventory items are ordered, nor does it identify the quantities and prices of items ordered. We will now show you how to create a Purchase Order-Materials Inventory relationship table to properly store this information.

The Purchase Order-Materials Inventory Table

If the Electric Controls Company only ordered one inventory item on each purchase order, they would not need this table. They could add fields for the inventory item, its quantity, and its price to *tblPurchaseOrder*. Unfortunately, Electric Controls and most other businesses would find themselves drowning in purchase orders if they adopted this approach. The Purchase Order-Materials Inventory table is a relationship table that models the many-to-many link between *tblPurchaseOrder* and *tblMaterialsInventory*. That is, each purchase order may have many materials inventory items and each materials inventory item may appear on many purchase orders. The Purchase Order-Materials Inventory table needs four fields to store the following values:

- Primary key of *tblPurchaseOrder*
- Primary key of *tblMaterialsInventory*
- Quantity of specific materials inventory items that appear on specific purchase orders
- Price of specific materials inventory items that appear on specific purchase orders

In the next exercise, we will show you how to create *tblPurchaseOrder-MaterialsInventory*, a relationship table for the Electric Controls Company that will provide these two links and store these four fields. To begin the exercise, close any tables or forms you have open on the desktop and open the Database window.

EXERCISE 8.12: BUILDING A PURCHASE ORDER-MATERIALS INVENTORY TABLE

1. Click the Table tab in the Database window, click the New button, and then double-click Design View in the New Table dialog box that appears.
2. Type ***PurchaseOrderNumber*** as the first Field Name. Leave its Data Type set to Text.
3. Set PurchaseOrderNumber's Field Size property to ***6***, its Input Mask property to ***######***, and its Caption property to ***P.O. Number***
4. Set the Indexed property to Yes (Duplicates OK).

   Remember that when we use entity table primary keys as part of the composite primary key in a relationship table, we always want an exact match on the Data Type and Field Size properties. We will simultaneously enter values into the PurchaseOrderNumber fields in this table and *tblPurchaseOrder* using the form described in the next section. A referential integrity link on this field back to *tblPurchaseOrder* would not act as a data input control because the value would not yet exist in *tblPurchaseOrder*. However, we will create a link with referential integrity on the PurchaseOrderNumber field because it will help Microsoft Access synchronize the two forms we will use to enter purchase order information. The other half of this table's composite primary key is *tblInventory's* primary key, MInvStockNumber.
5. Type ***MInvStockNumber*** as the first Field Name. Leave its Data Type set to Text.
6. Set MInvStockNumber's Field Size property to ***3*** and its Caption property to ***Item Number***
7. Set the Indexed property to Yes (Duplicates OK).

   The Materials Inventory table will contain inventory item values before purchase orders are entered. Therefore, we can use a referential integrity link on MInvStockNumber to prevent users from entering nonexistent stock numbers in this field. We will show you how to establish this link later in this exercise. Our next task is to make the first two fields of this table its composite primary key.
8. While holding down the Ctrl key, click the row selectors of the PurchaseOrderNumber field and the MInvStockNumber field.
9. Click the Primary Key toolbar button.

   The primary key symbol should appear in the row selectors of both fields, indicating the composite primary key. The next two fields will store the quantity and price, respectively, of each inventory item ordered on a particular purchase order.

10. Enter a Field Name of ***POMInvQuantity*** and set its Data Type to Number.
11. Set POMInvQuantity's Field Size property to Long Integer, its Decimal Places property to ***0***, and its Caption property to ***Quantity***
12. Enter a Field Name of ***POMInvPrice***, set its Data Type to Currency, and set its Caption property to ***Price***
13. To save *tblPurchaseOrder-MaterialsInventory*, press Ctrl+W and click the Yes button to save your changes. Enter a Table Name of ***tblPurchaseOrder-MaterialsInventory*** in the Save As dialog box, then click the OK button. A copy of *tblPurchaseOrder-MaterialsInventory* is included in the *Ch08.mdb* database on your Companion CD-ROM.

    Now that the table design is complete, we can create the links to *tblMaterialsInventory* and *tblPurchaseOrder*.
14. While in the Database window, click the Relationships toolbar button. The Relationships window will open and display all of the purchase cycle table links we have created.
15. Click the Show Table toolbar button to open the Show Table dialog box.
16. Double-click *tblPurchaseOrder-MaterialsInventory*, then click the Close button.
17. Click and drag the MInvStockNumber field from *tblMaterialsInventory* to the MInvStockNumber field in *tblPurchaseOrder-MaterialsInventory*.
18. Click the Enforce Referential Integrity check box, then click the Create button.
19. Click and drag the PurchaseOrderNumber field from *tblPurchaseOrder* to the PurchaseOrderNumber field in *tblPurchaseOrder-MaterialsInventory*.
20. Click the Enforce Referential Integrity check box, then click the Create button.
21. The Relationships window showing the two new links among the existing relationships appears in Figure 8.22. To close the Relationships window, press Ctrl+W and click the Yes button to save your changes.

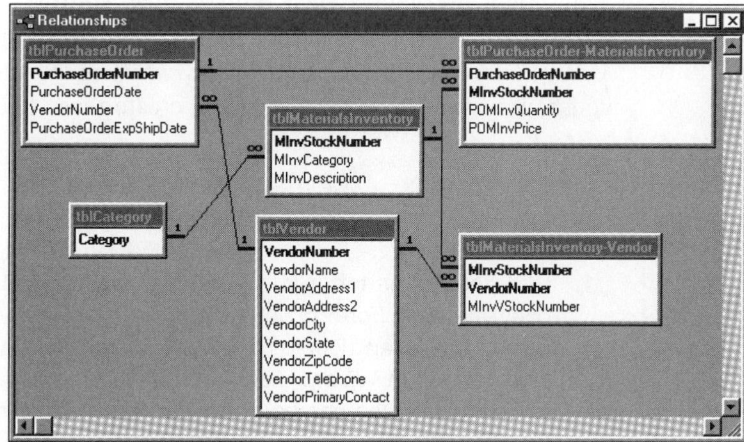

Figure 8.22 Adding links to *tblPurchaseOrder-MaterialsInventory* in the Relationships window.

Now that we have built the Purchase Order table and *tblPurchaseOrder-MaterialsInventory*, we can create a form that will enable the Electric Controls Company to enter its purchase orders. We show you how to create this Purchase Order Entry form in the next section.

The Purchase Order Entry Form

The Purchase Order Entry form is fairly complex. To enter purchase orders, we will need a form that links:

- The Purchase Order table to the Vendor table, to provide the vendor name.
- The Purchase Order table to the Purchase Order-Materials Inventory table, to provide a list of inventory items, quantities, and prices for each purchase order.
- The Purchase Order-Materials Inventory table to the Materials Inventory table, to provide a description and vendor stock number for each item on each purchase order.

A Purchase Order Entry form that meets these objectives will use four tables. The form must read from *tblVendor* and *tblMaterialsInventory* and will write to *tblPurchaseOrder* and *tblPurchaseOrder-MaterialsInventory*. Since the form will read data from *tblVendor* and *tblMaterialsInventory*, we will need to have data in these tables to test the form's operation as we build it. The versions of these two tables that we have included in the *Ch08.mdb* database on your Companion CD-ROM contain data. You can use these tables or copy the data from them to your own tables using the procedure we described in Exercise 5.4.

The Purchase Order Entry form will allow the Electric Controls Company to enter purchase order information simultaneously in *tblPurchaseOrder* and *tblPurchaseOrder-MaterialsInventory*. Microsoft Access handles this simultaneous data entry task best with a form-subform design. This design links *tblPurchaseOrder* to *tblVendor* in the main form and links *tblPurchaseOrder-MaterialsInventory* to *tblMaterialsInventory* in the subform. Exercise 8.13 shows you how to use the Form Wizard to create these two forms.

Exercise 8.13: Building the Purchase Order Entry Forms

1. Click the Forms tab in the Database window and click the New button to open the New Form dialog box. Enter ***tblPurchaseOrder*** in the source table combo box, then double-click Form Wizard in the list box.
2. The next Form Wizard dialog box should display Table: *tblPurchaseOrder* in its Tables/Queries combo box. Click the >> button to move all of the fields from the Available Fields list box to the Selected Fields list box.
3. Enter ***Table: tblVendor*** in the Tables/Queries combo box. Select VendorName in the Available Fields list box and click the > button to move it to the Selected Fields list box.

4. Enter ***Table: tblPurchaseOrder-MaterialsInventory*** in the Tables/Queries combo box. Using the > button, move the following fields to the Selected Fields list box: MInvStockNumber, POMInvQuantity, POMInvPrice.
5. Enter ***Table: tblMaterialsInventory*** in the Tables/Queries combo box. Using the > button, move the MInvCategory and MInvDescription fields to the Selected Fields list box.
6. Click the Next > button to continue. The Form Wizard presents a template of the form-subform design and main sort order in its next dialog box as shown in Figure 8.23.
7. Click the Next > button to accept the Form Wizard's design template and continue.
8. Click the Tabular layout option button, then click the Next > button.
9. Select the Standard style, then click the Next > button.
10. Enter a Form title of ***frmPurchaseOrder*** and a Subform title of ***fsubPurchaseOrder***. Click the Finish button to have the Form Wizard create the two forms.

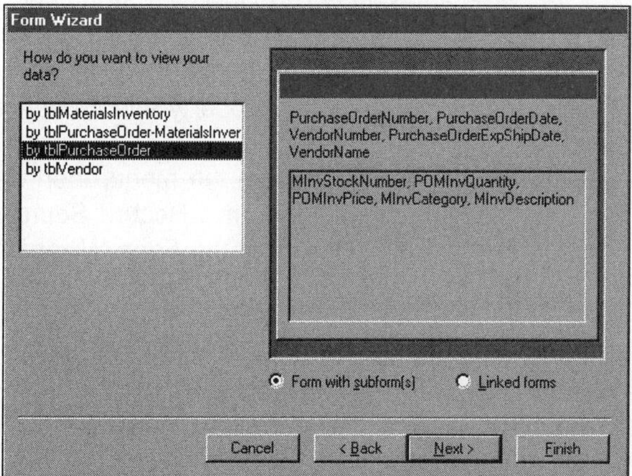

Figure 8.23 The Form Wizard's proposed template for the Purchase Order Entry form.

The Purchase Order Entry form generated by the Form Wizard appears in Figure 8.24 in Form view. We have included the main form and subform that comprise this form in the *Ch08.mdb* database on your Companion CD-ROM as *frmPurchaseOrder1* and *fsubPurchaseOrder1*. Although this design is a good start, we can enhance the form to make it more useful. We will show you several ways you can improve the form in Exercise 8.14.

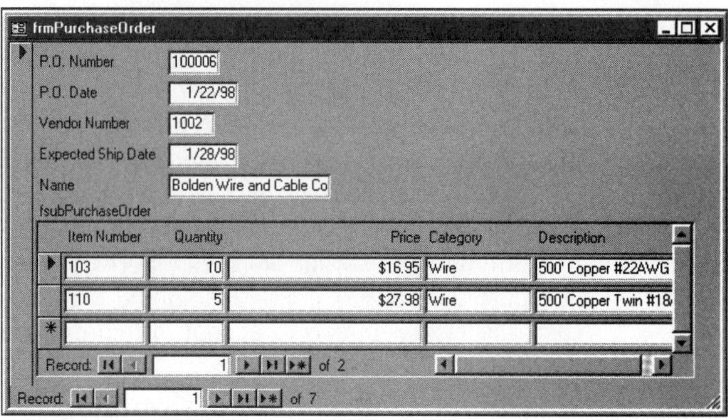

Figure 8.24 The Form Wizard-generated Purchase Order Entry form.

Exercise 8.14: Enhancing the Form Wizard's Purchase Order Entry Form

1. Open *frmPurchaseOrder* in Design view by selecting View, Form Design from the menu.
2. Click the Properties toolbar button to open the property sheet. We will assume that you have the property sheet open and available in Form Design view throughout this exercise.
3. Select Edit, Select Form from the menu, then click the Data tab in the property sheet. Select the form's Record Source property and click its Build button to open the query that the Form Wizard built behind the form.

   You may have noticed that the form opened with a display of PurchaseOrderNumber 100006, not PurchaseOrderNumber 100001. This happened because the Form Wizard did not set any sorting options in the query behind *frmPurchaseOrder*.
4. Enter ***Ascending*** in the PurchaseOrderNumber field's Sort cell in the first QBE grid column.
5. Press Ctrl+W to close the Query Builder window. Click the Yes button to save your change.
6. Double-click the *fsubPurchaseOrder* Subform/Subreport object at the bottom of the form. This should open *fsubPurchaseOrder*. Be sure that the object is not selected before you double-click it or it will not open.
7. With *fsubPurchaseOrder* open, click the Data tab in the property sheet, select the Record Source property, and click its Build button to open the query behind this form.
8. Enter ***Ascending*** in the MInvStockNumber field's Sort cell in the first QBE grid column.
9. Scroll the QBE grid to expose the first open Field cell, select it, then press Shift+F2 to open the Zoom box.

10. Enter ***Description: [MInvCategory] & ", " & [MInvDescription]*** in the Zoom box, then click the OK button.
11. Press Ctrl+W to close the Query Builder window. Click the Yes button to save your changes.
12. With *fsubPurchaseOrder* open in Form Design view, select the MInvCategory text box control and label. Press the Delete key to remove them from the form.
13. Select the MInvDescription text box control, click the Data tab in its property sheet, then change its Control Source property to ***Description***. Change the Enabled property to No and the Locked property to Yes.
14. Click on the property sheet Format tab and set the control's Back Style to Transparent, its Special Effect property to Flat, and its Border Style property to Transparent.
15. If you wish, you can click the Other tab and set its Name property to ***Description***
16. Select the label controls in the Form Header, then click the Bold button on the Formatting toolbar.
17. Change the size, alignment, and arrangement of the text box and label controls using Figure 8.25, which shows *fsubPurchaseOrder* in Form view, as a guide.

fsubPurchaseOrder

Item Number	Quantity	Price	Description
101	200	$8.45	Sheet Metal, 1/8" Steel 4x4 sheet
102	50	$14.96	Switch, DPDT 240v 100a
103	10	$16.95	Wire, 500' Copper #22AWG
104	100	$14.95	Sheet metal, 1/4" Steel 4x4 sheet
105	100	$9.47	Switch, SPDT 240v 100a
106	30	$32.89	Relay, SPDT 120v 40a Silver

Record: 1 of 14

Figure 8.25 Modifications to *fsubPurchaseOrder.*

18. Press Ctrl+W to close *fsubPurchaseOrder.* Click the Yes button to save your changes when prompted.
19. Select the Subform/Subreport object label and press Ctrl+X to delete it.
20. Select the VendorName label and press Ctrl+X to delete it.
21. Click and drag the VendorName text box control to a position to the right of the VendorNumber text box control. You may wish to use the Format, Align menu commands to ensure a precise alignment.
22. With the VendorName text box control still selected, click the Data tab in its property sheet, then change its Enabled property to No and its Locked property to Yes.

23. Click on the property sheet Format tab and set the control's Back Style to Transparent, its Special Effect property to Flat, and its Border Style property to Transparent.
24. Select the VendorNumber text box control and all of the label controls—you can do this by holding down the Shift key as you click each one—and click the Bold button on the Formatting toolbar.
25. Choose the Edit, Select Form command from the menu, click on the form's property sheet Format tab, change its Caption property to ***Purchase Order Entry***, and set the Record Selectors property to No.

We have made some additional adjustments to the alignment of the form controls to create the Purchase Order Entry form that appears in Figure 8.26. The form and subform shown in Figure 8.26 are included in the *Ch08.mdb* database on your Companion CD-ROM as *frmPurchaseOrder2* and *fsubPurchaseOrder2*, respectively. You can save your Purchase Order Entry forms by pressing Ctrl+W and clicking the Yes button to confirm your changes.

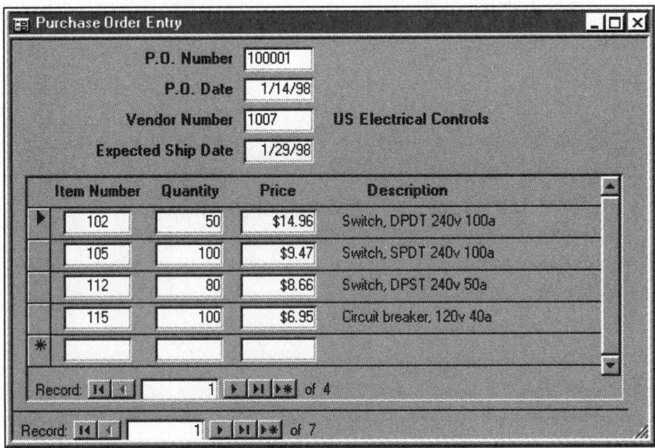

Figure 8.26 The completed Purchase Order Entry form.

As we explained in Chapter 5, you can add macros to this form's objects to make the form even more useful. You could use macros to provide detailed error messages, calculate a quantity × price extension, or create buttons to help users navigate among the purchase orders. We encourage you to experiment with the techniques you learned in Chapter 5 to make this form even more useful.

Printing Purchase Orders

In this section, we show you how to use the purchase cycle information gathered through the forms and stored in the tables that you have created. Entering purchase order information is an important step, but sending the printed purchase order out to vendors is one goal of this part of the purchase cycle. In Exercise 8.15, we show you how to use the Report Wizard to generate printed purchase orders.

EXERCISE 8.15: BUILDING A PURCHASE ORDER REPORT OBJECT

1. Click the Reports tab in the Database window, then click the New button to open the New Report dialog box. Enter ***tblPurchaseOrder*** in the source table combo box, then double-click Report Wizard in the list box.
2. The next Report Wizard dialog box should display Table: *tblPurchaseOrder* in its Tables/Queries combo box. Click the >> button to move all of the fields from the Available Fields list box to the Selected Fields list box.
3. Enter ***Table: tblVendor*** in the Tables/Queries combo box. Using the > button, move the following fields to the Selected Fields list box: VendorName, VendorAddress1, VendorAddress2, VendorCity, VendorState, and VendorZipCode.
4. Enter ***Table: tblPurchaseOrder-MaterialsInventory*** in the Tables/Queries combo box. Using the > button, move the following fields to the Selected Fields list box: MInvStockNumber, POMInvQuantity, POMInvPrice.
5. Enter ***Table: tblMaterialsInventory*** in the Tables/Queries combo box. Using the > button, move the MInvCategory and MInvDescription fields to the Selected Fields list box.
6. Click the Next > button to continue. The Report Wizard presents a template of the report-subreport design and main sort order in its next dialog box as shown in Figure 8.27.

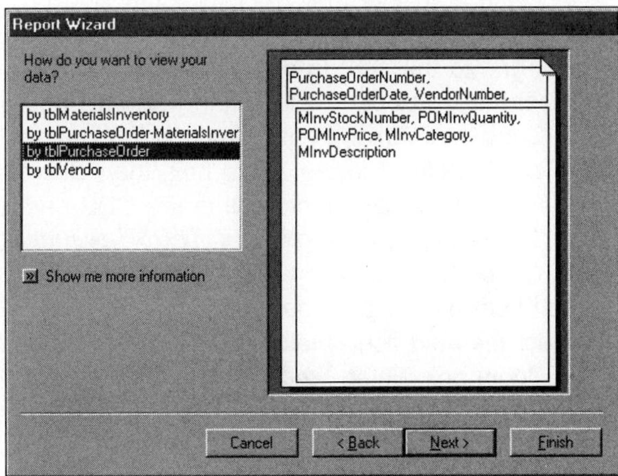

Figure 8.27 The Report Wizard's-proposed report template for *rptPurchaseOrder.*

7. To accept the Report Wizard's proposed design, click the Next > button.
8. To accept the Report Wizard's default grouping levels, click the Next > button.
9. Enter ***MInvStockNumber*** in the first sort order combo box, then click the Next > button.
10. Click the Outline 1 Layout option box control, then click the Next > button.
11. Select the Bold style, then click the Next > button.
12. Enter ***rptPurchaseOrder*** as the report title, then click the Finish button.

The report generated by the Report Wizard is in very rough form. It does not include the vendor's stock number, does not have a page break at the end of each purchase order, and does not include the Electric Controls Company's name or address. In Exercise 8.16, we will show you how to take this report object and transform it into a useful purchase order generator.

EXERCISE 8.16: IMPROVING THE PURCHASE ORDER REPORT OBJECT

1. Open the form in Design view. Click the Properties toolbar button to open the property sheet. We will assume that you have the property sheet open throughout this exercise.
2. Click the property sheet Data tab, select the Record Source property, and click on its Build button to open the query behind the report.
3. Click the Show Tables toolbar button, then double-click *tblMaterialsInventory-Vendor*. Click the Close button to dismiss the Show Table dialog box.
4. Enter ***Ascending*** in the first Sort cell in the QBE grid, under the PurchaseOrderNumber Field name.
5. Click and drag the MInvVStockNumber field from *tblMaterialsInventory-Vendor* to the first open Field cell in the QBE grid. You will need to scroll the QBE grid to the right to display this cell.
6. Select the next open Field cell in the QBE grid and press Shift+F2 to open the Zoom box. Enter ***Description: [MInvCategory] & ", " & [MInvDescription]*** in the Zoom box, then click the OK button.
7. Select the next open Field cell in the QBE grid and press Shift+F2 to open the Zoom box. Enter ***Extension: [POMInvQuantity]*[POMInvPrice]*** and click the OK button. This expression calculates the quantity × price extension for each item on the purchase order.
8. Select the next open Field cell in the QBE grid and press Shift+F2 to open the Zoom box. Enter ***VendorNameAndAddress: [VendorName] & Chr(13) & Chr(10) & [VendorAddress1] & Chr(13) & Chr(10) & IIf(IsNull([VendorAddress2]),"",([VendorAddress2] & Chr(13) & Chr(10))) & [VendorCity] & ", " & [VendorState] & " " & [VendorZipCode]*** in the Zoom box, then click the OK button. Press Ctrl+W to close the Query window. Click the Yes button to save your changes.

This expression combines the components of the vendor address into one field that we can print on the purchase order. The expression includes two interesting components. First, the expression uses the *Chr(13) & Chr(10)* characters to insert a carriage return and line feeds. Second, the expression uses an IsNull() function nested inside an IIF() function to test whether the VendorAddress2 field contains data. If it does, the expression prints it as the third line of the field.

Try it

You can learn more about these two functions in Microsoft Access on-line help. You may recall that we used four separate lines in Exercise 7.24 when we created the Invoice report. If you ran that report, you noticed that invoices for customers that did not have second address line information included a blank line in the address. Now that you have seen this more sophisticated use of the Chr(), IsNull(), and IIF() functions, you might want to try revising *rptInvoice*.

9. Change the label control text in the Report Header to ***Purchase Order***.
10. Click and drag the top of the Detail section bar down to make room in the PurchaseOrderNumber Header for a title and the Electric Controls Company name and address. Click and drag a marquee around all of the objects in the PurchaseOrderNumber Header, then click and drag the selected objects down to make room at the top of the section. You may find it easier to use the Ctrl+down arrow key to move the objects straight down. Figure 8.28 shows the Report Design View window at this point.

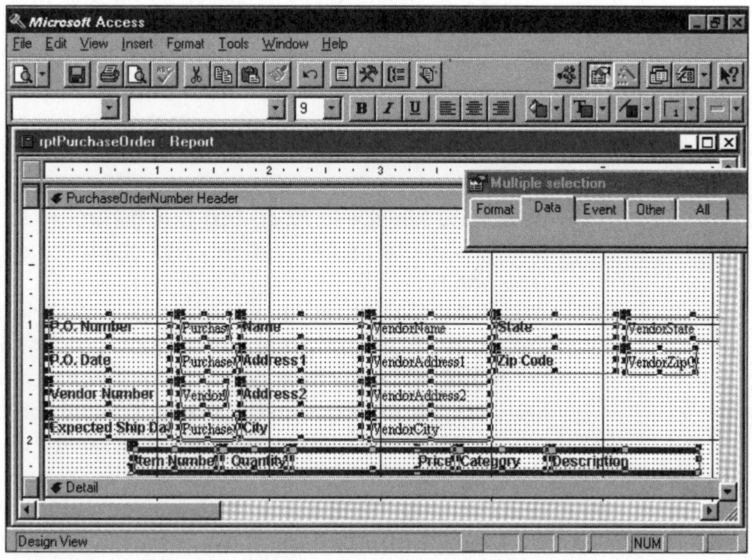

Figure 8.28 Moving objects in the PurchaseOrderNumber Header.

11. Select all three of the objects, the label control and the two lines, in the Report Header. The easiest way to do this and be sure to select all of the objects is to click and drag in the left ruler space from the top of the Report Header section to its bottom. Press Ctrl+X to cut these objects. If any objects remain visible in the Report Header, press Ctrl+Z to undo the cut and try again.
12. Select the PurchaseOrderNumber Header by clicking on its title bar, then press Ctrl+V to paste the objects from the Report Header.
13. Select View, Report Header/Footer from the menu to delete these sections. Select View, Page Header/Footer from the menu to delete these sections, also. Click the Yes button to confirm that we want to delete the controls in the Page Footer section.
14. Click the Toolbox button on the toolbar, then select the Label tool. Use it to draw a new label control near the top of the PurchaseOrderNumber Header. Enter the Electric Controls Company name and address in that label. Remember to use Ctrl+Enter to insert line breaks as you type in the label control. You can use the finished copy of *rptPurchaseOrder* that appears in Figure 8.29 as a guide.
15. Select the PurchaseOrderNumber, PurchaseOrderDate, VendorNumber, and PurchaseOrderExpShipDate fields, click on the Format tab in the property sheet and change the controls' Border Style to Transparent. Select the PurchaseOrderDate and PurchaseOrderExpShipDate fields, click the Format tab in the property sheet, and enter a Format property value of ***mmmm d ", " yyyy***
16. Change the text of the labels and arrange these controls as they appear in Figure 8.29. You can use the Toolbox label control to create the label with the text ***Please include this number on all invoices and shipping documents.***
17. Select and delete the six vendor name and address fields. Click the Field List toolbar button to open the Field List, then click and drag VendorNameAndAddress to the PurchaseOrderNumber Header section. Change the label control's text to ***To:*** and expand the text box control to accommodate the full vendor name and address. We used a 12-point bold Arial font for this text box.
18. Delete the MInvCategory text box control and its label.
19. Select the MInvDescription text box control in the Detail section, click on the Data tab in the property sheet, and change the Control Source property to ***Description***
20. Select the MInvStockNumber text box control in the Detail section, press Ctrl+C, then Ctrl+V to make a copy of the control. Align the new control to the left of MInvStockNumber and change its Control Source property (under the Data tab in the property sheet) to MInvVStockNumber. Use the same procedure to make a copy of the label control in the PurchaseOrderNumber Header section.
21. Use this copy-and-paste procedure to create another set of text box and label controls for the Extension field. With the Extension text box control selected, click the property sheet's Format tab and set its Format property to Currency, then click the Data tab and set its Decimal Places property to ***2***

Again, you can use Figure 8.29 as a guide for arranging these controls on the report.

22. Create a PurchaseOrderNumber Footer for the report by selecting the View, Sorting And Grouping menu command. In the Sorting and Grouping dialog box that appears, change the PurchaseOrderNumber's Group Footer property to Yes and its Keep Together property to Whole Group. You can close the dialog box by repeating the menu command you used to open it or by clicking the Sorting And Grouping toolbar button.
23. Click the new PurchaseOrderNumber Footer bar, then click the Format tab in the property sheet. Set the Force New Page property to After Section.
24. You can copy the line objects from the PurchaseOrderNumber Header section, or create your own footer design. The Footer needs only two controls, a text box control to total the Extension field and an accompanying label control. Copy the Extension text box to this section using the Ctrl+C and Ctrl+V cut-and-paste procedure. Click the Data tab in the property sheet and change the Control Source property to ***=Sum([Extension])***. Add a label control with the text ***Purchase Order Total*** to the Footer section.
25. To close the form, press Ctrl+W and click the Yes button to save your changes.

A copy of purchase order number 100001 generated by *rptPurchaseOrder* appears in Figure 8.29. The Purchase Order report, *rptPurchaseOrder*, is included in the *Ch08.mdb* database on your Companion CD-ROM.

RECORDING MATERIALS INVENTORY RECEIPTS

After the Electric Controls Company enters their purchase order data and mails the printed purchase orders to their vendors, *tblPurchaseOrder-MaterialsInventory* contains detailed line item information about what they expect vendors to ship. When materials arrive on the receiving dock, Electric Controls will want to record the quantity and identity of each item on each shipment. Dock personnel record this information on receiving reports. In the past, the receiving report was a paper form on which the dock worker wrote the information about items received. Today, dock workers can enter the receiving information directly into the firm's accounting database using a Microsoft Access screen form. This electronic receiving report enters data directly into the Inventory Receipt table.

One advantage of direct data entry into the Inventory Receipt table is that we can assign each item a unique receipt number. Many firms use bar code scanners that read inventory identification codes on inventory packages. These scanners also can date- and time-stamp the inventory receipt record. The accounts payable department collects other information about inventory received, including vendor invoice number and each item's price, from vendor invoices and can enter that information directly into the Inventory Receipt table.

Purchase Order

Electric Controls Company
12582 Camino Del Rio
San Diego, CA 92110-4264

To: US Electrical Controls
14878 Freemont Avenue
Suite 1800
St. Louis, MO 63127-5588

P.O. Number 100001

Please include this number on all invoices and shipping documents.

P.O. Date January 14, 1998

Vendor Number 1007

Expected Ship Date January 29, 1998

Your Item Number	Our Item Number	Quantity	Price	Description	Extension
240-100-SW284	102	50	$14.96	Switch, DPDT 240v 100a	$748.00
240-100-SW184	105	100	$9.47	Switch, SPDT 240v 100a	$947.00
240-50-SW236	112	80	$8.66	Switch, DPST 240v 50a	$692.80
120-40-CB79	115	100	$6.95	Circuit breaker, 120v 40a	$695.00
				Purchase Order Total	$3,082.80

Figure 8.29 The purchase order number 100001 printout generated by *rptPurchaseOrder*.

The Inventory Receipt Table

An Inventory Receipt table for the Electric Controls Company will require seven fields to store the following information attributes: a primary key for each receipt, the date of the receipt, Electronic Controls' materials inventory stock number, Electronic Controls' purchase order number, the vendor's invoice number, the quantity of the item received, and the price billed on the vendor's invoice for the item. In Exercise 8.17, we show you how to create *tblInventoryReceipt*, an Inventory Receipt table for the Electric Controls Company that meets these data storage requirements.

Exercise 8.17: Building an Inventory Receipt Table

1. Click the Tables tab in the Database window, click the New button, and then double-click Design View in the New Table dialog box that appears.

2. Enter the first Field Name, ***InventoryReceiptNumber***, and leave its Data Type set to Text.
3. Click on the Primary Key toolbar button to make this field the table's primary key.
4. Set its Field Size property to ***6***, its Input Mask Property to ***######;;_*** and its Caption property to ***Inventory Receipt Number***
5. Enter a Field Name of ***InventoryReceiptDate***, set its Data Type to Date/Time, its Format Property to Short Date, its Input Mask Property to ***99/99/00;;_*** and its Caption property to ***Date Received***

   The next two fields are the foreign key links to *tblPurchaseOrder* and *tblMaterialsInventory*, respectively.
6. Enter a Field Name of ***PurchaseOrderNumber*** and leave its Data Type set to Text. Set its Field Size to ***6***, its Input Mask Property to ***000000;;_*** and its Caption property to ***Purchase Order Number***
7. Enter ***MInvStockNumber*** as the next Field Name and leave its Data Type set to Text. Set its Field Size to ***3***, its Input Mask Property to ***000;;_*** and its Caption property to ***Stock Number***

   We will enforce referential integrity on each of the links from these fields back to the primary keys of *tblPurchaseOrder* and *tblMaterialsInventory*, respectively. The link to *tblPurchaseOrder* will prevent dock workers from erroneously entering nonexistent PurchaseOrderNumbers. The link to *tblMaterialsInventory* will prevent entry of nonexistent MInvStockNumbers. We will create these links later in this exercise.
8. Enter a Field Name of ***IRVendorInvoiceNumber*** and leave its Data Type set to Text. Set its Field Size to ***20***, and its Caption property to ***Purchase Order Number***

   Since the structure and size of vendor invoice numbers is not under our control, we must provide sufficient space to hold the longest number we might expect a vendor to use. We cannot set a meaningful Input Mask property for this field because we cannot predict or control what format vendors might use for their invoice identifiers.
9. Enter a Field Name of ***InventoryReceiptQuantity*** for the next field. Set its Data Type to Number, its Field Size property to Long Integer, its Decimal Places property to ***0***, and its Caption property to ***Quantity***
10. Enter a Field Name of ***InventoryReceiptPrice*** for the next field. Set its Data Type to Currency, its Decimal Places property to ***2***, and its Caption property to ***Price***
11. Press Ctrl+W to save your work and close the table. Enter ***tblInventoryReceipt*** as the Table Name in the Save As dialog box.

    Now that we have created the Inventory Receipt table, we must integrate it with the other purchase cycle tables. We can do this by creating links to the new table and setting referential integrity constraints on those links.
12. Select Tools, Relationships from the menu. The relationships window will appear with a display of the relationships we created earlier in this chapter.
13. Click the Show Table toolbar button.

14. Double-click *tblInventoryReceipt*, then click the Close button. You may want to resize and rearrange the tables in the Relationships window using Figure 8.30 as a guide.
15. Click and drag the PurchaseOrderNumber field from *tblPurchaseOrder* to the corresponding field in *tblInventoryReceipt*. Click the Enforce Referential Integrity check box, then click the Create button.
16. Click and drag the MInvStockNumber field from *tblMaterialsInventory* to the corresponding field in *tblInventoryReceipt*. Click the Enforce Referential Integrity check box, then click the Create button. The completed set of relationships appears in Figure 8.30.
17. Press Ctrl+W and click the Yes button to confirm the changes you have made. This will close the Relationships window and return you to the Database window.

Figure 8.30 shows the updated relationships among the purchase cycle tables. A copy of *tblInventoryReceipt* is included in the *Ch08.mdb* database on your Companion CD-ROM. Now that we have a table in which to store information about inventory receipts, our next task is to build a form that will make entering data into the table easy and effective.

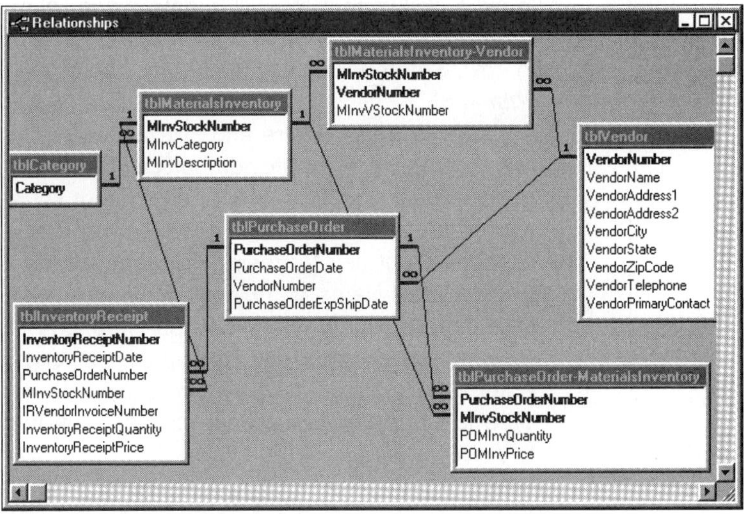

Figure 8.30 Connecting *tblInventoryReceipt* with the existing purchase cycle tables.

An Inventory Receipt Form

The Inventory Receipt form is simple and straightforward. Since we can rely on the referential integrity links to existing values in *tblPurchaseOrder* and *tblMaterialsInventory* for the foreign key fields, PurchaseOrderNumber and

MInvStockNumber, we can build the form based on *tblInventoryReceipt* alone. We do not need a complex form design or an underlying query. Exercise 8.18 shows you how to create *frmInventoryReceipt*, an Inventory Receipt Data Entry form for the Electric Controls Company sample data.

EXERCISE 8.18: BUILDING AN INVENTORY RECEIPT FORM

1. In the Database window, click the Forms tab, then click the New button.
2. Type ***tblInventoryReceipt*** in the table box or select it from the drop-down list in the New Form dialog box.
3. Double-click AutoForm: Tabular in the New Form dialog box.
   The AutoForm tool generates a simple tabular form. With a few minor changes, this form will work quite well for the Electric Controls Company.
4. Select View, Form Design from the menu.
5. Click the Properties toolbar button to open the property sheet.
6. Select Edit, Select Form from the menu, then click the Format tab in the form's property sheet and change the Caption property to ***Inventory Receipt Data Entry Form***
7. Select all of the label controls in the Form Header, then click the Bold button on the Formatting toolbar.
8. Click and drag the right side of the form's frame to make more room on the form, then drag the gray section background to fit the expanded frame.
9. Click and drag the top edge of the Detail section bar down to make more room in the Form Header.
10. Select the label controls in the Form Header, then press Shift+down arrow repeatedly to increase the height of the controls enough that two lines of text appear in the controls that the AutoForm tool made too small.
11. Using Figure 8.31 as a guide, adjust the arrangement, size, and alignment of the controls on the form. Remember, you can force a line break in a label control by pressing Ctrl+Enter.
12. To save the form, select File, Save As/Export and enter a New Name of ***frmInventoryReceipt*** in the Save As dialog box.

The completed form appears in Figure 8.31 in Form view displaying the Electric Controls Company sample data. This Inventory Receipt Data Entry form is included in the *Ch08.mdb* database on your Companion CD-ROM as *frmInventoryReceipt*. If you test the form, you will find that the foreign key links to *tblPurchaseOrder* and *tblMaterialsInventory* prevent you from entering a value for a purchase order number or stock number that does not already exist in the underlying entity table. Note that the Electric Controls Company assigns a unique inventory receipt number to each individual stock number received on a purchase order. Many firms still use a receiving report format in which they assign one

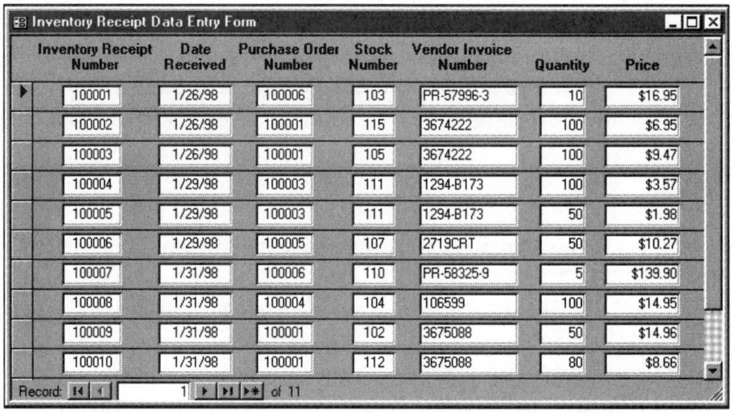

Inventory Receipt Data Entry Form

Inventory Receipt Number	Date Received	Purchase Order Number	Stock Number	Vendor Invoice Number	Quantity	Price
100001	1/26/98	100006	103	PR-57996-3	10	$16.95
100002	1/26/98	100001	115	3674222	100	$6.95
100003	1/26/98	100001	105	3674222	100	$9.47
100004	1/29/98	100003	111	1294-B173	100	$3.57
100005	1/29/98	100003	111	1294-B173	50	$1.98
100006	1/29/98	100005	107	2719CRT	50	$10.27
100007	1/31/98	100006	110	PR-58325-9	5	$139.90
100008	1/31/98	100004	104	106599	100	$14.95
100009	1/31/98	100001	102	3675088	50	$14.96
100010	1/31/98	100001	112	3675088	80	$8.66

Record: 1 of 11

Figure 8.31 The completed *frmInventoryReceipt* in Form view.

receiving report number to an entire shipment. This is, in many cases, a holdover from manual procedures. As computer facilities become increasingly available everywhere, even on the receiving dock, workers can easily enter atomic-level data. In the next section, we will show you what you might do with these inventory receipt data.

Inventory Receipt Reports

Standard reporting forms for inventory receipts do not exist, so you may create your own report designs to meet your needs or those of your clients. In this section we describe an Inventory Receipt report that calculates the price × quantity extensions for inventory received by the Electric Controls Company. The report groups inventory receipts by vendor to show what Electric Controls owes their vendors for materials they have received. To be even more useful, the report groups receipts by purchase order number within each vendor. Exercise 8.19 shows you how to use the Reports Wizard to select fields from Electric Controls' Inventory Receipt, Purchase Order, and Vendor tables. We also show you how to modify the Report Wizard-generated report to calculate price × quantity extensions for each materials inventory receipt.

Exercise 8.19: Building an Inventory Receipt Report

1. Click the Reports tab in the Database window, then click the New button to open the New Report dialog box. Enter ***tblInventoryReceipt*** in the source table combo box, then double-click Report Wizard in the list box.
2. The next Report Wizard dialog box should display Table: *tblInventoryReceipt* in its Tables/Queries combo box. Click the >> button to move all of the fields from the Available Fields list box to the Selected Fields list box.

3. Enter ***Table: tblPurchaseOrder*** in the Tables/Queries combo box. Using the > button, move the VendorNumber field to the Selected Fields list box.
4. Enter ***Table: tblVendor*** in the Tables/Queries combo box. Using the > button, move the VendorName field to the Selected Fields list box. Click the Next > button to continue.
5. Since we are going to create our own grouping design, we will not give the Report Wizard any instructions about how we wish to view the data. To accept the default design, data organized by *tblInventoryReceipt*, click the Next > button.
6. We want our report to group the inventory receipt data by vendor and, within each vendor, by purchase order number. Select VendorName in the grouping levels list box, then click the > button to modify the Report Wizard's template. Next, select PurchaseOrderNumber and click the > button. The Wizard will make the changes to the report design template shown in Figure 8.32.

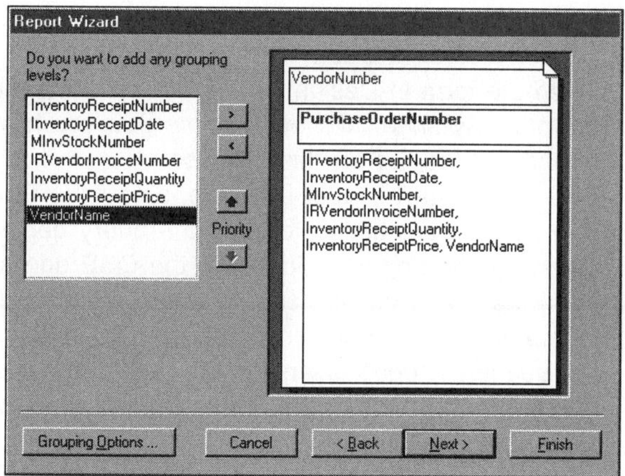

Figure 8.32 The Report Wizard's modified template for *rptInventoryReceipt.*

7. To accept the modified design, click the Next > button.
8. Enter ***InventoryReceiptNumber*** in the first sort order combo box.

Try it

At this point, we are going to play a little trick on the Report Wizard. We want to multiply the price by the quantity to obtain an extension value to include in the report. The Report Wizard does not offer this option, so we will need to add the extension field after the Report Wizard has created the report. We also want footers in the report that include text box controls with Sum() functions that subtotal the extension amounts for each purchase order and each vendor. To trick the Wizard into generating the footers and text box controls with Sum() functions, we can instruct it to sum the InventoryReceiptPrice fields. We will still have to edit the controls to change InventoryReceiptPrice to Extension, but the Report Wizard will do most of the work for us.

9. Click on the Summary Options button. In the next dialog box, click the Sum check box for InventoryReceiptPrice. Be sure that the Show Detail and Summary option button has been selected. Click the OK button to return to the previous dialog box.
10. Click the Next > button to proceed.
11. Select the Outline 1 Layout and the Corporate style in the next two dialog boxes, respectively.
12. Enter a report title of ***rptInventoryReceipt***, then click the Finish button.

    The report generated by the Report Wizard clearly needs some work. The Wizard made a few errors in judgment; for example, it placed the VendorName field in the Detail section of the table instead of in the VendorNumber Header.
13. Open the form in Design view. Click the Properties toolbar button to open the property sheet. We will assume that you have the property sheet open throughout the rest of this exercise.
14. Click the property sheet Data tab, select the Record Source property, and click on its Build button to open the query behind the report.
15. Select the first open Field cell in the QBE grid and press Shift+F2 to open the Zoom box. Enter ***Extension: [InventoryReceiptQuantity] * [InventoryReceiptPrice]*** and click the OK button. This expression calculates the quantity × price extension for each item received.
16. Press Ctrl+W to close the Query Builder window. Click the Yes button to save your changes.
17. Using Figure 8.33 as a guide, adjust the report layout using your own judgment.

The completed Inventory Receipt report, *rptInventoryReceipt*, is included in the *Ch08.mdb* database on your Companion CD-ROM. We encourage you to use Figure 8.33 and the report on the CD-ROM as springboards for experimenting with your own report design ideas.

CASH DISBURSEMENTS

Thus far in Chapter 8, we have shown you how the Electric Controls Company might maintain vendor records, materials inventory records, prepare purchase orders, and record receipts of ordered inventory items. Once they receive mate-

Inventory Receipts

By Vendor and by Purchase Order ***Electric Controls Company***

for internal use only

VendorNumber 1002 Bolden Wire and Cable Co.

Purchase Order Number *100006*

Inventory Receipt Number	*Date Received*	*Stock Number*	*Vendor Invoice Number*	*Quantity*	*Price*	*Extension*
100001	1/26/98	103	PR-57996-3	10	$16.95	$169.50
100007	1/31/98	110	PR-58325-9	5	$139.90	$699.50
			Total for this Purchase Order			$869.00
			Total for this Vendor			$869.00

VendorNumber 1005 Bomac Sheet Metal Co.

Purchase Order Number *100004*

Inventory Receipt Number	*Date Received*	*Stock Number*	*Vendor Invoice Number*	*Quantity*	*Price*	*Extension*
100008	1/31/98	104	106599	100	$14.95	$1,495.00
			Total for this Purchase Order			$1,495.00
			Total for this Vendor			$1,495.00

VendorNumber 1007 US Electrical Controls

Purchase Order Number *100001*

Inventory Receipt Number	*Date Received*	*Stock Number*	*Vendor Invoice Number*	*Quantity*	*Price*	*Extension*
100002	1/26/98	115	3674222	100	$6.95	$695.00
100003	1/26/98	105	3674222	100	$9.47	$947.00
100009	1/31/98	102	3675088	50	$14.96	$748.00
100010	1/31/98	112	3675088	80	$8.66	$692.80
			Total for this Purchase Order			$3,082.80

Purchase Order Number *100005*

Inventory Receipt Number	*Date Received*	*Stock Number*	*Vendor Invoice Number*	*Quantity*	*Price*	*Extension*
100006	1/29/98	107	2719CRT	50	$10.27	$513.50
			Total for this Purchase Order			$513.50
			Total for this Vendor			$3,596.30

Page 1 of 2

Figure 8.33 The completed Inventory Receipt report, *rptInventoryReceipt*.

rials inventory items, their vendors would like them to pay for the items. This section describes one way to use the information we have gathered in our purchase cycle tables to write checks. The approach we describe here is only one of many possible ways to do this. Since we have a record of materials received in our Inventory Receipt table, we can use that table as a basis for payments.

More elaborate systems might require us to compare purchase order terms to vendor invoice terms before payment. One way to do this is with a voucher system, in which accounting personnel compare purchase orders with vendor invoices, shipping documents, and receiving reports before authorizing payment. You can build on the tables and forms we describe in this section to create such a system; however, the details of a full voucher system are beyond the scope of this book.

The Cash Disbursements Table

The Cash Disbursements table must include fields that store the check number, date, and payee for each check. In Exercise 8.20, we show you how to create a Cash Disbursements table with these fields.

Exercise 8.20: Building a Cash Disbursements Table

1. Click the Tables tab in the Database window, click the New button, and then double-click Design View in the New Table dialog box that appears.
2. Enter ***CDCheckNumber*** as the first Field Name and click the Primary Key toolbar button. Leave its Data Type set to Text and set its Field Size property to ***5***, its Input Mask property to ***#####;;_*** and its Caption property to ***Check Number***
3. Next, enter a Field Name of ***CDDate*** and set its Data Type to Date/Time, its Format property to Short Date, its Input Mask property to ***99/99/00;;_*** and its Caption property to ***Date***
4. The payee field is a link to *tblVendor*, so enter its Field Name as ***VendorNumber*** and leave its Data Type set to Text. Set its Field Size property to ***4*** to match the value for VendorNumber in *tblVendor*, then set its Input Mask property to ***####;;_*** and its Caption property to ***Vendor Number***
5. Press Ctrl+W to save your work and close the table. Click the Yes button to confirm that you want to save your changes, then enter ***tblCashDisbursements*** as the Table Name in the Save As dialog box.

   Since *tblCashDisbursements* includes a foreign key link to *tblVendor*, we must establish that link in the Relationships window. We will also enforce referential integrity on the link to ensure that we do not erroneously write a check to a supplier that is not in our Vendor table.

6. Select Tools, Relationships from the menu. The relationships window will appear with a display of the relationship we have already created for the purchase cycle tables.
7. Click the Show Table toolbar button.
8. Double-click *tblCashDisbursements*, then click the Close button. You may want to resize and rearrange the tables in the Relationships window using Figure 8.34 as a guide.
9. Click and drag the VendorNumber field from *tblVendor* to the corresponding field in *tblCashDisbursements*. Click the Enforce Referential Integrity check box, then click the Create button. The completed set of relationships appears in Figure 8.34.
10. Press Ctrl+W and click the Yes button to confirm the changes you have made. This will close the Relationships window and return you to the Database window.

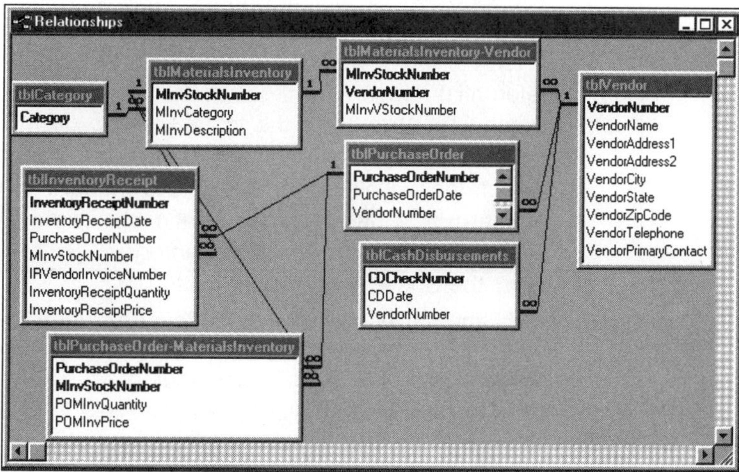

Figure 8.34 Adding *tblCashDisbursements* to the purchase cycle Relationships window.

The Cash Disbursements-Inventory Receipts Table

Since the Electric Controls Company often pays for more than one materials inventory receipt with each check and sometimes pays for one materials receipt with two or more checks, we need a relationship table to model the many-to-many link between the Cash Disbursements table and the Inventory Receipt table. Exercise 8.21 shows you how to build this Cash Disbursements-Inventory Receipts table. This table contains only two fields, the primary keys of *tblCashDisbursements* and *tblInventoryReceipt*, which combine to form this table's composite primary key.

Exercise 8.21: Building a Cash Disbursements-Inventory Receipts Table

1. Click the Tables tab in the Database window, click the New button, and then double-click Design View in the New Table dialog box that appears.
2. Enter a Field Name of ***CDCheckNumber*** and leave its Data Type set to Text.
3. Set its Field Size property to ***5***, its Input Mask property to ***#####;;_***, its Caption property to ***Check Number***, and its Indexed property to Yes (Duplicates OK).
4. Enter a second Field Name of ***InventoryReceiptNumber*** and leave its Data Type set to Text.
5. Set its Field Size property to ***6***, its Caption property to ***Inventory Receipt Number***, and its Indexed property to Yes (Duplicates OK).
6. While pressing the Ctrl key, click the row selectors for each of the two fields. While the two rows are selected, click the Primary Key toolbar button. The primary key symbol should appear in both row selectors.

   The *Ch08.mdb* database on your Companion CD-ROM includes *tblCashDisbursements-InventoryReceipts*. This table contains the Electric Controls Company's cash disbursements-inventory receipts information. To finish the table, we will create links back to the entity tables and enforce referential integrity on those links.
7. Press Ctrl+W to close the table. Enter ***tblCashDisbursements-InventoryReceipts*** as the Table Name and click the OK button.
8. Select Tools, Relationships from the menu. The relationships window will appear with a display of the relationship we created earlier between *tblCategory* and *tblMaterialsInventory*.
9. Click the Show Table toolbar button.
10. Double-click *tblCashDisbursements-InventoryReceipts*, then click the Close button. You may want to resize and rearrange the tables in the Relationships window using Figure 8.35 as a guide.
11. Click and drag the CDCheckNumber field from *tblCashDisbursements* to the corresponding field in *tblCashDisbursements-InventoryReceipts*. Click the Enforce Referential Integrity check box, then click the Create button.
12. Click and drag the InventoryReceiptNumber field from *tblInventoryReceipt* to the corresponding field in *tblCashDisbursements-InventoryReceipts*. Click the Enforce Referential Integrity check box, then click the Create button. The completed set of relationships appears in Figure 8.35.
13. Press Ctrl+W and click the Yes button to confirm the changes you have made and close the Relationships window.

You could build a form that would let you enter records simultaneously into the Cash Disbursements and Cash Disbursements-Inventory Receipts tables. Although the form design would be fairly complex—it would need to read from the Inventory Receipt, Purchase Order, and Vendor tables—it would resemble the Purchase Order Entry form-subform design we described in Exercise 8.13 earlier in this chapter.

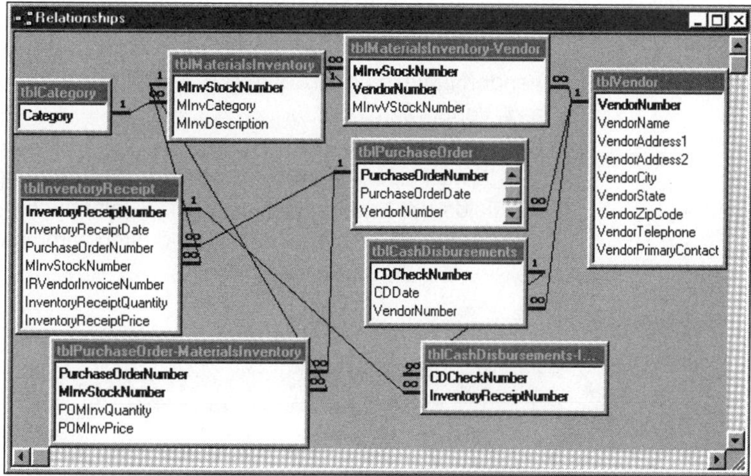

Figure 8.35 Adding *tblCashDisbursements-InventoryReceipts* to the purchase cycle Relationships window.

Printing Checks

We can use the cash disbursement information that we have stored to build a report that can print checks. Of course, the report formatting details will vary with the type of check used. Rather than focus our efforts on these formatting details, we will show you how to extract the essential information from the purchase cycle tables that a firm would need no matter what their check format was. In the next exercise, we will concentrate our attention on how to get the data out of the tables and onto paper rather than trying to produce the most attractive form.

Exercise 8.22: Extracting the Information Needed to Print a Check

1. In the Database window, click the Reports tab, then click the New button. In the New Report dialog box, select Report Wizard and choose *tblCashDisbursements* in the combo box. Click the OK button to proceed.
2. The Tables/Queries combo box should be displaying Table: *tblCashDisbursements*. Click the >> button to move all of the table's fields from the Available Fields box to the Selected Fields box. Click the Next > button to continue.
3. Enter or select ***Table: tblCashDisbursements-InventoryReceipts*** in the Tables/Queries combo box. Select InventoryReceiptNumber in the Available Fields list box, then click the > button to move that field to the Selected Fields list box.
4. Enter or select ***Table: tblInventoryReceipt*** in the Tables/Queries combo box. Select and use the > button to move the following fields to the Selected fields list box: PurchaseOrderNumber, MInvStockNumber, IRVendorInvoiceNumber, InventoryReceiptQuantity, and InventoryReceiptPrice.

5. Enter or select ***Table: tblVendor*** in the Tables/Queries combo box. Using the > button, move the following fields to the Selected Fields list box: VendorName, VendorAddress1, VendorAddress2, VendorCity, VendorState, and VendorZipCode.
6. Click the Next > button to continue.

    The Report Wizard prepares a design template for the report based on the fields we have selected and the relationships among the tables that we have included in the report. This design template appears in the next dialog box as shown in Figure 8.36.

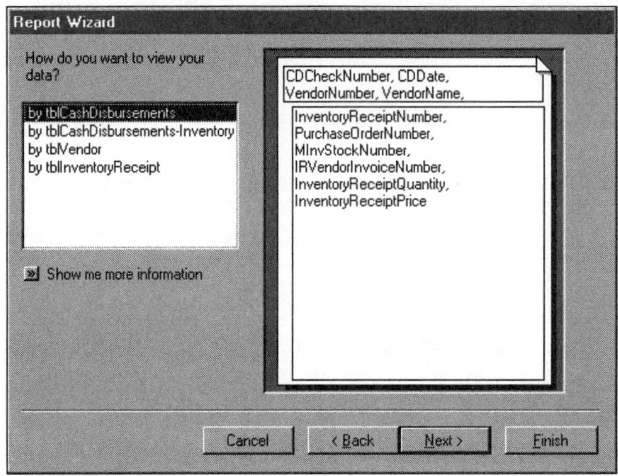

Figure 8.36 The Report Wizard's design template for the Check report.

Notice that the report design includes the check and vendor information in the Header section and all inventory receipt information in the Detail section. For example, each check will only have one vendor related to it, so the Wizard placed the VendorNumber field in the Header. The Wizard placed the PurchaseOrderNumber field in the Detail section because the Electric Controls Company may write one check for items from several different purchase orders.

7. Click the Next > button to continue. Enter or select ***InventoryReceiptNumber*** in the first sort order combo box, then click the Next > button to continue.
8. Select the Outline 1 Layout and the Corporate style in the next two dialog boxes, respectively.
9. Enter a title of ***rptCheck***, then click the Finish button.

    The Report Wizard creates a report that contains most of what we would like to appear on a check. We will describe some modifications you can make to the form. Remember, each firm will have specific formatting requirements so that the information will appear correctly on their printed checks. Our main goal here is to show you how to extract the information attributes from the four tables. Other than the information that appears on the Wizard-generated report, the Electric Controls Company will need a total dollar amount to print on the check. This amount does not exist in any of our tables because it is a calculation result. As you learned in Chapter 3, we try not to store calculation results in relational tables. The remaining steps in this exercise show you how to calculate and add the check amount to the report and give you some general formatting guidelines for other elements of the Check report. You can use the copy of the Check report printout that appears in Figure 8.37 as a guide for formatting details.

10. Select the View, Report Design menu command. Open the property sheet if it is not already open by clicking the Properties toolbar button. We will assume that you have the property sheet open throughout the remainder of this exercise.
11. Click the property sheet Data tab, select the Record Source property, and click on its Build button to open the query behind the report.
12. Select the next open Field cell in the QBE grid and press Shift+F2 to open the Zoom box. You will need to scroll the QBE grid to the right to find the next open column.
13. Enter ***Extension: [InventoryReceiptQuantity] * [InventoryReceiptPrice]*** and click the OK button. This expression calculates the quantity × price extension for each inventory receipt.
14. Select the next open Field cell in the QBE grid and press Shift+F2 to open the Zoom box. Enter *VendorNameAndAddress: [VendorName] & Chr(13) & Chr(10) & [VendorAddress1] & Chr(13) & Chr(10) & IIf(IsNull([VendorAddress2]),"",([VendorAddress2] & Chr(13) & Chr(10))) & [VendorCity] & ", " & [VendorState] & " " & [VendorZipCode]* in the Zoom box, then click the OK button.

    This expression combines the components of the vendor address into one field that we can print on the check. This expression is identical to the one we created for the *rptPurchaseOrder* in Exercise 8.16, so you can open that report and its query in Design view and copy the text of this expression instead of typing it in again.

Try it

As you work with Microsoft Access, you will develop a number of expressions that you use frequently. Since these expressions are all just plain text, you can store them in a word processor file or a text file. Whenever you need one of these expressions, you can simply open your word processor or text editor, make any changes to the expression, then copy and paste the expression into an Access control or property.

15. Change the label control text in the Report Header to ***Check Report***
16. Click and drag the top of the Detail section bar down to make room in the CDCheckNumber Header for the title and the Electric Controls Company name and address. Click and drag a marquee around all of the objects in the CDCheckNumber Header, then drag the selected objects down.

17. Select the label control and the two line objects in the Report Header, then press Ctrl+X to cut these objects. Select the CDCheckNumber Header by clicking on its title bar, then press Ctrl+V to paste the objects you cut from the Report Header.
18. Select View, Report Header/Footer from the menu to delete these sections. Select View, Page Header/Footer from the menu to delete these sections, too. Click the Yes button to confirm that you want to delete the controls in the Page Footer section.
19. Click the Toolbox button on the toolbar, then select the Label tool. Use it to draw a new label control for the Electric Controls Company name and address.
20. Select the CDDate text box control, click the Format tab in its property sheet, and enter a Format property value of ***mmmm d ", " yyyy***
21. Select and delete the five vendor address fields in the CDCheckNumber Header.
22. Click the Field List toolbar button to open the Field List, then click and drag VendorNameAndAddress to the PurchaseOrderNumber Header section. Change the label control's text to ***Mail Check to:*** and expand the text box control to accommodate the full vendor name and address. Click the Field List toolbar button to close the Field List.
23. Change the VendorName label control text to ***Pay to the Order of***
24. Select the InventoryReceiptPrice text box control in the Detail section and press Ctrl+C to copy the control. We chose to copy this control because it has the currency format settings that we would like to use for our Extension fields.
25. Press Ctrl+V to make a copy of the control in the Detail section. Align the new control as shown in Figure 8.37. Click the Data tab in the property sheet for the control and change its Control Source property to ***Extension***. Use the same procedure to make a copy of the label control in the CDCheckNumber Header section.
26. Use this copy-and-paste procedure to create a second copy of the new Extension control; however, paste this control into the CDCheckNumber Header.
27. With the new Extension control selected, click the Data tab in its property sheet and change the Control Source property to ***=Sum([Extension])***. This control will calculate and display the total amount of the check. Add a label control with the text ***In the Amount of*** to the CDCheckNumber Header section.
28. Click the CDCheckNumber Header bar, then click the Format tab in its property sheet. Set the Force New Page property to Before Section. This will put each check on a new page.
29. Arrange the report's controls to conform to the layout in Figure 8.37 or to your own design. To close the report, press Ctrl+W and click the Yes button to save your changes.

A printout generated by *rptCheck* that provides sufficient information to permit the Electric Controls Company to write check number 10001 appears in Figure

Check Report

Electric Controls Company
12582 Camino Del Rio
San Diego, CA 92110-4264

Check Number 10001

Date January 31, 1998

Pay to the Order of Bolden Wire and Cable Co.

In the Amount of $869.00

Mail Check to:

Bolden Wire and Cable Co.
2798 Larsen Road
Suite 400
Flint, MI 48502-2966

Inventory Receipt Number	*Purchase Order Number*	*Stock Number*	*Vendor Invoice Number*	*Quantity*	*Price*	*Extension*
100001	100006	103	PR-57996-3	10	$16.95	$169.50
100007	100006	110	PR-58325-9	5	$139.90	$699.50

Figure 8.37 The information generated by *rptCheck* for printing check number 10001.

8.37. The report *rptCheck* is provided on your Companion CD-ROM in the *Ch08.mdb* database.

PURCHASE CYCLE INFORMATION ON THE FINANCIAL STATEMENTS

In this chapter, we have described how you can use purchase cycle data to create purchase orders, checks, and other useful reports. This section discusses how accountants can extract the purchase cycle information for presentation on financial statements. The two main financial statement items that use purchase cycle information are the purchases account on the income statement and the accounts payable account on the balance sheet.

Purchases and Accounts Payable on the Financial Statements

The traditional function of an accounting system was to capture and store the information we needed to prepare financial statements and tax returns. The database approach to developing the purchase cycle accounting system that we presented in this chapter provides much more than that minimal level of information. However, the database approach does include the basic debit and credit accounting information that we need to prepare financial statements.

You can calculate the amount of the general ledger debit to Purchases, which is also the amount of the credit to Accounts Payable, by adding one text box control to the Report Footer section of *rptPurchaseOrder*. Set the control's Control Source property to the expression ***Sum([Extension])***. A Sum() function in a report footer will provide a grand total for the entire report. To obtain the amount for a particular period, you need to limit the purchase orders included to those that occurred in that period. You can do this in the query behind *rptPurchaseOrder* by setting the Criteria cell value in the QBE grid for the PurchaseOrderDate to a limited set of dates. We showed you how to set query Criteria values in Chapter 4. For example, to obtain the purchases general ledger debit for the year 1998, you would enter an expression of ***>=#1/1/98 And <=12/31/98*** in the Criteria cell.

You can also generate the amounts to debit the individual vendor accounts in the subsidiary accounts payable ledger. Simply add another grouping level on VendorNumber to *rptPurchaseOrder* and copy the Sum([Extension]) control we described in the preceding paragraph to the new VendorNumber Footer. The value in that control will be the debit to the subsidiary account for each vendor. Of course, you would not really need to maintain a subsidiary accounts payable ledger if you had a relational database purchase cycle system such as the one we described in this chapter, but we have seen old accounting habits linger before!

The general ledger and accounts payable subsidiary ledger account credits to Cash and debits to Accounts Payable are just as easy to extract from our purchase cycle relational database tables. Simply add a report footer to *rptCheck* and include a Sum([Extension]) control in it to calculate the general ledger amounts. To obtain the subsidiary account entry amounts, add a new grouping level on VendorNumber to *rptCheck* and copy the Sum([Extension]) control to the new VendorNumber Footer.

SUMMARY

In this chapter, we described how you might construct tables, forms, queries, and reports to use in the purchase cycle of an accounting information system. Tables are the basic building blocks of the purchase cycle and store information about vendors, materials inventories, and purchase cycle transactions. Forms make entering, editing, and deleting transaction information easier. Queries can simultaneously extract data from multiple tables to help answer complex questions about materials inventory, vendors, payments to vendors, and receipts of inventory. Queries also provide a basic building block on which you can construct purchase cycle reports. We showed you how to create typical purchase cycle printed outputs such as purchase orders and checks.

The purchase cycle begins with vendor records and materials inventory records. Production departments send materials requisitions to the purchasing department. Using these requisitions, purchasing agents negotiate price and delivery terms, then issue purchase orders to vendors. When materials inventory arrives at the receiving dock, dock workers enter inventory receipts information. Based on this receipts information and its agreement with purchase orders issued and invoices received from vendors, accounting prints checks that the treasurer will sign and mail to vendors. Finally, we summarize all this activity and create reports and journal entries that facilitate financial statement preparation.

REVIEW EXERCISES

MULTIPLE-CHOICE QUESTIONS

1. The Purchase Order-Materials Inventory table in this chapter is
   a. a referential integrity table.
   b. a query table.
   c. a relationship table.
   d. an entity table.
2. A good primary key for an inventory receipt table would be the
   a. remittance advice number.
   b. purchase order number.
   c. vendor invoice number.
   d. receiving report number.
3. The Purchase Order table described in this chapter, *tblPurchaseOrder*, is in first normal form because
   a. its primary key is unique.
   b. it contains no repeating fields.
   c. it contains a valid foreign key.
   d. its primary key exists for every record.
4. Purchase cycle activities include all of the following except
   a. keeping vendor information current.
   b. recording the cost of materials purchased.
   c. recording payments received from customers.
   d. printing purchase orders.
5. The purchase cycle uses a materials inventory table to provide
   a. descriptions of materials.
   b. purchase cost of materials.
   c. names of vendors that supply materials.
   d. quantity of materials purchased.
6. The VendorNumber field in *tblVendor* is a
   a. composite primary key.
   b. primary key.

c. foreign key.
d. relationship key.

7. In a materials requirements planning system,
   a. the master schedule replaces materials requisitions.
   b. inventory receipts are not recorded.
   c. the computer can generate materials requisitions.
   d. materials requisitions are generated daily.
8. Enforcing referential integrity on VendorNumber from *tblVendor* to *tblPurchaseOrder* is a good way to ensure that
   a. the VendorNumber in *tblVendor* is valid.
   b. the VendorNumber in *tblPurchaseOrder* is valid.
   c. the VendorNumber in both tables contains the right number of characters.
   d. both a and c are correct.
9. The list of materials that production sends to purchasing is called a
   a. request for quote.
   b. purchase order.
   c. bill of materials.
   d. materials requisition.
10. A sequential materials inventory item numbering scheme
   a. is easier to design than a mnemonic coding scheme.
   b. helps experienced employees identify inventory quickly.
   c. prevents data entry clerks from entering inventory codes quickly.
   d. is required by generally accepted accounting principles.

DISCUSSION QUESTIONS

1. In the Materials Inventory table for the Electric Controls Company, we used a Validation Rule property to control input to the MInvCategory field. In the Purchase Orders-Materials Inventory relationship table, we used a foreign key link with referential integrity on the MInvStockNumber field to the Materials Inventory table to accomplish a similar objective. Discuss the advantages and disadvantages of each approach.
2. Describe how you would design the Cash Disbursements Entry form mentioned in the chapter.
3. How would you modify the purchase cycle accounting system described in this chapter if you wished to include vouchers in the system?
4. How could you use the tables in this chapter to measure vendor price and delivery performance? What additional information would you like to add to the system design to make these measurements more effective?
5. How would you modify the purchase cycle system described in the chapter to include quality measurements?

EXERCISES

1. The Sheet Metal query described in this chapter provided information about vendors that supplied sheet metal products. Assume that the Electric Controls Company wanted to create a similar report that would list vendors that supplied *aluminum* sheet metal products. How would you change the structure of the query and its underlying tables to accomplish this task?
2. Create a report that uses the tables we designed in this chapter to print a check register report. Include check number, check date, payee, and amount in your report.
3. Create a report that lists materials inventory items sorted by category.
4. Modify the purchase cycle system presented in this chapter to include shipping information and freight costs on the Purchase Order form and report.
5. Create a query that will find items on purchase orders that vendors should have shipped seven days before today but that you have not received as of today. Hint: Microsoft Access includes a Date() function that you may find helpful.

9 Payroll Cycle

Objectives

The payroll cycle system calculates employee earnings, records payments to employees, and maintains payroll records. These records must satisfy a complex array of government regulations pertaining to time and pay records. Firms also use payroll cycle information to create management reports and financial statements. This chapter shows you how to use Microsoft Access tables, queries, forms, and reports to:

- Create and maintain employee records.
- Create and maintain records of time worked.
- Calculate gross and net pay.
- Prepare payroll registers.
- Prepare employee earnings reports.
- Print payroll check information.
- Calculate payroll expense and accruals.
- Calculate payroll tax expense and accruals.

The payroll cycle offers more opportunities to include internal control features than either the revenue cycle or the purchase cycle. Therefore, we will use the payroll cycle system components in this chapter to illustrate a number of data input and review procedure internal controls.

INTRODUCTION

This chapter shows how to use Microsoft Access to create the payroll cycle elements of accounting information systems. In many firms, the payroll cycle was the first part of the accounting information system to be automated because it involves complex, yet repetitive, calculations. As you may recall from Chapter 6, accountants sometimes consider the payroll cycle to be a part of the purchase cycle. The payroll cycle can also be integrated into the production cycle in manufacturing firms. However, treating the payroll cycle as separate from both purchasing and production cycles helps us highlight some interesting and unique characteristics of automated payroll systems. Designing and implementing a full-fledged integrated human resources-payroll system is a complex undertaking to which entire books have been devoted. Therefore, we will only illustrate fundamental payroll cycle system components in this chapter.

Manufacturing, merchandising, and service firms all have payroll cycle activity. In this chapter we will discuss the portions of the payroll activity that all firms undertake. In service and merchandising firms, payroll cost appears as an expense item on the income statement. In manufacturing firms, the portion of payroll expenditures that is related to manufacturing activities becomes a part of the cost of goods manufactured. This cost appears on the financial statements in the cost of goods sold and in the cost of finished goods and work in progress inventories. We will illustrate our discussion of the payroll cycle by using the Greenwood Lumber Company as an example. Greenwood Lumber employs 50 people that they pay at the end of each month. All of the employees are paid by the hour, none are paid a fixed salary. We will begin our tour through the payroll cycle by examining which information items we must record about our employees.

EMPLOYEE INFORMATION

The basic building block for any payroll system is employee information. At a minimum, we will need employee names, social security numbers, and pay rates. To calculate net pay amounts, we will need number of exemptions and marital status information. We will also need employee addresses to which we can mail paychecks and employee start dates to determine eligibility for pension and benefit plans. These are only a few examples of the types of employee information stored in payroll databases. Indeed, some firms track literally *hundreds* of individual data items for each employee!

Integrated human resources-payroll systems are the end product of an evolutionary process. Originally, human resources systems and payroll systems were separate in most companies. When firms began adopting database approaches to reduce data redundancy in their information processing activities, these two systems were ideal targets for integration. However, to enhance internal control, even today's integrated human resources-payroll systems limit accounting personnel's access to employee data—additions, deletions, and changes to employee records are typically handled by the human resources department.

The Employee Table

The first payroll cycle table that we will describe is the Employee table. The Employee table provides a central location for storing all information about each employee. This makes the human resources department's job of adding, deleting, and updating employee information easy and efficient. It also eliminates data redundancy; human resources creates and maintains data in this table, yet the accounting department can use information stored in the table to calculate payroll and print paychecks. The Employee table will include a fairly large number of fields. We will need to identify a good primary key field, then we will need fields to store employee names, addresses, social security numbers, pay rates, start dates, and other information (such as marital status and number of exemptions) that we need to calculate withholding taxes.

The first field we will design in the Employee table is its primary key, the employee number. Recall from Chapter 3 that a table's primary key must be a unique identifier that exists for every record in the table. One tempting primary key candidate for the Employee table is the employee social security number; however, privacy laws discourage firms from using social security numbers to identify employees. Also, large companies have found that the Social Security Administration occasionally assigns the same number to more than one person and sometimes assigns a person more than one number. By creating our own employee numbering scheme, we maintain complete control over the integrity of this primary key field.

Some firms use the employee number to store information implicitly. For example, a firm could make all salesperson employee numbers begin with the digit *4*. This approach breaks down, however, if employees transfer from one department to another. We will use a sequential number scheme to ensure that each employee number is unique and that the number contains no implicit information about an employee that might change. In a sequential number scheme, we assign each new employee a number that is one greater than the largest employee number already assigned. We do not reuse old employee numbers after employees leave because the employee number gives us a permanent access path to past employees' records. Although specific rules and practices vary, employers may be required to keep data about past employees for many years.

As we design the fields that will store employee names, we will keep in mind our discussion of good database design practice from Chapter 3 and store the name data in the most atomic form possible; that is, in the smallest possible logical chunks. Therefore, we will store each component of an employee's name in its three logical pieces: first name, middle initial, and last name. Some firms might also include separate fields to store titles, such as Mr. and Ms., or surname suffixes, such as Sr., Jr., and III.

The next set of fields in Greenwood's Employee table are the address and telephone number fields. Designing these fields should be a familiar task for you by now, since you have already created address and telephone number fields for customers and vendors in Chapters 7 and 8, respectively. This set of Employee table fields and their properties are quite similar to those of the Customer and Vendor tables you have already built.

The final group of fields will store information we need to calculate employees' gross and net pay. This information includes employees' pay rates, number of exemptions claimed, and marital status. We also use one field to store a record of employees' start dates. Greenwood Lumber organizes its management and supervision by department, so we will include a department identifier in the Employee table. Note that storing the department number in the Employee table assumes that Greenwood assigns employees to departments and that employees do not work in more than one department. If this assumption were not valid, we would need to store the employee-department link in a relationship table to accommodate the many-to-many relationship.

Exercise 9.1: Building an Employee Table

1. To create the Greenwood Lumber Company's Employee table, which we will title *tblEmployee*, click the Tables tab in the Database window, then click the New button. Double-click Design View in the New Table dialog box that appears.
2. To create the employee number field, type ***EmployeeNumber*** in the first row of the Field Name column. Since we will not be using EmployeeNumber in any calculations, we can leave its Data type set to Text. Click the Primary Key toolbar button to make this field the table's primary key.
3. When we use a sequential number coding scheme the size of the EmployeeNumber field will depend on how many employees we expect the business will have. Set the Field Size property to *3*. This will let us have up to 899 employees if we start with an EmployeeNumber value of 101.
4. Set the Input Mask property to ***000*** to limit EmployeeNumber entries to numbers and require an entry of exactly three digits. Set the Caption property to ***Employee #***

   The next four steps show you how to create the employee name fields and the social security number field.
5. Enter ***EmployeeLastName*** in the second row of the Field Name column and leave its Data Type set to Text. Set its Field Size property to ***30*** to accommodate the longest employee surname we expect to include in the table, and set its Caption property to ***Last Name***
6. Enter ***EmployeeFirstName*** in the next row of the Field Name column and leave its Data Type set to Text. Set its Field Size property to ***15*** to accommodate the longest first name we expect to include in the table, and set its Caption property to ***First Name***
7. Enter ***EmployeeMiddleInitial*** in the next row of the Field Name column and leave its Data Type set to Text. Set its Field Size property to *1* and its Input Mask property to *>L*. This will permit a one-letter middle initial and force it to be capitalized, even if a user enters it as lowercase. Set this field's Caption property to ***MI***

8. Enter a Field Name of ***EmployeeSSN*** for the social security number field and leave its Data Type set to Text. Set its Field Size property to ***11*** to store nine digits and two hyphens for each social security number. Set its Input Mask property to ***000\-00\-0000;0;_*** to help users enter the field values in the U.S. Social Security System's format and set its Caption property to ***SSN***

   The next five steps show you how to create the employee address and telephone number fields. The input mask and other property settings for these fields are similar to those of the Customer and Vendor tables in Chapters 7 and 8.
9. Enter ***EmployeeAddress*** in the next row of the Field Name column and leave its Data Type set to Text. Set its Field Size property to ***40*** and its Caption property to ***Address***
10. Enter ***EmployeeCity*** in the next row of the Field Name column and leave its Data Type set to Text. Set its Field Size property to ***20*** and its Caption property to ***City***
11. Enter ***EmployeeState*** in the next row of the Field Name column and leave its Data Type set to Text. Set its Field Size property to ***2***, its Input Mask property to ***>LL***, and its Caption property to ***State***
12. Enter ***EmployeeZipCode*** in the next row of the Field Name column and leave its Data Type set to Text. Set its Field Size property to ***10***, its Input Mask Property to ***00000\-9999;0;_*** and its Caption property to ***Zip Code***
13. Enter ***EmployeeTelephone*** in the next row of the Field Name column and leave its Data Type set to Text. Set its Field Size property to ***14***, its Input Mask property to ***!\(999") "000\-0000;0;_*** and its Caption property to ***Phone***. This Input Mask property lets the user enter an area code but does not require that an area code be entered. Remember, you can easily create these complex input masks by using the Build button to invoke the Input Mask Wizard.

   The last four fields will store tax-related information that we need to calculate net pay, pay rates, and employees' department affiliations.
14. Enter ***EmployeeMaritalStatus*** as the next Field Name. Leave its Data Type set to Text, set its Field Size property to ***1***, its Input Mask property to ***<L***, and its Caption property to ***Marital Status***. If an employee does not declare a marital status, U.S. law requires employers to withhold at the single person rate. Therefore, we can set the Default Value property to ***S***. Note that Microsoft Access automatically encloses the value with quotation marks when you leave the Default Value property.

   Since an employee must be either single or married, the only values we want to permit in this field are M and S. We can use the Validation properties to limit data entry to these values.
15. Set the Validation Rule property for the EmployeeMaritalStatus field to ***=M Or S***. Once again, quotation marks automatically enclose the stated values when you leave the property box.
16. Set the Validation Text property to ***Please enter an M for Married or an S for Single.***
17. Another information item that Greenwood needs to calculate its employees' federal income tax withholding amounts is the number of exemptions each

employee claims. In the next open row of the Field Name column, type ***EmployeeExemptions***

Try it

To save storage space and increase database access speed, you should always try to use the smallest storage space on the disk for number fields. In this case, a Byte field size is the most efficient. To learn more about the Field Size property settings that Microsoft Access provides for Number fields, select Help, Microsoft Access Help Topics from the menu, click the Index tab, enter ***FieldSize Property***, double-click on the selection, then double-click on FieldSize Property in the Topics Found dialog box. This Help Topic provides detailed information about the available Field Size property settings including range, decimal precision, and storage requirements.

18. Since we will use the EmployeeExemption value in calculating net pay, we must store it as a number. The value for this field will always be a whole number (an integer) and will never exceed 255. Set the EmployeeExemptions Data Type to Number, its Field Size property to Byte, and its Decimal Places property to ***0***. Set the field's Input Mask property to ***0*** and its Caption property to ***Exempts***
19. If an employee does not specify a number of exemptions, U.S. law requires withholding at the rate for zero exemptions; therefore, set the EmployeeExemptions Default Value property to ***0***

    Note that Microsoft Access does *not* automatically enclose the *0* in quotation marks because it is a Number Data Type, not a Text Data Type. The quotation marks are only necessary for character values, not number values. When we set the Default Value property for a field with a Number Data Type, Microsoft Access knows to store the default value as a number.

    To calculate employees' gross pay, we must know what their pay rates are. The Greenwood Lumber Company pays all of its employees by the hour, so we can store each employee's pay rate in an EmployeePayRate field.
20. In the next open row of the Field Name column, type ***EmployeePayRate***. Set its Data Type to Currency, its Decimal Places property to **2**, and its Caption property to ***Pay Rate***

    The U.S. government and many states have established minimum hourly wages. We can use the Validation Rule property to prevent entry of a value in the EmployeePayRate field that is less than the minimum wage. Using the Validation Rule property this way is an example of a *limit check*, an internal control procedure that limits the range of values that a field will accept. We can also use the Validation Rule property to set a maximum value on the field. One way that a data entry person can perpetrate payroll fraud is to change a confederate's pay rate to a large number and issue him or her one paycheck. The confederate then quits and disappears. A data entry person could also commit an unintentional error that overpaid an employee. Although we cannot completely prevent this type of fraud or error, we can mitigate its damage by setting a maximum limit on the EmployeePayRate value. If we assume that the legal minimum wage is $5.20 per hour and the highest wage we expect to pay is $40.00 per hour, we can set minimum and maximum limits on the EmployeePayRate field.

21. Set the EmployeePayRate Validation Rule property to ***> 5.19 And < 40.01***, and set its Validation Text property to ***The Pay Rate you have entered is not within the allowed range of Pay Rate values.*** This Validation Rule property requires that any EmployeePayRate value be within the limit check values. The Validation Text property includes the error message that will appear in a dialog box if a user attempts to enter an out-of-range value.

    Many firms will want to associate particular employees with jobs, projects, or departments. For example, the Greenwood Lumber Company assigns employees to departments. We will use a field to store department number rather than department name to avoid wasting storage space. Using a department number makes data entry easier and less error-prone. We will use a separate Department table to store the department names so that we can use a department number field in the Employee table. We will show you how to build the Department table and link it to the Employee table in the next exercise, but we can include the department number field in the Employee table design now.

22. Enter a Field Name of ***EmployeeDepartment*** and leave its Data Type set to Text. Set its Field Size property to ***2***, its Input Mask property to ***00***, and its Caption property to ***Dept***

    The last field in the Employee table will store the date each employee began work. Greenwood Lumber needs a permanent record of this date to determine its employees' eligibility for pension plans, vacation time, and other benefits.

23. Enter a Field Name of ***EmployeeStartDate***, set its Data Type to Date/Time, its Input Mask property to ***99/99/00;0;_*** and its Caption property to ***Start Date***
24. To save the Employee table, select the File, Save As/Export menu command and enter ***tblEmployee*** as the New Name in the Save As dialog box.

The *Ch09.mdb* database on your Companion CD-ROM includes an Employee table, *tblEmployee*, that includes sample employee records for the 50 Greenwood Lumber Company employees. This table appears in Figure 9.1 in Datasheet view in a maximized window displaying a partial view of the first few Greenwood employee records.

Although the Employee table you just built includes fifteen fields, it is actually less complex than the employee tables you will encounter in practice. In addition to the information included in our example, employee tables often include fields that store title, job skill, education level, insurance and pension plan participation codes, direct-deposit bank account number, and even the name of a person to call in case of an emergency.

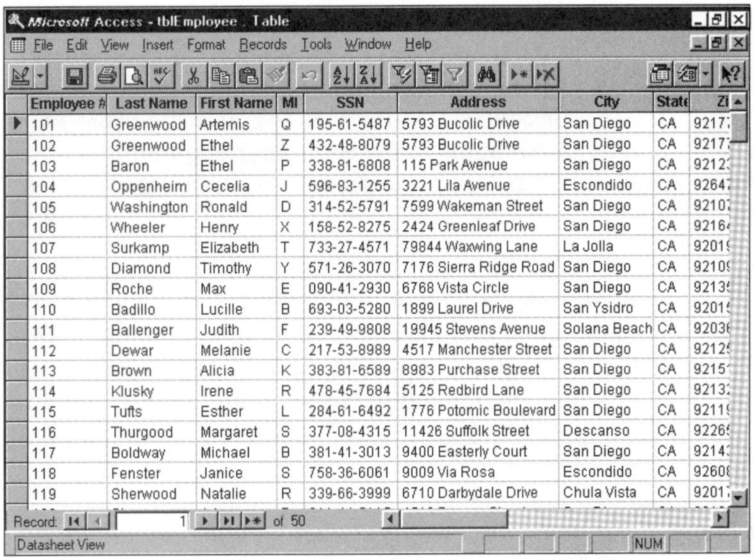

Microsoft Access - tblEmployee : Table

File Edit View Insert Format Records Tools Window Help

Employee #	Last Name	First Name	MI	SSN	Address	City	State	Zi
101	Greenwood	Artemis	Q	195-61-5487	5793 Bucolic Drive	San Diego	CA	9217
102	Greenwood	Ethel	Z	432-48-8079	5793 Bucolic Drive	San Diego	CA	9217
103	Baron	Ethel	P	338-81-6808	115 Park Avenue	San Diego	CA	9212
104	Oppenheim	Cecelia	J	596-83-1255	3221 Lila Avenue	Escondido	CA	9264
105	Washington	Ronald	D	314-52-5791	7599 Wakeman Street	San Diego	CA	9210
106	Wheeler	Henry	X	158-52-8275	2424 Greenleaf Drive	San Diego	CA	9216
107	Surkamp	Elizabeth	T	733-27-4571	79844 Waxwing Lane	La Jolla	CA	9201
108	Diamond	Timothy	Y	571-26-3070	7176 Sierra Ridge Road	San Diego	CA	9210
109	Roche	Max	E	090-41-2930	6768 Vista Circle	San Diego	CA	9213
110	Badillo	Lucille	B	693-03-5280	1899 Laurel Drive	San Ysidro	CA	9201
111	Ballenger	Judith	F	239-49-9808	19945 Stevens Avenue	Solana Beach	CA	9203
112	Dewar	Melanie	C	217-53-8989	4517 Manchester Street	San Diego	CA	9212
113	Brown	Alicia	K	383-81-6589	8983 Purchase Street	San Diego	CA	9215
114	Klusky	Irene	R	478-45-7684	5125 Redbird Lane	San Diego	CA	9213
115	Tufts	Esther	L	284-61-6492	1776 Potomic Boulevard	San Diego	CA	9211
116	Thurgood	Margaret	S	377-08-4315	11426 Suffolk Street	Descanso	CA	9226
117	Boldway	Michael	B	381-41-3013	9400 Easterly Court	San Diego	CA	9214
118	Fenster	Janice	S	758-36-6061	9009 Via Rosa	Escondido	CA	9260
119	Sherwood	Natalie	R	339-66-3999	6710 Darbydale Drive	Chula Vista	CA	9201

Record: 1 of 50

Datasheet View NUM

Figure 9.1 The Greenwood Lumber Company's *tblEmployee* in Datasheet view.

The number and size of the fields in this table make direct data entry into the table cumbersome. We will show you how to build a form for the Employee table that will make entering, changing, and deleting employee information much easier, but first we must create a Department table. The Department table will include the department descriptions we excluded from the Employee table and a department number field that will link it to the EmployeeDepartment field in the Employee table. You can press Ctrl+W to close *tblEmployee*.

The Department Table

The Greenwood Lumber Company Department table needs to include two fields. The first field will store a two-digit identifying number for each department. The second field will store the department descriptions. Exercise 9.2 provides step-by-step instructions for building this table.

Exercise 9.2: Building a Department Table

1. Click the Tables tab in the Database window, then click the New button. Double-click Design View in the New Table dialog box.
2. Enter ***DepartmentNumber*** as the first Field Name and leave its Data Type set to Text.
3. Click the Primary Key toolbar button, then set the following properties: Field Size, ***2***; Input Mask, ***00***; Caption, ***Dept #***; and Required, Yes.

4. Enter ***DepartmentDescription*** as the second Field Name and leave its Data Type set to Text.
5. Set its Field Size property to ***40*** and its Caption property to ***Description***
6. Select the File, Save As/Export menu command and type ***tblDepartment*** as the Table Name in the Save As dialog box.
7. Select View, Datasheet to open *tblDepartment* in Datasheet view.

The table shown in Datasheet view in Figure 9.2 is included as *tblDepartment* in the *Ch09.mdb* database on your Companion CD-ROM. With the table open in Datasheet view, you can enter Greenwood's department numbers and names. After entering the permitted values, you can follow the steps in Exercise 9.3 to create the link between *tblEmployee* and *tblDepartment*.

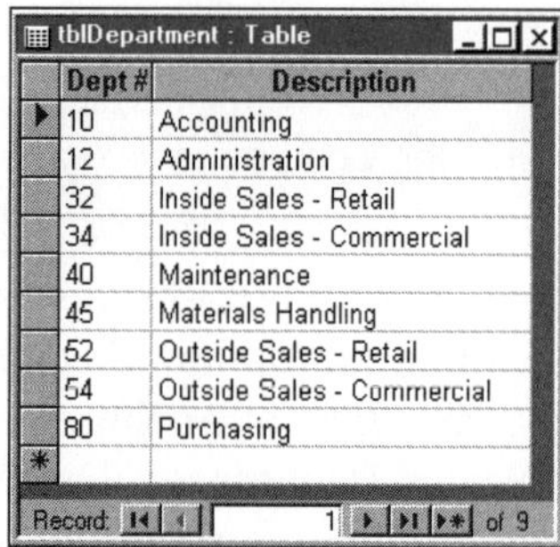

tblDepartment : Table

Dept #	Description
10	Accounting
12	Administration
32	Inside Sales - Retail
34	Inside Sales - Commercial
40	Maintenance
45	Materials Handling
52	Outside Sales - Retail
54	Outside Sales - Commercial
80	Purchasing

Record: 1 of 9

Figure 9.2 The Department table in Datasheet view.

Exercise 9.3: Linking *tblEmployee* and *tblDepartment*

1. Close *tblEmployee* and *tblDepartment* to return to the Database window.
2. Select the Tools, Relationships menu command to open the Relationships window and the Show Table dialog box.
3. Double-click *tblDepartment* and *tblEmployee* to place them in the Relationships window, then click the Close button.
4. Click and drag the DepartmentNumber field in *tblDepartment* to the EmployeeDepartment field in *tblEmployee*.
5. Click the Enforce Referential Integrity check box, then click the Create button.

The Relationship window showing the link appears in Figure 9.3.

To return to the Database window, select the File, Close menu command and click the Yes button to save the changes you have made to the table relationships. Now that we have completed the brief detour we took to build *tblDepartment* and

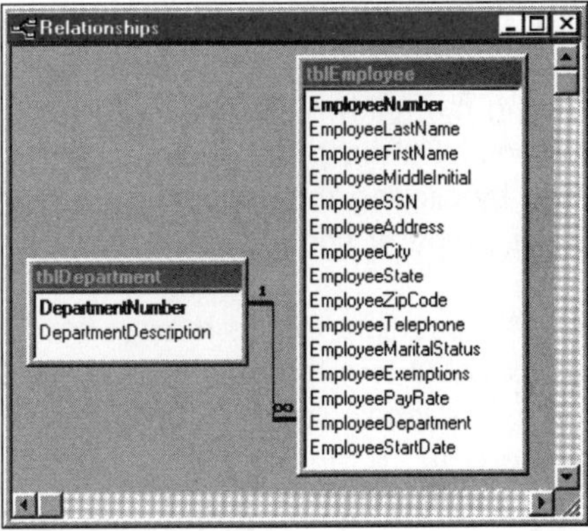

Figure 9.3 Linking the Employee table and the Department table.

link it to *tblEmployee*, we can turn our attention to designing a data entry form for Greenwood's employee information.

The Employee Information Entry Form

The Employee Information Entry form must include controls for the 15 fields in *tblEmployee*. One way to make data entry easier in a form with so many fields is to reduce visual clutter. We can do that on this form by grouping related fields into separate sections of the form. Greenwood's Employee table includes information that we can sort into four logical groups: employee identification fields, employee name fields, employee address fields, and payroll calculation information fields.

The employee identification fields are EmployeeNumber, EmployeeDepartment, and EmployeeStartDate. The employee name fields are EmployeeLastName, EmployeeFirstName, and EmployeeMiddleInitial. The employee address fields are EmployeeAddress, EmployeeCity, EmployeeState, EmployeeZipCode, and EmployeeTelephone. The payroll calculation fields are EmployeeSSN, EmployeeMaritalStatus, EmployeeExemptions, and EmployeePayRate.

We show you how to arrange controls in logical sections when building an Employee Information form in Exercise 9.4. This exercise will show you how to start with a blank form and construct all of the form elements without using the Form Wizard. You should close all tables and have the Database window open to begin this exercise.

Exercise 9.4: Building an Employee Information Entry Form

1. Click the Forms tab in the Database window, then click the New button. Select *tblEmployee* in the combo box, and then double-click Design View in

the New Form dialog box to open a blank form. You can use Figures 9.4 and 9.5 as guides for placing graphics objects, labels, and controls on the form when completing the following steps.

2. Open the toolbox by clicking the Toolbox toolbar button, then open the property sheet by clicking the Properties toolbar button. You should keep the toolbox and the property sheet open on the desktop throughout this exercise.
3. Use the toolbox Rectangle tool to draw a box for the identification fields.
4. Use the toolbox Label tool to create a label for the box and enter the text ***Identification*** in the label. Set the label's Text Align property to Center, its Font Size property to 10, and its Font Weight to Bold.
5. Select the box and the label (press the Shift key while clicking each object in succession), click the property sheet Format tab, then set both objects' Special Effect properties to Raised.
6. Draw a selection rectangle around both objects, press Ctrl+C to copy the object group, then press Ctrl+V three times to paste three copies of the object group to the form.
7. Change the label text in the three new groups to Payroll Calculation, Name, and Address as shown in Figure 9.4.

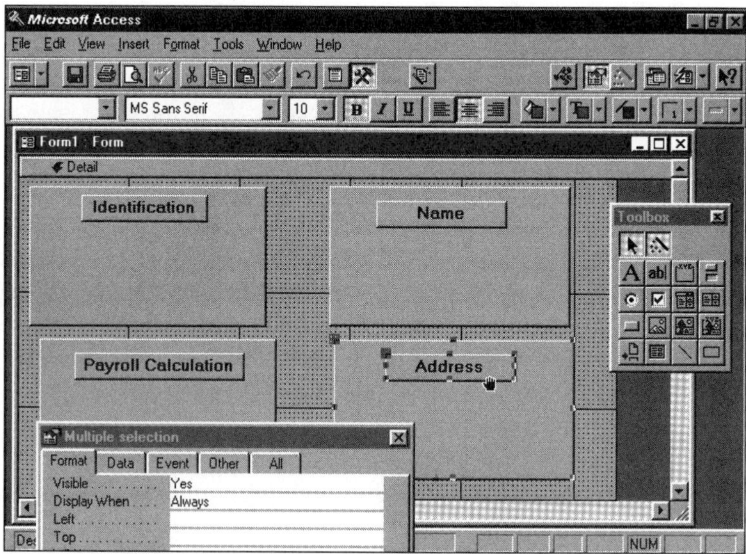

Figure 9.4 The Employee Information form under construction.

Note that Figure 9.4 shows the property sheet and the toolbox open. Now that you have a rough layout for the overall form, we can show you how to complete the design of each individual section.

8. Click the Field List toolbar button to open the *tblEmployee* field list.

9. Click and drag the EmployeeNumber and EmployeeStartDate fields to the first box you created.
10. Use the Combo Box tool from the toolbox to draw a field in the Identification section between the EmployeeNumber and EmployeeStartDate fields. After you draw the combo box control on the form, the first Combo Box Wizard dialog box appears.
11. Click the Next > button to accept the default option since we want to look up the values for this field in the Department table.
12. Select *tblDepartment* from the list box control, then click the Next > button.
13. Click the >> button to move both DepartmentNumber and DepartmentDescription from the Available Fields list box to the Selected Fields list box, then click the Next > button.
14. Click the "Hide key column (recommended)" check box to remove the check mark because we *do* want to display *tblDepartment's* key field in our form.
15. Reduce the first column's width and increase the second column's width so that the field values are displayed without extra unused space, then click the Next > button.
16. Double-click the DepartmentNumber field name in the Available Fields list box. This selects DepartmentNumber and opens the next Combo Box Wizard dialog box.
17. Click the "Store that value in this field" option button and enter ***EmployeeDepartment*** in the combo box control, then click the Next > button.
18. Enter ***Department Number*** as the combo box label name and click the Finish > button.
19. Using Figure 9.5 as a guide, adjust the size and spacing of the three controls in the Identification Box. You can also set the controls' Font Size, Font Weight, Special Effect, and other properties using Figure 9.5 and your own judgment.

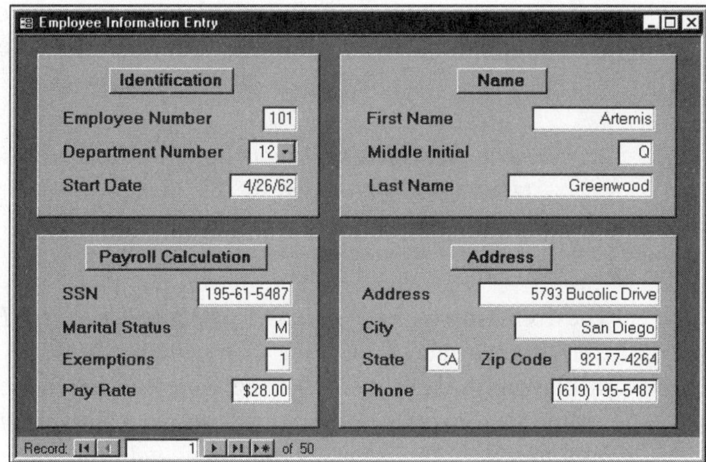

Figure 9.5 The completed Employee Information Entry form.

You can follow the same general procedure to click and drag the other *tblEmployee* fields to the appropriate sections of the form, set their properties, and adjust their sizes and spacing. As you refine the appearance of the form, you may find it helpful to toggle between Design and Form view.

Try it

You can move between the two View options for forms using the View menu command or the first button on the Form Design toolbar. This button has a drop button to its right, which makes it work much like a combo box control. Clicking on the drop button presents you with a choice of Design View, Form View, and Datasheet View.

20. Choose the Edit, Select Form menu command to select the form. Click the property sheet Format tab and change the form's Caption property to ***Employee Information Entry***, its Scroll Bars property to Neither, and its Record Selectors property to No.
21. Click the Detail section bar at the top of the form, then click the property sheet Format tab and change the Detail section's Back Color property to a color that contrasts with the rectangles that contain the text box controls.

Try it

When you select any Color property for a form object, a Build button appears to the right of the property box. You can click on this Build button to open a Color palette that offers you a choice of 48 colors and gives you the option of creating your own custom colors. After you choose a color and click the OK button, the number of the color you chose appears as the new property setting. We find this to be much easier than remembering that, for example, maroon is 4194432.

22. Select File, Save As/Export from the Design view menu and enter ***frmEmployeeInformation*** as the New Name in the Save As dialog box.

The form shown in Figure 9.5 is included as *frmEmployeeInformation* in the *Ch09.mdb* database on your Companion CD-ROM. In Figure 9.5, the form is displaying the first record of the Greenwood Lumber Company sample data. In addition to learning more about the payroll cycle in this exercise, you learned how to use color, control properties, and object grouping to create a form that contains many fields but is still easy to read and use.

Maintaining Employee Records

Now that we have an Employee table to store employee information and a form that makes using that table easy, we can efficiently and effectively maintain employee information. With the Employee Information Entry form, we can enter new employee information easily and update records as employees move, change their number of exemptions or marital status, get new telephone numbers, and change other information items we have entered in the Employee table.

Notice how the combo box control for the EmployeeDepartment field makes data entry easier. When you click the combo box button, a list of all the DepartmentNumber and DepartmentDescription values that are in the Department table appears as shown in Figure 9.6.

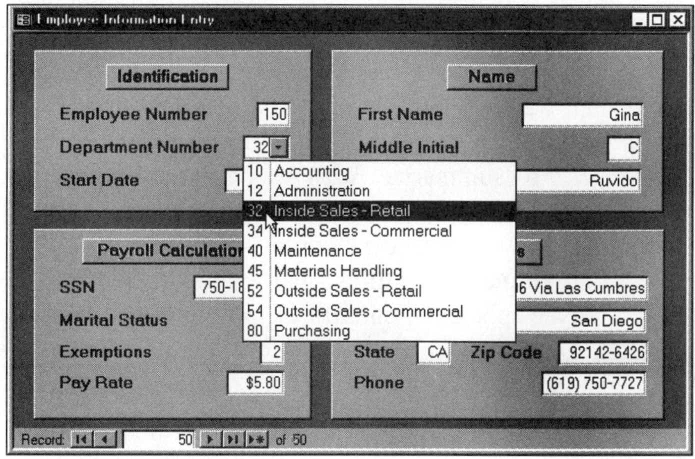

Figure 9.6 Using the combo box control to enter a department number.

By clicking the DepartmentDescription value we want, we enter the associated DepartmentNumber value into the EmployeeDepartment field of the Employee table. The advantages of using this combo box control here include:

- Data entry clerks do not need to memorize lists of department numbers.
- Only valid department numbers can be entered in the Employee table.
- The need to enter and store department names in the Employee table is avoided.
- New departments can be added easily to the Department table and they will automatically appear in the Employee Information Entry form combo box.

Note how the Default Value property settings we incorporated into the Employee table operate in the form. For example, immediately after you open a new record by adding a new EmployeeNumber, the EmployeeMaritalStatus value becomes *S* and the EmployeeExemptions value becomes *0*.

Try it

You can test the operation of the other internal control features we built into the table's design. For example, try entering illegal values in the EmployeePayRate field. If you attempt to enter a value less than *5.2* or greater than *40* in the field, a dialog box appears with the error message we entered as the Validation Text property. Note that the form will not permit you to leave the record until you enter an acceptable value in the EmployeeRateField.

Updating existing employee records to reflect pay rate changes, new addresses, new telephone numbers, and other changes is straightforward. The navigation buttons at the bottom of the form make it easy to find and display any employee record we want to change. The form will let a user move through the individual fields in the displayed record using the up and down arrow keys, the Tab and Shift+Tab keys, or the Enter key. Also remember that any internal control features that we built into the table's structure will limit changes to existing field values just as though you were entering new data.

To summarize, we now have a table that contains information about the Greenwood Lumber Company's employees. The table relates each piece of information to a particular employee through the employee number—a primary key that uniquely identifies each employee. All information about a particular employee appears in one row of *tblEmployee* and depends on the primary key value for that row. We also have a form that facilitates entering, deleting, and changing employee information. We will use the information in our Employee table as we construct payroll cycle forms, queries, and reports.

Employee Information Reports

We can build a variety of reports using the information in *tblEmployee*. We will describe an example report in the next exercise to show you one possibility. This example Employee Pay report will list employee names, start dates, and pay rates. The report will group employee records by department and show the average pay rate for each department.

Exercise 9.5: Building an Employee Pay Report

1. Click the Reports tab in the Database window, then click the New button. Enter ***tblEmployee*** in the combo box control and double-click Design View in the list box control.

   The report must obtain department names from the Department table. To add the Department table to the report, we must set the report's Record

Source property to a query. We can build this query by opening and editing the query behind the report.

2. Select Edit, Select Report from the menu, click the Properties toolbar button, select the Record Source property, then click the Build button to open the Query Builder window.
3. Add the Department table using the Show Table toolbar button.
4. Click and drag the DepartmentNumber field from *tblDepartment* to the first Field cell in the QBE grid and enter ***Ascending*** in its Sort cell.
5. Click and drag the DepartmentDescription field from *tblDepartment* to the second Field cell in the QBE grid.
6. Click and drag the EmployeeNumber field from *tblEmployee* to the third QBE grid Field cell and enter ***Ascending*** in its Sort cell.
7. Click and drag the asterisk from *tblEmployee* to the fourth QBE grid Field cell.
8. Click in the fifth QBE grid Field cell and enter ***EmployeeName: [EmployeeFirstName] & " " & [EmployeeMiddleInitial] & ". " & [EmployeeLastName]***
9. Select the File, Close menu command to return to the report Design window.

   Now that you have built the query, you can design the layout of the report. Begin by setting up a department group section on the report.
10. Click the Sorting and Grouping toolbar button and enter ***EmployeeDepartment*** in the first Field/Expression cell in the Sorting and Grouping dialog box. Press Tab and change the Group Header property to Yes. Set the Keep Together property to Whole Group, then press Alt+F4 to close the dialog box.

    You should now have four sections on the report: Page Header, EmployeeDepartmentHeader, Detail, and Page Footer. You can click and drag the bottom edges of these sections to change the size of each. This will let us accommodate the controls we must add to the report. You can refer to Figures 9.7 and 9.8 as you place controls, text boxes, and graphic objects on the report.
11. Click the Field List toolbar button, then click and drag the following fields to the Detail section: tblEmployee.EmployeeNumber, EmployeeName, EmployeeStartDate, and EmployeePayRate. Each of these fields will become a control on the report.
12. Draw a marquee around the control labels and press Ctrl+X. This will cut the labels from the text box portion of the control. Click the EmployeeDepartment Header bar, then press Ctrl+V to place the labels in that section. Using Figure 9.7 as a guide, align the labels and controls in two rows.
13. Click and drag the EmployeeDepartment and DepartmentDescription fields to the EmployeeDepartment Header section.

    To report an average pay rate for each department, add a calculating control to the EmployeeDepartment Header.
14. Open the toolbox, then use the Text Box tool to draw a new control in the EmployeeDepartment Header.

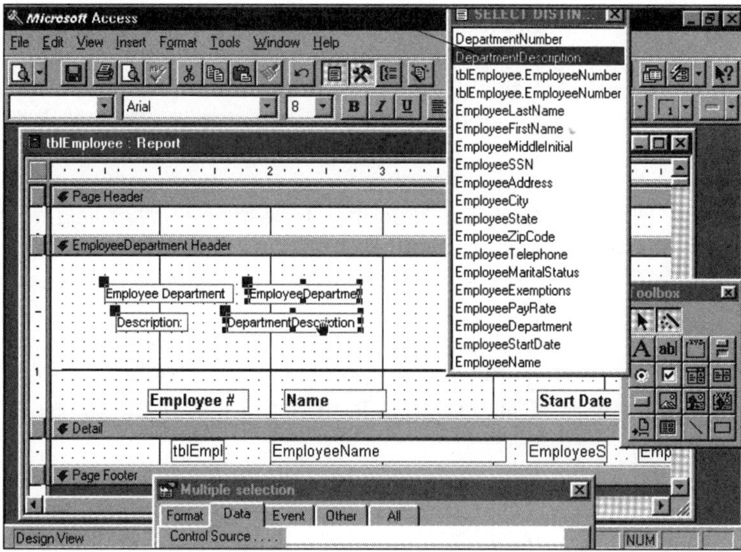

Figure 9.7 The Employee Pay report under construction in Design view.

15. Change the new control's Name property to ***Average Pay Rate***, its Control Source property to ***=Avg([EmployeePayRate])***, its Format property to Fixed, and its Decimal Places property to ***2***
16. Arrange the controls and add label controls and line objects to the Page Header section using Figure 9.8 and your own judgment. Figure 9.8 shows a printed page of the Employee Pay report for the Greenwood Lumber Company sample data.

Try it

As you make fine adjustments to objects' placement on the report, you may find it easier to work with Snap to Grid turned off. You can toggle this desktop setting by selecting Format, Snap to Grid from the menu. You may also find that you have more room to work if you turn the ruler off. You can do this by choosing View, Ruler from the menu.

Save the Employee Pay report by selecting File, Save As/Export from the Design view menu. Enter a New Name of ***rptEmployeePay*** in the Save As dialog box and click the OK button. The Employee Pay report shown in Figure 9.8 is included in the *Ch09.mdb* database on your Companion CD-ROM as *rptEmployeePay*.

Employee Pay Rates and Start Dates

By Department

Greenwood Lumber Company
for interal use only Page 3

Department Number 40 ***Maintenance***

Average Pay Rate $16.73

Employee #	Name	Start Date	Pay Rate
111	Judith F. Ballenger	1/21/68	$18.00
124	Louise K. Young	1/26/91	$14.20
142	Karl S. Smothers	6/15/94	$18.00

Department Number 45 ***Materials Handling***

Average Pay Rate $14.07

Employee #	Name	Start Date	Pay Rate
139	Edward G. Perciavalle	2/2/94	$16.20
115	Esther L. Tufts	10/31/77	$16.60
132	James R. Foster	12/1/92	$14.90
106	Henry X. Wheeler	8/3/64	$15.40
126	Colleen H. Ward	7/15/91	$12.20
143	Byron D. White	1/31/95	$9.10

Department Number 52 ***Outside Sales - Retail***

Average Pay Rate $9.43

Employee #	Name	Start Date	Pay Rate
149	Donald T. Forrest	6/17/97	$6.80
119	Natalie R. Sherwood	9/21/88	$12.80
146	Joel B. Blum	5/1/96	$6.60
131	Antonio N. Pelligrini	10/15/92	$11.50

Figure 9.8 The Employee Pay report.

RECORDING TIME WORKED

The second main entity in the payroll cycle often is some measure of the time that employees have worked because most employees are paid on that basis. However, not all employees are paid on the basis of time worked. For example, firms may pay salespersons a percentage of their sales as a commission and managers may earn a bonus based on their department's profit, production, or efficiency. Even when firms calculate pay using time worked, the methods they use to capture time data vary tremendously, ranging from workers punching a time clock to automated bar code scanners that read employee badges. Regardless of how firms capture time worked data, they must store the data by employee and by pay period before calculating payroll. This storage occurs in a Time Worked table.

The Time Worked Table

This section will explain how you can build a Time Worked table for the Greenwood Lumber Company that stores regular and overtime hours worked by each employee for each pay period. We have made two key simplifying assumptions: that Greenwood calculates all pay on an hourly basis, and that Greenwood pays all of its employees once each month. We will need a primary key that uniquely identifies each employee's time worked in each pay period. We could create a sequential number for each employee-pay period combination; however, we already have an employee number for each employee. If we add a field to identify the pay period we can build a composite primary key from the two fields.

Exercise 9.6 shows you how to create a Time Worked table for the Greenwood Lumber Company that accomplishes our data storage objectives. The Time Worked table also illustrates some internal control features that can help reduce potential losses from errors or irregularities.

EXERCISE 9.6: BUILDING A TIME WORKED TABLE

1. To create the Greenwood Lumber Company's Time Worked table, which we will title *tblTimeWorked*, click the Tables tab in the Database window, then click the New button. Double-click Design View in the New Table dialog box that appears.
2. Enter a Field Name of ***EmployeeNumber***, leave its Data Type set to Text, and set its Field Size to ***3***. Set its Input Mask property to ***000***, its Caption property to ***Employee #***, and its Indexed property to Yes (Duplicates OK).

   The second part of the primary key must identify the pay period. Since we are assuming that Greenwood pays once each month, we can use the last day of each month as the value for this field.
3. Enter ***TWPayPeriodEnded*** in the second Field Name row and set its Data Type to Date/Time. Set its Input Mask property to ***99/99/00;0;_***, its Caption property to ***Month Ended***, and its Indexed property to Yes (Duplicates OK).
4. To designate these fields as the composite primary key, hold down the Ctrl key and select both fields by clicking their row selectors. With both fields

selected, click the Primary Key toolbar button. The primary key symbol should appear in the row selectors of both fields.

The next two fields will store the hours that employees have worked—one field for regular hours, the other field for overtime hours. You can assume that Greenwood uses only one overtime rate and that it is one and one-half times the regular rate. Further, you can assume that when Greenwood's accounting personnel enter the time worked data in this table, regular and overtime hours have already been calculated from workers' time sheets. We could create a form that calculates regular time and overtime from time records using the Microsoft Access date/time and other functions; however, the details of those calculations are beyond the scope of this book.

5. Enter the next Field Name of ***TWRegularTime***. Set its Data Type to Number, its Field Size to ***Single***, and its Caption property to ***Regular Time***

   The greatest number of business days that ever occurs in any calendar month is 23. If Greenwood pays overtime for all hours over eight per day, the TWRegularTime field will never have a legitimate value greater than 184 (23 days × 8 hours per day). We will use the Validation Rule and Text property settings to enforce a limit check internal control on this field.
6. Set the TWRegularTime field's Validation Rule property to ***<185***
7. Set the TWRegularTime field's Validation Text property to ***The number of Regular Hours you have entered is too large.***

   The second hours field, TWOvertime, will store the overtime hours worked.
8. Enter a Field Name of ***TWOvertime***, set its Data Type to Number, its Field Size to ***Single***, and its Caption property to ***Overtime***

   We can establish a limit check internal control on the TWOvertime field, too. However, selecting the limit value is not as straightforward as it was for the TWRegularTime field. Since a Validation Rule property setting will absolutely prohibit any greater value, we must set it to accommodate any overtime that an employee might ever work.
9. Set the TWOvertime field's Validation Rule property to ***<200***
10. Set the TWOvertime field's Validation Text property to ***The number of Overtime Hours you have entered is too large.***
11. Save the table by selecting File, Save As/Export from the menu. Type ***tblTimeWorked*** as the New Name in the Save As dialog box. The table shown in Figure 9.9 is included as *tblTimeWorked* in the *Ch09.mdb* database on your Companion CD-ROM.

This Time Worked table needs a link to *tblEmployee* on EmployeeNumber. If we enforce referential integrity on this link, it will prevent users from entering time worked for employee numbers that do not exist in *tblEmployee*. This internal control feature, called an *existence check* or a *validity check*, can reduce the threat of errors and irregularities in payroll processing. Exercise 9.7 shows you how to create this link.

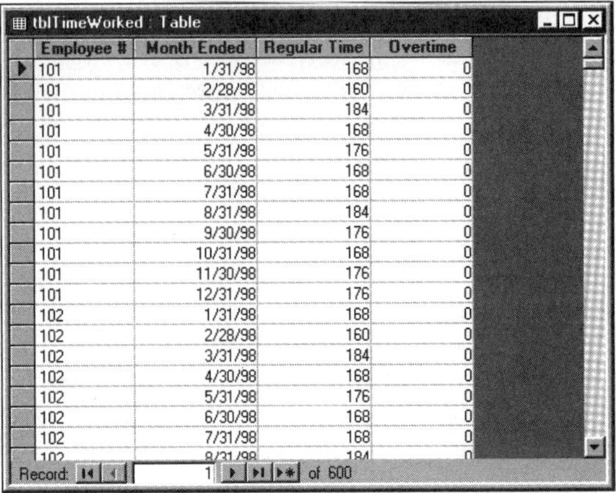

tblTimeWorked : Table

Employee #	Month Ended	Regular Time	Overtime
101	1/31/98	168	0
101	2/28/98	160	0
101	3/31/98	184	0
101	4/30/98	168	0
101	5/31/98	176	0
101	6/30/98	168	0
101	7/31/98	168	0
101	8/31/98	184	0
101	9/30/98	176	0
101	10/31/98	168	0
101	11/30/98	176	0
101	12/31/98	176	0
102	1/31/98	168	0
102	2/28/98	160	0
102	3/31/98	184	0
102	4/30/98	168	0
102	5/31/98	176	0
102	6/30/98	168	0
102	7/31/98	168	0
102	8/31/98	184	0

Record: 1 of 600

Figure 9.9 The Time Worked table in Datasheet view.

EXERCISE 9.7: LINKING *TBLTIMEWORKED* TO *TBLEMPLOYEE*

1. Press Ctrl+W to close *tblTimeWorked* if it is still open and return to the Database window.
2. Click the Relationships toolbar button to open the Relationships window. The existing relationship between the Department and Employee tables will appear in the Relationships window.
3. Use the Show Table toolbar button to open the Show Table dialog box. Double-click *tblTimeWorked* to add it to the Relationships window.
4. Click and drag the EmployeeNumber field in *tblEmployee* to the EmployeeNumber field in *tblTimeWorked*.
5. Click the Enforce Referential Integrity check box, then click the Create button. The Relationships window showing the new link appears in Figure 9.10.

To close the Relationships window and return to the Database window, select the File, Close menu command. Now we can build a data entry form through which we can enter and edit time worked data.

The Time Worked Entry Form

We can build a data entry form for the Time Worked table that will ease the task of entering employees' time records. The Time Worked Entry form will use the employee name fields in the Employee table to provide another validity check that can help data entry clerks detect errors. We can design the Time Worked form so that it displays the employee's name when a user enters an employee number.

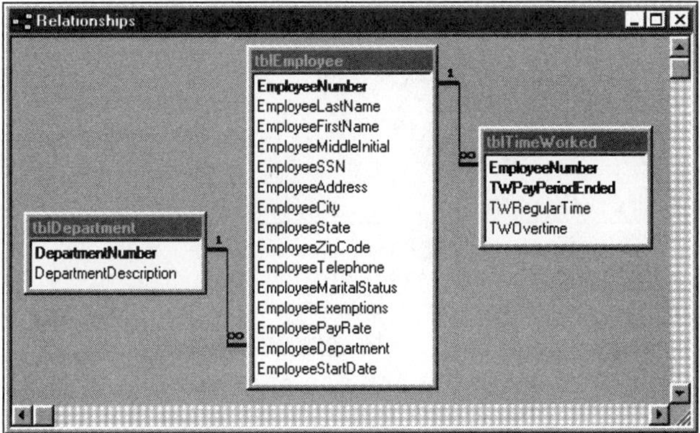

Figure 9.10 Linking the Time Worked table to the Employee table.

This lets the user check the displayed name against the employee name on the time sheet source document. Exercise 9.8 shows you how to create a Time Worked Entry form.

Exercise 9.8: Building an Entry Form for Time Worked

1. In the Database window, click the Forms tab, then click the New button.
2. In the New Forms dialog box, enter ***tblTimeWorked*** in the combo box control and double-click Form Wizard in the list box.
3. The Form Wizard dialog box will open with Table: *tblTimeWorked* selected in the Tables/Queries combo box.
4. Click the >> button to move all of the *tblTimeWorked* fields from the Available Fields list box to the Selected Fields list box.
5. Select or enter ***Table: tblEmployee*** in the Tables/Queries combo box.
6. Use the > button to move EmployeeFirstName, EmployeeMiddleInitial, and EmployeeLastName from the Available Fields list box to the Selected Fields list box. Figure 9.11 shows the Form Wizard dialog box at this point. Click the Next > button to continue.
7. Click the Next > button to accept the default of viewing the data by *tblTimeWorked*.
8. Click the Tabular option button, then click the Next > button to continue.
9. Click the Standard style, then click the Next > button.
10. Enter ***frmTimeWorked*** as the form title, then click the Finish button to have the Form Wizard create the form.

    We will now show you how to modify the Wizard-generated form to make it more useful.
11. Select View, Form Design from the menu. If the property sheet is not already open, click the Properties toolbar button.

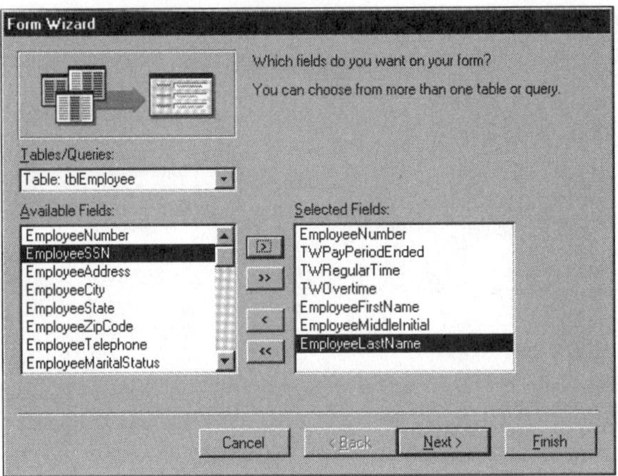

Figure 9.11 Selecting Fields in the Form Wizard dialog box.

12. Delete the EmployeeFirstName and EmployeeMiddleInitial text box controls and labels.
13. Choose Edit, Select Form from the menu, click the Data tab in the property sheet, then click the Build button for the form's Record Source property to open the query behind the form.
14. Select the second QBE grid column (the TWPayPeriodEnded field) and press the Delete key.
15. Click and drag the TWPayPeriodEnded field from *tblTimeWorked* to the first QBE grid Field cell and drop it on the EmployeeNumber field name in that cell. The EmployeeNumber field should move one cell to the left, leaving TWPayPeriodEnded in the first cell.
16. Enter ***Ascending*** in the first two columns' Sort cells.

    These Sort cell entries will cause the form to sort first by TWPayPeriodEnded and then by EmployeeNumber. This will allow a data entry clerk to add all of the time records for a particular month-end in employee number order.
17. Scroll to the right to find the first open QBE grid column and enter ***EmployeeName: [EmployeeFirstName] & " " & [EmployeeMiddleInitial] & ". " & [EmployeeLastName]*** in its Field cell.
18. Press Ctrl+W to close the Query Builder window. Click the Yes button to save your changes.
19. Select the EmployeeLastName text box control, click on the Data tab in its property sheet, and change its Control Source property to ***EmployeeName***. Click on the property sheet Format tab and change the Back Style property to Transparent, the Special Effect property to Flat, and the Border Style property to Transparent.
20. Using Figure 9.12 as a guide, you can make the final appearance modifications to the form, which include rearranging the controls, bolding the labels, and changing the form's Caption property to ***Time Worked Entry***. Remember

to set the EmployeeName control's Enabled, Locked, and Tab Stop properties to prevent a user from entering data in that field.

21. When you are satisfied with your form, you can save it by selecting File, Save As/Export from the Design view menu. Enter a Form Name of ***frmTimeWorkedEntry*** in the Save As dialog box and click OK.

frmTimeWorkedEntry

Employee #	Name	Month Ended	Regular Hours	Overtime Hours
101	Artemis Q. Greenwood	1/31/98	168	0
102	Ethel Z. Greenwood	1/31/98	168	0
103	Ethel P. Baron	1/31/98	168	0
104	Cecelia J. Oppenheim	1/31/98	168	4
105	Ronald D. Washington	1/31/98	168	8
106	Henry X. Wheeler	1/31/98	168	11
107	Elizabeth T. Surkamp	1/31/98	168	0
108	Timothy Y. Diamond	1/31/98	142	0
109	Max E. Roche	1/31/98	87	0
110	Lucille B. Badillo	1/31/98	168	0
111	Judith F. Ballenger	1/31/98	168	7
112	Melanie C. Dewar	1/31/98	126	0

Record: 1 of 600

Figure 9.12 The Greenwood Lumber Company's *frmTimeWorkedEntry* displaying sample records in Form view.

A version of this form is included in the *Ch09.mdb* database on your Companion CD-ROM as *frmTimeWorkedEntry*. Figure 9.12 shows the Time Worked Entry form displaying records from the Greenwood Lumber Company Time Worked and Employee tables.

Our example made some simplifying assumptions. The sample data includes only one year of data for 50 employees. We assumed an hourly pay basis for all employees, and we included only regular hours and one class of overtime hours. A more sophisticated payroll system would track accrual and use of vacation time, paid time off, unpaid time off, and sick days. Many payroll systems track several types of overtime and must calculate pay using measures other than hours. However, even with the limited example components we have illustrated here, we can generate some useful reports.

Time Reports

Firms regularly use many different reports built on time worked data. In our Greenwood Lumber Company example data, we included only regular and overtime hours in the Time Worked table. However, even in this simplified example, the Time Worked table combines with the Employee and Department tables to yield a total of 19 different fields that we can use in queries and reports. To illustrate how we can use these tables to build payroll cycle reports, this section describes how to create a report that displays total regular and overtime hours worked by department. This kind of report can help managers identify departments with staffing and work scheduling problems.

We will build the Time Worked report in two steps. First, we will design a query that links the Time Worked, Employee, and Department tables. In the second step, we will build a report based on the query. Exercise 9.9 shows you how to build the Time Worked query.

Exercise 9.9: Building the Time Worked Query

1. In the Database window, click the Queries tab and click the New button. Double-click Design View in the New Query dialog box.
2. In the Show Table box, hold down the Ctrl key and select *tblTimeWorked*, *tblEmployee*, and *tblDepartment*. Click the Add button, then click the Close button.
3. Click and drag the DepartmentDescription field from *tblDepartment* to the first Field cell in the QBE grid.
4. Double-click the TWRegularTime and TWOvertime fields to copy them to the next two QBE grid Field cells.
5. Click the Run toolbar button to test the query.

The dynaset resulting from this query should include the three fields we selected from *tblDepartment* and *tblTimeWorked*. Notice that we included *tblEmployee* in the Query window, but we did not use any fields from that table in the query. The Employee table provides the link between *tblDepartment* and *tblTimeWorked*; therefore, we must include it in the query model.

When you are satisfied that your Time Worked query is operating properly, you can save it as ***qryTimeWorked***. The *Ch09.mdb* database on your Companion CD-ROM includes *qryTimeWorked,* which you can use as a reference. You can close the query by pressing Ctrl+W.

Now we can build the Time Worked report using this query. The Time Worked query was a little unusual. The Time Worked report has a twist that makes it interesting, too. To find out more, follow the steps in Exercise 9.10.

Exercise 9.10: Building the Time Worked Report

1. In the Database window, click the Reports tab, then click the New button to open the New Report dialog box. Enter or select ***qryTimeWorked*** in the combo box control, then double-click Design View.

2. Drag the bottom edge of the Detail section up until the Detail section background grid disappears.
3. If the form does not open with a Page Header and Footer, use the Format, Page Header/Footer menu command to create them.

   The interesting twist to this report is that it contains no detail records! Everything on the form is either a header or a calculated total field.
4. Click the Sorting and Grouping toolbar button and enter ***DepartmentDescription*** in the first Field/Expression cell in the Sorting and Grouping dialog box. Change the Group Header property to Yes, then press Alt+F4 to close the dialog box.
5. Click the Field List toolbar button, then click and drag the DepartmentDescription field from the Field List to the DepartmentDescription Header. Delete the new control's label.
6. Open the toolbox and use the Text Box tool to create two controls in the DepartmentDescription Header section. Delete both new controls' labels.
7. Click the Properties toolbar button and set the Control Source property of the first control to ***=Sum([TWRegularTime])***. Set the Control Source property of the second control to ***=Sum([TWOvertime])***

   These controls will calculate subtotals of the TWRegularTime and TWOvertime values for each DepartmentDescription value. Using Figure 9.13 as a guide, you can arrange these controls, add label controls to the Page Header, and add line objects to the form's design.
8. The Time Worked report that appears in Figure 9.13 is included in the *Ch09.mdb* database on your Companion CD-ROM as *rptTimeWorked*. To save your Time Worked report, select File, Save As/Export from the menu. Enter a New Name of ***rptTimeWorked*** in the Save As dialog box and click the OK button.

This report illustrates how you can use the three payroll cycle tables to obtain some interesting information. It also demonstrates how to build a query that uses one table as a link between two other tables that contain data in which we are interested. The Time Worked report is an interesting example of a report that contains no detail records. By looking at the ratio of overtime hours to regular hours, managers at the Greenwood Lumber Company can identify departments that are improperly staffed or departments that have scheduling problems. Our next task is to use the information in the three payroll cycle tables to calculate payroll.

CALCULATING PAYROLL

Thus far in this chapter we have demonstrated how to enter and maintain payroll cycle information. We have used this payroll cycle information to produce two useful reports; however, the main transaction processing objective of the payroll

Time Worked in 1998
By Department

Greenwood Lumber Company
for interal use only

	Regular Hours	Overtime Hours
Accounting	8,836	24
Administration	5,852	8
Inside Sales - Commercial	10,936	33
Inside Sales - Retail	17,132	14
Maintenance	5,269	88
Materials Handling	11,043	110
Outside Sales - Commercial	8,869	32
Outside Sales - Retail	4,117	11
Purchasing	6,717	1

Figure 9.13 The Time Worked report.

cycle is to calculate payroll and print paychecks. Queries are very useful tools for performing payroll calculations. Indeed, if a relational database manager lacked a query language, we could not use it to calculate payroll. Since payroll calculations can be very complex, we will show you how to build several queries that each accomplish a step in calculating payroll. Then we will explain how you can use these queries to build payroll register reports, employee earnings record reports, and payroll check reports. You can extend this step-by-step approach to more complex payroll systems as you encounter them in your future studies or in your practice of accounting.

Payroll Calculation Queries

Our first payroll calculation is simple, we must calculate regular pay. All we must do is multiply each employee's pay rate times the number of regular hours he or she worked in the pay period. Since we have pay rates in *tblEmployee* and regular hours by pay period in *tblTimeWorked*, we can run a query on these two tables to calculate regular pay. We can use the Greenwood Lumber Company sample data to build these queries. Greenwood's Employee table has 50 employee records and their Time Worked table includes a full year of monthly pay period time data. We will use the January 31, 1998 payroll period for the example calculations. To calculate gross pay, just follow the steps in Exercise 9.11.

Exercise 9.11: Calculating Gross Pay

1. In the Database window, click the Queries tab, then click the New button. Click Design View in the New Query dialog box, then click the OK button. The Query Builder window will open along with the Show Table dialog box.
2. Double-click *tblEmployee* and *tblTimeWorked* in the Show Table dialog box, then click the Close button.
3. Click and drag the EmployeeNumber field from *tblTimeWorked* to the first QBE Field cell. Set the Sort cell to Ascending.
4. Click and drag the TWPayPeriodEnded field from *tblTimeWorked* to the second QBE Field cell.

   To have the query obtain only the records for the year's first payroll period, we must set a criterion for the TWPayPeriodEnded field that is equal to the date that the first payroll period ended.
5. Enter ***=#1/31/98#*** in the second Criteria cell in the QBE grid.

   The # symbols tell Microsoft Access to read the enclosed characters as a date. To calculate the regular and overtime pay amounts, we can use the pay rate field from *tblEmployee* and the time fields from *tblTimeWorked*.
6. Click in the third QBE Field cell and press Shift+F2 to open the Zoom box. Enter ***RegularPay: [TWRegularTime] * [EmployeePayRate]*** in the Zoom box, then click OK.
7. Click in the fourth QBE Field cell, press Shift+F2, enter ***OvertimePay: [TWOvertime] * [EmployeePayRate] * 1.5*** in the Zoom box, and click OK. These two calculations will compute the amounts of regular pay and overtime pay.
8. To check your work at this point, click the Run toolbar button. The query should produce the dynaset shown in Figure 9.14.

   Verify that the pay calculations are correct before you continue. The new RegularPay field should be the result of multiplying the TWRegularTime field from *tblTimeWorked* by the EmployeePayRate field from *tblEmployee*. The new OvertimePay field should equal the TWOvertime field times the EmployeePayRate field times 1.5 (to pay the overtime rate of one and one-half times the regular rate). For example, employees 104, 105, and 106 had overtime hours in January. You can use a calculator to check the OvertimePay calculations for those three employees. When building complex queries in steps, you should always check results after each step.
9. To create the field that will calculate gross pay, return to the Query window by selecting View, Query Design from the menu.

Query1 : Select Query

Employee #	Month Ended	RegularPay	OvertimePay
101	1/31/98	4704	0
102	1/31/98	4704	0
103	1/31/98	1377.6	0
104	1/31/98	1579.2	56.4
105	1/31/98	2066.4	147.6
106	1/31/98	2587.2	254.1
107	1/31/98	3763.2	0
108	1/31/98	1306.4	0
109	1/31/98	652.5	0
110	1/31/98	2167.2	0
111	1/31/98	3024	189
112	1/31/98	1234.8	0
113	1/31/98	1558.2	0
114	1/31/98	1512	0
115	1/31/98	2788.8	74.7
116	1/31/98	4032	0
117	1/31/98	1489.2	0

Record: 1 of 50

Figure 9.14 The regular pay and overtime pay query calculation results.

10. Once you have defined a calculated field in a query, Microsoft Access lets you use that new field in further calculations. Click in the fifth QBE grid Field cell, press Shift+F2 to open the Zoom box, enter ***GrossPay: [RegularPay] + [OvertimePay]***, and click OK.
11. To test the query, click the Run toolbar button. The dynaset resulting from the revised query appears in Figure 9.15.

Query1 : Select Query

Employee #	Month Ended	RegularPay	OvertimePay	GrossPay
101	1/31/98	4704	0	4704
102	1/31/98	4704	0	4704
103	1/31/98	1377.6	0	1377.6
104	1/31/98	1579.2	56.4	1635.6
105	1/31/98	2066.4	147.6	2214
106	1/31/98	2587.2	254.1	2841.3
107	1/31/98	3763.2	0	3763.2
108	1/31/98	1306.4	0	1306.4
109	1/31/98	652.5	0	652.5
110	1/31/98	2167.2	0	2167.2
111	1/31/98	3024	189	3213
112	1/31/98	1234.8	0	1234.8
113	1/31/98	1558.2	0	1558.2
114	1/31/98	1512	0	1512
115	1/31/98	2788.8	74.7	2863.5
116	1/31/98	4032	0	4032
117	1/31/98	1489.2	0	1489.2

Record: 1 of 50

Figure 9.15 The gross pay calculation results.

Once again, check the GrossPay field calculations with a calculator before you continue. You can save your query as ***qryGrossPay***. The *Ch09.mdb* database on your Companion CD-ROM includes *qryGrossPay,* which you can examine if you have trouble getting your query to work properly.

Of course, calculating gross pay is only the first half of the payroll calculation battle. The rest of the challenge is to calculate the deductions from gross pay that determine net pay. Our next step will be to revise *qryGrossPay* so that it calculates deductions and net pay. Payroll deductions include taxes, insurance, profit-sharing contributions, and many other items. The rules for calculating each of these deductions generally fall into one of three categories:

- *Fixed Amount Deductions*. These deductions are easy to calculate because they are a fixed amount each pay period. Examples of these include deductions for health insurance premiums, group life insurance premiums, and employee-approved donations to charitable organizations such as the United Way.
- *Fixed Percentage Deductions*. These deductions are a fixed percentage of gross income each pay period. Examples of these include deductions for employer-withheld city and county earnings taxes in many parts of the U.S. Some state income taxes are also calculated as a fixed percentage of all earned income.
- *Varying Percentage Deductions*. These deductions are similar to the fixed percentage deduction except that the percentage changes with variables such as level of income, marital status, and number of exemptions claimed. The U.S. federal income tax that employers must withhold is the best example of this type of tax. Many states have income tax withholding rules that are similar to the federal rules and, therefore, fall into this category.
- *Fixed Percentage Deductions Subject to a Ceiling*. These deductions are a fixed percentage of gross income each pay period until a ceiling amount is reached. The most common example of this deduction type are the deductions under the U.S. Federal Insurance Contributions Act (FICA), commonly called the social security tax. Employers deduct a fixed percentage of gross pay only until the FICA limit for the year is reached. Some states, such as California, require employee contributions to unemployment insurance funds that are calculated this way, too.

The first type of deduction, a fixed amount each pay period, is easy to model. We only need to add one Employee table field, a binary indicator of whether the employee was subject to the deduction, to trigger the calculation. The second type, a fixed percentage, is even easier. We simply build the fixed percentage into the payroll calculation query. The third type is fairly difficult to implement because it requires additional tables. The fourth type is even more difficult because it requires an additional table to store year-to-date amounts and a query that accesses that table.

Our example includes deductions for the second and third types. The fixed percentage calculation in our example is the social security, or FICA, tax. FICA tax is actually the fourth type of deduction, since it is a fixed rate up to a maximum pay amount per year. However, we have designed the Greenwood Lumber Company sample data so that none of the employees exceed the maximum.

Therefore, we can model the FICA tax for the Greenwood Lumber Company as a fixed percentage deduction. The deduction for employees' federal income tax, often called federal withholding tax (FWT), shows some of the intricacies of modeling the third type of deduction.

Please note that the tax deduction calculations we model in this chapter are not intended to be complete or accurate. Employer tax laws change constantly and vary by state. Our purpose here is to give you some practice building tables and queries that you can adapt to specific client or user needs—and to the ever-changing requirements of government regulators.

Before we create the query that will calculate net pay, we will build two tables that contain tax rates and exemption amounts. We could include these rates and amounts in the Net Pay query, but placing them in separate tables makes updating and modifying the rates and amounts much easier. And remember, tax laws change more frequently than software versions!

Exercise 9.12: Building the Marital Status Table

1. Click the Tables tab in the Database Window, then click the New button. Double-click Design View in the New Table dialog box.
2. Enter ***MSMaritalStatus*** in the first row of the Field Name column and leave the Data Type set to Text.
3. Click the Primary Key toolbar button.
4. Set the Field Size property to ***1***, the Input Mask property to *>L*, and the Caption property to ***Marital Status***
5. Set the Validation Rule property to ***="M" Or "S"***
6. Set the Validation Text property to ***Please enter an M for Married or an S for Single.***
7. Enter ***MSFWTRate*** in the second row of the Field Name column.
8. Set the Data Type to Number and the Caption property to ***FWT Rate***. Set the Field Size property to ***Single***
9. Save the Marital Status table by selecting the File, Save As/Export menu command. Enter ***tblMaritalStatus*** as the New Name in the Save As dialog box.

   The table shown in Figure 9.16 is included as *tblMaritalStatus* in the *Ch09.mdb* database on your Companion CD-ROM.
10. Click the Datasheet toolbar button to change the Marital Status table to Datasheet view to enter the two tax rates shown in Figure 9.16. After you enter the tax rates, close the table and return to the Database window by pressing Ctrl+W.

The Marital Status table stores the percentages that we will use in calculating federal withholding tax for the Greenwood Lumber Company. The next exercise

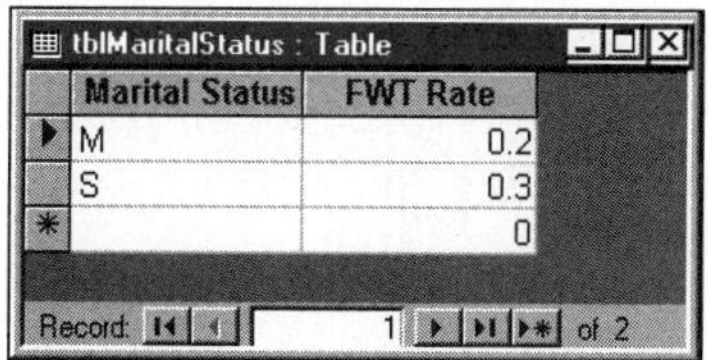

Marital Status	FWT Rate
M	0.2
S	0.3
*	0

Figure 9.16 The record values in *tblMaritalStatus.*

shows you how to build a second table that will store the exemption values for the deduction calculation. The exemption values are dollar amounts that the tax withholding calculation will deduct from gross pay before applying the percentages in *tblMaritalStatus*.

EXERCISE 9.13: BUILDING THE EXEMPTION TABLE

1. Click the Tables tab in the Database Window, then click the New button. Double-click Design View in the New Table dialog box.
2. Enter ***ExemptionNumber*** in the first row of the Field Name column and set its Data Type to Number.
3. Click the Primary Key toolbar button.
4. Set the ExemptionNumber's Field Size property to Byte, its Decimal Places property to ***0***, its Input Mask property to ***99***, and its Caption property to ***Number of Exemptions***
5. Enter ***ExemptionAmount*** in the second row of the Field Name column.
6. Set its Data Type set to Number, its Decimal Places property to ***0***, and its Caption property to ***Exemption Amount***
7. Select the File, Save As/Export menu command to save the new table. Type ***tblExemption*** as the New Name in the Save As dialog box. The table shown in Figure 9.17 is included as *tblExemption* in the *Ch09.mdb* database on your Companion CD-ROM.

You can click the Datasheet toolbar button to open the Exemption table in Datasheet view. Then you can enter the field values shown in Figure 9.17. The simplified tax system we assume for our example allows $200 per monthly pay period for each of the first five exemptions and $100 for each of the next five. Exemptions exceeding 10 do not have an additional allowance. After you enter the exemption values, close the table and return to the Database window by pressing Ctrl+W.

Next, we will show you how to create a Net Pay query that will calculate the two sample deductions, FICA and FWT, and net pay. The computation rules for the two simplified deductions are as follows:

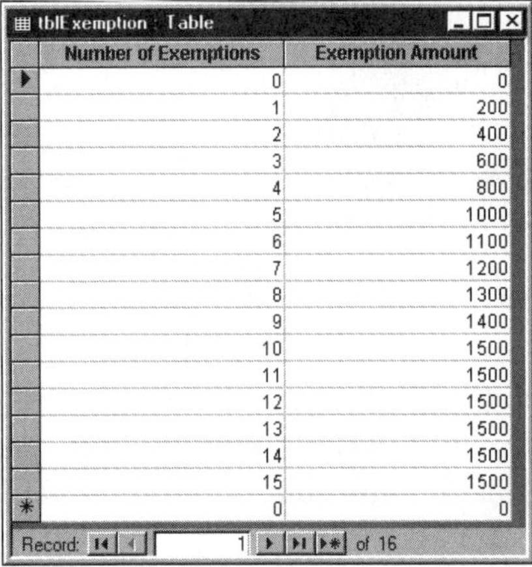

tblExemption : Table

Number of Exemptions	Exemption Amount
0	0
1	200
2	400
3	600
4	800
5	1000
6	1100
7	1200
8	1300
9	1400
10	1500
11	1500
12	1500
13	1500
14	1500
15	1500
0	0

Record: 1 of 16

Figure 9.17 The record values in *tblExemption*.

- *FICA*: A rate of 7% calculated on gross pay.
- *FWT*: A rate of 20% if married, 30% if single; calculated on gross pay less allowable exemptions.

The Net Pay query must link four tables: Employee, Time Worked, Exemption, and Marital Status. An easy way to create this Net Pay query is to modify the Gross Pay query we built in Exercise 9.11. In the next exercise, we show you how to design a Net Pay query that calculates the two deductions and net pay for Greenwood Lumber's December pay period.

Exercise 9.14: Calculating Net Pay

1. In the Database window, click the Queries tab, click *qryGrossPay* to select it, then click the Design button.
2. Click the Show Table toolbar button, double-click *tblExemption* and *tblMaritalStatus* to add them to the Query Builder window, then click the Close button in the Show Table dialog box.

   Note that the two tables we just added to the Query window are not linked to either *tblEmployee* or *tblTimeWorked*. To perform the inner joins required by the payroll deduction calculations, we must create links to *tblEmployee*.
3. Click and drag the MSMaritalStatus field from *tblMaritalStatus* to the EmployeeMaritalStatus field in *tblEmployee*.
4. Click and drag the ExemptionNumber field from *tblExemption* to the EmployeeExemptions field in *tblEmployee*.
5. Change the TWPayPeriodEnded Criteria cell contents to ***#12/31/98#***

Since you have modified the Gross Pay query, you should save it using the File, Save As/Export menu command. Give the new query a name of ***qryNetPay***. The query appears at this stage in Figure 9.18. Note that we have temporarily hidden the Query Design toolbar to display more of the table icons in the top pane of the Query Builder window.

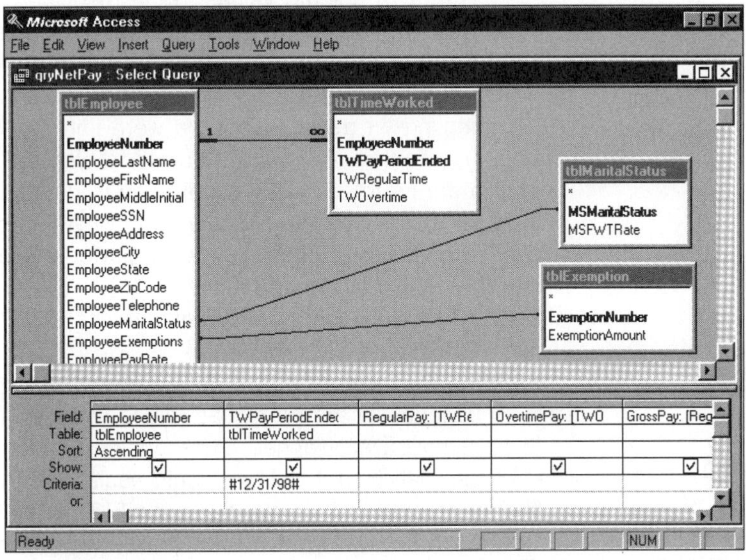

Figure 9.18 Adding tables and links to *qryNetPay*.

Try it

When you are modifying an existing query, form, report, or table that you want to keep, it is always a good idea to save the modified object under a new name immediately after making changes to it. Otherwise, you risk accidentally overwriting the existing object with the modified object.

6. Enter ***FICA: [GrossPay] * 0.07*** in the next open Field cell in the QBE grid.
7. Click the Run toolbar button to test the query.

   Notice that some of the calculated values for FICA have more than two decimal places. Rounding errors can create many hours of extra work in accounting systems, and payroll calculations are perhaps the most infamous source of rounding errors in accounting systems. To eliminate rounding errors at the calculation point, accounting system designers have developed a number of tricks. You can use one of these tricks to make sure FICA values are stored with two decimal places. The trick is to multiply the result by 100, use an integer function to round the value, then divide the rounded value by 100. You can incorporate this procedure in the FICA calculation with the next step.

8. Revise the FICA calculation so that it reads ***FICA: Int([GrossPay] * 0.07 * 100) / 100***
9. Run the query to test the revised expression.

   The FICA column values in the resulting dynaset should now have no more than two decimal places. We could have revised the expression to read: *FICA: Int([GrossPay] * 7)* and it would have worked just as well. However, the expression we did use has the advantage of being self-documenting—it reveals what we were thinking when we wrote the expression. This can be important if someone else may need to revise the expression in the future—a likely occurrence in payroll systems! Our next task is to build an expression that calculates the FWT deduction. The FWT deduction is each employee's gross pay less allowable exemptions multiplied by the tax rate for his or her marital status.
10. Enter ***FWT: ([GrossPay] - [ExemptionAmount]) * [MSFWTRate]*** in the next open QBE grid Field cell.
11. Click the Run toolbar button to test the query.

    Because of the particular values we used for our example tax rates and exemption allowances, the rounding problem does not appear in the FWT calculation. If it did, we could easily use the Int() function trick in this expression just as we did in the FICA calculation. The final step in the Net Pay query is, logically enough, the calculation of net pay. In our example, net pay is the remainder after subtracting FICA and FWT from gross pay.
12. Enter ***NetPay: [GrossPay] - [FICA] - [FWT]*** in the next open QBE grid Field cell.
13. Click the Run toolbar button to test the query.

    Again, you should use a calculator to check a few of the individual employee's net pay calculations. The Net Pay query's resulting dynaset appears in Figure 9.19. Once again, we have removed the toolbar to display more of the screen contents.

You can save your query as ***qryNetPay***. The *Ch09.mdb* database on your Companion CD-ROM includes *qryNetPay*. You can examine this query if you have trouble getting yours to work. Both *qryNetPay* and *qryGrossPay* include complex expressions that are easy to enter incorrectly. You can copy and paste expressions from the example queries to your queries if you wish.

This section demonstrated how to calculate gross pay, deductions, and net pay using Microsoft Access queries. You can use these queries to create useful payroll cycle reports and accounting entries.

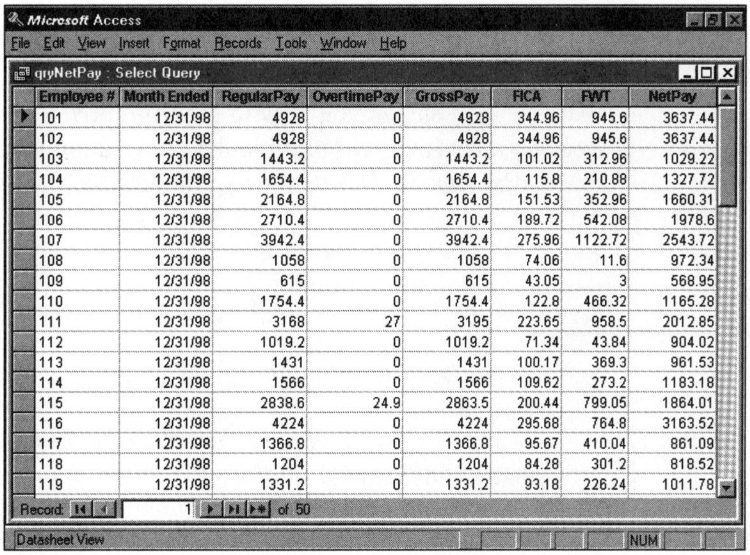

Microsoft Access

File Edit View Insert Format Records Tools Window Help

qryNetPay : Select Query

Employee #	Month Ended	RegularPay	OvertimePay	GrossPay	FICA	FWT	NetPay
101	12/31/98	4928	0	4928	344.96	945.6	3637.44
102	12/31/98	4928	0	4928	344.96	945.6	3637.44
103	12/31/98	1443.2	0	1443.2	101.02	312.96	1029.22
104	12/31/98	1654.4	0	1654.4	115.8	210.88	1327.72
105	12/31/98	2164.8	0	2164.8	151.53	352.96	1660.31
106	12/31/98	2710.4	0	2710.4	189.72	542.08	1978.6
107	12/31/98	3942.4	0	3942.4	275.96	1122.72	2543.72
108	12/31/98	1058	0	1058	74.06	11.6	972.34
109	12/31/98	615	0	615	43.05	3	568.95
110	12/31/98	1754.4	0	1754.4	122.8	466.32	1165.28
111	12/31/98	3168	27	3195	223.65	958.5	2012.85
112	12/31/98	1019.2	0	1019.2	71.34	43.84	904.02
113	12/31/98	1431	0	1431	100.17	369.3	961.53
114	12/31/98	1566	0	1566	109.62	273.2	1183.18
115	12/31/98	2838.6	24.9	2863.5	200.44	799.05	1864.01
116	12/31/98	4224	0	4224	295.68	764.8	3163.52
117	12/31/98	1366.8	0	1366.8	95.67	410.04	861.09
118	12/31/98	1204	0	1204	84.28	301.2	818.52
119	12/31/98	1331.2	0	1331.2	93.18	226.24	1011.78

Record: 1 of 50

Datasheet View NUM

Figure 9.19 The dynaset result of *qryNetPay*.

The Payroll Register

The payroll register is a columnar report that lists each employee's gross pay, deductions, and net pay for a particular pay period. Firms use payroll registers to reconcile paycheck totals to net pay and to support the period's payroll journal entries. Firms can also use information in the payroll register to calculate payroll taxes. We can build a Payroll Register report using the payroll calculation queries and tables that we have created.

We can base the Payroll Register report on a query that does the calculations since Microsoft Access does not support the summing of calculated fields in reports. We can modify *qryNetPay* to build a Payroll Register query that will extract some of the fields we need from tables and calculate the other fields we need. The fields we wish to include in the Greenwood Lumber Company's payroll register are as follows:

- Employee number
- Employee name
- Regular pay
- Overtime pay
- Gross pay
- FWT deduction
- FICA deduction

- Net pay
- Payroll period

Exercise 9.15 shows you how to modify *qryNetPay* and use it to build a Payroll Register query that will provide the information we need for the Payroll Register report. Exercise 9.16 then shows you how to build a report based on this query.

EXERCISE 9.15: BUILDING A PAYROLL REGISTER QUERY

1. Click the Queries tab in the Database window, click *qryNetPay*, then click the Design button.
   The Net Pay query includes all of the fields we need for the Payroll Register report except employee name. Since we stored the employees' names in three separate fields, we can combine them in different orders to suit different purposes. In this report, we would like the names to appear in a last-name-first order.
2. Click in the next open QBE Field, press Shift+F2 to open the Zoom box, then enter ***Name: [EmployeeLastName] & ", " & [EmployeeFirstName] & " " & [EmployeeMiddleInitial] & ". "***
3. Run the query to test the new field calculation.
4. When you are satisfied that your Payroll Register query operates properly, select File, Save As/Export, enter ***qryPayrollRegister*** as the query's New Name, and click the OK button.
5. Close the query by pressing Ctrl+W.

The *Ch09.mdb* database on your Companion CD-ROM includes a Payroll Register query, *qryPayrollRegister*, for your reference. The next exercise shows you how to build a Payroll Register report using this Payroll Register query.

EXERCISE 9.16: BUILDING A PAYROLL REGISTER REPORT

1. In the Database window, click the Reports tab, and then click the New button.
2. Enter ***qryPayrollRegister*** in the combo box control in the New Report dialog box, then double-click *qryPayrollRegister* in the list box control.
3. Use the Format, Page Header/Footer and the Format, Report Header/Footer menu toggles to include a Report Header and Footer instead of the Page Header or Footer on the blank report.
4. Click and drag the right edge of the report to the 6.5 inch mark on the top ruler.

5. Click the Field List toolbar button, then click and drag the following fields to the Detail section: EmployeeNumber, Name, RegularPay, OvertimePay, GrossPay, FICA, FWT, and NetPay. Each field will become a text box control with an attached label control in the Detail section of the report.
6. Click and drag the TWPayPeriodEnded field to the Report Header section of the report.
7. Draw a selection rectangle around the label controls that remain in the Detail section and press the Delete key.
8. Open the toolbox and use the Text Box tool to create a control in the Report Footer section. Open the new control's property sheet by clicking the Properties toolbar button and change its Control Source property to ***=Sum([RegularPay])***
9. Create similar total controls for the other five calculated fields in the report.
10. Use Figures 9.20 and 9.21 as guides in adding and arranging labels, line objects, and controls on the report.
11. To save your Payroll Register report, select the File, Save As/Export menu command and enter a New Name of ***rptPayrollRegister*** in the Save As dialog box. You can close the report by pressing Ctrl+W.

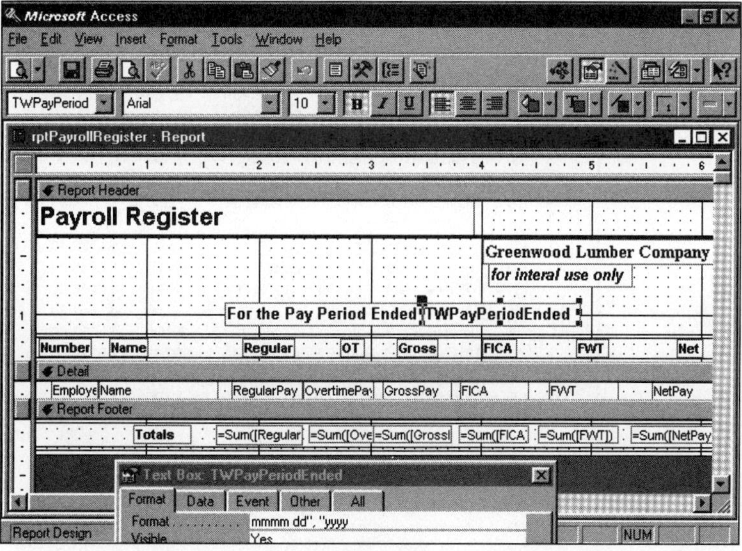

Figure 9.20 The Payroll Register report in Report Design view.

Figure 9.20 shows the Payroll Register report in Report Design view. Unfortunately, Microsoft Access does not permit us to adjust the size or spacing of report objects while in Print Preview. Therefore, as you refine the design of the Payroll Register report, you will find it helpful to toggle between Print Preview and

Payroll Register

Greenwood Lumber Company
for interal use only

For the Pay Period Ended December 31, 1998

Number	Name	Regular	OT	Gross	FICA	FWT	Net
101	Greenwood, Artemis	$4,928.00	$0.00	$4,928.00	$344.96	$945.60	$3,637.44
102	Greenwood, Ethel Z.	$4,928.00	$0.00	$4,928.00	$344.96	$945.60	$3,637.44
103	Baron, Ethel P.	$1,443.20	$0.00	$1,443.20	$101.02	$312.96	$1,029.22
104	Oppenheim, Cecelia	$1,654.40	$0.00	$1,654.40	$115.80	$210.88	$1,327.72
105	Washington, Ronald	$2,164.80	$0.00	$2,164.80	$151.53	$352.96	$1,660.31
106	Wheeler, Henry X.	$2,710.40	$0.00	$2,710.40	$189.72	$542.08	$1,978.60
107	Surkamp, Elizabeth	$3,942.40	$0.00	$3,942.40	$275.96	$1,122.72	$2,543.72
108	Diamond, Timothy Y	$1,058.00	$0.00	$1,058.00	$74.06	$11.60	$972.34
109	Roche, Max E.	$615.00	$0.00	$615.00	$43.05	$3.00	$568.95
110	Badillo, Lucille B.	$1,754.40	$0.00	$1,754.40	$122.80	$466.32	$1,165.28
111	Ballenger, Judith F.	$3,168.00	$27.00	$3,195.00	$223.65	$958.50	$2,012.85
112	Dewar, Melanie C.	$1,019.20	$0.00	$1,019.20	$71.34	$43.84	$904.02
113	Brown, Alicia K.	$1,431.00	$0.00	$1,431.00	$100.17	$369.30	$961.53
114	Klusky, Irene R.	$1,566.00	$0.00	$1,566.00	$109.62	$273.20	$1,183.18
115	Tufts, Esther L.	$2,838.60	$24.90	$2,863.50	$200.44	$799.05	$1,864.01
116	Thurgood, Margaret	$4,224.00	$0.00	$4,224.00	$295.68	$764.80	$3,163.52
117	Boldway, Michael B.	$1,366.80	$0.00	$1,366.80	$95.67	$410.04	$861.09
118	Fenster, Janice S.	$1,204.00	$0.00	$1,204.00	$84.28	$301.20	$818.52
119	Sherwood, Natalie R	$1,331.20	$0.00	$1,331.20	$93.18	$226.24	$1,011.78
120	Simon, Arlene P.	$3,150.40	$0.00	$3,150.40	$220.52	$945.12	$1,984.76
121	Morris, Anne F.	$850.00	$0.00	$850.00	$59.50	$195.00	$595.50
122	Clark, Carol C.	$1,115.20	$0.00	$1,115.20	$78.06	$63.04	$974.10
123	Smith, Dierdre R.	$3,784.00	$0.00	$3,784.00	$264.88	$676.80	$2,842.32
124	Young, Louise K.	$2,499.20	$0.00	$2,499.20	$174.94	$459.84	$1,864.42
125	Studd, Chester V.	$622.20	$0.00	$622.20	$43.55	$126.66	$451.99
126	Ward, Colleen H.	$2,147.20	$18.30	$2,165.50	$151.58	$649.65	$1,364.27
127	Johnson, Travis D.	$3,168.00	$0.00	$3,168.00	$221.76	$890.40	$2,055.84
128	Gonzales, David G.	$666.00	$0.00	$666.00	$46.62	$19.80	$599.58
129	Quinn, Charles H.	$1,307.20	$0.00	$1,307.20	$91.50	$41.44	$1,174.26
130	Flores, Hector L.	$2,868.80	$0.00	$2,868.80	$200.81	$740.64	$1,927.35
131	Pelligrini, Antonio N.	$2,024.00	$0.00	$2,024.00	$141.68	$324.80	$1,557.52
132	Foster, James R.	$2,622.40	$0.00	$2,622.40	$183.56	$726.72	$1,712.12
133	Schwartz, Harold T.	$4,048.00	$0.00	$4,048.00	$283.36	$1,214.40	$2,550.24
134	Jeffries, Mark T.	$1,276.80	$0.00	$1,276.80	$89.37	$323.04	$864.39
135	Andrej, Arthur R.	$2,851.20	$0.00	$2,851.20	$199.58	$795.36	$1,856.26
136	Klippenger, Steven	$1,584.00	$0.00	$1,584.00	$110.88	$316.80	$1,156.32
137	Beeler, Sheldon O.	$1,734.60	$0.00	$1,734.60	$121.42	$460.38	$1,152.80
138	Patel, Shantu L.	$2,481.60	$0.00	$2,481.60	$173.71	$684.48	$1,623.41
139	Perciavalle, Edward	$2,851.20	$0.00	$2,851.20	$199.58	$330.24	$2,321.38
140	Faumuina, Celestine	$2,205.00	$0.00	$2,205.00	$154.35	$601.50	$1,449.15
141	Ochoa, Raul V.	$4,576.00	$0.00	$4,576.00	$320.32	$1,312.80	$2,942.88
142	Smothers, Karl S.	$3,168.00	$0.00	$3,168.00	$221.76	$950.40	$1,995.84
143	White, Byron D.	$1,601.60	$0.00	$1,601.60	$112.11	$240.32	$1,249.17
144	Chalfonte, Yves M.	$1,708.00	$0.00	$1,708.00	$119.56	$452.40	$1,136.04
145	Applegate, Victor N.	$3,819.20	$0.00	$3,819.20	$267.34	$1,145.76	$2,406.10
146	Blum, Joel B.	$1,161.60	$0.00	$1,161.60	$81.31	$288.48	$791.81
147	Landers, Myra T.	$1,020.80	$0.00	$1,020.80	$71.45	$124.16	$825.19
148	Schumacher, Dirk S.	$974.40	$0.00	$974.40	$68.20	$232.32	$673.88
149	Forrest, Donald T.	$897.60	$0.00	$897.60	$62.83	$139.52	$695.25
150	Ruvido, Gina C.	$684.40	$0.00	$684.40	$47.90	$85.32	$551.18
	Totals	$108,816.00	$70.20	$108,886.20	$7,621.88	$24,617.48	$76,646.84

Figure 9.21 The Payroll Register report printout.

Report Design view using the toolbar button or the View menu commands to move between the two views. Of course, the Payroll Register report we have designed here is only one way to design the report. You can easily customize this report to meet the needs of specific users. The Payroll Register report shown in Figures 9.20 and 9.21 is included in the *Ch09.mdb* database on your Companion CD-ROM as *rptPayrollRegister*.

The Employee Earnings Report

A payroll register report lists *all* employees' earnings for *one* pay period. An employee earnings report lists *one* employee's earnings for *all* pay periods in a year. An employee earnings report provides information for unemployment tax calculations and the year-end W-2 form. We will show you how to build an Employee Earnings report for Esther Tufts, who is employee #115 in the Greenwood Lumber Company sample data. You can extend this example to generate similar reports for other selected employees, for groups of employees, or even for all employees. One way to build the Employee Earnings report is to modify the Payroll Register query and create the Employee Earnings report based on the new query. We will show you how to do this in the next exercise.

Exercise 9.17: Modifying *qryPayrollRegister* to Create *qryEmployeeEarnings*

1. In the Database window, click *qryPayrollRegister* to select it, then click the Design button.
2. To avoid accidentally overwriting your Payroll Register query with the modifications you make here, save the query now under its new name. Select the File, Save As/Export menu command and enter ***qryEmployeeEarnings*** as the New Name, then click the OK button.
3. Enter ***115*** in the first QBE grid Criteria cell to select only the payroll information for that EmployeeNumber record. Microsoft Access automatically encloses the text (remember, this field has a Text Data Type) in quotation marks when you leave the cell.
4. Delete the *#12/30/98#* entry in the second QBE grid Criteria cell that includes only the last pay period since we want all of the pay periods included in the Employee Earnings report.
5. Enter ***Ascending*** in the second QBE grid Sort cell to sort the resulting query dynaset by TWPayPeriodEnded.
6. Press Ctrl+S to save your changes to the query.

The modified query appears in Figure 9.22. This query will perform the same calculations as the Payroll Register query. The difference is that the Employee

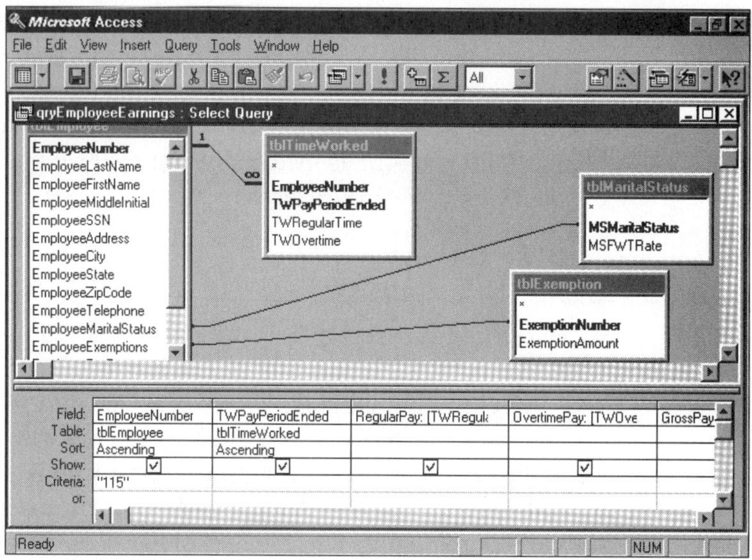

Figure 9.22 Modifying *qryPayrollRegister* to create *qryEmployeeEarnings.*

Earnings query will perform the calculations for *all* of the year's pay periods for *one* employee. The dynaset that results from running the Employee Earnings query appears in Figure 9.23. The *Ch09.mdb* database included on your Companion CD-ROM includes a query named *qryEmployeeEarnings* that you can use as an example to check your work in the preceding exercise. You can close *qryEmployeeEarnings* by pressing Ctrl+W.

qryEmployeeEarnings : Select Query

Employee #	Month Ended	RegularPay	OvertimePay	GrossPay	FICA	FWT	NetPay	Name
115	1/31/98	2788.8	74.7	2863.5	200.44	799.05	1864.01	Tufts, Esther L.
115	2/28/98	2622.8	0	2622.8	183.59	726.84	1712.37	Tufts, Esther L.
115	3/31/98	3054.4	99.6	3154	220.78	886.2	2047.02	Tufts, Esther L.
115	4/30/98	2788.8	74.7	2863.5	200.44	799.05	1864.01	Tufts, Esther L.
115	5/31/98	2921.6	24.9	2946.5	206.25	823.95	1916.3	Tufts, Esther L.
115	6/30/98	2788.8	74.7	2863.5	200.44	799.05	1864.01	Tufts, Esther L.
115	7/31/98	2788.8	74.7	2863.5	200.44	799.05	1864.01	Tufts, Esther L.
115	8/31/98	3054.4	49.8	3104.2	217.29	871.26	2015.65	Tufts, Esther L.
115	9/30/98	2921.6	49.8	2971.4	207.99	831.42	1931.99	Tufts, Esther L.
115	10/31/98	2788.8	124.5	2913.3	203.93	813.99	1895.38	Tufts, Esther L.
115	11/30/98	2838.6	24.9	2863.5	200.44	799.05	1864.01	Tufts, Esther L.
115	12/31/98	2838.6	24.9	2863.5	200.44	799.05	1864.01	Tufts, Esther L.

Record: 1 of 12

Figure 9.23 The dynaset results of running *qryEmployeeEarnings.*

Now we can show you how to build an Employee Earnings report based on *qryEmployeeEarnings.* The report that we describe in Exercise 9.18 includes a particularly interesting design feature. It uses the Group On property to generate quarterly subtotals.

EXERCISE 9.18: BUILDING *RPTEMPLOYEEEARNINGS* BASED ON *QRYEMPLOYEEEARNINGS*

1. In the Database window, click the Reports tab, and then click the New button.
2. Enter or select *qryEmployeeEarnings* in the combo box control in the New Report dialog box, then double-click Design View in the list box control.
3. Use the Format, Page Header/Footer menu command to delete the Page Header and Footer, then use the Format, Report Header/Footer menu command to add a Report Header and Footer.
4. Click and drag the right edge of the report's background out to the 6.5 inch mark on the top ruler.
5. Click the Sorting and Grouping toolbar button and enter *TWPayPeriod* as the first Field; the Sort Order will set itself to Ascending. Set both the Group Header and Group Footer properties to Yes and set the Group On property to Qtr.
6. In the second row of the Field/Expression column, enter *TWPayPeriod* again. Press Alt+F4 to close the Sorting and Grouping dialog box.
7. Click the Field List toolbar button, then click and drag the following fields to the Detail section: TWPayPeriodEnded, RegularPay, OvertimePay, GrossPay, FICA, FWT, and NetPay. When you release the mouse button, each field will become a text box control with an accompanying label control in the Detail section of the report.
8. Click and drag the EmployeeNumber and Name fields to the Report Header section of the report.
9. Click and drag a marquee around the control labels remaining in the Detail section and press the Delete key.
10. Open the toolbox and use the Text Box tool to add a new control in the Report Footer section.
11. With the new control still selected, click the Properties toolbar button to select the new control's property sheet and change its Control Source property to *=Sum([RegularPay])*
12. Create text box controls with similar =Sum() expressions for the other five calculated fields in the report.
13. Copy and paste the six total-calculating controls from the Report Footer to the TWPayPeriodEnded Footer. When these controls are placed in the group footer, they will compute quarterly subtotals.

    Figure 9.24 shows the Employee Earnings report in Report Design view. You can use Figures 9.24 and 9.25 as layout guides as you add the line objects to the report and arrange the controls on the report.
14. To save the Employee Earnings report, select the File, Save As/Export menu command and enter a New Name of *rptEmployeeEarnings* in the Save As dialog box. You can close the report by pressing Ctrl+W.

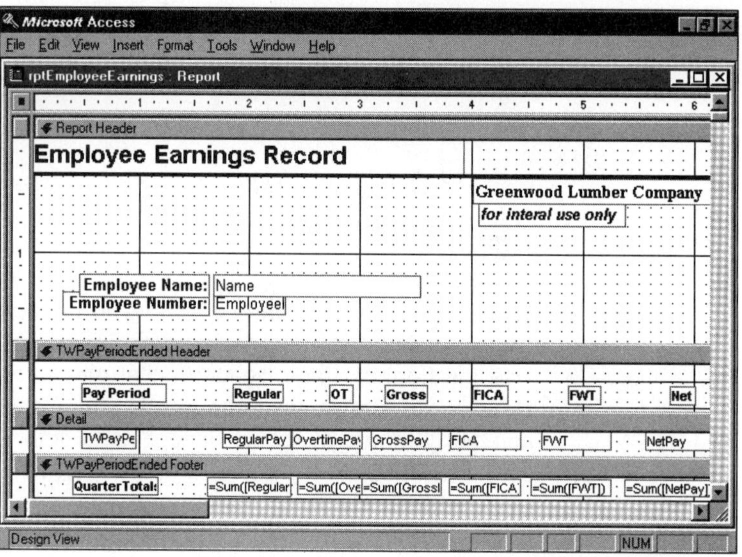

Figure 9.24 The *rptEmployeeEarnings* in Report Design view.

The Employee Earnings report that appears in Figure 9.24 is included in the *Ch09.mdb* database on your Companion CD-ROM as *rptEmployeeEarnings.* Figure 9.25 shows the Employee Earnings record that *rptEmployeeEarnings* generates for Greenwood Lumber employee Esther Tufts.

Printing Payroll Checks

The last payroll cycle report we will discuss is the payroll check itself. The payroll check should always include an earnings statement or pay stub that shows how the check was calculated. Payroll registers report payroll details for all employees for one pay period. Employee earnings records show one employee's payroll record for the year. The payroll check is one record from each of these reports.

We can use the same queries we built for the Payroll Register report and the Employee Earnings report to generate payroll checks. For example, we can add employee address fields to the information we already have in the Payroll Register query and build a report based on the query that includes page breaks between each employee record. Such a report would print all of the information we would need to include on a paycheck. The exact form of payroll checks and earnings statements will vary from firm to firm. Since we have already illustrated many report design techniques in this chapter, you are well-equipped to create your own paycheck reports for users or clients.

Employee Earnings Record

Greenwood Lumber Company
for internal use only

Employee Name: Tufts, Esther L.
Employee Number: 115

Pay Period	Regular	OT	Gross	FICA	FWT	Net
1/31/98	$2,788.80	$74.70	$2,863.50	$200.44	$799.05	$1,864.01
2/28/98	$2,622.80	$0.00	$2,622.80	$183.59	$726.84	$1,712.37
3/31/98	$3,054.40	$99.60	$3,154.00	$220.78	$886.20	$2,047.02
QuarterTotals	$8,466.00	$174.30	$8,640.30	$604.81	$2,412.09	$5,623.40

Pay Period	Regular	OT	Gross	FICA	FWT	Net
4/30/98	$2,788.80	$74.70	$2,863.50	$200.44	$799.05	$1,864.01
5/31/98	$2,921.60	$24.90	$2,946.50	$206.25	$823.95	$1,916.30
6/30/98	$2,788.80	$74.70	$2,863.50	$200.44	$799.05	$1,864.01
QuarterTotals	$8,499.20	$174.30	$8,673.50	$607.13	$2,422.05	$5,644.32

Pay Period	Regular	OT	Gross	FICA	FWT	Net
7/31/98	$2,788.80	$74.70	$2,863.50	$200.44	$799.05	$1,864.01
8/31/98	$3,054.40	$49.80	$3,104.20	$217.29	$871.26	$2,015.65
9/30/98	$2,921.60	$49.80	$2,971.40	$207.99	$831.42	$1,931.99
QuarterTotals	$8,764.80	$174.30	$8,939.10	$625.72	$2,501.73	$5,811.65

Pay Period	Regular	OT	Gross	FICA	FWT	Net
10/31/98	$2,788.80	$124.50	$2,913.30	$203.93	$813.99	$1,895.38
11/30/98	$2,838.60	$24.90	$2,863.50	$200.44	$799.05	$1,864.01
12/31/98	$2,838.60	$24.90	$2,863.50	$200.44	$799.05	$1,864.01
QuarterTotals	$8,466.00	$174.30	$8,640.30	$604.81	$2,412.09	$5,623.40

Year Totals	$34,196.00	$697.20	$34,893.20	$2,442.47	$9,747.96	$22,702.77

Figure 9.25 The *rptEmployeeEarnings* printout.

PAYROLL CYCLE INFORMATION ON THE FINANCIAL STATEMENTS

In this chapter, we have described how to use payroll cycle data to create data tables, track employee and time worked information, calculate payroll, and print a number of useful reports. This section discusses how payroll cycle information appears on firms' financial statements.

Accountants have always tracked the information needed to prepare financial statements and tax returns. Our database approach to developing payroll cycle accounting system elements provides a variety of information that managers can use to make better decisions. However, the database approach also provides everything that accountants need to calculate payroll cycle debits and credits.

Payroll Expense, Accruals, and Payables

The general ledger debit to Payroll Expense is the gross payroll total at the bottom of each payroll period's payroll register. The general ledger credit to Cash is included in the same report. By referring to Figure 9.21, the Payroll Register report for Greenwood Lumber Company, we can prepare the December 31, 1998 journal entry from the report totals:

Date	Account	Debit	Credit
Dec. 31, 1998	Payroll Expense	108,816.00	
	FWT Payable		24,617.48
	FICA Payable		7,621.88
	Cash		76,646.84

Since Greenwood Lumber pays on the last day of each month, our example firm conveniently avoids accruing payroll expenses. However, we could calculate accrued payroll using the same information we used to calculate payroll in this chapter. For example, if *tblTimeWorked* had included uncompensated time at the end of a reporting period, we could have run *rptPayrollRegister* to obtain the debits and credits for the accrual entry. This entry would be the same as the journal entry to record payroll expense except that the last credit in the entry would be to Accrued Payroll Expense or to Payroll Expense Payable instead of to Cash.

Payroll Tax Expense, Accruals, and Payables

Payroll tax calculations all use the current period payroll information included in the payroll register. Many payroll taxes require cumulative information, since the tax is payable only on earnings up to a fixed amount per employee each year. State and federal unemployment taxes are good examples of this type of payroll tax.

SUMMARY

In this chapter, we have described how to use payroll cycle data to track employee and time worked information, calculate payroll, and print employee information reports, time reports, payroll registers, and employee earnings reports. Many of these reports required you to construct queries and use the queries to build reports.

The payroll cycle begins with employee records and time worked records. Periodically, the firm pays employees and calculates payroll. Payroll calculation can be complex; employers must not only multiply pay rate times hours worked, but must comply with state and federal withholding regulations. Many firms also arrange to deduct charges for insurance and profit-sharing contributions from employees' pay. Employers must maintain payroll records to comply with numerous government regulations. Finally, accountants prepare financial statements and tax returns from the payroll cycle information.

REVIEW EXERCISES

MULTIPLE-CHOICE QUESTIONS

1. You can use queries in the payroll cycle to
   a. store time worked data.
   b. store employee pay rates.
   c. calculate payroll deductions.
   d. print an Employee Earnings report.
2. Payroll cycle activities include all of the following except
   a. recording office supplies expense.
   b. recording changes in employee pay rates.
   c. calculating overtime pay.
   d. keeping employee addresses current.
3. A good primary key for a time worked table in a firm that pays weekly would be the
   a. employee number.
   b. week.
   c. employee number *and* week.
   d. employee number *or* week.
4. A good way to make a data entry form that contains many fields easier to use would be to
   a. put the fields in alphabetical order.
   b. right-justify all of the fields.
   c. use a sharply contrasting background color.
   d. group related fields together on the form.

5. Setting the Validation Rule property that limits the minimum value that a user can enter in an employee pay rate field can help prevent
   a. violations of minimum wage laws.
   b. payment for regular hours at the overtime rate.
   c. payment for hours not actually worked.
   d. payroll tax fraud.
6. The EmployeeDepartment field in *tblEmployee* is a
   a. composite primary key.
   b. primary key.
   c. foreign key.
   d. relationship key.
7. A payroll register lists
   a. all wages paid to a single employee for the year.
   b. wages paid to all employees in a single pay period.
   c. all employees who received wages within the past year.
   d. accrued vacation time for all employees.
8. The Time Worked by Department report you built in this chapter could help managers
   a. identify employees that deserve raises.
   b. identify ineffective work scheduling.
   c. both a and b.
   d. neither a nor b.
9. We often design reports based on queries because in Microsoft Access
   a. a report cannot include field calculations.
   b. a query cannot include field calculations.
   c. a query cannot compute sums of fields.
   d. a report cannot sum calculated fields.
10. Setting a date field's Input Mask property to 99/99/00;1;_
    a. eases data entry by automatically inserting date separators.
    b. prevents entry of future dates in payroll records.
    c. prevents entry of non-existent dates such as 52/67/88.
    d. requires extra space in the data table to store the date separators.

DISCUSSION QUESTIONS

1. If you wanted to add employees to whom you pay a percentage commission to the payroll system described in the chapter, you would need to store the commission rate in a table. Discuss which table(s) you might use and why.
2. Describe how you could modify *tblTimeWorked* to include hourly time records. What would be candidates for the primary keys for the modified table?
3. Why are the purchase cycle and the payroll cycle often discussed separately?
4. How would you modify the Time Worked by Department report to make it more useful to Greenwood Lumber managers?

5. Discuss the advantages and disadvantages of storing employee names as three separate fields in *tblEmployee*.

EXERCISES

1. Write a query that independently verifies the gross pay calculation that *qryGrossPay* performs.
2. Create a report that uses tables from this chapter to print a payroll check and earnings statement for one employee.
3. Create any necessary tables and revise *qryNetPay* to include a deduction for medical insurance. Clearly state any assumptions you must make to accomplish this task.
4. Modify the payroll cycle system presented in this chapter to include employees that earn a fixed salary each pay period.
5. Modify the Payroll Register report so that it displays only the summary information that Greenwood Lumber Company needs to prepare its general ledger entry for payroll each month.

10 Production Cycle

Objectives

The production cycle includes all activities that convert raw materials, labor, and overhead into finished products. Therefore, some authors call this cycle the conversion cycle. The production cycle accounting system must trace or allocate manufacturing costs to products produced. The production cycle system must provide managers with information they can use to monitor the manufacturing process. It must also provide financial accountants with information they can use to value inventories and determine the cost of goods sold. This chapter will show you how to use Microsoft Access tables, queries, forms, and reports to:

- Track materials cost.
- Track labor cost.
- Allocate manufacturing overhead cost.
- Create a bill of materials.
- Accumulate costs in a job order cost system.
- Summarize and report job costs.

This chapter also explains how you can adapt the job order cost system examples presented here to build process, hybrid, and activity-based cost systems. Our discussion of the production cycle assumes that you have studied the purchase cycle in Chapter 8 and the payroll cycle in Chapter 9. We will show you how to modify some of the tables you created as you worked through those chapters. You can combine those modified tables with new tables, forms, queries, and reports to build the production cycle system components in this chapter.

INTRODUCTION

This chapter shows how to use Microsoft Access to create the elements of production cycle accounting systems. Although most accounting information systems textbooks use manufacturing firms to illustrate the production cycle, many service firms are beginning to examine their business processes using a product costing approach. In this approach, a service firm identifies specific components of the services it offers, then tracks and allocates costs to those service components—just as a manufacturing firm tracks and allocates costs to products. Some merchandising firms also track and allocate costs to specific product lines or customers. Therefore, the techniques you learn in this chapter will help you design accounting systems for all three types of firms, even though we use manufacturing examples only.

Chapter 8 showed you how to record the cost of materials purchased. Chapter 9 showed you how to record the cost of paying employees. This chapter describes how you can combine materials and labor costs with other manufacturing costs to determine the total cost of manufactured products. You will modify some of the Chapter 8 and 9 database objects as you work through this chapter. First, however, you need to understand the different ways that firms can accumulate costs in the production cycle.

COST ACCUMULATION APPROACHES

The goal of the production cycle accounting system is to assign costs to cost objects. If a firm is manufacturing airplanes, the ultimate cost object is *airplane*. If a firm is manufacturing tomato soup, the ultimate cost object is *can of tomato soup*. However, most production cost systems do not allocate costs directly to the ultimate cost object. Instead, they use a three-step approach:

1. Assign costs to intermediate-level cost objects.
2. Assign the intermediate-level cost objects to higher-level cost objects.
3. Assign higher-level cost objects to ultimate cost objects.

Logical intermediate-level cost objects for particular industries or product lines fall into two general categories: jobs and departments. The nature of the manufacturing process usually dictates which category of intermediate-level cost object is appropriate. Therefore, the nature of the manufacturing process typically determines which cost accumulation approach a firm will use. Firms that manufacture different types or quantities of products use a job order cost accumulation system. The intermediate-level cost objects in job order cost systems are jobs. Firms that manufacture one product or similar types of products that require the same processes and the same mix of labor and overhead use process cost accumulation systems. The intermediate-level cost objects in process cost systems are departments.

Job Order Cost Accumulation

Firms that produce many different products use *job* as the intermediate-level cost object in their cost accumulation systems. They break down their production processes into jobs, accumulate costs by job, then divide each job's cost by the number of units in each job to determine the cost of each unit. A job order system uses job numbers to track direct costs. Each raw materials inventory item that goes into production is assigned a job number. Each hour or other unit of labor is assigned a job number. Indirect manufacturing overhead costs are allocated to jobs using some rational allocation base, such as direct labor hours or machine hours. Figure 10.1 shows the job order approach to cost accumulation.

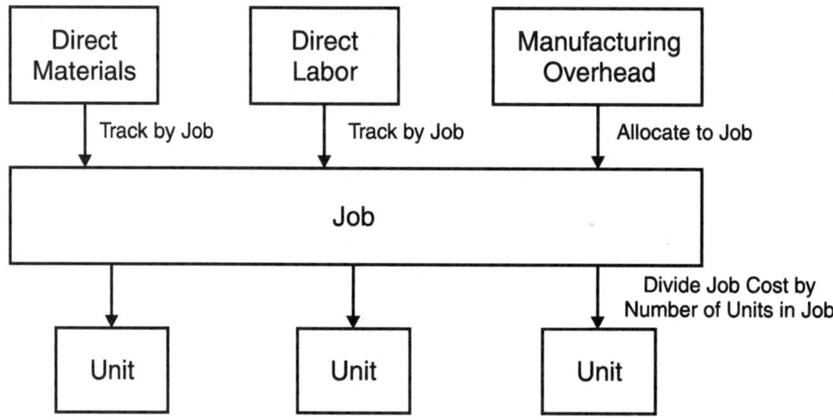

Figure 10.1 Job order cost accumulation.

Note that the ultimate cost object, such as *Unit* in Figure 10.1, can be a direct material item with respect to a subsequent job or process. For example, if the task represented in Figure 10.1 was to manufacture computer keyboards, the cost of each unit would include the direct materials, direct labor, and manufacturing overhead cost of one keyboard. If the firm were to then use these keyboards to build computers, the keyboard units would become a direct material in the computer assembly job.

Process Cost Accumulation

Firms that produce one product or similar products using the same manufacturing processes use *department* as the intermediate-level cost object in their cost accumulation systems. They organize their production processes by departments and accumulate costs by department. To obtain unit cost, they divide each department's monthly total cost by the number of units the department manufactured that month. Therefore, a process cost system uses department numbers to track direct costs. Each raw materials inventory item that enters production is tracked to a specific department. Some firms assign employees to particular departments. Other firms track each employee-hour worked to a specific department. Firms that use process cost systems allocate indirect manufacturing overhead costs to departments using some rational allocation base. Two common allocation bases are direct labor hours or machine hours. Figure 10.2 describes the process approach to cost accumulation.

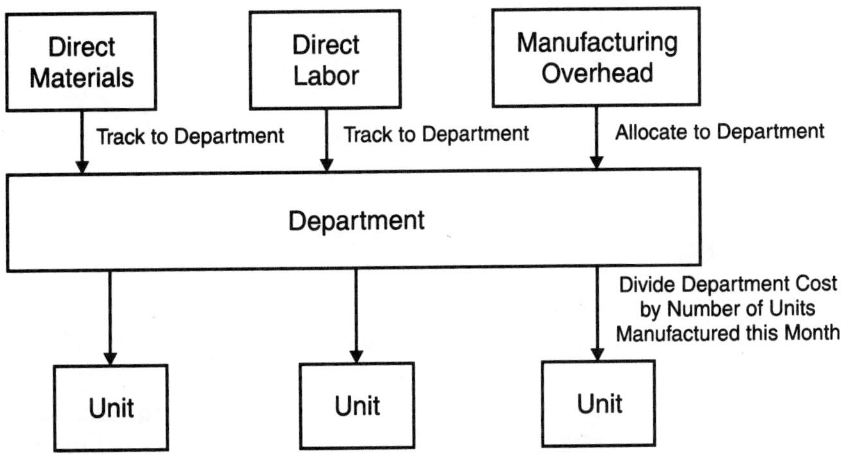

Figure 10.2 Process cost accumulation.

The ultimate cost objects in process cost systems, such as *Unit* in Figure 10.2, can be direct materials to a subsequent department. For example, if the job that is diagrammed in Figure 10.2 involved the manufacture of plastic soda bottles, the cost of each unit would include the direct material, direct labor, and manufacturing overhead cost of one bottle. If the firm were to fill these bottles with soda in a subsequent department, the bottles would be accounted for as a direct material in the bottle-filling department.

Hybrid Cost Accumulation

Some firms produce similar products using the same manufacturing processes, yet use different materials in different batches. For example, a clothing manufacturer may make cotton shirts and silk shirts. The manufacturing processes of cutting, sewing, and attaching buttons is similar for both kinds of shirts. However, the cost of cotton and silk differ considerably. *Department* would be an ineffective intermediate-level cost object for accumulating materials costs—since cloth costs would not be traced to specific batches, all shirts manufactured in a month would have the same cost.

The solution to this problem is a hybrid cost system. The clothing manufacturer can track the cost of direct materials by batch using a job order approach, and can track direct labor and overhead costs by department using a process approach. The job order part of the cost system would track the direct materials cost for each shirt in each batch. The process part of the cost system would track labor and allocate overhead cost for each shirt of either kind manufactured during the month. This particular hybrid system of using a job order approach for direct materials and a process approach for direct labor and manufacturing overhead is called *operation costing*.

Implications for Production Cycle Accounting Systems

Choosing between job order, process, and hybrid cost accumulation systems is an essential part of production cycle system design. The system must match the nature of the manufacturing process.

Firms that produce a variety of products or provide a variety of services use job order costing systems. These firms need a way to track costs as they flow in different amounts to different customized products or services. Examples of firms that typically use job order costing include aircraft manufacturers, auto repair shops, hospitals, and public accounting firms.

Process costing is the choice of firms that make one or only a few different products that are homogeneous in design and resource use. These firms do essentially the same things the same way every month. Examples of firms that typically use process costing include oil refineries, cement manufacturers, and some chemical manufacturers.

Operation costing is a blend of job order and process costing. Firms that use operation costing have some costs that flow evenly and regularly into their products or services and other costs that vary significantly by job, customer, or production batch. Examples of firms that use operation costing include jewelry manufacturers, garment manufacturers, luggage manufacturers, and auto manufacturers.

Although the meaning of information contained in reports and queries will vary with the accumulation system, table and form designs are surprisingly consistent across system types. In a job order system, all costs are traced or allocated using a job number. In a process system, all costs are traced or allocated using a department number. In both systems, tables and data entry forms must accommodate a number, but the design of the tables and forms is the same whether the number is a job number or a department number.

We will use a job order system example to illustrate production cycle elements in this chapter; however, remember that you can substitute *department number* for *job number* in a production cycle design to convert a job order accumulation system to a process accumulation system.

COST TRACING VS. COST ALLOCATION

Traditionally, accountants have divided manufacturing costs into two categories: direct and indirect. Direct costs are costs that accountants can easily track through the manufacturing process to ultimate cost objects. Accountants usually classify raw materials and labor costs of employees that work in the manufacturing process as direct costs—using the terms *direct materials* and *direct labor*, respectively. All other manufacturing costs are classified as indirect and referred to as *manufacturing overhead.*

Manufacturing Overhead Allocation

Manufacturing overhead includes all indirect manufacturing costs. Some raw materials costs are not significant enough to warrant the effort and expense of tracking them to jobs or departments. These indirect materials costs are part of manufacturing overhead. The labor costs of employees that do not work directly in the manufacturing process—such as maintenance, materials handling, and supervisory employees—are considered to be indirect labor and are included in manufacturing overhead. All other manufacturing costs—for example, insurance, rent, supplies, and utilities—are also included in manufacturing overhead.

To smooth out fluctuations in manufacturing overhead acquisition that might distort product costs, accountants have long followed a practice of normalizing manufacturing overhead costs. The most common normalization procedure is to apply manufacturing overhead costs using a predetermined overhead rate. This normalization procedure requires four steps:

1. Estimate the manufacturing overhead cost for the year.
2. Estimate usage of some activity base that is related to overhead consumption for the year. Common bases include direct labor hours, machine hours, and direct labor cost.
3. Divide the estimated manufacturing overhead cost by an estimate of activity base usage to obtain a predetermined overhead rate.
4. Each period, multiply the predetermined overhead rate by the actual amount of the activity base used in that period by each job or department.

Note that the manufacturing overhead cost for each job or department will vary with the amount of the activity base it consumes during the period. This approach to allocating manufacturing overhead is a *volume-based* approach, since the quantity of the activity base consumed by a particular job or department usually varies with its volume of production.

Activity-Based Costing

The volume-based approach to allocating manufacturing overhead has been criticized because it can lead to product cost distortions. An alternative procedure for allocating manufacturing costs is to measure activities and track costs for those activities. To perform this activity-based costing procedure, a firm follows four steps:

1. Track individual manufacturing process activities.
2. Record the costs of those activities.
3. Divide the activity cost by a physical measure of the activity to obtain the cost per activity unit.
4. Multiply the cost per activity unit times the quantity of the activity used by the job or department.

Note that these four steps are very similar to those in the normalization process we described earlier. In production cycle systems terms, activity-based costing simply adds another intermediate-level cost object to the cost flow. Figure 10.3 shows the job order cost accumulation system modified to include activity-based cost allocation.

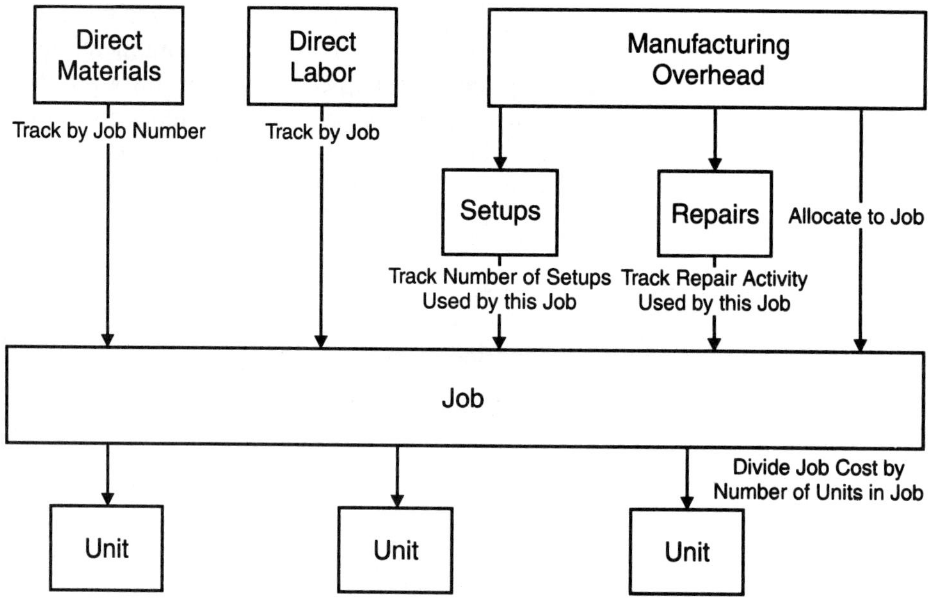

Figure 10.3 Activity-based job order cost system.

The two activities tracked in this system are machine setups and repairs. This system identifies machine setup and repair costs in the manufacturing overhead cost pool. These identified costs are then traced to the specific activity. Finally, using the number of setups and repair hours that each job requires, the activity costs are allocated to specific jobs. Note that other manufacturing overhead costs are still allocated using direct labor hours or machine hours. Even firms that adopt activity-based costing still have some manufacturing overhead costs that they cannot trace to specific activities.

Implications for Production Cycle Accounting Systems

Normalizing manufacturing overhead requires the accounting system to do double duty. The system must track the actual overhead costs *and* the applied overhead costs. Fortunately, we have already described a system for recording and paying actual costs in Chapter 8. Although we used materials acquisition to illustrate the purchase cycle in Chapter 8, those system elements require only minor modifications to accommodate actual manufacturing overhead costs. We explained how to record actual labor costs in Chapter 9. In this chapter, we will explain how you can perform overhead allocation tasks in a database accounting system.

Activity-based costing does not change the nature of cost allocation, it merely adds another layer to the allocation process. Therefore, you can easily extend the examples in this chapter to perform activity-based costing. All you need to do is replicate the cost tracking and allocation systems for each activity center in the system. For example, the cost system described in this chapter allocates manufacturing overhead cost using direct labor hours. You could add activity centers for machine setups and repairs to this system by building two additional tables to track machine setups by job number and repair hours by job number. Similarly, you could extend the job order system described in this chapter to allocate overhead using separate rates for each department instead of one rate for all departments.

TRACING AND ALLOCATING MANUFACTURING COSTS

To trace and allocate manufacturing costs to jobs, you must build a table that will store the individual job records. Each job record will have direct materials, direct labor, and manufacturing overhead costs related to it. Direct materials and direct labor each require a separate table because cost systems track these specific cost flows. Manufacturing overhead does not require its own table because it is an allocated cost. Remember, to use the components of this example system in a process accumulation system, you need only substitute *department number* for *job number*. You can also use these system components to perform activity-based costing by adding an additional table for each activity that the system must track or allocate.

The Job Table

The Job table must have a primary key field that uniquely identifies each job. The Job table must also include fields to store important job dates and foreign key fields that will be different for each firm. For example, one firm may want to relate each job to the customer that ordered the job. You can build this relationship by including a CustomerNumber foreign key field in the Job table that links to the primary key in the Customer table. Other firms might run jobs as production for inventory rather than for specific customers. These firms would want you to include an InventoryItemCode foreign key field in the Job table that would establish a link to the primary key in the Finished Goods Inventory table. Some firms might use both foreign key links.

Since you have already learned how to build Customer and Inventory tables in Chapter 7, we will not repeat that information here. However, we have included *tblCustomer* and *tblFinishedGoodsInventory* in the *Ch10.mdb* database on your Companion CD-ROM. These two tables appear in Datasheet view on the Microsoft Access desktop in Figure 10.4. They contain sample data that we will use in this chapter's examples.

Item Code	Description
100001	Model 100A Control Panel
100002	Model 200A Control Panel
100003	Model 300A Control Panel
100004	Model 400A Control Panel
100005	Model 450S Control Panel
100006	Model 470D Control Panel
100007	Model 500C Control Panel

Custom	Name	Address	City	State	Zip	Telephone
10001	Dunn Plumbing	2763 Cosgrove Blvd.	West Haven	CT	06516-1960	(203) 933-2063
10002	Ace Construction Co.	3788 Spring Grove Avenue	Cincinnati	OH	45217-1866	(513) 451-4264
10003	Bryant Boiler Repair	357 East Wentworth Drive	Chicago	IL	60629-1597	(312) 447-3198
10004	Bucknell Air Conditioning	3198 Storm Lake Road	Lewisburg	PA	17837-2933	(717) 938-4761
10005	Cole & Co.	720 Conover Court	Fargo	ND	58105-5137	(701) 565-3099
10006	Burch Builders' Supply	21887 Larwood Rd.	Reno	NV	89557-0014	(702) 784-1866
10007	Lin Plumbing Repair, Inc.	1297 Lambert Lane	New Orleans	LA	70148-4974	(504) 288-5869
10008	Mattison Maintenance Co.	7743 Van Meter Place	Bozeman	MT	59717-6206	(406) 994-2086
10009	Central Plumbing Supply	709 Baker St.	Baltimore	MD	21210-2768	(301) 233-8672
10010	Entero Construction	615 Lewis Ave.	Louisville	KY	40292-6788	(502) 585-7755

Figure 10.4 The Customer and Finished Goods Inventory tables in Datasheet view.

Exercise 10.1 shows you how to build a Job table that will work with the Finished Goods Inventory table and the Customer table in the production cycle. You should have Microsoft Access running with the Database window open as you begin the exercise. You may notice that we offer you an alternative to the Database window's New button as a way to open new database objects.

Exercise 10.1: Building a Job Table

1. To build the Job table, select the Insert, Table menu command and click Design View in the New Table dialog box.
2. Enter ***JobNumber*** in the first row of the Field Name column and leave its Data Type set to Text.
3. Click the Primary Key toolbar button.
4. Set the JobNumber's Field Size property to *4*, its Input Mask property to *0000*, and its Caption property to *Job #*

   Next, we will create two fields that will store key job dates: the date that each job is ordered and the date we expect to complete the job.
5. Enter ***JobOrderDate*** in the second row of the Field Name column and set its Data Type to Date/Time.
6. Set the JobOrderDate Input Mask property to *99/99/00;0;_* and the Caption property to ***Order Date***
7. Enter ***JobCompletionDate*** in the second row of the Field Name column and set its Data Type to Date/Time, its Input Mask property to *99/99/00;0;_* and its Caption property to ***Completion Date***

   The JobCompletionDate field will store the expected completion date for each job. Many firms also record an actual completion date to use in generating performance reports. To create the foreign key links to *tblCustomer* and *tblFinishedGoodsInventory*, we can add two fields that match these tables' primary key fields.
8. Enter ***CustomerNumber*** in the fourth row of the Field Name column and leave its Data Type set to Text.
9. Set the CustomerNumber Field Size property to *5*, its Input Mask property to *00000*, and its Caption property to ***Customer #***
10. Enter a Field Name of ***InventoryItemCode*** in the fifth row and leave its Data Type set to Text.
11. Set the InventoryItemCode Field Size property to *6*, its Input Mask property to *000000*, and its Caption property to ***Item Code***

Note that we cannot enforce referential integrity on either of the links from these two foreign key fields to their entity tables unless we know that every job will have a customer and a finished goods inventory item code when the job is entered. To save the Job table you have just completed, select the File, Save As/Export menu command and enter ***tblJob*** as the New Name in the Save As dialog box. The *Ch10.mdb* database on your Companion CD-ROM includes *tblJob,* which includes the job records shown in Figure 10.5.

We will use these sample job records for the queries and reports you will design later in this chapter. Note that the five jobs in *tblJob* include two that were completed in December and three that continue into January.

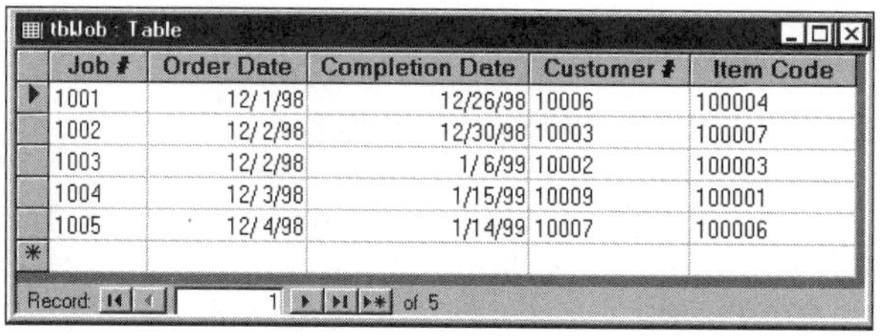

tblJob : Table

Job #	Order Date	Completion Date	Customer #	Item Code
1001	12/1/98	12/26/98	10006	100004
1002	12/2/98	12/30/98	10003	100007
1003	12/2/98	1/6/99	10002	100003
1004	12/3/98	1/15/99	10009	100001
1005	12/4/98	1/14/99	10007	100006

Record: 1 of 5

Figure 10.5 The *tblJob* records.

The Direct Materials Inventory Table

To track the cost of direct materials, we will need a to build a table much like the Materials Inventory table we created and used in Chapter 8 to record materials purchases. In the Chapter 8 purchase cycle system, we stored the cost of each inventory item in the Purchase Order-Materials Inventory table. This design allowed us to record different costs for the same inventory items purchased from different vendors, or from the same vendors purchased at different times. In this chapter, we want to focus on tracing direct materials costs into production. To simplify our example here, we will include the cost of direct materials in the Direct Materials Inventory table. Although a discussion of standard cost systems is beyond the scope of this book, such systems would also store the standard cost of each direct materials item in the Direct Materials Inventory table.

Since the Direct Materials Inventory table is so similar to the Materials Inventory table we created in Chapter 8, we can save some work by modifying that table instead of starting all over. You can import a copy of the Materials Inventory table from the *Ch08.mdb* database using the procedure described in Exercise 5.15. After you have imported a copy of *tblMaterialsInventory*, it should appear under the Tables tab in the *Ch10.mdb* file's Database window. Exercise 10.2 shows you how to modify this table for use in the production cycle.

EXERCISE 10.2 : CONVERTING *TBLMATERIALSINVENTORY* TO *TBLDIRECTMATERIALSINVENTORY*

1. In the Database window, click the Tables tab and click *tblMaterialsInventory*. Click the Design button to open the table in Design view.
2. Change the names of the three existing fields to ***DMStockNumber***, ***DMCategory***, and ***DMDescription***, respectively.
3. In the fourth row of the Field Name column, enter ***DMCost***
4. Set the new field's Data Type to Currency, its Decimal Places property to ***2***, and its Caption property to ***DM Cost***
5. Select the File, Save As/Export menu command and enter ***tblDirectMaterialsInventory*** as the New Name in the Save As dialog box. The

Ch10.mdb database on your Companion CD-ROM includes a Direct Materials Inventory table, *tblDirectMaterialsInventory*, that includes sample job records. This table appears in Figure 10.6.

6. Access deletes the records from the table when you save it under its new name. However, you can copy and paste the records from *tblMaterialsInventory*. You can then add the values for the DMCost field using Figure 10.6 as a guide.
7. You can return to the Database window by selecting File, Close from the menu.

tblDirectMaterialsInventory : Table

Stock #	Category	Description	DM Cost
101	Sheet metal	1/8" Steel 4x4 sheet	$8.45
102	Switch	DPDT 240v 100a	$14.96
103	Wire	500' Copper #22AWG	$16.95
104	Sheet metal	1/4" Steel 4x4 sheet	$14.95
105	Switch	SPDT 240v 100a	$9.47
106	Relay	SPDT 120v 40a Silver	$32.89
107	Circuit breaker	240v 40a	$10.27
108	Relay	TPST 240v 100a Mercury	$18.96
109	Sheet metal	1/8" Aluminum 4x4 sheet	$12.68
110	Wire	500' Copper Twin #18AWG	$27.98
111	Connector	F 240v 100a solderless	$3.57
112	Switch	DPST 240v 50a	$8.66
113	Connector	M 120v 40a clip	$1.98
114	Sheet metal	1/4" Aluminum 4x4 sheet	$19.49
115	Circuit breaker	120v 40a	$6.95
			$0.00

Record: 1 of 15

Figure 10.6 The populated Direct Materials Inventory table in Datasheet view.

Now we have a Job table with a record for each job and a Direct Materials Inventory table with a record for each materials inventory item that we might use in a particular job. To link these two tables and track the direct materials used on each job, we need a relationship table, the Job-Direct Materials Inventory table.

The Job-Direct Materials Inventory Table

Since each job can include many different direct materials and each direct materials item can be used in many different jobs, the Job table and the Direct Materials Inventory table have a many-to-many relationship. The Job-Direct Materials Inventory table is the relationship table that models this relation. The composite primary key for this relationship table will require two fields, the primary key fields of the two entity tables: the Job table and the Direct Materials Inventory table. The table also needs a field to store the quantity of each inventory item used on each job. Exercise 10.3 shows you how to build the Job-Direct Materials Inventory table for the production cycle.

Exercise 10.3: Building a Job-Direct Materials Inventory table

1. With the Database window open on the Microsoft Access desktop, select the Insert, Table menu command, then click Design View.
2. Enter the name of *tblJob's* primary key field, ***JobNumber***, as the first Field Name. Leave its Data Type set to Text and set its Field Size to ***4***

   Remember, when using entity table primary keys as part of the composite primary key in a relationship table, we always want to match Data Type and Field Size exactly.
3. Set JobNumber's Input Mask property to ***0000*** and its Caption property to ***Job #***
4. Set its Indexed property to Yes (Duplicates OK).
5. Enter ***DMStockNumber*** in the second row of the Field Name column. Leave its Data Type set to Text.
6. Set its Field Size property to ***3***, its Input Mask property to ***000***, and its Caption property to ***Stock #***
7. Set the Indexed property to Yes (Duplicates OK).
8. While pressing the Ctrl key, select both fields by clicking the row selectors for each field. With both fields selected, click the Primary Key toolbar button. The Primary key symbol should appear in the row selectors of both fields. The third field will store the quantity of each materials item used on each job.
9. Enter ***JobDMQuantity*** on the third Field Name line.
10. Set its Data Type to Number and its Caption property to ***Quantity***
11. Select the File, Save As/Export menu command. Type ***tblJob-DirectMaterialsInventory*** as the New Name in the Save As dialog box.
12. Select the File, Close menu command to close the table.

A copy of this table that includes the sample records we will use later in this chapter is included as *tblJob-DirectMaterialsInventory* in the *Ch10.mdb* database on your Companion CD-ROM. To ensure that any JobNumber value entered in the Job-Direct Materials Inventory table exists in *tblJob*, we can establish referential integrity between *tblJob-DirectMaterialsInventory* and *tblJob* on the JobNumber field. We can also ensure that each record in *tblJob-DirectMaterialsInventory* refers to an existing materials stock number by establishing referential integrity with *tblDirectMaterialsInventory* on the DMStockNumber field. To create these two links and enforce referential integrity on them, follow the steps in Exercise 10.4. To begin the exercise, you should close all open objects and have the Database window open on the desktop.

Exercise 10.4: Linking Job and Direct Materials Records

1. Click the Relationships toolbar button to open the Relationships window and the Show Table dialog box.

2. Double-click *tblDirectMaterialsInventory*, *tblJob-DirectMaterialsInventory*, and *tblJob* to place them in the Relationships window. Close the Show Table dialog box.
3. Click and drag the JobNumber field in *tblJob* to the JobNumber field in *tblJob-DirectMaterialsInventory*.
4. Click the Enforce Referential Integrity check box, then click the Create button.
5. Click and drag the DMStockNumber field in *tblDirectMaterialsInventory* to the DMStockNumber field in *tblJob-DirectMaterialsInventory*.
6. Click the Enforce Referential Integrity check box, then click the Create button.
7. The Relationship window showing these links appears in Figure 10.7. To return to the Database window, select the File, Close menu command. Click the Yes button to save your changes to the Relationships layout.

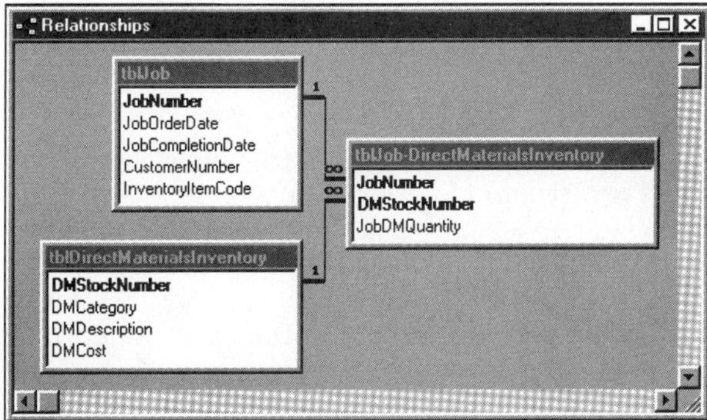

Figure 10.7 Creating referential integrity links for *tblJob-DirectMaterialsInventory*.

The Bill of Materials Form

Many firms use a bill of materials to organize the list of direct materials for each job. We can use this idea to create a form that will make entering records into *tblJob-DirectMaterialsInventory* easier and less prone to error. The Bill of Materials form is fairly complex. It must write records to *tblJob-DirectMaterialsInventory* and read records from:

- The Job table—to obtain the job order and completion dates.
- The Direct Materials Inventory table—to obtain the category, description, and cost of each materials item.
- The Customer table—to obtain the customer name.
- The Finished Goods Inventory table—to obtain the description of the finished goods inventory item that the job produces.

Since the form will read data from *tblCustomer* and *tblMaterialsInventory*, it is very important to have data in these tables. If you have not entered data in these tables yet, you can copy the sample records from the versions of these table objects that we have included in the *Ch10.mdb* database on your Companion CD-ROM.

We will use the Bill of Materials form to enter job information simultaneously in both *tblJob* and *tblJob-DirectMaterialsInventory*. As you have seen in earlier chapters, Microsoft Access handles this task best with a form-subform design. In our bill of materials design, we will link *tblJob* to *tblCustomer* in the main form section. We will link *tblJob-DirectMaterialsInventory*, the relationship table, to *tblDirectMaterialsInventory* in the subform section. Since you have had the experience of working with complex forms in Chapters 7 and 8, we will not use the Form Wizard to construct this form. We will show you how to build a form-subform combination from the blank forms. When you build complex forms in Access, you should always create the subform first. If you have a multiple subform design, you should start with the most deeply nested subform. In Exercise 10.5, we will show you how to create the Bill of Materials subform.

Exercise 10.5: Building the Bill of Materials Subform

1. Click the Forms tab in the Database window, then click the New button. Enter ***tblJob-DirectMaterialsInventory*** in the combo box control of the New Form dialog box, then double-click Design View in the list box control.
2. Select the View, Form Header/Footer menu command.
3. Select the Edit, Select Form menu command.
4. Click the Properties toolbar button, click the Data tab in the form's property sheet, then click the Record Source property's Build button to open the form's Query Builder window.
5. Click the Show Table toolbar button and double-click *tblDirectMaterialsInventory*.
6. Click the Close button. The Direct Materials Inventory table, linked on DMStockNumber to *tblJob-DirectMaterialsInventory*, should now appear in the top pane of the Query Builder window.
7. Click and drag the JobNumber field from *tblJob-DirectMaterialsInventory* to the first QBE grid Field cell, then set its Sort order to Ascending.
8. Click and drag the DMStockNumber field from *tblJob-DirectMaterialsInventory* to the second QBE grid Field cell, then set its Sort order to Ascending.
9. Click and drag the JobDMQuantity field from *tblJob-DirectMaterialsInventory* to the next open QBE grid Field cell.
10. Enter ***Description: [DMCategory] & " - " & [DMDescription]*** in the next open QBE grid Field cell.
11. Click and drag the DMCost field from *tblDirectMaterialsInventory* to the next open QBE grid Field cell. Press Ctrl+W to close the Query window. Figure 10.8

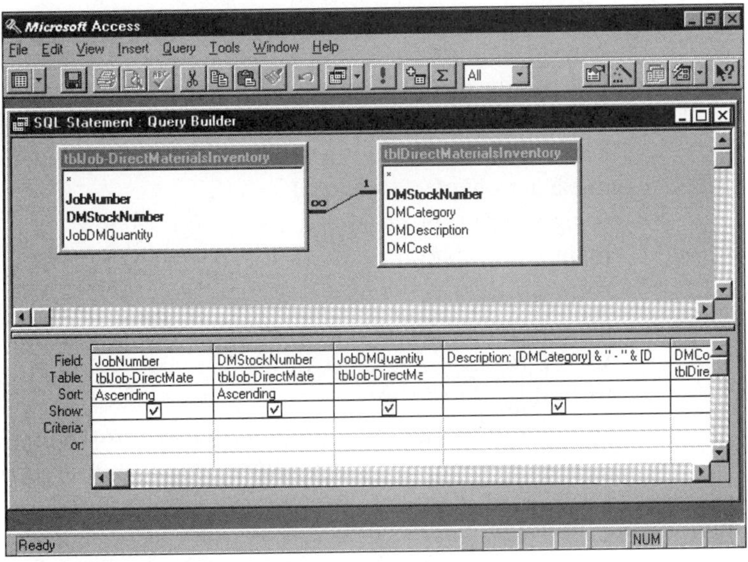

Figure 10.8 The Bill of Materials subform query.

shows the Bill of Materials subform query in the Query Builder window Design view.

Now we can place controls on the subform for the fields we have selected and calculated with the query.

12. Click the Field List toolbar button, then click and drag the DMStockNumber, JobDMQuantity, Description, and DMCost fields to the Detail section of the form.
13. Using Figure 10.9 as a guide, arrange the controls and labels on the form.
14. You can also change the form and control appearance properties as shown in the figure. Remember to set the Enabled, Locked, and Tab Stop properties for the Description and DMCost controls to prevent users from changing values in those fields.
15. Save the subform with the menu command File, Save As/Export and enter the name ***fsubBillOfMaterials***
16. Select File, Close from the menu to close the form.

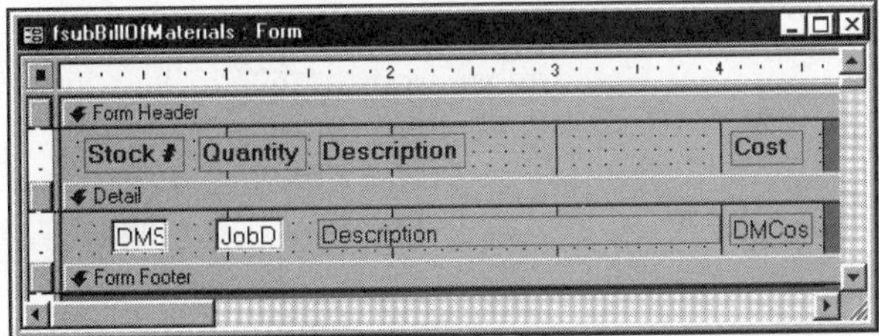

Figure 10.9 The Bill of Materials subform in Design view.

Exercise 10.6 shows you how to build the main Bill of Materials form. Since you have had considerable experience in designing and building forms as you worked through the exercises in the earlier chapters of this book, we encourage you to use your own ideas as you create this form. We do have an example form for your reference, but we encourage you to explore in this exercise.

Exercise 10.6: Building the Bill of Materials Main Form

1. Click the Forms tab in the Database window, then click the New button. Enter ***tblJob*** in the New Form combo box control, then double-click Design View.

   To have the form automatically look up the CustomerName when a user enters a CustomerNumber, we must include *tblCustomer* in the form's design structure. We will also need to include *tblFinishedGoodsInventory* to obtain the description of the item being manufactured on the job.
2. Open the form's property sheet by selecting the form, then clicking the Properties toolbar button.
3. Click the form's Record Source property Build button to open a query behind the form.
4. Click the Show Table toolbar button and add *tblCustomer*, *tblJob-DirectMaterialsInventory*, and *tblFinishedGoodsInventory* to the top pane of the Query Builder window.
5. Close the Show Table dialog box.

   Note that *tblCustomer*, linked on CustomerNumber to *tblJob*, and *tblFinishedGoodsInventory*, linked on InventoryItemCode, now appear in the Query Builder window. Also appearing in the window is *tblJob-DirectMaterialsInventory* with its referential integrity link on JobNumber to *tblJob*.
6. Click and drag the JobNumber field from *tblJob-DirectMaterialsInventory* to the first Field cell in the QBE grid, then enter ***Ascending*** in the first Sort cell.
7. Double-click the asterisk in *tblJob* to include all *tblJob* fields in the next QBE grid Field cell.
8. Double-click the CustomerName field in *tblCustomer* and double-click the InventoryDescription field in *tblFinishedGoodsInventory* to include those fields in the next two QBE grid Field cells.
9. Select File, Close from the menu to return to the form in Design view.
10. Click the Field List toolbar button, then click and drag the following fields to the form: JobNumber, JobOrderDate, InventoryDescription, CustomerName, and JobCompletionDate.
11. If the Toolbox is not already open, click the Toolbox toolbar button to open it.
12. Click the Subform/Subreport Toolbox button. Using Figure 10.10 as a guide, draw the outline of the subform at the bottom of the Detail section.
13. Select the subform's label and press the Delete key.
14. Click the Data tab in the subform's property sheet. Change its Source Object property to ***fsubBillOfMaterials***

Note that changing the Source Object property to *fsubBillOfMaterials* automatically changes both the Link Child Fields and the Link Master Fields property settings to JobNumber.

15. Using Figures 10.10 and 10.11 as guides, modify the controls' properties and add labels to the Bill of Materials form. Remember to set the Enabled, Locked, and Tab Stop properties for the CustomerName and InventoryDescription controls to prevent users from changing values in those fields.

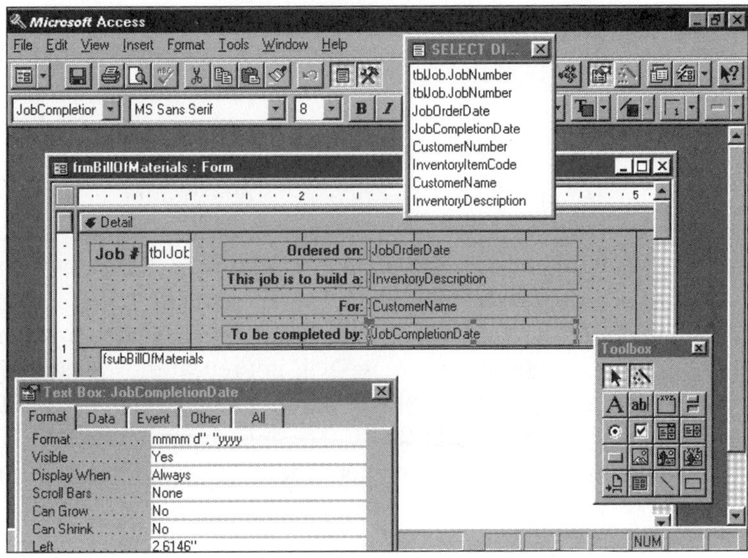

Figure 10.10 The Bill of Materials form in Design view.

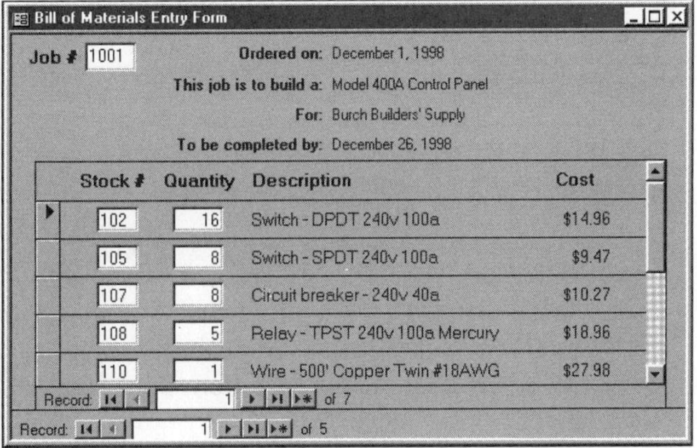

Figure 10.11 The Bill of Materials form in Form view.

16. To save your Bill of Materials form, select File, Save As/Export from the menu and enter ***frmBillOfMaterials*** as the New Name in the Save As dialog box.

The *Ch10.mdb* database on your Companion CD-ROM includes two forms, *frmBillOfMaterials* and *fsubBillOfMaterials*, that you can use as aids in designing your forms. Figure 10.11 shows the Bill of Materials form in Form view after a user has entered the materials for job number 1001 in the sample data.

In addition to its role as a useful data entry tool, this form provides a convenient way for managers to review the materials that have been charged to a job—although most firms would design a report for that purpose.

The Time Worked Table

To track labor costs into the production process, we need to know the number of hours each employee works on each job. Then we can multiply the hours times each employee's pay rate to determine the direct labor cost for the job. In Chapter 9, we described two tables that contain most of the information we will need to track direct labor. Since we have already shown you in Chapter 9 how to construct an Employee table, we will not repeat those instructions here. However, we have included an Employee table, *tblEmployee*, in the *Ch10.mdb* database on your Companion CD-ROM. The *tblEmployee* object contains the employee data we will use in this chapter. The Employee table structure appears in Figure 10.12.

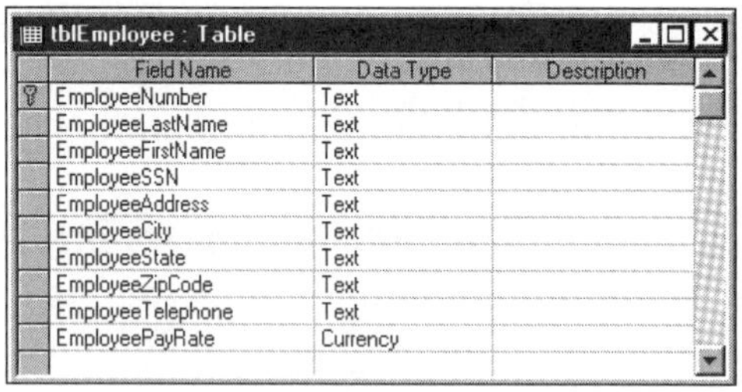

tblEmployee : Table

Field Name	Data Type	Description
EmployeeNumber	Text	
EmployeeLastName	Text	
EmployeeFirstName	Text	
EmployeeSSN	Text	
EmployeeAddress	Text	
EmployeeCity	Text	
EmployeeState	Text	
EmployeeZipCode	Text	
EmployeeTelephone	Text	
EmployeePayRate	Currency	

Figure 10.12 The Chapter 10 *tblEmployee* structure.

Note that we have simplified the table structure so that we can focus more easily on cost flow issues. For example, we have omitted the EmployeeDepartmentNumber field because we are tracking costs by job rather than by department in this chapter. This Chapter 10 version of *tblEmployee* includes only five employee records.

The Time Worked table requires such substantial modifications that creating a new table is easier than adapting *tblTimeWorked* from Chapter 9. To record time worked on each job in one-hour increments, the table will need a primary key that uniquely identifies each block of time that each employee works on each job—certainly a more difficult challenge than creating a primary key for the Chapter 9 Time Worked table. To avoid the details of time arithmetic, we will assume that each employee completes one time card for each week. Further, we will assume that each time card has preprinted sequential numbers for job time entries. An example of such a time card appears in Figure 10.13. We will use the sequence numbers on the time card as part of the unique identifier for each record in *tblTimeWorked*.

Name Ethel Baron | **Employee Number** 103 | **Pay Period Ending** 12/16/98

	Hours	Job Number
1	14	1002
2	8	1005
3	9	1001
4	6	1002
5	3	1005
6		
7		
8		
9		
10		

Figure 10.13 A sequentially numbered time card.

Exercise 10.7 will show you how to create *tblTimeWorked*. The primary key for the table will be a composite of three fields: pay period ended date, time card sequence number, and employee number. The Time Worked table must include these three fields to uniquely identify each bit of time worked by each employee on each job. The table will also need fields for number of hours and job number for each record. The JobNumber field is a foreign key and will link *tblTimeWorked* to *tblJob*. Close all database objects and have the Database window open to begin the exercise.

Exercise 10.7: Building a Time Worked Table for the Production Cycle

1. Select the Insert, Table menu command and double-click Design View in the New Table dialog box.

2. Enter ***EmployeeNumber*** as the first Field Name. Leave its Data Type set to Text.
3. Set its Field Size to ***3***, its Input Mask property to ***000***, and its Caption property to ***Employee #***
4. Set the Indexed property for EmployeeNumber to Yes (Duplicates OK).

   The second part of the composite primary key must identify the pay period. We can use the last day of each weekly pay period as the value for this field.
5. Enter ***TWPayPeriodEnded*** in the second row of the Field Name column and set its Data Type to Date/Time.
6. Set the field's Input Mask property to ***99/99/00;0;_*** and its Caption property to ***Week Ended***
7. Set the Indexed property for TWPayPeriodEnded to Yes (Duplicates OK).

   The third part of the composite primary key will identify the line on the time card using the preprinted sequence number.
8. Enter ***TWSequenceNumber*** in the third row of the Field Name column and set the Data Type to Number.
9. Since the time cards have only ten lines, we can set the Field Size to Byte.
10. Set the field's Decimal Places property to ***0***, its Input Mask property to ***99***, and its Caption property to ***Sequence #***
11. Set the Indexed property to Yes (Duplicates OK).
12. While pressing the Ctrl key, select all three fields by clicking the row selectors for each field.
13. With the fields selected, click the Primary Key toolbar button. The primary key symbol should appear in the row selectors of all three fields.

    Next, we can create a field that will store the number of hours recorded on the time card for each sequence number and create the foreign key field for job number.
14. Enter ***TWHours*** on the fourth row of the Field Name column.
15. Set its Data Type to Number, and its Caption property to ***Hours***
16. Enter ***JobNumber*** in the Field Name column. Leave its Data Type set to Text.
17. Set its Field Size property to ***4***, its Input Mask property to ***0000***, and its Caption property to ***Job #***
18. To save the table, select the File, Save As/Export menu command and enter ***tblTimeWorked*** as the New Name in the Save As dialog box.
19. You can close the table by pressing Ctrl+W.

The *Ch10.mdb* database on your Companion CD-ROM includes a Time Worked table, *tblTimeWorked*, that includes the sample data we will use later in this chapter. To ensure that each employee number entered in *tblTimeWorked* is for an employee that actually exists, we can build a referential integrity link to *tblEmployee*. We can also use referential integrity on the foreign key link to *tblJob*. This will ensure that any job number entered in *tblTimeWorked* is a valid job number that already exists in *tblJob*. Exercise 10.8 shows you how to add these links to *tblTimeWorked*.

EXERCISE 10.8: LINKING *TBLTIMEWORKED* TO *TBLJOB* AND *TBLEMPLOYEE*

1. Click the Relationships toolbar button to open the Relationships window, then click the Show Table toolbar button.
2. Double-click *tblEmployee* and *tblTimeWorked* to add these tables to the Relationships window, then close the Show Table dialog box.
3. Click and drag the JobNumber field in *tblJob* to the JobNumber field in *tblTimeWorked.*
4. Click the Enforce Referential Integrity check box, then click the Create button.
5. Click and drag the EmployeeNumber field in *tblEmployee* to the EmployeeNumber field in *tblTimeWorked.*
6. Click the Enforce Referential Integrity check box, then click the Create button.
7. Select File, Close from the menu to close the Relationships window and return to the Database window. Click the Yes button to save your changes. The Relationship window showing these links added to the existing production cycle system links appears in Figure 10.14.

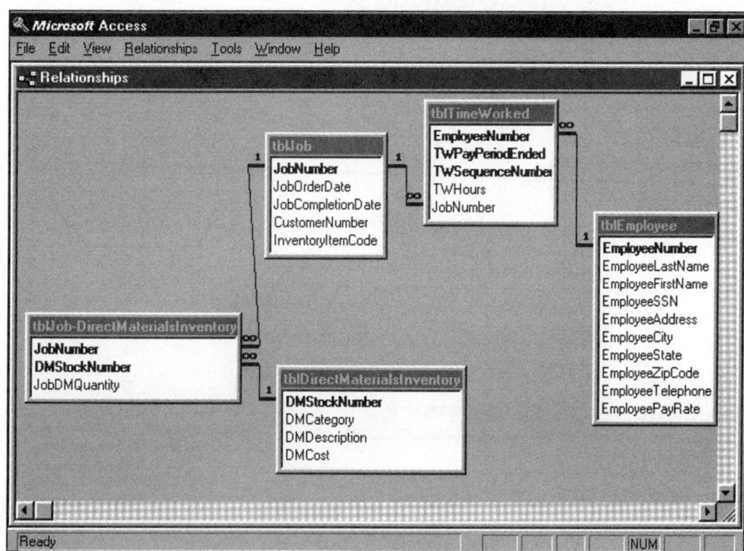

Figure 10.14 Adding referential integrity links to *tblTimeWorked.*

Managers and accountants can use the records in *tblTimeWorked* in many ways. For example, by multiplying the hours for a particular job from *tblTimeWorked* by the employee pay rates from *tblEmployee* for the employees who worked on that job, we can calculate the direct labor cost for a particular job. Exercise 10.9 shows you how you can build a query that calculates the direct labor cost for job number 1001 in the sample data.

EXERCISE 10.9: CALCULATING THE DIRECT LABOR COST FOR JOB NUMBER 1001

1. Select the Insert, Query menu command, then double-click Design View in the New Query dialog box.
2. Double-click *tblEmployee* and *tblTimeWorked* in the Show Table dialog box, then click the Close button.
3. Click and drag the JobNumber field from the *tblTimeWorked* box to the first QBE grid Field cell.
4. Enter ***1001*** in the first QBE grid Criteria cell. Microsoft Access encloses your entry with quotation marks as you leave the cell.
5. Enter ***DLCost: [EmployeePayRate] * [TWHours]*** in the second QBE grid Field cell.

   This field multiplies the employee pay rate times the hours that employee worked on job number 1001 and places the answer in a new field, DLCost.
6. Click the Run toolbar button to test the query. The resulting dynaset, which shows the direct labor costs for job number 1001, appears in Figure 10.15.

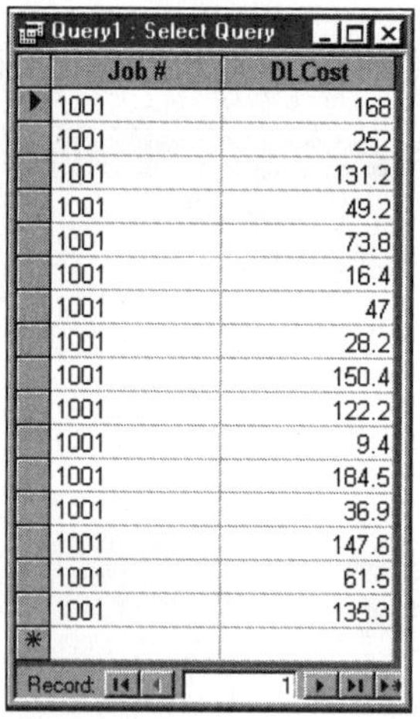

Query1 : Select Query

Job #	DLCost
1001	168
1001	252
1001	131.2
1001	49.2
1001	73.8
1001	16.4
1001	47
1001	28.2
1001	150.4
1001	122.2
1001	9.4
1001	184.5
1001	36.9
1001	147.6
1001	61.5
1001	135.3

Record: 1

Figure 10.15 Direct labor costs for job number 1001.

Of course, if we truly wanted to know the direct labor cost for job number 1001, the result shown in Figure 10.15 is probably not the answer we had hoped to get. We more likely wanted a single dollar amount rather than a column of numbers to enter into a calculator! The good news is that we can modify the query slightly to get the answer in a more useful form.

7. Return the desktop to Query Design View. Select View, Totals from the menu or click the Totals toolbar button. This adds a row of Total cells to the QBE grid between the Table cells row and the Sort cells row.
8. Enter ***Group By*** in the first Total cell, then enter ***Sum*** in the second Total cell. Figure 10.16 shows the Query window with these changes. The mouse pointer, activating the Totals button ToolTip, also appears in Figure 10.16.

9. Click the Run toolbar button to test the modified query.

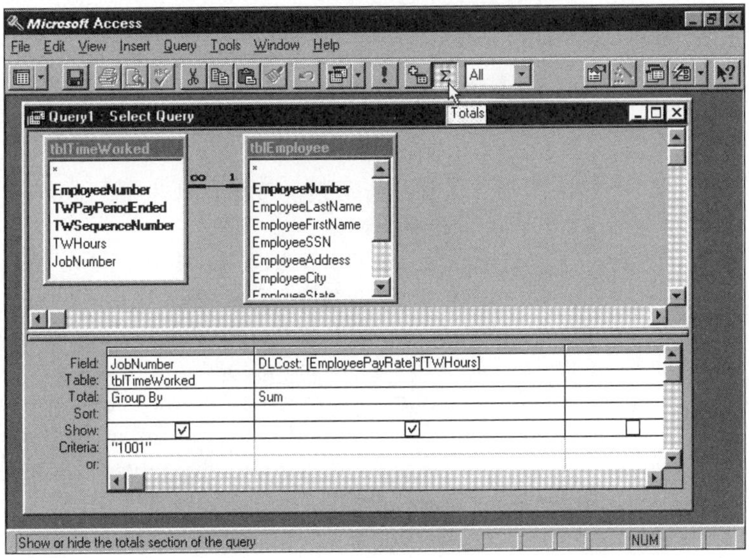

Figure 10.16 Summing the DLCost field.

The dynaset now includes only one row that contains one number, 1613.6, which is the total of all DLCost calculations for job number 1001 that are displayed in Figure 10.15. This query is included in the *Ch10.mdb* database on your Companion CD-ROM as *qryDirectLaborCostForJob1001*. This query is just one example of how you can use queries on various combinations of the Job, Time Worked, and Employee tables to answer a variety of questions about the use and cost of direct labor resources.

Allocating Manufacturing Overhead

Cost accounting systems do not track manufacturing overhead costs into production as they track direct materials and direct labor costs. At the beginning of the year, accountants and production managers get together and estimate the total manufacturing overhead costs they expect for the year. They also estimate the manufacturing activity level. The activity measure is usually volume-based; that is, the activity measure is expected to increase with higher manufacturing volume.

Firms often use direct labor hours, direct labor cost, or machine hours as activity measures. Cost accountants then divide the estimated manufacturing cost by the estimated activity measure to obtain a predetermined overhead rate. They use this rate to apply overhead to production throughout the year. For our example, assume that the estimates are:

Estimated manufacturing overhead cost	\$78,000
Estimated direct labor hours	4,800

The predetermined overhead rate is:

$78,000 ÷ 4,800 direct labor hours = $16.25 per direct labor hour

Therefore, our example production cycle accounting system must allocate $16.25 per direct labor hour to each job.

We have already captured the direct labor hours per job in *tblTimeWorked*. Production cycle systems that allocate manufacturing overhead using other allocation bases may need an additional table. For example, a firm that allocates manufacturing overhead using machine hours would need a machine hours table to store the number of machine hours used by each job. The structure of this machine hours table would be very similar to the structure of *tblTimeWorked*.

At this point, we have created tables that will track direct materials and direct labor costs. We have also described how we can allocate manufacturing overhead costs. Our next step is to use these tables to calculate job costs.

REPORTING JOB COSTS

The goal of tracking and allocating manufacturing costs is to provide information for calculating job or department costs. Since we have been using a job order cost accumulation system example in this chapter, we will now explain how we can calculate job costs. The Job Cost report summarizes direct materials, direct labor, and manufacturing overhead costs by job. This task requires a series of four queries and a report. The first three queries calculate and sum the direct materials, direct labor, and manufacturing overhead costs for each job. The fourth query combines these three summation queries and provides a basis for the Job Cost report.

Direct Materials Cost

The first step in building the Job Cost report is to calculate the total direct materials cost for each job. We show you how you can perform this calculation with a Direct Materials Cost query in Exercise 10.10.

EXERCISE 10.10: BUILDING THE DIRECT MATERIALS COST QUERY

1. Click the Queries tab in the Database window, then click the New button. Double-click Design View in the New Query dialog box.

2. In the Show Table dialog box, double-click *tblDirectMaterialsInventory*, *tblJob-DirectMaterialsInventory*, and *tblJob* to add these tables to the query. Click the Close button.
3. Click and drag the JobNumber field from *tblJob* to the first QBE grid Field cell.
4. Enter ***DM Cost: [DMCost] * [JobDMQuantity]*** in the second QBE grid Field cell.
5. Click the Totals toolbar button to open the Total line in the QBE grid.
6. Change the second QBE grid Total cell to ***Sum***
7. Select the File, Save As/Export menu command and enter ***qryDirectMaterialsCost*** as the Query Name. Figure 10.17 shows the query in Design view.

   When you run the query, it should return a dynaset with five direct materials cost values, one for each job. The *Ch10.mdb* database on your Companion CD-ROM includes a Direct Materials Cost query, *qryDirectMaterialsCost*, for your reference.
8. Close your query with the File, Close menu command.

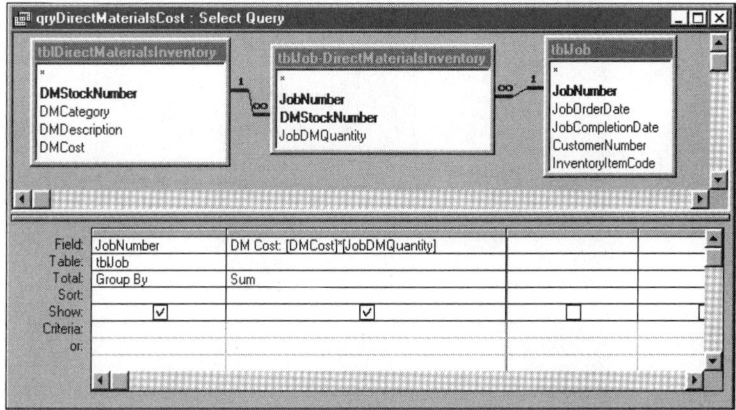

Figure 10.17 The Direct Materials Cost query in Design view.

Direct Labor Cost

The second step in building the Job Cost report is to calculate the total direct labor cost for each job. In Exercise 10.11, we show you how to do this with a Direct Labor Cost query.

Exercise 10.11: Building the Direct Labor Cost Query

1. Click the Queries tab in the Database window, then click the New button. Double-click Design View in the New Query dialog box.

2. In the Show Table dialog box, double-click *tblEmployee*, *tblTimeWorked*, and *tblJob* to add these tables to the query. Click the Close button.
3. Click and drag the JobNumber field from *tblJob* to the first QBE grid Field cell.
4. Enter ***DL Cost: [EmployeePayRate] * [TWHours]*** in the second QBE grid Field cell.
5. Click the Totals toolbar button to open the Total line in the QBE grid.
6. Change the second QBE grid Total cell to ***Sum***
7. Select the File, Save As/Export menu command and enter ***qryDirectLaborCost*** as the Query Name. Figure 10.18 shows the query in Design view.

   When you run the query, it should return a dynaset with direct labor values for the five jobs in *tblJob*. The *Ch10.mdb* database on your Companion CD-ROM includes a Direct Labor Cost query, *qryDirectLaborCost*, for your reference.
8. Close the query with the File, Close menu command. Click the Yes button to save any changes.

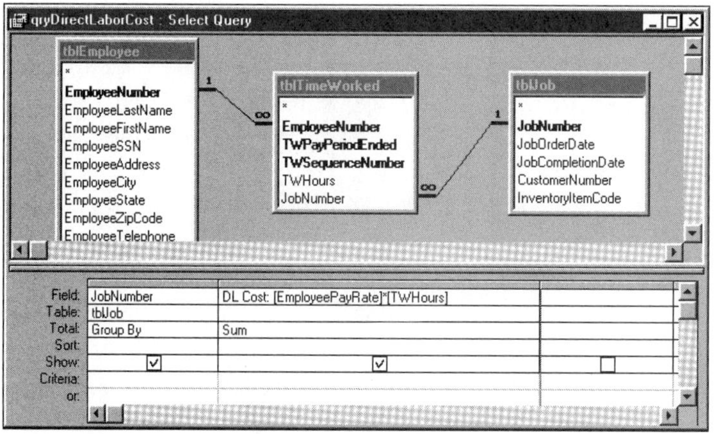

Figure 10.18 The Direct Labor Cost query in Design view.

Manufacturing Overhead Cost

The next step in building the Job Cost report is to calculate the total manufacturing overhead cost for each job. In the next exercise, we show you how to do this with a Manufacturing Overhead Cost query that uses the predetermined overhead rate we calculated earlier in this chapter.

Exercise 10.12: Building the Manufacturing Overhead Cost Query

1. Click the Queries tab in the Database window, then click the New button. Double-click Design View in the New Query dialog box.

2. In the Show Table dialog box, double-click *tblJob* and *tblTimeWorked* to add these tables to the query. Click the Close button.

   The manufacturing overhead calculation needs the hours worked on each job from *tblTimeWorked* because we are applying overhead using direct labor hours as the activity base. To use a different activity base, such as machine hours, we would need to include a table that contained information about how each job consumed that activity base.
3. Click and drag the JobNumber field from *tblJob* to the first QBE grid Field cell.
4. Enter ***MOH Cost: [TWHours] * 16.25*** in the second QBE grid Field cell.

   The *16.25* in the MOH Cost expression is the $16.25 per hour predetermined overhead rate we calculated earlier in the chapter.
5. Click the Totals toolbar button to open the Total line in the QBE grid.
6. Change the second QBE grid Total cell to ***Sum***
7. Select the File, Save As/Export menu command and enter ***qryManufacturingOverheadCost*** as the Query Name. Figure 10.19 shows the query in Design view.

   When you run the query, it should return a dynaset with manufacturing overhead values for the five jobs in the Job table. The *Ch10.mdb* database on your Companion CD-ROM includes a Manufacturing Overhead Cost query, *qryManufacturingOverheadCost*, for your reference.
8. Return to the Database window with the File, Close menu command.

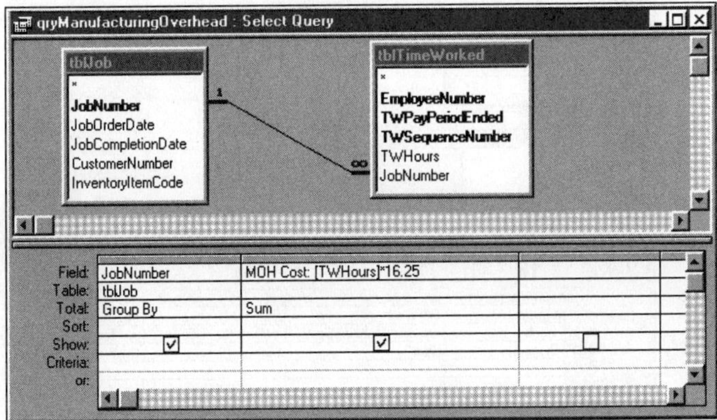

Figure 10.19 The Manufacturing Overhead Cost query in Design view.

Job Cost Calculation

Now we can build the summary query that will combine the results of the direct materials, direct labor, and manufacturing overhead queries. This Job Cost query provides the basis for the Job Cost report. The next exercise shows you how to build the Job Cost query.

Exercise 10.13: Building the Job Cost Query

1. Click the Queries tab in the Database window, then click the New button. Double-click Design View in the New Query dialog box.
2. In the Show Table dialog box, double-click *tblJob* to add the Job table to the upper pane of the Query Builder window.
3. Click the Queries tab of the Show Table dialog box.
4. Double-click *qryDirectMaterialsCost*, *qryDirectLaborCost*, and *qryManufacturingOverheadCost* to add these queries to the Job Cost query. Close the Show Table dialog box.

   This procedure of using one query to summarize other queries is sometimes called *nesting* queries.
5. Click and drag the JobNumber field from *tblJob* to the first QBE grid Field cell.
6. Click and drag the DM Cost, DL Cost, and MOH Cost fields to the next three open QBE grid Field cells.
7. Click the Totals toolbar button to open the Total line in the QBE grid.
8. Change the QBE grid Total cells for DM Cost, DL Cost, and MOH Cost to ***Sum***
9. Select the File, Save As/Export menu command and enter ***qryJobCost*** as the Query Name. Figure 10.20 shows the query in Design view.

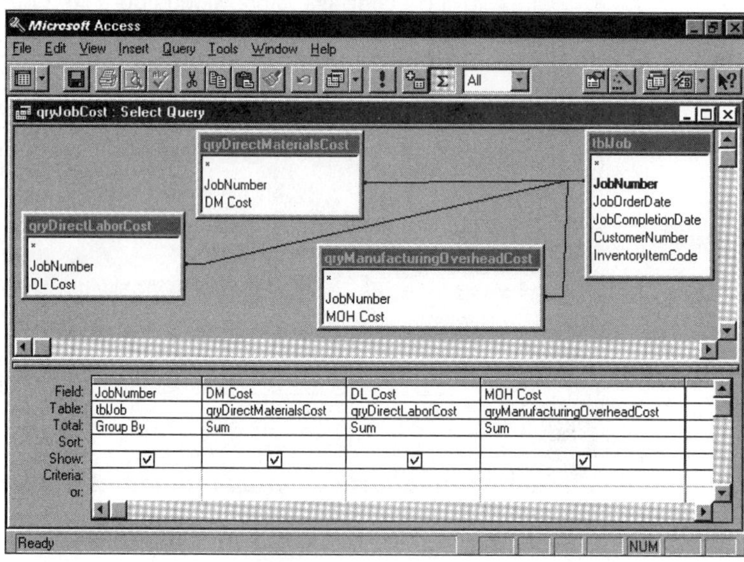

Figure 10.20 The Job Cost query in Design view.

When you run the query, it should return a dynaset with direct materials, direct labor, and manufacturing overhead values for the five jobs in *tblJob*. The query results appear in Figure 10.21. The *Ch10.mdb* database on your Companion CD-ROM includes a Job Cost query, *qryJobCost*, for your reference.

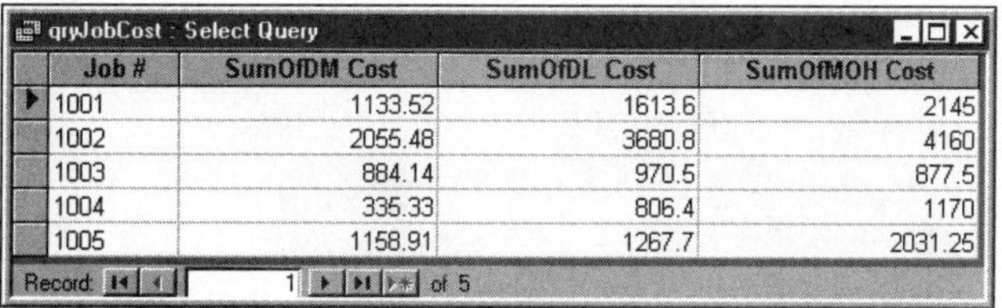

qryJobCost : Select Query

Job #	SumOfDM Cost	SumOfDL Cost	SumOfMOH Cost
1001	1133.52	1613.6	2145
1002	2055.48	3680.8	4160
1003	884.14	970.5	877.5
1004	335.33	806.4	1170
1005	1158.91	1267.7	2031.25

Record: 1 of 5

Figure 10.21 The Job Cost query results in Datasheet view.

The Job Cost Report

Now we can build a Job Cost report based on *qryJobCost*. Exercise 10.14 shows you how to use the *qryJobCost* calculations in a report design. To begin the exercise, close all tables, forms, and queries and open the Database window.

Exercise 10.14: Building a Job Cost Report

1. Click the Reports tab in the Database window, then click the New button.
2. Enter *tblJob* in the New Report combo box control, then double-click Design View in the list box control.
3. Click the Properties toolbar button and click the Data tab in the form's property sheet. Select the Record Source property, then click its Build button. Click the Yes button when prompted to open the Query Builder window.
4. The Query Builder window will open with *tblJob* in the top pane. Click the Show Table button, then double-click *tblFinishedGoodsInventory* to include it in the query.
5. Click the Queries tab on the Show Table dialog box.
6. Double-click *qryJobCost*, then click the Close button.
7. Click and drag the JobNumber field from *tblJob* to the first QBE grid Field cell. Set the Sort cell to Ascending. Click the check box in the Show cell to remove the selection.
8. Click and drag the asterisk from the *qryJobCost* to the second QBE grid Field cell.
9. Enter ***Total: [SumOfDM Cost] + [SumOfDL Cost] + [SumOfMOH Cost]*** in the third QBE grid Field cell.
10. Click and drag the InventoryDescription field from *tblFinishedGoodsInventory* to the fourth QBE grid Field cell. The Job Cost report design appears in the Query Builder window shown in Figure 10.22.
11. Click the Run toolbar button to test the query.
12. When you are satisfied that the query is operating properly, select the File, Close menu command to return to the Report Design window.

    Next, we will show you how to can use the query fields to build the Job Cost report. Use Figures 10.23 and 10.24 as guides in designing the report.

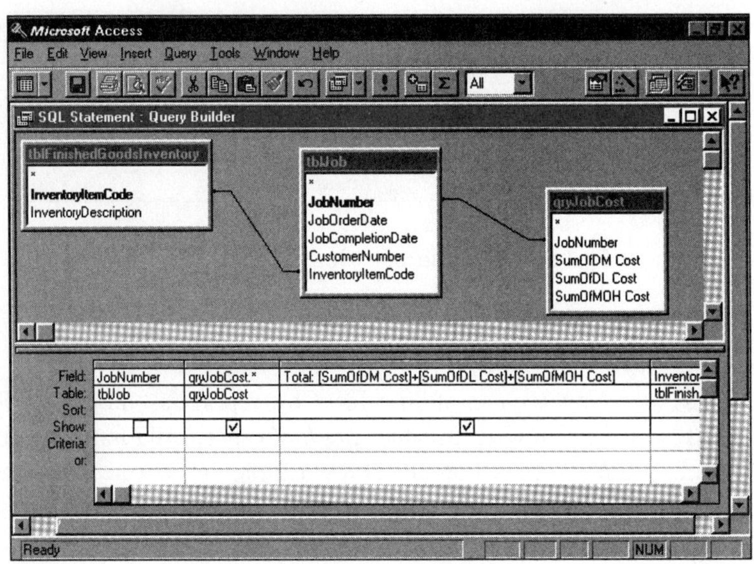

Figure 10.22 The Job Cost report design.

13. Click the Field List toolbar button, then click and drag all six fields to the Detail section of the report.
14. Click and drag a marquee around the label controls and press Delete.
15. Use the View menu command to delete the Page Header/Footer and add a Report Header/Footer.
16. Add descriptive labels for the column totals and the report title to the Report Header section.
17. Use the Text Box tool to create controls in the Report Footer.

    You can use the Sum() function to have these controls in the Report Footer sum the column amounts. For example, the Direct Materials total text box control contains the expression =Sum([SumOfDM Cost]). The square brackets are important here because the field names include a space. Figure 10.23 shows *rptJobCost* in Design view.
18. When you are satisfied with your report design, select the File, Save As/Export menu command and enter *rptJobCost* as the Report Name. The *Ch10.mdb* database on your Companion CD-ROM includes a Job Cost report, *rptJobCost*, that you can examine for details of the report's formatting and layout details.

SUMMARY

In this chapter we described how production cycle activities convert raw materials, labor, and overhead into finished products. We then explained how production cycle accounting traces and allocates manufacturing costs to products. The

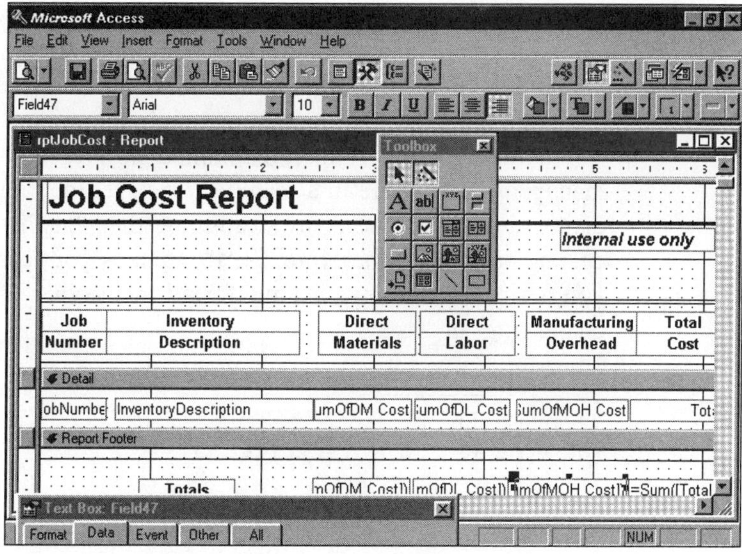

Figure 10.23 The Job Cost report in Design view.

Job Cost Report

Internal use only

Job Number	Inventory Description	Direct Materials	Direct Labor	Manufacturing Overhead	Total Cost
1001	Model 400A Control Panel	$1,133.52	$1,613.60	$2,145.00	$4,892.12
1002	Model 500C Control Panel	$2,055.48	$3,680.80	$4,160.00	$9,896.28
1003	Model 300A Control Panel	$884.14	$970.50	$877.50	$2,732.14
1004	Model 100A Control Panel	$335.33	$806.40	$1,170.00	$2,311.73
1005	Model 470D Control Panel	$1,158.91	$1,267.70	$2,031.25	$4,457.86
	Totals	$5,567.38	$8,339.00	$10,383.75	$24,290.13

Figure 10.24 The Job Cost report printout.

production cycle system elements you built as you worked through this chapter can provide managers with information for monitoring manufacturing processes. The production cycle system also provides financial accountants with information they need to value inventories and determine the cost of goods sold.

Although this chapter explained how to use Microsoft Access database management software in a manufacturing setting, a growing number of merchandising and service firms are examining their business processes using a product costing approach. Therefore, the techniques you learned in this chapter can help you design accounting systems for all three types of firms: manufacturing, merchandising, and service.

REVIEW EXERCISES

MULTIPLE-CHOICE QUESTIONS

1. You can use queries in the production cycle to
   a. calculate direct materials cost.
   b. calculate the predetermined overhead rate.
   c. store employee pay rates.
   d. store hours worked by job.
2. Production cycle activities include all of the following except
   a. allocating manufacturing overhead.
   b. calculating job costs.
   c. calculating payroll deductions.
   d. tracing direct materials costs to jobs.
3. In a process cost accumulation system
   a. direct materials costs are traced to departments.
   b. manufacturing overhead costs are traced to departments.
   c. both a and b.
   d. neither a nor b.
4. The InventoryItemCode field in *tblJob* is a
   a. composite primary key.
   b. relationship key.
   c. primary key.
   d. foreign key.
5. A time worked table's composite primary key that combines an employee number field with a job number field may not be a unique identifier because an employee may
   a. work on several jobs in a pay period.
   b. work on the same job more than once in a pay period.
   c. change employee numbers during the year.
   d. work on several jobs in different pay periods.

6. To measure the timeliness of job completions, you would need to add
   a. a time field to the Direct Materials Inventory table.
   b. a Standard Cost table.
   c. a date completed field to *tblJob*.
   d. an estimated time field to *tblJob*.
7. The Direct Materials Inventory table includes switches, relays, and connectors rated at 120 and 240 volts. You could improve this table by
   a. placing the voltage rating at the beginning of the description field.
   b. placing the voltage rating at the end of the description field.
   c. placing the voltage rating in a separate table.
   d. placing the voltage rating in a separate field in the same table.
8. The Employee table in Chapter 10 does not include a field for employee department because we accumulated costs using a
   a. job order system.
   b. process cost system.
   c. operation cost system.
   d. hybrid cost system.
9. Calculating job costs required a series of queries because in Microsoft Access
   a. a report cannot multiply by a constant.
   b. a report cannot compute sums of calculated fields.
   c. both a and b.
   d. neither a nor b.
10. In an activity-based job order cost system
   a. some manufacturing overhead costs are allocated to departments.
   b. all manufacturing overhead costs are traced to departments.
   c. some manufacturing costs are traced to activities, then allocated to departments.
   d. some manufacturing costs are traced to activities, then allocated to jobs.

DISCUSSION QUESTIONS

1. Describe the changes you would make to the production cycle system described in this chapter to convert it to a process cost accumulation system.
2. What tables and queries would you add to those described in this chapter to convert to an activity-based job order cost system?
3. Compare the Employee table in this chapter to the Employee table in Chapter 9. Explain the differences in the tables' structures.
4. Compare the Time Worked table in this chapter to the Time Worked table in Chapter 9. Explain the differences in the tables' structures.
5. Describe the modifications you would make to the production cycle elements described in this chapter to accommodate an operation cost accumulation system.

EXERCISES

1. Add a field to *tblJob* for budgeted cost. Create queries and a report that use this field to compute budget vs. actual differences by job.
2. Create a data entry form that would help persons enter time card data into the Time Worked table. Model the form after the time card shown in Figure 10.13 to make the data entry task easier.
3. Modify *rptJobCost* to display the customer name for each job.
4. Work-in-process inventory includes all jobs that have not been completed at month end. Modify the Job Cost queries and report to calculate the cost of December's work-in-process inventory.
5. Create a Job Cost Card form that facilitates the input of *budgeted* direct materials and direct labor cost data into Budgeted Direct Materials and Budgeted Time tables.

Index

A

B

C

N

O

P

Q

R

S

T